Student Learning

Equity

Curriculum, Instruction, Assessment

Critical Suppo[rt]

# USING DATA/ GETTING RESULTS:

A Practical Guide for
School Improvement in
Mathematics and Science

T E R C

# USING DATA/
# GETTING RESULTS:

A Practical Guide for
School Improvement in
Mathematics and Science

**Nancy Love**

Christopher-Gordon Publishers, Inc.
Norwood, Massachusetts

# Credits

This publication was developed by TERC through the work of the Eisenhower Regional Alliance for Mathematics and Science Education, one of the ten Eisenhower Regional Mathematics and Science Consortia established by the U.S. Department of Education. The National Network of Eisenhower Regional Consortia and the Eisenhower National Clearinghouse for Mathematics and Science Education form a coordinated, field based national infrastructure to promote systematic educational reform.

Based in Cambridge, Massachusetts, TERC is a not-for-profit educational research and development organization dedicated to improving mathematics and science learning.

This publication was supported by the Office of Educational Research and Improvement (OERI) of the U.S. Department of Education under grant number R168R50028, CFDA 84.164R. Any opinions, findings, conclusions, or recommendations expressed in this material are those of the author and do not necessarily reflect the views of OERI, the U.S. Department of Education, or any other agency of the U.S. government.

Chapter 2

*Selecting Evaluation Instruments, and Sample Data Organized by Question* from Tracking Your School's Success, by Joan L. Herman and Lynn Winters, 1994, Sage Publishing. Copyright 1994 by Sage Publications. Reprinted with Permission.

*Safety Regulations for Using Data* from Results: The Key to Continuous School Improvements (page 35-35) by Mike Schmoker, 1996, Alexandria, Virginia, Association for Supervision and Curriculum Development. Copyright 1996 by ASCD. All rights reserved. Adapted with permission.

"Organizing Data Driven Dialogue", from **Data Driven Dialogue: Tools for Collaborative Inquiry**, by Laura Lipton and Bruce Wellman, in press. To be published by MiraVia, LLC, Sherman, CT. Adapted with permission. Web Site: www.MiraVia.com.

*The Seven Norms of Collaborative Work* from The Adaptive School: A Sourcebook for Developing Collaborative Learning (pp. 37-47) by Robert Garmston and Bruce Wellman, 1999, Norwood, Massachusetts, Christopher-Gordon Publishers, Inc. Copyright 1999 by Christopher-Gordon Publishers, Inc. Reprinted with permission.

*Consensogram* based on the work of W. Edward Deming and Total Quality Management, by Laura Lipton and Bruce Wellman, Sherman, Connecticut, MiraVia LLC. Reprinted with permission.

*Data Matrix* from How to Conduct Collaborative Action Research by Richard Sago, 1992, Alexandria, Virginia, Association for Supervision and Curriculum Development. Copyright 1992 by ASCD. All rights reserved. Reprinted by permission.

*Finding Time*, from Designing Professional Development fore Teachers of Science and Mathematics (pages 226-27) by Susan Loucks-Horsley, Peter Hewson, Nancy Love, and Katherine E. Stiles, 1998, Corwin Press. Copyright 1998 by Corwin Press. Adapted by permission of authors.

Chapter 3

*Test Scores by Quartiles Over Three Years* from Setting Our Sights: Meeting Equity in School Change by Ruth S. Johnson, 1996, The Achievement Council. Copyright 1996 by Ruth Johnson. Reprinted with permission.

*SWINGS Task-* Examples of Student Work, from State Collaboration on Assessment and Student Standards of the Council of Chief State School Officers. Copyright CCSSOO/SCASS. Reprinted with permission.

*Pretest and Posttest Results on Performance Tasks* from A Comprehensive Guide to Designing Standards-Based Districts, School and Classrooms by Robert J. Marzano and John S. Kendall, 1996, McREL. Copyright 1996 by McREL (Mid-Continent Regional Educational Laboratory). Reprinted by permission.

Christopher-Gordon Publishers, Inc.

1502 Providence Highway, Suite 12

Norwood, MA 02062

1-800-934-8322

781-762-5577


Copyright 2002 by Christopher-Gordon Publishers, Inc.


Printed in the United States of America


10 9 8 7 6 5 4          07 06 05 04


Library of Congress: 2001091297


ISBN 1-929024-33-9

# Dedication

## For Susan Loucks-Horsley

This book is dedicated to my dear friend and colleague, Susan Loucks-Horsley. Her faith and love gave me the confidence to write a book. The doors she opened for me gave me the opportunity. Her brilliance, wisdom, and common sense inspired and shaped my thinking. I felt her presence throughout its writing . . . and feel it still.

# Table of Contents

# Extended Table of Contents

# Planning Tools

## Chapter 3

## Chapter 4

# Chapter 5

# Acknowledgments

This guidebook is not just *about* the process of collaborative inquiry. It is a product of my own process of collaborative inquiry. When I first was given the charge of developing a guidebook on systemic reform, I began a process of exploration that hasn't stopped yet. The questions came fast and furious. What is systemic reform? What fuels it? What stands in the way of schools achieving breakthrough results in mathematics and science achievement for all students? How can whole schools be as alive with inquiry as our best classrooms? What kind of resource can best support schools as they embark on a journey of discovery about improving student learning?

With tough questions like these to grapple with, I quickly and quite viscerally grasped the "collaborative" part of collaborative inquiry. Just as school staff can't go it alone, neither could I. Fortunately, I had many people who inspired, encouraged, confronted, informed, and supported me.

First and foremost, I want to thank Regional Alliance Director Mark Kaufman for giving me this opportunity and for his unflagging support, flexibility, sense of humor, integrity, and faith in me. Mark was with me every step of the way, offering conceptual and practical guidance, solving problems and running interference. I can think of no better person with whom to undertake an inquiry of this magnitude.

I am also indebted to each of the program staff of the Regional Alliance for their many contributions. Jeanne Harmon, Alliance Schools Coordinator, officemate and friend, read every line of every iteration of the guidebook. She offered timely and valuable feedback and advice and contributed immeasurably to the book's overall conceptualization and content, as well as to my emotional well-being. For input on "all things mathematical," including the mathematics resources, I thank Liz VanCleef and Myriam Steinback. Similarly, Marjorie Woodwell and consultant Page Keeley helped to shape the science resources section and "all things scientific." Mj Terry and Fred Gross provided valuable assistance with the issue of equity throughout the book and with the equity chapter in particular, and Mj designed and produced many of the Data Tools for investigating inequities in student learning and opportunities to learn. Molly Singsen brought her helpful lens as evaluator and writer to the task.

Special thanks to reviewers Arthur Baroody, Gay Gordon, Page Keeley, Susan Loucks-Horsley, Susan Mundry, Gail Paulin, Susan M. Remington, Joy Wallace, and Hubert M. Dyasi, whose thoughtful suggestions made this a better book, and to Anne Abeille, Bill Nave, and Elizabeth Rowe for their quality input on a quick turn-around.

The seeds for *Using Data/Getting Results* were actually planted several years ago, when the Regional Alliance (then based at the Northeast and Islands Regional Laboratory) supported a collaboration among the New England State Facilitators for the National Diffusion Network. In the course of that collaboration I was fortunate to work closely with my colleagues Richard Card, Susan Card, Jonathan Costa, Faith Fogle, Tondy Higginbotham, Laurie Rowe, and Howard Verman. Together we crafted a model for an action research approach to school improvement that served as a foundation and inspiration for this guidebook.

I have also drawn heavily on the work of many practitioners who have blazed the trail in using data, action research, and collaborative inquiry to foster equity and excellence in schools. Ruth Johnson, Michael Schmoker, and Victoria Bernhardt not only inspired me with their ideas, but offered their personal encouragement and assistance to me. *Using Data/Getting Results* was also influenced by Kati Haycock and the Education Trust's groundbreaking work in exposing inequities in our society and schools. Our guidebook is enhanced by their generous contribution of Data Tools. Iris Weiss of Horizon Research, Inc. and Rolf Blank of the Council of Chief State School Officers also kindly shared survey instruments and research expertise. From Laura Lipton and Bruce Wellman, I came to understand the role of dialogue as a precursor to decision making and the intersection between professional development and data use.

The guidebook did not truly come alive for me until I began to see collaborative inquiry in action, both in the schools we work with—the Alliance Schools—and in the many other schools and projects across the country that I visited and/or whose staff and students I interviewed: the Continuous Assessment in Science Project at Trinity College, Burlington, Vermont; Feinstein High School and EQUITY 2000, Providence, Rhode Island; Glendale (Arizona) Union High School District; Hall-Dale School District, Hallowell, Maine; Heinsberg (Vermont) Elementary School; Holaway Elementary School, Tucson, Arizona; Hudson (Massachusetts) Public Schools; Lawrence School, Brookline, Massachusetts; Mesa (Arizona) Unified School District; Norwood (New Hampshire) School; MSAD #52, Turner, Maine; Pomperaug Regional School District 15, Southbury and Middlebury, Connecticut; Souhegan High School, Amherst, New Hampshire; and Sutton Elementary School, Sutton, Massachusetts. Most of the examples, vignettes, and accounts in the guidebook come directly from my engagement with these many schools and districts. While other vignettes, especially those beginning the chapters and the long vignette woven throughout Chapter 4, are fictitious, they are based on the images gleaned from these and other schools I've come to know through my work.

In addition to these images, the guidebook is filled with the wisdom, experience, and words of the dozens of people whom I interviewed, either by phone or in person. I hope I am not overlooking anyone when I acknowledge Wende Allen, Mary Berle-Carmen, Sheldon Berman, Rolf Blank, Peg Bondorew, Sandra Campo, Ann Caren, Patricia Carini, Maura Carlson, Barry Carroll, Sonia Caus Gleason, John Correiro, Tim Craine, Nick Donohue, Hubert Dyasi, Paul Gammill, Dolores Grayson, Katherine Hanson, Michael Hibbard, Asa Hilliard, Don Horrigon, Greg Humphrey, Sharon Johnson, Roxanne Kapitan, Page Keeley, Sabra Lee, Leon Levesque, Ann Martin, Gary Marx, Robert McLaughlin, Judy Mumme, Susan Mundry, Patricia Nailor, Julia Phelps, Claire Pollard, Ewa Pytowska, Russ Quaglia, Sue Remington, Raymond Rose, Karl Stein, Anthony Terceira, Joy Wallace, Iris Weiss, Julian Weissglass, and Martha Williams.

While the guidebook was an exciting investigation into ideas, processes, and tools, it was also a product development effort. At some point, my inquiry had to be captured in words on pages—cogent words on carefully sequenced and designed pages. And for that process I have many other people to thank. Sue Martin, my developmental editor, has been my partner on the book for three years and my colleague and friend for many more. She reined me in, prodded and encouraged me, turned my explosion of ideas into a coherent book, and never gave up. Joyce Barnes, my research assistant, consistently exceeded my expectations, compiled virtually all of the resources, wrote the "Guidelines for Designing a School-Based Computer Database System," and did her best to keep me organized. She was preceded by Betty Lily and followed by Kate Blanchard and Tasha Morris, who helped assure the accuracy and timeliness of every resource entry.

Peggy Liversidge brought to the project the accuracy, precision, and patience for details that I lack. Those qualities, along with her conscientiousness and friendship, made her the perfect copy editor. Ken Mayer, ever calm and encouraging, shepherded the book through the preproduction process. And Jane Sherrill, with the flair, creativity, and dedication of the true artist that she is, transformed 400 pages of text and charts into a lively and highly readable prepublication edition. You will see many of her original design elements in this Christopher-Gordon edition.

One of the most onerous tasks in the production of the guidebook was the permissions, of which there were many—very many! No one knew this better than Bridget Mooney and Tasha Morris, who painstakingly obtained and catalogued every one. Thanks also to Robin Brown for her frequent permission consultations and her tenacious and conscientious support in bringing the book to publication. Chi-Yan Tsang produced the Data Tools, and did so with great care, efficiency, and accuracy, while Jana Marcotte edited copy and added her valuable design suggestions.

There is no greater compliment to an author than a high-quality publisher's enthusiastic support of her work. Sue Canavan and Hiram Howard, principals of Christopher-Gordon Publishers, Inc., immediately grasped my vision and goals for *Using Data/Getting Results* and worked with me as close collaborators to realize them. That same enthusiasm, commitment to quality, and collaboration characterized the marketing and production staff, Laurie Maker, Carol Treska, Judith Antonelli, and Chris Boyer, who moved the product from manuscript to market in record time.

Finally, I am grateful to Barbara Sampson, Chief Executive Officer of TERC, who, despite her frantically busy schedule, managed to make the publication of *Using Data/Getting Results* a personal priority. It touches me that she keeps a copy of the book on the windowsill in her office.

It is my hope that our collaborative inquiry and efforts in producing *Using Data/Getting Results* will contribute in some way to your collaborative inquiry into improving mathematics and science education. While the work of producing this edition of the guidebook has drawn to a close, our charge as educators to unearth the issues that underlie the data, to search our souls and our schools for ways to reach more students, and to achieve the results that every child deserves is neverending.

# Preface

*"We are surrounded by insurmountable opportunities."*

—Attributed to Pogo

As with many educational trends, the use of data to guide school improvement is touted as a panacea at the same time that it is distorted and abused. I worry, for example, that high-stakes tests, single and imperfect measures of student learning, are being used to size up the effectiveness of schools, dole out financial rewards and punishments, and determine students' futures. While accountability for student performance is not a bad idea, schools are now under enormous pressure to produce short-term gains in test scores rather than to build their capacity to sustain improvements in teaching and learning for all students. In this atmosphere, data are driving a frenzy of unfocused, knee-jerk activity—data-driven mania—producing more fatigue than results.

I worry, too, that useful data are cloistered in central office computer systems and research departments rather than shared broadly with teachers and parents to serve as a catalyst for inclusive dialogue, reflection, and professional and organizational growth. Even when data are available, school cultures, schedules, and mindsets may not support their being used to improve student learning. School staff are frequently isolated from each other with little time to reflect on their practice together. In the absence of a robust learning community, individual educators can remain data-immune, clinging to generalizations and assumptions about students, teaching, and learning that are not supported by local data or research. Above all, I worry that data will continue to be used to sort students rather than to better serve them, perpetuating racist, classist, and sexist policies and practices rather exposing them. In my worst moments, these challenges can seem insurmountable.

But the quote above reminds us that on the other side of "insurmountable" are "opportunities." The opportunities to use data as a catalyst to individual and organizational learning are many. We have the opportunity to rise above the data-driven mania and use data thoughtfully and carefully to inform the discourse about improving student learning. To do so requires that we provide teachers and administrators at every level with access to rich, disag-gregated data as well as the knowledge, skills, and time they need to use them well. It is the data-driven dialogue that goes on at grade-level, faculty, community, and committee meetings, not the rank-order listings of test results published in local newspapers, that holds out the greatest hope for schools. When the school community makes collective sense of multiple sources of data, owns problems, and embraces solutions together, then the wheels of school reform start turning.

In the context of a vibrant learning community, school staff are no longer data-immune, but seek out data to help them challenge their assumptions, investigate their own questions, uncover inequities, discover previously unrecognized strengths in their students, question their practice, improve instruction, and see their world anew. The community learns the value of bringing multiple perspectives to the table and the discipline of separating data from the "leaps of abstraction" we make from them. Then, as Peter Senge says, "conversations can produce genuine learning, rather than merely reinforcing prior views" (Senge 1990, 186). In short, schools are as alive with inquiry and discovery as our best science and mathematics classrooms.

This vision is what led me to write *Using Data/Getting Results: A Practical Guide to School Improvement in Mathematics and Science.* My passion is not for statistics, graphs, charts, or tables; I am neither a statistician nor a researcher. I am a teacher, professional developer, and activist for social and educational justice. My passion is unleashing the learning potential of students, teachers, and schools. Working in mathematics and science education reform for the last eight years, I have come to realize that the vision of the national mathe-matics and science education standards documents, with their emphases on equity, inquiry and investigation, discourse, and community, offers a power-ful image for revitalizing our schools. Through these lenses, I wrote *Using Data/Getting Results* not as a technical manual for crunching school data, but as a guide for engaging school communities in investigations that produce powerful learning for school staff as well as better results for students.

"Guide" is actually a good metaphor for the book. In much the same way as a mathematics or science teacher acts as a guide to students' inquiry and investigation in the classroom, *Using Data/Getting Results* is a guide for inquiry into improving mathematics and science teaching and learning. The book poses 12 challenging issues or problems upon which school commu-nities may want to focus their inquiry—problems that can lead to fruitful investigations, such as "to what extent are we implementing standards-based curriculum and assessment?" or "to what extent do some students (poor, minority, English-language learners, girls, others) have less opportunity to learn mathematics and science than others?" For each issue, the guidebook helps to answer the questions: What kind of data should we collect? How? For what purpose?

Recognizing that schools face many obstacles, including lack of time, to engaging in collaborative inquiry, the guidebook offers an array of tools and content to help make the process of using data and getting results accessible and practical for busy educators. You will find:

1. Narrative: describing principles, processes, and tools for effective data use and discussion of 12 problems for school teams to investigate related to mathematics and science education reform.

2. Planning Tools: including tools to help teams move from data collection and analysis to thoughtful planning and action. Data Collection Plan forms for each problem offer a menu of possible data sources and Data Tools contained in the book from which to choose.

3. Resources: fully annotated and located at the end of Chapters 2-5.

4. Reform in Action accounts: actual stories of local school districts that are using data and getting results, located in Chapter 6.

5. Data Tools: containing forms for disaggregating and analyzing data, survey instruments, interview and observation protocols, checklists, and other instruments to help school teams collect and analyze data.

6. CD-ROM: featuring an annotated listing of mathematics and science curriculum materials and Planning Tools and Data Tools in electronic format.

The content and structure of the book are discussed more fully in Chapter 1.

Just as skillful teachers help to create a safe learning environment and facilitate discourse in the classroom, so this guidebook suggests safety rules, collaborative norms, and a structure for orchestrating data-driven dialogue among teachers and administrators. Through the experience of inquiry and problem solving, both students in the classroom and educators and parents in the school community come to deep conceptual understandings as well as greater mastery of the process of framing questions, collecting data, formulating hypotheses, drawing conclusions, taking action, and monitoring results. They each become more capable masters and designers of their own learning. The scaffolding can fall away.

The product of the investigations proposed in *Using Data/Getting Results* is a systemic plan for improving student learning that is grounded in careful study of a problem and its possible solutions. Systemic action plans are multifaceted and long-term, based on the recognition that complex problems require complex, not simplistic, solutions. They enact our current theory about what will produce results for students and are rigorously tested as they are carried out.

The by-product, in my mind, is even more important: a learning community fortified by new understanding, fully committed to implementing the plan, and more skillful at collaborative inquiry. "It is less important," Senge says, "to produce perfect plans than to use planning to accelerate learning as a whole" (Senge 1990, 188). The accelerated learning of the school as an organization and of the staff as its lifeblood is what produces results for students. This is the insurmountable opportunity we face. The real high stakes are not how students will perform on a test, but whether we will squander or unleash the potential of the students whose education is in our hands.

My colleagues and I at the Regional Alliance for Mathematics and Science Education at TERC are eager to continue to learn from you about the process of using data and getting results. How are you putting the principles, processes, and tools discussed in this guidebook to work in your own school or district? What insurmountable opportunities are you facing? Please e-mail your comments and feedback to us at alliance@terc.edu.

Student Learning

# A FRAMEWORK FOR COLLABORATIVE INQUIRY AND SYSTEMIC REFORM

Curriculum, Instruction, Assessment

Equity

Critical Supports

**We thought we** were tracking students in or out of higher-level mathematics courses by their ability. Then we looked at the data on student achievement on standardized tests. We learned that African American and Latino students who scored as high as white students were getting tracked out of college-level courses. There was no more kidding ourselves. Our actions were based on false assumptions and now it was time for change. (Mathematics teacher, urban high school)

**For years our** school district did the innovation "du jour." One year it was a new mathematics program. The next year it was a new science program. We measured our success by how many things we had done. And yet we had no idea what, if anything, was making a difference in student learning. Now we have a set of clearly defined learning goals for all students based on national standards. We choose approaches that we think will help us meet those goals. We keep checking whether we are getting there or not by analyzing student learning results. We're not shooting in the dark anymore. (Curriculum coordinator, suburban school district)

**We didn't want** to believe that students were as poor at mathematics problem solving as they were until we looked at the results of the performance assessments all the fourth-grade teachers gave. At that point, we had no choice but to start thinking about strategies to improve. (Teacher, rural elementary school)

This guidebook is about a different road to change. It is the road that the schools in the examples above are taking. And, as the people involved will tell you, it is not for the faint of heart. It means going beyond paying lip service to "all students learning." It requires a willingness to let go of deeply held beliefs and practices if they are not serving all children. It demands the rigor of a good scientific investigation, using data to find out what is working and what is not and for whom. And it takes a commitment to tell the truth and take action based on it.

# Why a Different Road to Change?

When he entered first grade, Alec enjoyed mathematics immensely. His preschool years taught him to ask fascinating mathematical questions about Lego constructions and about the shapes necessary to build complex block structures. He learned to investigate proportion and ratio while playing with cars and to estimate how far his cars would go depending on how steep an incline they were on. Now, in third grade, after daily exposure to number drills, timed facts tests, and competitively graded assignments that discourage children more interested in questions than answers, Alec has been entirely "cured" of his love of math.

Ironically, Alec attends a model urban school where teachers have been working for years to improve their mathematics teaching. Various business partners have paid for many hours of staff development. Parents have been brought together in workshops to learn how to capitalize on "family math." Colleges compete for student-teaching slots in this school. Nevertheless, for three years Alec has brought home nothing but rote worksheets. His wonderful childlike capacity to generate mathematically meaningful questions is slowly giving way to the daily habits of memorizing and regurgitating the omnipresent math facts! I, an educator myself, have not been able to shield him from these mathematically obsolete habits. My attempts to nurture and protect Alec's sense of wonder have been futile in the face of the "right answer" orientation. As for

Alec, he sees no relation between what he likes to do and what mathematics is all about. He is slowly outgrowing Legos and cars. When he gets to high school physics and algebra, he will have forgotten the theories he so freely postulated in kindergarten, and his childhood sense of wonder will be strictly a memory of the past, not a measure of future possibilities.

(Alec's mother)

**M**any of you are working hard to reshape mathematics and science education in your schools and districts. National, state, and local standards have provided a major impetus for local reform. As you know, it is a bumpy ride over mostly uncharted territory. Some of the old ways of making change—adopting new textbooks or programs without sustained staff development and support for teachers, leaders defining problems and mandating solutions without teacher ownership, offering one-shot workshops and quick fixes, taking on too many changes at once—have not gotten us very far.

*"If what you are doing isn't working, try anything else."*

(Robert Garmston, workshop, 1994)

Despite the rhetoric of mathematics and science education reform and the call for "systemic change," we all know of too many students like Alec in the vignette above who have yet to benefit from any changes in the teaching and learning of mathematics and science. This is especially true for poor, minority, and female students. For example, the gap in mathematics achievement between minority and white students in the United States is not shrinking, but growing (Education Trust 1996, 4–5). And according to the Third International Mathematics and Science Study (TIMSS), the United States continues to weigh in with a pretty dismal performance in mathematics and science achievement when compared with students in other countries: by twelfth grade, even the best U.S. students performed among the lowest of the participating nations (U.S. Department of Education 1998). Belief systems that lead to damaging labeling and sorting of children persist. Widely discredited practices such as tracking prevail. And other barriers to change, such as teacher isolation and inadequate time for collaboration and professional development, seem as insurmountable as ever. Meanwhile, each day, we are leaving more students behind.

If you share our sense of urgency about these children, chances are you are looking for a different road to change. Not the path of quick fixes, which only leads to failure. Not the shortcuts to change that benefit some students while overlooking others. Not the road that meanders and never leads to results. *Using Data/Getting Results* is a guide for reform that has a clear destination—improved student learning—and a slow, steady process for getting there by unleashing the power of inquiry.

*The purpose of this book, then, is to support those who are leading mathematics and science reform at the school or district level to themselves become inquirers—inquirers into how best to improve student learning.* It is written for teachers, administrators, and community members who share some responsibility for school- or districtwide mathematics and science education reform and are actively engaged in facilitating change. In referring to our audience, we use the word "team" because we encourage teachers and administrators to work collaboratively to guide reform in their schools or districts. While we most often refer to the school as the unit of change, we recognize that mathematics and science education reform is often a district-level endeavor. The resources in this guidebook are equally applicable to school- or district-based initiatives. Also, although the book is tailored to mathematics and science reform, the processes and tools can easily be applied to other school reform efforts.

# On the Road to Results

*"You cannot fight what you cannot see."*

(Schmoker 1996, 38)

U*sing Data/Getting Results* is based on a set of principles and a conceptual framework that organize our thinking about inquiry as it applies to mathematics and science education reform. This approach emerged most directly from our work with the Alliance Schools, a group of 72 schools throughout the Northeast, Puerto Rico, and the Virgin Islands that are actively engaged in improving their mathematics and science education programs. Over the last few years, staff of the Regional Alliance for Mathematics and Science Education at TERC have piloted many of the ideas and tools we now share with you. But, like any way of thinking, this conceptual framework also grew out of our years of collective experience working in and thinking about school reform.

## Guiding Principles

The approach outlined in this guidebook is grounded in the following set of guiding principles or assumptions:

## Inquiry Fuels School Reform

The standards movement inspires us with a vision of mathematics and science classrooms that are alive with inquiry, where students ask questions,

## Guiding Principles for Our Work

▼ Inquiry fuels school reform. It is a process of exploring, questioning, discovering, and searching for new understandings. While inquiry is often thought of as a process by which scientists, young and old, come to know their world, we also think of inquiry as a process by which school staff learn how to better educate children.

▼ Rigorous use of data lies at the heart of the inquiry process.

▼ Inquiry is collaborative; it thrives within and helps to sustain a learning community.

▼ The focus of school-based inquiry is improving student learning.

▼ Improving student learning requires a systemic approach.

▼ Nothing changes if classrooms don't change; school reform must impact teaching and learning.

▼ Equity is not an incidental concern; rather, it is a central focus, embedded in all aspects of systemic reform.

▼ School reform is dependent on a set of critical supports. Factors such as effective professional development, leadership, school culture, partnerships, public engagement, policies, and use of technology create the essential context in which positive change takes hold and is sustained.

use data, examine their own assumptions, discuss with their classmates, solve challenging problems, and come to new and deeper understandings. But something troubles us about this vision. How can classrooms be alive with inquiry when schools are not?

We believe that the same process of inquiry that invigorates classrooms also breathes life into school reform. In inquiry-based schools, teachers and administrators continually ask questions about how to improve student learning, experiment with new ideas, and rigorously use data to uncover problems and monitor results. It's not that these schools have solved all of their problems. It's that they know how to tackle problems and continuously improve. Researchers in both business and education agree that these qualities are hallmarks of the most successful organizations (Fullan 1993; Senge 1990).

## Inquiry Relies on Rigorous Use of Data

Just as in mathematics or scientific inquiry, inquiry for school improvement relies on data. Imagine setting off in a car with no gauges, no windows, and no maps. You can't tell how much gas you have, how fast you are traveling, where you are, and if you are even headed in the right direction. You are data poor, not a smart way to travel. Yet this is the way many schools operate.

*"Inquiry is an approach to learning that involves a process of exploring the natural or material world, that leads to asking questions and making discoveries in the search for new understandings."*

(The Exploratorium Institute for Inquiry Web site [http://www.exploratorium.edu/IFI/about/inquiry.html])

It's not that schools don't have the data—they *have* lots of demographic information, standardized test scores, attendance records, dropout rates, grades, and more. They *give* data to state and federal government agencies, funding sources, and the media. Frequently, they *fear* data because they have been used so often as a club against schools, administrators, and teachers. But for a variety of reasons, including this fear, they often don't *use* data for their own purposes—to diagnose problems, spark action, and improve results. A major aim of this book is to reverse this situation, encouraging schools to become data users as well as data givers.

## Inquiry Is Collaborative

The process of inquiry we advocate and describe in this book is collaborative, involving teams of administrators and teachers working together to improve mathematics and science education in their schools or districts. We believe that the full power of the inquiry process is unleashed when school staff work together, not in isolation, when data become a catalyst for constructive dialogue, and when school communities develop shared understandings and ownership of problems and solutions being pursued.

When we were doing the research for this guidebook, we found many examples of individual superintendents or research departments doing a fantastic job of crunching numbers; but they were not using what they were learning to empower school staff to diagnose and solve problems. We also encountered inspiring examples of individual teachers conducting action research in their own classrooms. But unless action research catches on schoolwide, it has little impact beyond the individual teacher's classroom. The examples and cases used in this book are about schools and districts that are mobilized around a process of collaborative inquiry.

## The Focus of School-Based Inquiry Is Improving Student Learning

If mathematics and science education reform is to succeed, reformers must stay vigilantly focused on the results they want for students. The road to reform we describe in this guidebook may not have a definitive map, but it does have a clear destination—a set of learning goals that educators, parents, and the community are committed to achieving for all students. This isn't a joyride, although it can be joyous, especially as you see your goal getting closer. Rather, it is a trip with a clear and compelling purpose.

While the idea of focusing on student learning goals is simple, its implications are profound. It means turning most school improvement activities on

*Collaborative inquiry is a process by which all relevant groups construct their understanding of important problems and potential solutions through asking questions, carefully analyzing all relevant data, and engaging in constructive dialogue with colleagues.*

(Wagner 1998)

*"Most of what goes on in the name of innovation has limited impact on student learning."*

(Schmoker 1996, 26)

their heads. Frequently, school improvement begins with some activity such as implementing a new curriculum. Clearly, the planners want these innovations to improve student learning, but they are often unclear about what they mean by student learning, how they will measure it, and whether their actions are getting them where they want to go. The result is a vicious cycle of doing, doing, doing without knowing the effect on learning. No wonder school staff are often left feeling burned out and cynical. They've been riding the roads for years without ever knowing if they are getting closer to their destination. Students suffer too; they are losing out on the opportunity to learn while time and money are wasted chasing down the newest fad.

Change efforts that focus on student learning start and end in a different place. The cycle in Figure 1.1 illustrates a process that starts not with a particular program, but with a commitment to a vision of student learning and a set of standards. Once agreed upon, standards raise expectations for all students, focus improvement efforts on results, and offer a yardstick to measure improvement. Next steps are to collect and analyze a variety of data about student learning, define a learner-centered problem to solve, set student learning goals, plan for and take action to improve the system, and monitor results.

No program is implemented, no action is taken unless there is good reason to believe it will help students to reach a specific learning goal, such as improving their ability to reason better in mathematics. Once action is taken, teachers, students, and parents receive frequent feedback about how well students are performing in relation to that goal. If the changes are working, everyone knows it and can celebrate its success. On the other hand, if student learning is not increasing, planners try to find out why, make mid-course corrections, or abandon the program. The loyalty is not to a particular curriculum or instructional strategy; loyalty is to students and their learning.

**FIGURE 1.1: COLLABORATIVE INQUIRY INTO STUDENT LEARNING**

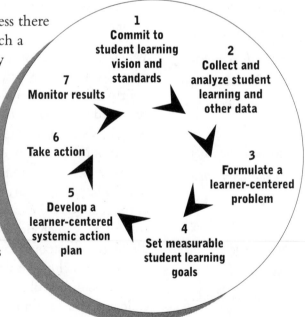

## Improving Student Learning Requires a Systemic Approach

A fifth principle underlying our approach is that producing learning results requires systemic, not piecemeal, change. In our view, improving student learning is integrally connected with improving the system as a whole, including schools' capacity to improve the quality of curriculum, instruction, and assessment, address equity issues, and provide critical supports. To illustrate our view of systemic reform, let's return to the car analogy. You wouldn't think of taking to the road in a car pieced together from random parts from different makes and models. And when the "patchwork" car doesn't go, your solution wouldn't be to change the oil, replace a single part, or blame your mechanic. The problem, obviously, is much deeper. The parts don't interconnect or work as a system. The car won't go anywhere until it is completely rebuilt.

Unfortunately, however, schools are trying to make their way down the road to reform in just such a vehicle. The parts of the educational system that need to work together are pulling in different directions. For example, on the one hand, national standards and some state frameworks call for an emphasis on students' complex reasoning and problem-solving abilities. On the other hand, standardized tests that measure recall of facts and procedures are still quite common, despite some progress in recent years. And although sustained, high-quality professional development is touted as the key to reform, school schedules, incentive systems, and contradictory local, state, and national policies often propel schools toward the widely discredited one-shot workshops. These and other "disconnects" in the system are all too familiar.

We take a rather pragmatic view of systemic reform. Just as you might rebuild your car piece by piece, day by day, your team can approach its reform efforts as a series of steps over a long time period. But to do this well, you need to understand all the parts and how they interconnect. As you work on one part of the system, you consider the impact it will have elsewhere and what else needs to change so that part can function. You always keep the big picture in mind and work on as many pieces at a time as you can. While there are many things you can change, others, like the condition of the roads or the climate (national or state policies), are beyond your control. So you change what you can and work around what you can't. No doubt, the constraints frustrate you. The complexity of the task can sometimes overwhelm or even paralyze you. But you know that piecemeal change doesn't work. If you want a car that runs (or schools that work for all children), you have no choice but to take action and think systemically.

## Nothing Changes If Classrooms Don't Change

While improving student learning requires a systemic approach, we also believe that change must reach down into the classroom. Mathematics and science education reform is at its core about transforming teaching and learning. A focused and coherent curriculum that emphasizes rigorous and developmentally appropriate content, complex reasoning, inquiry-based approaches to learning, and authentic and varied assessment strategies are essential components of this transformation. So is sustained and high-quality professional development for teachers, so that they can acquire the content knowledge and pedagogical skills they need to carry out such changes.

As they acquire this new knowledge, teachers need the opportunity to try out new curriculum and instructional practices in their classroom in a context of ongoing support from both colleagues and outside experts. This should include opportunities to engage deeply with the mathematics and science content they are teaching their students, to experience new approaches to teaching as learners themselves, to study student thinking, and to reflect on their beliefs about teaching, learning, the nature of mathematics and science, and their own practice. In addition, teachers need high-quality materials that align with their curriculum and with national, state, and local standards and strong administrative and policy-level support. Any reform effort that sidesteps these issues simply misses the point.

## Equity Is Center Stage

Significant improvements in teaching and learning will take you farther down the road to high levels of mathematics and science learning for all. But they won't take you all the way. To make schools work for all children, especially those who are poor and minority, requires directly confronting the very real obstacles to equity that stand in their way.

By equity, we mean the right of every student to achieve at high levels, a right many students still do not have. Ironically, the very students who need the best educational opportunities often get the worst; the very students who need their schools to hold out the highest expectations for them are often subjected to the lowest. Nowhere are these inequities more important to rectify than in the teaching and learning of mathematics and science, subjects that act as gatekeepers to college entrance and promising futures.

We believe that equity is not just an incidental part of the reform agenda, an afterthought or an issue for "other schools, not ours." It is a central issue for virtually every school in the United States and its territories. Certainly, equity issues are critical to urban schools with large poor and minority populations. But they are equally important in rural schools, where many poor students are underserved. Even in relatively well-off suburbs there are inevitably some less advantaged students who are often relegated to low tracks and second-rate educational opportunities. Moreover, gender inequities can arise in any school, regardless of its economic or racial composition.

When school staff take seriously the challenge of reaching all students, they don't just carry out one-size-fits-all reform. They use data to uncover who is being underserved, rigorously examine what school practices and beliefs may be preventing these students from achieving at their capacity, target reform activities to closing the achievement gap, and monitor their progress on that score.

## Critical Supports Can Make or Break Reform

Scaling the many obstacles to high levels of learning for all students is hard work. Reform teams can't go it alone. They need to have in place a set of supports that help to sustain positive change over the long haul. While these factors less directly affect student learning outcomes than, say, reforming curriculum or eliminating tracking, they create the conditions under which these reforms can succeed.

Topping the list is effective professional development, the major vehicle through which teachers transform their beliefs and gain the skills and knowledge they must have to improve teaching and learning in the classroom. Other critical supports are:

▼ school cultures that support risk taking, collegiality, and a focus on student learning;

▼ leadership that both guides and supports reform;

▼ technology in the service of student learning and organizational improvement;

▼ policies that work for, not against, reform;

▼ public engagement and support for mathematics and science education reform;

▼ partnerships with other organizations concerned with students and their well-being.

Because these critical supports can make or break the overall success of the effort, we believe that careful attention to them is an essential part of the work of the reform team.

## A Framework for Data-Driven, Systemic Reform

Based on the above principles, Figure 1.2 illustrates our view of how the pieces of systemic reform fit together. The triangle at the top (the roof of the structure) depicts the overarching goal of reform: high levels of mathematics and science learning for all students. The pillars represent two parts of the system we believe schools can and must affect to achieve that goal: curriculum, instruction, and assessment and equity. The foundation of the house is critical supports, which make continuous improvement in teaching, learning, and equity possible. Noted within each component of the framework are key issues for school-based inquiry.

The lines connecting all of these elements represent how integrally connected they are, both with student learning and with each other. Treating them in isolation is what has gotten schools in trouble. For example, a district may do a fantastic job building consensus around standards but be unwilling to tackle equity issues such as tracking, which poses a serious barrier to all students reaching those standards. Or a school may decide to implement a new curriculum but achieve little change in classroom practice because it does not have in place critical supports such as high-quality professional development, good leadership,

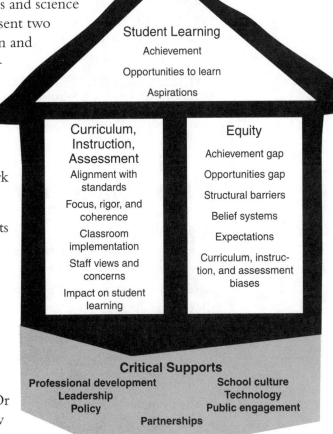

**Student Learning**

Achievement

Opportunities to learn

Aspirations

**Curriculum, Instruction, Assessment**

Alignment with standards

Focus, rigor, and coherence

Classroom implementation

Staff views and concerns

Impact on student learning

**Equity**

Achievement gap

Opportunities gap

Structural barriers

Belief systems

Expectations

Curriculum, instruction, and assessment biases

**Critical Supports**

Professional development
Leadership
Policy
Partnerships

School culture
Technology
Public engagement

**FIGURE 1.2: FRAMEWORK FOR DATA-DRIVEN SYSTEMIC REFORM IN MATHEMATICS AND SCIENCE EDUCATION**

and public support. Or a school improvement effort attends to these critical supports but never gets down to improving teaching and learning. Because of this piecemeal approach, the road to reform is strewn with many lost and stalled travelers.

On the other hand, thinking and acting systemically entails careful consideration of all the elements that impact student learning. In Chapter 3 we describe a planning process called "learner-centered systemic action planning." After studying student learning data and setting very specific goals to improve student learning, teams plan for action in each of the three major areas: classroom change, equity, and critical supports. Clearly, teams need to focus on one major area, for example, assessment reform. But they can't neglect other parts of the system as they plan.

In our model, thinking systemically goes hand in hand with the inquiry process and the focus on results. How do teams know what parts of the system need to change and how? Not by speculation or assumption, but by using data to understand current practices and problems and to test out solutions. And how do they know if what they are doing is working? By going back to the touchstone—student learning results. Trying to change the system without using data and inquiry is like trying to drive a car with no fuel or gauges. For each of the elements in our framework, we provide a set of indicators that teams can use to guide their inquiry and gauge their progress.

# What's Unique about This Guidebook?

Much has been written already about systemic mathematics and science reform, equity, and data-driven decision making. But no resource, as far as we know, has woven all of these together in a practical, hands-on guidebook. This book takes the process of data-driven decision making and shows how it can be used concretely to help meet three major challenges of systemic mathematics and science education reform: improving student learning, reforming curriculum, instruction, and assessment, and overcoming obstacles to equity. A discussion of another important facet of systemic reform, critical supports, is woven throughout the text, vignettes, and tools of the guidebook. However, a full treatment of this important topic would require a book in itself and is beyond the scope of this work.

Recognizing that schools face many obstacles to implementing data-driven systemic reform, we set out to make this guidebook straightforward and useful without oversimplifying the complexities of the issues involved. Each chapter is organized around a set of authentic problems reform teams face, such as broadening classroom reform beyond a small group of teachers or confronting belief systems that block equity. For each problem, you will learn how data can help, what kinds of data to use, and how to gather those data. In addition, you will gain practical tools for working with school-based inquiry (see "How to Use This Book (and Not Be Overwhelmed!)," page 19).

While this guidebook is problem-based and practical, we hope that it is also informative and provocative. That is, while it is rich with tools, it is much more than a toolkit. It provides a conceptual framework for thinking about the process of inquiry and systemic reform, discussions of the real problems involved, and vignettes about school districts that are successfully grappling with them. The text, in fact, provides a comprehensive overview of many of the complex issues surrounding systemic reform.

Another unique feature of the book is its scope. While *Using Data/Getting Results* is focused on improving student learning, it does not narrowly focus on student learning data. Unlike many other resources on data-driven school reform, we take a very broad view of data as any information that can guide decision makers as they work toward improving student learning. This includes, for instance, data about instructional practices, curriculum implementation, teachers' attitudes about reform, tracking practices, and expectations for students. We also define student learning data quite broadly to encompass performance assessments and examination of student work and thinking as well as more traditional test results.

Finally, while this guidebook outlines a process of inquiry and a framework for reform, it is not prescriptive. We encourage you to find your own route through it, focusing on the issues that are most important to you and selecting the tools that make sense in your own context. No one is expected to work through the book step by step. Rather, it is intended to be both a guide and a catalyst for your school's or district's own inquiry process in much the same way that teachers act as guides to students' inquiry in the classroom.

# The Content of the Guidebook

The content of *Using Data/Getting Results* emerges directly out of the principles and frameworks described above. Chapter 2, "Data and Inquiry: Turning the Wheels of Reform," focuses on the first three principles and deals with practicalities of making them work in a school context. It includes examples of data schools can use, 10 ways to use data as a lever for change, safety regulations for using data, and the dispositions that give life to the inquiry process. We explore the stages in working with data: framing problems, collecting data, analyzing data, organizing data-driven dialogue, drawing conclusions, taking action, and monitoring results. You will learn about the importance of disaggregating data—looking at how specific subgroups of students perform rather than lumping all students together—to surface problems

Framing the Question

Collecting Data

**Phases of Collaborative Inquiry**

Monitoring Results

Drawing Conclusions, Taking Action

Analyzing Data

Organizing Data-Driven Dialogue

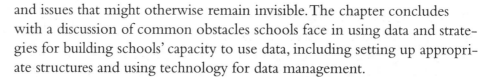

and issues that might otherwise remain invisible. The chapter concludes with a discussion of common obstacles schools face in using data and strategies for building schools' capacity to use data, including setting up appropriate structures and using technology for data management.

Chapter 3, "Keep Your Eyes on the Prize: Student Learning," is about how to keep school reform focused on student learning results. It fleshes out the cycle of collaborative inquiry into student learning illustrated in Figure 1.1 and equips teams with actual tools they can use to assess readiness for change, collect and analyze student learning data, formulate and prioritize problems, set measurable goals, develop learner-centered systemic action plans, and reflect on and monitor results. In addition, the chapter provides a set of indicators schools can use to monitor student learning as they implement reform, including gauges for achievement, opportunities to learn, and student aspirations.

Chapter 4, "Reforming Curriculum, Instruction, and Assessment," describes how data and inquiry can support the process of reforming teaching, learning, and assessing in the classroom. The chapter focuses on four problems that schools frequently encounter as they undertake classroom reform: how to align curriculum with standards; how to implement and sustain reform; how to broaden assessment practices to align with curriculum and instruction; and how to evaluate the impact of any of these changes on student learning. For each problem, we provide a brief overview, a discussion of what kinds of data and indicators to use, a form for a data collection plan, and relevant resources. In addition, readers will follow the story of a school team as it inquires into each problem and takes action, guided by data.

Chapter 5, "Overcoming Obstacles to Equity," profiles four common obstacles to equity that underlie performance gaps between rich and poor, white and minority, boys and girls: structural barriers such as tracking; underlying belief systems that contradict the stated belief that "all children can learn"; unequal expectations; and biases in curriculum, instruction, and assessment practices. Each problem includes a discussion of why it is an important equity issue, how to use data to help understand, assess, and overcome it, and where to find resources to help.

Chapter 6, "Reform in Action," contains five accounts of school districts that are making progress down the road to reform. You will learn about Glendale Union High School District, a large urban district outside Phoenix, Arizona, that is using districtwide performance and criterion-referenced assessments to fuel continuous improvement in student learning. The Providence (Rhode Island) Public Schools provide an inspiring example of another urban district's rigorous use of data to reform mathematics teaching and increase minority enrollment and success in algebra and geometry. In Hudson, Massachusetts, the story is about a small school district that has taken big steps to successfully implement a standards-based curriculum in mathematics and science, using data about implementation to guide their decision making. The Hall-Dale School District in Hallowell, Maine, shows us how building community-wide commitment to student learning goals and standards together with teacher leadership and involvement laid the groundwork for a successful curriculum development process. Finally, you will learn about Connecticut's Pomperaug Regional School District 15's highly acclaimed performance-based learning and assessment system that is driving districtwide improvements in teaching and learning.

# The Structure of the Guidebook

*Using Data/Getting Results* contains five distinct elements that act as a scaffold to support teams through the process of using data and getting results: narrative, Planning Tools, Resources, Reform in Action accounts (see description of Chapter 6 above), and Data Tools. Careful cross-referencing among these elements enables readers to follow a thread or story line and move purposefully from one element to another.

## Narrative

The narrative, the text of Chapters 2-5, is the glue that holds all these pieces together. As a problem is explored, relevant Planning Tools, Resources, Reform in Action accounts, and Data Tools are discussed and cross-referenced, with the icons illustrated below placed in the margins to serve as visual guides. Because the narrative is where the "story" starts, we recommend that readers begin with the chapter text and link to its tools and resources from there.

The narrative contains the following additional features:

▼ **On-time Resources:** These are short lists of resources that pertain to the topic being discussed. Most on-time resources are fully annotated in the Resources sections following the text.

▼ **Questions to Consider:** These are questions to stimulate further reflection and probing into a problem. They are marked with a question mark behind the text.

▼ **Warning Sign:** The stop sign in the margin indicates where teams might want to slow down and reflect in their inquiry process or heed a warning.

## Planning Tools: From Inquiry to Action

Following Chapters 3-5, Planning Tools are designed to help teams move from data collection to thoughtful planning and action. Planning Tools are also included in a form you can modify on the book's companion CD-ROM. When referenced in the narrative, they are marked in the margin with the Planning Tools icon. Planning Tools include:

▼ **Team Planning Questions:** These are prompts that teams can use to guide their planning. For each prompt, relevant Data Tools, Planning Tools, and Resources are noted.

▼ **Data Collection Plan Forms:** We consider these forms to be the core of the guidebook. They are designed to help guide your inquiry into the 12 powerful questions, listed in Figure 1.3, that are discussed in Chapters 3-5. Each form poses a question to investigate, such as "To what extent do some students (poor, minority, English language learners, girls, others) have less opportunity to learn mathematics and science than others?" and provides space for teams to consider what data they will collect and how. In addition, the form offers a menu of possible data sources, indicators, specific Data Tools in the guidebook, and, where relevant, disaggregation categories that can be used to inquire into that question. While the full-size forms can be found in the Planning Tools section that follows the chapter's narrative, you will find smaller versions illustrated in the text as each problem or question is discussed.

▼ Other aids to action planning, such as forms for writing goal statements, formulating problems, and planning for action systemically, are also included in these sections.

## Resources

Located at the end of Chapters 2-5 are fully annotated resources related to that chapter. When referenced within the chapter, they are marked with the Resources icon. In addition, an annotated list of mathematics and science curriculum materials is included on the accompanying CD-ROM.

## Reform in Action Accounts

Located in Chapter 6, these are actual stories of local school districts that are using data and getting results. The Reform in Action icon within chapters indicates where one of these examples illuminates what is being discussed in the narrative.

## Data Tools

Located as a separate section at the end of the guidebook and on the accompanying CD-ROM, Data Tools are provided for Chapters 2-5. Data Tools contain forms for disaggregating and analyzing data, survey instruments, interview and classroom observation protocols, checklists, and a variety of other instruments to help school teams collect and analyze data. When referenced in the narrative, they are marked with the Data Tools icon. They are also cross-referenced in the Team Planning Questions and on the Data Collection Plan forms.

# How to Use This Book (and Not Be Overwhelmed!)

We recognize that the sheer volume of material in *Using Data/Getting Results* can be overwhelming. Don't worry if you don't have the time or the inclination to read the book in its entirety. We do recommend that readers start with Chapters 1 and 2, which provide the foundation for understanding the process of collaborative inquiry. After that, the book can be used in a number of different ways, depending on your goals, immediate needs, and available time. Below we describe four possible scenarios for beginning to use the guidebook.

**Scenario 1: "We want to lay the foundation for effective use of data."**
Chapter 2 and the Glendale, Providence, and Pomperaug case studies from Chapter 6 provide a good starting point for teams that are just beginning to use data, for individual leaders who want to excite others about effective use of data, and for ongoing teams that wish to improve on their data use. These two chapters offer good background reading for group study and discussion and can help your team solidify a collaborative and inquiry-based approach to data use. Many teams we have worked with have used **Data Tools** such as the "Consensogram" (DT 2-3) and "Progress Toward Standards—A Self-Assessment" (DT 2-2) as a catalyst for reflection on their own data practices. The time frame for this scenario can be short—one or two half-day meetings—but the process can lead to more in-depth work.

**Scenario 2: "We're developing a data-driven action plan."** If your team is charged with developing an action or improvement plan based on student learning results, you can use the text and tools in Chapter 3 to guide you systematically through the process. This is for teams that are ready to devote considerable time—five to seven meetings over several months—to examining multiple measures of student learning data, carefully analyzing the possible causes for the results, and developing action plans. As you consider possible causes, this will naturally lead you into some of the issues in Chapters 4 and 5. Although time-consuming, this approach can help avoid some of the problems that result when teams jump to conclusions too quickly or rely on too few sources of data. Guidebook tools can help you streamline the planning process.

**Scenario 3: "We're thinking about equity or about curriculum, instruction, and assessment reform."** A third scenario is that your team is concerned about a specific dimension of reform, either equity or curriculum, instruction, and assessment. Perhaps you have analyzed disaggregated student achievement data and uncovered performance gaps between white children and African American and Latino children. You want to know where to go from here and are aware that equity issues can be very sensitive. In this case, Chapter 5 is a good starting point for reading and discussion. The section of Chapter 3 entitled "Assessing Opportunities to Learn" is also pertinent. This scenario could involve several study meetings before you actually choose a focus for further inquiry.

This same approach can be used for terms that want to broadly explore issues related to reforming curriculum, instruction, and assessment. Perhaps you are just beginning to implement a standards-based curriculum and want to think about how and what kind of data might be useful. You can start off by studying Chapter 4.

**Scenario 4: "We're ready to investigate a problem."** A fourth approach is to start with one of the 12 problems in the guidebook (summarized in Figure 1.3) that is most pressing for your team. For instance, if you are one or two years into implementing a standards-based curriculum and need to better understand if and how it is being used, you would choose question 6 from Figure 1.3 and begin with the pages listed there. The guidebook provides four different kinds of material to support you in investigating each question. First, the narrative in Chapters 3-5 discusses each question or problem, provides examples of how it manifests in schools, and offers suggestions about what kind of data can help schools better understand and improve in this area. Second, in the **Planning Tools** section for each of the three chapters is a Data Collection Plan form. As described above, these forms help users plan for data collection for each of the 12 problem areas by referencing data sources and **Data Tools**, a third aid to inquiry. Finally, Chapter 6, "Reform in Action," features short accounts of schools that have grappled with some of these

questions. By providing examples of actual questions and the tools to investigate them, the guidebook aims to help busy educators get started with the complex and oftenintimidating process of using data to support decision making. While it can takeseveral months to collect and analyze data related to any of these questions, the guidebook's "one-stop shopping" can save you many hours of work. Regardless of your entry point, we encourage you to follow your own path through the book as you make your way down the road to reform. It is our hope that with the ideas and tools provided in *Using Data/Getting Results* you will head down that road with a renewed sense of purpose, direction, and optimism.

**FIGURE 1.3: MATRIX FOR USING THE GUIDEBOOK TO INVESTIGATE 12 POWERFUL QUESTIONS ABOUT YOUR SCHOOL**

| Question | Narrative | Data Collection Plan Form | Reform in Action Vignette |
|----------|-----------|---------------------------|---------------------------|
| 1. What are our strengths and weaknesses in mathematics and science achievement? | pages 76–93 | pages 121–122 | Glendale (page 327) |
| 2. To what extent do performance gaps in mathematics and science exist among racial, class, cultural, or gender groups in our school? | pages 76–93 | pages 123–124 | Glendale (page 327), Providence (page 333) |
| 3. To what extent do some students (poor, minority, English language learners, girls, others) have less opportunity to learn mathematics and science than others? | pages 94–100 | pages 125–126 | Glendale (page 327), Providence (page 335) |
| 4. How do student aspirations impact on student success in mathematics and science? | pages 100–101 | pages 127–128 | |
| 5. How good is our written curriculum? | pages 161–166 | pages 219–220 | Hall-Dale (page 343); also see vignette, pages 159–160 |
| 6. To what extent is standards-based mathematics and science curriculum and instruction beingimplemented in our school/district? | pages 168–186 | pages 221–222 | Hudson (page 340); also see vignettes, pages 167–168 and 188–193 |
| 7. To what extent is standards-based assessment being implemented in our school/district? | pages 194–201 | pages 223–224 | Pomperaug (page 336); also see vignettes, pages 201–203 |

| Question | Narrative | Data Collection Plan Form | Reform in Action Vignette |
|---|---|---|---|
| 8. What is the impact of curriculum, instruction, and assessment reform on student learning outcomes, opportunities, and aspirations? | pages 203–212 | pages 225–226 | Glendale (page 327); also see vignettes, pages 201–203 and 212–214 |
| 9. To what extent do structural barriers result in some students (poor, minority, English language learners, girls, others) having less opportunity to learn mathematics and science than others? To what extent is tracking (de facto or intentional) practiced in our school? | pages 94–100 and 257–267 | pages 301–302 | Glendale (page 327), Providence (page 335) |
| 10. How prevalent are beliefs that block equity in our school? How do they manifest in school and classroom practices? How can individuals come to grips with their own prejudice and its effect on their lives? Who are our students? How can we better understand their cultural backgrounds? How can we learn to recognize students' strengths? | pages 268–280 | pages 303–304 | Glendale (page 327), Providence (page 335) |
| 11. To what extent do unequal expectations affect how we treat students? | pages 281–285 | pages 305–306 | Glendale (page 327), Providence (page 335) |
| 12. To what extent does racial, class cultural, or gender bias manifest in our curriculum, instruction, and assessment materials and practices? | pages 286–293 | pages 307–308 | |

**Framing the Question** 2

**Monitoring Results**

**Collec Dat**

# DATA AND INQUIRY:
# TURNING THE
# WHEELS OF REFORM

**Drawing Conclusions, Taking Action**

**Analy Da**

**Organizing Data-Driven Dialogue**

**2** **Our school just** received the students' results on the new state mathematics and science assessments. They were disappointing. What do they mean? How can we use these results to improve mathematics and science education? (Teacher, urban elementary school)

**We are members** of the mathematics curriculum committee that has been overseeing the implementation of a problem-based mathematics program for the last two years. Some teachers love it. Others complain that students are not getting the basics anymore. How can the committee make a fair assessment about the program's effectiveness? (Curriculum committee member, rural school district)

**We have been** appointed to a school-based team charged with taking a look at our mathematics and science programs and making recommendations for improvements. Where do we start? (Science teacher, suburban high school)

**Our middle school** team is debating whether or not to eliminate remedial mathematics and institute heterogeneous grouping in mathematics. How can we make the best decision for all students? (Mathematics teacher, urban middle school)

Each of the schools in the preceding examples is in a different place. But they have one thing in common: they each are ripe to use the process of collaborative inquiry to help them solve their problems. Mathematics and science teachers know this process well. It involves framing a question to investigate, collecting and analyzing data, drawing conclusions, and sharing results.

This chapter describes that same process scaled up from the classroom to the school and to the district. It is about putting collaborative inquiry to work to improve mathematics and science education. Your team will learn why inquiry is a powerful process, not just for students in classrooms but for school improvement in general and mathematics and science education reform in particular. You will explore the phases of inquiry, including organizing data-driven dialogue; common obstacles that schools and districts face in using inquiry and data; and strategies to overcome them. The processes and principles discussed here lay the foundation for the inquiry into virtually any aspect of systemic reform.

# The Inquiry Process: From the Classroom to the School

*"Knowledge is power."*

(Francis Bacon 1597)

Think about classrooms where students are engaged in authentic inquiry. Students begin by exploring a phenomenon or problem, thinking about their assumptions, and posing questions they want to investigate further. Then they set out systematically to answer their questions. They collect and analyze data and draw conclusions. As you watch students conduct the investigations, you can see prior assumptions fading and new and deeper understandings taking shape. The classroom is alive with excitement. Students love learning and feel responsible, invested, in charge.

*"What separates the schools that will be successful in their reform efforts from the ones that won't is the use of one, often neglected, essential element—data."*

(Bernhardt 1996, 1)

Now translate that image from the classroom to the whole school. Instead of students, it is teachers and administrators who are engaged in inquiry. They are not investigating scientific phenomena, but rather their school and how to improve it. Just as in the classroom, they begin by exploring a problem and posing questions, such as "Which students are doing poorly in mathematics or science? Why? What can we do to help them improve?" The "researchers" state their hypotheses, systematically collect data to confirm or refute them, and talk with colleagues about what the data mean. Based on what they learn, they rally around a decision and a course of action.

As the school staff take action, they continue their investigation, asking, "Is this working? Are we getting the results we hoped for? What do we need to do differently or better?" School-based inquiry is about continuously learning and using what is learned to continuously improve. Just as inquiry-based classrooms are energized and revitalized, so are inquiry-based schools. It's not that these schools don't face problems. They do. But they know how to work together to solve them—learning every step of the way.

## Data: The Heart of Inquiry

At the heart of the inquiry process is the use of data—the compelling evidence that grounds conclusions in actual results, not in speculation. Data can be either quantitative or qualitative. They are quantitative when they take numerical form and are collected using standardized instruments. Whether the data come from test scores, course enrollments, interviews, observations, or surveys, they are considered quantitative when they are analyzed and reported in this way. Data are qualitative when unstructured interviewing or observational techniques are used and analysis and reporting take the shape of narrative rather than numbers (Weiss 1998, 82–83). Whatever the type, data are the essential pieces of information needed to better understand and solve problems.

The kind of data that mathematics and science improvement teams will want to use depends on the problems they are investigating. Some examples are listed below. When and how your team might want to use these data are discussed throughout this guidebook.

If all this talk about data is making you nervous, you are not alone. For most schools, data are those annoying statistics they turn over to the state or federal government in a confusing tangle of reporting requirements. Or, worse than a nuisance, data are a club used against schools and teachers to show how bad they are or to compare them with others. When it comes to using data for the school's own purposes, to uncover and understand problems, target improvements, or monitor progress, schools are ill-equipped. They lack good data management systems along with the will, skill, time, and organizational structures to use data effectively.

So why fight this uphill battle? Why make the transformation from "data giver" to "data user"? Data offer a powerful tool for school change that educators can no longer afford to ignore. Without data,

> *"Data enable us to be educational detectives. We are 'Columbos.' We get clues as to how students are doing. We look at how to improve."*
>
> (Joe O'Reilly, Director of Research, Mesa Unified School District, Mesa, Arizona, interview, 1998)

### Examples of Useful Data

▼ Standardized test results

▼ State assessment results

▼ Performance assessment results

▼ Examples of student work

▼ Teacher surveys on classroom practice

▼ Teacher surveys on concerns and needs

▼ Surveys on student aspirations

▼ Records of use of science kits or manipulative materials

▼ Master schedules showing mathematics and science course offering

▼ Demographic breakouts of students taking algebra or geometry

▼ Interviews with teachers, administrators, students, parents

▼ Demographic breakouts of students participating in mathematics and science clubs

▼ Checklist of tracking practices

▼ Mathematics and science classroom observations

schools are blindsided, making decisions based on perceptions and opinions rather than the best possible information. Don't students, whose lives are profoundly affected by these decisions, deserve better?

## The Regional Alliance's Top 10 Ways to Use Data as a Lever for Change

1. **Data can uncover problems that might otherwise remain invisible.** When data are disaggregated (separated) by student groups, they can be especially helpful. For example, the Providence (Rhode Island) Public Schools took a close look at what mathematics courses they were offering and which students were taking them. When they disaggregated the data by racial groups, they realized that the majority of minority students did not have access to the "gatekeeper" courses of algebra and geometry. The problem suddenly hit them right between the eyes, and they realized they could do something about it. (See **Reform in Action,** page 335.)

2. **Data can convince people of the need for change.** Compelling data can stop people in their tracks, break through denial, and motivate change. For example, teachers at an elementary school in California decided to visit the middle and high schools in their district to see how their former students were faring. When they learned that most of their English language learners were forever tracked in special or bilingual education programs, they were motivated to double the amount of time they spent teaching English and to monitor student progress (Bernhardt 1998, 4). In cases like this, data, especially about one's own students, can act as wake-up call, alerting people that "it *is* broke and *does* need to be fixed!" Sometimes, powerful national and international data, such as the results of the Third International Mathematics and Science Study (TIMSS) can have a similar effect. (See **Resources**, page 70).

3. **Data can confirm or discredit assumptions about students and school practices.** Many school practices are based on false premises. Data can help people reexamine their beliefs and change their practices. For example, Glendale (Arizona) Union High School District, like many across the country, offered low-achieving students an array of remedial mathematics courses because they assumed these students would fail in more challenging courses. One high school in the district decided to test that assumption. They eliminated remedial mathematics and enrolled "low-track" students in a challenging algebra course while providing them with additional support. Not only did these students

*"Data keep the conversation focused on instruction. Wilted lettuce is not what we talk about."*

(Sid Bailey, Principal, Washington High School, Glendale, Arizona, interview, 1998)

avoid failure, but they performed better than they had in remedial mathematics. The data convinced the district to eliminate tracking thoroughly and permanently. (See **Reform in Action**, page 327.)

4. **Data can get to the root cause of problems, pinpoint areas where change is most needed, and guide resource allocation.** For years, teachers and administrators at a school district in northern California watched 95 percent of their graduates drop out of college. They assumed that the problem was the students' lack of social skills and undertook a school reform effort to develop these skills. Only after teachers conducted a survey of graduates did they learn the real cause: students' poor writing skills. This information prevented them from spending thousands of dollars solving the wrong problem (Bernhardt 1998, 2).

5. **Data can help schools evaluate program effectiveness and keep the focus on student learning results.** Under constant pressure from inside and out, schools are prone to jump on the newest bandwagon without being clear why they are doing a program and what results they hope to achieve. Before things settle down, the program is gone and another one is under way, and no one knows if students actually benefited. But if schools have effective ways of tracking student learning, they can take action with the goal of improving specific learning outcomes, monitor results, and evaluate programs. And they don't have to rely on outside evaluators. The Hudson (Massachusetts) Public Schools are taking this approach as they implement their new elementary mathematics program. They piloted the program in a few classrooms. Then by tracking student achievement and surveying teachers, they decided to expand the program based on positive results. (See **Reform in Action**, page 340.)

*"Effective use of data helps schools develop site-based capacity to evaluate the effects of policies, programs, and practices on student performance. They don't have to rely on outside evaluators to answer these questions."*

(Martha Williams, Vice President, CRM, Inc., South Hampton, New Hampshire, interview, 1998)

6. **Data can provide the feedback teachers and administrators need to keep going and stay on course.** One surefire recipe for burnout is being in the dark about the consequences of your actions. Data about results can energize and empower staff. For example, fourth-grade teachers at Holaway Elementary School in Tucson, Arizona, use a rubric to test their students' mathematics problem-solving skills four times a year. When scores go up, they celebrate and continue doing what is working. When scores go down, they brainstorm new strategies.

7. **Data can prevent overreliance on standardized test scores.** Standardized test scores are often the only data schools pay much attention to. But they provide only one view of a school's success or

failure. Without other good data—performance assessments, disaggregated results, mathematics/science enrollment figures, or information about classroom practice—schools can be baffled by standardized test score fluctuations, devastated by poor results, or lured into a false sense of security with high scores.

8.  **Data can prevent one-size-fits-all and quick-fix solutions.** In a rush to "do" something, schools may latch onto popular or simplistic solutions to resolve complex problems. Data help school staff dig deeper, consider the local context, and more fully understand a problem before jumping into action. The solution is more likely to be on target for the particular situation. For example, buying hands-on science kits for elementary teachers may not be the answer to improving science instruction. While good materials are necessary, they won't help if teachers don't feel comfortable with the science content or classroom inquiry. In this case, understanding and addressing teachers' professional development needs will do more to improve instruction than an infusion of materials.

9.  **Data can give schools the ability to respond to accountability questions.** More and more, schools are under fire to produce results and be accountable to organizations that provide them with grants and to the community at large. The standards movement has upped the ante. As schools commit themselves to high levels of learning for all students, they need effective ways to assess and communicate about student learning; in other words, they need data. Good examples of data for this purpose are the school reports being used in Vermont. They provide the community with data about school performance, including results on SATs, Advanced Placement Tests, and Vermont's New Standards Assessments. (For further information, access http://crs.uvm.edu.)

10. **Data can help build a culture of inquiry and continuous improvement.** Data don't change schools, people do—people who are committed to working together and doing whatever it takes to improve learning. But they need to be armed with good data if they are going to uncover and understand problems, test the best solutions, and learn as they go. Data use and inquiry are inseparable companions on the road to reform and hallmarks of the most successful schools.

*"From a teacher's perspective, we get excellent diagnostic information on individual students. I can look at how each student performed on each outcome so I can focus improvement on each individual student."*

(Teacher, Holaway Elementary School, Tucson, Arizona, interview, 1998)

## Handle Data with Care

While data can be a positive force for school change, they must be handled with care. Data are like fire. They have the power to illuminate and be put to many good uses. But people can and have gotten burned when data are used carelessly. Michael Schmoker offers the following suggestions to reduce the threat of misusing data.

## The Spirit of Inquiry

Data are at the heart of the inquiry process, but inquiry also has a spirit—a set of dispositions that give it life. Just as in successful inquiry-based classrooms, schools that foster genuine inquiry into student learning nurture and support these habits of mind:

### Safety Regulations for Using Data

▼ Do not use data primarily to identify or eliminate poor teachers.

▼ Do not introduce high stakes prematurely, for example, performance assessments as graduation requirements.

▼ Inundate practitioners with success stories that include data.

▼ Try to collect and analyze data collaboratively and anonymously by team, department, grade level, or school.

▼ Be cautious in implementing pay-for-performance schemes, especially in the beginning.

▼ Allow teachers, by school or team, as much autonomy as possible in selecting the kind of data they think will be most helpful.

---

▼ **A desire to continuously improve.** No matter where we are, we know we can get better.

▼ **Collaboration and discourse.** We need to work together, build broad support, listen to and learn from diverse perspectives.

▼ **Skepticism.** We are open to calling into question assumptions that have guided our actions if they don't stand up to the test of inquiry.

▼ **A hunger for knowledge.** We are never done learning. Learning is what keeps our organization alive.

▼ **A willingness to make mistakes.** We can only learn from taking risks and making mistakes. Risk taking should be rewarded.

▼ **Focus.** We never lose sight of student learning. No inquiry, no action is worth pursuing if it does not directly affect student learning.

▼ **Use of data.** Whenever possible, we will base decisions on compelling evidence, not on assumptions.(See also the National Center for Improving Science Education 1989, 18–19.)

# The Phases of Inquiry

Inquiry has a heart (data) and a spirit (a set of dispositions). It also has a method or sequence of steps. In this section, we describe six phases of the collaborative inquiry process and some general principles that pertain to each: framing a question or problem; collecting data; analyzing data; organizing data-driven dialogue; drawing conclusions and taking action; and monitoring results. Although we describe these steps in a linear fashion, the process of inquiry is often messy and recursive. It can start with taking action and cycle back to framing a question or problem. Or, in the throes of data collection, your team may decide it needs to reframe the problem. Wherever you start, you can expect the inquiry process to be continuous because new problems inevitably emerge on the road to reform.

**Framing the Question**

**Collecting Data**

**Phases of Collaborative Inquiry**

**Monitoring Results**

**Analyzing Data**

**Drawing Conclusions, Taking Action**

**Organizing Data-Driven Dialogue**

The phases of collaborative inquiry described below are generic, that is, they can be applied to inquiry into virtually anything, including any of the dimensions of reform discussed in this guidebook. In Chapters 1 and 3, we offer an expanded and adapted version of this cycle, tailored to the process of planning for improved student learning.

*"Be patient toward all that is unsolved in your heart and try to love the questions themselves."*

(Rainer Maria Rilke)

*The root word for question is "quest."*

## Framing the Question

Just as in scientific inquiry, school-based inquiry most often begins with a question, a problem, or a hypothesis. The first challenge improvement teams face is finding and framing that question or problem, "What do we need to know more about?" Joan L. Herman and Lynn Winters suggest in their book *Tracking Your School's Success: A Guide to Sensible Evaluation* (1992) two different approaches to framing a question: "wide angle" or "close-up."

Wide angle is for teams that want to start by looking at the big picture. They are wondering, "What is the quality of our mathematics and science program as a whole? What are its strengths and weaknesses? What are the biggest obstacles to all students achieving at high levels? Where are our priorities for improvement?" They are, in effect, looking for a needs assessment.

This guidebook offers a variety of tools for teams that want to look at their mathematics and science program as a whole. We suggest that teams begin by taking a comprehensive look at student learning, using the processes and tools described in Chapter 3. In addition, the **Data Tools** section of this

chapter includes two tools for self-assessing your overall mathematics and science programs. "A District Self-Assessment Guide for Improving Mathematics Teaching and Learning" from the U.S. Department of Education (DT 2-1) helps you rate curriculum, instruction, and assessment, professional development, and public engagement and identify areas of need. The other, "Progress Toward Standards—A Self-Assessment" (DT 2-2), uses stages for gauging your progress toward standards-led reform. Either of these tools can be a catalyst for "wide-angle" inquiry, especially if you gather evidence to document your areas of need.

Other teams are ready to take a close-up view and are less interested in the big picture. They have already identified a problem and are taking action to improve a particular outcome or practice. Now they want to know what the effect has been. They are asking evaluation questions such as "Is the change actually happening? What needs to happen to foster that change? Is the change having the intended effect on students and teachers? Are we reaching our goals?"

This guidebook frames 12 different questions that schools may choose to inquire into related to student learning, curriculum, instruction, assessment, and equity, along with possible indicators, data sources, and tools to aid your inquiry. We offer these as examples of important questions rather than as a comprehensive list or a prescription for your school or district. It is, of course, the real and pressing questions that are unique to your school or district that bring the inquiry process to life.

Regardless of the kind of question(s) your team may ask, you will need to choose a clear focus for your inquiries before starting to collect data. If the question is too vague, too complex, or too big, teams will surely get bogged down and discouraged. For example, "What is required to improve student achievement in mathematics and science?" is too broad a question. Equally important, teams need to home in on important questions—ones that relate closely to goals, affect student learning, and motivate people to take action. See the "Decision-Making Matrix for Choosing a Problem" in **Planning Tools**, page 129, for help in choosing a learner-centered problem.

## Collecting Data

Once your team has framed a question, the next step is to figure out how to answer it. Just as the punishment should fit the crime, the evidence or data should fit the question. Nobody has time to collect and analyze data that, in the end, won't be helpful. So consider carefully what kind of data

## FIGURE 2.1: SELECTING EVALUATION INSTRUMENTS

|  | Advantages | Limitations |
|---|---|---|
| **Questionnaires** | • Can probe several aspects of the program on one measure<br>• Can get candid, anonymous comments and suggestions if space provided for comments<br>• Questions are standardized for all respondents<br>• Questions can be made selected response for quick, machine scoring<br>• Gives respondents time to think | • Not as flexible as interviews<br>• People often express themselves better orally than in writing<br>• Responding is tedious and people forget to return questionnaires<br>• People may give "socially desirable" responses<br>• Requires literacy<br>• Depth of information sometimes sacrificed for breadth |
| **Interviews** | • Can do by phone at respondents' convenience<br>• Allows people who can't read or write to answer<br>• Can be conducted in respondents' native language<br>• Flexible; can pursue unanticipated lines of query<br>• Depth; can probe responses<br>• Persistence can yield high return rates | • Time-consuming, thus costly<br>• Possible for interviewer to (consciously or unconsciously) influence responses<br>• People may give "socially desirable" responses |
| **Observations** | • Can use required observations (such as teacher evaluation) for other purposes<br>• Observers can see what teachers or others actually do, not what they say they do | • Time needed to develop observation procedure, train observers, and conduct interviews<br>• Presence of observers may influence classroom behavior<br>• Scheduling problems<br>• Costly |
| **Performance Tests**<br>**Essays**<br>**Demonstrations**<br>**Projects**<br>**Performances** | • Provide actual sample of student work<br>• Can provide diagnostic information about student performance and about instruction<br>• Available for all subjects (unlike standardized tests)<br>• Credible method for assessing complex skills and processes<br>• Contextualized and relevant to real-life situations | • Criteria for judging needs to reflect subject matter standards yet be understandable and usable by all<br>• Need many samples to draw conclusions about one individual; classroom/school inferences require fewer samples<br>• Scoring process is time-consuming<br>• Finding scorers may be difficult given the time commitment to training and scoring<br>• Costly if you pay scorers or use release time |
| **Portfolios** | • Provide a broader range of student work than one sample<br>• Can be used for many purposes<br>• Provide students opportunities to observe own growth and reflect on work<br>• Encourage integration of instruction and assessment | • What constitutes a portfolio must be defined<br>• Methods for scoring and interpreting must be developed<br>• Costly to score |
| **Archival Information**<br>**Past test scores**<br>**Attendance**<br>**Discipline**<br>**Teacher records** | • Records already exist<br>• No administrative or development costs | • Gathering information takes clerical time<br>• May be incomplete, inconsistent<br>• May not have exactly the information you need |
| **Published Achievement and Attitude Measures** | • No development costs<br>• Information available about validity and reliability<br>• Most are quickly scored<br>• Clear methods for interpreting results<br>• Inexpensive to score | • May not match local goals<br>• Item formats often don't match real-life tasks<br>• Provides little diagnostic information |

writing or familiarity with the dominant culture as well? Or is a standardized test measuring students' achievement or their ability to deal with stress or take tests? Or are the survey questions so easily misconstrued that they actually tell you very little about what you thought you were asking? To avoid these validity problems, we recommend using professionally developed instruments that have been well tested, including many of the surveys and protocols in Data Tools.

Finally, you will need to take care that you are drawing valid conclusions from the data you have available. One important consideration is how representative the data are of what you want to measure. For example, TIMSS video researchers wanted to draw some conclusions about the quality of typical eighth-grade mathematics lessons in three countries. They realized that the presence of the video camera in the classroom might alter the lesson and result in unrepresentative data. They were careful to incorporate elements into the design to minimize this problem, giving them greater confidence in their conclusions (U.S. Department of Education 1999, 36). For more on drawing valid conclusions from data, see "Avoiding the Wrong Conclusions" in Chapter 4.

Reliability is another test of how trustworthy your data are. Reliability means that the instrument could be administered again and again and produce the same result. You will want to check for reliability in three different ways, depending on the type of measure. One check is for test-retest reliability, which means that you can give the same people the same or similar test or instrument at different times and still get the same result. A second check is for internal consistency, meaning that people respond similarly to items within a test or survey that measure the same thing. For example, if several items on a survey measure students' self-esteem, you would expect that an individual who rated one of these items high would rate other similar items high as well. Finally, check for inter-rater reliability: different raters should judge the same work in the same way. Inter-rater reliability is especially relevant when observing classrooms or scoring performance assessment tasks (Light, Singer, and Willett 1990, 166). While you most likely will not be conducting all of these tests for reliability yourselves, you will want to make sure that you use instruments that have been tested for reliability and that your raters or scorers have been thoroughly trained.

Even though you want the best quality data possible, data collection must be feasible; practical considerations like time and money weigh in heavily. Here are some suggestions to lighten the load. First, make use of what data you already have or what can be easily collected. For example, Mesa (Arizona) Public Schools were already tracking which science kits went in and out of their resource center. From there, they could easily advance to the next step—analysis of these data to learn more about how teachers were using the kits and to plan professional development.

If you don't already have the data available, consider whether you want to make or buy other instruments and assessments. Since many inexpensive and even free survey instruments are now available in mathematics and science (some are in this guidebook), buying or even borrowing may be a real option.

Finally, some informal methods like "one-legged" interviews (interviews that last as long as you can stand on one leg) and group surveys, can yield information as rich and timely as expensive surveys would. The Consensogram, a tool we learned from educational consultants Laura Lipton and Bruce Wellman, is one such method. Consensograms are an easy and fast way to get a sense of a group, create a vivid display of the data, and engage the group in dialogue about their data. First, participants fill out a questionnaire with a small number of questions that can be rated on a scale. A sample we created for science education reform is illustrated in Figure 2.2. Questions can pertain to the group's perceptions, commitment, beliefs, interests, knowledge, or skill level. By placing self-stick notes, color-coded by question, in the appropriate column on a large wall chart, the group efficiently generates a colorful graph of its own data, which they can then analyze together. (See **Data Tools**, DT 2-3, for the full directions for the Consensogram.)

---

**Figure 2.2: Consensogram Questionnaire**

Please respond on a scale from 0 to 100 in increments of 10.

1. To what degree do you understand inquiry-based science teaching and learning?

   0   10   20   30   40   50   60   70   80   90   100

2. Where on the scale would you rate your own skills in facilitating inquiry in the classroom?

   0   10   20   30   40   50   60   70   80   90   100

3. To what degree are you implementing an inquiry-based approach in your classroom?

   0   10   20   30   40   50   60   70   80   90   100

4. To what extent are you getting the support, professional development, and resources you need to effectively implement inquiry-based teaching and learning in your classroom?

   0   10   20   30   40   50   60   70   80   90   100

---

## Triangulate, Triangulate, Triangulate

Another important principle in data collection is triangulation. Triangulation means using three independent sources of data about the same issue or problem. Why bother with the extra work of triangulating? Richard Sagor offers the analogy of a third-grade science lesson on observing a terrarium:

The teacher asks Mary to look through the front panel of the classroom terrarium and list or draw everything she sees. Mary, being a diligent student, writes up a thorough list. She's just about to go back to her seat when the teacher asks her to take a look through the side panel of the terrarium. Mary does, and immediately sees several plants and animals that had been obscured from view in the front panel by rocks and shrubs. By using this second "window" on the phenomenon (the terrarium), Mary now has a more complete picture.

Although Mary feels that her work is now done, the teacher makes one last request. She asks Mary to peer through the top of the terrarium to see if there is anything else she has missed. Mary adds to her list and then sits down. Although Mary may still have failed to observe something of importance, her three windows reveal a far more comprehensive picture than any one window alone could have. (1992, 43–44)

The notion of multiple windows or perspectives applies just as well to understanding what is happening with student achievement or classroom practice. In Chapter 3, we describe several windows into understanding student learning in mathematics and science, including standardized tests, performance assessments, and student work, any one of which alone may provide too narrow a view. Similarly, if you want to understand the extent to which data collection and analysis is being practiced in the mathematics classroom, you may gain one perspective from teacher surveys. What students say may offer a different perspective, either supporting or contradicting teachers' views. And classroom observations yield still richer descriptions of how students are working with data. The form "Additional Sources of Data" in **Data Tools**, DT 2-4, and discussed on page 46, prompts you to test out possible explanations before taking action.

According to Sagor, triangulation has the following benefits: it compensates for the imperfections of data-gathering instruments; when multiple measures yield the same results, it can increase confidence in the results; and, when multiple measures fail to yield the same results, it can raise important follow-up questions.

## Disaggregate, Disaggregate, Disaggregate

If you want to tap one of the most powerful uses of data, disaggregate! Disaggregation means looking at how specific subgroups of students perform rather than lumping all students together. Typically, student achievement data come "aggregated," reported for the population as a whole. Disaggregating can bring to light critical problems and issues that might otherwise remain invisible.

For example, your district's eighth-grade mathematics test scores may have improved over previous years. But by disaggregating those data, you may discern that boys' scores improved while girls' scores went down, pointing to the need to provide special encouragement to girls at this critical age. Or science club participation may be on the increase as a whole. That appears to be good news until you look more closely and see that African American students aren't signing up.

In the hypothetical example in Table 2.1, you can see how aggregated data paint a rosy picture of freshman enrollment in algebra. The number of students taking algebra has almost doubled over a three-year period.

*"Disaggregation is a practical, hands-on process that allows a school's faculty to answer the two critical questions: 'Effective at what? Effective for whom?' It is not a problem-solving but a problem-finding process."*

(Lezotte and Jacoby 1992, 114)

**TABLE 2.1: NUMBER & PERCENTAGE OF FRESHMEN ENROLLED IN ALGEBRA**

| School Year | Number of Freshmen in Algebra | Total Number of Freshmen | Percentage of Freshmen in Algebra |
|---|---|---|---|
| 1994-95 | 27 | 303 | 8.9% |
| 1995-96 | 48 | 318 | 15.1% |
| 1996-97 | 58 | 322 | 18.0% |

But when the data are disaggregated by gender (see Table 2.2), we see the gap between boys and girls taking algebra is getting wider—not so rosy a picture.

**TABLE 2.2: FRESHMAN ENROLLMENT IN ALGEBRA BY GENDER**

| School Year | Number of Freshman Boys in Algebra | Number of Freshman Boys | Percentage of Freshman Boys in Algebra | Number of Freshman Girls in Algebra | Number of Freshman Girls | Percentage of Freshman Girls in Algebra |
|---|---|---|---|---|---|---|
| 1994-95 | 20 | 140 | 19.4% | 7 | 163 | 4.3% |
| 1995-96 | 41 | 140 | 29.0% | 6 | 171 | 3.5% |
| 1996-97 | 52 | 147 | 35.0% | 6 | 175 | 3.4% |

Here are some questions that disaggregated data can help answer:

▼ Is there an achievement gap in mathematics and science among different groups? Is it getting bigger or smaller?

▼ Are minority or female students enrolling in higher-level mathematics and science courses at the same rate as other students?

▼ Are poor or minority students overrepresented in special education or underrepresented in gifted and talented programs?

▼ Are students at certain grade levels doing better in mathematics and science than students at other grade levels?

▼ Is transience a factor in mathematics and science achievement?

▼ Are all students getting access to top-quality mathematics and science instruction, or do some student groups have less of an opportunity to learn?

▼ Are students whose teachers participate in ongoing professional development in mathematics or science doing better than students whose teachers do not?

▼ Are the improvements we are making in our mathematics and science program improving the performance of students in the lowest quartile?

▼ Does English proficiency affect student achievement in mathematics or science? If so, what does this tell us about our bilingual program?

To answer these or other questions your team may have, give careful consideration to what disaggregated data you already have available and what additional data you need. As you develop your data collection plan, keep in mind that a wide variety of data—from performance on standardized, state, or local performance assessments, to enrollment in mathematics and science courses, to participation in special programs, to survey results—can be disaggregated. See the **Data Tools** for Chapter 3 for examples of forms you can use to disaggregate these and other data. Figure 2.3 illustrates one of these, a sample form for disaggregating norm-referenced mathematics achievement results.

FIGURE 2.3

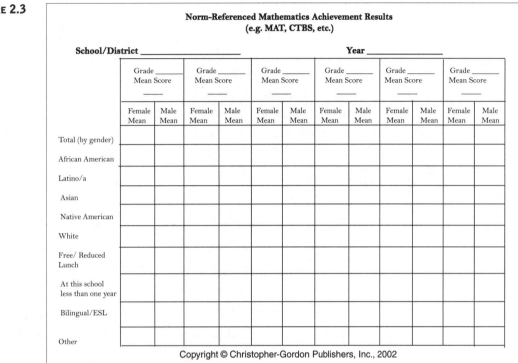

**Norm-Referenced Mathematics Achievement Results**
**(e.g. MAT, CTBS, etc.)**

School/District _____              Year _____

| | Grade _____ Mean Score ____ | | Grade _____ Mean Score ____ | | Grade _____ Mean Score ____ | | Grade _____ Mean Score ____ | | Grade _____ Mean Score ____ | | Grade _____ Mean Score ____ | |
|---|---|---|---|---|---|---|---|---|---|---|---|---|
| | Female Mean | Male Mean | Female Mean | Male Mean | Female Mean | Male Mean | Female Mean | Male Mean | Female Mean | Male Mean | Female Mean | Male Mean |
| Total (by gender) | | | | | | | | | | | | |
| African American | | | | | | | | | | | | |
| Latino/a | | | | | | | | | | | | |
| Asian | | | | | | | | | | | | |
| Native American | | | | | | | | | | | | |
| White | | | | | | | | | | | | |
| Free/ Reduced Lunch | | | | | | | | | | | | |
| At this school less than one year | | | | | | | | | | | | |
| Bilingual/ESL | | | | | | | | | | | | |
| Other | | | | | | | | | | | | |

There are many ways to disaggregate data. Each school and district needs to think about what variables are most important to them. The box to the right lists some options to consider.

Often, you may need to disaggregate data even further within certain groups. For example, a middle school in Boston took a closer look at how bilingual students were faring and discovered an alarming trend: Puerto Rican students who were born in this country were not doing as well as recent arrivals. The teachers quickly realized that a single approach for all of these students was not working and that special attention to the literacy needs of U.S.-born Puerto Rican students was required. In this case, teachers needed to further unbundle the category "Puerto Rican" to surface the problem.

## Possible Ways to Disaggregate Data

▼ Schools within a district

▼ Grade level

▼ Proficiency in English

▼ Length of time in the district

▼ Race

▼ Gender

▼ Quartiles

▼ Socioeconomic status using indicators such as students receiving free or reduced lunch or mother's level of education

▼ Course-taking experience

▼ Amount or type of training the teacher has received

▼ Participation in programs such as special education, bilingual, or Title I

Similarly, lumping together other racial and ethnic groups can cover up important differences within those groups (Johnson 1996, 27). The Asian community is tremendously diverse, spanning students from many different countries and cultural and economic backgrounds. So too is the black population, in which important differences in school performance often emerge among African Americans, West Indians, and African-born students (Ogbu and Matute-Bianchi 1990). Disaggregating data both among and within student groups is an important way to better understand and serve the needs of diverse students.

Here are some tips to help you get started with disaggregating test data:

▼ Make sure you have a thorough understanding of your school's demographics so you can choose the most relevant variables.

▼ Ask for standardized and state test data to be disaggregated as available and relevant to your student population.

▼ Explore technology tools that will help you collect, analyze, and report disaggregated data more easily.

▼ Remember to ask students for relevant demographic data as you collect other data about student learning.

▼ Select the most important variables, but don't choose too many; otherwise you may be overwhelmed with data.

▼ Pay attention to who actually takes tests. Sadly, schools have been known to exclude certain student groups from taking tests in order to raise test scores.

▼ Get your hands dirty—dive into the data—but get help from experts in your research department, if you have one, or from professionals at the testing companies.

## Develop a Data Collection Plan

Once your team has reviewed the options for data collection, weighed the important considerations of validity, reliability, feasibility, and triangulation, and decided on which data to disaggregate and how, you are ready to create a plan for data collection. You will need to include a statement of the problem or question, the sources of data, how the data will be collected, and who will be responsible for each task. Different team members may take responsibility for different parts of the plan, but one team member needs to be in charge of the overall plan. The basic form included here can help you develop a data collection plan.

Throughout the rest of this guidebook, we provide specific data collection forms for investigating 12 questions related to mathematics and science education reform. These are included in the **Planning Tools** for Chapters 3–5.

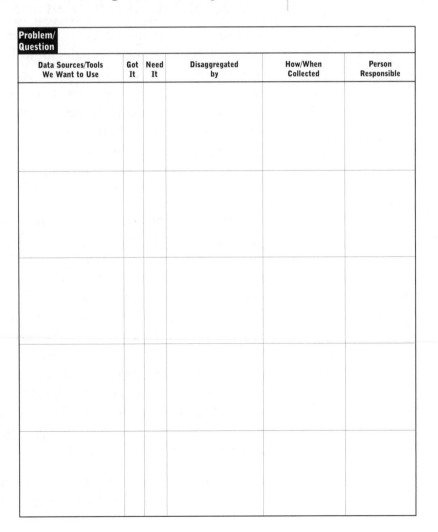

| Problem/Question | | | | | | |
|---|---|---|---|---|---|
| **Data Sources/Tools We Want to Use** | **Got It** | **Need It** | **Disaggregated by** | **How/When Collected** | **Person Responsible** |
| | | | | | |
| | | | | | |
| | | | | | |
| | | | | | |
| | | | | | |

## Analyzing the Data

*"Information is power, but only if it is understood and accepted."*

(Johnson 1996, 31)

Test scores, survey results, observation records—what do they all mean? Once the data are collected, you have to make sense of them all. Analyzing data is no more mysterious than that—a process of sense making. It involves looking for trends, plausible explanations, clusters of information that fit together, meanings, and implications for action. The tools of the trade can be as simple as colored markers or bins of sorted information or as complex as the software programs that researchers use. While you don't need to be a formally trained researcher to analyze data, you will need some skills, frameworks, and tools to guide you, many of which can be found in this book. Also valuable are the perspective and knowledge that those close to the situation, such as classroom teachers, parents, or students, can bring to data analysis.

## Organizing Data-Driven Dialogue

Just as in scientific inquiry, discourse is a vital part of the learning process. Data can provide rich opportunities for dialogue, sense making, and learning. Too often, however, these opportunities are short-circuited in schools and other organizations, where the temptation is great to use data to justify prior assumptions and jump to premature explanations and decisions. This rush to "data-driven decision making" is problematic for at least two reasons. One, it can result in poor decisions. And two, it often leaves teachers and other key constituents out of the loop as they are encouraged to "buy into" a solution before they even understand or agree on what the problem is.

To avoid this unhappy outcome, it is important for the team to structure opportunities for key constituencies—staff, parents, school boards, students—to engage with and make sense of the data through what educational consultants Laura Lipton and Bruce Wellman call "data-driven dialogue." Dialogue, a process where groups create shared meaning through respectful sharing and listening, is an important precursor to decision making. Lipton and Wellman encourage groups to "hang out in uncertainty," allowing adequate time to explore assumptions, predictions, questions, and observations before offering explanations or solutions. In doing so, groups not only reach sounder conclusions but also build their capacity to inquire and learn together. Their three-phase process for organizing data-driven dialogue, illustrated in Figure 2.4, suggests questions groups might explore in three distinct phases of engaging with data.

Ideally, in the "activating and engaging" phase, groups have not even seen the data yet. This is the time for participants to activate prior knowledge, surface assumptions, and make predictions to create the readiness to talk about the data. For example, if the group is about to see student learning data, they may surface their criticisms of the test itself or their skepticism about data in general. Just as in an inquiry-based classroom, it is important that all assumptions and predictions are honored and heard, as they are the building blocks for new learning.

In phase 2, "exploring and discovering," participants engage with the actual data. Lipton and Wellman recommend that groups work with one or two significant pieces of data that are clearly and vibrantly displayed rather than with pages and pages of tables that are difficult to read. Large wall displays of data can be very effective in focusing the whole group's attention. They also have the advantage of physically separating the data from the people discussing them, which can reduce defensiveness and keep the conversation on "that data" rather than "us teachers." Phase 2 questions encourage exploration of observations and trends. The word "because" is off-limits.

In phase 3, "organizing and integrating," groups begin to generate possible explanations for the results. This is a good time to use some of the tools in Chapter 3 (see "Formulating a Learner-Centered Problem") for analyzing root causes or a range of factors that might influence outcomes. Once possible explanations are generated, it is often necessary for groups to collect more data to validate them.

For example, say the school staff has looked at a variety of mathematics performance data over time. They observe that many high- and mid-range-achieving students have improved their performance since the implementation of the new curriculum, but low achievers have not improved at all. They suspect this group includes many Title I and English language learners who have been pulled out of the regular classroom and are not studying the same curriculum as other students. This is a hypothesis that will require additional data to test out, such as who are the students who have not

**FIGURE 2.4: ORGANIZING DATA-DRIVEN DIALOGUE**

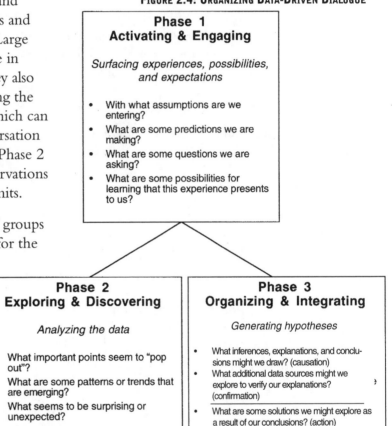

**Phase 1
Activating & Engaging**

*Surfacing experiences, possibilities, and expectations*

- With what assumptions are we entering?
- What are some predictions we are making?
- What are some questions we are asking?
- What are some possibilities for learning that this experience presents to us?

**Phase 2
Exploring & Discovering**

*Analyzing the data*

- What important points seem to "pop out"?
- What are some patterns or trends that are emerging?
- What seems to be surprising or unexpected?
- What are some things we have not yet explored?

**Phase 3
Organizing & Integrating**

*Generating hypotheses*

- What inferences, explanations, and conclusions might we draw? (causation)
- What additional data sources might we explore to verify our explanations? (confirmation)

- What are some solutions we might explore as a result of our conclusions? (action)
- what data will we need to collect to guide implementation? (Calibration)

improved and what mathematics curriculum are they being taught. The form "Additional Sources of Data," in **Data Tools**, DT 2-4, and illustrated here, can help you think about where to take your inquiry next. Only after multiple perspectives about data have been explored and possible explanations generated and verified is the group ready to consider solutions and ways to calibrate implementation, the second part of the "organizing and integrating" phase.

The three-phase process for organizing data-driven dialogue can be a very useful way to structure constructive conversations. But it is also important that group leaders develop skills in managing, modeling, mediating, and monitoring effective group process and that groups develop strong collaborative norms (Lipton and Wellman, workshop, 1998). Norms, such as those listed below, create a context for effective group learning.

---

**Additional Sources of Data**

———————————

Data Source 1

**Possible Explanation**

———————————                    ———————————

Data Source 2                          Data Source 3

## Seven Norms of Collaborative Work

**Pausing:** Pausing before responding or asking a question allows time for thinking and enhances dialogue, discussion and decision-making.

**Paraphrasing:** Using a paraphrase starter that is comfortable for you: "So..." or "As you are..." or "You're thinking...." and following the starter with a paraphrase assists members of the group to hear and understand each other as they formulate decisions.

**Probing:** Using gentle open-ended probes or inquiries such as "Please say more..." or "I'm curious about..." or "I'd like to hear more about..." or "Then, are you saying...?" increases the clarity and precision of the group's thinking.

**Putting ideas on the table:** Ideas are the heart of a meaningful dialogue. Label the intention of your comments. For example, you might say, "Here is one idea..." or "One thought I have is..." or "Here is a possible approach...."

**Paying attention to self and others:** Meaningful dialogue is facilitated when each group member is conscious of self and of others and is aware of not only what she/he is saying but how it is said and how others are responding. This includes paying attention to learning styles when planning for, facilitating, and participating in group meetings. Responding to others in their own language forms is one manifestation of this norm.

**Presuming positive presuppositions:** Assuming that others' intentions are positive promotes and facilitates meaningful dialogue and eliminates unintentional put-downs. Using positive presuppositions in your speech is one manifestation of this norm.

**Pursuing a balance between advocacy and inquiry:** Pursuing and maintaining a balance between advocating a position and inquiring about one's own and others' positions assists the group to become a learning organization.

## Having the Tough Conversations

The phases of data-driven dialogue, collaborative groups norms, and skilled facilitation are all preventive medicine—creating the best possible context for what are often difficult conversations. Bad news can cause defensiveness, denial, and finger pointing, especially when racial, ethnic, or gender disparities are exposed. Depending on people's beliefs, interpretations of the data can vary widely, from blaming "those kids" to proclaiming that "mediocre is good enough" to constructively questioning the quality of teaching.

Sharp differences can also arise around the impact of a new program. Often several years must be spent carefully supporting implementation before achievement gains are realized. Moreover, to be a fair measure, assessments have to match what is being taught. Supporters of the program understand this; adversaries, on the other hand, can use the lack of early results as an excuse to drop a program before it has been fully implemented.

Defensiveness and conflict are not the only pitfalls. Many school staff don't trust data or they fear reprisals. While the specifics of each circumstance need to be considered, here are some general suggestions for having the tough conversations:

▼ Remember the safety rules for data use (see "Safety Regulations for Using Data," page 31). If you can't provide a safe environment for the staff, don't play with data "fire."

▼ Make sure the data are as accurate as possible. Any mistake can discredit the whole process.

▼ Keep the focus on improvement, not on blame. Set ground rules for the discussions that make finger pointing off-limits, and enforce them!

▼ Use brief, simple, and graphic reports of data.

▼ Balance bad news with good. Emphasize strengths as well as weaknesses.

▼ Provide training in data use to the staff.

▼ If serious conflict is anticipated, consider bringing in a skilled outside facilitator.

▼ Cultivate the group's communication skills by explicitly teaching, modeling, and practicing collaborative group norms.

▼ Provide adequate time for dialogue. Without time to hash out disagreements, you will have difficulty reaching common understandings.

▼ Don't force-feed conclusions. This can make people feel manipulated. Present the data and allow open discussion about the implications.

▼ Be sure that administrators and decision makers are involved in the process from the beginning.

▼ Use the three-phase process for organizing data-driven dialogue (page 45).

While sharing data can be difficult, it also provides the catalyst for important dialogue that might not happen otherwise—dialogue that challenges beliefs, calls traditions into question, builds commitment to change, and forges a common action agenda.

## More In-Depth Data Analysis

Organizing data-driven dialogue and having the tough conversations with multiple stakeholders are important parts of the data analysis. However, more in-depth data analysis may, of necessity, happen in smaller groups, who will then need to plan for how to bring key constituencies back into the dialogue. Below we offer some additional suggestions for working with lots of data:

1. **Go back to the original question.** It is easy to get lost in all the numbers and words swirling around you. To help focus your analysis, return to your original question. What are you trying to find out? Herman and Winters (1992) suggest organizing the data not by instrument but by question (see Figure 2.5).

**FIGURE 2.5: SAMPLE DATA ORGANIZED BY QUESTION**

**Question: Are we implementing the math program as planned?**
**Teacher Interview Summaries (20 teachers)**

| What new strategies used: | What problems are we having? |
|---|---|
| Cooperative learning; n = 20 | Need more planning time; n = 18 |
| Student math projects; n = 14 | No time for writing essays; n = 14 |
| Math essays; n = 2 | Kids don't know math facts; n = 7 |

**Student Survey Summary (Grade 6 = 310; Grade 7 = 331; Grade 8 = 312)**

I usually understand how to do my math assignments and homework.

| Grade | Boys | Girls |
|---|---|---|
| 6 | 75% | 77% |
| 7 | 78% | 56% |
| 8 | 79% | 43% |

**Grade 8 Mathematics Portfolio Summaries**
**(random sample of 50; 10 per classroom)**

| Class | Papers | Essay | Problems | Mean Rating 1-6 | ITBS Concepts Mean SS |
|---|---|---|---|---|---|
| 1 | 40 | 2% | 10% | 2.3% | 210 |
| 2 | 17 | 30% | 45% | 4.7% | 245 |
| 3 | 10 | 20% | 50% | 4.2% | 234 |
| 4 | 4 | 0 | 1% | 1.2% | 195 |
| 5 | 12 | 3% | 10% | 2.1% | 200 |
| Average | 16.60 | 11.00 | 23.20 | 3.10 | 216.80 |

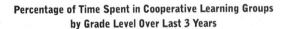

**Percentage of Time Spent in Cooperative Learning Groups by Grade Level Over Last 3 Years**

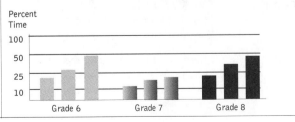

2. **Use Statistics 101.** When working with numerical data, you may need to get somewhat technical to summarize the data in useful ways. If you need help, check around your school or district. Usually, you can find someone familiar with statistics and data analysis.

3. **Look for common themes or trends.** When dealing with a lot of data, Richard Sagor suggests that teams scan all the information first to try to get a sense of the big picture. In this phase, you are looking for items that come up repeatedly or items that come up infrequently but seem important. Some themes that your team can analyze more systematically in the next phase should emerge from this process.

4. **Test your hunches.** It's time to test those hunches you made about important themes. Here is one way to organize this process: Use a matrix with the themes you identified listed along the top and the sources of information you collected listed down the left (Sagor 1992, 49), as illustrated in Figure 2.6. Now go through the data systemati-

**FIGURE 2.6: DATA MATRIX**

| | Previous Experience | Parent Involvement | Relationships with Teachers |
|---|---|---|---|
| **Surveys** | | | |
| **Interviews** | | "It's very important to my parents that I do well in school. My father thinks that an education is the only way out of this neighborhood." (Subject 3)<br><br>"My parents don't care about my grades. They said once I'm sixteen, if I can find a job, I can drop out." (Subject 7) | "I work hard for the teachers who show an interest in me. If a teacher talks to me in the halls and seems to recognize that I'm a human being, I'm willing to work for them. The others can go to hell as far as I'm concerned." (Subject 6)<br><br>"When teachers relate the work to my life, I'm interested. If I can't see how it applies to my life I'm bored." (Subject 9) |
| **Archival Evidence** | Eighty-five percent of the students who had GPAs of 3.5 or above in junior high school had GPAs of 3.5 or above in high school.<br><br>Ninety-one percent of the students who had received remedial services in elementary school also received them in high school. | | |

cally. Every time you find a piece of evidence related to one of the themes, record it in the appropriate box along with its source. With a quick scan, you can see how much data support each theme. Be ready to add new themes as they emerge.

When analyzing open-ended surveys, journals, or interview or observation transcripts, you do not have to have expensive equipment. Color markers, for instance, can be your best friends. Use them to color code common themes or issues that come up, remembering to label the sources before collating the data so that you can go back to them if you need to.

Of course, computers can also be very helpful for sorting data. In "Use Technology for Data Management," page 57, we offer detailed suggestions for those schools and districts that have the resources for computer-generated data analysis.

## Drawing Conclusions, Taking Action

All of your work with data has a single purpose—to take the best-informed actions you can to improve student learning. After hypotheses are generated, then validated or invalidated with more data, it is time to draw some conclusions and plan a course of action. Good, healthy, data-driven dialogue eventually leads to data-driven decisions (see following vignettes). And if you do the painstaking work of organizing data-driven dialogue among stakeholders within the school community, it is likely that more people will feel a sense of ownership in the solutions chosen. But it is equally critical in this phase to engage key constituencies in dialogue about possible solutions and action plans.

**In Hudson, Massachusetts,** some teachers wondered if their new, problem-based mathematics curriculum was effective for students who hadn't done well in a more traditional curriculum. The district collected a variety of different data to assess the program's effectiveness, including teacher surveys, standardized test results, and an assessment aligned with the new curriculum. In analyzing the data, staff saw that all three sources pointed to gains for all students and particular benefits to previously low performers. Based on this, the district made a data-driven decision to expand implementation of the new mathematics program. (See **Reform in Action**, page 340.)

will shed light on your question. If you want to know how your new mathematics program is affecting classroom teaching, for example, classroom observations, interviews with teachers, and surveys would be appropriate sources of information. If your question is whether the new program is improving student learning, performance assessment results and examples of student work might fill the bill.

When choosing what kind of data to collect, it is a good idea to consider the variety of different sources that are available (see "Examples of Useful Data," page 27). Each source has its purposes and pros and cons, as detailed in Figure 2.1.

## Consider Validity, Reliability, and Feasibility

When deciding what data to collect and how, you will also need to juggle three other important considerations: validity, reliability, and feasibility.

Careful consideration of validity is one way to help assure that your data are trustworthy. When checking for validity, you ask yourself, how do I know that the measure I am using is telling me what I want to know? You wouldn't want to use a person's annual salary, for example, as a measure of their self-worth. Nor would you want to use standardized tests as a measure of students' ability to conduct inquiry. In choosing valid measures, you need to first be as clear as you can about what you want to measure. Then you can find appropriate measures. For example, if your team wants to know to what extent inquiry-based instruction is going on, you will need to be very clear about what constitutes inquiry-based instruction and how you will know it when you see it. It is important that your measure include the full range of factors that constitute inquiry. Just looking at the use of inquiry-based materials in the classroom will not be sufficient. Teachers may be using these materials, but not actually promoting students' ability to plan and carry out investigations, propose explanations, raise questions, or critique their practice. Inquiry encompasses a wide range of teacher and student behaviors as well as numerous characteristics of the classroom environment. (See "Defining the Change: Will We Know It When We See It?" in Chapter 4 and **Data Tools**, DT 4-5.)

In addition to checking to see if your measures are complete and consistent with what you want to measure, you will want to make sure that they measure just what you want and not something else. For example, is a particular performance assessment task measuring just students' knowledge of the science content and their inquiry abilities, or is it measuring reading or

**When teachers in** the Hall-Dale School District in Hallowell, Maine, took a hard look at their science curriculum, they saw how some topics were repeated year after year while other important ones were completely ignored. With this information, they knew they had to put serious effort into reworking their curriculum. (See **Reform in Action**, page 343.)

We suggest that action plans address, first and foremost, goals for improving student learning. From there, you can delineate what specific actions you will take to achieve those results and how you will know when you have.

We also advocate systemic action planning. This means that while your action plans will focus on a particular area, such as curriculum reform, they will also deal with other parts of the system essential to the success of your plan, such as effective professional development and public engagement. For a fuller discussion of action planning, see "Developing a Learner-Centered Systemic Action Plan" in Chapter 3.

## Monitoring Results

Using data does not stop once action is taken. Now your questions are about what effect your actions are having. Are you getting the results you want? What do you need to do differently to assure the success of the plan? How will you use data to judge how well you are doing? The key to good monitoring is to agree upon some good success indicators in the planning phase. Then it is simply a matter of checking those indicators periodically to make sure you are on course.

Indicators are the specific measures or evidence used to track progress on goals. For example, the Providence (Rhode Island) Public Schools, through their work with EQUITY 2000, had a goal of eliminating tracking in high school mathematics over a five-year period. How would they know if they were moving toward that goal? They agreed on three measures: the numbers taking algebra, disaggregated; students' algebra grades, disaggregated; and teachers' and guidance counselors' expectations, measured in a survey. (See **Reform in Action**, page 335.) Deciding on indicators forces teams to be concrete about what success actually looks like. Throughout this guidebook, we suggest indicators to monitor progress in student learning, curriculum, instruction, assessment, and equity.

# Overcoming the Obstacles: Building Capacity for School-Based Inquiry

As powerful as the inquiry process might be, it won't do anybody any good if it is not put into practice. Right now, serious obstacles prevent many schools from using data and inquiry. The list to the right notes some of those obstacles. You may certainly add your own.

Overcoming these obstacles defies simple solutions. But many schools are surmounting them by slowly building their capacity to use data and inquiry. We suggest six steps that schools can take to create the conditions for successful inquiry. Some schools are already well organized for continuous improvement and will need to pay less attention to these steps. For others, laying a strong foundation now, even though it is labor intensive, can accelerate positive change later.

## Create an Inquiry-Friendly Culture

Classrooms that are completely teacher-directed, discourage risk taking, frown on questioning, and punish mistakes are poor places for inquiry. So too are schools with these characteristics. For inquiry to thrive, school leaders must nurture and model the habits of mind and collaborative norms associated with inquiry (see "The Spirit of Inquiry," page 31, and the "Seven Norms of Collaborative Work," page 47), create a safe environment for working with data (see "Safety Regulations for Using Data," page 31), and never use data in a punitive manner. For example, at Glendale Union, a data-driven school district near Phoenix, Arizona, test results cannot be part of teacher evaluation by agreement with the teachers association. Principals receive special training in how to discuss results sensitively, build trust, and promote improvement, not fear. (See **Reform in Action**, page 327.) Besides these features, all the other elements discussed below are incorporated by an inquiry-friendly culture.

## Allocate Time and Money

Anyone who has ever used inquiry in the classroom knows how time-consuming it is. How can schools possibly use the inquiry process to foster dialogue and improve decision making? Given the frantic pace of the school day and the school year, finding time in schools, even for the most worthwhile activities, can seem almost impossible. Here's what schools committed to inquiry say about time.

**Obstacles to School-Based Inquiry**

▼ Antidata school cultures

▼ Time

▼ Lack of training and experience dealing with data

▼ Lack of good data

▼ Poor to nonexistent data management systems

▼ "It's nobody's job"

▼ Fear of reprisals

▼ Fear of increased accountability

▼ Bad experiences with data

▼ Lack of effective leadership

*"Good seeds grow in strong cultures."*

(Saphier and King 1985, 1)

First, they concede that they do spend more time planning up front, but the time is well spent. They don't waste time solving the wrong problem or taking actions that won't get results. Also, setting up good data management systems initially can be very time-consuming. But once they are in place, less time is needed. So think of time spent as an investment.

Second, school teams need to be selective about what they inquire into. Save the inquiry process for the most critical issues that affect student learning and for the big changes you can plan. Every change cannot or should not be the subject of a major investigation. Some change results from capitalizing on opportunities as they arise. For instance, a grant possibility emerges and you go for it. Sometimes change is unplanned, such as when the principal misses a meeting and strong teacher leadership emerges for the first time. Some decisions have to be made on the fly or with the best information you have at the time.

Even so, there is no way to have an inquiry-friendly culture without allocating time to plan, use data, and reflect. For most schools, that requires rethinking how time is allocated during the school day and the school year (a potential focus for inquiry). For example, at Souhegan High School in Amherst, New Hampshire, teachers have at least one period a day to work together reflecting on student work and thinking about how to improve instruction. Teachers at Holaway Elementary School in Tucson, Arizona, meet four times a year after school to discuss the data they are collecting on their mathematics program. Because they recognize the power of inquiry to improve learning, schools like these are finding creative solutions to the time crunch. For other ideas on using available school time more effectively, see the box below.

Using data well takes money as well as time. Budget items to consider are release time, consultants, professional development, books, and computer hardware and software. Eventually, funds for developing and administering a school's or district's own assessments may be required. At the high end, Glendale Union High School District spends about 1 percent of its budget for an instructional management system, which administers district multiple-choice and performance tests and rigorously uses results to foster improvement. Obviously, schools or districts just beginning will start smaller—with one segment of the curriculum, one grade level, a few outcomes, or a particular student population.

## Finding Time

### Freed-up time

This strategy entails freeing teachers from their regular instructional time to participate in professional development activities. This can be achieved by hiring substitute teachers or recruiting principals or administrators and parents or volunteers to serve as substitute teachers.

### Restructured or rescheduled time

This solution requires formally altering overall instructional time—the school day, the school year, or teaching schedules. Examples of this time-creating strategy are a move to a team-teaching approach, a year-round school schedule, or a revised weekly schedule that allows for early student release one day a week.

### Common time

Many schools are encouraging common teacher preparation and planning time, instead of individual preparation time. This enables teachers to meet according to common grade level or subject area, or as interdisciplinary teams. Meeting times, when coupled with a lunch hour, for example, can result in approximately 90 minutes of uninterrupted development time.

### Better-used time

This refers to schools' efforts to reduce the amount of time teachers spend on administrative-related activities. Examples of strategies used to increase the professional development value of teachers' time and meetings are the regular use of electronic mail for routine communication about administrative issues, moving nonessential student-oriented activities (such as assemblies) to after-school time, and comprehensive reassessment of the value of existing professional development plans to assure that teachers' needs are being fulfilled.

### Purchased time

Schools can find ways to reallocate existing funds to provide time for professional development. Some schools and districts have established a pool of permanent substitutes and, though not encouraged as a permanent solution, provide stipends for teachers to attend professional development activities outside the school day.

# Build Structures for Collaborative Inquiry

## Form or Retool the Mathematics/Science Leadership Team

*"Collecting data by [itself] does not drive reform. It is looking at data as a group."*

(Rosemary Beck, Holaway Elementary School, Tucson, Arizona, interview 1998)

Many schools already have a team charged with the responsibility of improving mathematics and science education. If your school has such a team, your work may need to focus on building the team's capacity to use the inquiry process. If it does not, decide if your school can benefit from one. Look at what other structures are already in place. Is there an existing group or subset of a group, like a school improvement team, for instance, that can take charge of mathematics/science improvement? Or will you need to constitute a new group?

While team structure and composition may vary greatly, it is generally recommended that teams include both teachers and administrators, reflect the gender and racial diversity of the staff, and have the authority to act on their decisions. At the middle and high school levels, mathematics and science teachers often find value in working together. Effective teams can range in size from three to 12 members.

When you say teamwork or collaboration, some school staff shudder. In some cases, the school culture has not been conducive to teachers and administrators working collaboratively. Effective cross-role teams often have to work hard initially to establish norms of collaboration and transform power relationships into collegial ones. On other cases, staff have too many memories of painful meetings, unresolved conflicts, or group exercises in futility. But the answer is not for teachers and administrators to retreat into isolation. Effective collaboration first requires a genuine reason for working together. Using data and inquiry to improve student learning provides such a purpose. Second, it takes skill and practice.

Teams often benefit from putting effort into learning about effective communication, teamwork, and facilitation skills. Protocols for group problem solving and examining teacher and student work, such as the Tuning Protocol or the Descriptive Review Process, can be effective in structuring productive collaboration (see **Data Tools**, DT 2-5 and DT 2-6). Data collection instruments, such as "A Yardstick for Measuring the Growth of a Team," can also help teams focus on and improve their group process (see **Data Tools**, DT 2-7). Finally, good resources on effective teamwork, such as *The Adaptive School: A Sourcebook for Developing Collaborative Groups* (see **Resources**, page 63), are readily available.

Besides learning about effective teamwork, you will probably need to devote a few sessions to learning more about inquiry, data, and change. Along with this guidebook, you can use some of the materials listed in **Resources**, beginning on page 65, visit schools that are using data well, and attend workshops on using data, action research, and school change.

## Designate Responsibility for Data

Teams that work with data recommend that responsibility for collecting, analyzing, and presenting data be clearly designated. Some members may already have interest and expertise in data use. Capitalize on that! Your team may choose to form a data subcommittee. Or, if the change effort is districtwide, a whole committee devoted to working with data may be warranted. As the school or district builds its data management system, staff resources must be allocated to maintain them. Somebody needs to enter the data, produce the charts, and offer technical support. However responsibilities get allocated, the data have to be somebody's job.

## Build Teacher Ownership

We've all seen students go through the motions of an investigation that has been fully orchestrated by the teacher. The excitement and the learning are rarely as great as when students are posing and researching their own questions. The same is true regarding inquiry for school change. When teachers and even students are asking the questions, collecting and analyzing the data, and suggesting improvements, the process comes alive. Curriculum committee, faculty, grade-level, and department or team meetings are possible venues for bringing teachers into the process. Selecting or developing and scoring assessments are other important activities in which to involve teachers.

## Use Technology for Data Management

Most school teams interested in using data will quickly grow frustrated with their current data management systems. They can't easily access useful data because they are in a variety of places. They can't disaggregate data or monitor the performance of specific groups or individuals. They can't link various types of information such as demographics or participation in a particular program with student learning outcomes. If schools are going to be data-driven, they must have easy access to helpful data.

Carefully implemented, a computerized student database system can fill the bill. It can ensure accuracy and consistency of record keeping, allow ease of

*"Our use of data was not as strong as in previous years because nobody took charge. I used to produce the graphs for everybody, but I just didn't have time this year. You need to have a designated leader to make this happen."*

(Rosemary Beck, Holaway Elementary School, Tucson, Arizona, interview 1998)

data retrieval, increase capacity for data storage exponentially, and, most important, allow for speed and power of data analysis never before possible with paper records. Five years ago, widespread use of the Internet in schools was a pipe dream. Today, it is reality for more and more schools. The use of more sophisticated data management systems can become a reality as well. As schools become more accountable and focused on student learning results, these systems will be as much of a necessity as other technologies we have come to take for granted.

Schools and districts that are ready and can afford a computer database system may want to examine the guidelines on the next two pages. Others not yet able can still continue the journey to school improvement without a database system.

## Use Data to Monitor Your Use of Data

As circular as it sounds, data can be a tool for your team to assess, monitor, and improve the inquiry process. For example, you can start collecting data right away to find out about your school's or district's use of data and its capacity to produce and manage data. What kinds of data are currently available? Who has responsibility for data? Who has the expertise? What computer hardware and software are required? What are the prevailing attitudes about data use? What obstacles might the team face? What will work in its favor?

Both the "Progress Toward Standards—A Self-Assessment" (**Data Tools**, DT 2-2) and the "Information and Analysis" rubric (**Data Tools**, DT 2-8) can help teams self-assess their data use. Consider revisiting this periodically to track progress and target areas for improvement.

## Guidelines for Designing a School-Based Computer Database System

**1. Design the database.**

▼ Define the uses of the student record system. Clearly define the purpose of the system and questions that need to be answered through data. Care in planning at this stage will save potential system redesign and, therefore, time and money later in the process.

▼ Select the software system. There are a number of essential characteristics to look for when selecting database software. First, the database should be relational; that is, it should offer the potential for multidimensional analysis, as opposed to the two-dimensional limitation of most spreadsheet programs. Here are other characteristics to consider:

- Longitudinal capability (ability to track student data year to year). This capability is difficult to come by but can be customized into the larger, server-based systems.

- Integrated (ability to include all relevant student data, such as student performance, demographic, and program and practice data).

- Ability to disaggregate data for meaningful analysis.

- Ability to import and export data easily into a variety of database formats.

- Cross-platform support, for linking systems such as Macintosh, Windows, Unix.

- Flexibility (through options for user-definable fields and variables).

- Expandability (ability to grow with your expanding needs).

- User-friendly interface.

- Programmability. The more powerful the database tool, the more programming and maintenance will be required of your staff.

- Technical support. Quality, availability, and cost can vary significantly from vendor to vendor.

- Cost.

One recommended approach to building a database system is to start with a good office software suite, such as Microsoft Office or Corel Suite (each includes database, word processing, and spreadsheet), then build upon the basic system with advanced add-on statistical packages to analyze the data you've stored (see **Resources**, page 68).

▼ Standardize software districtwide. Make decisions districtwide on what software all schools will use and on how to report. This standardizes analysis and saves training, energy, and money systemwide.

▼ Select an appropriate storage medium and hardware. The systems should be expandable since the database will grow much larger over time.

▼ Adopt standard database fields and variables. This step fosters the sharing of school statistics with other schools and facilitates state and national reporting. When information about students is available to school officials in a standardized format, it can help in the following ways:

- aid in the comparison of information among communities and among states;

- facilitate rational decision making about curriculum development and change;

- enhance program evaluation by easy cross-tabulation of individual-level student data;

- enhance reporting to the public about the condition and progress of education.

For a standardized database field, see the information on the *Student Data Handbook for Early Childhood, Elementary, and Secondary Education* in **Resources**, page 67.

**2. Analyze the task of building the database.**

▼ Determine what staff resources are needed. You will probably need a systems analyst/data specialist on staff or as a consultant. Also, additional personnel resources will be required for the initial data collection and entry.

▼ Articulate the regulations, laws, rules, and policies with which the system must be designed to comply (federal, state, city/town).

▼ Clearly define roles for accessing and processing data in the system, and standardize procedures for doing so.

▼ For security and to ensure privacy, protect access privileges.

**3. Collect and prepare to import data.**

▼ Systematically and consistently collect data from manual and electronic archives for all variables for all students.

▼ Modify existing electronic files for importation into new databases.

▼ Clean data (spot check for accuracy and identify inconsistencies).

**4. Enter and import data.**

▼ Input data into the database, either manually record by record, or import from existing electronic sources.

**5. Generate initial reports and analyze the data.**

▼ Run pilot reports to test the integrity of the system.

▼ Analyze the data. Did the database generate useful reports?

**6. Modify the system as needed.**

▼ Based on the results of the initial reports, modify the database's variables or structure, if necessary.

**7. Train staff.**

▼ Provide training for all staff you expect to use the database. Ensure that ongoing support is available.

**8. Use the data to improve programs and practices.**

▼ Apply results of data analysis directly to improve programs and practices. Make sure all appropriate stakeholders are involved in the review of data and the decision-making process.

Information for these guidelines was based on interviews with Karl Stein, Vermont Department of Education, Montpelier, VT; Paul Gammill, Prince George's County (Maryland) Schools; Gerry Paquin, President, Edustar, Inc., Londonderry, NH; and Martha Williams, Vice President, CRM, Inc./Socrates, South Hampton, NH.

## Attend to Critical Supports for Systemic Change

The same factors that are critical to supporting systemic change are equally important in building the capacity for inquiry: effective professional development, public engagement, partnerships, culture, leadership, and technology.

# Conclusion

Ultimately, the goal of mathematics and science education reform is classrooms alive with inquiry and learning for all students. By building your school's capacity to use data and inquiry for dialogue and decision making, you will be helping your school to reach that goal. Data and inquiry make the wheels of systemic mathematics and science education reform turn. The remainder of this guidebook is about how to put the principles and processes discussed in this chapter to work to investigate and improve three key dimensions of mathematics and science education reform: student learning results; curriculum, instruction, and assessment; and equity. We begin this investigation with the heart of the matter—student learning results.

# Resources for Data and Inquiry

## Books

***The Adaptive School: A Sourcebook for Developing Collaborative Groups***, by Robert J. Garmston and Bruce M. Wellman (Norwood, MA: Christopher-Gordon), 1999

This book presents numerous innovative ideas and insights to help educators work successfully together. Drawing on a number of sources and disciplines, including organizational development, cognitive psychology, group dynamics, and new sciences such as chaos theory, the authors give a rich perspective for viewing work with groups and the work of groups. The techniques are school and group tested; there are practical solutions to real problems; and a unique "problem locator" gives the reader quick access to concerns of specific interest. The book provides a wealth of specific tools that can be used to develop collective understanding, make decisions, respond to conflict, and develop high-performance groups.

**Contact**: Christopher-Gordon Publishers, Inc., 1502 Providence Highway, Suite 12, Norwood, MA 02062-4643; (800) 934-8322

***Change in Action: Navigating and Investigating the Classroom Using Action Research***, edited by De Tonack and Ceri Dean (Aurora, CO: McREL), 1997

*Change in Action* highlights 22 teacher-research projects conducted in the Nebraska schools. Action research was the tool for these investigations, and Richard Sagor's *How to Conduct Collaborative Action Research* (1992) was the guidebook for the research process. The results reflect on many issues critical to educators, including assessment, the use of portfolios, communication with parents and the community, the effectiveness of peer mentoring, the impact of computer use, and gender equity in mathematics and science instruction.

**Contact:** Mid-continent Research for Education and Learning (McREL), 2550 South Parker Road, Suite 500, Aurora, CO 80014-0162; (303) 337-0990; fax: (303) 337-3005; e-mail: info@mcrel.org; Web site: http://www.mcrel.org/

***Change Forces: The Sequel***, by Michael Fullan (Bristol, PA: Falmer), 1999

This sequel to *Change Forces: Probing the Depths of Educational Reform* (1993) extends and expands the use of chaos theory as a lens through which to view and comprehend change. Covering new aspects of this science of complexity, this volume helps educators gain further insights into moral purpose and the forces of change.

**Contact**: Routledge New York, 29 West 35th Street, New York, NY 10001-2299; (212) 216-7800; fax: (212) 564-7854; Web site: http://www.routledge-ny.com/

***Data Analysis for Comprehensive Schoolwide Improvement***, by Victoria Bernhardt (Larchmont, NY: Eye on Education), 1998

The author presents practical tools to help educators make better decisions based on data. Targeted at nonstatisticians, this book demonstrates how to gather, analyze, and use information to improve schools. All the examples given are based on data collected from schools at both the elementary and the high school levels.

**Contact:** Eye on Education, 6 Depot Way West, Larchmont, NY 10538-0300; (914) 833-0551; fax: (914) 833-0761; e-mail: order@eyeoneducation.com; Web site: http://www.eyeoneducation.com

***Education Watch: The Education Trust Community Data Guide***, by The Education Trust (Washington, DC: Education Trust), [1996]

This companion guide to *The Education Trust State and National Data Book* is designed to help local communities pull together important data about their own children and schools. The guide emphasizes using data in the conversation among all stakeholders in communities to help close the achievement gap and build stronger schools.

**Contact:** The Education Trust, 1725 K Street N.W., Suite 200, Washington, DC 20006-1409; (202) 293-1217; fax: (202) 293-2605; Web site: http://www.edtrust.org/

***Education Watch: The 1996 Education Trust State and National Data Book***, by The Education Trust (Washington, DC: Education Trust), 1996

Based on nationwide data assessing student achievement by race, ethnicity, and income, this book presents an overview of the condition of the nation's educational system and argues for a two-pronged campaign to raise the achievement of students at all grade levels and to improve the performance of schools and colleges serving low-income and minority students. The book also provides a state-by-state examination of trends in funding, school and course enrollment, teaching, and student achievement and ranks the performance of each state on 17 indicators.

**Contact:** The Education Trust, 1725 K Street N.W., Suite 200, Washington, DC 20006-1409; (202) 293-1217; fax: (202) 293-2605; Web site: http://www.edtrust.org/

***How to Conduct Collaborative Action Research***, by Richard Sagor (Alexandria, VA: ASCD), 1992

In this practical book, Richard Sagor describes how teachers can use a process called collaborative action research to improve the teaching-learning process and make meaningful contributions to the development of the teaching profession. Sagor takes readers through the five steps of collaborative action research, emphasizing that the process is one that will pull teachers out of the isolation of their classrooms and enable them to consult and work collegially with one another.

**Contact:** Association for Supervision and Curriculum Development (ASCD), 1703 North Beauregard Street, Alexandria, VA 22311-1714; (800) 933-2723; fax: (703) 575-5400; e-mail:member@ascd.org; Web site: http://www.ascd.org/

*Improving Student Learning: Applying Deming's Quality Principles in Classrooms*, by Lee Jenkins (Milwaukee: ASQC), 1997

Nationally renowned for his work in education and for using quality practices in his school district, Lee Jenkins brings Edward Deming's theory to educators. He provides a wealth of actual examples of statistical quality tools that have been successfully applied to K–12 classrooms. This book answers the critical question of how to measure improvement and gives direct and important information about what to measure. Numerous examples and activities are presented that can be used in the classroom.

**Contact:** ASQC Quality Press, P.O. Box 3005, Milwaukee, WI 53201-3005; (800) 248-1946; Web site: http://www.asq.org/

*Results: The Key to Continuous Improvement*, by Michael J. Schmoker (Alexandria, VA: ASCD), 1996

The author examines the conditions and the theory behind successful school improvement efforts. Using many examples from schools, he demonstrates that meaningful teamwork, when combined with setting clear, measurable goals and regularly collecting and analyzing performance data, provides the foundation that leads to results.

**Contact:** Association for Supervision and Curriculum Development (ASCD), 1703 North Beauregard Street, Alexandria, VA 22311-1714; (800) 933-2723; fax: (703) 575-5400; e-mail: member@ascd.org; Web site: http://www.ascd.org/

*The School Portfolio: A Comprehensive Framework for School Improvement*, by Victoria L. Bernhardt (Larchmont, NY: Eye on Education), 1994

A school portfolio is an effective, nonthreatening self-assessment tool that exhibits a school's goals, progress, achievements, and vision for improvement. Using examples from schools that have already established and maintained them, this comprehensive book demonstrates how to develop a school portfolio specifically tailored to a school's continuous improvement efforts.

**Contact:** Eye on Education, 6 Depot Way West, Larchmont, NY 10538-0300; (914) 833-0551; fax: (914) 833-0761; e-mail: order@eyeoneducation.com; Web site: http://www.eyeoneducation.com/

***Schools That Learn: A Fifth Discipline Fieldbook for Educators, Parents, and Everyone Who Cares About Education,*** by Peter Senge et al. (New York: Doubleday), 2000

*Schools That Learn* offers much-needed material for the dialogue about the education of children in the twenty-first century. The book features articles, studies, and anecdotes from prominent educators such as Howard Gardner, Jay Forrester, and 1999 U.S. Superintendent of the Year Gerry House, as well as from impassioned teachers, administrators, parents, and students. The book offers a wealth of practical tools and advice that can be used to help schools, classrooms, and communities learn to learn.

***Contact:*** Random House, Inc., 1540 Broadway, New York, NY 10036; (212) 782-9000; fax: (212) 302-7985; e-mail: customerservice@randomhouse.com; Web site: http://www.randomhouse.com/

***The Self-Renewing School***, by Bruce Joyce, James Wolf, and Emily Calhoun (Alexandria, VA: ASCD), 1993

The authors present the "self-renewing school" through the actions of a district restructuring committee that is looking at ways to improve student learning. In Part I, they describe the rationale and design to transform a school system into an "academy," in which everyone is involved in action research on school improvement. Part II presents a scenario in which the restructuring committee considers the overall purposes of education and surveys the literature on change and curricular and instructional options while gradually organizing the district faculty to create a self-renewing organization.

**Contact:** Association for Supervision and Curriculum Development (ASCD), 1703 North Beauregard Street, Alexandria, VA 22311-1714; (800) 933-2723; fax (703) 575-5400 e-mail: member@ascd.org; Web site: http://www.ascd.org/

***Setting Our Sights: Measuring Equity in School Change***, by Ruth Johnson (Los Angeles: Achievement Council), 1996

Inviting schools to use data as a lens through which to examine counterproductive and unequal school practices and to remedy those inequalities, Ruth Johnson guides schools and districts in developing the skills they need for reform that is focused on the creation of a culture of high standards and equity. This book provides ways of thinking about change in a new light, methods of challenging the beliefs and attitudes that get in the way, and a toolbox full of practical ideas and instruments that can be used to prompt and measure change. The book is designed specifically for the schools most likely to be left behind in "generic" reform efforts: those serving African American, Latino, Native American, and low-income students.

**Contact:** The Achievement Council, 3460 Wilshire Boulevard, Suite 420, Los Angeles, CA 90010; (213) 487-3194; fax: (213) 487-0879; Web site: http://www.achievementcouncil.com/

*Student Data Handbook for Early Childhood, Elementary, and Secondary Education: 2000 Edition* (NCES 2000343), by the Education Data Systems Implementation Project, Council of Chief State School Officers (Washington, DC: National Center for Education Statistics), 2000

Addressing the importance of consistency in how data are defined and maintained within the educational system to support ongoing decision making, this handbook aims to

▾ provide common language and definitions;

▾ promote standard maintenance of student data;

▾ promote the development of policies to safeguard the confidentiality and ensure appropriate use of student data;

▾ describe how data can be maintained in a way that promotes appropriate and flexible usage by all relevant parties;

▾ encourage automation of student data.

An electronic version of the handbook has been developed to make the product more useful to state and local education agencies, as well as to the public (http://www.nces.ed.gov). The handbook is free; other education-related data and statistical publications are also available.

**Contact:** Education Publications Center (ED Pubs), P.O. Box 1398, Jessup, MD 20794-1398; (877) 433-7827; fax: (301) 470-1244; Web site: http://www.ed.gov/pubs/edpubs.html.

*A Toolkit for Using Data to Improve Schools: Raise Student Achievement by Incorporating Data Analysis in School Planning*, by Marguerite Roza (Newton, MA: New England Comprehensive Assistance Center), 1998

*A Toolkit for Using Data to Improve Schools* provides a dynamic context and process for data-driven decision making to sustain continuous school improvement and allow students to achieve at higher levels. Detailing a six-step, inquiry-based process for identifying which students are not succeeding and which aspects of the school program need improvement, it includes a variety of print tools and electronic templates to facilitate the compilation, disaggregation, analysis, and communication of student data.

**Contact:** New England Comprehensive Assistance Center (NECAC), Education Development Center, Inc., 55 Chapel Street, Newton, MA 02158; (800) 225-4276 ext. 2536; fax: (617) 965-6325; e-mail: CompCenter@edc.org; Web site: http://www.edc.org/NECAC/

*Tracking Your School's Success: A Guide to Sensible Evaluation*, by Joan L. Herman and Lynn Winters (Newbury Park, CA: Corwin), 1992

This comprehensive guide offers educators the step-by-step procedures and practical advice needed to conduct sensible assessment and evaluation, record and measure progress, and communicate in credible terms what they are trying to accomplish and how well they are doing it. The book instructs the reader on how to configure evaluation strategies sensitive to the unique needs, priorities, and goals of individual schools and to use evaluation information to aid school planning and improve management decisions.

**Contact:** Corwin Press, Inc. (a Sage Publications Company), 2455 Teller Road, Thousand Oaks, CA 91320-2218; (800) 818-7243; fax: (800) 417-2466;
e-mail: order@corwin.sagepub.com; Web site: http://www.corwinpress.com/

## Commercial Software

### Apple Computer, Inc.

Apple Works

One Infinite Loop, Cupertino, CA 95014; (800) 692-7753; Web site: http://www.apple.com/

### Chancery Software

Site- and district-based student data management software, including District Data Integrator, MacSchool, Open District, WinSchool

3001 Wayburne Drive, Suite 275, Burnaby, BC V5G 4W3, Canada; (800) 999-9931; fax: (604) 294-2225; Web site: http://www.chancery.com/

### Corel Corporation

Paradox

1600 Carling Street, Ottawa, ON KIZ 8R Canada; (800) 772-6735; fax: (716) 447-7366; Web site: http://www.corel.com/

### FileMaker, Inc.

FileMaker Pro, FileMaker Server

P.O. Box 58168, Santa Clara, CA 95052-8168; (800) 325-2747; Web site: http://filemaker.claris.com/

### IBM

DB2, data warehousing software (DataAtlas, DataGuide, DataJoiner, Data Propagator, TeamConnection, Visual Warehouse)

New Orchard Road, Armonk, NY 10504; (888) 746-7426; fax: (877) 441-1329; Web site: http://www.ibm.com/

### Microsoft

Microsoft Access, Microsoft SQL Server, Visual FoxPro

(800) 426-9400; Web site: http://msdn.microsoft.com/

### Oracle

Oracle

500 Oracle Parkway, Redwood City, CA 94065-1765; (888) 422-6924; fax: (650) 506-7200; Web site: http://www.oracle.com/

## Educational Systems and Software

### EASE-e™, developed by the TetraData Corp.

EASE-e™ is a data analysis suite of products and services that empowers educators to make decisions about curricula and education programs. Data Analyzer is a data warehouse, mining, analysis, and reporting system. Data Manager imports data from multiple file formats and exports data to any number of database formats, including Microsoft SQL Server, dBase, and any ODBC-compliant database. Data Services personnel guide you through the design, data gathering, and loading of your district's data warehouse, help build your initial data warehouse, and remain available to help you keep data current.

**Contact:** TetraData Corp., 1200 Woodruff Road, Suite A-16, Greenville, SC 29607; Web site: http://www.ease-e.com/

### Edustar, Inc.

Edustar is a company of educators and school administrators helping schools to automate systems. Specifically, they provide implementation consulting services for the Chancery Software suite of school data management products: MacSchool, Open School Data Integrator, WinSchool, and associated products. Edustar assists schools in integrating their existing technology, while helping them plan future technologies in compliance with standards; they have developed a "district codebook" to support this effort. Using Open School Data Integrator, Edustar helps schools build a bridge between their existing data systems and more powerful reporting databases such as Filemaker Pro or FoxPro.

**Contact:** Gerry Paquin, President, Edustar, Inc.; (800) 421-8775 (offices in Londonderry, NH; Lakeville, MA; Springfield, VT)

### Quality School Portfolio, developed by the National Center for Research on Evaluation, Standards and Student Testing (CRESST)

The Quality School Portfolio software consists of two distinct applications that together offer schools one solution for collecting in one place all the student data that can best inform their practices.

**Contact:** CRESST/UCLA, 301 GSE&IS, Mailbox 951522, 300 Charles E. Young Drive North, Los Angeles, CA 90095-1522; (310) 206-1532; fax: (310) 825-3883; Web site: http://cse.ucla.edu/

**Socrates**, developed by CRM, Inc.

Socrates is a highly versatile relational database system that integrates data from school or district information systems, state assessments, testing programs, and other data files. By linking data on student performance, demographics, and school programs and practices, Socrates allows virtually unlimited data disaggregation and produces data displays that answer a wide range of questions about student performance trends on multiple measures over time. CRM offers a Socrates "Data Web" component that allows users to easily access data organized around an extensive number of queries and to link to a wide range of support materials. CRM also provides tailored services to build the capacity of schools and districts to use data for planning and program improvement.

**Contact:** Martha Williams, CRM, Inc./Socrates, 2 Highland Road, South Hampton, NH 03827-3607; (603) 394-7040; fax: (603) 394-7483; e-mail: socrates@crminc.com

## Web Sites

**Eisenhower National Clearinghouse's TIMSS Web Page**

Web site: http://www.enc.org/topics/timss/

This Web site is maintained by the Eisenhower National Clearinghouse for Mathematics and Science Education (ENC), which serves a national audience of teachers, teacher educators, parents, students, and other education stakeholders in the endeavor to improve teaching and learning in K–12 mathematics and science. It contains many resources for learning about and discussing TIMSS (Third International Mathematics and Science Study), including Facilitation Tools VI, which offers interactive strategies to engage educators with TIMSS. TIMSS included a comparative achievement test of mathematics and science at grades 4, 8, and 12 and examined classroom practice, teachers' and students' lives, curriculum materials, and policy issues in the participating countries.

**Contact:** Eisenhower National Clearinghouse, 1929 Kenny Road, Columbus, OH 43210-1079; (800) 621-5785; fax: (614) 292-2066; e-mail: info@enc.org

# KEEP YOUR EYES ON THE PRIZE: STUDENT LEARNING

Achievement

Opportunities to learn

Aspirations

# 3

"I know one thing we did right
Was the day we started to fight.
Keep your eyes on the prize,
Hold on, hold on."

(from a traditional Civil Rights song)

In the fight for better schools, student learning is the prize. It is the reason for school reform and the measure of its success. And yet, despite decades of spending reform dollars, spouting rhetoric, and implementing new programs, the promise of "high levels of learning for all students" rings hollow —especially for poor and minority students. How can we make sure the mathematics and science education reform movement, unlike those that have preceded it, delivers on its promise for mathematical and scientific literacy for all?

The Civil Rights slogan "keep your eyes on the prize" suggests at least part of the answer. If the prize is student learning, school reformers must never lose sight of it, pursuing it with the dogged determination of the freedom fighters. Few things in life are accomplished without goals. Improved student learning is no exception. That's the lesson researchers have gleaned from studying wave after wave of school reform: "We did not find a single case in the literature where student learning increased but had not been a central goal" (Joyce, Wolf, and Calhoun 1993, 19).

In fact, it is impressive how much schools can accomplish when they stay focused on improving student learning. For example, in 1990 the Providence (Rhode Island) Public Schools had a typical urban tracking system for algebra, which meant that only 43 percent of students made it through the gate. Most of the minority students didn't. After six years of focused, data-driven reform, 99 percent of all students were taking algebra and faring better as a group than the "select" students of the past. (See **Reform in Action,** page 335.)

Similar success stories are being told nationwide, such as in Oak Park, Michigan, an urban/suburban district north of Detroit. After five years of a systemwide school improvement effort focused on student achievement, the district has gone from one of the worst in Michigan to among its most improved (National Staff Development Council 1997, 1).

The above examples offer inspiration and hope, but we don't want them to be misinterpreted. It is true that these districts were focused on improving student learning. But they accomplished that goal by improving the system as a whole: instituting high-quality professional development, reforming classroom practice, and building broad support for change. While this guidebook is clearly advocating a focus on producing learning results, we caution against a narrow and short-sighted focus on improving test scores, an approach that can actually be harmful to students and schools.

Take the following familiar scenario. A school learns of poor standardized test results. School administrators, feeling the pressure to raise scores, encourage teachers to do more drill with students on test-like items. Next year, test scores improve slightly. But this narrow, short-term approach to school improvement has a price. For one thing, standardized tests are not the only, or necessarily the best, indicators of student learning. And even if aggregate test scores increase, poor and minority students can still be losers. Curriculum and instruction have not been improved; professional development is not aligned with learning goals. As a result, the system has not increased its capacity to produce results for all students in the long run.

Our conclusion, in short, is that if student learning is the prize, it will not be won without a systemic approach to change. That's why, in the framework for this book, student learning results are integrally connected with other parts of the system, including capacity to address equity issues, quality of curriculum, instruction, and assessment, and critical systemic supports such as a high-quality professional development.

**FIGURE 3.1: COLLABORATIVE INQUIRY INTO STUDENT LEARNING**

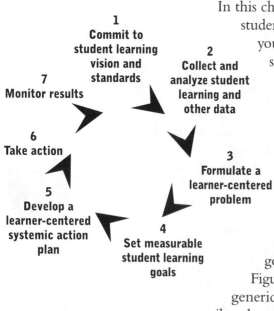

In this chapter you will learn about a process for improving student learning in mathematics and science by "keeping your eyes on the prize." The process begins by mobilizing school communities around a common vision for student learning in mathematics and science—the prize. Next steps are to collect and analyze data about student learning, define a learner-centered problem to solve, set student learning goals, plan for and take action to improve the system, and monitor results. Based on feedback about results, the team makes changes, uncovers new problems, and continues the improvement cycle. While the initial vision is long-term (and evolves as you work), the day-to-day business is about moving toward it, inch by inch, goal by goal, problem by problem. This process is illustrated in Figure 3.1. Note that this is a modified version of the generic inquiry cycle, described in Chapter 2, which we have tailored to the process of planning for improved student learning. Also, note that we use the term "learner-centered" to emphasize that the goal is to improve student learning, not to imply that the learner is the problem.

# Committing to Student Learning Vision and Standards

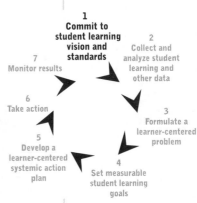

In the introduction to this guidebook, we said that while the road to reform does not have a map, it does have a clear destination: attainment of a set of clearly defined goals for student learning. That's because we believe that the best assurance of getting results is knowing the results you want and publicly committing to them.

Public commitment to a set of results is the essence of the standards movement. Standards offer a vision for student learning as the focal point for change. They are a set of clearly defined, desired results—the important knowledge and skills all students should acquire. Once agreed upon, standards raise expectations for student learning, focus improvement efforts on results, and offer a yardstick to measure progress.

While this may sound simple, mobilizing school communities around a common vision for student learning is a complex and long-term undertaking. It involves getting important conversations going among teachers, administrators, students, and community members about what is important for all students to know and be able to do. It requires serious study of state and national standards documents and careful scrutiny of a school's or district's programs and values. It takes artful orchestration of stakeholders. And, once the vision has been articulated, the process of using standards to improve learning has just begun.

To further complicate matters, the vision will change as you go—just as when you are on a trip and decide to alter your destination based on what you have learned along the way. In fact, Michael Fullan argues that "vision emerges from, more than it precedes, action" (1993, 28). Like everything else about change, vision building is messy and recursive despite our fondest wish that it be lock-step and neat.

Guiding schools through the process of developing a vision and using standards to drive change is beyond the scope of this guidebook. Fortunately, many good resources are available for this purpose. In the **Resources on Standards**, beginning on page 143, we list ones we think are most helpful. Also, see **Reform in Action**, page 340, for an example of how the process unfolded in one school district. Finally, the **Data Tools** contain three instruments related to committing to standards: "A District Self-Assessment Guide for Improving Mathematics Teaching and Learning" (DT 2-1) and "Progress Toward Standards—A Self-Assessment" (DT 2-2) are for assessing your school's progress toward becoming a standards-led system; the third, "Perceptions of Attitudes, Readiness and Commitment to Change" (DT 3-1), is for assessing readiness for change.

*"Begin with the end in mind."*

(Covey 1989, 95)

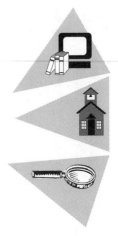

This chapter deals with one essential part of the process of standards-led reform: using data about student learning, opportunities to learn, and aspirations to help close the gap between standards and reality. Once student learning becomes the focal point, the best place to start is to take a closer look at what needs improving.

# Collecting and Analyzing Student Learning and Other Data

O nce your school and district have a common vision about student learning, you know where you want to go. Now it is important to find out where you are. Student learning data can offer important clues about what problems need to be solved in order to improve learning results. Common wisdom urges us not to go fishing for trouble because we might find it. This chapter urges us to fish for trouble precisely because we will find it! Uncovering real problems is the only way to create real solutions.

In the section that follows, we take you fishing for trouble. We describe how to "sink your hooks" into a variety of data about student learning. You can start with readily available data like grades, standardized tests results, or dropout rates, but look at them with fresh eyes. You can dig deeper, using performance assessments and student work, observations, and interviews to uncover more clues. See what light they can shed on the data you already have. Round out the picture with information about students' opportunities to learn and their aspirations and opinions about school. Then put all the pieces together to see what they tell you.

Admittedly, collecting and analyzing multiple sources of student learning data is time-consuming and difficult work. But we believe it will be well worth it. First, because of the insights you will gain and the mistakes you will prevent. Second, because it will keep student learning front and center as you shape improvement plans. Third, because once you do the work, you will have established baseline indicators from which to monitor improvement over time.

## Making the Most of What You've Got: Standardized Tests, Grades, State Assessments

All schools have plenty of data about student performance: standardized tests scores such as achievement tests and SATs, grades, and, increasingly, state assessment results. We suggest starting with what you have. Clearly,

1
Commit to
student learning
vision and
standards

2
Collect and
analyze student
learning and
other data

7
Monitor results

3
Formulate a
learner-centered
problem

6
Take action

5
Develop a
learner-centered
systemic action
plan

4
Set measurable
student learning
goals

*"Problems are our friends."*

(Fullan 1993, 21)

each of these sources has limitations. Standardized test scores have been widely criticized for their one-size-fits-all approach, their bias against low-income, disabled, and minority students, their failure to predict student success, and the limited slice of information they provide about student learning (Sacks 2000, 7–9). In mathematics and science, they fall short of measuring deep understanding of ideas or complex reasoning skills. Grades, typically, are quite subjective and unreliable as a data source.

State assessments vary widely in their quality and alignment with national mathematics and science standards. Some, like the New Standards Reference Exam (See **Resources**, page 150), have a strong performance-assessment component and more closely reflect National Council of Teachers of Mathematics (NCTM) standards. Others, however, are based on state standards, which may depart significantly from the national standards and emphasize multiple-choice questions and recall of facts. In addition, they typically test only certain grade levels, making it difficult to pinpoint problems or assess the impact of a new program. And, as with any standardized test, they often reveal more about the socioeconomics of the students tested than the quality of the program (Meyer 2000, 2). Our experience has been that state assessments can be a good place to begin a dialogue, but they will need to be supplemented with performance-based and other classroom assessments collaboratively used to guide improvement (see page 83).

While it is important to recognize the limitations of standardized tests so that you don't overrely on them, you can still learn a lot from these sources,

## Types of Assessments

▼ Standardized tests are uniform in content, administration, and scoring, allowing for comparisons of results across classrooms, schools, and school districts (Bernhardt 1998, 65). Two types of standardized tests are norm-referenced and criterion-referenced.

▼ Norm-referenced tests compare student test performance against that of other students, using a national sample. NRTs usually report student performance as a percentile score and rely on multiple-choice questions. Examples include the Iowa Test of Basic Skills and the SATs.

▼ Criterion-referenced tests measure student performance on an agreed-upon set of skills and against an agreed-upon criterion (Marzano and Kendall 1996, 90). Standards-based assessments, which measure student performance against a set of standards, are one kind of criterion-referenced test.

▼ Performance assessments require students to generate rather than choose a response. Students must bring prior and recent knowledge and relevant skills to bear to accomplish complex tasks or solve realistic, authentic problems (Herman, Aschbacher, and Winters 1992, 2).

especially when these data are disaggregated, tracked over time, and supplemented with other information. The box below briefly describes some of the common types of assessments that are used to measure student performance.

*The achievement gaps between white and minority, rich and poor, which were narrowing until 1988, are widening again.*

(Education Trust 1996, 5)

## Disaggregating: Shedding New Light on Student Learning

Disaggregating means looking at how specific subgroups of students perform rather than just at the big picture. Typically, student achievement data come "aggregated," in other words, reported for the population as a whole. The problem is that aggregated data can mask important trends and issues. (For a more in-depth discussion on disaggregating data, see "Disaggregate, Disaggregate, Disaggregate" in Chapter 2.) If your school is at all typical, you are likely to find some gaps in performance between low-income students and others, among different racial groups, and possibly between girls and boys. Uncovering these differences is critical to beginning a dialogue about what practices and beliefs might be perpetuating these gaps and how to better serve children who are falling behind (see Chapter 5).

Figure 3.2 illustrates one urban middle school's 2001 results on the New Standards Reference Exam (NSRE) in mathematics problem solving. The NSRE results are reported disaggregated by gender, race, Limited English Proficiency (LEP), and special and general education. If educators from this school were having a dialogue about these results, using the three-phase process described in Chapter 2 (see Figure 2.4), they might make some of the following observations in the exploring and discovering phase:

▼ overall, students are not performing well in mathematics problem solving;

▼ no special education students meet the standard in mathematics problem solving;

▼ white students slightly outperform black and Hispanic students;

▼ students with Limited English Proficiency are the most successful at meeting the standards;

▼ no gender gap is evident;

▼ Asian Pacific Islander students perform slightly better than white and somewhat better than black or Hispanic students.

As they begin to ask why and formulate hypotheses in the next phase of their dialogue, they might generate several questions for further investigation: What opportunities do students have to engage with complex mathematics problems in their middle school? Are students tracked? Are blacks or Hispanics disproportionately represented in the lower tracks?

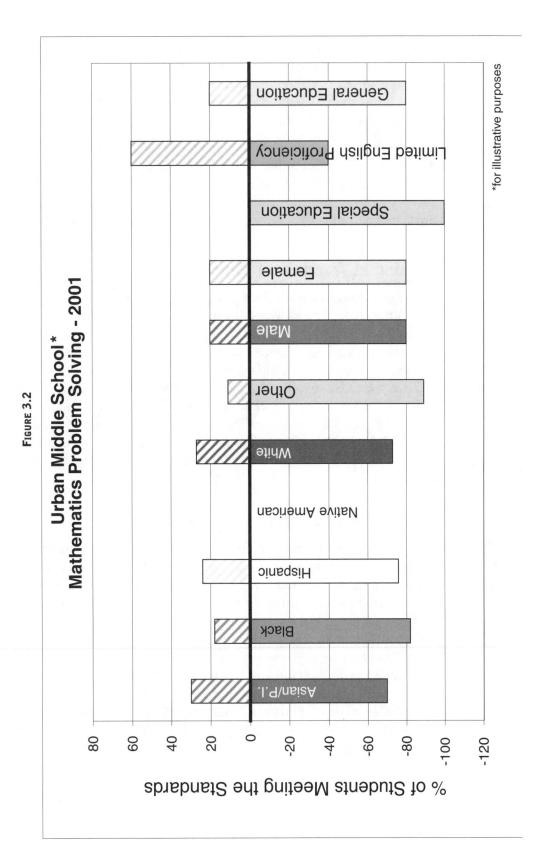

FIGURE 3.2

**Urban Middle School***
**Mathematics Problem Solving - 2001**

*for illustrative purposes

What is the quality of the mathematics instruction they are receiving? What is happening in special education? Why are a higher percentage of LEP students meeting the standards? Disaggregated data such as these can help schools begin to talk about problems that might otherwise be overlooked and to probe more deeply into opportunities to learn and other equity issues discussed in Chapter 5.

Many testing companies will provide schools with a variety of disaggregated data upon request. The **Data Tools** contain forms for collecting demographic data (see "Who's in Our School/District?" DT 3-2) and for analyzing disaggregated mathematics and science achievement data, both norm-referenced and standards-based (see DT 3-3 through DT 3-6).

## Looking at Trends over Time

Drawing valid conclusions from just one year's worth of data can be difficult. But studying several years of data can uncover important trends, such as how a particular group of students performs over time. This information can provide additional clues about where problems lurk. The forms for comparing two years of standards-based assessment results, in **Data Tools**, DT 3-5 and DT 3-6, offer one way to help you look at trends over time. Below, we offer a menu of other ideas about how to track data over time. Some of these data may be readily available; some will be more difficult to compile. You don't need to go for it all. Eventually, when you develop your monitoring plan, you can choose the most important pieces of data to track over time.

*Quartiles divide norm-referenced test scores into four equal parts. The highest quartile consists of the highest 25 percent of the scores of the norm group.*

*The lowest quartile represents the bottom 25 percent of the norm group scores.*

(Vermont Department of Education 1998, 3.20)

### Looking for Movement in the Lowest Quartile

A lot can be learned from analyzing standardized test data by quartiles. For example, Ruth Johnson suggests looking at whether students are moving out of the bottom quartile over time. As can be seen in Table 3.1, the percentage of students in the top quartile in mathematics increases from 17.1 percent to 38.5 percent over a three-year period. But very little change takes place at the bottom: "The middle rises but the bottom sticks," as Johnson puts it (1996, 236). These data raise questions about whether improvement efforts were targeted for all students. It can also be useful to look at which students are falling into the bottom quartile and whether they have access to the same curriculum as other students. The form "Analyzing Norm-Referenced Test Results by Quartile," in **Data Tools**, DT 3-7, can help your team take a closer look at these questions.

## Table 3.1: Test Scores by Quartiles Over Three Years

| School: Grade 4 | Read Vocab | Read Comp | Read Total | Lang Mech | Lang Expr | Lang Total | Math Comp | Math C&A | Math Total |
|---|---|---|---|---|---|---|---|---|---|
| Number of Students in 1993 | 75 | 76 | 75 | 76 | 76 | 76 | 76 | 76 | 76 |
| Quartiles (%/Quarter) | | | | | | | | | |
| 76–99 | 0.0 | 2.6 | **1.3** | 3.5 | 1.3 | **1.3** | 28.9 | 10.5 | **17.1** |
| 51–75 | 17.3 | 18.5 | 17.3 | 13.2 | 17.1 | 3.9 | 32.6 | 23.7 | 32.9 |
| 26–50 | 26.7 | 28.9 | 30.7 | 25.0 | 28.9 | 21.1 | 15.8 | 30.3 | 17.1 |
| 01–25 | 56.0 | 52.6 | 50.7 | 57.9 | 53.9 | 73.7 | 23.7 | 35.5 | **32.9** |
| Number of Students in 1994 | 84 | 85 | 84 | 84 | 84 | 84 | 84 | 83 | 83 |
| Quartiles (%/Quarter) | | | | | | | | | |
| 76–99 | 7.1 | 5.9 | 4.8 | 17.9 | 4.8 | 10.7 | 27.4 | 12.0 | 21.7 |
| 51–75 | 21.4 | 23.5 | 22.6 | 21.4 | 17.9 | 19.0 | 16.7 | 19.3 | 16.9 |
| 26–50 | 27.4 | 30.6 | 31.0 | 27.4 | 39.3 | 28.6 | 27.4 | 28.9 | 25.3 |
| 01–25 | 44.0 | 40.0 | 41.7 | 33.3 | 38.1 | 41.7 | 28.6 | 39.8 | 36.1 |
| Number of Students in 1995 | 78 | 78 | 78 | 78 | 78 | 78 | 78 | 76 | 78 |
| Quartiles (%/Quarter) | | | | | | | | | |
| 76–99 | 17.9 | 10.3 | **15.4** | 23.1 | 15.4 | **19.3** | 39.7 | 37.2 | **38.5** |
| 51–75 | 15.4 | 21.8 | 17.9 | 23.1 | 17.9 | 16.7 | 9.0 | 17.9 | 17.9 |
| 26–50 | 14.1 | 30.8 | 26.9 | 21.8 | 38.5 | 35.9 | 25.6 | 12.8 | 11.5 |
| 01–25 | 52.6 | 37.2 | 39.7 | 32.1 | 28.2 | 28.2 | 25.6 | 32.1 | **32.1** |

Good news: Reading, Language and Mathematics scores indicate increases in the top quartile by year three.

Bad news: By year three, the bottom quartile percent in math is similar to year one.

81

## Following a Cohort of Students

Another interesting way to look at achievement data over time is to follow the same group of students, or cohort. Typically, when test data are reported from year to year, the students being compared are different. For example, fourth-grade students from 1996–97 are compared with students who were in fourth grade in 1997–98. The differences in students undoubtedly account for at least some of the variation. By tracking the same student group from year to year, that variable is eliminated. Then the data can reveal more about the effect of changes in programs and practices on a particular cohort of students.

Following the same cohort of students over time requires converting standardized test scores to Normal Curve Equivalents (NCEs). An annotated chart in **Data Tools**, DT 3-8, illustrates how to use NCEs to track the same group of students over time.

## Selecting and Tracking Test Items That Matter to Your Team

For many teachers, the most useful information that standardized tests provide for diagnostic purposes is the item analysis. Available from most major testing companies, these analyses show how individual students performed on a cluster of test items related to the same skill. Often, clusters are cross-referenced with activities from major publishers' textbooks so teachers have some specific ideas on how to refocus instruction.

Improvement teams can take advantage of item analysis data by tracking student performance on clusters of items that are particularly relevant to their local standards-led reform effort. In this way you can use standardized tests selectively for information that is valuable to you. See **Data Tools**, DT 3-9, for an example of an item analysis.

## Comparing Grades with Standardized Test Data

What does it mean when students are earning high grades but scoring poorly on standardized tests? It could mean that teachers are grading too easy, expecting too little of their students, or not reaching all of their students. This is an example of what can be learned from comparing grades with standardized test data. The **Data Tools**, DT 3-10, contain a form, "Grades and Test Performance," to help facilitate such comparisons. While grades alone are unreliable measures of student performance, comparing them with other achievement data can uncover discrepancies and lead to improvements in grading practices.

## Tapping Other Available Data about Student Performance

In addition to standardized tests and grades, school improvement teams can tap other readily available data about student performance, such as dropout, retention, and attendance rates and numbers of discipline referrals and overage students. While not direct measures of mathematics or science performance, these data provide additional indicators of how students are faring, who is in trouble, and what factors might be affecting their academic performance. For example, students absent more than 15 percent of the time during a school year often end up dropping out (Education Trust [1996], 26). So do students who are two years overage for their grade level. Contrary to the intent of retention, retained students tend to fall further and further behind, never to catch up (Education Trust [1996], 12). Other red flags are dropout rates that surge at a particular grade level or a disproportionate number of minority discipline referrals. To the right are some questions to consider when looking at these types of data.

Forms are provided in **Data Tools**, DT 3-11 through 3-15, for disaggregating and analyzing retention, overage student, dropout, absenteeism, and discipline referral data.

### ANALYZING RETENTION, OVERAGE STUDENT, DROPOUT, ABSENTEEISM, AND DISCIPLINE REFERRAL DATA: QUESTIONS TO CONSIDER

▼ Which groups of students appear to be at risk of school failure, based on a combination of excessive absence, retention, and dropout rates?

▼ What percentage of the student population has been suspended or involved in disciplinary action?

▼ What are the characteristics of students with high absence, discipline, retention, or dropout rates? (Lachat and Williams 1996)

## Using Performance Assessments to Learn More about Student Learning

We began this section by suggesting that your team start painting a picture of student learning by using readily available achievement and performance data, disaggregating that data, and tracking them over time. But don't stop there. These data provide a thin, one-dimensional view of student learning. To fill out the picture, your team will eventually want to draw on multiple assessments, such as performance tasks, portfolios, close examination of student work, observations, and self-assessments.

For a number of reasons, these assessment strategies are an integral part of mathematics and science reform. They are far more effective than standardized testing at measuring the kind of learning called for in the standards. They are learning experiences in themselves and promote high-quality classroom instruction. They help teachers gain rich insights into their students' thinking. And, when collected and analyzed by grade level, subject, school, or district, multiple assessment data add the necessary depth, texture, and color to the picture you are painting of student learning. (For more on assessment as it relates to curriculum and instruction, see "Problem Three: Implementing Assessment Reform" in Chapter 4.)

## Performance Assessment Tasks

For the purposes of schoolwide mathematics and science improvement, performance assessment tasks are an essential complement to short-answer and multiple-choice test data. Performance tasks focus on important content and performance goals, giving students an opportunity to demonstrate their understanding of concepts and ability to conduct scientific inquiry or apply mathematics in complex or new situations (NCTM 2000, 24, and National Research Council (NRC) 1996, 38). For example, the Swings Task, a fourth-grade performance task from the Council of Chief State School Officers/ State Collaborative on Assessment and Student Standards (CCSSO/ SCASS), asks students to "investigate variables which may seem to affect the movement of a pendulum, or 'swing.' Students are then asked to interpret their observations and come to a conceptual discovery of the pendulum" (CCSSO/ SCASS, from Center for Technology and Learning Web site [http://www. ctl.sri.com/pals/tasks/k-4/Swings/]). To be successful, students must understand concepts related to the position and motion of objects as well as be able to conduct an investigation; use equipment; gather, organize, and represent data; formulate conclusions; and apply scientific principles to develop explanations and solve new problems. Scoring student work such as that generated by the swings task requires the development of a rubric—standards or criteria for judging performance. The annotated example of student work on this task, illustrated in Figure 3.3, was scored according to the following criteria:

Criterion 1: In either question one or two, score one point for noticing that the swings with shorter strings (A and B) went faster, OR if the student correctly identifies the model as a pendulum.

Criterion 2: In either question one or two, score one point for a statement of the underlying concept: that shorter-stringed pendulums go faster because they are shorter.

Criterion 3: Score one point if, in question two, the student cites the result of the experiment in order to make a clear connection to the model of the tire swing.

Criterion 4: One point for coming to the logical conclusion in either question one or two that weight is irrelevant to the speed of the swing (CCSSO/SCASS, from Center for Technology and Learning Web site [http://www.ctl.sri.com/pals/tasks/k-4/Swings/]).

**FIGURE 3.3**

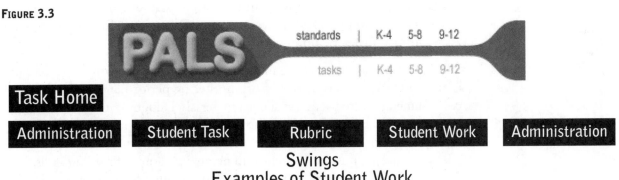

## Swings
### Examples of Student Work
Contributed by: Council of Chief State School Officers (CCSSO/SCASS)

**Question 1 and Question 2: Event Score = 3**

1. Which two swings go back and forth the fastest? What do the fastest two swings have in common? How do the fastest two swings differ from the slowest two swings?

2. Tell Jodi and Eduardo how to make Jodi's swing go faster. Tell them about results as you give your answer.

### Questions

*Please answer the following questions by yourself*

1. **Which two swings go back and forth the fastest? What do the fastest two swings have in common? How do the fastest two swings differ from the slowest two swings?**

> The short and light and short and heavy washers went the most times. The fastest to strings both have a short string. The faster to strings have a short string and the slowest two string have long

2. **Tell Jodi and Eduardo how to make Jodi's swing go faster. Tell them about results as you give your answer.**

> You should make your rope shorter. Because I notesed that the Shorter the string the faster it will go.

> Score 3
> meets CRITERION ONE in the first ANSWER and CRITERIA TWO and THREE in the second answer:
> "Because I noticed [CRIT 3] that the shorter the string the faster it will go" [CRIT 2]

Many quality performance assessments tasks in mathematics and science are now published in print and on the web (see **Resources for Performance Assessment Tasks**, beginning on page 146).

While performance tasks have many advantages, they are difficult to administer, construct, and score reliably. Administering performance tasks is time-consuming and often requires special materials. Designing valid assessments, ones that actually measure what they intend, is another challenge. For example, the intention might be to measure students' understanding of science concepts, but the task ends up being a measure of reading skills. Reliability is equally important and challenging in at least two ways. First, students should perform similarly on two or more tasks that claim to measure the same aspect of student achievement. Moreover, scoring assessments reliably, so that several scorers give the same result, requires a great deal of training and experience. Finally, assuring that assessments are free from bias demands careful scrutiny for use of stereotypes, contexts that may be unfamiliar to a particular group, or offensive or exclusionary language (NRC 1996, 84-85). All of these challenges suggest that great care should be taken in designing or selecting performance tasks and scoring them, that multiple assessments should be used to assess the same skill, and that performance assessments should be one more piece of the puzzle, not the sole measure of success or failure.

## Grade-Level or Subject-Area Performance Assessments

When first beginning to use performance assessment data for school improvement, we urge teams to start small. Integrating performance assessment strategies into the classroom is enough of a challenge! One approach is to start with one grade level or one subject. Target one or two key concepts or skills in the curriculum. Many of the new curriculum materials in mathematics and science include performance tasks that could be used for this purpose. Teachers can work together to administer performance tasks—two, three, or four times a year—and track students' performance in these areas. The leadership team can collaborate with teachers to collect and analyze the data, uncover problems, and improve instruction.

This is the approach that fourth-grade teachers at Holaway Elementary School in Tucson, Arizona, used. They wanted to increase students' mathematical thinking and problem-solving abilities. Every four to six weeks, they administered performance assessments and scored them using rubrics for logical reasoning, demonstration, and computation. Then they combined their data, reflected on them, and decided on a course of action to improve student learning. In one meeting, for instance, the team noticed that the same students were remaining at low levels of performance, even though aggregate performance was increasing. They decided to try out prompts to probe and guide students' thinking as they solved problems. Six weeks later they had feedback to show that their approach was working. Figure 3.4 shows how the teachers at Holaway reported their data on the students' logical reasoning skills. The numbers 0–6 indicate scores on their rubric.

## Schoolwide Performance Assessments

Increasingly, school staff involved in standards-led reform are recognizing the need for collecting and analyzing performance assessment data schoolwide. Table 3.2 shows the results of one such effort in an elementary school. Teachers in grades 1–5 gave their students performance tasks that assessed two skill areas—problem solving and ability to communicate mathematically—at the beginning and end of the school year. During the year, students practiced with performance tasks and worked hard on their thinking and reasoning skills, with satisfying results.

**FIGURE 3.4: GRADE-LEVEL PERFORMANCE ASSESSMENT RESULTS SCORED WITH RUBRIC**

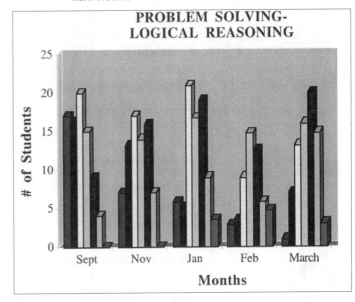

**TABLE 3.2: SAMPLE: SCHOOL PERFORMANCE ASSESSMENT RESULTS**

### Pretest and Posttest Results on Performance Tasks

| Ethnicity | A<br>Pretest Problem Solving | B<br>Posttest Problem Solving | C<br>Pretest Communication | D<br>Posttest Communication |
|---|---|---|---|---|
| Asian<br>(25) | 16.0%<br>(4) | 68.0%<br>(17) | 12.0%<br>(3) | 44%<br>(11) |
| African American<br>(130) | 8.3%<br>(11) | 50.8%<br>(66) | 12.3%<br>(16) | 32.3%<br>(42) |
| Hispanic<br>(31) | 3.2%<br>(1) | 77.4%<br>(24) | 0%<br>(0) | 48.4%<br>(15) |
| White<br>(116) | 29.3%<br>(34) | 78.4%<br>(92) | 24.1%<br>(28) | 62.9%<br>(73) |
| Grand Total<br>(302) | 16.6% | 65.6% | 15.6% | 46.7% |

Note: From R.J. Marzano and J.S. Kendall, 1992, unpublished data, Aurora, CO: Mid-continent Educational Laboratory

## Districtwide Performance Assessments

Requiring even more commitment and coordination are districtwide performance assessments. A good example of effective use of these comes from the Glendale Union High School District outside of Phoenix, Arizona, which has been at the business of designing and administering such assessments since 1995. Data from these tests, along with district criterion-referenced test data, then become the basis for improvement planning at the district, school, and department level. Figure 3.5 offers a summary of the chemistry course and assessments, and Figures 3.6 and 3.7 illustrate a sample report of results. **(See Reform in Action**, page 327.)

If your district doesn't have the resources that Glendale did to develop your own performance assessments, don't despair. Many excellent assessment tasks are now available either as part of a standards-based curriculum program or from commercial and other sources. Consider shopping for already existing assessments that match your curriculum rather than reinventing the wheel (see **Resources for Performance Assessment Tasks**, beginning on page 146.) This is the approach that Fresno (California) Unified School District takes. They use the assessments that are part of the Full Option Science System (FOSS) program (see Mathematics and Science Curriculum Materials on the accompanying CD-ROM) for their district science assessment. Each year, K-6 teachers administer portions of one FOSS assessment, including hands-on, pictorial, and reflecting sections that cover an entire unit, to their students for district assessment purposes. Teachers then submit

### FIGURE 3.5: CHEMISTRY COURSE DESCRIPTION

This course is a lab-oriented class with emphasis on the students

- Becoming aware of chemistry-related societal issues.
- Focusing on current chemistry-related issues.
- Using scientific/technological information in the decision-making process.
- Doing data analysis and scientific inquiry.

These outcomes are measured by a performance-based assessment over a four day period.

Outcomes assessed by a multiple choice assessment include

- Chemical nomenclature
- Mole problems
- Gas laws
- Stoichiometry
- Interpretation of data

### FIGURE 3.6: CHEMISTRY LABORATORY ASSESSMENT

| Distrct | | | |
|---|---|---|---|
| Level of Achievement | Problem & Purpose 546 Assessed | Data Collection 546 Assessed | Analysis & Conclusion 546 Assessed |
| % Students Successful or Better | 82% | 89% | 85% |
| Not Yet Successful | 16% | 9% | 13% |
| Prereq. Not Met | 2% | 2% | 2% |

the students' assessments to the district, which has teams of trained teachers score them in the summer. This assessment program has the advantage of being tied directly to the curriculum, giving teachers some choice in what assessments are used, providing a valuable professional learning experience for teachers scoring the work, and generating useful data about student learning in science.

| FIGURE 3.7: PERCENT OF STUDENTS BY LEVEL OF ACHIEVEMENT | |
| --- | --- |
| Level of Achievement | District 546 Assessed |
| % Students Successful or Better | 68% |
| Outstanding | 4% |
| Highly successful | 14% |
| Successful | 50% |
| Not Yet Successful | 30% |
| Prereq. Not Met | 2% |

## Looking at Student Work: "A Treasure Trove of Insights"

Analyzing grade-level, school, or district performance assessment results is one way to use alternative assessment data. Closely examining students' work offers another powerful, yet largely untapped, source of information about student learning. Student work can include journals, projects, mathematics problems, laboratory reports, drawings, writings, and exhibitions. When done well, discussing student work can lead to deeper understandings about individual students, insights about students' thinking, and a wealth of ideas about how to improve teaching and learning. It can also provide information about the quality of assignments provided. And, perhaps most important of all, it provides a rich professional learning opportunity for teachers.

## Searching for Evidence of Student Learning

In their book *Active Assessment for Active Science*, George Hein and Sabra Price identify two approaches to interpreting students' work (1994, 87). One approach is to search for evidence of specific criteria, set in advance, such as how well students are measuring and using instruments or communicating mathematically. This is the approach that teachers involved in the professional portfolio project at Souhegan High School in Amherst, New Hampshire, use. They pose a question about student learning that they want to investigate and examine student work to help them answer that question.

For example, mathematics teacher Jim Bosman wanted to know if students were making connections between the mathematics they were doing in school and the world around them. As he examined samples of student work on tides, location of solar bodies, airline flight, and predator/prey relations, he was pleased to see his students applying the trigonometry concepts and skills he was teaching in his eleventh-grade classroom to real-world problems. "It feels good to see that students' work reflects my values and goals as a teacher," Bosman commented.

*"Looking closely together at student work can unveil a treasure trove of insights to guide school communities as they reflect on their purpose, assess their progress, and plan strategies for reaching all children better. It's scary work, though, and respectful protocols can help."*

(Cushman 1996, 1)

Science lends itself equally well to looking at student work against set criteria. A good example is the work teachers at Heinsberg (Vermont) Elementary School are doing with student journals. Through their participation in the Vermont Continuous Assessment in Science Project at Trinity College in Burlington (now the Center for Science Education and Professional Development in Williston, Vermont), these teachers learned how to examine student journals to assess students' skills in using the scientific process. Fifth-grade teacher Lauren Kogge explained, "We used journaling to determine if students were using the scientific process, setting up fair experiments, understanding the idea of variables, drawing scientifically valid conclusions. One thing we noticed was that students were trying to draw conclusions on not-so-good data. We had to go back and work on accurate data collection."

## Learning More about Student Thinking

A second approach to looking at student work is to view it without any predetermined criteria—just for the purpose of learning more about what students think, what their deepest understandings are, and what they feel. By better grasping how students are making sense of mathematics or science concepts or approaching skills, teachers can help deepen students' understandings and also gain insights into how to improve their own curriculum and instruction.

For example, examination of student work is a regular activity for teachers using the Investigations in Number, Data, and Space mathematics curriculum (see Mathematics and Science Curriculum Materials on the accompanying CD-ROM). When doing written work, students are often required to record their strategies for problem solving, as illustrated in Figure 3.8. As teachers examine what strategies students use, they learn about individual students' strengths and preferences as well as about how to redirect instruction.

Investigations curriculum developers Jan Mokros, Susan Jo Russell, and Karen Economopoulos offer the following suggestions on what to look for when examining student work in mathematics:

▼ the extent to which the students' use of mathematics was effective in helping them solve a problem;

▼ the flexibility and appropriateness of the students' strategies for solving a problem;

▼ whether the students make use of traditional algorithms, and if they can explain why they work;

**FIGURE 3.8: STRATEGIES FOR PROBLEM SOLVING**

I have 12 crayons. I have some red, some green and some blue. How many of each could I have? Find as many solutions as you can!! Show your answers with numbers, pictures or words.

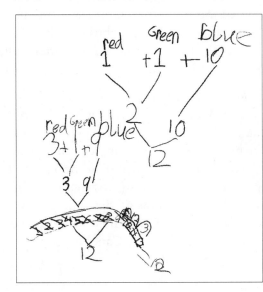

A teacher-developed problem based on the Grade 1 *Investigations in Number, Data, and Space* curriculum.

▼ the extent to which the students' explanations, representations, or drawings of their solutions clearly communicate their mathematical thinking;

▼ the accuracy of the students' work;

▼ whether the students were able to use "false starts" or mistakes in order to get on the right track;

▼ how the students used tools to solve a problem (Mokros, Russell, and Economopoulos 1995, 96).

Examining student work in these ways not only produces insights into student learning; it promotes powerful, ongoing professional growth for teachers if it is done well. For teachers, who are accustomed to the privacy of their own classrooms, putting their own students' work on the table for colleagues to critique can be scary business. It is important that discussions of student work take place in a safe environment, where participants will not be judged or threatened.

The Coalition of Essential Schools based at Brown University, the Prospect School in North Bennington, Vermont, the ATLAS Project at Harvard University, and others have developed protocols, or step-by-step procedures, that help ensure that reflecting on student work takes place in a risk-free climate. These protocols, including the Tuning Protocol (Coalition) and the Descriptive Review Process (Prospect School), carefully structure listening, sharing different points of view, and giving productive feedback and require skilled facilitators. (For more on these protocols, see **Data Tools**, DT 2-5 and DT 2-6, and "How Can We Learn to Recognize Students' Strengths?" in Chapter 5.)

**Souhegan High School**, a member of the Coalition of Essential Schools in Amherst, New Hampshire, is a great place to go to see the Tuning Protocol and other structures for examining student work in action. At Souhegan, collegial reflection is as much a part of school life as buses or chalkboards. Teachers have two unassigned periods a day, time they commit to working together. Grade-level teams typically meet daily; most departments meet monthly; and teacher groups, such as teacher advisors and Critical Friends Groups (groups committed to working together to improve student learning), meet regularly as well.

No doubt, these teachers are fortunate to have time to work together. But they also work hard, using structures such as those mentioned above to make their time together productive—so productive, in fact, that Souhegan teachers can hardly imagine life without them. Ninth-grade mathematics teacher Kristen Gallo explained, "When I started working with my colleagues, discussing students' work and reflecting on our teaching, that's when I really started growing. It's easy to allow kids to fall through the cracks. But when my colleagues ask me to reflect, it's hard to ignore any one student. My team meets on a daily basis; they hold me responsible for all kids. I now know it doesn't work to teach as an island."

## Assessing the Quality of Work in Relation to Standards

Another way for improvement teams to make effective use of examples of student work is to examine the quality of assignments students are receiving. Do assignments give students the opportunity to gain important knowledge called for in local, state, or national standards? Do they require students to use complex reasoning skills? Are they worth the time they take to do for the quality of learning produced? Are certain student groups receiving more interesting and challenging assignments than others?

Ruth Mitchell, in her book *Front-End Alignment: Using Standards to Steer Educational Change* (1996), offers a process for teams to examine teacher assignments and student work in relation to standards; it is outlined in the box below.

Obviously, examining student work in any of the ways described above is very time-consuming. So for schoolwide improve-

### Process for Examining Teacher Assignments and Student Work in Relation to Standards

1. Every member of the team does the assignment as given to the students.

2. The group generates a rough scoring guide from the standards and the assignment.

3. The group scores the student papers, using the guide.

4. The recorder writes the group's answers to these questions: What does this student work tell us about student learning? What do students know and what are they able to do? Was the assignment well-designed to help students acquire knowledge and exercise skills?

5. The recorder writes the group's answers to this question: What needs to happen in the classroom, school, and district so that all students can do this and similar tasks well?

6. The group plans action to improve student learning.

ment efforts, the bulk of the data on student learning will, of necessity, be quantitative. But we urge improvement teams to incorporate some analysis of student work, particularly as it sheds light on areas targeted for improvement. For example, if improving students' ability to communicate in mathematics is a priority, look at samples of student work in this area only.

## Developing a Data Collection Plan

The different data sources discussed above can help you answer two questions that will be critical to improving mathematics and science learning in your school or district: (1) What are our strengths and weaknesses in mathematics and science achievement? (2) To what extent do performance gaps in mathematics and science exist among racial, class, cultural, or gender groups in our school? In the **Planning Tools**, pages 121–122 and 123–124, are forms that can help you organize your plan for collecting data about these two questions. A sample is illustrated here.

## Surveying Student Learning Results

| Problem/ Question | *What are our strengths and weaknesses in mathematics and science achievement?* | | | | |
|---|---|---|---|---|---|
| Data Sources/Tools We Want to Use | Got It | Need It | Disaggregated by | How/When Collected | Person Responsible |
| | | | | | |

## Summarizing and Analyzing Student Learning Data

In the section above, we discussed how to mine a variety of sources of data about student performance, from standardized test scores to dropout rates to analysis of student work. The form "Putting It All Together—Student Learning Data Summary Sheet" in **Data Tools**, DT 3-16, can help your team summarize the variety of student learning data you have gathered so far.

As you "put it all together," analyzing the multiple measures of student learning you have collected, avoid the temptation to rush to conclusions about causality— "Our students are doing poorly at mathematics because. . ." This is a good time to remember the "hang out in uncertainty" principle discussed in Chapter 2 (page 44). Use this time to reach out to more people and engage in constructive and open-ended dialogue about what the data might mean. Also, don't be afraid to explore additional sources of data to validate your conclusions, using the "Additional Sources of Data" form in **Data Tools**, DT 2-4. Later in this chapter we will discuss how to formulate a problem statement based on what you have learned.

To summarize, while student learning data can begin to point to problem areas, it does not necessarily tell you what actions to take. For that, you will need to dig deeper, considering, among other issues, whether all students have the opportunity to learn challenging, high-quality mathematics and science content.

## Assessing Opportunities to Learn

Imagine a school where some students don't get to learn with qualified teachers. Or they don't have access to computers, high-quality instructional materials, or rigorous curriculum. Or they don't get to take algebra or geometry, even though they may have good enough grades or scores on standardized tests. Or they aren't taught challenging science, not because they don't have the ability, but because they don't speak English well. Unfortunately, these conditions are prevalent in U.S. schools (see Figures 3.9, 3.10, and 3.11). And the victims, most often, are poor and minority students. Many students are not learning well simply because they are not given the opportunity.

FIGURE 3.9

## Teachers in High Poverty Schools Spend Less Time Developing Reasoning Skills

| | % Teachers Who Spend a Lot of Time on Reasoning Skills |
|---|---|
| High Poverty Schools | 39% |
| More Affluent Schools | 55% |

Source: NAEP 1996 Math Data Tables (NCES, US Department of Education)

Many national and state standards include Opportunities to Learn (OTL) standards, a set of recommended practices to support all students in achieving learning standards. OTL standards attempt to resolve the contradiction between talk about high standards for all and practices that prevent students from achieving them. A list of OTL standards is given in the box to the left.

What practices might be preventing students from learning at high levels in your school or district? Here are some places to look:

**Course enrollment**: Who is enrolled in the gatekeeper courses such as algebra and geometry? What is the selection process? Can students enroll or do they have to be selected? Who is taking advanced mathematics and science courses? Who drops out? Why? Who doesn't take mathematics and/or science in their senior

### Opportunities to Learn Standards

All students have access to:

▼ quality instructors;

▼ rigorous content;

▼ ample resources, including technology;

▼ effective use of time;

▼ relevant curriculum;

▼ effective instruction and assessment practices;

▼ family and community collaboration (Vermont Department of Education 1996, 8.0).

year? Peer into any physics or calculus class. Do the students there look like the student body as a whole? How many girls, boys, African Americans, Asians, Hispanics, whites move up a level (from regular to honors) or down a level? Does your school offer remedial mathematics? What is the curriculum? Who is taking it? Does it lead every student to algebra? (Campbell and Storo 1996.) These are some important questions to ask as you investigate possible inequities in course enrollment. The forms in **Data Tools**, DT 3-17 and DT 3-18, can help you disaggregate and begin to analyze course enrollment trends in mathematics and science.

**Course enrollment and test performance:** Are minorities who score well on tests not being placed in algebra or geometry? (See Figure 3.10.) The form "Performance on Standardized Tests and Course Placement, by Race and Ethnicity" in **Data Tools**, DT 3-19, can help you organize your data to answer this question.

**FIGURE 3.10**

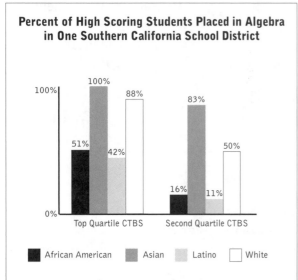

Percent of High Scoring Students Placed in Algebra in One Southern California School District

- African American
- Asian
- Latino
- White

**Master schedules:** These can also offer valuable information about course offerings and enrollment. Figure 3.12 illustrates course offerings in the Providence (Rhode Island) Public Schools before EQUITY 2000, a College Board-sponsored initiative to increase minority students' access to higher levels of mathematics, was implemented. Note the tangled web of courses, including remedial, basic, applied, and consumer math, few of which led to algebra and geometry. Figure 3.13 shows the changes in course offerings after reform. It illustrates four clear pathways for students, all of which eventually lead to algebra or geometry. (See **Reform in Action**, page 335.)

**Special programs placement:** Who is placed in special education, gifted and talented programs, and bilingual and ESL programs? What is the quality of

the mathematics and science these students are offered and how are they faring? See the form in **Data Tools**, DT 3-20, for disaggregating student placement in special programs.

**Tracking:** Is tracking in any of its many forms being practiced? Which students are in the low tracks? What is the quality of instruction they are receiving? (Tracking, the sorting of students by categories, is one of the most significant barriers to equal learning opportunities. Schools committed to high levels of learning for all students will need to thoroughly investigate tracking practices and their impact on student learning. For a fuller treatment of this topic, see "Structural Barriers to Equity" in Chapter 5.)

**Teachers' qualifications:** Are teachers without at least a minor in mathematics or science teaching these courses? Are a disproportionate number of poor or minority students taking courses with underprepared teachers? See Figure 3.13, Figure 4.6, and the form "How Well Are Teachers Prepared?" in **Data Tools**, DT 3-21.

**Quality of curriculum, instruction, and assessment:** What is being taught in mathematics and science and how? How is learning being assessed? Are all students gaining equal access to the best practices? For a fuller discussion of ways of assessing classroom practice, see Problems Two and Three in Chapter 4.

## Access to technology:

Where are computers? Who is using them? How often and for what purposes? Are computers used by all students in mathematics and science? Who is participating in computer clubs and after-school activities? See "Equity and Technology Checklist" (DT 3-22), Computer Laboratory Usage Forms 1 and 2 (DT 3-23 and DT 3-24), "Technology Course Enrollment Form" (DT 3-25), and the Surveys of Classroom Practices (DT 4-7 and DT 4-8) in **Data Tools** to help you investigate these questions.

**FIGURE 3.11**

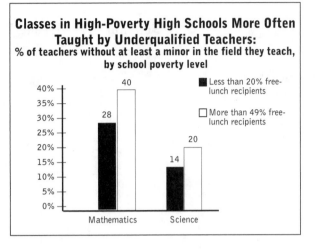

Classes in High-Poverty High Schools More Often Taught by Underqualified Teachers:
% of teachers without at least a minor in the field they teach, by school poverty level

■ Less than 20% free-lunch recipients
□ More than 49% free-lunch recipients

**College-going and graduation rates:** Are some student groups under-represented? Why? What factors seem to be associated with college entrance and completion? See **Data Tools**, DT 3-26 and DT 3-27, for a sample survey and a form to help with this analysis.

Especially when student achievement data is low, as a whole or for particular groups, data about these potential gaps in learning opportunities can point to important leverage points for change. So can students' voices about their aspirations, as you will see in the section that follows.

---

**RESOURCES FOR EXPLORING PERFORMANCE AND OPPORTUNITIES GAPS**

*Closing the Achievement Gap: A Vision to Guide Change in Beliefs and Practice,* edited by Belinda Williams, 1995 (see **Resources**, Chapter 5)

*Education Watch: The Education Trust Community Data Guide,* by The Education Trust, [1996] (see **Resources**, Chapter 2)

*Education Watch: The 1996 Education Trust State and National Data Book,* by The Education Trust, 1996 (see **Resources**, Chapter 2)

*Setting Our Sights: Measuring Equity in School Change,* by Ruth Johnson, 1996 (see **Resources**, Chapter 2)

FIGURE 3.12: SCHEDULE A

## SCHEDULE A—BEFORE EQUITY 2000

Providence School Department
Secondary Mathematics
Grades 9–12

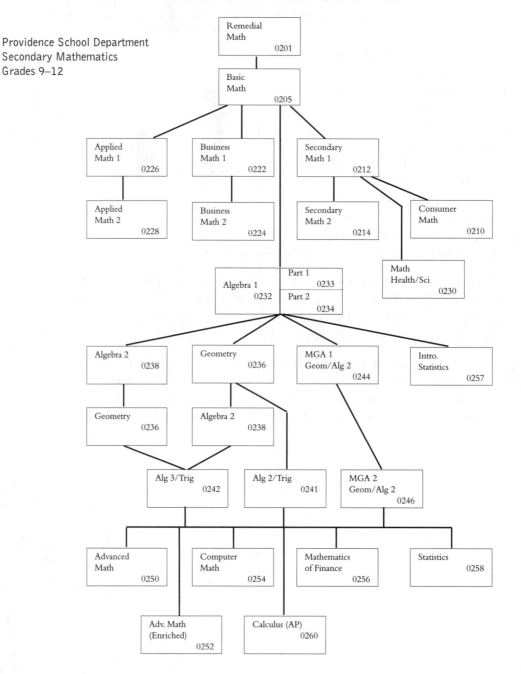

**FIGURE 3.13: SCHEDULE B**

## SCHEDULE B—AFTER EQUITY 2000

### Mathematics Division Courses

| Course Sequence—Providence Public Schools 1994–95 | | | | |
|---|---|---|---|---|
| | The top 10% of 6th graders are ready to take Transition Mathematics in 6th grade. | Students in the 30th–70th percentile on a grade 7 standardized test are ready to take Transition Mathematics in grade 7. | Those 7th grade students requiring 3 semesters to complete Transition Mathematics should begin Algebra in the second semester of grade 8. | Those students who will require two full years to complete Transition Mathematics should begin Algebra 1 in 9th grade. |
| Grade | Option 1 | Option 2 | Option 3 | Option 4 |
| 5 | Exploring Math | | | |
| 6 | Transition Math (Pre-Algebra) | Exploring Math | | |
| 7 | Algebra | Transition Math I (Pre-Algebra) | Transition Math I (Pre-Algebra) | Transition Math I (Pre-Algebra) |
| 8 | Geometry | Algebra | Transition Math IX Algebra I | Transition Math II (Pre-Algebra) |
| 9 | Advanced Algebra | Geometry | Algebra IX | Algebra I |
| 10 | Pacesetter-Pre Calculus From a Modeling Perspective | Advanced Algebra | Geometry X | Geometry |
| 11 | AP Calculus AB | Pacesetter-Pre Calculus From a Modeling Perspective | Advanced Algebra X | Advanced Algebra |
| 12 | AP Calculus BC | AP Calculus AB | Pacesetter-Pre Calculus From a Modeling Perspective | Pacesetter-Pre Calculus From a Modeling Perspective |

## Developing a Data Collection Plan

The form in **Planning Tools**, pages 125–126, and illustrated below can help you plan which data sources and tools you will use to explore possible gaps in opportunities to learn.

KEEP YOUR EYES ON THE PRIZE: STUDENT LEARNING

Data Collection Plan

### Exploring Gaps in Opportunities to Learn

| Problem/ Question | *To what extent do some students (poor, minority, English language learners, girls, others) have less opportunity to learn mathematics and science than others?* | | | | |
| --- | --- | --- | --- | --- | --- |
| Data Sources/Tools We Want to Use | Got It | Need It | Disaggregated by | How/When Collected | Person Responsible |
| | | | | | |

## Listening to Student Voices: Measuring Aspirations

*"Student aspirations, after all, are the source and substance of dreams and achievement."*

(Quaglia n.d., 6)

As your team works to unravel the puzzle of student learning, they may have noticed that one important piece is missing: how students feel about themselves, about the relevance of mathematics and science to their lives, and about school in general. No doubt, these feelings have a lot to do with how well students perform. Narrowly focusing on academics will not necessarily open the door to high levels of learning for all students. Students need to believe in themselves, set challenging but attainable goals for the future, and be inspired in the present to go for them. These qualities, known as aspirations, are critical ingredients for success in school and life.

But how can teams get a handle on something as amorphous as aspirations? Russell Quaglia and his colleagues at the Center for Student Aspirations at the University of Maine in Orono have figured out a way. They have identified eight conditions that affect student aspirations: achievement, belonging, curiosity, empowerment, excitement, mentoring, risk taking, and self-confidence. Using an 84-item student survey, they help schools measure student aspirations and the conditions that support them (see sample "Students Speak: My Education and My Future, Grades 3–5" in **Data Tools**, DT 3-28). These data allow schools to see themselves "through the eyes of their students" and provide another window into understanding and improving student learning. Many schools that have worked with the Center to assess and improve students' aspirations are now enjoying impressive gains in student achievement, such as 150 percent increases on national proficiency test scores and 50 percent increases in grades (Russ Quaglia, telephone conversation, 1998).

**RESOURCE ON STUDENT ASPIRATIONS**

National Center for Student Aspirations, University of Maine, Orono, ME (see **Resources**, page 152)

## Developing a Data Collection Plan

School teams that want to investigate student aspirations and their impact on mathematics and science learning may want to use the form in **Planning Tools**, pages 127–128 and illustrated below.

KEEP YOUR EYES ON THE PRIZE: STUDENT LEARNING

Data Collection Plan

### Investigating Student Aspirations

| Problem/ Question | How do student aspirations impact on student success in mathematics and science? | | | | |
|---|---|---|---|---|---|
| **Data Sources/Tools We Want to Use** | **Got It** | **Need It** | **Disaggregated by** | **How/When Collected** | **Person Responsible** |
| | | | | | |

# Formulating a Learner-Centered Problem

In the section above, we suggested many different places to look for gaps between what is actually happening in your school or district and what you desire to be happening. Chances are that as your team examined the data, you unearthed some areas of concern. Maybe mathematics achievement took a dip for eighth-grade girls. Or fourth-graders scored well on science performance assessments but eighth-graders did poorly. Or students who were not doing well in science also expressed feelings of not belonging. As you analyze your data, you may also have considered possible implications for action (see "Putting It All Together—Student Learning Data Summary Sheet" in **Data Tools**, DT 3-16).

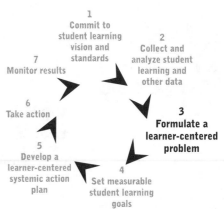

1 Commit to student learning vision and standards

2 Collect and analyze student learning and other data

3 Formulate a learner-centered problem

4 Set measurable student learning goals

5 Develop a learner-centered systemic action plan

6 Take action

7 Monitor results

*"A problem exists only if there is a difference between what is actually happening and what you desire to be happening."*

(Blanchard and Johnson 1982, 31)

Now your team may have a new problem: too many problems to solve. You cannot possibly pursue them all at once. Focus is critical to success. Here are some guidelines for choosing a problem on which to focus:

▼ **Make it manageable and feasible.** Narrow the scope so you can experience some early successes. Focus on one school, a particular grade level, a particular group of students, or a particular learning outcome. Michael Schmoker argues for a focus on rapid results and notes that "impact does not need to be dramatic; continuous, incremental improvements are the building blocks of sweeping systemic change that is rapid—and attainable" (1996, 51).

▼ **Make it important.** The counterbalance to making it manageable and feasible is that it also be significant: a problem that, when solved, will move you toward your vision for mathematics and science education.

▼ **Make sure enough people have the energy and commitment to follow it through.** Is this an issue that deeply concerns people? Can you activate a critical mass to do the work it will take to address it?

▼ **Be as clear as possible about the problem.** "Teams who began their work with a clear idea of what they were studying and why they were studying it tended to find the motivation to complete their work. Conversely, the teams who lacked clarity on what they were about tended to lose interest in their collaborative work," warns Richard Sagor (1992, 23). The form "Decision-Making Matrix for Choosing a Problem" in **Planning Tools**, page 129, can help teams rank problems and determine top priorities.

## Digging Deeper into the Problem: Look Before You Leap

Once a team chooses a problem on which to focus, they are often ready to leap into action to solve it. You are now at a point in the process where you are ready to assign causality, unlike in the earlier phases of exploration and discovery. But you want to be certain you are assigning the right causality. Otherwise, your team may be very busy solving the wrong problem. So it is wise to slow down the process again by taking stock of what you already know about the problem and what else you need to know in order to better understand it and take effective action. Often it is important to involve other staff and stakeholders in this analysis. Four tools to help you dig deeper into problems—graphic reconstruction, root-cause analysis, fishbone cause-and-effect analysis, and questions for digging deeper—are described below. Whichever tools you use, additional data will often be needed to verify your hunches about the nature of the problem. (See the "Additional Sources of Data" form in **Data Tools**, DT 2-4.)

## Graphic Reconstruction

Richard Sagor, in his book *How to Conduct Collaborative Action Research* (1992), offers a technique for planners to map their understanding of a problem. Called "graphic reconstruction," it involves graphically illustrating a problem by showing the relationship among variables, as illustrated in Figure 3.14. The steps involved are:

▼ brainstorming all the relevant factors, variables, and context;

▼ arranging relevant factors in relational order;

▼ evaluating your knowledge base (what you are sure and unsure of);

▼ surfacing questions for further research (Sagor 1992, 17–23).

**FIGURE 3.14: GRAPHIC RECONSTRUCTION**

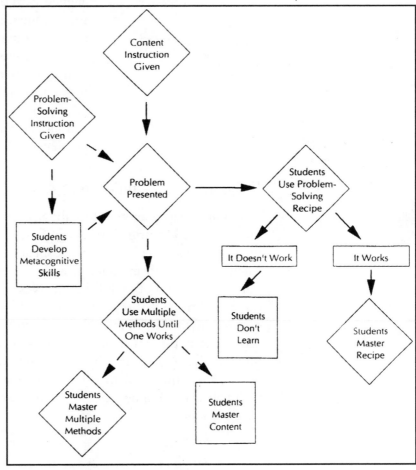

## PROBLEM IDENTIFICATION FORM

Problem Identification Form

| Problem/Barrier/Issue #1 | Problem/Barrier/Issue #2 |
|---|---|
| | |
| *Why?* | *Why?* |
| Because: | Because: |
| | |
| *Why?* | *Why?* |
| Because: | Because: |
| | |
| *Why?* | *Why?* |
| Because: | Because: |

2.  Ask of each problem, up to three times, "Why?" and answer,
    "Because ——————————————." Stop asking
    Why? when you reach consensus on the underlying cause of the
    problem.

## Root-Cause Analysis

Another technique for digging deeper is root-cause analysis. Root-cause analysis helps a group look beyond symptoms to underlying causes by taking the identified problem and asking why it exists three different times, each time probing more deeply.

For example, your team has learned that mathematics scores on the state test improved a lot overall except for the bottom-quartile students. On the first round of "why?" team members respond that many of these students are special education and Title I students. On the second round, they speculate that the new mathematics curriculum, which is closely aligned with the state test, is just too hard for some students. On the third round, they consider that often these students are pulled out of the regular classroom for mathematics instruction and may not even be getting access to the new curriculum. The form in **Planning Tools**, page 130 and illustrated here, offers an example of a process for identifying possible causes of problems.

## Fishbone Cause-and-Effect Analysis

A fishbone chart is another tool for analyzing the causes of a problem. Using the form in **Planning Tools**, page 131, and illustrated here, a group writes the problem or effect in the blank square at the far right labeled "Problem." Then they brainstorm about possible causes in the categories identified (or others) at the end of each fishbone. Next they identify the most significant causes and those that they are most likely to be able to act upon. At the end of this analysis the group is likely to find that they need to collect additional data to verify the causes they have identified. The advantage of this process is that it gives school staff the opportunity to surface all of the factors they believe affect the problem, even those they can do little to change. Often, such beliefs need to be expressed and heard before staff can mobilize for effective action.

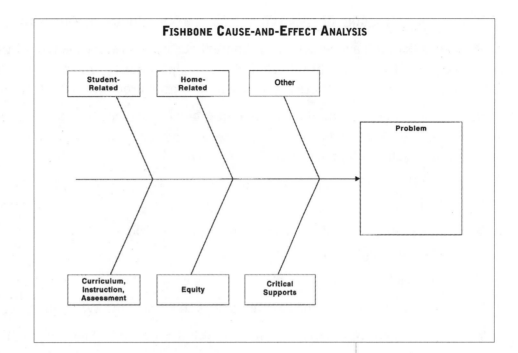

## Questions for Digging Deeper into a Problem

A fourth technique is to ask yourselves a series of questions about the problem, such as those listed below. Often, answering these questions will require more data collection. Where relevant, recommended data sources are suggested.

**DIGGING DEEPER INTO A PROBLEM: QUESTIONS TO CONSIDER**

▼ How is the problem perceived by different constituencies—parents, students, teachers, administrators, others? What kind of support does your team have? What obstacles might you face? (Possible data sources: focus groups, interviews.)

▼ How does the problem impact different groups of students (by economic status, race, gender, etc.)? What equity obstacles need to be confronted? (Possible data sources: disaggregated data, focus groups, interviews. Also see Chapter 5.)

▼ How is the problem impacted by curriculum, instruction, or assessment practices? (See Chapter 4.)

▼ What beliefs and assumptions may underlie this problem? (See "Beliefs that Block Equity" in Chapter 5.)

▼ What does the research say about this problem?

▼ What has been done in the past to address this problem? What happened and why?

▼ What are some alternatives for action? What are other schools doing to address this problem?

▼ What other systemic factors will most greatly impact this problem area and how can we consider them in our planning?

▼ What action makes the most sense to us?

## Writing a Problem Statement

The final step in formulating the problem is to write a clear, succinct problem statement that answers the following questions:

▼ What is the problem with student learning you want to address?

▼ How do you know you have this problem? What evidence do you have?

▼ Who is affected?

▼ What do you think is causing the problem? What evidence do you have?

▼ What is the learning goal targeted for improvement?

▼ What do you plan to do about it? What evidence do you have that this plan can in fact solve the problem? (Sagor 1992, 23)

The fourth and fifth items above are the beginning of your action plan. Remember that inquiry is an evolving process. The question you start off with might not be the one you end up with. Be open to reframing the question and focusing on new problems as you learn. Also, continue to dig for information from research and practice about which actions are likely to be most effective in solving the problem. (See **Planning Tools**, page 132, for the form "Formulating a Learner-Centered Problem.")

# Setting Measurable Student Learning Goals

Even teams that use data about student learning to identify problems can lose their focus on learning when they plan for action. That's why we suggest that the next step in planning is to formulate one or two clear goals for improving student learning. If the vision you have for student learning is the prize, these goals are the checkpoints along the way. They will shape what actions you plan. And because improving student learning requires improving the system as a whole, they will guide you toward a systemic approach. This approach, which we have dubbed "learner-centered systemic action planning," is described below.

There was a reason why you spent all that time studying learning results and formulating a problem. A clear statement of a learner-centered problem leads naturally to clear learning goals. Take the following problem statement:

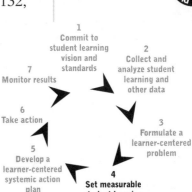

▼ Only 30 percent of our fourth-grade students are proficient at mathematics problem solving and communication. A disproportionate number of the other 70 percent are economically disadvantaged.

▼ Our goal is to increase the number of students reaching proficiency in mathematics problem solving and communication each year for five years until all students reach at least this level.

▼ We propose to thoroughly review our curriculum, incorporate a greater emphasis on mathematics problem solving, and provide extensive, long-term professional development to teachers in both mathematics content and effective teaching strategies. We also will address equity issues such as expectations for students through our professional development program.

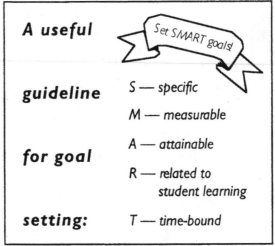

**A useful**

**guideline**

**for goal**

**setting:**

Set SMART goals

S — specific

M — measurable

A — attainable

R — related to student learning

T — time-bound

The goal expressed in the second bullet above is an example of a SMART goal—one that is specific, measurable, attainable, related to student learning, and time-bound. These criteria provide a useful guideline for goal setting.

Setting SMART goals can be tricky. You may encounter what Boston-based education consultant Sonia Caus Gleason calls the "Goldilocks" problem: goals can be "too big" or "too small" or "just right."

A goal that is too big doesn't meet the "attainable" criterion. It's like saying "I'm going to lose 30 pounds in the month before Christmas," or declaring that the United States will be number one in mathematics and science by the year 2000. While the intent of such goals is to motivate people to make dramatic changes, the result is often to let people off the hook. Why should they work hard to achieve a goal that is totally unrealistic? They couldn't possibly be held accountable for it.

A goal that is too small is equally ineffective. These are goals that everyone knows can easily be achieved or have already been achieved. It's like Arnold Schwarzenegger setting a goal to be physically fit. Often, goals that are too small are set in schools where staff aren't ready to take risks and fear reprimand for "failure," or where many staff haven't embraced the desire to change or don't feel comfortable pressuring their colleagues to change.

A goal that is "just right" poses enough of a challenge to motivate action but is attainable within a reasonable time frame. One way to frame a "just-right" goal is to set a long-term goal, such as the one in the second bullet above, and then aim for incremental change each year. Some teams find that actual numbers, such as "10 percent of students will move out of the lowest quartile in problem-solving proficiency this year," are effective. Others prefer to shoot for "improvement" in a specific area, such as gradually increasing the number of minority students who take algebra each year. But it is important to put a time limit on achieving a quantitative goal. As Anthony Terceira, formerly of the Providence (Rhode Island) Public Schools, says, "There has to be a D-day or it never comes." (See **Reform in Action**, page 335.)

The box on the next page provides examples of some SMART goals, as well as some not-so-SMART ones. Also see the form "Setting SMART Goals" in **Planning Tools**, page 140.

## SMART Goals

**You've got it! These work:**

▼ To have 80 percent of students reach proficiency level at mathematics problem solving over the next two years.

▼ To increase students' ability to formulate a scientific hypothesis, collect data accurately, analyze them, and draw sound conclusions this year.

▼ To increase minority enrollment in algebra so that within three years all students will complete the course successfully.

▼ To improve the performance of the bottom quartile of students in numbers and operations over the next two years.

▼ To have all eighth-graders understand the concept of "systems" by the end of this school year.

▼ To increase the number of students who can demonstrate mastery of principles of technology design from 10 percent to 50 percent over the next three years.

**These need improvement:**

▼ To improve student learning in mathematics and science. (This is too general, although worthy.)

▼ To introduce technology in mathematics and science classrooms. (This is a means to an end, not an end in itself.)

▼ To provide professional development to teachers in effective mathematics teaching strategies. (This is a means to an end, not an end in itself.)

▼ To improve our school's scores on the Iowa Basic Skills Mathematics Test by 3 percent next year. (This is focused on one measure, not a goal.)

▼ To motivate students by improving teachers' teaching styles. (This is too vague and is difficult to measure.)

# Developing a Learner-Centered Systemic Action Plan

With SMART learning goals, your team has a clear idea of its next milepost on the road to improving student learning. Action plans are the specific steps you will take to reach the milepost. The analysis you have already done about the causes of the problem can guide you in generating possible solutions and courses of action. Initially, we suggest that you cast the net broadly, generating a range of possible solutions from which to choose. It is a good idea, for example, to look into what other schools or districts have done to tackle similar problems and to consult relevant research. The same matrix for choosing a problem can also be adapted to help you settle on a course of action (see "Decision-Making Matrix for Choosing a Problem," **Planning Tools**, page 129).

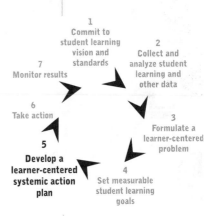

1
Commit to student learning vision and standards

2
Collect and analyze student learning and other data

3
Formulate a learner-centered problem

4
Set measurable student learning goals

5
Develop a learner-centered systemic action plan

6
Take action

7
Monitor results

*"None of us can expect to act on more than a tiny corner of the great complexity. But in our interrelated society, itself part of an uncompromisingly interdependent world, we have to think about the whole complexity in order to act relevantly on any part of it."*

(Cleveland 1985, 17)

Clearly, in mathematics and science education reform there are a few obvious paths to take: reforming curriculum, instruction, and assessment, confronting barriers to equity, and building systemic supports, such as school culture, professional development, public engagement, partnerships, and technology. Because these elements are so interconnected, action plans should address all of them. While it is impossible to act on all aspects of the system at once, it is counterproductive to focus myopically on only one aspect of the system, such as reforming curriculum, while ignoring the rest. Systemic action plans operationalize Harlan Cleveland's advice to think about the whole in order to act on any part of it.

For example, let's say your learning goal is to have all students successfully complete algebra by tenth grade. You know you have to change the way algebra is being taught to make it culturally relevant and engaging for more students—a curriculum and instruction issue. That's where you decide to focus your efforts. But you also know that teachers' and counselors' expectations of students are an important factor and that no change in classroom practice or expectations will happen without high-quality, sustained professional development. Moreover, as you focus on classroom change, you are aware of the need to engage the public about the reasons for the change. So, to achieve your primary action goal—improving the teaching of algebra—your team will have to take action on several fronts simultaneously.

Action goals are different from learning goals, although they too should meet the SMART criteria. They pertain to implementing a new program or practice for the purpose of achieving the learning goal. For example, an action goal in the curriculum arena would be to have in place a well-articulated and coordinated mathematics curriculum that sets high academic standards for all students (see **Reform in Action**, page 343). An example of an action goal in the equity arena would be to implement long-term professional development in equity issues in mathematics by participating in the Equity in Mathematics Education Leadership Institute (EMELI) (see **Resources**, page 319).

Whatever direction your team decides to take, the challenge will be to weave together the different elements of systemic reform into a cohesive, doable action plan. The form "Systemic Mathematics and Science Action Goals" in **Planning Tools**, page 141 and illustrated below, is designed to assist teams in building systemic action plans. It keeps the learning goal front and center as teams set goals for curriculum, instruction, and assessment, equity, and critical supports that will advance their student learning goal. The accompanying

"Systemic Mathematics and Science Action Plan" forms in **Planning Tools**, pages 133, 134, and 135, can be used to help teams flesh out more detailed plans, including designating responsibility for carrying out actions and timelines, in each of these three major areas. We also provide a separate form for professional development planning (page 136), even though it is one of the critical supports, because of its central importance. All of these action plans, however, are in the service of the same SMART student learning goal. The planning form for equity is illustrated below.

**Systemic Mathematics and Science Action Goals**

| | | |
|---|---|---|
| Student Learning | SMART Student Learning Goals | |
| Curriculum Instruction Assessment / Equity | Curriculum/Instruction?Assessment Goals | Equity Goals |
| Critical Supports | Critical Support Goals | |

The remainder of this guidebook is set up to help you investigate and address common problems that emerge in each of these three areas: curriculum, instruction, and assessment; equity; and critical supports. For example, say that your inquiry into student learning has uncovered serious disparities in mathematics and/or science achievement among racial, class, cultural, or gender groups. Your team decides that confronting barriers to equity is the most pressing issue. Chapter 5 deals with issues such as lack of understanding and appreciation of students' diverse cultures, low expectations for certain student groups, and structural barriers such as tracking.

Or your team may have decided on a different direction. After studying the data, you are not happy with students' scientific inquiry skills. You believe that the problem is that the curriculum overemphasizes facts and underemphasizes scientific processes. Chapter 4 provides tools for understanding current classroom practice and monitoring improvements.

**Systemic Mathematics and Science Action Plan-Equity**

| SMART Student Learning Goals | | | | |
|---|---|---|---|---|
| **Equity Goals** | **Steps to Reach Goal** | **Person Responsible** | **Documentation for Action Taken** | **Timeline** |
| | | | | |
| | | | | |
| | | | | |
| | | | | |

Regardless of which area your team chooses to focus on, it is important that you not lose sight of other aspects of the system that directly impact the problem you are working on. Issues such as public engagement, leadership, and professional development will all come into play as you attempt to solve a particular problem.

Your work in systemic reform will undoubtedly lead you down many different roads. Some of these are described in this book, while others you will be discovering on your own. But all roads lead home—back to your goals for student learning.

# Taking Action and Monitoring Results

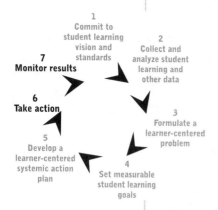

**A**ll the work your team has been doing has been building toward taking action—action that leads to results. While this guidebook emphasizes the importance of using data about student learning as a basis for careful goal setting and planning, we share with Susan Loucks-Horsley and Leslie Hergert, authors of *An Action Guide for School Improvement* (1985), a bias toward action. Nothing will change if teams use up all their energy planning and assessing and never get to doing. On the other hand, jumping into action without understanding the problem or setting learning goals is equally unproductive. Planning and doing are a careful balancing act.

*"When you have a choice between planning and doing, choose doing."*

(Loucks-Horsley and Hergert 1985, 13)

Once your team swings into action, it is easy to become consumed by the implementation frenzy. As busy as you are, it is important to check the gauges that monitor where the trip is going. Are the actions being carried out? What kind of results are you getting? What new problems are coming up? What are you learning? What new directions do you need to consider? Now the challenge is to balance doing with monitoring and reflecting.

At one level, monitoring is about gauging where you are in the change process, whether the reforms you are implementing are actually sticking, and what interventions are most appropriate to move the enterprise forward. Just keeping your eyes and ears open, chatting with teachers, parents, or students, and visiting classrooms are all ways to assess progress. But you will also want to rely on more formal methods as well. Each of the subsequent chapters in this guidebook contains tools, such as survey instruments, observation protocols, and interviews, for monitoring implementation of curriculum, instruction, and assessment reform (Chapter 4) and progress in confronting barriers to equity (Chapter 5). But eventually, once your team has some evidence that the change is being implemented, you will be ready to ask the big question: What has been the impact of reform activities on student learning?

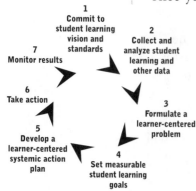

# Coming Home to Student Learning

**Y**ou started off the planning process by carefully analyzing student learning data, followed by identifying a learner-centered problem, setting SMART goals, and taking action to improve the system and achieve those goals. How will you know if all your effort produced any benefit for students? Did you achieve the results you intended? Did you "win the prize"?

To answer these questions, your team will need to select a set of indicators by which to measure progress toward your SMART learning goal. Given the limitations of any one source of data, it is wise to agree on multiple indicators. For example, take a goal we referred to earlier in this chapter: to increase the number of students reaching proficiency in mathematics problem solving and communication each year for five years until all students are proficient. What indicators could this team use to measure proficiency?

They might, for instance, decide on a combination of three indicators: state test results, which report proficiency levels in those areas; rubric scores on grade-level performance assessments administered by teachers and aligned with their curriculum; and item analysis results on problem solving from the standardized tests the district administers. In addition, because of this school's concern about the performance of low-income students, they will want to disaggregate results to ensure that these students are benefiting from reform.

As the example above illustrates, the work you have already done analyzing student learning data and setting SMART goals lays the groundwork for a monitoring plan. SMART goals are, by definition, measurable and will lend themselves easily to a set of relevant indicators. And the student learning data you have already collected can often provide baseline data from which to measure progress. For example, you might have analyzed standardized and standards-based tests by quartiles and now want to monitor whether students move out of the bottom quartile over time. Just be sure your team uses the same sources from year to year so comparisons are useful. For example, make sure ethnic categories or dropout rates are defined in the same way (Johnson 1996, 205).

Even with the groundwork laid, deciding on success indicators can be difficult and controversial. It requires being very specific about what you think success will actually look like, in concrete, measurable terms. Different stakeholders are likely to disagree about what constitutes evidence of success. For some, standardized tests tell it all. For others, they are worse than useless. Having these conversations can help build common ground.

Another issue to consider is when to collect data. Some data you have no control over. School districts and states test on their own schedule. Sometimes teachers don't learn about a group of students' results until the next year, after those students have moved on. So your team may want to consider collecting more targeted, timely information. For example, you can collect grade-level data on performance tasks quarterly or examine student work twice a year. These data will then complement the standardized test scores when they become available.

### Plan for Monitoring the Impact of Reform Activities on Student Learning

| Problem/ Question | What is the impact of reform activities on student learning outcomes, opportunities, and aspirations? | | | | | |
|---|---|---|---|---|---|---|
| SMART Student Learning Goals | Indicators (disaggregated by race, ethnicity, free/reduced lunch, gender, etc.) | Data Collection | | | How Will Data Be Analyzed? | How Will Data Be Reported/ Disseminated? |
| | | How? | When? | By Whom? | | |
| | | | | | | |
| | | | | | | |
| | | | | | | |

All of these considerations go into the development of a monitoring plan, which includes the specific indicators as well as how and when data will be collected, analyzed, and reported. As with other plans, it is important to designate clear responsibilities for this important work, so that it doesn't fall through the cracks. The form "Plan for Monitoring the Impact of Reform Activities on Student Learning" in **Planning Tools**, page 137 and illustrated here, provides a simple organizer for a learner-centered monitoring plan. Monitoring plans for curriculum, instruction, and assessment activities and for equity-related activities can be found in **Planning Tools**, pages 225 and 309.

As your team monitors student learning results, make sure you allocate time to reflect on what the data are telling you. This is the time to see what the indicators are saying. Are they showing gains, losses, or no change? How can the team explain the results? What new questions have arisen? What additional data are needed? And, most important, what are the implications for action? The form "SMART Student Learning Goals—Data Reflection Form" in **Planning Tools**, page 139 and illustrated here, can help your team organize this process of reflection.

### SMART Student Learning Goals–Data Reflection Form

| SMART Student Learning Goals | | | | |
|---|---|---|---|---|

| Indicators (disaggregated by race, ethnicity, free/reduced lunch, gender, etc.) | Results: + = increase − = decrease 0 = no change | Possible Explanations | New Questions/ New Data Needed | Implications for Action |
|---|---|---|---|---|
| Group 1: | | | | |
| Group 2: | | | | |
| Group 3: | | | | |
| Group 4: | | | | |
| Group 5: | | | | |
| Aggregate Results: | | | | |

# Striving for Continuous Improvement

Monitoring improvements involves the same kind of detective work your team was engaged in early on. Now you are looking for evidence that the problem you identified is being solved and that student learning is improving. If your gauges are telling you that you are moving toward the checkpoint handily, click on the cruise control and enjoy the ride! It is important to publicize and celebrate success. This provides the fuel for what undoubtedly will be a long, hard trip to future checkpoints.

But always be on the lookout for problems. Even when indicators are looking good, new challenges arise, such as dealing with public opinion or finding more time for professional development. If results are not forthcoming, it is important to dig deeper to find out why. It may be that the goals and plans are good, but you hit a roadblock in implementation. Or poor results may be an indication that you are heading in the wrong direction and need to change course. Or your vision has changed and you need to rethink your goals. At this stage in the game, it is most important to be flexible. It is rare, in fact, that any change is ultimately carried out exactly as planned.

The point is not to create the perfect plan. The point is to create the best plan you can based on careful analysis of student learning and other data. Then take bold, but focused, action to improve the system, monitor results, and learn as you go. You continuously strive to improve because you've got your eyes on that prize: high levels of mathematics and science learning for all students.

# Chapter 3 Planning Tools: From Inquiry to Action

## Team Planning Questions

The following are questions for your team to consider as you plan, based on the process outlined in the chapter. You will also find cross-references to relevant text, Data Tools, and Resources.

1. Where are we in the process of becoming a standards-led system? What are our strengths? (evidence) What areas need improvement? (evidence) What additional information do we need? What are the implications for action? (See "Progress Toward Standards—A Self-Assessment: Student Learning," page 119.)

2. How ready are we to undertake reform in mathematics and science education? (See "Perceptions of Attitudes, Readiness and Commitment to Change," DT 3-1.) What are the implications for action?

3. What do we know about the status of student performance in mathematics and science? What data do we have?

4. What do we want to know? How can we find out? (See "Data Collection Plan: Surveying Student Learning Results," page 121, and "Data Collection Plan: Exploring the Performance Gap," page 123.)

5. What are some different ways of looking at student learning data that might be helpful to us? (See "Collecting and Analyzing Student Learning Data," page 76.)

6. To what extent do some students (poor, minority, English language learners, girls, others) have less opportunity to learn mathematics and science than others? (See "Assessing Opportunities to Learn," page 94.)

7. What student learning problem do we want to focus on? How can we better understand that problem so we can take effective action? (See "Decision-Making Matrix for Choosing a Problem," page 129; "Problem Identification Form," page 130; "Fishbone Cause-and-Effect Analysis," page 131; and "Formulating a Learner-Centered Problem," page 132.)

8. What are our SMART student learning goals? (See "Setting SMART Goals," page 140.)

9. If these learning goals are to be achieved, what needs to happen relative to equity, curriculum/instruction/assessment, and critical supports such as professional development and public engagement? (See "Systemic Mathematics and Science Action Goals," page 141, and "Systemic Mathematics and Science Action Plans" for Curriculum/Instruction/Assessment, Equity, Critical Supports, and Professional Development, pages 133–136.)

10. How can we track our progress? What indicators can we use? (See "Plan for Monitoring the Impact of Reform Activities on Student Learning," page 137.)

11. What support and resources do we need to carry out our plans? (See Chapter 3 Resources, pages 143–152.)

## Progress Toward Standards—A Self Assessment: Student Learning

SCHOOL/DISTRICT:_____          DATE:_____          __Math     __Science     __Both

Directions: Mark the box in each row that most accurately describes your school at the present time. Mark only one box in each row.

| Maintenance | Awareness | Transition | Emergence | Predominance |
|---|---|---|---|---|
| 1 ☐ Educators do not share a vision for student learning. | ☐ Educators are aware of the importance of a shared vision for student learning. | ☐ The school is developing a common vision for student learning based on a study of standards. | ☐ The school articulates a common vision for student learning based on a study of standards. | ☐ The school embraces a common vision for student learning based on careful study and extensive dialogue about standards. |
| 2 ☐ Educators are not aware of the need to provide all students the opportunity to achieve standards through quality instruction, rigorous content, ample resources, and qualified teachers. | ☐ Educators are aware of the need to provide all students the opportunity to achieve standards through quality instruction, rigorous content, ample resources, and qualified teachers. | ☐ The school is developing a plan to provide all students the opportunity to achieve standards through quality instruction, rigorous content, ample resources, and qualified teachers. | ☐ The school has begun to implement a plan to provide all students the opportunity to achieve standards through quality instruction, rigorous content, ample resources, and qualified teachers. | ☐ The school provides all students the opportunity to achieve standards through quality instruction, rigorous content, ample resources, and qualified teachers. |
| 3 ☐ Educators are not aware of the potential of collaborative study to improve student learning. | ☐ Educators are aware of the need to collaborate to study student learning data, reflect on practice, and improve instruction. | ☐ Groups of educators in the school occasionally collaborate to study student learning data, reflect on practice, and improve instruction. | ☐ A majority of school staff often collaborate to study student learning data, reflect on practice, and improve instruction. | ☐ School staff consistently collaborate to study student learning data, reflect on practice, and improve instruction. |
| 4 ☐ School improvement plans are not based on student learning data. | ☐ Educators are aware of the need to base school improvement plans on student learning data. | ☐ School improvement plans are based on standardized state and national test data. | ☐ School improvement plans are based on national, state, and local sources of student learning data. | ☐ School improvement plans are based on multiple sources of disaggregated student learning data, including performance assessments. |
| 5 ☐ School administrators do not understand or promote standards-based reform. | ☐ School administrators are aware of standards-based reform and recognize the need to promote it. | ☐ School administrators understand standards-based reform and are taking steps to implement it. | ☐ School administrators endorse standards-based reform and promote its implementation. | ☐ School administrators are committed to standards-based reform and systematically promote its full implementation. |

Christopher-Gordon Publishers, Inc. © 2002

Evidence:

1

2

3

4

5

# Surveying Student Learning Results

| Problem/ Question | What are our strengths and weaknesses in mathematics and science achievement? | | | | |
|---|---|---|---|---|---|
| **Data Sources/Tools We Want to Use** | **Got It** | **Need It** | **Disaggregated by** | **How/When Collected** | **Person Responsible** |
| | | | | | |
| | | | | | |
| | | | | | |
| | | | | | |
| | | | | | |

## Possible Indicators and Data Sources/Tools

❑ Mathematics/science standardized test scores (DT 3-3, DT 3-4, DT 3-7)

❑ Mathematics SAT scores

❑ Grades (DT 3-10)

❑ Mathematics/science state assessments (DT 3-5, DT 3-6)

❑ Grade-level performance assessments

❑ School performance assessments

❑ District performance assessments

❑ Quality of student work (DT 2-5, DT 2-6)

❑ Retention rates (DT 3-11)

❑ Overage students (DT 3-12)

❑ Dropout rates (DT 3-13)

❑ Absenteeism (DT 3-14)

❑ Discipline referrals (DT 3-15)

❑ College-going and graduation rates (DT 3-26, DT 3-27)

**3** Planning Tools

## Possible Disaggregation Categories

❑ Grade level

❑ Proficiency in English

❑ Gender: ❑ Male   ❑ Female

❑ Race:  ❑ African American   ❑ Latino
❑ Native American   ❑ White   ❑ Asian
❑ _____   ❑ _____

❑ Socioeconomic status (e.g., free/reduced lunch recipient; mother's level of education)

❑ Amount of time in country

❑ Amount of time at our school

❑ Course-taking experience

❑ Amount or type of training the teacher has received

❑ Quartiles

❑ Participation in programs such as special education, bilingual, Title I

❑ Other _____

# Exploring the Performance Gap

| Problem/ Question | To what extent do performance gaps in mathematics and science exist among racial, class, cultural, or gender groups in our school? | | | | | |
|---|---|---|---|---|---|---|
| **Data Sources/Tools We Want to Use** | **Got It** | **Need It** | **Disaggregated by** | **How/When Collected** | **Person Responsible** | |
| | | | | | | |
| | | | | | | |
| | | | | | | |
| | | | | | | |
| | | | | | | |

## Possible Indicators and Data Sources/Tools

❏ Mathematics/science standardized test scores (DT 3-3, DT 3-4, DT 3-7)

❏ Mathematics SAT scores

❏ Grades (DT 3-10)

❏ Mathematics/science state assessments (DT 3-5, DT 3-6)

❏ Grade-level performance assessments

❏ School performance assessments

❏ District performance assessments

❏ Quality of student work (DT 2-5, DT 2-6)

❏ Retention rates (DT 3-11)

❏ Overage students (DT 3-12)

❏ Dropout rates (DT 3-13)

❏ Absenteeism (DT 3-14)

❏ Discipline referrals (DT 3-15)

❏ College-going and graduation rates (DT 3-26, DT 3-27)

**3** *Planning Tools*

## Possible Disaggregation Categories

❏ Grade level

❏ Proficiency in English

❏ Gender: ❏ Male ❏ Female

❏ Race: ❏ African American ❏ Latino
❏ Native American ❏ White ❏ Asian
❏ _____ ❏ _____

❏ Socioeconomic status (e.g., free/reduced lunch recipient; mother's level of education)

❏ Amount of time in country

❏ Amount of time at our school

❏ Course-taking experience

❏ Amount or type of training the teacher has received

❏ Quartiles

❏ Participation in programs such as special education, bilingual, Title I

❏ Other _____

Data Collection Plan

# Exploring Gaps in Opportunities to Learn

| Problem/ Question | To what extent do some students (poor, minority, English language learners, girls, others) have less opportunity to learn mathematics and science than others? | | | | |
|---|---|---|---|---|---|
| Data Sources/Tools We Want to Use | Got It | Need It | Disaggregated by | How/When Collected | Person Responsible |
| | | | | | |
| | | | | | |
| | | | | | |
| | | | | | |
| | | | | | |

## Possible Data Sources/Tools

❏ Disaggregated course enrollment data (DT 3-17–DT 3-19)

❏ Disaggregated special program placement data (DT 3-20)

❏ Tracking practices (DT 5-1)

❏ Teacher qualifications (DT 3-21)

❏ Access to rigorous, hands-on instruction and alternative assessment, disaggregated (DT 4-3–DT 4-10, DT 4-12, DT 4-13, DT 4-15, DT 4-16, DT 4-19–DT 4-21)

❏ Access to technology, disaggregated (DT 3-22–DT 3-25)

❏ College-going and graduation rates, disaggregated (DT 3-26, DT 3-27)

## Possible Disaggregation Categories

❏ Grade level

❏ Proficiency in English

❏ Gender: ❏ Male   ❏ Female

❏ Race:  ❏ African American   ❏ Latino
❏ Native American   ❏ White   ❏ Asian
❏ _____   ❏ _____

❏ Socioeconomic status (e.g., free/reduced lunch recipient; mother's level of education)

❏ Amount of time in country

❏ Amount of time at our school

❏ Course-taking experience

❏ Amount or type of training the teacher has received

❏ Quartiles

❏ Participation in programs such as special education, bilingual, Title I

❏ Other _____

**3** Planning Tools

# Investigating Student Aspirations

| Problem/ Question | How do student aspirations impact on student success in mathematics and science? | | | | |
|---|---|---|---|---|---|
| **Data Sources/Tools We Want to Use** | **Got It** | **Need It** | **Disaggregated by** | **How/When Collected** | **Person Responsible** |
| | | | | | |
| | | | | | |
| | | | | | |
| | | | | | |
| | | | | | |

## Possible Data Sources/Tools

❏ Student aspirations data (DT 3-28)

## Possible Disaggregation Categories

❏ Grade level

❏ Proficiency in English

❏ Gender: ❏ Male  ❏ Female

❏ Race:  ❏ African American  ❏ Latino
❏ Native American  ❏ White  ❏ Asian
❏ _____  ❏ _____

❏ Socioeconomic status (e.g., free/reduced lunch recipient; mother's level of education)

❏ Amount of time in country

❏ Amount of time at our school

❏ Course-taking experience

❏ Amount or type of training the teacher has received

❏ Quartiles

❏ Participation in programs such as special education, bilingual, Title I

❏ Other _____

*3 Planning Tools*

## Decision-Making Matrix for Choosing a Problem

**Directions:**

Step 1. Weight the criteria from 1-3, with the highest rating indicating the criteria that are most important to you.
Step 2. Rank each problem by the extent to which it meets the criteria, with 3 being the problem that best meets the criterion.
Step 3. Assign a number to each box by multiplying the weight times the rank. (For example, if "manageable" is weighted a 3, and a particular problem is seen as highly manageable and ranked a 3, the number in the box for that criterion and that problem is "3x3=9".
Step 4. Add total for each problem.

| Problems ↓ | Manageable and Doable<br>Weight = (STEP 1) | Important<br>Weight = | People are Committed<br>Weight = | Clear<br>Weight = | Other<br>Weight = | Other<br>Weight = | |
|---|---|---|---|---|---|---|---|
| | (STEP 1) (STEP 2) | | | | | | Total |
| | (STEP 3) | | | | | | (STEP 4) |
| | | | | | | | Total |
| | | | | | | | |
| | | | | | | | Total |
| | | | | | | | |
| | | | | | | | Total |
| | | | | | | | |
| | | | | | | | Total |
| | | | | | | | |

**Criteria ↓**

# PROBLEM IDENTIFICATION FORM

| Problem/Barrier/Issue #1 | Problem/Barrier/Issue #2 |
|---|---|
| | |

*Why?*

Because:

*Why?*

Because:

*Why?*

Because:

*Why?*

Because:

*Why?*

Because:

*Why?*

Because:

2.  Ask of each problem, up to three times, "Why?" and answer, "Because _____ ." Stop asking Why? when you reach consensus on the underlying cause of the problem.

# Fishbone Cause-and-Effect Analysis

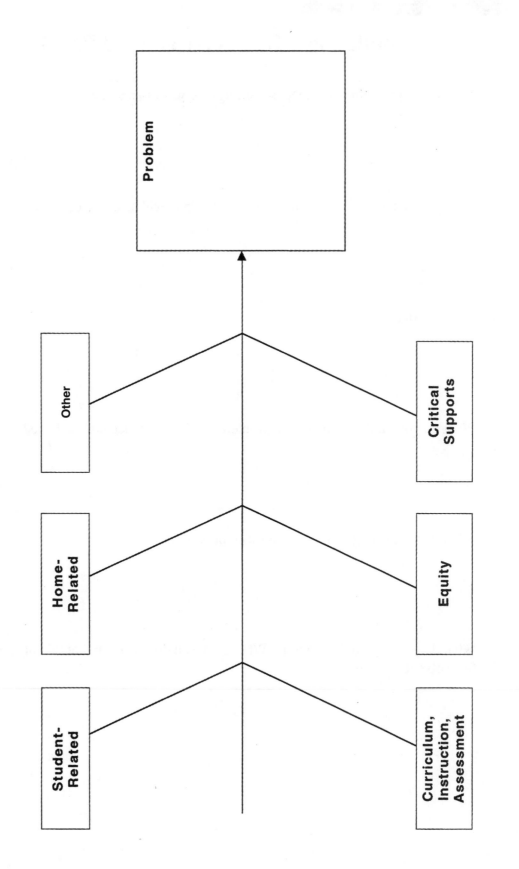

# Formulating a Learner-Centered Problem

1. What is the problem with student learning you want to address?

2. How do you know you have this problem?  What evidence do you have?

3. Who is affected?

4. What do you think is causing the problem?  What evidence do you have?

5. What is the learning goal targeted for improvement?

6. What do you plan to do about it?  What evidence do you have that this plan can in fact solve the problem?

# Systemic Mathematics and Science Action Plan–Curriculum/Instruction/Assessment

**SMART
Student
Learning
Goals**

| Curriculum/Instruction/Assessment Goals | Steps to Reach Goal | Person Responsible | Documentation for Action Taken | Timeline |
|---|---|---|---|---|
| | | | | |
| | | | | |
| | | | | |
| | | | | |

Planning Tools 3

# Systemic Mathematics and Science Action Plan–Equity

| SMART Student Learning Goals | | | | | |
|---|---|---|---|---|---|
| **Equity Goals** | **Steps to Reach Goal** | **Person Responsible** | **Documentation for Action Taken** | **Timeline** | |
| | | | | | |
| | | | | | |
| | | | | | |
| | | | | | |

# Systemic Mathematics and Science Action Plan–Critical Supports

**SMART Student Learning Goals**

| Critical Supports Goals | Steps to Reach Goal | Person Responsible | Documentation for Action Taken | Timeline |
|---|---|---|---|---|
| | | | | |
| | | | | |
| | | | | |
| | | | | |

Planning Tools 3

# Systemic Mathematics and Science Action Plan–Professional Development

**SMART Student Learning Goals**

| Professional Development Goals | Steps to Reach Goal | Person Responsible | Documentation for Action Taken | Timeline |
|---|---|---|---|---|
|  |  |  |  |  |
|  |  |  |  |  |
|  |  |  |  |  |
|  |  |  |  |  |

# Plan for Monitoring the Impact of Reform Activities on Student Learning

| Problem/ Question | *What is the impact of reform activities on student learning outcomes, opportunities, and aspirations?* | | | | | | |
|---|---|---|---|---|---|---|---|
| **SMART Student Learning Goals** | **Indicators** (disaggregated by race, ethnicity, free/reduced lunch, gender, etc.) | **Data Collection** | | | **How Will Data Be Analyzed?** | **How Will Data Be Reported/ Disseminated?** | |
| | | **How?** | **When?** | **By Whom?** | | | |
| | | | | | | | |
| | | | | | | | |

**Planning Tools 3**

## Outcomes

❏ Mathematics/science standardized test scores (DT 3-3, DT 3-4, DT 3-7)

❏ Mathematics SAT scores

❏ Grades (DT 3-10)

❏ Mathematics state assessments (DT 3-5)

❏ Science state assessments (DT 3-6)

❏ Grade-level performance assessments in mathematics/science

❏ School performance assessments in mathematics/science

❏ District performance assessments in mathematics/science

❏ Quality of student work (DT 2-5, DT 2-6)

❏ Retention rates (DT 3-11)

❏ Overage students (DT 3-12)

❏ Dropout rates (DT 3-13)

❏ Absenteeism (DT 3-14)

❏ Discipline referrals (DT 3-15)

❏ College-going and graduation rates (DT 3-26, DT 3-27)

## Opportunities

❏ Disaggregated course enrollment data (DT 3-17– DT 3-19)

❏ Disaggregated special program placement data (DT 3-20)

❏ Tracking practices (DT 5-1)

❏ Teacher qualifications (DT 3-21)

❏ Access to rigorous, hands-on instruction and alternative assessment, disaggregated (DT 4-7–DT 4-10, DT 4-12, DT 4-13, DT 4-15, DT 4-19–DT 4-21)

❏ Access to technology, disaggregated (DT 3-22–3-25)

❏ College-going and graduation rates, disaggregated (DT 3-26, 3-27)

## Aspirations

❏ Student aspirations data (DT 3-28)

# SMART Student Learning Goals–Data Reflection Form

| SMART Student Learning Goals | | | | |
|---|---|---|---|---|
| **Indicators** (disaggregated by race, ethnicity, free/reduced lunch, gender, etc.) | **Results:** + = increase – = decrease 0 = no change | **Possible Explanations** | **New Questions/ New Data Needed** | **Implications for Action** |
| Group 1: | | | | |
| Group 2: | | | | |
| Group 3: | | | | |
| Group 4: | | | | |
| Group 5: | | | | |
| **Aggregate Results:** | | | | |

# Setting SMART Goals

A useful

guideline

for goal

setting:

Set SMART goals!

S — specific

M — measurable

A — attainable

R — related to
student learning

T — time-bound

Write your goal statement here:

_____

_____

_____

_____

_____

_____

_____

_____

Planning Tools 3

# Systemic Mathematics and Science Action Goals

| SMART Student Learning Goals | | |
|---|---|---|
| Curriculum/Instruction/Assessment Goals | | Equity Goals |
| Critical Supports Goals | | |

Student Learning

Curriculum Instruction Assessment

Equity

Critical Supports

Planning Tools 3

141

# Resources for Student Learning

## Resources on Standards

### Standards Documents

**American Association for the Advancement of Science (AAAS)**, **Project 2061**, *Benchmarks for Science Literacy*, 1993

**Contact:** AAAS, 1200 New York Avenue N.W., Washington, DC 20005; (202) 326-6666; fax (202) 842-5196; Web site: http://www.aaas.org/

**National Council of Teachers of Mathematics (NCTM)**, *Principles and Standards for School Mathematics*, 2000

**Contact:** NCTM, 1906 Association Drive, Reston, VA 20191-9988; (800) 235-7566; fax: (703) 476-2970; e-mail: orders@nctm.org; Web site: http://www.nctm.org/

**National Research Council (NRC)**, *National Science Education Standards* (Washington, DC: National Academy Press), 1996

**Contact:** NRC, 2101 Constitution Avenue N.W., Washington, DC 20418-0006; (202) 334-2000; Web site: http://www.nas.edu/nrc/

**National Staff Development Council**, *Standards for Staff Development*, 1995 (elementary and high school editions) and 1996 (middle school edition)

**Contact:** National Staff Development Council, P.O. Box 240, Oxford, OH 45056; (513) 523-6029; e-mail: nsdcoffice@aol.com; Web site: http://www.nsdc.org/

### Other Books/CD-ROMs

*A Comprehensive Guide to Designing Standards-Based Districts, Schools, and Classrooms*, by Robert J. Marzano and John S. Kendall (Alexandria, VA: ASCD and Aurora, CO: McREL), 1996

This volume begins with a complete history and rationale behind the standards movement and continues with analyses of the impact of standards on national, state, and local benchmarks, student assessment, reporting, and accountability. A nine-step process is provided to help teachers at the classroom level, and four approaches are outlined to assist schools or districts in designing their own standards-centered models. The appendices also provide indispensable information and resources to support these efforts.

**Contacts:** Association for Supervision and Curriculum Development (ASCD), 1703 North Beauregard Street, Alexandria, VA 22311-1714; (800) 933-2723; fax (703) 575-5400; e-mail: member@ascd.org; Web site: http://www.ascd.org/

Mid-continent Research for Education and Learning (McREL), 2550 South Parker Road, Suite 500, Aurora, CO 80014; (303) 337-0990; fax: (303) 337-3005; e-mail: info@mcrel.org; Web site: http://www.mcrel.org

*Content Knowledge: A Compendium of Standards and Benchmarks for K–12 Education* (3rd ed.), by John S. Kendall and Robert J. Marzano (Alexandria, VA: ASCD and Aurora, CO: McREL), 2000

The information contained in this book is the result of a seven-year project to survey and consolidate the many national- and state-level efforts to identify what K–12 students should know and be able to do in a variety of subject areas. To accomplish this goal, McREL researchers consulted 116 national- and state-level documents that address standards and benchmarks in various subject areas. This effort produced the 255 standards with their accompanying 3,968 benchmarks that are detailed in this text. This document is intended as a resource and reference for schools and entire districts that are attempting to generate their own standards and benchmarks, or to revise and augment those provided by their state department of education. In short, this document can be a valuable tool in the design of a standards-based system.

**Contacts:** Association for Supervision and Curriculum Development (ASCD), 1703 North Beauregard Street, Alexandria, VA 22311-1714; (800) 933-2723; fax (703) 575-5400; e-mail: member@ascd.org; Web site: http://www.ascd.org/

Mid-continent Research for Education and Learning (McREL), 2550 South Parker Road, Suite 500, Aurora, CO 80014; (303) 337-0990; fax: (303) 337-3005; e-mail: info@mcrel.org; Web site: http://www.mcrel.org

*Front-End Alignment: Using Standards to Steer Educational Change*, by Ruth Mitchell (Washington, DC: Education Trust), 1996

This manual was developed to help educators use standards to positively impact education at all levels, from kindergarten to graduate school. *Front-End Alignment* is designed as a tool to help schools and districts gain the involvement of all stakeholders in the community at the development stage of the standards process and throughout the transition to a standards-based model.

**Contact:** The Education Trust, 1725 K Street N.W., Suite 200, Washington, DC 20006-1409; (202) 293-1217; fax: (202) 293-2605; Web site: http://www.edtrust.org/

*How to Bring Vision to School Improvement Through Core Outcomes, Commitments and Beliefs*, by Jon Saphier and John D'Auria (Carlisle, MA: Research for Better Teaching), 1993

This "how-to" booklet helps schools and districts unify their vision for educating students around three core values: outcomes for students, commitments about internal operations, and beliefs about learning. A process is detailed for achieving community-wide consensus around outcomes and taking action. Additional resources are provided.

**Contact:** Research for Better Teaching, Inc., One Acton Place, Acton, MA 01720-3951; (978) 263-9449; fax: (978) 263-9959; e-mail: info.@rbteach.com; Web site: http://www. rbteach.com/

*NSTA Pathways to the Science Standards: Guidelines for Moving Vision into Practice (Elementary School Edition)*, edited by Lawrence F. Lowery (Arlington, VA: NSTA), 1997

*NSTA Pathways to the Science Standards: Guidelines for Moving Vision into Practice (Middle School Edition)*, edited by Steven Rakow (Arlington, VA: NSTA), 1998

*NSTA Pathways to the Science Standards: Guidelines for Moving Vision into Practice (High School Edition)*, edited by Juliana Texley and Ann Wild (Arlington, VA: NSTA), 1996

This series of *NSTA Pathways* books support efforts to incorporate the National Science Education Standards into real-world teaching, professional development, assessment, content, programs, and systems. Each book contains a chapter devoted to content standards as well as corresponding appendices. A CD-ROM collection is also available as a companion for each book.

**Contact:** National Science Teachers Association (NSTA), 1840 Wilson Boulevard, Arlington, VA 22201-3000; (703) 243-7100; fax (703) 243-7177; Web site: http://www.nsta.org

**Resources for Science Literacy: Curriculum Evaluation**, developed by Project 2061 of the AAAS

This CD-ROM and its print companion volume contain detailed instructions for evaluating curriculum materials in light of Project 2061's Benchmarks for Science Literacy and other national standards. Included are case studies illustrating the application of the analysis procedure to a variety of curriculum materials, a utility for relating findings in the case studies to state and district learning goals, and a discussion of issues and implications of using the procedure.

**Contact:** Oxford University Press, Order Department, 2001 Evans Road, Cary, NC 27513-2010; (800) 451-7556; e-mail: custserv@oup-usa.org; Web site: http://www.oup-usa.org/

*Standards for Our Schools: How to Set Them, Measure Them, and Reach Them*, by Marc S. Tucker and Judy B. Codding (San Francisco: Jossey-Bass), 1998

In *Standards for Our Schools*, Tucker and Codding focus on empowering both students and adults by emphasizing high student expectations and by giving school professionals the information, skills, authority, and resources needed to do the job. They advocate building a standards-based instructional system, creating a results-oriented culture devoted to continuous improvement, and making the institution and the people in it accountable for reaching the goals set by the standards. The book lays out a step-by-step plan to bring all students up to high standards as well as to improve the performance of high-achieving students.

**Contact:** National Center on Education and the Economy (NCEE), Order Department, P.O. Box 10391, Rochester, NY 14610; (888) 361-6233; fax: (716) 482-1284; Web site: http://www.ncee.org/

## Web Sites

### Achieve Standards Database

**Web site:** http://www.achieve.org/

The Achieve Standards Database is a searchable database of state and international academic standards in English language arts, mathematics, science, and social studies, conveniently organized by subject, state, grade level, topic, and keyword. The Achieve Standards Database is unique in bringing these standards together in one place and organizing them in a way that allows for sophisticated searches and side-by-side comparisons.

**Contact:** Achieve, Inc., 8 Story Street, First Floor, Cambridge, MA 02138; (617) 496-6300; fax: (617) 496-6361

### Developing Educational Standards

**Web site:** http://www.putnamvalleyschools.org/standards.html

This Web site provides an annotated list of Internet sites with educational standards and curriculum frameworks documents.

**Contact:** Putnam Valley Central Schools, 171 Oscawana Lake Road, Putnam Valley, NY 10579-3050

## Resources for Performance Assessment Tasks

## Books

*A Collection of Performance Tasks and Rubrics* (Larchmont, NY: Eye on Education), 1998: *High School Mathematics*, by Charlotte Danielson and Elizabeth Marquez

*Middle School Mathematics*, by Charlotte Danielson
*Upper Elementary School Mathematics*, by Charlotte Danielson

*A Collection of Performance Tasks and Rubrics* is a series of three books for different grade levels, each of which provides performance tasks and scoring rubrics for important topics in mathematics. Included are many samples of student work that clarify the tasks and anchor the points of the scoring rubrics. Chapters are also included to guide educators in constructing their own performance tasks and rubrics.

**Contact:** Eye on Education, 6 Depot Way West, Larchmont, NY 10538-0300;
(914) 833-0551; fax: (914) 833-0761; e-mail: order@eyeoneducation.com;
Web site: http://www.eyeoneducation.com/

*Puddle Questions: Assessing Mathematical Thinking*, developed by Creative Publications

Challenge students in grades 1–8 with the absorbing investigations in this series and watch the ideas come in waves. Open-ended questions such as "How would you measure a puddle?" motivate students to think critically and to communicate what they know. Each book gives you everything you need for authentic assessment. Key mathematics ideas at each grade level focus on probability, measurement, reasoning, geometry, mathematics language, and visual thinking. Open-ended investigations show how students think, use tools, and communicate ideas. Ideas and follow-up activities introduce investigations, stimulate discussion, and extend learning.

**Contact:** Creative Publications, 5623 West 115th Street, Alsip, IL 60803; (800) 624-0822;
fax: (800) 624-0821; e-mail: deborah_olszewski@mcgraw-hill.com;
Web site: http://www.creativepublications.com/

*Puddle Questions for Science*, developed by Creative Publications

Open-ended investigations for grades 2–6 motivate critical thinking and communication to help teachers assess students' science skills. Each resource book contains proven Puddle Question features: key science skills at each grade level; open-ended investigations; assessment criteria and a scoring rubric for each problem; and ideas and follow-up activities to introduce investigations, stimulate discussion, and extend learning.

**Contact:** Creative Publications, 5623 West 115th Street, Alsip, IL 60803; (800) 624-0822;
fax: (800) 624-0821; e-mail: deborah_olszewski@mcgraw-hill.com;
Web site: http://www.creativepublications.com/

# Organizations

## Exemplars

Exemplars was founded to assist teachers, schools, and districts in implementing authentic assessment and problem solving in their classrooms in order to meet the challenging new standards developed in mathematics and science at the national, state, and local levels. It does this by providing high-quality teacher-developed and classroom-tested assessment problems in mathematics for grades K–2, 3–5, 6–8, and 9–12 and in science for grades K–2, 3–5, and 6–8. Each problem comes with rubrics based on national standards and benchmark papers and is keyed to the national mathematics and science standards and the basic skills that are required for successful completion. Exemplars also provides books on mathematics portfolios and workshops to help schools and districts begin to assess and implement the standards. The Exemplars Web site features a "Preview Kit" with examples of their Mathematics, Science, and Humanities Exemplars.

**Contact:** Exemplars, 271 Poker Hill Road, Underhill, VT 05489; (800) 450-4050; e-mail: exemplars@sover.net; Web site: http://www.exemplars.com/

## National Center for Research on Evaluation, Standards, and Student Testing (CRESST)

Funded by the U.S. Department of Education, CRESST conducts research on important topics related to K–12 educational testing and offers assistance in the form of guidebooks, videos, and online access to assessment databases and sample assessments. CRESST's Alternative Assessments in Practice Database will be of special interest to teachers, school districts, and assessment developers who are looking for new methods to assess student growth; it can be found on the Web at http://www.cse.ucla.edu/cresst/sample/aaip.pdf. The database contains listings of over 300 developers of new assessments and presents detailed information about their type and purpose, scoring and availability, subject matter, and skills measured.

**Contact:** CRESST/UCLA, 301 GSE&IS, Mailbox 951522, 300 Charles E. Young Drive North, Los Angeles, CA 90095-1522; (310) 206-1532; fax: (310) 825-3883; Web site: http://www.cse.ucla.edu/

## Northwest Regional Educational Laboratory (NWREL)

NWREL's mission is to improve educational results for children, youth, and adults by providing research and development assistance in delivering equitable, high-quality educational programs. Although NWREL provides assistance primarily to the states of Alaska, Idaho, Montana, Oregon, and Washington, all educators can access the helpful resources and programs/services information on their Web site. Included are an assessment program and an assessment resource library, which includes the Regional Educational Laboratory's *Improving Classroom Assessment: A Toolkit for Professional Developers (Toolkit98)*.

**Contact:** NWREL, 101 S.W. Main Street, Suite 500, Portland, OR 97204-3297; (503) 275-9500; Web site: http://www.nwrel.org/

### WestEd

WestEd is a nonprofit research, development, and service agency dedicated to improving education and other opportunities for children, youth, and adults. They work with practitioners and policy makers to address critical issues in education and related areas, from early childhood intervention to school-to-work transition, from curriculum, instruction, and assessment to safe schools and communities. WestEd has numerous publications on assessment, standards, and accountability, including Learning from Assessment: Tools for Examining Assessment Through Standards and Assessment Alternatives for Diverse Classrooms. In addition, the Center for Science Education and Professional Development, based in Williston, Vermont, is dedicated to helping teachers use continuous assessment to facilitate science inquiry. This center is a part of Learning Innovations, a division of WestEd in Stoneham, Massachusetts.

**Contact:** WestEd, 730 Harrison Street, San Francisco, CA 94107-1242; (415) 565-3000; Web site: http://www.wested.org/

## Assessment Series and Software

*Balanced Assessment for the Mathematics Curriculum*, by Alan Schoenfeld, Hugh Burkhardt, Judah Schwartz, and Sandra Wilcox (Columbus, OH: Dale Seymour), 1999

Supported by a grant from the National Science Foundation, this unique program offers a series of units containing field-tested assessment tasks. Designed to prepare students for the New Standards Testing at grades 4, 8, 10, and 12, each task contains a description, a sample solution, a set of suggestions for characterizing student performance, and several renderings of typical student work at various levels of achievement. Four packages are available for elementary, middle school, high school and advanced high school assessment.

**Contact:** ETA/Cuisenaire, 500 Greenview Court, Vernon Hills, IL 60061; (800) 445-5985; fax: (800) 875-9643; Web site: http://www.etacuisenaire.com/

**Connecticut Academy Science Assessment Project© (CASAP)**, developed by the Connecticut Academy for Education in Mathematics, Science & Technology, Inc.

CASAP combines written and performance assessment components to provide local districts with information about the performance of their students in science at grades 3, 5, and 8. In addition to learning how well students are performing "overall" in science, CASAP provide results that address performance in specific topic areas, e.g., electricity in physical science or the solar system in earth science. The assessments also provide a means to see how well students are using science skills such as observation, classification, measurement, recording, graphing and interpreting data, making inferences or predictions, and drawing conclusions. While tailored to Connecticut's standards, assessments are aligned with national science standards and applicable to other states.

**Contact:** Connecticut Academy for Education in Mathematics, Science & Technology, Inc., 211 South Main Street, Middletown, CT 06457-3769; (860) 346-1177; fax: (860) 346-2157; Web site: http://www.ctacad.org/Science/casap.htm

### New Standards Reference Examinations: Mathematics

Available in English and Spanish for students in grades 4, 8, and 10, these exams include extended open-ended and short-answer items measuring conceptual understanding, mathematical skills and tools, problem-solving ability, and reasoning and mathematical communication. Many tasks are derived from real-life situations. The exams are based on the New Standards Performance Standards, developed as a collaborative effort of the Learning Research and Development Center of the University of Pittsburgh and the National Center on Education and the Economy in Washington, D.C.

**Contact:** Harcourt Educational Assessment, (800) 211-8378; fax: (800) 232-1223; e-mail: customerservice@harcourt.com; Web site: www.hbem.com/

### TechPaths for Math, developed by Technology Pathways

Technology Pathways develops software that organizes the vast array of materials and data associated with curriculum, instruction, and assessment and creates easy-to-use tools that help schools reach their goal: improving student performance. TechPaths for Math is a complete mathematics assessment software system that helps analyze and track student performance. It consists of four user-friendly, integrated software programs—Planner, Task Selector, Task Designer, and Performance Assessor—designed to help teachers to use their time and resources for teaching and assessment mathematics performance. All four programs come on a single CD-ROM with a comprehensive guide to using TechPaths for Math. A training video is also available.

**Contact:** Technology Pathways, 1304 West Street, Guilford, CT 06437; (866) 457-1990; fax: (203) 457-1990; e-mail: info@techpaths.com; Web site: http://www.techpaths.com/

### TerraNova®, The Second Edition, developed by CTB/McGraw-Hill

TerraNova's second edition, the CAT (California Achievement Test) series, has the same content structure and score scale as the earlier CTBS (Comprehensive Test of Basic Skills) series. These two series can be used together as alternate forms for tracking student achievement results. The new series offers a wide range of content and assessment options in mathematics and science, as well as in reading/language arts and social studies. Content is aligned with national standards, instructional practices, and curricula. The tests integrate selected-response and open-ended questions and utilize multiple measures to ensure reliable assessment of a wide range of skills and proficiency levels. The process is facilitated by CTB's scoring teams, which work with customers to plan, prepare for, and manage the scoring process, identify and create the most useful types of score reports, and interpret the results.

**Contact:** CTB/McGraw-Hill, 20 Ryan Ranch Road, Monterey, CA 93940-5703; (800) 538-9547; fax: (800) 282-0266; Web site: http://www.ctb.com/

## Web Sites

### Best Practice Resources

**Web site:** http://www.teachermentors.com/

Developed and maintained by consultant and author Barry Sweeny, this Web site provides educators with resources on new-teacher mentoring and induction, peer observation, authentic performance assessment, and school improvement and staff development. The performance assessment section provides many links to organizations, written materials, research, software, and actual performance assessments.

**Contact:** Barry Sweeny, 26 W 413 Grand Avenue, Wheaton, IL 60187; (630) 668-2605; fax (630) 752-9941; e-mail: barry@teachermentor.com; Web site: http://www.teachermentors.com

### Performance Assessment Links in Science (PALS)

**Web site:** http://www.ctl.sri.com/pals/

PALS is an online, standards-based resource bank of science performance assessment tasks indexed according to the National Science Education Standards (NSES) and various other standards frameworks. The tasks, collected from numerous sources and continually updated, include student directions and response forms, administration procedures, scoring rubrics, examples of student work, and technical quality data calculated from field testing. Online rater training packs have also been created for some tasks.

**Contact:** Center for Technology in Learning, SRI International, 333 Ravenswood Avenue, Menlo Park, CA 94025; (650) 859-4826; e-mail: contact_pals@www.ctl.sri.com/

# Resources on Student Aspirations

## Organizations

### National Center for Student Aspirations (NCSA)

Student and teacher aspirations increasingly are viewed as important and identifiable components of quality schools. Under the direction of Russell Quaglia at the University of Maine, the National Center for Student Aspirations provides leadership, research, assessment, and interventions to help schools cultivate environments in which student aspirations can flourish. NCSA has designed the Aspirations Assessment Survey to measure conditions affecting student aspirations. Using the survey data, NCSA targets areas for improvement in the schools and districts in which they work and helps them to implement solutions, such as professional development for school staff or programs to enhance student leadership. NCSA also disseminates information about their aspirations research to students, parents, and policy makers.

**Contact:** NCSA, University of Maine, 5766 Shibles Hall, Orono, ME 04469-5766; (207) 581-2492; fax: (207) 581-2423; e-mail: aspire@umit.maine.edu; Web site: http://www.studentaspirations.org

# REFORMING CURRICULUM, INSTRUCTION, AND ASSESSMENT

Alignment with standards

Focus, rigor, and coherence

Classroom implementation

Staff views and concerns

Impact on student learning

# 4

# Problem One:

**Students came into** our middle schools from 10 different elementary schools. Some had studied dinosaurs for three years in a row but had never encountered a single physical science concept. Some had dabbled with the scientific inquiry process, while others knew only "textbook" science. And some, sadly, had had almost no science at all. How could we bring some coherence and consistency to our science curriculum and align it with our new vision of science education?

# Problem Two:

**We knew there** were pockets of teachers who were excited about the National Science Education Standards and inquiry-based science. Others were unfamiliar with the idea of standards and inquiry or uncomfortable with change. Still others were hoping that "this too shall pass." How could we get more to buy in? How could we get our curriculum off the shelves and alive in every classroom? How could we spread high-quality science teaching throughout the district and sustain the changes over time?

# Problem Three:

**We were not** sure whether students were learning the knowledge and skills we committed to in our curriculum frameworks. We had made changes in our curriculum and instruction but were still using mostly traditional assessments. These didn't give us a good picture of how students were learning skills such as data collection and analysis, problem solving, or complex reasoning or how well they really understood important concepts. How could we change assessment practices to better measure the concepts, skills, and dispositions that were important to us?

# Problem Four:

**We couldn't afford** to hire expensive program evaluators, and we didn't have time to be full-time program evaluators ourselves. But we did want to know if our new science program was improving student learning. Were all students benefiting in the ways we had hoped for? Were we getting the results we wanted? Was this plan working? It was time to find out.

If one or more of these problems hits close to home, read on. Together they illustrate four common problems schools and districts face as they reform mathematics and science curriculum, instruction, and assessment:

▼ how to develop coherent curricula aligned with national, state, and/or local standards;

▼ how to effectively implement, sustain, and monitor curriculum and instruction reform;

▼ how to broaden assessment practices to align with curriculum and instruction and standards;

▼ how to evaluate the impact of the changes on student learning.

In this chapter you will learn how to approach each of these problems by asking good questions, using reliable data to guide decision making, taking thoughtful action, and monitoring results. You will follow the progress of a fictitious district science reform team that is, in large part, an amalgam of the many school teams we visited and interviewed. Many of the same issues apply to school-based efforts and also to mathematics. As the team winds its way through the process of reforming their science curriculum, instruction, and assessment, its members encounter each of the four problems described above. As they confront each problem, they pause, ask questions, use data, take action, and reflect on what they have learned. They aren't perfect; they are learning as they go. But they give us a glimpse into inquiry in action.

At each critical juncture in their journey, we divert from the vignette to provide the reader with some background information on the problem, questions to consider in order to dig deeper into it, sources of data and tools to help answer those questions, and other helpful resources. The purpose of the vignette and the text in this chapter is not to provide you with solutions but to help guide your inquiry into these complex issues.

# Overview of Curriculum, Instruction, and Assessment: The Heart of Systemic Reform

Chapter 3 was about schools and communities committing to a vision of student learning and a set of high standards for each and every student. If student learning is the goal or destination of reform, then curriculum, instruction, and assessment is the vehicle. Virtually every national standards document, every state framework, and every local set of standards calls for fundamental changes in what teachers teach and how content is organized (curriculum), how they teach (instruction), and how student learning is monitored, evaluated, and reported (assessment). Everyone seems to agree on one thing: if change does not reach the classroom level, all the talk of reform is for naught.

The challenge, of course, is to effectively implement the vision for mathematics and science classrooms called for in the standards. This vision:

▼ emphasizes high expectations for all students;

▼ focuses on in-depth learning of a limited number of powerful concepts, emphasizing understanding, reasoning, and problem solving rather than memorization of facts, terminology, and algorithms;

▼ integrates scientific and mathematical inquiry with knowledge of science and mathematics concepts and principles;

▼ engages students in meaningful activities that enable them to construct and apply their knowledge of key science and mathematics concepts;

▼ reflects sound principles from research on how students learn; uses cooperative learning and techniques for asking questions that promote interaction and deeper understanding;

▼ features appropriate, ongoing use of calculators, computers, and other technologies;

▼ empowers students by enabling them to do science and mathematics, and increases their confidence in their ability to do so;

▼ develops in students the scientific and mathematical literacy necessary to make informed decisions and to function as full participants in society;

▼ assesses learning as an integral part of instruction;

▼ ensures that teachers have a deep understanding of their subject matter;

▼ provides ongoing support for classroom teachers, including continuing opportunities for teachers to work together to plan curriculum and instruction (Weiss 1997, 1; adapted by permission of Iris Weiss).

Note that the standards talk about curriculum, instruction, and assessment together, as a single vehicle. This reflects a new understanding of the three as an integrated system, not as independent activities. What unites them is a common focus on student learning. Standards shape what is being taught and how. Assessment provides evidence for attainment of standards.

What's nice about the unity of the three is that you can enter any door to start the change process. If you keep the focus on learning, any change in one area will inevitably lead to change in another. For example, if you decide to move first to performance-based assessments, curriculum and instruction will have to change if students are going to perform well on the new assessments. On the other hand, if you implement a new inquiry-based science curriculum, traditional short-answer and multiple-choice testing will soon be rendered inadequate to assess students' inquiry skills or the depth of their conceptual understanding. The key is to start somewhere!

In the vignette that follows, our hypothetical district begins by deciding to implement curriculum reform, a common starting point for many reform efforts. But their approach is far from common, as you will soon find out.

# Part One: Getting Started

**Our middle school** science team came home from the science leadership institute all fired up. We had experienced inquiry-based science as learners and loved it! Some of us felt for the first time as if we understood what the National Science Education Standards and our state frameworks were all about. We also learned a lot about systemic change. We received some training in how to plan effectively for change, including how to stay focused, set goals, make plans and implement them, and monitor progress. And we heard about the importance of using data as a tool for planning and decision making.

Now we were ready for the hard part: taking what we had learned and implementing it successfully in our three middle schools and across the district. When we arrived back from the institute, the district formed a science committee made up of our middle school team (six teachers and two administrators), additional teachers from the elementary and high schools in our district, the science and technology coordinators, the principals, the assistant superintendent, and a school board representative. The superintendent gave her blessing to the committee and officially charged us with the task of aligning our science curriculum with state and national frameworks, selecting appropriate materials, and developing a plan for improving science districtwide.

The first year got off to a good start. The committee began by reviewing our district's overall vision and goals. Then we asked ourselves what kind of science curriculum fit with that mission. With that question in mind, we began poring over the national and state standards documents. Sometimes we would spend a whole session just trying to understand one or two standards. We argued about what "inquiry" really meant, whether "less is really more," what were the important "big ideas" for students to understand in science, and whether interdisciplinary science was the way to go.

As we discussed and debated, a consensus started to emerge about the importance of providing a high-quality science education for all students. We made some broad decisions about the key science concepts they should understand to be prepared for life and work in the 21st century while affirming a commitment to actively engage students in the scientific inquiry process.

But our district's vision was a far cry from our reality. Five years ago, a science curriculum committee put together a written science curriculum—a list of topics from the textbook series we adopted. But that document sat on some administrator's shelf somewhere. Nobody had paid any attention to it then, and now it was totally out of sync with our new thinking about science. Our current science curriculum was really pretty much "every teacher for him- or herself"!

We could see the negative effect of this on our students. They came into our middle schools from 10 different elementary schools. Some had studied dinosaurs for three years in a row but had never encountered a single physical science concept. Some had dabbled with the scientific inquiry process, while others knew only "textbook" science. And some, sadly, had had almost no science at all. How could we bring some coherence and consistency to our science curriculum and align it with our new vision of science education?

# Problem One: Developing a Standards-Based Curriculum

## Overview of the Problem

Traditionally, we have thought about curriculum as lists of textbook topics or scope and sequences. Written plans for curriculum, if they existed at all, were often better at collecting dust on shelves than giving coherence to instruction. But all of this changes once schools commit to high levels of learning for all students. Suddenly, what is being taught and how matters—matters a lot—if students are going to reach those standards. We can no longer afford to have students missing out on important concepts and skills while others are repeated over and over. The desire to reach standards drives the need to bring coherence and alignment to the curriculum.

And that means doing the hard work of studying the standards and developing, revising, or adopting a written curriculum based on them that:

▼ makes crystal clear what the expectations are for students and teachers at each grade level;

▼ helps assure that students learn the concepts and skills everyone agrees are essential;

▼ drives the selection of textbooks and other curriculum materials (rather than having those drive the curriculum);

▼ is alive in classrooms, not sitting on a shelf somewhere;

▼ builds ownership by actively involving teachers throughout the process.

Ideally, this process is coordinated districtwide. But if necessary, individual schools can take the initiative to give coherence to their own mathematics and science curricula. For a good example of how to go about developing curriculum, see **Reform in Action**, page 343.

Developing a standards-based curriculum is very different from traditional curriculum writing in at least two ways. First, it's not about dusting off the curriculum document every five years for another go-round. Instead, it's about continuously improving the curriculum in order to continuously improve student learning. As Page Keeley, former Hall-Dale Science

*"A curriculum is an operational plan for instruction that details what . . . students need to know, how students are to achieve the identified curricular goals, what teachers are to do to help students develop their . . . knowledge, and the context in which learning and teaching occur."*

(National Council of Teachers of Mathematics 1989, 1)

Curriculum Coordinator from Hallowell, Maine, explains, "Our curriculum work is always evolving. Even after two years of curriculum development work, a lot of things still need to happen. We need to develop standards-based units, connections among the disciplines, tasks that go with indicators, and ways to infuse technology. The process doesn't stop."

In addition to being a continuous and evolving process, curriculum writing is most successful when it grows out of the curriculum committee's deep understanding of mathematics and science content and pedagogy described in national standards. For example, in Turner, Maine, the K–12 mathematics curriculum committee, made up of representatives of each of the seven schools in the district, is, with support from staff of the Regional Alliance for Mathematics and Science Education, undertaking a study of NCTM's *Principles and Standards for School Mathematics* (2000), using a three-step process: (1) read and discuss each of the major content strands in the document; (2) as a group, do mathematics problems related to each strand; and (3) examine their own students' work on problems dealing with the same concepts. The combination of these experiences gives them the opportunity to reflect deeply on the nature of mathematics, to envision how students' understanding of a particular concept might develop from kindergarten to 12th grade, and to consider the implications for their curriculum. "Having K–12 teachers doing the same mathematics problems together has already sparked discussion about the use of hand-ons approaches for older students," commented Assistant Superintendent Linda Parkin. Through this process, the committee will be better prepared not only to craft a curriculum but also to provide leadership in its implementation.

Both the Hall-Dale and the Turner examples illustrate some of the key features of a successful curriculum development process: support and involvement of both administrators and teachers; allocation of sufficient time and resources to carefully study state and national standards and develop a common vision for mathematics and science education; and a timely product.

In some cases, the product is a written curriculum document with all of the features described in the chart "Basic Elements of a Good Written Curriculum" on page 164. Many schools take this approach, and then adopt, adapt, or piece together curriculum materials. This method has the advantage of having the committee fully invested in a curriculum that they developed together. Their curriculum, not a textbook or any particular set of materials, drives what is taught. A possible disadvantage, however, is that the committee invests all of its time developing a curriculum document and then can't find any comprehensive, standards-based materials that align with it. Then they have to cobble together a set of curriculum materials from a variety of sources, sacrificing some of the coherence and strength of the available programs.

Another scenario can be equally effective and more efficient. Rather than investing considerable time into writing their own document, the committee can decide to develop a general framework or adopt national or state standards. Then they adopt an excellent set of standards-based curriculum materials and spend the district's time and money on helping teachers learn to use them well. This approach has been easier in mathematics, where there are comprehensive standards-based programs and curricula for all levels, K–12. Science requires more planning and coordination because there are more gaps in available standards-based curricula. Regardless of which scenario you choose, many mathematics and science curriculum materials, both comprehensive and supplementary, are available; the accompanying CD-ROM contains an annotated list of many of these.

## Taking Stock of Your Existing Curriculum

If schools are going to continuously improve their curriculum, they need to know how good it is and how to make it better. For many schools and districts, the first questions are "Do we have a written curriculum at all? And if so, is it based on standards?" If the answer to either question is no, the next step is to organize a good curriculum development or revision process using either of the approaches described above. What follows are some processes to help you take stock of your existing curriculum.

### Mapping the Curriculum

Often districts (and schools) find that a useful first step in curriculum development or revision is to map what is currently being taught. Curriculum mapping is a process of collecting and analyzing data about what content and skills teachers are teaching, at what depth, and how they are assessing that knowledge. When teachers are involved in the process, it can be a powerful tool for communicating about what they are teaching, uncovering gaps and redundancies, and generating ideas for the new curriculum plan. But since revealing what you are or are not teaching can be threatening, it is important that curriculum mapping be well structured and safe for teachers. Heidi Hayes Jacobs, in her book *Mapping the Big Picture: Integrating Curriculum and Assessment K–12* (1997), offers one such process, a low-risk, practical way to go about mapping based on the school calendar. (See **Data Tools**, DT 4-1, for a sample high school physics curriculum map based on calendar mapping and DT 4–7 and DT 4–8 for surveys on topic coverage and expectations.) Another curriculum mapping process is available online from the North Central Regional Educational Laboratory, which uses TIMSS curriculum surveys to generate analyses of the breadth, depth, flow, and rigor of your mathematics and science curricula (see **Resources**, page 227).

## Assessing the Written Curriculum

What makes for a good written curriculum? The box below identifies some key components, which can guide you as you develop a new curriculum or assess and revise your current one.

### Basic Elements of a Good Written Curriculum

▼ A district mission statement or philosophy

▼ District student outcomes—five or six broad statements about what students should know and be able to do by graduation

▼ Content standards—descriptions of what all students should know and be able to do in each content area

▼ Key concepts and critical content, listed by topics or thematic units, that form the core content curriculum at each grade level

▼ Benchmarks—statements that indicate what students should know and be able to do at various developmental levels, such as K–2, 3–5, 6–8, 9–12

▼ Scope and sequence for the process development areas only— reading, writing, mathematics

▼ A plan for measuring progress through the grades on the district student outcomes

In addition to looking at its components, it is important to assess how well your written curriculum aligns with your local, state, and national frameworks and standards. Many of the state frameworks documents or accompanying handbooks provide checklists or rubrics to help you do this. A sample from the state of Connecticut is included in **Data Tools**, DT 4-2.

A third check on your written curriculum is to assess its focus. Focus refers to the depth with which topics in the curriculum are treated within and across classes. Recent findings of the Third International Mathematics and Science Study (TIMSS) show that curricula in the United States cover more topics in less depth than some countries that outperform our students. For example, the typical eighth-grade mathematics curriculum in

Japan covers 17 topics, versus 31 in the United States (Schmidt, McKnight, and Raizen 1997, 55). How many topics are included in your school's or district's curriculum? Is your curriculum sacrificing depth for breadth?

Another measure of focus that TIMSS used was how much attention priority topics received in the curriculum. In Japan, for example, the five most heavily emphasized fourth-grade science topics accounted for 40 to 45 percent of the total curriculum. In the United States, the five most emphasized topics accounted for about 25 percent of the curriculum (Schmidt, McKnight, and Raizen 1997, 58). Which topics are emphasized most heavily in your curriculum? How much of the curriculum do they account for?

Related to focus is rigor. How rigorous are the expectations for a particular topic? Are students expected, for example, to memorize an idea or procedure? deeply understand it? use complex reasoning? use the knowledge to solve new problems or create original solutions or products? A strong curriculum includes expectations at all of these levels. How rigorous is your curriculum? The Subject Content sections of the Surveys of Classroom Practices in **Data Tools** (DT 4-7 and DT 4-8), and the NCREL Curriculum Mapping Web Site (see **Resources**, page 233) can also be used to examine the focus and rigor of your written curriculum.

Another consideration is the coherence of your curriculum. Coherence refers to the connectedness of the ideas and skills presented to students over an extended period of time (National Research Council 1999, 1). A coherent curriculum tells a story, artfully sequencing segments, elaborating on central themes and concepts, and building toward a conclusion. According the National Research Council (NRC) to achieve coherence, a curriculum must (1) focus on important ideas and skills; (2) help students develop an understanding of these ideas and skills over several years in ways that are logical and developmentally appropriate; (3) explicitly establish connections among ideas and skills in ways that enable students to understand both the ideas and the connections; and (4) assess and diagnose what students understand to determine next steps in instruction (NRC 1999, 9–11).

**RESOURCES FOR DEVELOPING A COHERENT CURRICULUM ALIGNED WITH NATIONAL STANDARDS**
(full listings at end of this chapter)

*Atlas of Science Literacy*, by the American Association for the Advancement of Science (Project 2061) and the National Science Teachers Association, 2000

*Designing Mathematics or Science Curriculum Programs: A Guide for Using Mathematics and Science Education Standards*, by the Committee on Science Education K–12 and the Mathematical Sciences Education Board, National Research Council, 1999

*Designs for Science Literacy*, by the American Association for the Advancement of Science (Project 2061), 2000

NCREL Curriculum Mapping Web Site (North Central Regional Educational Laboratory)

See also **Resources on Standards** in **Resources**, Chapter 3

TIMSS researchers found that U.S. textbooks and tests added fragmentation rather than coherence to our curriculum. One recent report describes U.S. textbooks as "voluminous, unselective, and filled with redundant content over the grades." As a result, teachers are often left "trying to accomplish a mosaic of fragmented, small tasks. . ." (Schmidt et al. 1998, 49). How coherent is your curriculum? Does it develop a "story" or does it suffer from repetition and fragmentation?

One last key question a curriculum committee should ask is whether students could achieve a particular standard or goal through their curriculum. This is a superb test of whether they have assembled the right concepts, performance standards, and teaching units at all grade levels (Susan Loucks-Horsley, personal communication, 2000). And it is critical to use this test for all students. A focused, rigorous, and coherent curriculum should be accessible to all students, providing multiple entry points for students with gaps in their knowledge to engage in inquiry and learn rigorous content (NRC 1999, 12).

## Developing a Data Collection Plan

The form in **Planning Tools**, page 219–220 and illustrated below, can assist you in developing a plan for taking stock of your written curriculum.

### Assessing the Written Curriculum

| Problem/Question | How good is our written curriculum? | | | | |
|---|---|---|---|---|---|
| Data Sources/Tools We Want to Use | Got It | Need It | Disaggregated by | How/When Collected | Person Responsible |
| | | | | | |

# Part Two: Developing a Curriculum, Developing a Professional Culture

**After looking over** our current science curriculum and talking more about what was going on in classrooms, the science committee knew we had to start from scratch building a new science curriculum for all grade levels. We decided to get some help from an outside science consultant. She led us through a curriculum mapping exercise where we honestly looked at what was being taught at each grade level. Elementary teachers were shocked to learn that some "pet" topics like plants, dinosaurs, and the solar system were repeated year after year, while important science concepts such as force, energy, and gravity were completely ignored. In the middle and high schools, we also learned for the first time what everyone was teaching. After identifying gaps and overlaps, we talked more about how to build a curriculum that emphasized important science concepts, science processes, and complex reasoning, not just facts.

The more we talked, the more excited we became. Not only were we developing a curriculum framework; we were developing a professional culture. We were getting together to talk about things besides "Johnny was a pain." We were discussing teaching and learning. We realized we had brilliant people in our district and that we could really learn from each other. Committee members started to look forward to our bimonthly meetings. Sometimes we met as a whole group; sometimes we broke out into elementary, middle, and high school groups.

After six months, the committee completed a draft of our district's science curriculum frameworks. While based on state and national standards, it was "our" document, complete with content standards for K–3, 4–6, 7–9, and 10–12 and benchmarks for each grade band. We were really excited about the product we had created but knew that our work had only begun. Now it was time to present it to the staff.

This was a critical juncture. We had spent six months working together as a committee, studying, arguing, debating, and consolidating our understanding of and commitment to inquiry-based science. But the rest of the staff had not been through this process. How could we bridge the gap?

We knew there were pockets of teachers who were excited about the National Science Education Standards and inquiry-based science. Others were unfamiliar with the idea of standards and inquiry or uncomfortable with change. Still others were hoping that "this too shall pass." How could we get more to buy in? How could we get our curriculum off the shelves and alive in every classroom? How could we spread high-quality science teaching throughout the district and sustain the changes over time?

# Problem Two: Implementing Standards-Based Curriculum and Instruction Reform

## Overview of the Problem

*"Schools don't pilot anything. They just send ideas and innovations on and wave at them from the pier, never to be seen again."*

(Wiggins 1998, 3)

Having a good map, a coherent plan for instruction, can certainly help teachers find their way on the road to reform. But it is no guarantee. Actually implementing that curriculum in the classroom is where the rubber hits the road. And sadly, this is often where the change process breaks down.

For many teachers, what follows is all too familiar a scenario. The school or district launches a new program with a great deal of energy and fanfare. A small group of innovative teachers eagerly jumps on the bandwagon. Another group watches and waits to see how they fare. Still others, hoping that "this too shall pass," are determined to sit this one out.

A year or two or three later, the administration starts to wonder, "Whatever happened with that new curriculum? Did it improve student learning? What did we get for our time and money?" Those questions, however, are meaningless without first knowing if and how the change was ever implemented. For lasting change to take hold, reform leaders have to pay close

attention to the process of change and to the people implementing it. Researchers and practitioners have learned a lot from decades of making and studying change. Some important general principles are summarized in the box below. (For more information about the change process, see **Resources for Managing Change/ Monitoring Implementation**, beginning on page 245.)

## Principles of Change

▼ Change is both an individual and an organizational phenomenon.

▼ Change is a process that takes time and persistence.

▼ As individuals progress through a change process, their needs for support and assistance change.

▼ Change efforts are effective when the change to be made is clearly defined, support and assistance are available, and leaders and policies support the change.

▼ Most systems resist change.

▼ Organizations that are continuously improving have ongoing mechanisms for setting goals, taking actions, assessing the results of their actions and making adjustments.

▼ Change is complex because it requires people to communicate with one another about complex topics in organizations that are, for the most part, large and structured.

While general principles about change are useful, the real trick is applying them to your own specific situation. To do that well, school reform teams have to stay closely attuned to how teachers are responding. What are they actually doing with the new curriculum? How are they feeling about the change? What kind of support do they need most now? Once a change effort is launched, it is not too early to ask if your program is going down a road that is likely to lead to your desired outcomes. That's better than waiting until the momentum has stalled because of problems that have not been addressed.

This section offers tools for collecting and analyzing data about the implementation of changes in curriculum and instruction. Because of its scope and importance, assessment reform is treated separately later in the chapter. Implementation data can be a great aid to your team. They can provide you with information vital to your planning, such as which components of the program teachers are using, which they are not, and why. They can help you diagnose and even prevent problems and target the best interventions. For example, if you find out early on that teachers are

## WARNING!

**Collecting data about implementation is not to be used to single out, punish, or "remediate" teachers who "aren't doing it." Using data for these purposes can set implementation back decades! Rather, data collection is for the purpose of improving the system as a whole.**

not comfortable with the science content they are now expected to teach, you can offer appropriate professional development up front, cutting the problem off at the pass.

Tracking implementation also gives you baseline data from which to measure progress. This is important not only for planning but also for morale and public relations. For instance, a school board is getting impatient with lack of improvement on mathematics test scores. With implementation data, you can show that while scores have not increased yet, progress is being made. For example, you may be able to report that this year, 35 percent more teachers are using research-based mathematics problem-solving strategies with their students.

These and other vital questions that can be answered with implementation data are summarized on page 171.

## Defining the Change: Will We Know It When We See It?

A first challenge in assessing the implementation of standards-based curriculum and instruction is defining what you are looking for. Even though you may have a beautifully written curriculum document, that doesn't mean everyone agrees on exactly what that curriculum looks like in action. Clearly defining a desired practice, such as "standards-based instruction," is as complex as it is critical, both for building understanding of and commitment to change and for assessing progress.

Let's take one important dimension of standards-based instruction: inquiry. Notions about what inquiry is vary widely depending on educators' experiences and beliefs about teaching and learning. For some, the use of hands-on materials and cooperative groupings constitutes inquiry. For others, inquiry has more to do with how students are engaged in asking questions, formulating explanations, and coming to deep understandings of important mathematical or scientific ideas. What are the essential features of inquiry and how can your team as well as teachers and administrators in your school or district come to some shared understandings about what it is?

## Inquiring into Inquiry

The NRC's publication *Inquiry and the National Science Education Standards: A Guide for Teaching and Learning* (2000) provides a rich discussion of inquiry and a useful resource for sharpening your vision of inquiry in the

*"Nothing blocks communication, inhibits evaluation, hampers staff development, and thwarts improvement more than a program that is not clearly defined."*

(Crandall and Loucks 1982, 1)

## GATHERING CURRICULUM IMPLEMENTATION DATA: QUESTIONS TO CONSIDER

▼ What is actually being taught and how? What instructional materials are being used? What resources and equipment are available? How are they being allocated? How closely linked are curriculum and instruction with standards and assessments? What kinds of assessments are being used?

▼ Where are our pockets of success? What factors lead to successful practices? How can improvement teams build on successes and learn from them? What are the most important areas where improvement is needed?

▼ To what extent are curriculum materials and instructional practices free of racial, class, cultural, and gender biases? (See "Racial, Class, Cultural, and Gender Bias in Curriculum, Instruction, and Assessment" in Chapter 5.)

▼ What groups of students are getting access to high-quality mathematics and science curriculum, instruction, and assessment opportunities? What groups are not? Do gaps in opportunity help explain gaps in achievement?

▼ What relationships seem to exist between student achievement and inquiry-based instruction?

▼ What are key stakeholders' (teachers, administrators, students, parents, school board, community) perceptions/ concerns about curriculum reform? How can our implementation plan take these into consideration?

▼ What kind of professional development do teachers need to support them in implementing curriculum reform?

▼ What policies and practices in the district, state, or country as a whole support or undermine our local curriculum reform efforts? What critical supports are most important right now?

science classroom. The NRC defines inquiry as having certain essential features but acknowledges that these features can vary widely in their implementation. "For example, every inquiry engages students in scientifically oriented questions. However, in some inquiry, students pose the initial question. In others, students choose alternatives or sharpen the initial question, and in others the students are provided with the question" (NRC 2000, 28). Figure 4.1 illustrates these essential features and their variations. Over the course of their science learning, the NRC recommends, students should have opportunities to engage in all types of inquiry, from the most open-ended to the most guided.

**FIGURE 4.1: ESSENTIAL FEATURES OF CLASSROOM INQUIRY AND THEIR VARIATIONS**

| Essential Feature | Variations | | | |
|---|---|---|---|---|
| 1. Learner engages in. scientifically oriented questions | Learner poses a question | Learner selects among questions, poses new questions | Learner sharpens or clarifies question provided by teacher, materials, or other source | Learner engages in question provided by teacher, materials, or other source |
| 2. Learner gives priority to **evidence** in responding to questions | Learner determines what constitutes evidence and collects it | Learner directed to collect certain data | Learner given data and asked to analyze | Learner given data and told how to analyze |
| 3. Learner formulates **explanations** from evidence | Learner formulates explanation after summarizing evidence | Learner guided in process of formulating explanations from evidence | Learner given possible ways to use evidence to formulate explanation | Learner provided with evidence |
| 4. Learner connects explanations to scientific knowledge | Learner independently examines other resources and forms the links to explorations | Learner directed toward areas and sources of scientific knowledge | Learner given possible connections | |
| 5. Learner communicates and justifies explanations | Learner forms reasonable and logical argument to communicate explanations | Learner coached in development of communications | Learner provided broad guidelines to use sharpen communications | Learner given steps and procedures for communication |

More————————————————— **Amount of Learner Self-Direction**—————————————Less
More—————————————— **Amount of Direction from Teacher or Materials** ————————————Less

## Myths about Inquiry

According to the NRC, several myths about inquiry "threaten to inhibit progress in science education reform either by characterizing inquiry as too difficult to achieve or by neglecting the essential features of inquiry-based learning" (NRC 2000, 35):

▼ Myth 1: All science subject matter should be taught through inquiry.

▼ Myth 2: True inquiry occurs only when students generate and pursue their own questions.

▼ Myth 3: Inquiry teaching occurs easily through use of hands-on or kit-based instructional materials.

▼ Myth 4: Student engagement in hands-on activities guarantees that inquiry teaching and learning are occurring.

▼ Myth 5: Inquiry can be taught without attention to the subject matter. (NRC 2000, 36)

Confronting myths about inquiry and embracing and practicing it well in the classroom often require deep changes in teachers' beliefs about teaching and learning. Change at this deep level is a process that unfolds over time when teachers have had the opportunity to:

▼ experience cognitive dissonance between old and new beliefs, most often through learning mathematics and science in new ways themselves;

▼ resolve the dissonance and revise their thinking over time through ongoing collegial support, reading, writing, discussing;

▼ develop skills in implementing new teaching practices that support their new understandings;

▼ expand their repertoire of practice to support new understandings;

▼ receive continued help surfacing and learning from new issues and problems as they arise. (Thompson and Zueli 1999, 355–357)

Short-circuiting this process can result in superficial change rather than the deep and sustained transformation that emerges out of a new set of beliefs about teaching and learning. You may see a teacher "going through the motions," using some of the features of inquiry, such as use of hands-on materials or cooperative groups, while missing its essence. Moreover, it is important that not just teachers, but also administrators and others responsible for leading reform and evaluating teachers, go through a similar process so that they develop the "lens" for observing and assessing inquiry-based teaching and learning.

Presuming the kind of in-depth professional learning described above as a necessary backdrop, some of the guidebook tools that you can later use to assess implementation of reform can also help your team achieve clarity and consensus about the change you are looking for. For example, Horizon Research, Inc., evaluators for the National Science Foundation's Local Systemic Change sites, uses classroom videotapes to train evaluators to use their observation protocol and to help build consensus about what a good lesson looks like. Even without the goal of becoming evaluators, the exercise of viewing video lessons as a team, using an observation protocol to rate their effectiveness, and then comparing individuals' ratings can be a powerful learning experience. (See "2000-2001 Local Systemic Change Classroom Observation Interviews and Protocol," **Data Tool**s, DT 4–16, and Teaching Math: A Video Library, **Resources**, page 233.)

## FIGURE 4.2: WHAT ARE STUDENTS DOING [IN MATH CLASS]?

Some things one might observe in an inquiry-based classroom:

1. Interacting with each other, as well as working independently, just as adults do.

2. Working in teams to challenge and defend possible solutions. Students help each other to learn.

3. Working in groups to test solutions to problems, with each group member highly involved.

4. Communicating mathematical ideas to one another through examples, demonstrations, models, drawings, and logical arguments.

5. Using textbooks as one of many resources. Students also should know how and when to use manipulatives (such as blocks and balances) and technology (such as calculators and computers) as problem-solving tools.

6. Applying math to real-life problems and not just practicing a collection of isolated skills. Students spend lots of time solving complex problems.

7. Seeking a best solution among several solutions to a problem. Students can explain the different ways they reach these solutions and can defend the choice of one over another.

Another approach is to create (or borrow) your own detailed checklists or rubrics of the key features of your mathematics or science program. When written in concrete, observable terms, checklists can build common understanding while serving as yardsticks against which to measure actual classroom practice. Several examples are included in **Data Tools**, DT 4–3 through DT 4–5; one is illustrated in Figure 4.2.

A third approach is to use the Innovation Configuration methodology, developed by the CBAM Project at the University of Texas to help educators create precise descriptions of a program or practice. Innovation Configurations describe key components of a practice and possible variations ranging from ideal to unacceptable. They are useful both for helping developers and implementers gain clarity about what a program actually looks like and for monitoring implementation. (See

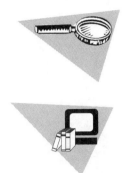

**Data Tools**, DT 4-6, for a sample Innovation Configuration for the NCTM Standards and **Resources**, page 246.)

## Choosing Indicators

Drawing on the work of the National Science Foundation, Horizon Research, Inc., the Council of Chief State School Officers, and the Concerns-Based Adoption Model (CBAM) Project, we have compiled a list of possible indicators (summarized on page 182) that you might use to help track your progress toward implementation of standards-based curriculum and instruction reform. For each indicator, you will need to fill in more specific criteria or targets that you agree are important. Many of the Data Tools contain detailed indicators and checklists that can help you with this task.

## Time Spent on Instruction

For elementary schools, simply looking at how much time teachers spend teaching science and mathematics relative to other subjects can be informative (see Figure 4.3). For elementary schools where little science instruction is taking place, increasing time spent teaching science may be an important measure of progress. At the high school level, the number of years students study mathematics and science versus other subjects can be revealing. (See **Data Tools**, DT 4-7, DT 4-8, and DT 4-18.)

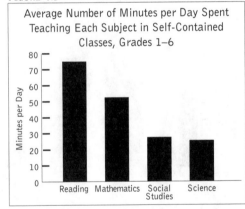

**FIGURE 4.3**

Average Number of Minutes per Day Spent Teaching Each Subject in Self-Contained Classes, Grades 1–6

## Use of Problem-Solving and Inquiry-Based Instructional Strategies

Of course, it is important to consider not just the quantity but also the quality of mathematics and science instruction. One indicator of quality is the extent to which problem-solving and inquiry-based instructional strategies are being used and used well (see discussion above). The National Science Foundation publication *Foundations* ([1997]) offers one set of inquiry indicators based on what students are doing, what teachers are doing, and how the environment supports inquiry (see **Data Tools**, DT 4-5). Another similar framework is Horizon Research, Inc.'s, which creates composites of the "investigative culture" and "investigative practices" from their survey data (see "Local Systemic Change Through Teacher Enhancement: 2001 Teacher Questionnaire, 6–12 Mathematics," **Data Tools**, DT 4-12). Investigative culture includes strategies used by the teacher to facilitate

exploration by the students, such as arranging seating to facilitate student discussion, using open-ended questions, requiring students to supply evidence to support their claims, and encouraging them to consider alternative explanations. Investigative practices pertain to what students are doing in the classroom, including engaging in hands-on mathematics and science activities, working on models or simulations, conducting extended investigations, and writing reflections in notebooks or journals. (See also Figure 4.1 and **Data Tools**, DT 4-3, DT 4-4, DT 4-6, DT 4-7, DT 4-8, DT 4-13B, and DT 4-15, DT 4-16, and DT 4-18 through DT 4-21.)

## Inquiry for Everyone?

Another important question to consider is whether all students are being given the same opportunities to participate in inquiry-based learning. The 1993 National Survey of Science and Mathematics Education found that ability grouping, especially in high school mathematics, was still widely practiced and that students in low-ability classes had fewer opportunities to do inquiry-based science or to write about reasoning when problem solving in mathematics (See Figure 4.4). In addition, the survey found that classes with high minority enrollment emphasized preparing students for standardized tests rather than for future study of mathematics or science (Weiss, Matti, and Smith 1994, as cited in Weiss 1997, 4–5).

**FIGURE 4.4**

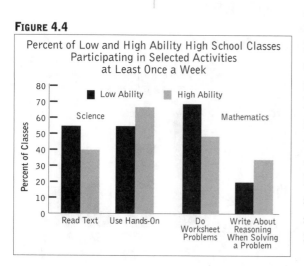

Percent of Low and High Ability High School Classes Participating in Selected Activities at Least Once a Week

As you consider not just inquiry but each of the first nine indicators we discuss, it will be important to disaggregate data to see if all students have equal access to rigorous content, quality lessons, effective assessment practices, good materials, and qualified and prepared teachers.

## Focused, Rigorous, and Coherent Content

While use of problem-solving and inquiry-based instructional strategies gets at how the content is delivered, this indicator considers the nature of that content. Are the concepts and skills identified in your written curriculum actually being taught, and to all students? Are they being taught accurately, at the appropriate developmental level, and coherently across the grade levels? At what level of expectation? Are students expected mostly to memorize facts and formulas? Or are they challenged to deeply understand, reason, and create novel solutions and products? Is the curriculum focused,

that is, are important ideas treated in depth? One of the findings of Horizon Research, Inc.'s study of the Local Systemic Change (LSC) sites was that elementary teachers heavily involved in LSC professional development activities did not teach more science units, but increased the length of time spent on a typical science unit, an indicator of increased focus (Weiss, Arnold, Banilower, Soar 2000, 37). (See NCREL Curriculum Mapping Web, **Resources**, page 231, and **Data Tools**, DT 4-6, DT 4-7, DT 4-8, DT 4-13A, DT 4-15, DT 4-16, and DT 4-18.)

## Quality Lessons

**FIGURE 4.5**

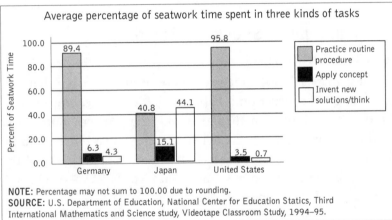

Average percentage of seatwork time spent in three kinds of tasks

NOTE: Percentage may not sum to 100.00 due to rounding.
SOURCE: U.S. Department of Education, National Center for Education Statics, Third International Mathematics and Science study, Videotape Classroom Study, 1994–95.

Assessing the quality of lessons taught requires having a keen eye and a deep understanding of standards-based reform. The TIMSS videotape study of eighth-grade mathematics classrooms in the United States, Japan, and Germany suggests some interesting dimensions of a classroom to explore, including how lessons are structured and delivered, what kind of mathematics is presented, and what kind of mathematical thinking students are engaged in. The study found significant differences between the United States and Japan in each of these areas. For example, teachers in the United States emphasized skill development, short student responses, and one-solution methods, while Japanese classrooms emphasized thought-provoking problems, more in-depth discussions, and alternative solution methods (U.S. Department of Education 1996, 42). During seat work, students in the United States spent 95.8 percent of their time practicing routine procedures, while Japanese students balanced this kind of practice with applying concepts and inventing new solutions (see Figure 4.5). What are teachers emphasizing in your classrooms? Is there a balance among instructional approaches such as lecture, hands-on work,

individual seat work, and nonlaboratory group work, and are these approaches used appropriately? (See **Data Tools**, DT 4-7, DT 4-8, and DT 4-12.)

Another lens for looking at lessons are the indicators Horizon Research, Inc. uses in their classroom observation protocol. These are organized around the design of the lesson, its implementation, the mathematics and science content, and the classroom culture (see **Data Tools**, DT 4-16). **Data Tools**, DT 4-6, "Innovation Configuration Continuum: NCTM Evaluation Standard—Instruction," offers a third tool, focused on mathematics lessons, by identifying five key components of instruction and four variations, rubric-style, on each. (See also **Data Tools**, DT 4-3 through DT 4-8, DT 4-12, DT 4-13B, DT 4-15, and DT 4-18 through DT 4-21.)

## Use of High-Quality, Standards-Based Instructional Materials

Use of these materials does not assure good instruction, but they are often in use when good instruction is happening. (See the accompanying CD-ROM for descriptions of mathematics and science curriculum materials.) In addition, if you are looking at whether a particular curriculum program is being used well, you will want to find out what materials from that program are being used and how. (See **Data Tools**, DT 4-9, DT 4-10, DT 4-14 through DT 4-16, and DT 4-21.)

## Use of Multiple Classroom Assessment Strategies

The use of portfolios, performance tasks, journals, observations, and examination of student work to assess understanding and skill development is another feature of standards-based instruction. This feature is treated more fully later in this chapter. (Also see **Data Tools**, DT 4-7, DT 4-8, DT 4-12, DT 4-15, DT 4-16, DT 4-18, DT 4-21, and DT 4-25.)

## Teacher Qualifications

Do all students have equal access to mathematics and science instructors with majors in the fields? Researchers have found that classes with high percentages of minority students tend to have less qualified teachers (Weiss, Matti, and Smith 1994, as cited in Weiss 1997, 5)(see Figure 4.6). Your team may want to investigate if this trend is true in your middle or high school. (See **Data Tools**, DT 3-21.)

## Teacher Preparedness

Even when teachers are certified in mathematics or science, that doesn't mean that they feel prepared to teach these subjects in the ways advocated by the national standards. This kind of teaching requires deep knowledge of the mathematics and science being taught, a wide repertoire of instructional and assessment strategies, and an understanding of how children think and develop mathematical and scientific understandings. How prepared are teachers to teach their content? Are there some content areas in which they feel better prepared than others? How prepared are they to use problem-solving and inquiry-based strategies or materials from a program you have adopted? How deep is their understanding of student thinking in mathematics and science? What kind of ongoing professional development, such as workshops, study groups, coaching, and time to reflect and plan, are provided to support teacher preparation? In addition to using self-report surveys (see **Data Tools**, DT 4-12 and DT 4-13B), you can ask teachers to listen to student dialogue or review student work to identify areas where understanding of content was incorrect or incomplete; other ways of assessing teacher preparedness are interviewing or observing teachers, reviewing lesson plans, and administering content assessments (Weiss 1999).

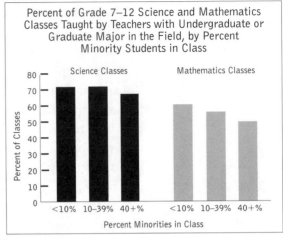

**FIGURE 4.6**

Percent of Grade 7–12 Science and Mathematics Classes Taught by Teachers with Undergraduate or Graduate Major in the Field, by Percent Minority Students in Class

## Support for Reform

Closely connected to knowledge and skills are beliefs and opinions about standards-based reform. Underlying and driving what people do is what they believe. Changing beliefs can be a good indication that reform is progressing. For example, teams may want to know if support for inquiry is growing, if staff believe that computers or calculators are important for instruction, or if they think ability grouping is the best way for students to learn. It is also important to assess the understanding and support for reform among the other stakeholders and leaders—administrators, parents, the school board, and the community as a whole. These data help leaders take beliefs and attitudes into account as they plan and support implementation. (See **Data Tools**, DT 4-7, DT 4-8, DT 4-12, DT 4-13B, and DT 4-18.)

## Levels of Use

The tracking strategies described above are specific to mathematics and science. Reform teams may also want to consider a widely used tool for

assessing implementation of any particular innovation, known as Levels of Use. Developed by the Concerns-Based Adoption Model (CBAM) Project at the University of Texas in the 1970s, Levels of Use looks at what teachers are actually doing with a new program or practice, such as a mathematics replacement unit or a kit-based science program. Typically, as teachers work with a new program over time, they progress in their skill and comfort. Through a series of interviews, evaluators can determine where teachers are in their use, ranging from early levels of preparation to more sophisticated integration and renewal (see Figure 4.7). This information can help planners target support appropriate to teachers' needs. Training and materials are available for teams that want to learn more about this approach. (For more on CBAM, see *Implementing Change: Patterns, Principles, and Potholes* by Shirley Hord and Gene Hall (2001) and Deborah S. Roody, Educational Consultant and CBAM Trainer in **Resources**, pages 245–246 and "Evaluation of Staff Development: How Do You Know It Took?" in **Data Tools**, DT 4-11.)

**FIGURE 4.7**

| Levels of Use of the Innovation: Typical Behaviors | |
|---|---|
| **Levels of Use** | **Behavioral Indices of Level** |
| VI    Renewal | The user is seeking more effective alternatives to the established use of the innovation. |
| V    Integration | The user is making deliberate efforts to coordinate others in using the innovation. |
| IVB    Refinement | The user is making changes to increase outcomes. |
| IVA    Routine | The user is making few or no changes and has an established pattern of use. |
| III    Mechanical use | The user is using the innovation in a poorly coordinated manner and is making user-oriented changes. |
| II    Preparation | The user is preparing to use the innovation. |
| I    Orientation | The user is seeking out information about the innovation. |
| 0    Nonuse | No action is being taken with respect to the innovation. |

CBAM Project, Research and Development Center for Teacher Education, The University of Texas at Austin

## Stages of Concern

Research on change tells us that it is important to pay attention to how teachers feel as they implement a new program or practice. Another tool developed by the CBAM Project, Stages of Concern, enables change facilitators to better understand and measure teachers' concerns ("perceptions, feelings, motivations, frustrations and satisfactions") about an innovation (Hall and Loucks 1978, 38). CBAM researchers learned that individuals go through predictable stages in their perceptions and feelings about change, starting with concerns about self, progressing to concerns about the task itself, and eventually moving on to concerns about impact (see Figure 4.8). They developed three tools for assessing concerns: a 35-item Stages of Concern questionnaire, an Open-Ended Statement of Concerns, and an informal interview (see **Data Tools**, DT 4-11 and DT 4-17). By assessing concerns, reform teams can target interventions to help teachers resolve their most pressing concerns. Training in the use of these instruments is recommended.

**FIGURE 4.8**

| Stages of Concern: Typical Expressions of Concern about the Innovation | |
|---|---|
| **Stages of Concern** | **Expressions of Concern** |
| 6  Refocusing | I have some ideas about something that would work even better. |
| 5  Collaboration | I am concerned about relating what I am doing with what other instructors are doing. |
| 4  Consequence | How is my use affecting kids? How can I refine it to have more impact? |
| 3  Management | I seem to be spending all my time in getting material ready. |
| 2  Personal | How will using it affect me? |
| 1  Informational | I would like to know more about it. |
| 0  Awareness | I am not concerned about it (the innovation). |

CBAM Project, Research and Development Center for Teacher Education, The University of Texas at Austin

## Innovation Configurations

The third tool developed by the CBAM Project is the Innovation Configuration, descriptions of key components of a particular practice and their variations (ranging from unacceptable to ideal). Innovation Configurations provide another set of indicators by which teams can monitor implementation of a new curriculum. Through interviews and observations, reform teams can assess how these components are being implemented. This information can then be used to help you determine what aspects of your program are not being implemented well and direct your support to those areas. For example, the Innovation Configuration may reveal that

teachers are doing well at engaging students with materials and structuring group interaction but have not yet implemented alternative assessments that are part of the program. For more on Innovation Configurations, see **Data Tools**, DT 4-6 and **Resources**, page 245. All of the indicators above are summarized in the following box.

---

### Possible Indicators for Tracking Implementation of Mathematics and Science Curriculum Reform

▼ Time spent on mathematics and science instruction

▼ Use of problem-solving and inquiry-based instructional strategies

▼ Focused, rigorous, coherent, accurate, and developmentally appropriate content taught across grade levels

▼ Quality lessons

▼ Use of high-quality, standards-based instructional materials

▼ Use of multiple classroom assessment strategies

▼ Teachers qualified to teach rigorous mathematics and science

▼ Teachers prepared to teach rigorous mathematics and science

▼ Equal access to each of the above indicators for all students (disaggregating data collected by high- and low-achieving classrooms or minority enrollment)

▼ Stakeholders' support for reform

▼ Levels of Use

▼ Stages of Concern

▼ Innovation Configurations

---

## Collecting Implementation Data

Once your team has identified what indicators you will use to track implementation of curriculum reform, you are ready to choose data collection methods. Below, we describe six ways to collect data and specific instruments to use for each.

## Teacher and Student Surveys

Teacher surveys provide a relatively quick way to collect information about many of the indicators summarized in the box above. Several samples that can be used for this purpose are found in the **Data Tools** of this chapter. One series, from Horizon Research, Inc. and originally designed for

National Science Foundation Local Systemic Change Projects, gathers in-depth information about classroom practice, teachers' opinions, and professional development from teachers, K–12, in both mathematics and science (see DT 4-12 for the 6–12 mathematics questionnaire). Another in-depth series of questionnaires comes from the Science Education Assessment Project of the Council of Chief State School Officers' State Collaborative on Assessment and Student Standards (SCASS). We have included excerpts from their teacher surveys for elementary school mathematics and middle school science (DT 4-7 and DT 4-8); teacher surveys at other grade levels and student surveys are also available. Finally, we include excerpts from the questionnaire used in the TIMSS study of classroom practices in eighth-grade science ("Section C: Opportunity to Learn [Science]" and "Section D: Pedagogical Approach," DT 4-13A and DT 4-13B), which includes questions about which topics are taught and in how much depth, as well as questions about teachers' beliefs and instructional practices. A comparable mathematics survey is also available from TIMSS. Because these surveys are quite long and include information you might not need, consider lifting specific questions out that give you just the data you can use.

We also include a simpler teacher survey, developed by a local school district. The "1998 *Investigations* Survey" (DT 4-14) is a good example of how to monitor the implementation of a particular program, in this case a new mathematics curriculum, and could easily be adapted for a program your school is implementing. For collecting Stages of Concern data, you can use the questionnaire in DT 4-17.

## Classroom Observations

Observations are a rich source of information about classroom practice, providing observers are clear about what they are looking for and know how to use observation protocols. Two sample observation protocols are included in **Data Tools**: the CAMS "Classroom Observation Protocol" for mathematics (DT 4-15) and Horizon Research's three-part observation protocol (DT 4-16). In addition, the same checklists and rubrics you may have used to help define the change can also act as guides for observation (see DT 4-3 through DT 4-6).

Richard Sagor, in his book *How to Conduct Collaborative Action Research* (1992), offers another approach to classroom observation using open-ended checklists. Every 30 seconds, the observer records "snapshots" of what he or she sees going on in the classroom. See the example in Figure 4.9.

**FIGURE 4.9**

Example of Open-Ended Checklist

643 Snapshots of Student Activities

| Activity | No. of snapshots where observed | Percentage of total snapshots |
|---|---|---|
| Seatwork | 142 | 22% |
| Listening to teacher | 112 | 17% |
| Responding to questions from teacher | 91 | 14% |
| Lab work | 88 | 14% |
| Taking tests | 65 | 10% |
| Visiting with each other | 25 | 4% |
| Performing | 18 | 3% |
| Reciting | 14 | 2% |
| Asking the teacher questions | 14 | 2% |
| Watching or listening to audio-visual materials | 13 | 2% |
| Getting out materials | 12 | 2% |
| Group work | 10 | 2% |
| Clean-up | 10 | 2% |
| Observing performance | 8 | 1% |
| Discussion | 8 | 1% |
| Responding to questions in writing | 5 | .8% |
| Responding to management questions | 4 | .6% |
| Observing teacher demonstrations | 2 | .3% |
| Waiting | 2 | .3% |

## Interviews

Iris Weiss, President of Horizon Research, Inc., prefers in-depth interviews with teachers as a data collection method, particularly for getting a fix on teachers' professional development needs. "It is especially interesting to follow the same group of teachers over time to see longitudinal growth," Weiss notes (interview 1998). Horizon's sample teacher interview protocol is in **Data Tools**, DT 4–18. Levels of Use data is also collected through interviews. Interviewing students is another important way to learn about classroom practice. Two sets of questions for students, the "Student Interview Protocol" and "Sample Student Interview Questions," are included in **Data Tools**, DT 4–19 and DT 4–20. To use these interview protocols, training is recommended.

## Classroom Artifacts

Classroom artifacts, such as lesson plans, sample assessments, and examples of student work, offer yet another lens on current practice. Supplementing surveys, classroom observations, and interviews, artifacts provide additional evidence of inquiry and problem-solving approaches, attention to equity and different learning styles, and understanding and use of alternative assessments. One protocol for collecting and analyzing these artifacts, developed by Horizon Research, is included in **Data Tools**, DT 4-21. A fuller discussion of looking at student work is included in "Looking at Student Work: 'A Treasure Trove of Insights' " in Chapter 3.

## Materials Use

Mesa (Arizona) Unified School District boasts one of the most sophisticated science (and social studies) resource centers in the country, complete with a fully computerized materials distribution system. While the main purpose of the system is to deliver fully stocked science kits to the district's elementary teachers, resource center staff take advantage of the data they collect to monitor implementation of their science program. When the kits are returned, teachers fill out usage surveys that include information about materials used, number of student content hours, student achievement of unit goals and outcomes, and difficulties with the material. Center staff collect and analyze the data and generate reports for each building. The data has helped them decide which units to revise and where to target professional development. See the sample of one school's usage summary in Figure 4.10; Mesa's usage survey, "Science and Social Sciences Program Assessment," is included in **Data Tools**, DT 4-9.

> ### RESOURCES FOR MONITORING CURRICULUM IMPLEMENTATION
> (full listings in Resources at end of this chapter)
>
> Horizon Research, Chapel Hill, NC
>
> Deborah S. Roody, Educational Consultant and CBAM Trainer, Bedford, NH
>
> *Facilitating Systemic Change in Science and Mathematics Education: A Toolkit for Professional Developers*, by the Regional Educational Laboratory Network, 1995
>
> *Implementing Change: Patterns, Principles, and Potholes*, by Shirley Hord and Gene Hall, 2001
>
> *Tracking Your School's Success: A Guide to Sensible Evaluation*, by Joan L. Herman and Lynn Winters, 1992

## Self-Assessments

Self-assessments can be a catalyst for reflection and discussion about curriculum, instruction, and assessment practices and a way to get a sense of progress over time. Their effectiveness is enhanced by using other data sources discussed above as evidence for the judgments made. The **Data Tools** contain two self-assessment tools. One, the "Progress Toward Standards—A Self-Assessment" (DT 2-2), is for evaluating the curriculum-instruction-assessment aspect of a systemic reform effort. The other, the "Peer Review and Self-Assessment Checklist" (DT 4-22), helps an individual teacher to examine curriculum materials that he or she is designing and to reflect on them with a colleague.

## Developing a Data Collection Plan

Teams can choose from among the indicators and data collection strategies described above to develop their own data collection plans using the form in **Planning Tools**, page 221–222 and illustrated below.

KEEP YOUR EYES ON THE PRIZE: STUDENT LEARNING

Data Collection Plan

## Implementing Standards-Based Curriculum and Instruction

| Problem/ Question | To what extent is standards-based mathematics and science curriculum and instruction being implemented in our school/district? | | | | |
|---|---|---|---|---|---|
| Data Sources/Tools We Want to Use | Got It | Need It | Disaggregated by | How/When Collected | Person Responsible |
| | | | | | |

FIGURE 4.10

## Unit Usage Summary

Date: 5/22/97

This report includes all SSRC materials used as of the end of the second grading period. This reflects two quarters of this year's curriculum completed by your teachers.

### Grade 5

**507 Mystery Powders**
Usage: **Used**
Student Contact Hours: **15**   Comment:

**Evaluation Not Req'd**
Class Success Rate: **91–95%**

Delivered: **8/12/96**
Due: **9/20/96**
Returned: **4/22/96**

### Grade 5

**507 Mystery Powders**
Usage: **Used**
Student Contact Hours:   Comment

**Evaluation Not Req'd**
Class Success Rate: **91–95%**

Delivered: **8/12/96**
Due: **9/20/96**
Returned: **9/22/96**

**503 \*\*Flight & Space Exploration\*\***
Usage: **Used**
Student Contact Hours:   Comment

**Evaluation Required**
Class Success Rate:

Delivered: **9/17/96**
Due: **10/18/96**
Returned: **10/13/96**

### Grade 5

**507 Mystery Powders**
Usage: **Used**
Student Contact Hours:   Comment

**Evaluation Not Req'd**
Class Success Rate: **91–95%**

Delivered: **8/12/96**
Due: **9/20/96**
Returned: **9/30/96**

### Grade 5

**510 HAP: Sight & Sound**
Usage: **Used**
Student Contact Hours:   Comment

**Evaluation Not Req'd**
Class Success Rate: **91–95%**

Delivered: **8/12/96**
Due: **9/20/96**
Returned: **9/22/96**

# Part Three: Implementing the New Middle School Science Program

**The science committee** had spent the last six months working on our science curriculum frameworks. But as we prepared to introduce them to our staff, we felt like our work was just beginning. When we sat down to plan the kick-off meetings that we would be conducting at each school, we remembered what we had learned about the Concerns-Based Adoption Model (CBAM) last summer: that people go through a developmental progression of concerns as they approach something new. So we decided that first collecting data about teachers' concerns would help us plan better. Since we didn't have much time before the meeting, we decided to use CBAM's quick Open-Ended Statement of Concerns.

After collecting the concerns data, it was clear that teachers needed a lot of accurate information about the new curriculum frameworks and how they would be implemented. Rumors and half-truths were already spreading. They also needed time to understand what the curriculum changes were and why. And they needed a whole array of supports—from quality professional development to administrative support. Many teachers were nervous about their lack of preparation in science content. They were also concerned about what parents would say about the changes. Most important, they needed to feel a sense of ownership and involvement.

We were glad we had these data since we could now speak to their concerns at the upcoming meetings. We asked the superintendent to begin each of the presentations with a message about her support and the priority and resources that were going to be devoted to science reform over the next several years.

After all of the school meetings were completed, the committee met to discuss them. The feedback was unanimous. Teachers were impressed that we cared enough about what they said to bring their data to the meeting and to ask for their own analysis and recommendations. As a next step, most of the staff said they wanted to participate in school-based study groups to discuss the new curriculum frameworks.

So that's what we did. Each school formed a study group, facilitated by a committee member from that school. The study groups were voluntary, but most teachers opted to participate. Principals were strongly urged to participate and most did. Two meetings were held during release days, several more after school. After just a few meetings, we were excited to see the study groups get into the same kinds of debates and discussions as we did on the science committee. Participants began sharing lesson ideas and materials and discovering, as we had, how much they could learn from each other. As questions came up about the curriculum, we published a question-and-answer bulletin and circulated it to all the study groups.

At the same time we were launching the study groups, the science committee heeded the teachers' advice about outreach to parents and the school board. Each school held a community forum. Our purpose was to help parents, the school board, and community members understand what standards were, why they were beneficial to children, what inquiry-based science was, what changes they might expect, and how they could help. We didn't just talk to parents about inquiry-based science; we actually had them do an activity. We left plenty of time for questions and, in the end, felt as if some of the fear and resistance had begun to subside. Not that there wasn't more work to do, but it was a good start. More parent meetings were planned for the future.

## Selecting Materials

While the study groups were digging into the curriculum frameworks, the science committee set to work selecting materials that aligned with our frameworks—no small task, we soon discovered, and a far cry from the old textbook selection process. Plenty of textbooks were presented as being "aligned with standards." They had the right buzzwords, but if you scratched the surface, you could see they didn't really capture the spirit of our frameworks. Through our local educational collaborative, we found a listing and samples of high-quality, standards-based curriculum materials along with a tool for evaluating materials. Whenever possible, we shared these with the study groups and asked for their input. In the end, we on the middle school leadership team settled on an integrated, inquiry-based science program for grades 7–8; compatible programs were decided upon at the other grade levels.

## Professional Development

Drawing on the interview data from the spring and additional input from the study groups, our leadership team devised a plan for gradually phasing in the new program at the middle schools—one or two modules at a time over the next three years. Good professional development was the centerpiece of the plan. We would launch the program with a three-day summer institute where teachers would focus on one module. They would experience each of the activities in the module, learn more about inquiry-based science in general and the related science content, and deal with issues of classroom and materials management. As follow-up, we planned three workshops during the school year on release half-days. We also would encourage the study groups to continue, although finding time during the school day was going to be a problem. Over the next two years, we would offer similar training and follow-up in the additional three modules of the program.

## Measuring Improvement

Once the implementation plan was developed, we started to think about how we could monitor and measure our progress over time. Data collection was a sensitive issue with the staff. In the past, data had hardly ever been used, and if it was, it was to make teachers and schools look bad. So we decided to involve staff from the outset in shaping a monitoring plan, using the study groups as a forum to discuss the idea. At the study group meetings, representatives from the leadership team emphasized that the purpose of tracking implementation was not to monitor individual teachers, but to have some way to measure the program's success and to facilitate improvement. All data would be shared with participants for their own analysis.

We were pleasantly surprised at the richness of the discussion. Thinking about how to measure change forced everyone to be very concrete. We asked ourselves, "If we are really doing inquiry, what will we see? How can we translate the inquiry standards into specific success indicators that we can track and measure?" We set goals to increase the amount of time students would spend conducting investigations and expressing their ideas and to decrease lecture time. Actually, the discussion about assessing implementation resulted in more clarity about our goals than our initial goal-setting conversations had.

Encouraged by the discussion, teachers agreed to open up their classroom for implementation data collection with a few stipulations. First, they wanted their data to be anonymous. Second, they felt that if their practice was going to be scrutinized, so should school climate and support systems for teachers.

The leadership team looked over several survey instruments we had received at the leadership institute last summer. We settled on two different surveys: one that would give us a quick snapshot of classroom practice and system support from the teachers' point of view and another that would collect similar data from the students' viewpoint. Since the district was doing its own surveys on parents' perceptions of the schools, we didn't concern ourselves directly with that. Our team decided to administer the two surveys at the end of the school year, before the program kick-off at the summer institute, so that we would have some good baseline data. Then we could re-administer them each year for the next few years to see how much practice was changing.

## Collecting, Analyzing, and Reporting on Baseline Data

With a little help from the computer, the leadership team crunched the survey numbers and produced some charts to report the data. We decided to present the data at the summer institute, where both principals and teachers from each school would be present.

We had no idea what a catalyst for discussion the data would be. Here's a snapshot from one of the discussion groups at the institute:

"I never realized we were lecturing that much!" one teacher observed. "And look at this chart. The kids think they spend more time listening than the teachers think," another added. "I don't believe the issue is so much how much we lecture, but when," observed another team member. "Are we lecturing first, or after students have explored enough to understand the ideas we then lecture about?" What followed was a lively discussion about the learning cycle, when and how to engage students in asking questions and making their own observations, and when to provide direct instruction through lecture and other methods.

We were starting to realize that the power of data wasn't in the charts and graphs and numbers themselves. It was in the reflections and discussions they sparked. Teachers were really analyzing their teaching and thinking together about how to improve. By the end of the three days, plans were hatched for study groups to continue at each school. Principals committed to hiring roving subs so teams could meet for two hours monthly. And teachers set individual goals for increasing students' active participation in the science classroom. Spirits were high.

## Keeping Up the Momentum—Monitoring Implementation

Now our challenge was to keep up the momentum and the support. Over the next year, the leadership team kept the communication lines open with the study groups and continued tracking concerns using the Open-Ended Statement of Concerns. As CBAM predicted, management concerns—dealing with time and materials, simply managing the task—were in the forefront. It's a good thing we had scheduled those follow-up sessions with the trainer from the summer institute, who helped us troubleshoot some of the logistics. She also worked with teachers in science content they were not familiar with since they were now teaching integrated units that covered more than one discipline. At two of our middle schools, study groups thrived. But at the third, roving subs never materialized and study groups didn't meet.

The results of the survey administered at the end of the first year of implementation validated our informal observations. Classroom practice was improving, as was systems support, especially at the two schools where study groups were going strong. And concerns were shifting, just as CBAM predicted. As teachers' management concerns resolved and they gained experience and confidence with the program, they started wondering what impact the new curriculum was having on student learning. As one concerns survey respondent put it, "We are not sure whether students are learning the knowledge and skills we committed to in our curriculum frameworks. We've made changes in our curriculum and instruction but are still using mostly traditional assessments. These don't give us a good picture of how students are learning skills such as data collection and analysis, problem solving, or complex reasoning or how well they really understand important concepts. How can we change assessment practices to better measure the concepts, skills, and dispositions that are important to us?"

# Problem Three: Implementing Assessment Reform

## Overview of the Problem

At some point, schools involved in mathematics and science education reform face the challenge of rethinking assessment. Traditional multiple-choice and short-answer tests simply do not adequately measure the kind of learning called for in the standards and that many schools and communities value. And nothing will derail change faster than assessments that do not measure what is valued or taught. According to a recent National Science Foundation-funded publication, *Foundations: The Challenge and Promise of K–8 Science Education Reform*, "pure, multiple choice, factual recall tests offer strong disincentives to adopting an inquiry approach to teaching and can render inquiry-based reform programs impotent. Those planning a reform process must examine existing policies and tests to see how they align with the goals of the effort" (National Science Foundation [1997], 23). If teaching and learning in mathematics and science are going to change, so too must assessment practices.

Concerns for the learning of all students also compel us to rethink assessment practices. Because of bias in design and scoring, traditional assessments have been particularly unfair measures of poor, minority, and female students' learning. And yet these assessments continue to be used to make critical judgments about these students' capabilities and their futures. (See "Racial, Class, Cultural, and Gender Bias in Curriculum, Instruction, and Assessment" in Chapter 5.)

Another impetus for changing assessment practices is the need for better data about student learning to inform school and district decision making and planning (the whole point of this book!). Standardized tests offer much too limited a view of student learning for these purposes. The richer the picture of student learning school staff can paint, the better the decisions they can make about how to help students improve. Assessment has a unique place in data-driven reform: it is both a way to measure change and a measure that needs to be changed. That is, good data about student learning is critical to making good decisions about how and what to change. But assessment practices themselves need to be reformed.

For all of these reasons, a new vision of assessment is gathering steam across the country. That vision calls for measuring not just what is easy, but what is important: students' deep understandings of ideas, their ability to apply what they learn to real-world problems, to reason, solve difficult problems, communicate, and use productive habits of mind. To do so requires not one but many ways of gathering evidence about student learning, including day-to-day observations and documentation of students' work, portfolios, and performance-based tasks. These approaches supplement traditional tests with a variety of ways to gather evidence about student learning, including tasks that resemble real-life situations and are meaningful and engaging to students. (See "Using Performance Assessments to Learn More about Student Learning" in Chapter 3.)

> ### The Assessment Dictionary
>
> **Alternative**—any type of assessment in which students create a response to a question (for example, short-answer questions, essays, performance assessments, oral presentations, demonstrations, exhibitions and portfolios) instead of choosing a response from a given list (for example, multiple-choice, true-false or matching).
>
> **Authentic**—assessment tasks in which students demonstrate their knowledge and skills in ways that resemble "real life" as closely as possible are engaging for students and reflect sound instructional practice.
>
> **Performance**—direct, systematic observation of actual student performances and judging the quality of the performances according to pre-established performance criteria.

Central to this new vision is the understanding that assessment is not something that happens when instruction is over but is an ongoing, integral part of the learning experience. Students extend and stretch their learning through assessment activities and learn how to assess their own work as well. And teachers use the results of assessments to guide next steps in instruction.

Moving from this vision of assessment to reality is one of the major challenges of education reform. As long as high-stakes assessments, such as those used for course or program placement or for college entrance, remain traditional, it is difficult for school districts to fully commit themselves to alternative approaches. Even when they do, they face many other obstacles. High-quality performance assessments are not readily available. Staff frequently lack the knowledge and skill needed to develop, use, or score them. And the public can be skeptical of changes in testing and reporting, especially if they don't understand their purpose or benefit. Lasting assessment reform will require thoughtful implementation at the local level, public engagement, and coordination of local, state, and national policies.

*"assess" is from the root* assidére, *which means "to sit beside."*

Despite these obstacles, many schools and districts are taking on the challenges of assessment reform at the local level. In this section, we will explore how asking hard questions and using data can help.

## What Kinds of Assessments Do You Want?

While there are no cookbook answers about how to implement standards-based assessments, the process of inquiry can help your team design, implement, and monitor assessment reform. Just as with curriculum reform, one of the first questions your team will ask is "What kinds of assessments do we want?" Since your team is most likely not in a position to shape national, state, or possibly even district policy, your focus will be on classroom assessments. How do you want them to change? How will you know good assessment practices when you see them? As with curriculum reform, the challenge is to be specific and clear. Listed below are some questions you might need to ask at this time.

### DEFINING THE CHANGE: QUESTIONS TO CONSIDER

▼ What knowledge do we want to assess? What do we think is important for students to know and be able to do?

▼ What is the purpose of assessment? What kinds of assessments will best help us improve student learning?

▼ Who are the assessments for? What audiences?

▼ What kinds of assessments "measure what we treasure"? meet our purpose? communicate to the appropriate audiences? are fair, reliable, and bias-free?

▼ How cognitively demanding should assessments be?

▼ If we want assessments to be more authentic, what does that really look like? What are the key elements of an authentic performance task? How frequently should performance tasks be used?

▼ How many different kinds of assessments would we like students to be using? For what purposes?

▼ How would we like to see assessment practices evolve over time?

The same tools discussed earlier in this chapter under Problem Two, "Defining the Change: Will We Know It When We See It?" can help your team and staff to clearly define the changes in assessment that you want. In addition, the Center for Science Education and Professional Development, a part of Learning Innovations at WestEd, has created a useful map for assessment planning, "Assessment: The 'Big Picture'" (see Figure 4.11). We also suggest careful study of standards on assessment and a number of excellent resources on the subject (see list on this page). Clarity at this stage will help students, teachers, administrators, and parents know what is expected of them and make the next steps in the process easier.

## Assessing Current Assessment Practices

Once your team has a clear idea of what kinds of changes in assessment practices you want, it is time to start planning for implementation. Just as with curriculum implementation, gathering data about current practices and needs can help you plan, carry out, and monitor changes. Some questions to consider are listed below.

---

**RESOURCES FOR ASSESSMENT REFORM**
(full listing in **Resources** at end of this chapter)

*Educative Assessment: Designing Assessments to Inform and Improve Student Performance,* by Grant P. Wiggins, 1998

*Improving Classroom Assessment: A Toolkit for Professional Developers (Toolkit98),* by the Regional Educational Laboratories, 1998

*A Teacher's Guide to Performance-Based Learning and Assessment,* by K. Michael Hibbard et al., 1996

See also other **Assessment Resources**

**FIGURE 4.11: ASSESSMENT: THE "BIG PICTURE"**

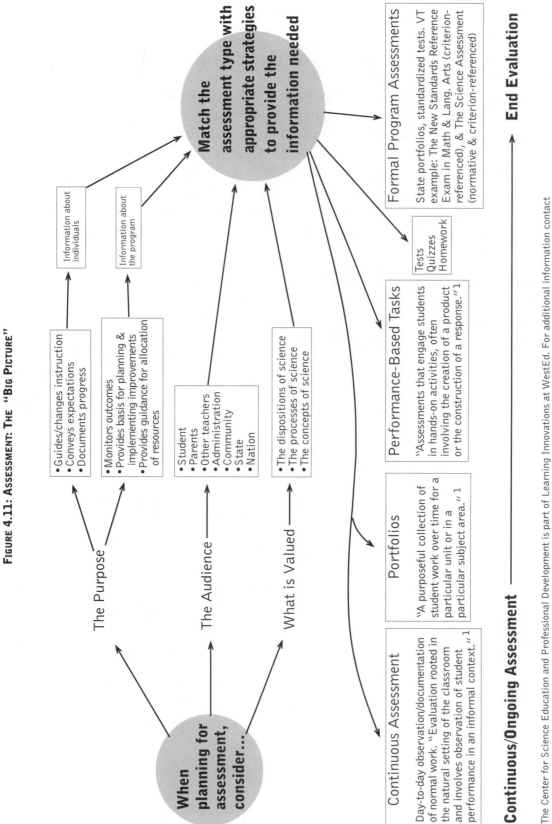

The Center for Science Education and Professional Development is part of Learning Innovations at WestEd. For additional information contact Maura O. Carlson, Director, at 802-951-8201, mcarlso@west.org or 20 Winter Sport Lane, Williston, VT 05495. This material is based on work supported by the National Science Foundation under Grant No. ESI 9550020, November 1996.

[1] ETS, Focus, "Capturing the Power of Assessment," Princeton, NJ

## GATHERING ASSESSMENT IMPLEMENTATION DATA: QUESTIONS TO CONSIDER

▼ What kinds of classroom assessments are currently being used? What kinds of knowledge and skills do they measure? How cognitively demanding are they? How closely linked are learning assessments with standards, curriculum, and instruction? How authentic are they? How varied are the types of assessments being used?

▼ Where are our pockets of success? What factors lead to successful assessment practices? How can we build on successes and learn from them? What are the most important areas where improvement is needed?

▼ To what extent are assessments free from racial, class, cultural, and gender biases? (See "Racial, Class, Cultural, and Gender Bias in Curriculum, Instruction, and Assessment" in Chapter 5.) To what extent are they valid? reliable? of high technical quality?

▼ For what purpose are assessments being used? To what extent are they used to categorize and place students in tracks, label them unconstructively, or retain them?

▼ What is the impact of these practices on racial, class, cultural, or gender groups? How frequently are assessments used to better understand student thinking? to improve curriculum and instruction?

▼ What groups of students are getting access to high-quality, authentic assessment tasks? cognitively demanding tasks? varied assessments? What groups are not?

▼ What relationships seem to exist between student achievement and the use of multiple assessments?

▼ What are key stakeholders' (teachers, administrators, students, parents, school board, community) perceptions/concerns about assessment? assessment reform? How can our implementation plan take these into consideration?

▼ What kind of professional development do teachers need to support them in implementing assessment reform?

▼ What policies and practices in the district, state, or country as a whole support or undermine our local assessment reform efforts? How consistent are report cards with standards-based assessment? What critical supports are most important right now?

## Choosing Indicators

In the box below we suggest some possible indicators to help you answer some of the above questions and monitor the progress of assessment reform. Some are generic indicators that overlap those given in Problem Two, but we have added others that are more specific to assessment.

---

### Possible Indicators for Monitoring Assessment Reform

▼ Number of different types of assessments used, disaggregated by high- and low-achieving classes or minority enrollment

▼ Frequency of use of portfolios, authentic tasks, and other alternative assessments, disaggregated by high- and low-achieving classes or minority enrollment

▼ Cognitive complexity of assessments (using Dimensions of Learning, Bloom's Taxonomy, or other frameworks), disaggregated by high- and low-achieving classes or minority enrollment

▼ Authenticity of the tasks

▼ Fairness and lack of bias in assessment tasks

▼ Stakeholder support for assessment reform

▼ Report cards that reflect student progress in reaching standards

▼ Levels of Use

▼ Stages of Concern

▼ Innovation Configurations

---

Two tools are included in **Data Tools** for analyzing your assessments. One, the "Alternative Assessment Evaluation Form" (DT 4-23), can help you evaluate fairness and rater bias, among other features. A second, "Stimulus Questions Derived from the Reasoning Processes of Dimensions 3 and 4" (DT 4-24), is based on Dimensions of Learning, a model for instruction developed by Robert Marzano, Debra Pickering, and others. Their table contains a list of questions that require students to use complex reasoning rather than just recall information (Dimensions 3 and 4 in their model). By comparing questions asked in your performance assessments to these, you can evaluate how challenging your tasks are. Readers may also want to refer to Grant Wiggins' "Peer Review and Self-Assessment Checklist" in **Data Tools**, DT 4-22 to evaluate authenticity of tasks. Also included in **Data Tools** (DT 4-25) is a sample of a report card that evaluates students' performance on standards, one indicator of movement toward a standards-based assessment system.

## Developing a Data Collection Plan

The form in **Planning Tools**, pages 223–224 and illustrated below, can help your team organize its plan for assessing assessment.

Data Collection Plan

## Implementing Standards-Based Assessment

| Problem/ Question | To what extent is standards-based assessment being implemented in our school/district? | | | | |
|---|---|---|---|---|---|
| Data Sources/Tools We Want to Use | Got It | Need It | Disaggregated by | How/When Collected | Person Responsible |
| | | | | | |

# Part Four: Implementing Performance-Based Assessments

**We on the middle** school leadership team were glad the assessment issue was on the table, but we also realized that changing assessment practices was not going to be easy. There were parents' attitudes to contend with, and teachers would need a whole new set of knowledge and skills. And how were the students going to respond? In some ways, we seemed to be starting the cycle of change all over again—building support for the change, planning, collecting data, and implementing yet another major change. "It seems like we just start to address one problem when another one pops up," one member of the team complained. So goes the business of continuous improvement!

Before jumping into anything, we realized the importance of getting a better handle on current assessment practices—both for the purpose of planning for and monitoring change and to stimulate reflection and discussion. We wondered what kind of assessments were currently being used and how well they reflected the spirit of the standards and our own curriculum. To answer these questions, we summarized the data on assessment from the surveys we had been administering for the last two years and presented it to a combined meeting of the study groups for their analysis.

We started the session by brainstorming about the purposes of and audiences for assessment and the types of assessments that best fit these. Participants then took the list and made it into a pie chart that reflected the relative importance that they thought each assessment approach merited in terms of time, resources, and influence on our judgments about students. Then a team member shared the data on our current assessment practices, using the same pie chart format. It was instantly apparent that our current assessment practices were out of line with our priorities.

That led us to a plan for integrating the use of authentic performance assessments into our classrooms. Again, professional development was the centerpiece—a five-day summer institute where participants would learn about using authentic performance tasks, developing and scoring rubrics, and examining student work. Follow-up sessions and study groups would focus on troubleshooting and sharing throughout the school year. We also organized another forum for parents to learn more about the purposes of performance assessments and what it would mean for their children.

Over the next year, teachers struggled with the many difficulties of using performance assessments well. Sometimes they found their tasks were not really assessing the important learning they wanted to measure. Or important content got lost as students focused exclusively on process and product. Sometimes the tasks took more time than they were worth. Often teachers discovered they weren't clear enough up front about what they wanted from the task and ended up with less than quality work. In addition, there was always the challenge of scoring rubrics fairly and consistently.

Nonetheless, with support from their study groups, administrators, and the leadership team, most teachers stuck with it. As they became more practiced, they saw the potential of these assessments for helping teachers communicate more clearly about desired outcomes, motivating students, and improving learning.

Improving learning . . . That was the whole reason for the changes we initiated three years ago. As the leadership team sat down to reflect on the third annual survey of classroom practice and system support, we could, in fact, document some pretty important changes in practice. Students' active involvement in science inquiry in the classroom was on the rise. So was collegial sharing. From the concerns statements, we noted that impact concerns were also increasing. Teachers' concerns echoed those of the leadership team: What effect were all these changes having on student learning? We couldn't afford to hire expensive program evaluators, and we didn't have time to be full-time program evaluators ourselves. But we did want to know if our new science program was improving student learning. Were all students benefiting in the ways we had hoped for? Were we getting the results we wanted? Was this plan working? It was time to find out.

# Problem Four: Evaluating the Impact of Reform on Student Learning

## Overview of the Problem

Being ready to ask the question "What impact are changes in curriculum, instruction, and assessment having on student learning?" is a good place to be. It indicates both that the team has implemented reforms and that it has its focus in the right place—on improving student learning. Improved student learning is the goal of any and all reform activities and thus the measure of their success. If a particular initiative improves student learning, it is worthy of resources and support. If it doesn't, then either the initiative itself or its implementation needs to be reconsidered. Student learning results provide the ultimate test of any program or practice.

*"When used for most educational settings, evaluation means to measure, compare, and judge the quality of student work, schools, or a specific educational program."*

(CRESST Web site [http://www.cse.ucla. edu/cresst/pages/ glossary.htm])

Nonetheless, evaluating the impact of changes in curriculum, instruction, and assessment on student learning can be complex and intimidating. Most schools can't afford to hire outside evaluators or must minimize such expenditures. Staff are too busy and often don't believe that they have the expertise to be program evaluators. Worse yet, the data on student achievement most districts have available is of limited value for measuring achievement of mathematics and science standards. As one leader of a National Science Foundation-funded Local Systemic Change site put it, "How do you measure change while changing the measures?"

## What Schools Can Do Without Outside Evaluators

School staff can do a lot to evaluate their own programs, especially if they take time up front to set up a database to track student learning results over time, disaggregate data, and relate those results to the variables they decide are important. If their budgets allow it, schools or districts may decide that it is a good investment to hire a consultant to help set up the system and teach the staff so they can eventually evaluate their own programs and practices. (See "Use Technology for Data Management" in Chapter 2.)

That's what the Northwood (New Hampshire) School, a small, rural elementary school, did. Several years ago, in conjunction with a state-funded school-improvement effort, the school-improvement team worked with professional evaluators to set up a relational database, which enables them to track student learning in relation to a number of other variables. "We have many sources of information and can look at all of them. We don't have to paw through piles of data. The power of the information we now have at our fingertips is limitless," says fourth-grade teacher and improvement team member Gale Lucy.

Even without a good relational database, schools can design and conduct their own evaluations; they are just more time-consuming. For example, the Poudre School District in Fort Collins, Colorado, implemented an intensive elementary mathematics professional development program. The program involved teams of teachers from individual schools in a total of 75 hours of training over the course of a school year. Determined to track the program's impact on student learning, the program coordinator manually pored over the district's mathematics level test results (criterion-referenced tests that measure student growth from year to year in mathematics content, knowledge, and process skills). Though tedious, it was worth the effort. He found that students whose teachers participated in the program increased their

*"Give a man [sic] a fish and you feed him for a day; teach a man to fish and you feed him for a lifetime."*

(Chinese proverb)

achievement by more than 10 points over students whose teachers did not participate. With these results, he was able to convince the district to continue its major investment in this program.

## Finding the Time to Be Both Leaders and Evaluators

Most teachers and administrators are doers; they like to take charge and take action. The very idea of taking time to collect and analyze data and reflect on it may seem like a luxury at best, a waste of time at worst. And even if they wanted to take the time, where would they get it?

There is both a philosophical and a practical answer to this question. The philosophical answer is that systemic change demands a redefinition of leadership to embrace both doing and reflecting. Otherwise, schools are doomed to continue doing, doing, doing, with dubious results. Reform leaders need to understand that their role is not just to initiate change, but to focus on results. And that means pausing to reflect, collect data, monitor implementation, and evaluate student learning.

The more practical answer is to reallocate time, involve more people as leaders, and divide labor intelligently. For more information on reallocating time, see "Finding Time," page 55. As for dividing the labor, capitalize on the strengths of the various individuals involved. If your strength as a leader is offering vision and inspiration, great! Or you may be great at thinking of the questions to investigate or drawing conclusions from the data. Find others whose strengths are number crunching and presenting the data. Finally, keep the scale of the evaluations small and rely, when you can, on data you already have.

## Measuring Change While Changing the Measures

Lack of good measures of student learning is a big problem for schools that are implementing challenging, inquiry-based mathematics and science curricula. The ever-popular norm-referenced tests fail to measure the depth of students' understanding of concepts or the more complex process skills emphasized in national standards. Moreover, they are commonly available in mathematics but scarce in science. State tests based on state frameworks may provide more useful data on student achievement but still have their limitations as one-shot tests that rely mostly on short-answer and multiple-choice questions. Some experts argue that many of the state tests, while improved, still emphasize too much factual content. Finally, grades, because of their subjectivity, have not proven a very useful measure of student achievement.

What are results–driven schools and districts to do? Some are devoting their resources to developing their own district criterion-referenced and/or performance assessments. For example, the Glendale (Arizona) Union High School District has devoted 10 years to developing, revising, and refining its own high-quality, criterion-referenced tests and, more recently, performance assessments in all major academic areas (see **Reform in Action**, page 327). The Poudre School District in Fort Collins, Colorado, bought a pre-existing database of mathematics assessment problems from which they developed their own district-based level tests. (For information on where to find performance assessments and tasks, see **Resources for Performance Assessment Tasks**, beginning on page 146.)

Still, many school districts are without such tests. That doesn't mean, though, that they can't devise creative and inexpensive ways of evaluating student learning results. One solution is to have teachers who teach the same course or grade work together to develop or adopt a few high-quality performance tasks that measure students' mastery of important mathematics problem-solving or science inquiry skills. Many curriculum materials now include such assessments. By administering the assessments periodically and collectively analyzing results, both teachers and planners can gain a fuller picture of student learning results over time for the purpose of evaluating and improving programs and practices. (See Fresno example under "Districtwide Performance Assessments" in Chapter 3.)

The multiple forms of assessments discussed in Chapter 3 can offer invaluable information about student learning. When analyzed and discussed collectively, these sources of evidence of student learning can foster deep reflection and change in teaching practices.

## Deciding When to Start

Looking for impact on student learning before a new practice or program is fully implemented can be detrimental. Too often people blame the program rather than poor or incomplete implementation for the lack of results. It is also important to keep in mind the "implementation dip," a phrase coined by Michael Fullan (2001, 92) to describe the common experience of things getting worse before getting better when implementing a new program. On the other hand, when planning for implementation, it is not too soon to start thinking about how impact on student learning will be measured and to gather baseline data if possible. When you have evidence that the new curriculum is being taught or new assessments are being used, then you can begin to look at impact on student learning.

## Avoiding the Wrong Conclusions

Student learning results can easily be misinterpreted. That's why the more sources of data you can use to validate conclusions, the better (see "Triangulate, Triangulate, Triangulate" in Chapter 2). Basing important programmatic decisions on one set of test results can be a big mistake. Joan Herman and Lynn Winters (1992, 23) offer the example of a school in the first year of implementing a whole language program, which emphasizes literature and word meaning. The school experienced a drop in standardized test scores in those classrooms where teachers were using whole language techniques. These teachers were providing no drill in test taking while other teachers were. A simplistic look at this data alone could have led to the decision to eliminate whole language teaching and increase drill in testlike activities. But because school staff believed there were other benefits to whole language, they also conducted parent surveys. These revealed that students in the classes using more whole language were voluntarily reading more at home and improving their attitudes toward reading. With the additional data, they were able to draw better conclusions about how to improve their program. Traditional teachers, they decided, might benefit from using more whole language techniques, while the whole language teachers could provide at least some practice in test taking.

> **RESOURCES FOR EVALUATING THE IMPACT OF CURRICULUM, INSTRUCTION, AND ASSESSMENT REFORM ON STUDENT LEARNING**
> (full listings in Chapter 2 Resources)
>
> EASE-e™, TetraData Corp., Greenville, SC
>
> Quality School Portfolio, CRESST, Los Angeles, CA
>
> Socrates (a school-based information system), CRM, Inc., South Hampton, NH
>
> *Data Analysis for Comprehensive Schoolwide Improvement*, by Victoria Bernhardt, 1998
>
> *Tracking Your School's Success: A Guide to Sensible Evaluation*, by Joan L. Herman and Lynn Winters, 1992

In this case, and in general, it is important to look at standardized test results in the context of other data on student learning; student demographics; student, parent, and teacher attitudes and perceptions; opportunities to learn; and other practices. Also, make sure data is accurate, valid, and reliable. And, whenever possible, look at trends over time rather than one year's results, and disaggregate by looking at how specific subgroups of students perform. Aggregate data can be misleading, masking low performance, low enrollment, or other trends among poor, minority, or female students. These precautions can help prevent misusing data and jumping to the wrong conclusions. (See "Consider Validity, Reliability, and Feasibility," "Triangulate, Triangulate, Triangulate," and "Disaggregate, Disaggregate, Disaggregate" in Chapter 2.)

## Determining Cause and Effect

How do you know if the results you see are attributable to changes you implemented or something else? You don't, unless you can design a highly controlled study, which is often difficult in a school situation. What you can establish are compelling, but not necessarily cause-and-effect, relationships. Take, for example, the relationship between professional development and improved student learning. Thomas Guskey and Dennis Sparks have explored this relationship in depth for years. While they cannot establish a direct link, they can show a number of factors that affect the relationship, the "most immediate and significant being changes in teacher knowledge and practice. Clearly, if staff development does not alter teachers' professional knowledge of their classroom practices, little improvement in student learning can be expected" (1996, 36). A similar link can be made between changes in curriculum, instruction, and assessment: no significant change in student learning is likely without changes in classroom practice.

Isolating a single variable that caused a particular result is difficult even in the most rigorous, academic studies. Moreover, student learning is complex, influenced by many different and interrelated factors. As you go about the work of systemic reform, you undoubtedly are making more than one change simultaneously, such as improving school climate, providing high-quality professional development, and introducing new teaching methods and materials in the classroom. What matters is not which particular change is having an impact on student achievement but whether, as many changes are taking place, student learning is increasing. If it is, that fact can provide enough evidence that you are on the right track. If it isn't, then understanding the many factors at play can help you interpret results and take appropriate action. Remember that your purpose for tracking results is not to publish academic studies or validate a particular program, but to inform decision making in your own school.

For example, Pomperaug Regional School District 15 in Middlebury and Southbury, Connecticut, was looking for evidence of the impact of their performance-based learning and assessment program on student achievement. They constructed a timeline of events important to the implementation of their program, a 10-year journey (see Figure 4.12). They also looked at a variety of measures of student performance over the same time period, including SAT scores, Advanced Placement scores, the Connecticut Mastery Test (CMT), and the Connecticut Academic Performance Test (CAPT), supplemented by surveys of graduating seniors and local citizens. Over the same period of time that the district was implementing performance-based learning, the data showed that student learning was strong and improving, even when Pomperaug was compared with other similar districts on the CAPT (see Figure 4.13). Taken together, these data made a strong case that changes in assessment practices were positively influencing student learning. (See **Reform in Action**, page 346.)

**FIGURE 4.12**

| Creating and Implementing Performance-Based Learning and Assessment in Region 15 |
| --- |

| 1987 | 1988 | 1989 | 1990 | 1991 | 1992 | 1993 | 1994 | 1995 | 1996 |
| --- | --- | --- | --- | --- | --- | --- | --- | --- | --- |

National Standardized Test, Grades 3, 5, and 7

SAT

AP Tests

CMT, Grades 4, 6, and 8

CAPT, Grade 10

Process Writing

Cooperative Learning, Including Issue Controversies in Social Studies

Integrated Language Arts

Performance-Based Learning Strategies Across the Disciplines and Grade Levels

Writing Portfolio for All Students

Social Studies, Themes, and Essential Questions

Math, Content and Problem Solving

Science, Content and Process

Computer Technology to Support Learning

**Note:** Dotted lines indicate small-scale pilot projects.

**FIGURE 4.13**

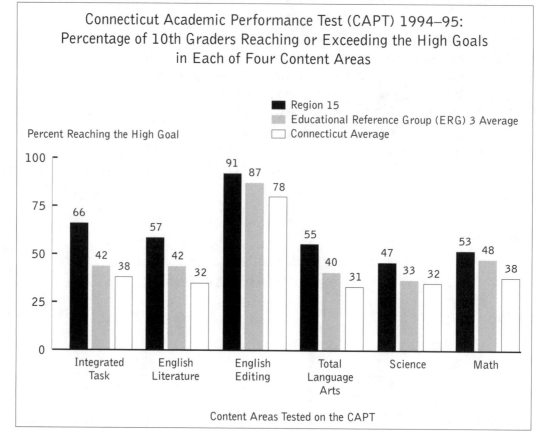

Connecticut Academic Performance Test (CAPT) 1994–95:
Percentage of 10th Graders Reaching or Exceeding the High Goals
in Each of Four Content Areas

## Getting Started

The learner-centered systemic action planning process outlined in Chapter 3 suggests a straightforward way to get started. The key is setting SMART goals—specific, measurable, attainable, related to student learning, and time-bound—from the outset. For example, a SMART goal might be to have all students reach a proficiency level in mathematics problem solving within the next five years. Next, you formulate what actions you will take to achieve the goal, such as implementing a new elementary mathematics curriculum that emphasizes problem solving and includes performance assessments for each unit. Along with SMART goals and action plans, the team settles on a set of indicators by which to measure progress toward these goals. In this case, for instance, you decide on three indicators: results of performance assessments from the new curriculum that all teachers agree to implement twice a year; problem-solving results on state assessments for fourth graders; and the quality of problem solving reflected in examples of student work collected quarterly. As you implement the new mathematics curriculum, you study the indicators to see if you are getting the results you want. No fancy evaluation studies, no expensive evaluators—just school reformers who are "keeping their eyes on the prize."

As your team digs deeper into evaluating the effect of changes in curriculum, instruction, and assessment on student learning, consider the questions below.

### EVALUATING THE IMPACT OF REFORM ON STUDENT LEARNING: QUESTIONS TO CONSIDER

▼ How broadly and deeply has reform been implemented? (See Problems Two and Three.)

▼ What specific results do we hope to achieve for students by implementing a particular curriculum, instruction, or assessment reform?

▼ How can we best measure these results?

▼ What data do we already have?

▼ What additional data do we need?

▼ What variables will we need to track?

▼ How should we disaggregate the data?

▼ What other data sources can we use to triangulate and validate our findings?

## Developing a Data Collection Plan

Your plan for monitoring the impact of curriculum, instruction, and assessment reform on student learning should be based on the SMART goals you set and the indicators you chose for those goals. The form in **Planning Tools**, pages 225–226 and illustrated below, is provided to help you develop this plan.

## Plan for Monitoring the Impact of Reform Activities on Student Learning

| Problem/ Question | What is the impact of curriculum, instruction, and assessment reform on student learning outcomes, opportunities, and aspirations? | | | | | |
|---|---|---|---|---|---|---|
| **SMART Student Learning Goals** | **Indicators** (disaggregated by race, ethnicity, free/reduced lunch, gender, etc.) | **Data Collection** | | | **How Will Data Be Analyzed?** | **How Will Data Be Reported/ Disseminated?** |
| | | **How?** | **When?** | **By Whom?** | | |
| | | | | | | |
| | | | | | | |
| | | | | | | |

# Part Five: Taking a Closer Look at Student Learning

**Good data on** student learning in science were nonexistent in our district. State tests weren't going to be administered until next year, and since every teacher graded differently, grades weren't going to tell us much. While individual teachers had begun experimenting with performance assessments, they were using them primarily to glean information about individual students, not to evaluate the curriculum.

The truth was that three years after initiating curriculum reform, we still had no systematic way of evaluating its impact on student learning. Now that we realized how essential this was, however, there was no getting around it—we were going to have to create our own assessments. And given teachers' negative experiences with other kinds of assessments, we knew it was important to approach this carefully.

We thought about what had worked so far: getting teachers involved in choosing how data would be collected; sharing data with all participants for their own reflection; using data for improvement, not punishment; staying focused on our purpose—scientific literacy for all of our students; and taking it slowly. We also remembered two important lessons we had learned in our leadership institute three years ago: triangulating—using more than one source of data—and disaggregating—looking at how subgroups of students performed. Considering these lessons, the leadership team created a plan for involving teachers in developing or adapting a small number of performance assessments—three or four—providing opportunities in the study groups for teachers to reflect together on these assessment results as well as on examples of student work. We would not go public with individual teacher results; rather, we would use the data solely for the purpose of analyzing the strengths and weaknesses of our new middle school science curriculum.

Our third annual summer institute focused on these goals. We brought the developer of the science modules in to present the new performance assessments she had developed for each of the modules. The teachers actually did the tasks themselves and, with minor changes, agreed to try one assessment for each of four modules. While the tasks dealt with different content, the skills of organizing and displaying data, making predictions, and drawing conclusions cut across all of them. This would enable us to measure improvement over the school year.

Then the teachers practiced scoring the rubrics, comparing their scores, and striving toward increasing reliability. As they examined different samples of students' work, they gained insights not only into scoring but into students' thinking and their own instruction. "This has been one of the best staff development experiences we've ever had," several teachers commented enthusiastically. More and more, they could see the potential of assessment to improve their own teaching. But they also saw how difficult and time-consuming good scoring was and were relieved that for the district and school profiles, they would only have to score a random sample.

The good professional development experience in the summer prepared us pretty well for administering and scoring the performance assessments. Knowing that assessments were coming, teachers pushed even harder on inquiry skills. Needless to say, everyone was eagerly anticipating the first-quarter results.

At first glance, the data didn't shock us, even though our students were scoring at the "below proficiency" level. But when we disaggregated the data, a discrepancy jumped out at us: overall, our middle school girls clearly were not doing as well as the boys. How could this be? Was there gender bias in our curriculum, instruction, or assessment that was depressing girls' performance? How could we find out and what could we do about it?

"This can't be right." "Something must be wrong with these assessments." "Are you sure you got the numbers right?" "A lot of good all these changes in the science curriculum are doing us!" After a flurry of defensive reactions and just plain shock, most members of the study groups settled into the kind of upset that leads to constructive action and inquiry.

They started by looking at some of the research on gender bias in the classroom, including the American Association of University Women's studies *How Schools Shortchange Girls* and *Girls in the Middle: Working to Succeed in School*. As they thought about how the research might apply in our situation, two issues struck them as particularly important. The new curriculum had very little about women in science today and throughout history. And, while most teachers were trying out cooperative learning and other more active instructional strategies, they weren't paying much attention to the dynamics between boys and girls in the classroom. They decided that both of these issues warranted further attention.

With this input, the leadership team worked out a three-pronged plan:

▼ review all curriculum and assessment materials for gender and other forms of bias;

▼ collect data on classroom interactions between boys and girls through videotapes and classroom observations of science experiments;

▼ encourage study groups to learn more about teacher-student interactions and their effect on girls.

"We've come a long way since that first institute," one leadership team member reflected. "But it seems like it is only now that we are getting to the real issues—who is learning and who isn't and why. I guess they were right when they said that change takes time. We may not be where we want to be, but at least we are learning how to get better."

# Conclusion

If student learning in mathematics and science is going to improve, what we teach, how we teach it, and how learning is assessed have got to change. This chapter has examined problems schools often encounter as they set out to make these changes: how to align curriculum with standards; how to broaden and deepen curriculum reform; how to implement alternative assessments; and how to evaluate the impact of reform on student learning. For each problem, we raise important questions for inquiry and suggest indicators and data sources to help teams answer these questions. Data about the implementation of reform as well as its impact can help reform teams make better decisions, keep reform on track, and deliver on student learning gains.

# Chapter 4 Planning Tools: From Inquiry to Action

## Team Planning Questions

The following are questions for your team to consider as you plan, based on the process outlined in the chapter. You will also find cross-references to relevant text, Data Tools, and Resources.

1. Where are we in the process of reforming curriculum, instruction, and assessment? What are our strengths? (evidence) What areas need improvement? (evidence) What additional information do we need? What are the implications for action? (See "Progress Toward Standards—A Self-Assessment: Curriculum, Instruction, and Assessment," page 217.)

2. Do we have written curriculum plans for mathematics and science that are aligned with standards and frameworks? If not, what plans are in place or can we make for developing them? (See "Wagons Heading West in Hallowell, Maine," page 343.)

3. How strong is our written curriculum plan? Does it have the elements of a good plan? Is it aligned with standards and frameworks? Is it coherent and focused? (See "Data Collection Plan: Assessing the Written Curriculum," page 219.)

4. What is our vision of what standards-based classrooms look like? How will we know it when we see it? (See "Things I Expect to See the Students Doing in Mathematics Classroom," Data Tools, DT 4-3; "What Are Students Doing [in Math Class]?" Data Tools, DT 4-4; "Inquiry Indicators," Data Tools, DT 4-5; and "Innovation Configuration Continuum: NCTM Evaluation Standard—Instruction," Data Tools, DT 4-6.)

5. Have we selected curriculum materials aligned with our vision and curriculum plan? If not, what criteria will we use? What materials will we review? (See list of mathematics and science curriculum materials on the accompanying CD-ROM.)

6. To what extent is standards-based curriculum, instruction, and assessment being implemented in classrooms? (See "Data Collection Plan: Implementing Standards-Based Curriculum and Instruction," page 221, and "Data Collection Plan: Implementing Standards-Based Assessment," page 223.)

7. What are our goals and plans for extending the implementation of curriculum/instruction/assessment reform? (See "Systemic Mathematics and Science Action Plan: Curriculum/Instruction/Assessment," page 227.) How will they address overcoming racial, class, cultural, and gender bias in curriculum, instruction, and assessment practices? (See "Data Collection Plan: Assessing Racial, Class, Cultural, and Gender Bias in Curriculum, Instruction, and Assessment," page 307.)

8. What knowledge and skills do teachers need to implement reform? What kind of professional development will best support teachers? (See "Systemic Mathematics and Science Action Plan—Professional Development," page 136.)

9. How can we track the implementation of standards-based reform in the classroom? What indicators can we use? (See "Data Collection Plan: Implementing Standards-Based Curriculum and Instruction," page 221 and "Data Collection Plan: Implementing Standards-Based Assessment," page 223.)

10. How can we track the impact of curriculum, instruction, and assessment reform in student learning? (See "Plan for Monitoring the Impact of Reform Activities on Student Learning," page 225.)

11. What support and resources do we need to carry out our plan? (See Chapter 4 Resources.)

# Assessing the Written Curriculum

| Problem/Question | How good is our written curriculum? | | | | |
|---|---|---|---|---|---|
| **Data Sources/Tools We Want to Use** | **Got It** | **Need It** | **Disaggregated by** | **How/When Collected** | **Person Responsible** |
| | | | | | |
| | | | | | |
| | | | | | |
| | | | | | |
| | | | | | |

Planning Tools 4

| Possible Indicators | Possible Data Sources/Tools |
|---|---|
| ❏ Contains basic elements of a good written curriculum | ❏ Curriculum documents <br><br> ❏ Basic Elements of a Good Written Curriculum (p. 164) |
| ❏ Aligns with standards | ❏ Checklists for standards alignment (DT 4-2) <br><br> ❏ Curriculum maps (DT 4-1) |
| ❏ Is focused, rigorous, and coherent | ❏ Curriculum documents <br><br> ❏ CCSSO surveys (Content sections) (DT 4-7, DT 4-8) <br><br> ❏ Section C: Opportunity to Learn (Science) (DT 4-13A) <br><br> ❏ NCREL curriculum mapping Web site (p. 233) |
| ❏ Enables students to achieve standards K–12 | ❏ Curriculum documents |

4 Planning Tools

# Implementing Standards-Based Curriculum and Instruction

| Problem/ Question | To what extent is standards-based mathematics and science curriculum and instruction being implemented in our school/district? | | | | |
|---|---|---|---|---|---|
| **Data Sources/Tools We Want to Use** | **Got It** | **Need It** | **Disaggregated by** | **How/When Collected** | **Person Responsible** |
| | | | | | |
| | | | | | |
| | | | | | |
| | | | | | |
| | | | | | |

| Possible Indicators | Possible Data Sources/Tools |
|---|---|
| ❏ Time spent on mathematics and science instruction | ❏ DT 4-7 ❏ DT 4-, ❏ DT 4-18 |
| ❏ Use of problem-solving and inquiry-based instructional strategies | ❏ Figure 4.1 ❏ DT 4-3–DT 4-8 ❏ DT 4-12 ❏ DT 4-13B ❏ DT 4-15 ❏ DT 4-16 ❏ DT 4-18–DT 4-21 |
| ❏ Focused, rigorous, coherent, accurate, and developmentally appropriate content taught across grade levels | ❏ NCREL Curriculum Mapping Web Site (p. 233) ❏ DT 4-6–DT 4-8 ❏ DT 4-13A ❏ DT 4-15 ❏ DT 4-16 ❏ DT 4-18 |
| ❏ Quality lessons | ❏ DT 4-3–DT 4-8 ❏ DT 4-12 ❏ DT 4-13B, ❏ DT 4-15 ❏ DT 4-16 ❏ DT 4-18–DT 4-21 |
| ❏ Use of high-quality, standards-based instructional materials | ❏ DT 4-9 ❏ DT 4-10 ❏ DT 4-14 ❏ DT 4-15 ❏ DT 4-16 ❏ DT 4-21 |
| ❏ Use of multiple classroom assessment strategies | ❏ DT 4-7 ❏ DT 4-8 ❏ DT 4-12 ❏ DT 4-15 ❏ DT 4-16 ❏ DT 4-18 ❏ DT 4-21 ❏ DT 4-25 |
| ❏ Teachers qualified to teach rigorous mathematics and science | ❏ DT 3-21 |
| ❏ Teachers prepared to teach rigorous mathematics and science | ❏ DT 4-12 ❏ DT 4-13B |
| ❏ Equal access to each of the above indicators for all students (disaggregating data collected by high- and low-achieving classrooms or minority enrollment) | |
| ❏ Stakeholders' support for reform | ❏ DT 4-7 ❏ DT 4-8 ❏ DT 4-12 ❏ DT 4-13B ❏ DT 4-18 |
| ❏ Levels of Use | ❏ DT 4-11 |
| ❏ Stages of Concern | ❏ DT 4-11 ❏ DT 4-17 |
| ❏ Innovation Configurations | ❏ DT 4-6 ❏ *Implementing Change*, by Shirley Hord and Gene Hall (p. 245) |

Planning Tools 4

# Implementing Standards-Based Assessment

| Problem/ Question | To what extent is standards-based assessment being implemented in our school/district? | | | | |
|---|---|---|---|---|---|
| **Data Sources/Tools We Want to Use** | **Got It** | **Need It** | **Disaggregated by** | **How/When Collected** | **Person Responsible** |
| | | | | | |
| | | | | | |
| | | | | | |
| | | | | | |
| | | | | | |

**Planning Tools 4**

223

| Possible Indicators | Possible Data Sources/Tools |
|---|---|
| ❏ Number of different types of assessments used, disaggregated by high- and low-achieving classes or minority enrollment | ❏ DT 4-7  ❏ DT 4-8  ❏ DT 4-12  ❏ DT 4-18 |
| ❏ Frequency of use of portfolios, authentic tasks, and other authentic assessments, disaggregated by high- and low-achieving classes or minority enrollment | ❏ DT 4-7  ❏ DT 4-8  ❏ DT 4-12  ❏ DT 4-18 |
| ❏ Cognitive complexity of assessments, disaggregated by high- and low-achieving classes or minority enrollment | ❏ DT 4-24 |
| ❏ Authenticity of the tasks | ❏ DT 4-22 |
| ❏ Fairness and lack of bias in assessment tasks | ❏ DT 4-23  ❏ Assessment questions (p. 290) |
| ❏ Stakeholder support for assessment reform | ❏ DT 4-7  ❏ DT 4-8  ❏ DT 4-12  ❏ DT 4-18 |
| ❏ Report cards that reflect student progress in reaching standards | ❏ DT 4-25 |
| ❏ Levels of Use | ❏ DT 4-11 |
| ❏ Stages of Concern | ❏ DT 4-11  ❏ DT 4-17 |
| ❏ Innovation Configurations | ❏ DT 4-6  ❏ *Implementing Change*, by Shirley Hord and Gene Hall (p. 245) |
| ❏ Overall progress toward standards-based curriculum, instruction, and assessment | ❏ Progress Toward Standards—A Self-Assessment: Curriculum, Instruction, and Assessment (p. 217) |

**4** Planning Tools

# Plan for Monitoring the Impact of Reform Activities on Student Learning

| Problem/ Question | *What is the impact of curriculum, instruction, and assessment reform on student learning outcomes, opportunities, and aspirations?* | | | | | | |
|---|---|---|---|---|---|---|---|
| **SMART Student Learning Goals** | **Indicators** (disaggregated by race, ethnicity, free/reduced lunch, gender, etc.) | **Data Collection** | | | **How Will Data Be Analyzed?** | **How Will Data Be Reported/ Disseminated?** |
| | | **How?** | **When?** | **By Whom?** | | |
| | | | | | | |

**⌐ PLAN FOR MONITORING THE IMPACT OF REFORM ACTIVITIES ON STUDENT LEARNING, P. 2**

## Outcomes

❑ Mathematics/science standardized test scores (DT 3-3, DT 3-4, DT 3-7)

❑ Mathematics SAT scores

❑ Grades (DT 3-10)

❑ Mathematics state assessments (DT 3-5)

❑ Science state assessments (DT 3-6)

❑ Grade-level performance assessments in mathematics/science

❑ School performance assessments in mathematics/science

❑ District performance assessments in mathematics/science

❑ Quality of student work (DT 2-5, DT 2-6)

❑ Retention rates (DT 3-11)

❑ Overage students (DT 3-12)

❑ Dropout rates (DT 3-13)

❑ Absenteeism (DT 3-14)

❑ Discipline referrals (DT 3-15)

❑ College-going and graduation rates (DT 3-26, DT 3-27)

**Planning Tools 4**

## Opportunities

❑ Disaggregated course enrollment data (DT 3-17–DT 3-19)

❑ Disaggregated special program placement data (DT 3-20)

❑ Tracking practices (DT 5-1)

❑ Teacher qualifications (DT 3-21)

❑ Access to rigorous, hands-on instruction and alternative assessment, disaggregated (DT 4-3–DT 4-10, DT 4-12, DT 4-13, DT 4-15, DT 4-16, DT 4-19–DT 4-21)

❑ Access to technology, disaggregated (DT 3-22–DT 3-25)

❑ College-going and graduation rates disaggregated (DT 3-26, DT 3-27)

## Aspirations

❑ Student aspirations data (DT 3-28)

# Systemic Mathematics and Science Action Plan–Curriculum/Instruction/Assessment

**SMART Student Learning Goals**

| Curriculum/Instruction/Assessment Goals | Steps to Reach Goal | Person Responsible | Documentation for Action Taken | Timeline |
|---|---|---|---|---|
| | | | | |
| | | | | |
| | | | | |
| | | | | |

**Planning Tools 4**

# Resources for Curriculum, Instruction, and Assessment

## Curriculum and Instruction Resources

Author's note: The following listing contains books, videos, Web sites, and organizations related to curriculum, instruction, and assessment reform. It does not include mathematics and science curriculum materials and programs. For a listing of these materials, see the accompanying CD-ROM.

### Books

***Atlas of Science Literacy***, by the American Association for the Advancement of Science (Project 2061) and the National Science Teachers Association (Washington, DC: AAAS and Arlington, VA: NSTA), 2000

Project 2061's *Atlas of Science Literacy* is a collection of nearly 50 strand maps that show how students' understanding of the ideas and skills that lead to literacy in science, mathematics, and technology might grow over time. The book also discusses the intent and meaning of the maps, describes some uses for maps, and considers some of the implications of mapping for teaching and learning.

**Contact**: AAAS Project 2061, 1333 H Street N.W., P.O. Box 34446, Washington, DC 20005; (202) 326-6666; fax: (202) 842-5196; e-mail: project2061@aaas.org; Web site: http://www.project2061.org/

***Choosing a Standards-Based Mathematics Curriculum,*** by Lynn T. Goldsmith, June Mark, and Ilene Kantrov (Portsmouth, NH: Heinemann), 2000

This guide offers a comprehensive view of the issues involved in the selection and implementation of a standards-based mathematics curriculum. Beginning with an explanation of what a standards-based curriculum is, the book presents principles for adoption of standards-based curricula, outlines of a curriculum selection process, and details the critical issues of curriculum implementation.

**Contact**: Heinemann, 88 Post Road West, P.O. Box 5007, Westport, CT 06881; (800) 793-2154; Web site: htpp://www.heinemann.com/

*Designing Mathematics or Science Curriculum Programs: A Guide for Using Mathematics and Science Education Standards,* by the Committee on Science Education K–12 and the Mathematical Sciences Education Board, National Research Council (Washington, DC: National Academy Press), 1999

This guidebook has been developed to help state- and district-level education leaders create coherent, multi-year curriculum programs that provide students with opportunities to learn both mathematics and science in a connected and cumulative way throughout their schooling.

**Contact**: National Academy Press, 2101 Constitution Avenue N.W., Lockbox 285, Washington, DC 20055; (888) 624-8373; fax: (202) 334-2451; Web site: http://www.nap.edu/

*Designs for Science Literacy*, by American Association for the Advancement of Science (Project 2061) (Oxford, England: Oxford University Press), 2000

Project 2061 has developed *Designs for Science Literacy*, a new print and CD-ROM tool. Designs deals explicitly with strategies and techniques for aligning the entire K–12 curriculum to specific learning goals, such as Project 2061's benchmarks, national standards in science and mathematics, or state and local frameworks. In doing so, it addresses many of the considerations and constraints that attend curriculum design.

**Contact**: AAAS Project 2061, 1333 H Street N.W., P.O. Box 34446, Washington, DC 20005; (202) 326-6666; fax: (202) 842-5196; e-mail: project2061@aaas.org; Web site: http://www.project2061.org/

*Exemplary and Promising Mathematics Programs* (Washington, DC: Office of Educational Research and Improvement, U.S. Department of Education), 1999

In 1997, the U.S. Department of Education's Office of Educational Research and Improvement convened an Expert Panel on Mathematics and Science Education to develop a selection process and to identify exemplary and promising programs. This publication describes the criteria and the programs that were selected.

**Contacts**: Mathematics and Science Expert Panel, Office of Educational Research and Improvement, U.S. Department of Education, 400 Maryland Avenue S.W., Washington, DC 20202-0498; (877) 433-7827

Eisenhower National Clearinghouse, 1929 Kenny Road, Columbus, OH 43210; (800) 621-5785; fax: (614) 292-2066; e-mail: info@enc.org; Web site: http://www.enc.org/professional/federalresources/exemplary/promising/documents/

*Foundations: Inquiry Thoughts, Views, and Strategies for the K–5 Classroom*, by the National Science Foundation (Arlington, VA: National Science Foundation), 2000

*Foundations* examines opportunities and challenges for those directly involved in science education at the elementary and middle school levels. Designed as a resource for teachers and adminstrators interested in inquiry-based science education, this book is a short introduction to the complex process of reforming science education based on the experience of educators working in the inquiry field today. It is can be downloaded from the National Science Foundation Web site (report no. nsf 99148).

**Contact**: National Science Foundation, 4201 Wilson Boulevard, Arlington, VA 22230; (703) 292-5111; Web site: http://www.nsf.gov/pubsys/#reports/

***Guiding Curriculum Decisions for Middle-Grades Mathematics***, by Lynn Goldsmith and Ilene Kantrov (Newton, MA: Education Development Center, Inc.), 2000

***Guiding Curriculum Decisions for Middle-Grades Science***, by Barbara Brauner Berns et al. (Newton, MA: Education Development Center, Inc.), 2000

*Guiding Curriculum Decisions for Middle-Grades Mathematics* and *Guiding Curriculum Decisions for Middle-Grades Science* are part of a series of curriculum guides for middle-grades language arts, mathematics, science, and social studies. These guides offers a set of principles for making curriculum decisions and illustrates these principles with practitioners' descriptions of their experiences in implementing standards-based curricula. These guides can be downloaded from the Web site below.

**Contact**: Education Development Center, Inc., 55 Chapel Street, Newton, MA 02458-1060; (800) 225-4276 ext. 2541; Web site: http://www.middleweb.com/EDC/EDCmain.html

***How People Learn: Brain, Mind, Experience, and School*** (expanded edition), by the Committee on Developments in the Science of Learning, with additional material from the Committee on Learning Research and Educational Practice, National Research Council (Washington DC: National Academy Press), 2000

This popular trade book, originally released in hardcover in 1999, has been newly expanded to show how the theories and insights from the original book can translate into actions and practice, making a real connection between classroom activities and learning behavior. This paperback edition includes far-reaching suggestions for research that could increase the impact that classroom teaching has on actual learning.

**Contact**: National Academy Press, 2101 Constitution Avenue N.W., Lockbox 285, Washington, DC 20055; (888) 624-8373; fax: (202) 334-2451; Web site: http://www.nap.edu/

***Inquiry and the National Science Education Standards: A Guide for Teaching and Learning***, by the National Research Council (Washington, DC: National Academy Press), 2000

This is a practical guide to teaching inquiry and teaching through inquiry, as recommended by the National Science Education Standards. It is an important resource for educators who must help school boards, parents, and teachers understand "why we can't teach the way we used to." The book explores the dimensions of teaching and learning science as inquiry for K–12 students across a range of science topics.

**Contact**: National Academy Press, 2101 Constitution Avenue N.W., Lockbox 285, Washington, DC 20055; (888) 624-8373; fax: (202) 334-2451; Web site: http://www.nap.edu/

***Making Sense of Integrated Science: A Guide for High Schools***, by Biological Sciences Curriculum Study (Colorado Springs, CO: BSCS), 2000

The interconnectedness of natural science disciplines has become increasingly obvious of late. The "high ground" perspective of observing Earth from space allows us to see that the individual "-ologies" are really part of a unified whole: integrated science. This guide, funded by the National Science Foundation, describes how high school teachers can best use this concept to enhance their students' understanding of their natural world, and how schools might go about implementing such a program. The guide can be downloaded from the BSCS Web site.

**Contact**: BSCS, 5415 Mark Dabling Boulevard, Colorado Springs, CO 80918-3842; (719) 531-5550; fax: (719) 531-9104; e-mail: info@bscs.org; Web site: http://www.bscs.org/

***Selecting Instructional Materials: A Guide for K–12 Science***, edited by Maxine Singer and Jan Tuomi (Washington, DC: National Academy Press), 1999

*Selecting Instructional Materials* presents a procedure to help educational decision makers evaluate and choose materials for science classrooms; this procedure is also relevant to selecting mathematics materials. The book outlines the evaluation process for school district facilitators and provides review instruments for each step.

**Contact**: National Academy Press, 2101 Constitution Avenue N.W., Lockbox 285, Washington, DC 20055; (888) 624-8373; fax: (202) 334-2451; Web site: http://www.nap.edu/

## Videos

***Science K–6: Investigating Classrooms***, produced by WGBH Boston

*Science K–6: Investigating Classrooms* is a library of nine videos and supporting print publications designed to illustrate effective inquiry-based science teaching at the elementary school level. Produced with a grant from the National Science Foundation, the videos provide resources for professional development, allowing teachers to examine a range of flexible models for inquiry-based teaching and the promotion of scientific discourse.

**Contact**: WGBH Boston Video/Investigating Classrooms, P.O. Box 2284, South Burlington, VT 05407-2284; (800) 959-8670; Web site: http://main.wgbh.org/wgbh/learn/

*STREAM*, produced by COMAP

*STREAM* is a set of video and supporting materials designed to engage facilitators, parents, administrators, and school boards in discussion and action about secondary mathematics education reform. The six-video set contains an introductory video and five videos that show NSF-funded high school mathematics programs in action, including *Mathematics: Modeling Our World, Contemporary Mathematics in Context, Interactive Mathematics Program, Integrated Mathematics: A Modeling Approach Using Technology,* and *Math Connections: A Secondary Mathematics Core Curriculum.* Also included is a User's Guide with facilitator and participant materials.

**Contact**: COMAP, Inc., 57 Bedford Street, Suite 210, Lexington, MA 02420; (800) 772-6627; fax: (781) 863-1202; e-mail: info@comap.com; Web site: http://www.comap.com/

*Teaching High School Science*, produced by WGBH Boston

This series of six videotapes, plus print materials, provides visual examples of high school teachers using inquiry to promote student learning in science. Featured teachers share goals and strategies for promoting inquiry-based learning.

**Contact**: Annenberg/CPB, 401 9th Street N.W., Washington, DC 20004; (800) 532-7637 (orders); fax: (802) 846-850 (orders); e-mail: info@learner.org; Web site: http://www.learner.org/catalog/science/

*Teaching Math: A Video Library*, produced by WGBH Boston

This video library documents effective teaching and learning in many schools: small, large, rural, suburban, inner-city, with and without technology. The videos cover the NCTM content and evaluation standards in lessons targeted to specific grade levels (K–4, 5–8, and 9–12). Examples of effective teaching and learning help teachers, administrators, and policy makers examine the issues associated with improving mathematics in their schools and to witness the positive results for a broad range of children.

**Contact**: Annenberg/CPB, 401 9th Street N.W., Washington, DC 20004; (800) 532-7637 (orders); fax: (802) 846-850 (orders); e-mail: info@learner.org; Web site: http://www.learner.org/catalog/math/

## Web Site

### NCREL Curriculum Mapping Web Site

**Web site**: http://currmap.ncrel.org/

The North Central Regional Educational Laboratory (NCREL) has developed an online tool for curriculum mapping and analysis based on the TIMSS curriculum survey. Users are prompted to map out their mathematics and science curriculum by indicating what topics are being taught at which grade level across a framework of 44 mathematics and 79 science topics. Four types of analyses are available, including breadth (the number of topics being taught at each grade level), duration (the length of time topics are retained in the curriculum), flow (a combination of number, placement, and duration of topics), and rigor (which includes the interplay of breadth, duration, and flow as well as at what grade particular topics are introduced). Each analysis generates a set of displays that superimpose the particular curriculum being mapped against that of the top-achieving TIMSS nations.

**Contact**: North Central Regional Educational Laboratory (NCREL), 1120 East Diehl Road, Suite 200, Naperville, IL 60563; (800) 356-2735; fax: (630) 649-6700

## Assessment Resources

### Books

*Active Assessment for Active Science: A Guide for Elementary School Teachers*, by George E. Hein and Sabra Price (Portsmouth, NH: Heinemann), 1994

This book focuses on authentic and performance-based assessment for hands-on science education and provides essential guidelines for interpreting and scoring these new assessments. The book combines practical discussion with theoretical information on the rationale for active assessment and enables classroom teachers to develop and score their own assessments. The numerous classroom examples of assessments and student work provide teachers and staff developers with materials for workshops as well as for individual reflection.

**Contact**: Heinemann, P.O. Box 5007, Westport, CT 06881-5007; (800) 793-2154; fax: (800) 847-0938; e-mail: custserv@heinemann.com; Web site: http://www.heinemann.com/

*An Assessment Sampler: A Resource for Elementary School Teachers, Administrators, and Staff Developers*, by Edward Chittenden, Rosalea Courtney, and Carole Stearns (Rahway, NJ: Merck Institute for Science Education), 1999

Compiled to disseminate the design and outcomes of the Assessment Project, a collaboration between school districts and Merck Institute for Science Education, this book provides an overview of the project, analysis of participating teachers' reflections, and examples of assessment tasks they designed as part of their inquiry-based instruction.

**Contact**: Merck Institute for Science Education, P.O. Box 2000, Rahway, NJ 07065; (732) 594-3443

*Assessment Standards for School Mathematics*, by the Assessment Standards Working Groups of the NCTM (Reston, VA: National Council of Teachers of Mathematics), 1995

This book, the third in the NCTM Standards series, was developed as a guide for examining current assessment practices and planning new ones. It is based on extensive research and development in national efforts to reform the teaching and learning of mathematics in grades K–12.

**Contact**: National Council of Teachers of Mathematics, 1906 Association Drive, Reston, VA 20191-9988; (800) 235-7566; fax: (703) 476-2970; e-mail: orders@nctm.org;

Web site: http://www.nctm.org/

*Educative Assessment: Designing Assessments to Inform and Improve Student Performance*, by Grant P. Wiggins (San Francisco: Jossey-Bass), 1998

*Educative Assessment* furnishes the information needed to design performance-based assessments, craft performance tasks that meet rigorous educational standards, score assessments fairly, and structure and judge student portfolios. It also shows how performance assessment can be used to improve curriculum and instruction, grading, reporting, and teacher accountability. The book includes numerous design templates and flowcharts, strategies for design and trouble-shooting, and myriad examples of assessment tasks and scoring rubrics that Wiggins has developed and repeatedly refined using feedback from clients in schools, districts, and state departments of education.

**Contact**: Jossey-Bass, 350 Sansome Street, San Francisco, CA 94104; (800) 956-7739; fax: (800) 605-2665; Web site: http://www.jbp.com/

*Improving Classroom Assessment: A Toolkit for Professional Developers (Toolkit98)*, by Regional Educational Laboratories (Portland, OR: NWREL), 1998

Developed for trainers who lead or coordinate professional development and in-service sessions for teachers, the two-volume *Toolkit98* contains current findings and approaches to blending assessment with instruction in order to improve student learning. First published in 1995, this revised and updated edition addresses all content areas, including mathematics and science, and contains new sample assessments and training activities (complete with overheads, handouts, and presenter's outlines). Volume One contains professional development activities and readings organized into four chapters: "Standards-Based Assessment—Nurturing Learning," "Integrating Assessment with Instruction," "Designing High-Quality Assessments," and "Grading and Reporting—A Closer Look." Volume Two includes a sampler of alternative assessments from nearly 50 projects at all grade levels; samples of student responses to various performance tasks; papers and articles about grading and reporting; sample training agendas that illustrate how various activities in the book could be sequenced; and a glossary of assessment-related terms.

**Contact**: NWREL Document Reproduction Service, 101 S.W. Main Street, Suite 500, Portland, OR 97204; (503) 275-9500; fax: (503) 275-0458; e-mail: products@nwrel.org

*Learning and Assessing Science Process Skills* (3rd ed.), by Richard J. Rezba, Constance Sprague, Ronald L. Fiel, and H. James Funk (Dubuque IA: Kendall/Hunt), 1995

*Learning and Assessing Science Process Skills* is intended to make science in the classroom more interesting for students. The process skills discussed in this book are the vehicles for generating content and a means by which concepts are formed, helping students in science as well as other subjects.

**Contact**: Kendall/Hunt Publishing Co., 4050 Westmark Drive, P.O. Box 1840, Dubuque, IA 52004-1840; (800) 228-0810; fax: (800) 772-9165; Web site: http://www.kendallhunt.com/

*Learning About Assessment, Learning Through Assessment* (Compass Series), by Mark Driscoll and Deborah Bryant (Washington, DC: National Academy Press), 1998

The Compass Series consists of three booklets that explore the implications of standards-based mathematics reform initiatives on curriculum, instruction, and assessment. The text is based on recent staff development literature and the personal experiences of teachers. Its goal is to define professional development that can support teachers in all grades in becoming more effective users of assessment.

**Contact**: National Academy Press, 2101 Constitution Avenue N.W., Lockbox 285, Washington, DC 20055; (888) 624-8373; fax: (202) 334-2451; Web site: http://www.nap.edu/

*Learning from Assessment: Tools for Examining Assessment Through Standards*, by Tania J. Madfes and Ann Muench (San Francisco: WestEd and Reston, VA: National Council of Teachers of Mathematics), 1999

Professional developers and teacher leaders can use this kit to help middle school teachers bridge standards and classroom practice. The kit contains materials for three modules with two-hour sessions in which teachers examine the interrelationships among assessment, standards, and instruction to improve student achievement in grades 5–8 mathematics.

**Contact**: WestEd, Publications, 730 Harrison Street, San Francisco, CA 94107-1242; (415) 565-3044; fax: (415) 565-3012; Web site: http://www.wested.org/

*Measuring What Counts: A Conceptual Guide for Mathematics Assessment*, by the Mathematical Sciences Education Board, National Research Council (Washington, DC: MSEB), 1993

To achieve national goals for education, we must measure the things that really count. *Measuring What Counts* establishes crucial research-based connections between standards and assessment. Arguing for a better balance between educational and measurement concerns in the development and use of mathematics assessment, this book sets forth three principles related to content, learning, and equity that can form the basis for new assessments that support emerging national standards in mathematics education

**Contact**: Mathematical Sciences Education Board, National Research Council, 2101 Constitution Avenue N.W. (HA 450), Washington, DC 20418-0006; (202) 334-3294; fax: (202) 334-1453; e-mail: mseb@nas.edu; Web site: http://www.nas.edu/mseb/

***Science Educator's Guide to Assessment***, by Rodney Doran, Fred Chan, and Pinchas Tamir in collaboration with the National Science Teachers Association (Arlington, VA: NSTA), 1998

*Science Educator's Guide to Assessment* links a rationale for assessment reform with specific alternative assessment methods and then incorporates both into more than 50 ready-to-use, curriculum-based science classroom and laboratory activities for biology, chemistry, earth science, and physics. It is geared directly to the National Science Education Standards and was field-tested over a period of 10 years. Four comprehensive chapters discuss the important aspects of a rationale for assessment; how to develop new assessments; alternative assessment formats; and using the results of performance assessment. The guide also includes an appendix containing the most complete bibliography of assessment-related works and materials to date, a glossary of assessment terminology, and the National Science Education Standards for Assessment.

**Contact**: National Science Teachers Association (NSTA), 1840 Wilson Boulevard, Arlington, VA 22201-3000; (703) 243-7100; fax: (703) 243-7177; Web site: http://store.nsta.org/default2g.asp

***A Teacher's Guide to Performance-Based Learning and Assessment***, by K. Michael Hibbard et al. (Alexandria, VA: ASCD), 1996

This book describes the approach of educators in Connecticut's Pomperaug Regional School District 15 to teaching and learning which balances basic instruction with performance-based learning and assessment using tools such as performance tasks, benchmarks, assessment lists, rubrics, and portfolios. Tasks are engaging and are well connected to the content, process skills, and work habits of the K–12 curriculum in many subject areas. Analytical assessment tools foster teacher dialogue, improve communication with students, encourage self-assessment, and help parents support learning. Student performance in this district was improved, as measured by standardized achievement tests, district measures, and the regionwide student portfolio.

**Contact**: Association for Supervision and Curriculum Development (ASCD), 1703 North Beauregard Street, Alexandria, VA 22311-1714; (800) 933-2723; fax: (703) 575-5400; e-mail: member@ascd.org; Web site: http://www.ascd.org/

## Videos

***Classroom Assessment Training***, produced by NWREL

NWREL has developed this set of trainer's instructional packages based on extensive research conducted over several decades. Video module titles include "Developing Assessments Based on Observation and Judgment," "Understanding Standardized Tests," "Assessing Mathematical Power," "Assessment in the Science Classroom," "Using Portfolios in Assessment and Instruction," "How Do You Spell Parallel? Visiting Middle School Math," and "Why Won't You Tell Me the Answer? Inquiry in the High School Classroom." The series may be purchased, but it is also available for borrowing from NWREL's Assessment Resource Library.

**Contacts**: To purchase: IOX Assessment Associates, 5301 Beethoven Street, Suite 190, Los Angeles, CA 90066-7061; fax: (310) 822-0269

To borrow: Northwest Regional Educational Laboratory (NWREL), 101 S.W. Main Street, Suite 500, Portland, OR 97204; (503) 275-9500; e-mail: arl@nwrel.org; Web site: http://www.nwrel.org/

*Look at Children's Thinking Series*, produced by Kathy Richardson and Jeannie Brunnick

Teachers in grades K–2 can use these two videos as a model for assessment techniques to explore children's thinking and to discover their level of understanding of number concepts. The videos are based on the belief that understanding children's thinking enables teachers to provide the kinds of experiences students need in order to make sense of numbers and build a solid foundation for future success in mathematics.

**Contact**: Educational Software Institute, 770 West Rock Creek Road, P.O. Box 1524, Norman, OK 73070; (800) 292-6022; fax (800) 292-8846; e-mail: sheryl@telepath.com

*Mathematics: Assessing Understanding,* produced by Marilyn Burns

This series of three videos and a discussion guide is a resource for planning and delivering workshops for educators interested in assessing students in grades K–7 in accordance with recommendations found in the NCTM Standards. Interviews with students illustrate the kinds of questions that can reveal what students do and do not understand, including their ability to apply numerical understanding to problem-solving situations and to explain their reasoning. The discussion guide describes the problems used for individual assessments, presents analyses of each interview, and provides guidelines for teacher discussion.

**Contact**:  Dale Seymour Publications, 4350 Equity Drive, Columbus, OH 43228; (800) 321-3106; Web site: http://www.pearsonlearning.com/

*Mathematics Assessment: A Video Library, K-12*, produced by WGBH Boston

The K–12 case studies in this professional development video library illustrate a range of assessment approaches based on NCTM's *Assessment Standards for School Mathematics* (1995). The five videos and related guidebook are designed to prompt discussion and reflection about changing assessment practices and to help viewers see the link between instruction and assessment.

**Contact**: Annenberg/CPB, 401 9th Street N.W., Washington, DC 20004; (800) 532-7637 (orders); fax: (802) 846-850 (orders); e-mail: info@learner.org; Web site: http://www.learner.org/ catalog/math/

## Organizations/Web Sites

### Centers for Curriculum Implementation

### BSCS High School Science Curriculum Implementation Center

The BSCS High School Science Curriculum Implementation Center assists high school teachers, schools, and districts to learn about, select among, and implement standards- and inquiry-based curriculum programs developed with NSF funding. The Center's work is organized around three topics: evaluating and selecting curriculum materials; designing professional development and support for teachers implementing new materials; and special issues in high school science reform (including assessment, college entrance requirements, and tracking). The Center also has established an Academy for Curriculum Leadership, a two-year intensive program for selected school and district teams. In addition to its emphasis on curriculum reform, the Center is developing and piloting institutes for teachers teaching out-of-field in both earth science and physics.

**Contact**: BSCS High School Science Curriculum Implementation Center, 5415 Mark Dabling Boulevard, Colorado Springs, CO 80918-3842; (719) 531-5550; fax: (719) 531-9104; e-mail: info@bscs.org; Web site: http://www.bscs.org/

### Center for the Enhancement of Science and Mathematics Education (CESAME)

The Center for the Enhancement of Science and Mathematics Education (CESAME) is a nonprofit K–12 mathematics and science education reform organization supported by the National Science Foundation, Northeastern University, and other public and private organizations. CESAME has gained recognition locally, regionally, and nationally for its efforts in creating awareness and supporting implementation of standards-based curricula and for providing high-quality professional development in mathematics and science. IMPACT, one of the CESAME-supported projects, promotes the successful evaluation, selection, and implementation of standards-based mathematics and science instructional materials in local school districts through regional curriculum implementation centers throughout New England.

**Contact**: CESAME, Northeastern University, 716 Columbus Avenue, Suite 378, Boston, MA 02120; (617) 373-8380; fax: (617) 373-8496; Web site: http://www.dac.neu.edu/cesame/

### Consortium for Mathematics and Its Applications (COMAP)

Since 1980, COMAP's mission has been to improve mathematics education for students of all ages. The organization has worked with teachers, students, and business people to create learning environments where mathematics is used to investigate and model real-world issues. The Web site offers information on curriculum products and services for elementary, high school, and undergraduate levels as well as materials and support services to assist teachers, parents, and administrators in reform efforts. Elementary services include Bridges to Classroom Mathematics, a project developed to help elementary schools prepare for NCTM Standards implementation, and The ARC Center (Alternatives for Rebuilding Curriculum), a resource for mathematics curricula. High school products include Mathematics: Modeling Our World, a rigorous curriculum focused on integration of real-world themes; Geometry and Its Applications (Geomap), a free collection of supplementary units that focus on innovations in geometry in the last 50 years; and *STREAM*, a proactive set of videos and supporting materials designed to engage facilitators, parents, administrators, and school boards in discussion and action about secondary mathematics education reform.

**Contact**: COMAP, Inc., 57 Bedford Street, Suite 210, Lexington, MA 02420; (800) 772-6627; fax: (781) 863-1202; e-mail: info@comap.com; Web site: http://www.comap.com/

## Curricular Options in Mathematics Programs for All Secondary Students (COMPASS)

The mission of COMPASS is to focus specifically on the implementation of five multi-year high school curriculum development projects. The curricula provide a wide range of options in high school mathematics and have been designed to address the challenges of the NCTM Standards. The Web site provides comprehensive information on the five projects supported by COMPASS: Applications Reform in Secondary Education (ARISE), Core-Plus Mathematics Project (CPMP), Interactive Mathematics Program (IMP), MATH Connections Project, and Systemic Initiative in Montana Mathematics and Science Project (SIMMS).

**Contact**: COMPASS, Williams Hall 306, Ithaca College, Ithaca, NY 14850; (800) 688-1829; fax: (607) 274-3054; e-mail: compass@ithaca.edu; Web site: http://www.ithaca.edu/compass/frames.htm

## The EDC K–12 Science Curriculum Dissemination Center

The EDC K–12 Science Curriculum Dissemination Center is part of a nationwide effort to introduce school districts to exemplary science instructional materials that were developed with funding from the National Science Foundation (NSF). The Center targets school districts with limited previous exposure to NSF curricula and/or little experience with NSF or other national science education reform efforts. The Center is working with underserved communities through 10 regional centers, or "hubs," located at school districts, universities, and affiliates of the Eisenhower Regional Consortia.

**Contact**: Center for Science Education, Education Development Center, Inc., 55 Chapel

Street, Newton, MA 02458-1060; (617) 618-2570; fax: (617) 630-8439: Web site: http://www.edc.org/cse/

## K–12 Mathematics Curriculum Center

This NSF-funded Mathematics Curriculum Center informs and assists school districts as they select and implement standards-based mathematics curricula. They provide a series of seminars, resource guides, case studies, and other written material, referrals, and phone consultations to help facilitate discussion and decision making among stakeholders within school districts. The Web site provides general information about the Center, timely updates about upcoming events, and links to publishers, developers, and other sources of information and services. The site also features summaries of each of the 13 affiliated K–12 curriculum programs, including teacher support material and student resources.

**Contact**: K–12 Mathematics Curriculum Center, Education Development Center, Inc., 55 Chapel Street, Newton, MA 02458-1060; (800) 332-2429; e-mail: mcc@edc.org; Web site: http://www.edc.org/mcc/

## Show-Me Center

The Show-Me Center, in partnership with five NSF-sponsored middle grades curriculum development satellites and their publishers, provides information and the resources needed to support selection and implementation of standards-based middle grades mathematics curricula. To this end, the center sponsors conferences, supports professional development, and offers consulting services for schools and districts. The Web site provides information on five mathematics curricula: Connected Mathematics, Mathematics in Context, MathScape, MATH Thematics, and Pathways to Algebra and Geometry™.

**Contact**: Show Me Center, University of Missouri, 303 Townsend Hall, Columbia, MO 65211; (573) 884-2099; e-mail: center@showme.missouri.edu; Web site: http:// showmecenter.missouri.edu/

# Eisenhower Regional Consortia

Funded by the U.S. Department of Education, each of the 10 Eisenhower Regional Consortia serves a different geographic region of the country. They provide technical assistance and professional development on issues in mathematics and science education important to their region and the nation and disseminate effective materials and instructional methods.

## Northeast and Islands Region

Eisenhower Regional Alliance for Mathematics and Science Education, TERC, 2067 Massachusetts Avenue, Cambridge, MA 02140; (617) 547-0430; fax: (617) 349-3535; e-mail: alliance@terc.edu; Web site: http://www.ra.terc.edu/

## Mid-Atlantic Region

Mid-Atlantic Eisenhower Consortium for Mathematics and Science Education, Research for Better Schools, 444 North Third Street, Philadelphia, PA 19123-4107; (215) 574-9300 ext. 277; (215) 574-0133; Web site: http://www.rbs.org/ec.nsf/

## Appalachia Region

Eisenhower Regional Consortium for Math and Science Education, Appalachia Regional Educational Laborary (AEL), P.O. Box 1348, Charleston, WV 25325-1348; (800) 624-9120; fax: (304) 347-0487; Web site: http://www.ael.org/eisen/

## Southeast Region

Southeastern Eisenhower Regional Consortium for Mathematics and Science Education at SERVE, 1203 Governor's Square Boulevard, Suite 400, Tallahassee, FL 32301; (800) 854-0476; (850) 671-6010; Web site: http://www.serve.org/Eisenhower/

## North Central Region

North Central Mathematics and Science Consortium (NCMSC), North Central Regional Educational Laboratory (NCREL), 1120 East Diehl Road, Suite 200, Naperville, IL 60563; (800) 356-2735; fax: (630) 649-6700; e-mail: ncmsc@contact.ncrel.org; Web site: http://www.ncrel.org/msc/

## Mid-continent Region

Eisenhower High Plains Consortium for Mathematics and Science (HPC), Mid-continent Research for Education and Learning (McREL), 2550 South Parker Road, Suite 500, Aurora, CO 80014-1678; (800) 949-6387; fax: (303) 337-3005; Web site: http://www.mcrel.org/hpc/

## Southwest Region

Southwest Consortium for the Improvement of Mathematics and Science Teaching (SCIMAST), Southwest Educational Development Laboratory (SEDL), 211 East 7th Street, Austin, TX 78701-3281; (512) 476-6861; fax: (512) 476-2286; Web site: http://www.sedl.org/pitl/scimast/

## Northwest Region

Northwest Consortium for Mathematics and Science Teaching (Northwest CMAST), Mathematics and Science Education Center, Northwest Regional Educational Laboratory (NWREL), 101 S.W. Main Street, Suite 500, Portland, OR 97204; (503) 275-9594; fax: (503) 275-0445; Web site: http://www.nwrel.org/msec/

## Far West Region

WestEd Eisenhower Regional Consortium for Science and Mathematics (WERC), 730 Harrison Street, San Francisco, CA 94107-1242; (415) 241-2730; fax: (415) 512-2024; Web site: http://www.wested.org/werc/

## Pacific Region

Pacific Mathematics and Science Regional Consortium, Pacific Resources for Education and

Learning (PREL), Ali'i Place, 1099 Alakea Street, Suite 2500, Honolulu, HI 96813-4513; (808) 441-1300; fax: (808) 441-1385; Web site: http://www.prel.org/programs/ms/ms.asp

## Other Organizations/Web Sites

### The American Association for the Advancement of Science (AAAS)

AAAS is the world's largest general science organization and publisher of the peer-reviewed journal *Science*. With more than 138,000 members and 275 affiliated societies, AAAS serves as an authoritative source for information on the latest developments in science and bridges gaps among scientists, policy makers, and the public to advance science and science education. Project 2061, the long-term initiative of AAAS working to reform K–12 science, mathematics, and technology education nationwide, developed *Benchmarks for Science Literacy* and publishes many other related resources.

**Contact**: AAAS Project 2061, 1333 H Street N.W., P.O. Box 34446, Washington, DC 20005; (202) 326-6666; fax: (202) 842-5196; e-mail: project2061@aaas.org; Web site: http://www.project2061.org/

### Association for Supervision and Curriculum Development (ASCD)

ASCD, founded in 1943, is an international nonprofit and nonpartisan education association that provides professional development in curriculum and supervision, initiates and supports activities to provide educational equity for all students, and serves as a leader in education information services. ASCD distributes a variety of journals, newsletters, books, and audio- and videotapes each year. Regular publications include *Educational Leadership, The Journal of Curriculum and Supervision,* and *Education Update.*

**Contact**: ASCD, 1703 North Beauregard Street, Alexandria, VA 22311-1714. (800-933-2723; fax: (703) 575-5400; e-mail: member@ascd.org; Web site: http://www.ascd.org/

### Eisenhower National Clearinghouse for Mathematics and Science Education (ENC)

ENC online provides K–12 teachers with a central source of information on mathematics and science curriculum materials as well as information about free publications, CD-ROMs, and professional development activities.

**Contact**: Eisenhower National Clearinghouse, 1929 Kenny Road, Columbus, OH 43210; (800) 621-5785; fax: (614) 292-2066; e-mail: info@enc.org; Web site: http://www.enc.org/

### The Math Forum

The Math Forum's goal is "to build an online community of teachers, students, researchers, parents, educators, and citizens at all levels who have an interest in math and math education." They provide summaries of mathematics education research published on newsgroups, school networking support, the Elementary Problem of the Week, Web-based lessons, and classroom materials.

**Contact:** The Math Forum, 101 South Chester Road, Suite 400, P.O. Box 156, Swarthmore, PA 19081-0156; (800) 756-7823; fax: (610) 544-1358; Web site: http://forum.swarthmore.edu/

### National Academy of Sciences (NAS) and National Research Council (NRC)

The National Academy of Sciences was established by Congress in 1863 to further scientific and technical knowledge and advise the federal government in these areas. The NAS includes the National Research Council, which carries out or coordinates most of the scientific and technical studies requested by Congress and federal agencies. Many NAS and NRC publications are available free online. Of particular interest to K–12 mathematics and science teachers are the National Science Education Standards, published by the NRC; the National Science Resources Center, which sponsors the Science and Technology for Children™ and Science and Technology Concepts for Middle Schools curriculums; and the Resources for Involving Scientists in Education (RISE) project.

**Contact:** NRC, 2101 Constitution Avenue N.W. (HA 450), Washington, DC 20418-0006; (202) 334-3294; fax: (202) 334-1453; e-mail: mseb@nas.edu; Web site: http://www.nas.edu/

### National Council of Teachers of Mathematics (NCTM)

For more than 75 years the NCTM has been dedicated to improving the teaching and learning of mathematics. It is a recognized leader in efforts to ensure an excellent mathematics education for all students as well as an opportunity for every mathematics teacher to grow professionally through annual, regional, and leadership conferences. NCTM publishes four professional journals plus the *NCTM News Bulletin*, more than 250 educational books, videos, and other materials, and the Addenda Series, which brings the message of the NCTM Standards documents to the classroom. The Web site offers information about the organization and its programs, publications, and professional development opportunities.

**Contact:** NCTM, 1906 Association Drive, Reston, VA 20191-9988; (703) 620-9840; fax: (703) 476-2970; Web site: http://www.nctm.org/

### National Science Teachers Association (NSTA)

The NSTA, founded in 1944, is the largest organization in the world committed to promoting excellence and innovation in science teaching and learning for all. NSTA provides many programs and services for science educators, including awards, professional development workshops, and educational tours, and offers professional certification for science teachers in eight teaching-level and discipline-area categories. NSTA's newest and largest initiative to date, Building a Presence for Science, seeks to improve science education and align science teaching to the National Science Education Standards nationwide. The Web site provides links to state, national, and international science education organizations, an online catalog of publications, and two "discussion rooms" to foster interaction and ongoing conversations about science education.

**Contact**: NSTA, 1840 Wilson Boulevard, Arlington, VA 22201-3000; (800) 722-6782; fax: (703) 841-8329; Web site: http://www.nsta.org/

### National Staff Development Council (NSDC)

The National Staff Development Council (NSDC), founded in 1969, is the largest nonprofit professional association committed to ensuring success for all students through staff development and school improvement. The Council views high-quality staff development programs as essential to creating schools in which all students and staff members are learners who continually improve their performance. NSDC publishes the *Journal of Staff Development* as well as other newsletters and publications.

**Contact**: NSDC, P.O. Box 240, Oxford, OH 45056; (513) 523-6029; e-mail: nsdcoffice@aol.com; Web site: http://www.nsdc.org/

## Resources for Managing Change/Monitoring Implementation

### Books

*Facilitating Systemic Change in Science and Mathematics Education: A Toolkit for Professional Developers*, by the Regional Educational Laboratory Network (Andover, MA: Regional Laboratory for Educational Improvement of the Northeast and Islands), 1995

Two critical, interrelated themes weave throughout this book: using a systemic approach to change in order to ensure equitable access and achievement of science and mathematics for all students. The book is structured as a set of learning activities that help those supporting reform to deepen their knowledge about mathematics and science education, dissemination, professional development, and the change process. Additional activities suggest strategies for engaging all of the necessary people and resources needed for reform to succeed. Masters for transparencies, handouts, and readings that are called for by specific activities are also included.

**Contact**: Learning Innovations (a division of WestEd), 91 Montvale Avenue, Stoneham, MA 02180-3616; fax: (781) 279-8220; Web site: http://www.wested.org/

*Implementing Change: Patterns, Principles, and Potholes*, by Shirley Hord and Gene Hall (Needham Heights, MA: Allyn & Bacon), 2001

If the focus of change is solely on technology and if the personal side is not addressed, the result is resistance and implementation failure. This book addresses those concerns using the

Concerns-Based Adoption Model (CBAM) in a useful and immediately applicable format. Chapter 3 focuses on the innovation configurations of change, including the concept of describing an innovation and its variations, applications, and implications.

**Contact**: Allyn & Bacon/Longman, 160 Gould Street, Needham Heights, MA 02494; (781) 455-1250; Web site: http://www.ablongman.com/

## Organizations/Consultants

### Council of Chief State School Officers (CCSSO)

The Council of Chief State School Officers is a nationwide, nonprofit organization that represents chief education administrators and works on behalf of the state agencies that have primary authority for education in each state. One of their programs, the State Collaborative on Assessment and Student Standards (SCASS), is designated to assist states in developing needed student standards and assessments in conjunction with other states expressing similar needs. This program developed the Measures of the Enacted Curriculum Surveys, field-tested instruments designed to collect data on curriculum content and instructional practices in elementary, middle, and high school science. Surveys are available upon request along with a paper entitled "Measures of Enacted Curriculum in Science: A Guide for K–12 Educators" by Megan Martin, Rolf Blank, and John Smithson (1996).

**Contact**: State Collaborative on Assessment and Student Standards, Council of Chief State School Officers (CCSSO), One Massachusetts Avenue N.W., Suite 700, Washington, DC 20001-1431; (202) 408-5505; fax: (202) 408-8072; Web site: http://www.ccsso.org/

### Horizon Research, Inc.

HRI is a private research firm specializing in mathematics and science education. HRI's expertise is diverse, encompassing such areas as survey design and analysis, policy research, development of in-service materials for teachers, information dissemination, and evaluation of and technical assistance to educational reform initiatives.

**Contact**: Horizon Research, Inc., 326 Cloister Court, Chapel Hill, NC 27514; (919) 489-1725; fax: (919) 493-7589; e-mail: hri@horizon-research.com; Web site: http://www.horizon-research.com/

### Deborah S. Roody, Educational Consultant and CBAM Trainer

Deborah S. Roody is an educational consultant providing services to educators both nationally and internationally. Her work focuses on training and facilitating individuals and school teams in the issues and implementation of school change. Deborah is a certified trainer in the Concerns-Based Adoption Model (CBAM) and in the facilitation of the Making Change for School Improvement and Systems Thinking/Systems Changing simulation games developed at The NETWORK, Inc. As a consultant, she has worked with many schools not only introducing this material but working with staff to implement new programs and practices.

**Contact**: Deborah S. Roody, 3 Alder Way, Bedford, NH 03110-5501; (603) 472-2062; fax: (603) 471-0280; e-mail: deb1roody@aol.com

## Games

**Making Change for School Improvement: A Simulation Game**, developed by Leslie Hergert, Susan Mundry, Frances Kolb, Ray Rose, and Jo Corro at The NETWORK, Inc.

This training tool, based on the Concern-Based Adoption Model of change, provides an active and exciting simulation of school-based change. With the goal of implementing a new program in a school district, teams play this simulation game and earn credit for their progress. The object is to convince fictional administrators, parents, and teachers to implement proposed changes and generate benefits for students.

**Contact**: Learning Innovations and WestEd, 91 Montvale Avenue, Stoneham, MA 02180; (617) 279-8210; Web site: http://www.wested.org/

**Systems Thinking/Systems Changing: A Simulation Game for Transforming School Communities**, developed by Susan Mundry and Carol Bershad at The NETWORK, Inc.

Systems Thinking/Systems Changing is a challenging and fun simulation game for educators designed to provide training and experience in planning for and managing continuous improvement of schools. Participants in the simulation build their awareness of change principles based on Systems Thinking, Total Quality Management in Schools, the Concerns-Based Adoption Model for Change, Adopter Types, Diffusion of Innovations, and Knowledge Dissemination and Use. The game simulates a school community that is learning to use these important tools to make positive changes in schools. Systems Thinking/Systems Changing is intended for individuals involved in planning and managing ongoing improvements in educational organizations, including community members, teachers, administrators, parents, students, and business representatives.

**Contact**: Carol Bershad/Susan Mundry, ST&C Associates, 25 Hammond Road, Natick, MA 01760-1101; (508) 652-9954; fax: (508) 652-9954; e-mail: cbers@mediaone.net

# OVERCOMING OBSTACLES TO EQUITY

Achievement gap

Opportunities gap

Structural barriers

Belief systems

Expectations

Curriculum, instruction,
and assessment biases

**5**

**Our mathematics/science** reform team was at a planning session at a summer institute, where we were encouraged to examine equity issues in our school. At first we were convinced we didn't have any problems. But we soon realized that we had never considered our small Native American population. Now we are going to take a hard look at whether their needs are being met in our school. (Mathematics/science reform team, rural elementary school)

**When we disaggregated** the data on enrollment in algebra, we couldn't deny the problem. The composition of our algebra classes, mostly white, didn't look anything like our school population, which was mostly minority. Our tracking system was sorting students by race. (Mathematics chair, urban high school)

**Our elementary school** is virtually all white. At first, we resisted any discussion about equity as irrelevant to us. But with encouragement from our mathematics/science reform network, we started looking at our special education and Title I programs. Many of these students were being pulled out during science, where some of the best hands-on, project-based learning happens. Now we are working on an inclusion program, where these students stay in the regular classroom and the special needs and regular education teachers work together to integrate language arts and mathematics skills with the science lessons. (Mathematics/science reform team, suburban elementary school)

**I always hated** any conversations about equity or racial differences; I believed I treated all my students equally. Then our school got involved in a program where we started to look at prejudice from a personal standpoint. Ultimately, I came to realize some of the more subtle elements of racism that resulted in my treating black students differently, expecting less of them, overlooking their strengths. It's been both a painful and exhilarating process. I now know that if our school is going to change, I have to change. (Teacher, urban middle school)

# Overview of Equity

As the above examples illustrate, when schools proceed down the road to reform, they inevitably encounter a major roadblock. School reformers may get as far as making mathematics and science education better for some; but they won't reach all students without breaking the silence about racism, classism, and sexism and actively confronting the barriers to equity. While the road to mathematics and science education reform is fraught with many challenges, none is as great or as important as this one.

With the standards movement, equity has come to mean much more than just equal access to schools and classrooms. It implies the right of all students to reach high standards of performance. And that means their right to a rigorous curriculum, high-quality materials and equipment, a positive learning environment, and teachers who both believe in their potential and are qualified to teach mathematics and science. The true measure of equity is when race, class, cultural background, gender, or physical challenges are no longer a factor in student achievement—when all students are achieving at their capacity. By this measure, virtually every school in the United States has equity work to do.

## "All Students Can Learn" Means All!

Equity work is about reaching all children, especially those who are currently cut out of the best that this country's educational system has to offer. Who are these children? They are:

▼ poor and minority students, who, in disproportionate numbers, are receiving a second-class mathematics and science education. The achievement gaps between white and minority, rich and poor have been widening in the last decade (National Center for Education Statistics 1994, as cited in Education Trust 1996, 5);

▼ English language learners, who rarely have access to mathematics or science instruction appropriate to their grade level or in their primary language, simply because they do not speak fluent English;

▼ special education students, who, because of the damaging effects of labeling, segregating, and ineffective mainstreaming, are often deprived of high-quality mathematics and science instruction;

*"Equity is the right to achieve at levels sufficient to participate productively, and in a rewarding way, economically and civically."*

(Lauren Resnick, as cited in Rothman 1994, 2)

▼ girls, who receive less and poorer quality attention in mathematics and science classrooms than boys (National Science Foundation [1997], 79–81; see also Grayson and Martin 1997, 24–25).

They are, in fact, a growing majority of our children, and our educational system is failing them.

No one is denying that many of these students come to school with the deck stacked against them. But what prevents them from reaching their capacity is not their poverty, their IQ, their parents, their skin color, their gender, or their native language. It is, as Asa Hilliard (1991) implies, our lack of will to educate all children. This manifests in belief systems that blind us to students' strengths and fixate us on sorting and labeling; in structures like tracking, whose negative impact on poor and minority students is well documented; in the subtle and not-so-subtle ways that we communicate lower expectations for these students, especially when it comes to mathematics and science; and in curriculum, instruction, and assessment practices geared to a majority culture, rendering others irrelevant or invisible.

The truth is that mathematics and science education reform can proceed—states and schools can adopt standards for "all students"; schools can implement new, more challenging inquiry-based mathematics and science programs—yet little will change for these disenfranchised students unless we directly confront racial, class, cultural, and gender biases and the inequitable practices they spawn. Reform that does not put equity center stage has not and will not bring about high levels of mathematics and science achievement for all.

On the other hand, when individuals, schools, and districts have confronted obstacles to equity, they have achieved stunning results. A good example is the College Board's EQUITY 2000 reform initiative. Through this program, teachers and guidance counselors in seven participating urban districts have confronted low expectations for minority students, enrolled them in algebra and geometry in record numbers, and improved instructional practices. As a result, many EQUITY 2000 schools are close to their goal of 100 percent enrollment in algebra and are making progress in geometry. In more than half of the participating districts, two-thirds of the students enrolling in Algebra I passed; nearly one in four earned Bs or better (Everson and Dunham 1996). (See **Reform in Action**, page 335, and Figures 5.1, 5.2, and 5.3.)

*"We have one and only one problem: Do we truly will to see each and every child in this nation develop to the peak of his or her capacities?"*

(Hilliard 1991, 36)

FIGURE 5.1: CHANGE IN NINTH-GRADE ENROLLMENT IN ALGEBRA I OR HIGHER FOR EACH SITE

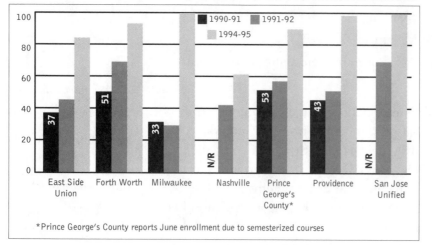

*Prince George's County reports June enrollment due to semesterized courses

FIGURE 5.2: CHANGE IN TENTH-GRADE ENROLLMENT IN GEOMETRY OR HIGHER FOR EACH SITE

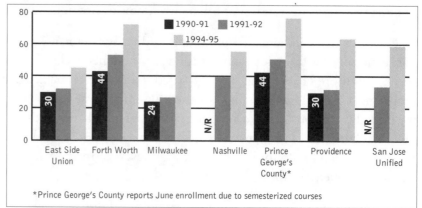

*Prince George's County reports June enrollment due to semesterized courses

Another example is the teachers who have worked with the Generating Expectations for Student Achievement (GESA) program. Teachers in the program have, in fact, reduced the disparity in their treatment between boys and girls while their students overall have made gains in standardized test scores, especially in classes with large minority enrollments (Grayson and Martin 1997). These and other similar examples are part of a small but growing trend among education reformers to confront head-on the barriers that have made "high levels of mathematics and science achievement for *all*" such an elusive goal.

Now more than ever, realizing this goal is imperative, because of the incalculable human costs of prejudice—children whose self-esteem is shattered,

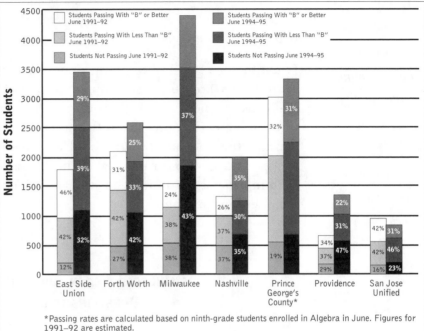

**FIGURE 5.3: NINTH-GRADE STUDENTS IN ALGEBRA I PASSING AND RECEIVING A GRADE OF B OR BETTER**

*Passing rates are calculated based on ninth-grade students enrolled in Algebra in June. Figures for 1991–92 are estimated.

whose hopes for the future are dashed—and, increasingly, because of the economic costs. As more jobs require more sophisticated mathematics and science knowledge and skills, our economy simply cannot thrive by educating only the elite well.

## The Role of Data in Equity Reform

Ruth Johnson, The Education Trust, The College Board and EQUITY 2000, and others have helped us to understand the especially important role that data can play in equity reform as a guide and a catalyst. Data can help schools cut through the denial that "we don't have an equity problem here" and begin a dialogue about how to better serve all children.

Even so, this topic inevitably triggers strong emotions. Educators often avoid discussing racial, class, cultural, or gender issues because of feelings of fear, insecurity, and pain. That's why, as school communities take on equity issues, it is important to support staff in facing these emotions by respecting divergent opinions, listening well to each other, avoiding finger pointing and blame, agreeing to put the welfare of students first, and using inquiry and data, not assumptions, to guide reform.

> *"Confronting these data is often uncomfortable, even painful. Yet without an open and thoughtful examination of these patterns, you will never identify the practices and beliefs that perpetuate the achievement gap. And these are the very practices and beliefs that must be changed if we are to eliminate the achievement gap, once and for all."*
>
> (Education Trust 1996, 2)

Inequities are a reality of education in the United States. Acknowledging this fact does not create the problem; it brings the problem to light so that all children can be served, not in the identical way, but equitably, with equal opportunity to succeed.

Often the first step in beginning a constructive dialogue about equity is to find out who is underserved in your school district and how. In virtually every school across the country, urban, suburban, or rural, some students are performing at less than their capacity. To begin this process, consider the students at your school who, because of race, class, cultural background, gender, or physical challenges, are likely to be underserved, both in general and in mathematics and science specifically. The following questions may help.

### WHO IS UNDERSERVED IN OUR SCHOOL/DISTRICT? QUESTIONS TO CONSIDER

▼ Who are our students? What is an accurate picture of the demographics in our school or district? (See **Data Tools**, DT 3-2.)

▼ Are some groups of students performing more poorly than others?

▼ Is tracking practiced? If so, what groups are disproportionately represented in the low track? How does being in a low track affect their opportunity to learn mathematics and science?

▼ Are English language learners or special education students being pulled out during science lessons? How much quality mathematics and science are they receiving?

▼ How are girls treated in mathematics and science classrooms? How much advanced mathematics and science are they taking? What practices might be discouraging them from doing their best?

In previous chapters, we have prompted your exploration into these and other questions. For example, in Chapter 3 we discussed how to use disaggregated data about student learning, opportunities to learn, and student aspirations to surface two kinds of gaps: performance gaps and unequal learning opportunities. In Problems Three and Four of Chapter 4, we showed you ways to measure whether standards-based curriculum, instruction, and assessment were equally accessible to low-track and minority groups and discussed ways that gender inequities might manifest in the classroom.

The next step, once performance or opportunities gaps are identified, is to ask what beliefs and practices in your school might be perpetuating these inequities. This chapter offers a guide to help teams investigate more deeply the obstacles to equity in their own schools. It is organized around four possible obstacles your school may face: structural barriers such as tracking; belief systems; unequal expectations; and biases in curriculum, instruction, and assessment practices. You will learn why each is an important equity issue, how to use data to better understand how they may operate in your own school, and where to find resources to help.

Before diving into any one of these issues, your team may want to begin your investigation by using the "Focus Statements: Obstacles to Equity" in **Planning Tools**, page 297. These statements are designed to stimulate dialogue about obstacles to equity and to identify issues for further inquiry.

# Structural Barriers to Equity

One of the most serious barriers to equity is school structures that deny some students the opportunity to learn mathematics and science. In this section, we explore four such structures: tracking, programs for English language learners, special education programs, and gifted and honors programs.

## Intractable Tracking

The student quoted on the next page is the lucky exception. She had the chance to move from a tracked to a heterogeneous mathematics class that offered a rich, challenging curriculum. But for many students the story doesn't have a happy ending. Low-track education is notoriously boring, repetitive, and second-rate; and once assigned to a low track, students rarely move up. Yet in most high schools and many elementary and middle schools, tracking is still the dominant practice.

*"Systemic reform means taking responsibility to serve, not to sort."*

(Robert McLaughlin, Director, National Institute for Community Innovation, Montpelier, Vermont, interview, 1998)

*"Tracking is like separating the good from the bad and not making the bad any better. I got a D in the lower-track class because it was so boring. In this class I got a B. I have the most fun when I'm in the most diverse class. I meet new people and people are more supportive. Higher-track teachers look after you and give you more encouragement. They ask questions. Grades are not so important. It's good to feel good about yourself, to feel you really understand it, not that you just memorized it."*

(Student in a college-preparatory mathematics class, as cited in Linn 1992, 25)

Tracking takes various forms, and it may or may not be labeled as such. It can start in kindergarten, where students are often separated into academic (for more advanced students) and developmental (for less advanced) classes. These labels can follow students throughout their school careers. In elementary school, students may be assigned to a classroom or a special program based on their perceived abilities. In middle school come the honors and remedial tracks, where students of similar perceived abilities are assigned to the same block of teachers and move together from class to class throughout the school day. In high school, curriculum tracking is most common, with students being assigned by ability or achievement to tracks such as college-preparatory, general, or vocational (Adelman 1995, 32; O'Neil 1992, 19–21). Sometimes tracking is planned; sometimes it is de facto, resulting from what Jeannie Oakes calls the "inflexibilities and idiosyncrasies of 'master' schedules" (Oakes 1986, 13). For example, students who don't take algebra may be unable to schedule challenging academic courses in other content areas, which locks them into a low-track experience all day long.

Not all ability grouping is harmful, according to Robert Slavin and other researchers. Slavin draws a distinction between "within-class" and "between-class" ability grouping. Within-class ability grouping occurs in a heterogeneous classroom, is flexible, groups students based on current levels of skill in a particular content area (such as reading or mathematics), and does not result in different quality instruction for different groups. This kind of ability grouping can actually be beneficial (Slavin 1988). The problem comes with ability grouping that is based on global judgments about how smart students are, locks them into their place in the hierarchy, is a public feature of a school's culture, and results in a very different experience for students in different groups (O'Neil 1992). This kind of "between-class" ability grouping, tracking, has two major problems.

First, it is fundamentally unfair, especially to poor and minority students, who are disproportionately represented in low tracks. Students from minority groups are seven times more likely than whites to be placed in low tracks (Powell 1994, 2.2). And it is not unusual to find African American and Latino students placed in these low tracks who scored as well or better on standardized tests than their white or Asian peers (Education Trust [1996], 32). Moreover, once relegated to a low track, students are taught a thinner curriculum, "oversimplified, repetitive, and fragmented," by less qualified teachers than their high-track peers (Oakes 1990, 89). As a result, they are effectively cut off from academic content that could prepare them for later success in school and in life. This is especially true when it comes to mathematics, as Eleanor Linn explains:

In the "tracked" schools of America, algebra acts as the switching station. Students who learn algebra early typically get switched onto the fast track that prepares students for college, and in the long run, good jobs. Students who don't learn algebra early get switched onto the slower vocational or general track. In today's high-tech economy, those tracks lead mainly to low-level jobs and sometimes to no job at all. And they are loaded with African Americans and Latinos. . . .(1992, 23)

On the other hand, when given the opportunity to take higher-level mathematics, students of all races perform better on national tests. The more mathematics students take, the better they perform (see Figure 5.4).

*"Tracking involves the categorization of students according to particular measures of intelligence into distinct groups for purposes of teaching and learning. Once they have been sorted and classified, students are provided with curricula and instruction deemed suited to their ability and matched to spoken or unspoken assessments of each student's future."*

(Wheelock 1993, 44)

**FIGURE 5.4: A RIGOROUS MATH CURRICULUM IMPROVES SCORES FOR ALL STUDENTS**

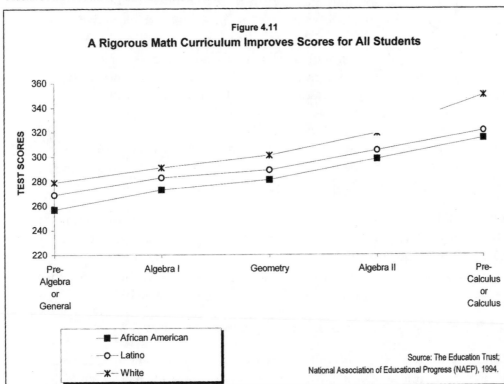

Figure 4.11
**A Rigorous Math Curriculum Improves Scores for All Students**

Source: The Education Trust;
National Association of Educational Progress (NAEP), 1994.

Tracking is not just unfair; it is ineffective. According to Robert Slavin and other researchers, "evidence has not been found to support the notion that [between-class] ability grouping produces greater overall student achievement" (Century 1994, 44). Many of the assumptions upon which tracking has been based—that it would benefit both high and low achievers, that all students could receive a good education at their appropriate level—have been seriously challenged by decades of research (see box below).

## Tracking: Point—Counterpoint

**Point:** Tracking can provide low-track students with just as good an education as high-track students.

**Counterpoint:** This has not been the case. Oakes and others have found that low-track students are denied equitable access to qualified teachers and resources, making it almost impossible for them to ever move out of the low tracks. What's more, low-track classes offer a second-class curriculum that neglects important concepts and skills, use less effective instructional strategies, and offer poorer learning environments. Rather than helping low-track students, tracking has been found to lower their self-esteem and aspirations and promote misbehavior and dropping out (Oakes 1985, 1986, 1990; Gamoran 1992).

**Point:** Tracking is the best way to meet individual students' needs. How can teachers possibly meet the individual needs of a wide range of heterogeneous students? Sorting by ability simply makes teaching manageable.

**Counterpoint:** There is no such thing as a homogeneous group. Any group of 20 students will require a variety of instructional approaches to meet their needs. Tracking distracts us from this fact and leads to blaming failure on the student or his or her placement. Even if tracking does make teaching easier for some teachers, that does not mean it is best for students (Oakes 1986).

**Point:** Detracking hurts high-achieving students.

**Counterpoint:** While students in high tracks have enjoyed some advantage, they can achieve at least as well in heterogeneous classrooms. High-track students can learn well without low-track students paying a heavy price (Oakes 1986).

**Point:** Mathematics is different from other subjects. It is more sequential and requires mastery of one set of skills before proceeding to the next. How can students learn algebra if they don't even know their multiplication tables?

**Counterpoint:** No doubt, students need better preparation in mathematics in elementary and middle school. But that preparation has to go far beyond mastery of basic computation, much of which can be done with a hand-held calculator. So why make mastery of multiplication tables a prerequisite for algebra and lock students into the boring, repetitive, and mostly unsuccessful "drill and kill" of general mathematics classes? Instead, children from early elementary school need to be engaged in building understandings of numbers, data, geometry, and algebra that will provide them with a strong foundation for more advanced mathematics. Moreover, when high school mathematics curricula are relevant, interactive, engaging, and problem-based, such as the Interactive Mathematics Program (IMP), heterogeneous student groups are enjoying great success. (See Mathematics and Science Curriculum Materials on accompanying CD-ROM).

## English Language Learners: Caught in the Invisible Track

Students with linguistic and cultural backgrounds different from mainstream English-speaking students experience their own unique structural barriers to quality mathematics and science instruction. They are caught in what one researcher calls an "invisible track" (Adler 1992, 1), where they receive "a steady diet of basic skills instruction in place of regular curriculum content" (Wong-Filmore and Meyer 1992, 649). This is particularly true in mathematics and science, where they rarely receive high-quality, inquiry-based instruction in their native language. This is despite the fact that several research studies indicate that performance in mathematics improves when students are instructed in their native language (Powell 1994, 109). How does this happen?

One common cause is culturally and linguistically biased intelligence and placement tests. Often students are tested soon after they come to the United States or long before they understand the nuances of the language. With poor English language skills and little knowledge of this country's culture, they test poorly. As a result, they are placed in a vocational track or even diagnosed as "mentally retarded" simply because of their lack of English language proficiency. Even after these students are mainstreamed, their English proficiency is often confused with their academic ability. "This results in practices such as reducing the number of subjects a student studies, limiting the scope of material covered, or offering instructional materials below the student's grade level" (Adler 1992, 12).

## The Special Education Track

Another structural barrier to equity is the special education system. Despite advances in special education legislation and research, current policy and practice raise serious equity concerns. Take the referral process. Often students end up in special education because their behavior or academic progress varies from the norm, the assumption being that something is wrong with the student. The result is too many students in special education, especially boys, minorities, and English language learners (Gartner and Lipsky 1987; Greenbaum 1992). One researcher found that even when lower-class, African American boys scored the same on standardized tests as middle-class, white girls, the African American boys were more likely to be referred to special education (Powell 1994).

Another problem is how well served students are in special education programs, which are, as Greenbaum put it, "for all intents and purposes, low level tracks" (1992, 19). Often these programs are characterized by low expectations for students, slow progress in pull-out programs, and ineffective mainstreaming practices. For many special needs students, mathematics instruction consists of constant drill and practice in arithmetic with little opportunity to use mathematics to solve meaningful problems. And they may not even see a science classroom because their program focuses so heavily on basic skills.

## Access to Gifted, Honors, and Advanced Placement Programs

While poor and minority students are overrepresented in special education programs, they are underrepresented in gifted, honors, and advanced placement programs. According to Powell, "educators and parents tend to construct mental images of gifted students—images reflecting the characteristics of white, middle-class students—that can blind them to the actual abilities of children from minority, poor, and other underrepresented groups" (1994, 2.2). These same students are often discouraged from pursuing honors and advanced placement courses by biased counseling practices and by restrictive policies such as grade requirements and inflexible schedules. Offering such courses does not pose an equity problem; unfairly restricting access to them does. Figure 5.5 illustrates the results of EQUITY 2000 school districts' efforts to increase minority participation in Advanced Placement courses.

**FIGURE 5.5: AP AT ALL EQUITY 2000 SITES**

| | 1990 | 1994 | % Increase |
|---|---|---|---|
| Total Exams Administered | 4,383 | 6,254 | 42.69 |
| Total Exam Candidates | 3,097 | 4,074 | 31.55 |
| Exams per Candidate | 1.42 | 1.54 | 8.47 |
| **Exams Taken By:** | | | |
| Native American | 14 | 28 | 100.00 |
| African American | 349 | 666 | 90.83 |
| Mexican American | 138 | 280 | 102.90 |
| Asian American | 702 | 1,427 | 103.28 |
| Puerto Rican | 7 | 33 | 371.43 |
| Other Hispanic | 49 | 204 | 316.33 |
| White | 2,449 | 3,093 | 26.30 |
| Other | 65 | 523 | 704.62 |

# Investigating Structural Barriers to Equity

The structural barriers described above—tracking, English language learner, special education, and gifted and honors programs and practices—result in unequal opportunities for some students to learn mathematics and science. Investigating which structures in your school district might act as barriers to equity and how is an important first step to removing them. It will help you build a case for change and better understand the nature of the problem(s) so you can take appropriate and effective action.

**RESOURCES ON TRACKING**
(full listings in **Resources** at end of this chapter)

*Crossing the Tracks: How "Untracking" Can Save America's Schools*, by Anne Wheelock, 1992

*Multiplying Inequalities: The Effects of Race, Social Class, and Tracking on Opportunities to Learn Mathematics and Science*, by Jeannie Oakes, 1990

In "Assessing Opportunities to Learn" in Chapter 3 we offered several suggestions about where to begin your inquiry into possible inequitable opportunities by:

▼ examining disaggregated enrollment data to see if patterns emerge in course taking, especially in algebra and geometry and in higher-level sciences;

▼ comparing enrollment with test performance to see if minority students who score well are being excluded from high-level courses;

▼ looking at master schedules to see if some course sequences never lead to algebra or geometry;

▼ disaggregating special education and gifted program placement data to see who might be over- or underrepresented;

▼ seeing if low-track teachers are as experienced or as qualified to teach matematics or science as high-track teachers;

▼ checking for equal access to computers and other technology.

In addition, you can focus your investigation on the extent to which standards-based instruction is available to all students with tools offered in Chapter 4.

Because ability grouping takes many forms, some intentional and some not, it is often difficult to sort out which grouping practices in your school are inequitable and which are actually beneficial to diverse learners. Robert Slavin (1988) and Jeannie Oakes (O'Neil 1992) offer some helpful guidelines: be suspicious of equity problems if ability-grouping is occurring between classes as opposed to within classes, if students are in low-ability groups for a good part of the day, and if they are stigmatized by their placement and receiving a substantially different curriculum than other students. In the following section, we take a look at some common examples of ability grouping in schools and, with Slavin's and Oakes' guidelines in mind, offer some questions for further inquiry.

## Is This Tracking?

**1. A middle school has a remedial and/or an honors group, but all other classes are heterogeneous.**

Are students in remedial and/or honors groups together in their ability groups most of each day? Is the curriculum substantially different between remedial and other groups? What is the quality of teaching in each group? of the learning environment? Are better qualified, more experienced teachers teaching the honors group? Are students in the low track stigmatized? How are judgments made about who is in each group? What is the racial and economic composition of each group? What are the long-term implications of being in the remedial group? What happens to these students later in school and after?

**2. A high school offers a special course in remedial mathematics for students who are judged as not ready for algebra.**

How are these judgments made? Are students encouraged to try algebra with additional support? What are the actual prerequisite skills and knowledge for success in algebra? What specific skills and concepts do these individuals need? Does the remedial course help them acquire these skills and concepts? Can students transition to algebra when ready? Is remedial mathematics a bridge to higher-level mathematics or a life sentence to a low-track experience? How can algebra be taught in ways that engage students with different learning styles, such as using manipulatives, technology, and real-world problems familiar to diverse students' experience? How can students who need help in specific areas get that help when they need it without being labeled "remedial" and becoming dependent on remediation?

**3. A high school is considering expanding its science course offerings to attract students who are not currently taking three or four years of science.**

Is the course rich in science content, inquiry-based, relevant to students' future career or higher education aspirations, engaging for a wide range of students? Does the school encourage a wide range of students, including those taking other academic science courses, to enroll?

4. **A high school offers honors and Advanced Placement mathematics and science courses that attract the "brightest" students.**

Are honors and Advanced Placement viewed as the exclusive realm of the "elite" rather than as an opportunity for those students who want the challenge and are ready to work hard? Are some students who have the desire discouraged from taking an honors course because of past grades even though they want to give it a try? Do unnecessary barriers block access to these courses, such as grade requirements or pressure to pay for Advanced Placement tests? To what extent does honors and Advanced Placement enrollment reflect the diversity of your student body?

As you inquire into tracking practices in your own school, you can supplement quantitative data with qualitative data about how students in different tracks experience their school day. Shadowing, a research technique that involves actually following a student, one-on-one, through their school day, can be a powerful tool for capturing this kind of information. Teachers and administrators who have shadowed students, especially those in low tracks, report that it is an eye-opening experience. Interviewing or conducting focus groups with students and their parents is another way to gain more perspective on the impact of grouping practices on students' lives.

In addition to these qualitative data collection ideas, the **Data Tools** contain two checklists that can help you self-assess your tracking practices. One, entitled "The Checklist: Assessing the Tracking Practices in Your School" by Eleanor Linn and Norma Barquet (**Data Tools**, DT 5-1), examines broad issues related to tracking, such as policies, culture evaluation procedures, and the needs of special education students and English language learners.

We also include Anne Wheelock's assessment of readiness for untracking and an accompanying action planning form ("Get Ready, Get Set: A Readiness Assessment for Untracking," **Data Tools**, DT 5-2). Wheelock's assessment reminds us that while untracking is a worthy goal, it needs to be approached thoughtfully and with critical supports such as ongoing professional development in place. Schools and districts are taking many creative and successful approaches to untracking: making curriculum and instruction more engaging and relevant for all students, involving parents, implementing cooperative and project-based learning, and restructuring vocational education. We urge teams inquiring into tracking and untracking to consult the growing body of research on these topics (see **Resources on Tracking** and **Resources for Winning Approaches to Untracking**, pages 263 and 264).

## Developing a Data Collection Plan

The form in **Planning Tools**, page 301 and illustrated below, can help you develop a data collection plan for examining structural barriers to equity.

Data Collection Plan

### Looking at Structural Barriers to Equity

| Problem/ Question | *To what extent do structural barriers result in some students (poor, minority, English language learners, girls, others) having less opportunity to learn mathematics and science than others? To what extent is tracking (de facto or intentional) practiced in our school?* | | | | |
|---|---|---|---|---|---|
| **Data Sources/Tools We Want to Use** | **Got It** | **Need It** | **Disaggregated by** | **How/When Collected** | **Person Responsible** |
| | | | | | |

## Taking Action and Digging Deeper

What if your inquiry uncovers structural barriers to equity in your school? Using the process outlined in Chapter 3, you will want to research possible solutions and develop systemic action plans focused on eliminating these barriers. But often these structural barriers signal the presence of another problem: deep-seated racist, classist, and sexist belief systems that are incompatible with "success for all." In the next section, we explore these beliefs.

*Untracking: "Dismantling unproductive grouping practices that have undermined education for all but a few students."*

*(Wheelock 1992, 1)*

# Beliefs That Block Equity

Why, despite overwhelming evidence that tracking does not work, does it prevail? Why do gaps in mathematics and science achievement between rich and poor, white and minority, persist despite decades of reform? Why do practices like cooperative learning fail to catch on widely despite their well-documented success for all students?

The answer to these questions lies in deep-seated beliefs that perpetuate unequal opportunities and outcomes—beliefs that are incompatible with success for all. This section examines three sets of beliefs that are pervasive in our society and our schools, so pervasive that, like the air we breathe, we may not even be aware of them. They are not the beliefs we espouse or put in our mission statements. But, intentional or not, they shape the way we treat children. These include beliefs about the nature of intelligence and the purpose of schools, the abilities of poor, minority, and female students, and the nature of mathematics and science.

## "There Are Only So Many 'Smarts' to Go Around"

Jeff Howard, a social psychologist and founder of the Efficacy Institute in Waltham, Massachusetts (see **Resources**, page 318) gets right to the point: "Our approach to educating children is failing because the attitudes that underlie it are wrong" (1991, 1). He describes these attitudes as the "innate ability paradigm," which is based on three simple (and false!) assumptions:

▼ There is a distribution of intelligence in the population ranging from "very smart" to "sorta smart" to "kinda dumb" (in kid terms).

▼ How much intelligence you have determines what you can learn and what you can be in life.

▼ All this can be sorted out through standardized testing and teacher observation (1991, 4).

One outgrowth of this paradigm is our educational system's obsession with testing and labeling. Think of all the labels you may hear in the course of a school day: ADD, LD, LEP, SPED, gifted, at risk, Title I . . . Even before kindergarten, children are subjected to testing that is specifically designed to shake out differences, identify deficiencies, and compare one child to another. Minor differences in performance, representing only a few months'

---

*"A major obstacle to equity is that we keep trying to avoid seeing children. We want to resort to some way of sorting and classifying. We are insistent in making truer their deficiencies than their capacities."*

(Patricia Carini, former Director, Prospect Archive and Center for Education and Research, North Bennington, Vermont, interview, 1998)

*"No matter what their socioeconomic background, race, or gender, babies of similar ages tend to perform similarly on the basic [cognitive] test."*

(Denton 1990, as cited in Hilliard 1991, 34)

difference in cognitive development, can determine what label a child may get tagged with for his or her entire school career (Howard 1991, 5).

Anne Martin, a kindergarten teacher in Brookline, Massachusetts, expressed her dismay and anger at the effect of testing on children just entering school, many of whom are quickly identified as "at risk" on highly dubious grounds:

> These young children, often not yet five years old, were being sorted out and categorized with little allowance for the infinite variety of their learning styles and developmental patterns . . .

> . . . there is no way that twenty minutes of contact and a set of test scores can adequately describe a child's potential to learn. All children come to school as complex persons with their own unique backgrounds and sets of experiences. For me the fascination of each new school year is the gradual revelation of this complexity . . . (1988, 489–90)

If all this sorting helped so-called "slow" learners catch up, that would be one thing. But the opposite is true. Once a child is labeled as slow, teachers, counselors, and administrators start expecting less. Low expectations undermine confidence; lack of confidence undercuts performance; and the downward spiral of self-fulfilling prophecy begins. Any small gap in performance that may have existed initially tends to grow over the years, despite special services students may receive (Howard 1991). And, saddest of all, the children themselves come to believe the labels.

## "All Kids Can Learn Except . . .": The Devastating Effects of Racism, Classism, and Sexism

*"I have heard teachers say that math is a good indicator of how successful students will be and that some have it and some don't. Until we question that assumption, nothing is going to change."*

(Joy Wallace, Equity Specialist, Columbia Education Center, Portland, Oregon, interview, 1998)

---

**"During a science** lesson, a primary school teacher asked students to brainstorm what they knew about eggs as she held up a sample. Some students offered characteristics such as 'oval,' 'white,' and 'gooey on the inside' and were praised for their answers. A Latina student offered an example of a time she had cooked eggs with her grandmother. Her answer was ignored, considered irrelevant by the teacher."

(Presenter, Institute on Cultural and Linguistic Diversity, 1997)

> **"A fourth-grade** teacher stood in shock when she learned that an African American student who was failing mathematics was single-handedly managing the family budget. 'How could I have overlooked her obvious strengths in mathematics?' "
>
> (Panelist, Institute on Cultural and Linguistic Diversity, 1997)

*"Prejudice is a preconceived judgment or opinion, usually based on limited information."*

(Tatum 1997, 5)

When the innate ability paradigm meets racism, classism, and sexism, the results are devastating for poor, minority, and female students; they are the ones most often judged as less intelligent. These ideologies are more than individual prejudices: they involve a whole system of cultural messages and institutional policies and practices, such as tracking, differential allocations of resources, and unequal access to jobs, housing, and power (Tatum 1997, 7; Weissglass [1997], 102). Eliminating individual prejudices is a necessary but not sufficient condition for equity. These deeply ingrained institutional practices and power relationships have also got to go.

One of the most pernicious forms of institutional racism, classism, and sexism is the way in which children are sorted in schools by their supposed "intelligence." Society's image of the "very smart" student is one with white, middle-class behaviors and values. If students don't fit that image, if they are culturally different, they are judged to be less intelligent. "There is a rumor of inferiority that follows minority children to school," says Jeff Howard (1991, 6–7). Students who have not yet mastered English are also judged less capable, especially when it comes to mathematics and science. Girls are considered to be not as smart as boys in these subjects, and the poor are judged to be inferior by almost any measure to the rich.

"Children from middle class homes tend to do better in school than those from non-middle class homes because the culture of school is based on the culture of the upper and middle classes of those in power," explains Lisa Delpit (1995, 25). For Delpit, the culture of power consists of ways of talking, writing, dressing, and interacting; success is based on learning the rules and codes of the dominant society. She advocates explicitly teaching students these rules and codes, acknowledging the power relationships that exist, while encouraging students to express their own culture and language style.

Cultural differences emerge in subtle ways in the classroom. For instance, students from different cultures have different styles of recounting events, writing, and arguing, all important activities in mathematics and science classrooms. Without understanding these differences, teachers may judge certain students as having nothing to contribute, missing important steps in a procedure, or being disorganized (Estrin 1993).

Take the example of the Latina in the vignette above. When asked what she knew about eggs, she offered a story about making eggs with her grand-mother. In Latino culture, social relationships are an important way that children experience and understand their world (Sinha and Tripahti 1994). She was, as the teacher invited, connecting the egg to *her* prior knowledge and experience. The teacher, however, was looking for more objective descriptions of the egg—oval, white, has a shell—but never specified that that was what she expected. She was operating out of the dominant culture's assumptions without teaching culturally different children what the rules were. The result was to discount the child's response and teach her that her contributions have no value in that classroom.

The second example, about the fourth-grader who managed the family budget, illustrates another way racism blinds us to students' strengths. Many poor and minority students are successfully running households and busi-nesses at very young ages. Outside school, they use mathematics, verbal, reasoning, and management skills on a daily basis. They are, as Connecticut equity activist Mj Terry remarked ironically, "only dumb in school."

*". . . racism [is] a 'system of advantage based on race.'"*

(Wellman 1977, as cited in Tatum 1997, 7)

## Mathematics and Science: The Special Realm of the "Very Smart"

"'**What do you** think you are not smart enough to do?' Jeff Howard asked a group of Efficacy Workshop participants seated around a giant conference table. An uncomfortable silence took over the room as participants realized that they themselves, a group of adult educators, had been victims of the innate ability paradigm. Some wept, others spoke with anger as they recalled vividly when and where it was—Mrs. Kramer's fourth grade, geometry class, the guidance coun-selor's office—that they learned they were not smart enough. For virtually every African American and female participant, the answer was higher-level mathematics or science."

(Participant, Efficacy Institute workshop, 1986)

A third set of beliefs comes into play specifically in relation to mathematics and science: that these subjects are the special realm of the "very smart." This is based on a view of science as a set of authoritative facts accessible only to experts. Those who do well in science tend to be students who can "talk. . . like science books do" (Lemke 1990, as cited in Warren and Rosebery 1993, 3). A similar view of mathematics is that it too is a static body of knowledge. If mathematics is viewed as memorizing formulas and giving quick responses to lots of questions that have right answers, then students who do that well are considered to be good at mathematics (Julian Weissglass, interview, 1997).

These views of mathematics and science contrast sharply with those put forward in the national standards. The standards advocate for mathematics and science as dynamic pursuits involving asking questions that may never be answered, making meaning, solving problems, discussing ideas with peers, and using common sense. This view is potentially more inclusive of diverse students (if other barriers to equity are addressed), as the vignette below illustrates.

---

**"I was observing** a child who had difficulty with computation. That was disturbing to him and his family. Then we started to notice some things. In almost any kind of discussion, he would be a person who would state a point of view and then argue it from another angle and subvert his own statement. We looked at his writing. He wrote about knights and warriors' adventures. In one story, he wrote about how many heartbeats it took them to get to the cave. That reminded us that he was a good estimator. We began to put things together about this child. He didn't trust absolutes. He saw a more complicated picture—much more mathematical than numerical. He saw complicated relations and patterns, so we thought it better to start from geometry, patterns, approximation and not keep beating away at computation. It is so important that we have a larger picture of what math and science are. The bigger the picture, the more children we can include."

(Patricia Carini, former Director, Prospect Archive and Center for Education and Research, North Bennington, Vermont, interview, 1998)

Right now our picture of mathematics and science, of schools, and of human potential is still too small to include *all* children. The belief systems described above—the innate ability paradigm; racism, classism, and sexism; and elitist views of mathematics—continue to have a strong hold on our schools, our policies, and our practices. Making schools work for all children will require honest examination of these belief systems and a concerted effort to eradicate them in all of their manifestations.

## Examining Belief Systems

Examining belief systems takes courage and conviction. It is a true measure of our "will to educate all children," for it is only by breaking the silence about racism, classism, and sexism that we can begin to break their grip on our society and our schools. Because beliefs are intangible, examining them is much more complex than collecting and analyzing student learning data, although it may begin there. How can teams begin to gain a better understanding of these powerful, yet elusive, belief systems and how they influence what we do? In this section we offer four questions to guide your inquiry into beliefs, with suggested approaches and relevant resources for each.

## How Does Racial, Class, Cultural, and Gender Bias Manifest in School and Classroom Practices?

Although beliefs themselves are invisible, they nonetheless manifest in what we do and say. One window into beliefs is the more objective forms of data collection about student performance and school policies and practices discussed above. For example, gaps in student performance and opportunities to learn signal the prevalence of certain assumptions about students and their potential. As you look at practices such as tracking or course enrollment and counseling procedures, you can also ask yourself what beliefs drive these practices. As you evaluate special education or English language learners programs, consider the deeper assumptions that underlie them. Classroom practice offers another window into belief systems. Later in this chapter we discuss how to monitor unequal expectations and treatment in the classroom and how to scrutinize curriculum, instruction, and assessment practices for overt and subtle biases—two other avenues for exploring belief systems in practice.

*". . . To really examine my class and how I deal with the students and other people, it changes you. I think that there's a lot of lip service. . . To really be conscious of equity and effectively deal with equity in the classroom, you have to open yourself up and look at yourself."*

(European American teacher, as cited in Weissglass [1997], 122)

## How Can Individuals Come to Grips with Prejudice and Its Effect on Their Lives?

Another whole avenue of investigation into beliefs is far more subjective and personal. It involves looking at our own beliefs and experiences and how prejudice and discrimination have affected us. "Although we may feel afraid," says Julian Weissglass, Director of the Equity in Mathematics Education Leadership Institute (EMELI), "avoiding the issues through denial or intellectualization will be harmful in the long run" (Weissglass [1997], 122). (For more on EMELI, see **Resources**, page 319.)

Weissglass believes that addressing prejudice and discrimination can be productive if it focuses on people telling their personal stories, listening intently to each other, and avoiding blaming, criticizing, and analyzing. In his work with mathematics educators, he uses such structures as dyads ("the exchange of constructivist listening between two people" [p. 45]), support groups, and personal experience panels to facilitate constructive and deep dialogue about equity issues. Guidelines for structuring this dialogue are summarized in the box below.

### Principles for Dialogue about Prejudice and Discrimination

1. Only one form of discrimination is addressed at a time.

2. Everyone in the group is listened to attentively about their own experiences, beliefs, thoughts, and feelings.

3. Participants have the opportunity to reflect deeply in dyads (pairs) on their assumptions about equity.

4. It is recognized that the origin of present interpersonal difficulties is often in early distress experiences, cultural and racial biases, and societal discrimination.

5. Those who have not experienced a particular form of discrimination listen respectfully (without analysis or debate) to the personal experiences of people who have been discriminated against.

6. Listeners get a chance (in dyads, support groups, discussions) to talk about how they found out about prejudice toward or mistreatment of the group in question and their own experiences at the time.

7. All participants have the opportunity to talk about their common mistreatment as learners and as children.

8. Participants have the opportunity to talk or write about what they have learned and their next steps (or goals) in working for social justice in their personal lives, classrooms, or schools (Weissglass [1997], 122).

Using these principles, you can engage in productive conversations about questions such as those below.

### EXPLORING PREJUDICE AND DISCRIMINATION: QUESTIONS TO CONSIDER

▼ What personal experiences have helped you understand your own prejudices? What has helped you understand better how inequity and discrimination affect education?

▼ What productive educational experiences that address prejudice and discrimination have you participated in? What has been ineffective?

▼ What support do teachers, parents, administrators have in your school district to address equity issues? What else is needed?

▼ From your experience, what do people have trouble listening to concerning prejudice and discrimination? What do you think is the source of their difficulty?

▼ What can you do to see that equity is addressed productively in your school community? Take some time to write down some short-range and long-range goals for yourself in this area.

▼ How did you first learn about the mistreatment of someone different (racial, gender, economic class, physical difference) from yourself? Who was this person? How did you feel? What were the questions you wanted to ask? (Weissglass [1997], 124)

## Who Are Our Students? How Can We Better Understand and Appreciate Their Cultural Backgrounds?

A third avenue for inquiry into belief systems is to learn more about your students and their cultural backgrounds. If you have not done this already, first collect and analyze straight demographic data about your school's student population (see **Data Tools**, DT 3–2). For many schools, like the one in the first example at the beginning of this chapter, having a realistic picture of who your students are can be a real eye-opener. Also gather information about demographic trends in your area so you can project what your student population might look like in the future. Figure 5.6 illustrates national demographic trends. How do trends in your area compare?

**FIGURE 5.6: PERCENT CHANGE IN 0- TO 24-YEAR-OLDS, BY RACE/ETHNICITY AND AGE: 1993 TO 2000**

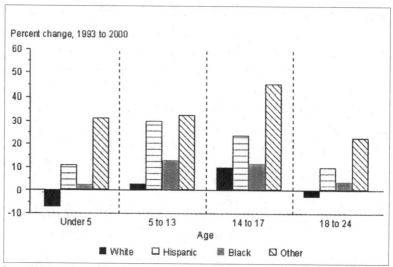

Source: U.S. Department of Commerce, Bureau of the Census, Current Population Reports, Population Projections of the United States, by Age, Sex, Race, and Hispanic Origin: 1993 to 2050 and U.S. Population Estimates, by Age, Sex, Race, and Hispanic Origin: 1990 to 1994, PPL–21.

The school-age population (ages 5 to 17) is expected to increase through the end of the century. Increasing numbers of minorities are expected in all age groups. The white non-Hispanic population will decrease by about 7 percent in the preschool age range and by about 3 percent in the college age range between 1993 and 2000. The population of Asians and American Indians in the high school age range is expected to increase even more rapidly than other groups.

Once you know your school's demographics, the next challenge is to understand more about the culture of the children those numbers represent. What are their traditions and languages? How does their culture shape the way they make sense of the world and experience school? Inquiring into your students' cultures requires going much deeper than learning about food or music or dress. It involves, as Lisa Delpit puts it so eloquently,

> . . . seeking out those whose perspectives may differ most, by learning to give their words complete attention, by understanding one's own power, even if that power stems merely from being in the majority, by being unafraid to raise questions about discrimination and voicelessness with people of color, and to listen, no, to hear what they say. (1995, 47)

*"By culture, we mean traditions, language, and daily experiences of the home and community."*

(Williams and Newcombe 1994, 76)

By carefully listening to and observing students in a nonjudgmental way, teachers can learn a great deal about their students' cultural backgrounds, what knowledge and experience they bring to school, and how they learn best (see information about Descriptive Processes, page 275). Ewa Pytowska, Assistant Superintendent of Schools in Central Falls, Rhode Island, where 70 percent of students speak another language at home, uses culturally meaningful literature as a way to give voice to children and promote teachers' understanding:

> Multicultural literature can turn teachers' negative perceptions of children into positive appreciation of their language, culture, and learning capacities. When I read children books which are familiar to them and congruent with their sense of the world, they know what questions to ask, what to pay attention to, and what statements to make about the stories. This is true of all children, but especially those with limited formal schooling, just learning English, or placed in special education. When teachers see this happening with a child they perceive as a problem, they begin to question themselves. They are more likely to ask "What's wrong with my teaching?" than "What's wrong with this child?" Multicultural literature helps teachers to see how much their children already know, but cannot share in a standard American classroom. (Ewa Pytowska, interview, 1999)

Other ways to deepen your understanding of your students' cultures are to talk to parents, visit their communities, and read about their cultures. You can also survey or interview students and parents to learn more about how they perceive themselves, their children's future, and their school (see "Listening to Student Voices: Measuring Aspirations" in Chapter 3). Taking the time to investigate your students' cultures can help bridge the gap between teachers and their increasingly diverse students.

**RESOURCES FOR LEARNING ABOUT STUDENTS' CULTURES**
(full listings in **Resources** at end of this chapter)

*Connecting Cultures: A Guide to Multicultural Literature for Children,* by Rebecca L. Thomas, 1996

*Multicultural Literature for Children and Young Adults: Volume 2, 1991–1996,* by Ginny Moore Kruse, Kathleen T. Horning, and Megan Schliesman, 1997

*Multicultural Teaching: A Handbook of Activities, Information, and Resources,* by Pamela L. Tiedt and Iris M. Tiedt, 1995

## How Can We Learn to Recognize Students' Strengths?

**A group of** seven teachers from the Lawrence School in Brookline, Massachusetts, squeezes around a child-size table in a primary school classroom after school one afternoon to do something they have been doing on a monthly basis for years: working together to better understand their students' strengths. Today a kindergarten teacher is presenting drawings done by a student whose impulsive outbursts have been upsetting her and the classroom. "These sessions give me hope," she explains. "I see things about the children I never saw before. Then, instead of giving up on them, I have an idea of how I can build on their strengths." The meeting follows a set structure, with a facilitator guiding participants through a sequence of activities and carefully summarizing after each. Most of the time is spent in a go-round, where participants describe what they see in Adam's drawings without judging, classifying, or using clinical terms or labels—just their impressions. "I'm struck by the fish." "I see a lot of attention to what color is being used." Each go-round probes a little deeper, revealing more about the patterns, symmetry, use of color, attention to detail, and variations in the child's work.

A fourth area of inquiry, closely related to understanding students' cultural backgrounds, is recognizing diverse students' strengths. The teachers in the vignette above are using a method called the "Prospect Center's Description of Work Process," one of three Descriptive Processes developed by the Prospect School in North Bennington, Vermont (see **Data Tools**, DT 2-6, and the Prospect Archive and Center for Education and Research in **Resources**, page 321). The Descriptive Processes provide a structure for teachers to come together to discuss their observations of students and their work in a descriptive rather than a judgmental way. Structured group processes such as these can help teachers discard cultural biases and discover students' strengths.

Fully appreciating diverse students' strengths requires a shift from the innate ability paradigm to a new set of assumptions about learners and schools. Research for Better Schools in Philadelphia, in their framework for working with urban students, offers some guiding principles for building on the strengths of urban (and other underserved) learners:

▼ Urban students bring to schools cultural strengths and learning experiences that must be reflected in curriculum, instruction, and school routines.

▼ Culture plays a fundamental role in cognitive development. While many of us were taught that intelligence is genetically determined, unitary, and fixed at birth, psychologists now argue that intelligence is modifiable, multi-faceted, and mediated by the cultural environment.

▼ Motivation and effort are as important to learning as are innate abilities. Urban students will benefit from school environments in which they can learn from their mistakes, are effortful in their learning, and fully engage themselves (Bernal 1992 and Stevenson and Stigler 1992, as cited in Williams and Newcombe 1994).

▼ Resilience is a characteristic of urban learners. Despite adverse conditions, many urban children grow into healthy, responsible, productive adults. These "resilient" children display characteristics of social competence, autonomy, problem solving, and a sense of the future (Williams and Newcombe 1994, 76).

Based on these assumptions, we offer the following questions to guide your inquiry into diverse students' strengths:

---

**RESOURCES FOR EXAMINING BELIEF SYSTEMS**
(full listings in **Resources** at end of this chapter)

"Building on the Strengths of Urban Learners," by Belinda Williams and Ellen Newcombe, *Educational Leadership* 51(8) (1994): 75–78

"Do We Have the Will to Educate All Children?" by Asa Hilliard, *Educational Leadership* 49(1) (1991): 31–36

*Other People's Children: Cultural Conflict in the Classroom*, by Lisa Delpit, 1995

*Ripples of Hope: Building Relationships for Educational Change*, by Julian Weissglass, [1997]

The Efficacy Institute, Waltham, MA

Equity in Mathematics Education Leadership Institute (EMELI), University of California, Santa Barbara, CA

The Prospect Archive and Center for Education and Research, North Bennington, VT

### INQUIRING INTO STUDENTS' STRENGTHS:
### QUESTIONS TO CONSIDER

▼ What are the strengths of our diverse students? Do we recognize their resilience, social competence, autonomy, and problem-solving abilities?

▼ How do our curriculum, instruction, and school routine reflect the strengths of diverse students?

▼ To what extent do we believe that intelligence is not fixed at birth, but changeable based on the cultural environment? How would our school practices change if we fully embraced this belief?

▼ How do we encourage students to learn from mistakes and connect effort to achievement?

▼ What structures, such as the Tuning Protocol or the Descriptive Review Process (see **Data Tools**, DT 2-5 and DT 2-6), for collegial reflection can we use to support us in discarding cultural biases and recognizing students' strengths?

## Developing a Data Collection Plan

The form in **Planning Tools**, page 303 and illustrated below, summarizes possible data sources for each of the four questions about beliefs posed in the section above. You can use it to develop your own data collection plan.

Data Collection Plan

## Examining Beliefs That Block Equity

| Problem/ Question | *How prevalent are these belief systems in our school? How do they manifest in school and classroom practices? How can individuals come to grips with their own prejudice and its effect on their lives? Who are our students? How can we better understand their cultural backgrounds? How can we learn to recognize students' strengths?* | | | | |
|---|---|---|---|---|---|
| **Data Sources/Tools We Want to Use** | **Got It** | **Need It** | **Disaggregated by** | **How/When Collected** | **Person Responsible** |
| | | | | | |

## Taking Action and Digging Deeper

Examining beliefs that block equity in itself represents important action. By beginning a constructive dialogue about them, your school community will already have taken significant steps toward change. But exploration of equity is a multilayered process; initial questions inevitably lead to more questions, such as how beliefs affect our expectations and treatment of students. We address this subject in the next section.

# Unequal Expectations and Treatment

Most educators believe that their expectations for children have a strong influence on students' confidence and performance. They are right. Most also believe that teachers have the same expectations for all children, regardless of class, color, or gender. They, unfortunately, are wrong. We now have decades of research that show that teachers tend to expect less of poor, minority, and female students and treat them differently in the classroom. These students receive less attention, praise, "wait time," and feedback than their white and male peers (see vignette and box below). And, because "what you expect is what you get," students quickly learn to sink to the teachers' lower standards.

*"A lot of what happens in a classroom boils down to teacher expectations."*

(Joy Wallace, Equity Specialist, Columbia Education Center, Portland, Oregon, interview, 1998)

*"Our current ceiling for students is much closer to where the floor ought to be."*

(Hilliard 1991, 35)

**Recently, the Montgomery** County (Maryland) Schools completed an analysis of its eighth-grade mathematics test scores and the likelihood of success in ninth-grade algebra. The study showed that white and Asian students who scored 650 or above on the eighth-grade test were more likely to pass ninth-grade algebra than African American or Latino students who scored just as well in eighth grade. The administration identified teacher expectations as the "driving factor" in the mathematics achievement gap and is instituting programs to raise them, including providing teachers with more data about student performance and encouraging them to adapt instruction to reach all students in their classes.

(*Washington Post*, Dec. 9, 1998)

## The Expectations Gap: What Research Shows

### Teacher-student interactions

▼ Teachers initiated significantly more mathematics interactions with males than females (Fennema and Peterson, as cited in Grayson and Martin 1997, 24).

▼ African American girls had fewer interactions with teachers than did white girls, despite evidence that they attempted to initiate interactions more frequently (AAUW 1992, 70).

▼ African American and Latino males were interacted with at a deficit rate of 27% less than their class representation (Grayson, as cited in Grayson and Martin 1997, 24).

### Wait time

▼ The average time that a teacher waited for a student to respond to a question was 2.6 seconds. The teacher waited an average of 5.0 seconds if a correct response was anticipated and less than 1.0 second if the student was expected to give an incorrect response or not to respond at all (Grayson and Martin 1997, 47).

▼ Perceived low-achieving students received an average of 0.9 seconds of wait time (Sadker and Sadker, as cited in Grayson and Martin 1997, 47).

▼ Even when high- and low-achieving students exhibited the same behavior—frowning, scratching their heads, asking the question to be repeated—teachers assumed the high achiever was thinking through the problem but reprimanded the low achiever for not having the answer (Good and Brophy, as cited in Grayson and Martin 1997, 47).

### Discipline

▼ Even when males and females were misbehaving equally, the males were more likely to get harsher reprimands (Serbin et al., as cited in Grayson and Martin 1997, 71). If the offenders were mixed by race or ethnicity, an African American or Latino student received a harsher reprimand than a white student.

▼ Minority students, especially African Americans, were the most harshly treated, especially when measured by school suspension records or referrals (Grayson and Martin 1997, 69).

### Quality of feedback

▼ Teachers were more likely to say "o.k." to African American students (females and males) than to European American students, whether or not their answer was correct, thus leaving the African American student with little information about the quality of his or her performance (Sadker and Sadker, as cited in Grayson and Martin 1997, 106).

▼ When students responded correctly in high-level mathematics, teachers ignored the females more often than they did males (Fennema and Peterson, as cited in Grayson and Martin 1997, 25).

# From Gatekeeper to Advocate for All Students: Reforming the Role of the Guidance Counselor

Outside the classroom, guidance counselors' expectations are another powerful influence on students. But many counselors, unfortunately, help to perpetuate the practice of tracking poor and minority students into dead-end courses and second-class futures. They also tend to try to "protect" girls from too much academic pressure by not "pushing" higher-level mathematics and science (Campbell and Storo 1996). Because of their influential gatekeeper role, however, counselors are in an equally powerful position to become positive forces for change and should be included in mathematics and science education reform efforts.

EQUITY 2000, a district-based reform initiative of the College Board, makes the following recommendations for reforming guidance practices:

- ▼ start in the elementary and middle school to provide information to parents and students about careers and college;

- ▼ work as an integral part of an instructional team;

- ▼ use data to analyze and improve student learning;

- ▼ use group counseling and classroom guidance sessions;

- ▼ encourage all students to enroll in rigorous academic courses;

- ▼ build support systems with colleges, businesses, and community organizations (Lennon et al. 1996).

It is also critical that principals and other administrators consider how bias may influence their treatment of students and staff and take a leadership role in promoting equity at all levels. The Generating Expectations for Student Achievement (GESA) program has developed a special program for administrators for this purpose. See **Resources**, page 320).

## Investigating Unequal Expectations and Treatment

Since most school staff are not aware that they treat students differently, data about the use of praise, wait time, discipline, feedback, and other specific interactions can help raise awareness about unequal expectations and treatment. Classroom observations are probably the best way to collect data about teacher expectations in your own school, especially when staff development is provided in what to look for, how to collect data, and how to process what you learn. The Generating Expectations for Student Achievement (GESA) program is a wonderful example of a staff development program that helps teachers use classroom observations to confront bias in the classroom (see **Resources**, page 320). The **Data Tools**, DT 5-3, contain a sample form for collecting classroom observation data, "Observation Sheet for Verbal Interaction Assessment," which is also illustrated below (Figure 5.7). This sheet could be adapted to observe interactions with racial and ethnic groups as well.

**FIGURE 5.7: OBSERVATION SHEET FOR VERBAL INTERACTION ASSESSMENT**

```
Directions
     For each category indicated, tally the teacher comments
directed at boys and girls.  Refer to the definition of each
category if necessary (see page 89).
```

|  | Teachers Comments Directed at: | | | |
|---|---|---|---|---|
|  | Boys | Total | Girls | Total |
| **I. Praise** | | | | |
| A. Academic | ___ | ___ | ___ | ___ |
| B. Nonacademic | ___ | ___ | ___ | ___ |
| **II. Academic Criticism** | | | | |
| A. Intellectual quality | ___ | ___ | ___ | ___ |
| B. Effort | ___ | ___ | ___ | ___ |
| **III. Nonacademic Criticism** | | | | |
| A. Mild | ___ | ___ | ___ | ___ |
| B. Harsh | ___ | ___ | ___ | ___ |
| **IV. Questions** | | | | |
| A. Low level | ___ | ___ | ___ | ___ |
| B. High level | ___ | ___ | ___ | ___ |
| **V. Academic Intervention** | | | | |
| A. Facilitative | ___ | ___ | ___ | ___ |
| B. Disruptive | ___ | ___ | ___ | ___ |

Surveys can also be useful in gathering information about teacher and guidance counselor expectations and practices. Three sample surveys are included in the **Data Tools** of this chapter; one focuses on teacher expectations, "Survey of Mathematics Teachers" (DT 5-4), one on guidance counselor expectations, "Survey of Milwaukee Guidance Counselors" (DT 5-5), and one on counseling practices, "Characteristics of High-Performing and Low-Performing Counseling Programs" (DT 5-6). A fourth survey including information on teachers' expectations, "Perceptions of Attitudes, Readiness and Commitment to Change," can be found in the **Data Tools** of Chapter 3 (DT 3-1). Finally, going to the source, by shadowing, interviewing, or surveying students, can also be very revealing. (See sample student surveys, "Student Gender Equity Survey," in **Data Tools**, DT 5-7, and "Student Speak: My Education and My Future, Grades 3–5," **Data Tools**, DT 3-28.)

## INVESTIGATING UNEQUAL EXPECTATIONS AND TREATMENT: QUESTIONS TO CONSIDER

▼ What can we learn about teacher expectations for students by examining classroom behaviors such as teacher-student interactions, wait time, discipline, and quality of feedback?

▼ What guidance counselor practices may be perpetuating low expectations for some students?

▼ What can students tell us about how they experience teacher and guidance counselor expectations?

▼ What administrative practices and policies reinforce low expectations for students?

## Developing a Data Collection Plan

The form in **Planning Tools**, page 303 and illustrated below, can help you plan for collecting data to probe the problem of unequal expectations.

Data Collection Plan

## Investigating Unequal Expectations and Treatment

| Problem/ Question | To what extent do unequal expectations affect how we treat students? | | | | |
|---|---|---|---|---|---|
| Data Sources/Tools We Want to Use | Got It | Need It | Disaggregated by | How/When Collected | Person Responsible |
| | | | | | |

## Taking Action and Digging Deeper

As you probe the problem of unequal expectations, your team may be surprised to learn what a strong grip unconscious biases have on how school staff treat children. When these inequities are brought to light through your

**RESOURCES FOR INVESTIGATING EXPECTATIONS**

(full listings at end of this chapter in **Resources**)

*Whose Responsibility Is It? The Role of Administrators and Guidance Counselors* (part of *Math and Science for the Coed Classroom* pamphlet series), by Patricia B. Campbell and Jennifer N. Storo, 1996

Generating Expectations for Student Achievement (GESA), Canyon Lake, CA

EQUITY 2000 (The College Board), New York, NY

data collection, you can then take steps toward fairer treatment of all students. In the next section, you will learn how biases permeate curriculum, instruction, and assessments and how to use data to move toward more inclusive classrooms.

# Racial, Class, Cultural, and Gender Bias in Curriculum, Instruction, and Assessment

There is no doubt that wide-scale implementation of the kind of reform called for in the national standards documents will benefit many students. Curriculum that emphasizes topics that affect students' lives, draws on their immediate environment, develops higher-order thinking and problem-solving abilities, and is rich with challenging and interconnected concepts extends the opportunity to learn to more children. So does a wide repertoire of instructional strategies, including cooperative and experiential learning. Assessment practices that are aligned with curriculum and instruction and provide multiple ways for students to demonstrate their knowledge are much fairer to diverse students than traditional testing. But these reforms will not go far enough if racial, class, cultural, and gender biases are not directly challenged.

For example, it is crucial to carefully screen curriculum materials for biases. These biases show up in mathematics and science curriculum materials in what *is* and *is not* included. What is included may be discriminatory language and stereotypes. What is left out may be important ways that culturally different students can "see themselves" in the curriculum. For example, they need to see references to people like themselves who have contributed to mathematics and science. They need to see ways that they can apply what they are learning to careers to which they can realistically aspire. Equally important, they need to see examples from their own daily lives in the curriculum. We know that to learn something new, students must connect new learning to prior knowledge. But what happens to a Latina student, for example, who can see little of herself or her own life in the science or mathematics curriculum? How likely is she to make those essential connections?

Hubert Dyasi, who works with teachers and students in Harlem through the Workshop Center at the City College of New York, explains:

We haven't looked where the students live. Just look at the examples used in physics. They are common to white males. The concepts of heat, electricity, or magnetism are not necessarily racist or sexist. But when the example used is a 12-volt car battery, children from different contexts can't deal with it. The same concepts can be taught using the example of flashlights or boom boxes. It's in the examples that you see gross injustice. (Hubert Dyasi, interview, 1996)

Just as with curriculum, instructional reforms such as implementing cooperative learning or inquiry-based approaches are not enough. Teachers have to consciously struggle against the many ways that their prejudices distort how they view and treat children in the classroom. And they need to create zero tolerance for students' racist or sexist mistreatment of each other. Truly inclusive instruction requires not just effective instructional strategies, but continuous monitoring of racist and sexist teacher-student and student-student interactions.

The same vigilance is necessary when it comes to assessment, which Dyasi describes as "a bedrock of inequity." Even though traditional assessments are riddled with biased content and encourage rote memorization, they are continually used to sort and label students.

> It is no secret that scores on ability and achievement tests are highly correlated with socioeconomic status and with the quality of schooling to which children have access. Tests can thus compound the inequities endured by poor children by foreclosing to them additional learning opportunities. (Hubert Dyasi, interview, 1996)

Even alternative forms of assessment, while potentially more equitable, can be biased and misused. For example, raters can be biased, allowing extraneous factors like handwriting or unconscious judgments about students' abilities to affect their ratings. Or the tasks themselves can be biased when they are embedded in a context that is unfamiliar to a particular cultural or gender group, such as a football game (Regional Educational Laboratories 1998).

In addition, deep-seated attitudes about language, culture, and assessment put nondominant groups at a distinct disadvantage, even with alternative assessments. For example, the very idea of displaying competence through formal, timed, and often public assessments is incompatible with some students' cultures (Estrin 1993). Another issue is the increased language

**RESOURCES FOR ASSESSING RACIAL, CLASS, CULTURAL, AND GENDER BIAS IN CURRICULUM, INSTRUCTION, AND ASSESSMENT**
(full listings at end of this chapter in **Resources**)

*Improving Classroom Assessment: A Toolkit for Professional Developers (Toolkit 98),* by Regional Educational Laboratories, 1998

*Multicultural and Gender Equity in the Mathematics Classroom: The Gift of Diversity (1997 Yearbook),* edited by Janet Trentacosta and Margaret J. Kenney, 1997

Making Schools Work for Every Child CD-ROM and Web site

demands of alternative assessments, making them all the more formidable for English language learners. And different communication styles, including varied ways of reciting, recounting, writing, interacting with peers, discussing, and debating have serious implications for how children will perform and be rated on alternative assessments. All of these issues confound the fairness of alternative assessments and point to the need to carefully monitor all assessment practices for cultural bias.

## Assessing Racial, Class, Cultural, and Gender Bias in Curriculum, Instruction, and Assessment

Assessing bias in your own curriculum, instruction, and assessment practices is as tough as it is important. It will require openly and honestly investigating to what extent racial, class, cultural, or gender bias in curriculum, instruction, and assessment practices is a factor in the performance of particular groups of students in your school or district.

To help you answer this overarching question, we break it down into a number of related sub-questions. Some of these questions are addressed elsewhere in this or other chapters of this guidebook, but because they directly relate to curriculum, instruction, and assessment, we include them here as well.

### CURRICULUM AND INSTRUCTION

1. Have we fully reviewed all mathematics and science curriculum materials for overt bias, including stereotyping, invisibility of certain groups, and distorted or selective presentation of issues, situations, people, and use of language?

2. To what extent does our curriculum use examples and contexts relevant to our students' lives and cultures? (See "Who are Our Students? How Can We Better Understand and Appreciate Their Cultural Backgrounds?" above.) How does our curriculum capitalize on diverse students' prior knowledge and strengths? (See "How Can We Learn to Recognize Students' Strengths?" above.)

3. To what extent does our curriculum explicitly teach students about the "culture of power"—ways of talking, writing, and interact-

ing that are associated with success in the dominant culture and in mathematics and science—while honoring their own languages and cultures?

4. To what extent is high-quality curriculum, consistent with national and state standards, being implemented? Which students are getting access to that curriculum? Which students aren't? (See "Structural Barriers to Equity" above and "Problem Two: Implementing Standards-Based Curriculum and Instruction Reform" in Chapter 4.)

5. To what extent are a variety of challenging and interactive instructional strategies being used? Which students are getting access to these approaches? Which students are not? Why? (See "Problem Two: Implementing Standards-Based Curriculum and Instruction Reform" in Chapter 4.)

6. Who are our students? What are their cultural backgrounds? How does their culture affect their ways of learning, interacting, communicating, presenting, discussing, and writing? To what extent does our instruction acknowledge, build on, and even celebrate our students' strengths? (See "Who are Our Students? How Can We Better Understand and Appreciate Their Cultural Backgrounds?" and "How Can We Learn to Recognize Students' Strengths?" above.)

7. To what extent do teacher-classroom interactions exemplify high expectations for all students? To what extent do racist, classist, and sexist attitudes affect teachers' treatment of students? (See "Unequal Expectations and Treatment" above.) How do teacher-classroom interactions affect student performance?

8. What is the nature of student-student interactions in the classroom? Which students are participating actively? using computers? science equipment? Which aren't? What roles are students playing in small groups? Are some groups of students acting in ways that discourage the learning of other groups of students? How do these factors affect the performance of particular groups of students, such as minorities or girls?

## ASSESSMENT

1. To what extent have alternative assessments been implemented? Who is getting access to alternative assessment approaches? Who is not? How does this affect student performance? Do our reporting systems reflect students' strengths and abilities on a range of assessments? (See "Problem Four: Evaluating the Impact of Reform on Student Learning" in Chapter 4.)

2. Who are our students? What are their cultural backgrounds? How do these affect their attitudes toward assessment and the ways they perform certain tasks, such as recounting events, writing, public speaking, debating, and discussing? What are their strengths and how can they be capitalized on in our assessment practices?

3. To what extent are our assessments free from racial, class, cultural, and gender stereotypes? Do they reflect content and contexts that are equally familiar, acceptable, and appropriate for all groups of students? Do they assess knowledge and skills that all students have had equal opportunity to acquire (Regional Educational Laboratories 1998, 35)? Do they offer reasonable accommodations for students' special needs, such as untimed testing for students who need it or special equipment for physically challenged students? Is racial, class, cultural, or gender bias a factor in particular student groups' performance on assessments?

4. How are we dealing with rater prejudgments about features such as spelling or handwriting, knowledge of the type of student or of the individual student, etc.? Is rater bias a factor in the performance of particular student groups (Regional Educational Laboratories 1998, 35)?

The **Data Tools** contain instruments that can help teams unearth answers to many of these questions. We include:

▼ three checklists for reviewing curriculum materials, "Guidelines for Evaluating Mathematics Books for Bias," "Guidelines for Evaluating Science Books for Stereotyping," and "Diversity in the Classroom: A Checklist," which looks at teaching materials and more broadly at issues of student-teacher interaction (**Data Tools**, DT 5-8, DT 5-9, and DT 5-10);

▼ "Equity in Mathematics and Science Checklist," which focuses on classroom as well as schoolwide issues (**Data Tools**, DT 5-11);

▼ "Profile of an Equitable Math and Science Classroom and Teacher," which defines seven dimensions of equity and a description of their ideal form (**Data Tools**, DT 5-12).

▼ "Alternative Assessment Evaluation Form," which assesses fairness of assessments (**Data Tools**, DT 4-23).

Checklists such as these typically use self-reporting but can be strengthened by including others' perceptions (such as students' and parents'), videotaping, and classroom observations. For observation protocols, see the GESA program (**Resources**, page 318) and the "Observation Sheet for Verbal Interaction Assessment" in **Data Tools**, DT 5-3. For an example of how these data sources can be combined in a study of students' classroom interactions, see the vignette below.

**Frank Tworek,** a middle school teacher in Omaha, Nebraska, wanted to find out more about the interactions between boys and girls in his science classes. Specifically, he set out to investigate whether either gender dominated an activity when boys and girls were lab partners. To do this, he looked at his students' interactions during a two-day laboratory, using a combination of open-ended surveys administered to

118 students with videotaping of and personal interviews with four students (two boy-girl pairs).

After examining the videotapes of the four students and considering their interview responses, Tworek diagrammed three patterns of sharing lab equipment that he observed (with the tray placed equidistant between partners, offering equal access; with the tray passed back and forth as needed; and with the tray in front of one partner, who dominated the activity) and calculated and graphed each student's percentage of total participation. He also graphed the responses, by gender, to each of the 14 survey questions he asked of the other 118 students.

After sifting through all his data, he observed: "The videotapes and interviews proved to me that I, as the gender equity researcher, was not even aware of some of the inequities taking place in front of me until I had the opportunity to examine the videotapes and other data at a later time." He also concluded that in his sample "There was not enough evidence to suggest that females and males should be separated for science class at the seventh-grade level, but there was plenty of evidence to suggest that students and teachers should both be given opportunities to become more alert to gender inequities, to recognize those inequities when they do develop, and to practice strategies to remedy the problems."

(Mid-continent Regional Educational Laboratory [1997, May]. *Change in Action: Navigating and Investigating the Classroom Using Action Research. Reports of Twenty-Two Teacher Research Projects*, edited by De Tonack and Ceri Dean, pp. 79–104, Aurora, CO: McREL. adapted with permission of McREL.)

## Developing a Data Collection Plan

The form in the **Planning Tools**, page 307 and illustrated here, can help you map out your data collection plan for assessing racial, class, cultural, and gender bias in curriculum, instruction, and assessment practices.

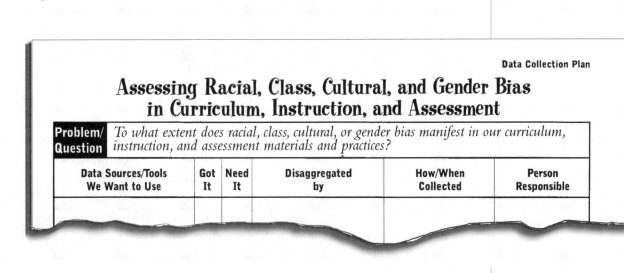

Data Collection Plan

### Assessing Racial, Class, Cultural, and Gender Bias in Curriculum, Instruction, and Assessment

| Problem/ Question | To what extent does racial, class, cultural, or gender bias manifest in our curriculum, instruction, and assessment materials and practices? | | | | |
|---|---|---|---|---|---|
| **Data Sources/Tools We Want to Use** | **Got It** | **Need It** | **Disaggregated by** | **How/When Collected** | **Person Responsible** |
| | | | | | |

# Conclusion

Equity problems often first surface in racial, economic, or gender gaps in student achievement and unequal opportunities to learn. In this chapter, we profiled four common and interconnected obstacles to equity that may underlie gaps in performance and opportunities: structural barriers, belief systems, unequal expectations, and bias in curriculum, instruction, and assessment. These are, however, by no means an exhaustive list of equity issues to consider. For example, if you are working at the district level, unequal resource allocations among schools within the district can be a problem. Or staffing can be an issue because professionals from diverse backgrounds are often underrepresented in mathematics and science teaching positions and in school leadership. While we do not address these directly, we hope that the chapter provides a model for how reform teams can use data to tackle these or other equity issues you may identify as important.

Whatever obstacles to equity you take on, the painstaking work you do to collect data and deepen your understanding of the problem has a big payoff: once underlying equity problems are brought to light you can take appropriate steps to solve them. As you move from research to action, we suggest that you follow the process outlined in Chapter 3: clearly define the problem you want to solve, set specific goals to close the achievement gap, and establish equity action plans.

But remember that, because of the systemic nature of change, it will be important to address how other parts of the system need to improve to realize your equity goals. For example, you will need to rally critical supports, such as parent engagement, professional development, policy, and leadership, to implement your equity plan. And any work you are doing on curriculum, instruction, and assessment should be aligned with and in support of your equity goals. Removing the roadblocks to equity will take all parts of the system working together!

The **Data Tools** of other chapters contain two additional instruments to help you examine equity within the larger context of systemic reform. One is the "Progress Toward Standards—A Self-Assessment," which encourages reform teams to self-assess progress toward a standards-led system on a number of dimensions, including Student Learning, Curriculum, Instruction, and Assessment, Equity, and Professional Development (see DT 2-2). Another tool, developed by Ruth Johnson, helps schools to assess readiness for change by surveying staff's, parents', and students' perceptions of beliefs, practices, and support for collegiality (see "Perceptions of Attitudes, Readiness and Commitment to Change," **Data Tools**, DT 3-1). Either tool can help school reform teams to focus on immediate next steps as well as to develop long-range plans for systemic reform. In addition, you can use the systemic action planning forms provided in **Planning Tools**, pages 133–136, to plan for equity reform in the context of reforming curriculum, instruction, and assessment, building critical supports, and keeping the focus on improved student learning.

Once your plans are in place, you can swing into action. But, as always, the research doesn't stop when the action begins. You will continue to use your SMART goals, the baseline data you collected, and other indicators you agree on to monitor your progress (see **Planning Tools**, "Plan for Monitoring the Impact of Reform Activities on Student Learning," page 141). By using data as your "eyes," you will see gains as well as new problems to solve, new challenges to meet. Making a commitment to equity means that you won't rest until every child is achieving to his or her peak capacities.

# Planning Tools: From Inquiry to Action

## Team Planning Questions

The following are questions for your team to consider as you plan, based on the process outlined in the chapter. You will also find cross-references to relevant text, Data Tools, and Resources.

1. How well is our school serving all students? What are our strengths? (evidence) What areas need improvement? (evidence) What additional information do we need? What are the implications for action? (See "Progress Toward Standards—A Self-Assessment: Equity," page 296.)

2. What are the obstacles to equity in our school? Which are the most important to focus on and why? (See Focus Statements: Obstacles to Equity, page 297.)

3. What additional information do we need to better understand equity issues in our school and plan for action? How can we get it? What Data Tools can we use? (See "Looking at Structural Barriers to Equity," page 301; "Examining Beliefs That Block Equity," page 303; "Investigating Unequal Expectations and Treatment," page 305; and "Assessing Racial, Class, Cultural, and Gender Bias in Curriculum, Instruction, and Assessment," page 307.)

4. What are our equity goals? What steps can we take to reach those goals? (See "Systemic Mathematics and Science Action Plan—Equity," page 311.)

5. How can we track our progress? What indicators can we use? (See "Plan for Monitoring the Impact of Reform Activities on Student Learning," page 309.)

6. What kind of professional development will help us meet our equity goals? (See "Systemic Mathematics and Science Action Plan—Professional Development," page 136.)

7. What support and resources do we need to carry out our equity plans? (See Chapter 5 Resources.)

# Focus Statements: Obstacles to Equity

Consider the following statements. Think about how your school compares. How do you know?

## The Performance Gap

The achievement gaps between white and minority, rich and poor, which were narrowing until 1988, are widening again (Education Trust 1996, 5).

How does our school compare?

## Tracking and Sorting Students

Even before kindergarten, children are subjected to testing that is specifically designed to shake out differences, identify deficiencies, and compare one child to another. Minor differences in performance, representing only a few months' difference in cognitive development, can determine what label a child may get tagged with for his or her entire school career (Howard 1991, 5).

How does our school compare?

" 'We don't have tracking in our school. All our classes are heterogeneous—except for the advanced placement and remedial ones' " (The tracking wars 1992, 1).

How does our school compare?

"...the schedule often creates de facto tracking—a student who takes practical math may end up in remedial English simply because it's all that is available at the time he [or she] has open" (The tracking wars 1992, 1).

How does our school compare?

"Studies...reveal crucial differences in the kinds of instruction offered in different tracks. Instruction in the low tracks tends to be fragmented, often requiring students to memorize small bits of information and fill out worksheets. Although many upper-track classes share some of these traits, they are more likely to offer opportunities for discussion, writing, and other meaning-making activities" (The tracking wars 1992, 3).

How does our school compare?

## Beliefs That Block Equity

▼ There is a distribution of intelligence in the population ranging from "very smart" to "sorta smart" to "kinda dumb" (in kid terms).

▼ How much intelligence you have determines what you can learn and what you can be in life.

▼ All this can be sorted out through standardized testing and teacher observation (Howard 1991, 4).

How does our school compare?

Society's image of the "very smart" student is one with white, middle-class behaviors and values. If students don't fit that image, if they are culturally different, they are judged to be less intelligent.

How does our school compare?

Mathematics and science are the special realm of the "very smart."

How does our school compare?

## Unequal Expectations and Treatment

We now have decades of research that show that teachers tend to expect less of poor, minority, and female students and treat them differently in the classroom. These students receive less attention, praise, "wait time," and feedback than their white and male peers.

How does our school compare?

## Bias in Curriculum, Instruction, and Assessment

Racial, class, cultural, and gender biases show up in mathematics and science curriculum materials in what *is* and *is not* included. What is included may be discriminatory language and stereotypes. What is left out may be important ways that culturally different students can "see themselves" in the curriculum.

How does our school compare?

Just as with curriculum, instructional reforms such as implementing cooperative learning or inquiry-based approaches are not enough. Teachers have to consciously struggle against the many ways that their prejudices distort how they view and treat children in the classroom.

How does our school compare?

Deep-seated attitudes about language, culture, and assessment put nondominant groups at a distinct disadvantage, even with alternative assessments.

How does our school compare?

# Looking at Structural Barriers to Equity

| Problem/ Question | *To what extent do structural barriers result in some students (poor, minority, English language learners, girls, others) having less opportunity to learn mathematics and science than others? To what extent is tracking (de facto or intentional) practiced in our school?* | | | | | |
|---|---|---|---|---|---|---|
| Data Sources/Tools We Want to Use | Got It | Need It | Disaggregated by | How/When Collected | Person Responsible |
| | | | | | |
| | | | | | |
| | | | | | |
| | | | | | |
| | | | | | |

## Possible Data Sources/Tools

❏ Disaggregated course enrollment data (DT 3-17–DT 3-19)

❏ Disaggregated special program placement data (DT 3-20)

❏ Tracking practices (DT 5-1)

❏ Teacher qualifications (DT 3-21)

❏ Access to rigorous, hands-on instruction and alternative assessment, disaggregated (DT 4-3–DT 4-10, DT 4-12, DT 4-13, DT 4-15, DT 4-16, DT 4-19–DT 4-21)

❏ Access to technology, disaggregated (DT 3-22–DT 3-25)

## Resources

### Print

▼ *Closing the Achievement Gap: A Vision to Guide Change in Beliefs and Practice*, edited by Belinda Williams

▼ *Crossing the Tracks: How "Untracking" Can Save America's Schools*, by Anne Wheelock

▼ *Education Watch: The 1996 Education Trust State and National Data Book**

▼ *Education Watch: The Education Trust Community Data Guide**

▼ *Setting Our Sights: Measuring Equity in School Change*, by Ruth Johnson*

### Projects and Programs

▼ The Algebra Project, Inc., Cambridge, MA

▼ EQUITY 2000, The College Board, New York, NY

▼ Global Systems Science, Berkeley, CA (CD-ROM)

▼ The Interactive Mathematics Program, (CD-ROM)

▼ Pacesetter, The College Board, New York, NY

All resouces are listed at the end of this chapter except *, which are listed at the end of Chapter 2.

# Examining Beliefs That Block Equity

| Problem/ Question | *How prevalent are beliefs that block equity in our school? How do they manifest in school and classroom practices? How can individuals come to grips with their own prejudice and its effect on their lives? Who are our students? How can we better understand their cultural backgrounds? How can we learn to recognize students' strengths?* |
|---|---|

| Data Sources/Tools We Want to Use | Got It | Need It | Disaggregated by | How/When Collected | Person Responsible |
|---|---|---|---|---|---|
| | | | | | |
| | | | | | |
| | | | | | |
| | | | | | |
| | | | | | |

## Possible Data Sources/Tools

❏ Enrollment data (DT 3-17, DT 3-18)

❏ Course enrollment and test performance data, disaggregated (DT 3-19)

❏ Tracking practices (DT 5-1)

❏ Teacher qualifications (DT 3-21)

❏ Master schedules (pp. 3.32–3.33)

❏ SPED placement (DT 3-20)

❏ Gifted and talented placement (DT 3-20)

❏ Access to technology, disaggregated (DT 3-22–DT 3-25)

❏ Disaggregated student performance data (DT 3-3–DT 3-7)

❏ Demographic data (DT 3-2)

❏ Observations of classroom interactions (DT 5-3)

❏ Student Aspirations Survey (DT 3-28)

❏ Interviews with parents, students

❏ Descriptive Review Process (DT 2-6)

❏ Surveys of attitudes and practices (DT 5-4, DT 5-5, DT 5-7)

❏ Other _____

## Resources

### Print

▼ *Multicultural Education: Issues and Perspectives,* edited by James A. Banks and Cherry A. McGee

▼ *Multicultural Teaching: A Handbook of Activities, Information, and Resources,* by Pamela L. Tiedt and Iris M. Tiedt

▼ *Other People's Children: Cultural Conflict in the Classroom,* by Lisa Delpit

▼ *Science in the Multicultural Classroom: A Guide to Teaching and Learning,* by Robertta H. Barba

▼ *Ripples of Hope,* by Julian Weissglass [Note: This is not a separate book description; it is mentioned in the EMELI description.]

### Projects and Programs

▼ The Efficacy Institute, Waltham, MA

▼ Equity Assistance Centers

▼ Equity in Mathematics Education Leadership Institute (EMELI), Santa Barbara, CA

▼ The Prospect Archive and Center for Education and Research, North Bennington, VT

All resources are listed at the end of this chapter.

**5** Planning Tools

# Investigating Unequal Expectations and Treatment

| Problem/ Question | To what extent do unequal expectations affect how we treat students? | | | | | |
|---|---|---|---|---|---|---|
| **Data Sources/Tools We Want to Use** | **Got It** | **Need It** | **Disaggregated by** | **How/When Collected** | **Person Responsible** |
| | | | | | |
| | | | | | |
| | | | | | |
| | | | | | |
| | | | | | |

## Possible Data Sources/Tools

❏ Observations of teacher-student interactions, including numbers of interactions, wait time, discipline referrals, and quality of feedback (DT 5-3)

❏ Surveys of staff expectations and practices (DT 3-2, DT 5-4–DT 5-6)

❏ Shadowing, interviewing, surveying students (DT 5-7, DT 3-28)

❏ Other _____

## Resources

### Print

▼ *Math and Science for the Coed Classroom*, by Patricia B. Campbell and Jennifer N. Storo

### Projects and Programs

▼ EQUITY 2000, The College Board, New York, NY

▼ Generating Expectations for Student Achievement (GESA), Canyon Lake, CA

All resources are listed at the end of this chapter.

# Assessing Racial, Class, Cultural, and Gender Bias in Curriculum, Instruction, and Assessment

| Problem/ Question | *To what extent does racial, class, cultural, or gender bias manifest in our curriculum, instruction, and assessment materials and practices?* | | | | |
|---|---|---|---|---|---|
| **Data Sources/Tools We Want to Use** | **Got It** | **Need It** | **Disaggregated by** | **How/When Collected** | **Person Responsible** |
| | | | | | |
| | | | | | |
| | | | | | |
| | | | | | |
| | | | | | |

## Possible Data Sources/Tools

❏ Curriculum materials (DT 5-8, DT 5-9)

❏ Assessments (DT 4-23)

❏ Classroom observations (DT 4-15, DT 4-16)

❏ Surveys, checklists, profiles (DT 5-10, DT 5-11, DT 5-12)

## Resources

### Print

▼ *Improving Classroom Assessment: A Toolkit for Professional Developers (Toolkit98)*, by Regional Educational Laboratories*

▼ *Multicultural and Gender Equity in the Mathematics Classroom*, edited by Janet Trentacosta and Margaret Kenney

### CD-Rom/Web Site

▼ Making Schools Work for Every Child

All resources are listed at the end of this chapter except *, which is listed at the end of Chapter 4.

# Plan for Monitoring the Impact of Reform Activities on Student Learning

| Problem/ Question | *What is the impact of equity reform on student learning outcomes, opportunities, and aspirations?* | | | | | |
|---|---|---|---|---|---|---|
| **SMART Student Learning Goals** | **Indicators** (disaggregated by race, ethnicity, free/reduced lunch, gender, etc.) | **Data Collection** | | | **How Will Data Be Analyzed?** | **How Will Data Be Reported/ Disseminated?** |
| | | **How?** | **When?** | **By Whom?** | | |
| | | | | | | |
| | | | | | | |

Planning Tools 5

## Outcomes

❏ Mathematics/science standardized test scores (DT 3-3, DT 3-4, DT 3-7)

❏ Mathematics SAT scores

❏ Grades (DT 3-10)

❏ Mathematics state assessments (DT 3-5)

❏ Science state assessments (DT 3-6)

❏ Grade-level performance assessments in mathematics/science

❏ School performance assessments in mathematics/science

❏ District performance assessments in mathematics/science

❏ Quality of student work (DT 2-5, DT 2-6)

❏ Retention rates (DT 3-11)

❏ Overage students (DT 3-12)

❏ Dropout rates (DT 3-13)

❏ Absenteeism (DT 3-14)

❏ Discipline referrals (DT 3-15)

❏ College-going and graduation rates (DT 3-26, DT 3-27)

## Opportunities

❏ Disaggregated course enrollment data (DT 3-17–DT 3-19)

❏ Disaggregated special program placement data (DT 3-20)

❏ Tracking practices (DT 5-1)

❏ Teacher qualifications (DT 3-21)

❏ Access to rigorous, hands-on instruction and alternative assessment, disaggregated (DT 4-3–DT 4-10, DT 4-12, DT 4-13, DT 4-15, DT 4-16, DT 4-19–DT 4-21)

❏ Access to technology, disaggregated (DT 3-22–DT 3-25)

❏ College-going and graduation rates, disaggregated (DT 3-26, DT 3-27)

## Aspirations

❏ Student aspirations data (DT 3-28)

**5** *Planning Tools*

# Systemic Mathematics and Science Action Plan–Equity

**SMART Student Learning Goals**

| Curriculum/Instruction/Assessment Goals | Steps to Reach Goal | Person Responsible | Documentation for Action Taken | Timeline |
|---|---|---|---|---|
| | | | | |
| | | | | |
| | | | | |
| | | | | |

Planning Tools 5

# Resources for Equity

## Books and Pamphlets

*Beyond Tracking: Finding Success in Inclusive Schools*, edited by Harbison Pool and Jane Page (Bloomington, IN: Phi Delta Kappa Educational Foundation), 1995

This collection of papers addresses the various issues around tracking, such as whether tracking should be abolished, the movement toward inclusiveness in schools, and the process of untracking.

**Contact:** Phi Delta Kappa Educational Foundation, P.O. Box 789, Bloomington, IN 47402-0789; (800) 766-1156; fax: (812) 339-0018; Web site: http://www.pdkintl.org/

*Closing the Achievement Gap: A Vision to Guide Change in Beliefs and Practice*, edited by Belinda Williams (Philadelphia: Research for Better Schools), 1995

*Closing the Achievement Gap* examines what it will take to close the current achievement gap between urban students and suburban students and offers a vision of community-wide involvement to integrate change in six areas: school-linked community service; culturally compatible schools and classrooms; caring teachers with high expectations and cultural sensitivity; opportunities to learn; school environments that foster resilience; and teacher engagement. The book has recommendations for implementation action in all of these areas.

**Contact:** Research for Better Schools, 444 North Third Street, Philadelphia, PA 19123; (215) 574-9300 (cite order no. RS-895-RD); e-mail: info@rbs.org; Web site: http://www.rbs.org/

*Connecting Cultures: A Guide to Multicultural Literature for Children*, by Rebecca L. Thomas (New Providence, NJ: R. R. Bowker), 1996

This guidebook provides information on more than 1,600 recent books of fiction, folk tales, poetry, and songs to use with children from kindergarten through sixth grade.

**Contact:** R. R. Bowker, 121 Chanlon Road, New Providence, NJ 07974; (888) 269-5372

*Connecting with the Learner: An Equity Toolkit*, by the Michigan Department of Education and the North Central Regional Educational Laboratory (Lansing, MI: Michigan Department of Education and Oak Brook, IL: NCREL), 1998

The *Toolkit* was designed to facilitate systemic change in order to create and maintain supportive learning environments where all students have equal opportunity to achieve science and mathematics literacy. Activities, information, and resources are provided for varied professional development experiences and formats (e.g., learning communities, workshops, study groups, action research teams) focused on equity in learning. The issues addressed in the book's chapters are "Examining Beliefs and Defining Equity," "Designing Equitable Curriculum," "Linking Teaching With Learning," "Exploring Instructional Strategies," "Building Upon Successful Model Programs," and "Projects for Forming Partnerships with Families and the Community." The activities were designed from a constructivist perspective, allowing each participant to become actively engaged in the learning and change process.

**Contacts:** Michigan Department of Education, 608 West Allegan Street, Lansing, MI 48909; (517) 373-4224; fax: (517) 355-2374

North Central Regional Educational Laboratory (NCREL), 1120 East Diehl Road, Suite 200, Naperville, IL 60563; (800) 356-2735; fax: (630) 649-6700; e-mail: info@ncrel.org; Web site: http://www.ncrel.org/

***Crossing the Tracks: How "Untracking" Can Save America's Schools***, by Anne Wheelock (New York: New Press), 1992

*Crossing the Tracks* begins with an overview of the components of successful untracking in schools and districts, utilizing case studies of specific schools to explore the components in greater depth. Other chapters highlight innovative practices in parent involvement and in the reform of school culture, curriculum, instruction, assessment, and counseling that together and separately support untracking to improve learning.

**Contact:** The New Press, 450 West 41st Street, 6th Floor, New York, NY 10036; (800) 233-4830 (orders), (212) 629-8802 (inquiries); Web site: http://www.thenewpress.com

***Gender Gaps: Where Schools Still Fail Our Children***, by the AAUW Educational Foundation (Washington, DC: AAUW Educational Foundation), 1998

In *Gender Gaps: Where Schools Still Fail Our Children*, the AAUW documents the progress and failure of schools in providing equitable education since their 1992 publication of *How Schools Shortchange Girls*. The new report focuses on emerging gaps in areas such as technology and school-to-work programs that threaten to disadvantage girls. Based on 1,000 research studies, this report finds some gains in girls' achievement, some areas where boys lag, and some areas, like technology, where needs have not yet been addressed. *Gender Gaps* offers more than 35 recommendations for action by states, local school districts, educators, and researchers to achieve gender equity in education.

**Contact:** American Association of University Women Educational Foundation, 1111 16th Street N.W., Washington, DC 20036; (800) 326-2289; Web site: http://www.aaww.org

***Math and Science for the Coed Classroom***, by Patricia B. Campbell and Jennifer N. Storo (Groton, MA: Campbell-Kibler Associates), 1996

*Math and Science for the Coed Classroom* is a collection of four pamphlets for educators, administrators, counselors, parents, and community programs that are working to increase gender and race equity in mathematics, science, and technology education. Each pamphlet offers practical strategies for changing classroom and school climates and motivating students to succeed. Individual pamphlet titles are *Why Me? Why My Classroom? The Need for Equity in Coed Math and Science Classes; Whose Responsibility Is It? The Role of Administrators and Counselors; Girls Are . . . Boys Are . . . : Myths, Stereotypes and Gender Differences;* and *Making It Happen: Pizza Parties, Chemistry Goddesses & Other Strategies that Work for Girls and Boys.* Also provided are "next steps," a good set of references for continuing and furthering reform efforts, and helpful advice for systemic reform. These pamphlets can be downloaded, at no cost, from the Campbell-Kibler Associates Web site (http://www.tiac.net/users/ckassoc).

**Contacts:** To order packets of pamphlets: WEEA/EDC-C97, P.O. Box 1020, Sewickley, PA 15143; (800) 793-5076; fax: (412) 741-0609; e-mail: EDCorders@abdintl.com

For additional information and technical assistance: Women's Educational Equity Act (WEEA) Equity Resource Center, Education Development Center, Inc., 55 Chapel Street, Newton, MA 02158; (800) 225-4276 ext. 2326; e-mail: weeactr@edc.org; Web site: http://www.edc.org/womensequity

**Multicultural Education: Issues and Perspectives** (4th ed.), edited by James A. Banks and Cherry A. McGee-Banks (Somerset, NJ: John Wiley & Sons), 2000
This useful reference is designed to help present and future educators acquire the concepts, paradigms, and explanations needed to become effective practitioners in culturally, racially, and language diverse classrooms and schools. The fourth edition reflects current and emerging research, concepts, and debates about the education of students of both genders from different cultural, racial, ethnic, and language groups.

**Contact:** John Wiley & Sons, Inc., One Wiley Drive, Somerset, NJ 08875-1272; (800) 225-5945; fax: (732) 302-2300; Web site: http://www.wiley.com/

**Multicultural and Gender Equity in the Mathematics Classroom: The Gift of Diversity (1997 Yearbook)**, edited by Janet Trentacosta and Margaret J. Kenney (Reston, VA: NCTM), 1997

The NCTM's *1997 Yearbook* presents a vision of how research and classroom practices related to multicultural diversity and gender equity can reinforce each other to ensure a powerful mathematics program for all students. Through essay contributions from a wide range of experts, chapters explore issues around diversity and equity in the mathematics classroom as they relate to classroom culture, to curriculum, assessment, and instruction, and to professional development.

**Contact:** National Council of Teachers of Mathematics (NCTM), 1906 Association Drive, Reston, VA 20191-9988; (800) 235-7566; fax: (703) 476-2970; e-mail: orders@nctm.org; Web site: http://www.nctm.org/

*Multicultural Literature for Children and Young Adults: Volume 2, 1991-1996*, by Ginny Moore Kruse, Kathleen T. Horning, and Megan Schliesman (Madison, WI: The Cooperative Children's Book Center), 1997

This is an annotated bibliography of books by and about people of color for children up to age 14; it is the companion to an earlier volume covering 1980–90.

**Contact:** CCBC, 4290 Helen C. White Hall, 600 North Park Street, Madison, WI 53706; (608) 263-3720; Web site: http://www.soemadison.wisc.edu/ccbc/public2.htm

*Multicultural Teaching: A Handbook of Activities, Information, and Resources*, by Pamela L. Tiedt and Iris M. Tiedt (Needham Heights, MA: Allyn & Bacon), 1995

*Multicultural Teaching* provides activities and information to help teachers explore the many kinds of diversity in the classroom, such as family arrangements, naming customs, and ways of handling conflict. This book conveys to both preservice and in-service teachers the practical knowledge needed to create curricula that combine multicultural teaching practices with multicultural content. Two main thrusts of the text are teaching teachers how to present multicultural concepts and providing equity for children with diverse needs.

**Contact:** Allyn & Bacon Publishers, 160 Gould Street, Needham Heights, MA 02194; (800) 852-8024; fax: (781) 455-7024; e-mail: ABSales@abacon.com; Web site:\http://www.abacon.com/

*Multiplying Inequalities: The Effects of Race, Social Class, and Tracking on Opportunities to Learn Mathematics and Science*, by Jeannie Oakes (Santa Monica, CA: RAND Corp.), 1990

This book explores the social/historical underpinnings of tracking and discusses the extensive reforms needed to successfully dismantle existing systems. Oakes recommends a reconstructed and expanded curriculum, new provisions for special-needs students, alternative forms of assessment, and administrative commitment.

**Contact:** RAND Corp., 1700 Main Street, P.O. Box 2138, Santa Monica, CA 90407-2138; (310) 393-0411; fax: (310) 393-4818; Web site: http://www.rand.org

*Other People's Children: Cultural Conflict in the Classroom*, by Lisa Delpit (New York: New Press), 1995

In a groundbreaking analysis of what is going on in American classrooms today, the author suggests that many of the academic problems attributed to children of color are actually the result of miscommunication as schools and "other people's children" struggle with the imbalance of power and the dynamics of inequality in our system. Delpit unravels the threads of the debate through a series of provocative essays, drawing upon her own work in a variety of classroom settings from Philadelphia to Alaska to New Guinea, and finishes with recommendations for the future directions of education.

**Contact:** The New Press, 450 West 41st Street, 6th Floor, New York, NY 10036; (800) 233-4830 (orders), (212) 629-8802 (inquiries); Web site: http://www.thenewpress.com

*Science in the Multicultural Classroom: A Guide to Teaching and Learning* (2nd ed.), by Robertta H. Barba (Needham Heights, MA: Allyn & Bacon), 1998

A revision of this popular methods text reinforces the need to approach teaching with reflective practice to better help every child excel in the science classroom. Organized into four parts, the book helps readers address diversity in the classroom, construct knowledge of science, develop pedagogical content knowledge, and teach with thematic units. Instructional strategies throughout each chapter support educators in addressing the needs of all children.

**Contact:** Allyn & Bacon Publishers, 160 Gould Street, Needham Heights, MA 02194; (800) 852-8024; fax: (781) 455-7024; e-mail: ABSales@abacon.com; Web site:http://www.abacon.com/

## Projects and Programs

**The Algebra Project**, developed by Bob Moses

The Algebra Project is an interactive curriculum designed to help inner-city and rural students better understand abstract mathematical concepts. Developed by mathematician and civil rights leader Bob Moses, The Algebra Project uses physical surroundings as tangible references for mathematical ideas. After a field trip, for instance, students might be asked to create a model or picture of the event, write a creative essay describing their experience, then develop a symbolic representation using mathematical concepts.

**Contact:** The Algebra Project, Inc., 99 Bishop Allen Drive, Cambridge, MA, 02139; (617) 491-0200; Web site: http://www.algebra.org

**The Collaboration for Equity: Fairness in Science and Mathematics Education**

The Collaboration for Equity, a project of the AAAS, works with policy makers, leaders of reform efforts, educators, researchers, and equity advocates to ensure that efforts to reform mathematics and science education benefit all students. The Collaboration's products include tools for monitoring the equity impact of reformed practices and policies, summaries of research about equity in mathematics and science, and analysis of data on enrollment and achievement. Valuable resources are available via the Web site.

**Contact:** AAAS, Directorate for Education and Human Resources Programs, 1200 New York Avenue N.W., Washington, DC 20005; (202) 326-6670; fax (202) 371-9849 Web site: http://ehrweb.aaas.org/ehr/

## The Education Trust

Established in 1990, the Education Trust promotes high academic achievement for all students at all levels, kindergarten through college. The organization places special emphasis on schools and colleges serving low-income and minority students. Education Trust staff work with policy makers, education professionals, and community and business leaders to implement and support high academic standards for all students at all levels; establish rigorous and challenging instruction; support teacher and higher education faculty with preservice and professional development; shift more decision-making authority to principals, teachers, and parents at the school-building level; and link standards reform efforts to consequences for teachers, schools, and students. The Education Trust offers a number of publications on topics such as student achievement data, setting and using standards, and implementing new Title I strategies, as well as the periodic publication *Thinking K-16*. In addition, the Education Trust sells sets of data graphics especially suited for use in meeting and conference presentations.

**Contact:** The Education Trust, 1725 K Street N.W., Suite 200, Washington, DC 20006-1409; (202) 293-1217; fax: (202) 293-2605; Web site: http://www.edtrust.org

## The Efficacy Institute

"Envision a nation of gifted and talented. We won't settle for anything less," says the cover of the Efficacy Institute brochure. The Efficacy Institute is a nonprofit organization committed to raising the academic outcomes and quality of life for children, especially children of color. The core of the program is a four-day seminar for educators that offers a highly experiential process designed to give participants the tools to engage their students in focused, committed, and consistent effort. At the heart of the training process is an examination of how beliefs about intellectual development structure educational policies and practices, particularly in the areas of curriculum, instruction, assessment, and discipline. Other services include workshops for administrators, staff developers, parents, families, and community organizations and a curriculum and workshop for students. Active in many urban areas across the country, including Detroit, Boston, and New York, Efficacy has research documenting improvements in students' reading and mathematics test scores, attitudes about school, and social behavior.

**Contact:** The Efficacy Institute, Inc., 182 Felton Street, Waltham, MA 02453; (781) 547-6060; fax: (781) 547-6077; Web site: http://www.efficacy.org/

## EQUALS and Family Math

The innovative Family Math program is designed to teach mathematics skills by having children in grades K–8 and their parents join together in informal, enjoyable activities that demonstrate the role mathematics plays in their daily lives. The program pays particular attention to encouraging girls and minorities to enter careers in mathematics and science. EQUALS offers classroom materials, computer activities, handbooks, assessment materials, and workshops. EQUALS and Family Math have workshop and in-service sites across the country, which are listed at their Web site..

**Contacts:** EQUALS, Lawrence Hall of Science, University of California, Berkeley, CA 94720-5200; (510) 642-1823; fax: (510) 643-5757; e-mail: equals@uclink.berkeley.edu; Web site: http://equals.lhs.berkeley.edu

## Equity Assistance Centers

The Equity Assistance Centers are funded by the U.S. Department of Education under Title IV of the 1964 Civil Rights Act. They provide assistance in the areas of race, gender, and national origin equity to public schools to promote equal educational opportunities. Ten regional centers are located in California, Colorado, Florida, Kansas, Maryland, Michigan, New York, Oregon, Rhode Island, and Texas. Visit the Equity Centers Web site for links to these centers.

**Contact:** Web site: http://www.equitycenters.org/

## Equity in Mathematics Education Leadership Institute (EMELI)

"We try to have educators look at equity issues in mathematics more deeply and in a different way," says EMELI Director Julian Weissglass. EMELI workshops offer an environment in which educators can reflect on and discuss equity issues at both a personal and an intellectual level. Participants look at how class, race, gender, and other forms of bias affect the teaching and learning of mathematics, learn leadership skills, and plan future actions. A newsletter, articles and reports, a resource manual, and Internet discussions provide additional support to participants. EMELI is also the publisher of *Ripples of Hope: Building Relationships for Educational Change*, a guidebook for implementing the institute's principles and strategies.

**Contact:** EMELI, CEDIMS, University of California, Santa Barbara, CA 93106; (805) 893-7722; fax: (805) 893-3026; Web site: http://www.math.ucsb.edu/EMELI/index.htm

## EQUITY 2000

Launched in 1990 by the College Board, EQUITY 2000 is a pilot program aimed at increasing enrollment in algebra and geometry classes among minority and disadvantaged students in middle and high schools. The program provides for all aspects of a child's education: curriculum, quality of instruction, environment, equal access, parental involvement, and adequate precollegiate counseling. A recent study showed a 72 percent increase in enrollment rates in algebra classes among Latino students at the program's Providence, Rhode Island, site.

**Contact:** The College Board, 45 Columbus Avenue, New York, NY 10023; (212) 713-8000; Web site: http://www.collegeboard.org

### Generating Expectations for Student Achievement (GESA)

GESA is a staff development program that helps schools directly confront gender, race, ethnic, and other forms of bias in teachers' interactions with students. Teachers observe themselves and one another in a nonthreatening manner in order to discover what disparities may occur in their treatment of different students. These include noting who receives more teaching attention, who is criticized for incorrect responses, who gets harsher reprimands, who gets more instructional contact, and who gets rewarded more for creative behavior. Once teachers have examined their own biases, they look at what changes they can make in their interactions as well as in instruction and curriculum. A special program called the Equity Principal supports administrators in taking leadership to support equity.

**Contact:** GrayMill, 22821 Core View Street, Canyon Lake, CA 92587; (909) 246-2106; fax: (909) 246-2107

### Family Science

Family Science is designed to teach science skills and increase intergeneration family learning by having children in grades K–8 and their family members join together in informal, enjoyable activities that demonstrate the role science plays in their daily lives. The program pays particular attention to encouraging girls and minorities to enter mathematics and science careers. Family Science is implemented by teachers, parents, and community members who have attended a two-day facilitator workshop in which they learn hands-on science activities designed for families, strategies to recruit families to attend a series of four to six sessions, and why family involvement is important to science education.

**Contacts:** For workshops: Columbia Family Science, 3838 N.E. Prescott, Portland, OR 97211; (503) 284-2613; e-mail: joywallace@home.com/

For books: David Heil and Associates, 6420 S.W. Macadam Avenue, Suite 208, Portland, OR 97201; (503) 245-2102

### Pacesetter, developed by the College Board

Pacesetter is a fourth-year mathematics course aimed at making the high-standards curriculum, strong teaching, and performance assessment associated with the College Board's Advanced Placement Program a part of all high school students' learning. A rigorous curriculum, Pacesetter draws on students' previous mathematics training to solve complex, multifaceted problems by applying linear, exponential, and logarithmic functions to real-world case studies. Pacesetter also eliminates tracking and designs much of its curriculum for group learning. The College Board offers summer institutes and mid-year refresher courses for teacher training and development.

**Contact:** The College Board 45 Columbus Avenue, 9th Floor, New York, NY 10023-6992; (800) 416-5137; fax: (212) 713-8304; Web site: http://www.collegeboard.org/index_this/pace/html/p_info.html

### Prospect Archive and Center for Education and Research

The Prospect Archive and Center for Education and Research is committed to observation and description as the ground for teaching and inquiry. The archive includes extensive longitudinal collections of individual children's art, writing, and other work, much of which has been published. Observations about children's work, shared and accumulated through Prospect's descriptive and archival processes, demonstrate a respectful approach to understanding a child's characteristic interests, concerns, approach, and way of thinking. These observations in turn help adults support and further children's learning and thinking, both individually and collectively. Prospect also includes a nationwide network of preschool through university educators, researchers, and others and offers a wide range of publications, institutes, conferences, and consultation services based on the center's research and methodology.

**Contact:** Prospect Archive and Center for Education and Research, P.O. Box 326, North Bennington, VT 05257; (802) 442-8333; fax (802) 442-8444

### SCORE... For College and Career

SCORE is a highly successful, nationally validated program committed to improving the achievement of students who might not ordinarily go on to college. "Given the right skills, tools, and support...every student can and will succeed," is SCORE's credo, which is supported by the fact that SCORE students have increased graduation and college enrollment rates and are more likely to test out of Limited English Proficiency (LEP) programs. Through the program, administrators, counselors, teachers, parents, and students become partners in a comprehensive support system that provides students with the skills and the self-esteem they need to succeed academically. Trainers assist schools in designing and implementing customized curricula and provide staff development, materials, and follow-up consultation.

**Contact:** SCORE, PMB 379 30100 Town Center Drive, Suite O, Laguna Niguel, CA 92677; (949) 363-6764; fax: (949) 363-6764; e-mail: sharonmarjo@earthlink.net; Web site: http://www.score-ed.com

## Web Sites

### American Association for the Advancement of Science (AAAS)

**Web site:** http://ehrweb.aaas.org/ehr/

This is one of the best Web sites for mathematics and science teachers. For information on curriculum, equity, reform, and just about anything else to do with mathematics and science education, this is the place to start.

**Contact:** AAAS, Directorate for Education and Human Resources Programs, 1200 New York Avenue N.W., Washington, DC 20005; (202) 326-6670; fax (202) 371-9849

### Eisenhower National Clearinghouse for Mathematics and Science Education (ENC)

**Web site:** http://www.enc.org/

The ENC provides K–12 teachers with a central source of information on mathematics and science curriculum materials. A publication from the Clearinghouse called *Equity in the Reform of Mathematics and Science Education* provides a thorough review of the literature on equity in mathematics; use the Web site's search function to locate more information and an abstract of this title.

**Contact:** Eisenhower National Clearinghouse, 1929 Kenny Road, Columbus, OH 43210; (800) 621-5785; fax: (614) 292-2066; e-mail: info@enc.org

### Making Schools Work for Every Child

**Web site:** http://enc.org/focus/equity

The Eisenhower National Clearinghouse for Mathematics and Science Education (ENC) worked with the Equity Task Force of the National Network of Eisenhower Regional Consortia and Clearinghouse (NNERCC) to produce this CD-ROM and Web site to serve as a resource for educators who are concerned about creating equitable conditions in which every child can succeed at school. Included are resources aimed at strengthening skills in serving students with diverse needs; gaining insights into our cultural frameworks; examining school structures and mechanisms that promote or inhibit the participation of members from diverse communities; examining district, state, and federal policies; strengthening preservice programs' preparation of teachers, guidance counselors, and administrators; forming local learning communities to determine how best to serve students with diverse needs; and examining classroom mathematics and science assessment practices.

**Contact:** Eisenhower National Clearinghouse, 1929 Kenny Road, Columbus, OH 43210 (800) 621-5785; fax: (614) 292-2066; e-mail: info@enc.org

### North Central Regional Educational Laboratory (NCREL)

**Web site:** http://www.ncrel.org

NCREL's goal is to help students, teachers, and policy makers apply proven practices to create productive schools where all students can develop to their fullest potential. To this end, the organization provides research-based resources and assistance to educators, policy makers, and communities. The Web site offers product and service information as well as resources in the areas of educational leadership, technology, evaluation and policy, and mathematics and science. The NCREL Web site also features access to the Pathways to School Improvement Internet Server (http://www.ncrel.org/sdrs/pathways.htm), which offers easy-to-find, concise, research-based information on school improvement. A number of Pathways Web pages are focused specifically on critical issues of equity:

Ensuring Equity with Alternative Assessments
(http://www.ncrel.org/sdrs/areas/issues/methods/assment/as800.htm);
Ensuring Equity and Excellence in Mathematics
(http://www.ncrel.org/sdrs/areas/issues/content/cntareas/math/ma100.htm);
Ensuring Equity and Excellence in Science
(http://www.ncrel.org/sdrs/areas/issues/content/cntareas/science/sc200.htm); and
Ensuring Equitable Use of Education Technology
(http://www.ncrel.org/sdrs/areas/issues/methods/technlgy/te400.htm).

**Contact:** NCREL, 1120 East Diehl road, Suite 200, Naperville, IL 60563; (800) 356-2735;
fax: (630) 649-6700; e-mail: info@ncrel.org; Web site: http://www.ncrel.org/

### Women's Educational Equity Act (WEEA) Equity Resource Center

**Web site:** http://www.edc.org/womensequity

This Web site has information on the WEEA Equity Resource Center and its initiatives, list-ings of WEEA materials, services, and resources, and links to other equity and diversity sites.

**Contact:** WEEA Equity Resource Center, Education Development Center, Inc., 55 Chapel
Street, Newton, MA 02158; (800) 225-3088; e-mail: weeactr@edc.org;
Web site: http://www.edc.org/womensequity

# REFORM IN ACTION

# Data Fuels Continuous Improvement in Glendale, Arizona

It's hard to argue with success at Glendale (Arizona) Union High School District. Glendale is an ethnically diverse school community comprising nine high schools, three located in Glendale and six in Phoenix. Over the last 25 years, student achievement has steadily improved. Pick your measure—standardized tests, the district's own criterion-referenced tests, or performance assessments. All of them show steady growth in student learning in mathematics, science, and other subjects. When the state of Arizona administered performance testing from 1990 to 1994, Glendale scored the highest in the state. Just about the only time you see test scores go down in Glendale is when the district decides to challenge students even more by raising content standards.

There's more good news. Student success at Glendale is not about success for some, but success for all. The district completely eliminated tracking in mathematics and scores still went up. Enrollment in higher-level mathematics and science courses has increased while the dropout rate has decreased from 8.6 percent in 1993 to 6.5 percent in 1997. Any relationship between student achievement and socioeconomic status is shrinking. The district measures this relationship using an Equity Index, a figure that correlates student achievement with mother's education. Under .15 is considered excellent, an indication that students are succeeding regardless of their backgrounds. In Glendale, the Equity Index has been as low as .07.

Sid Bailey, principal of Glendale Union's Washington High School, described the change in attitude in his staff that coincided with improved student learning: "I used to hear a lot of complaining about the kids. 'Sid, you don't understand the kind of kids we have; the neighborhood has gone down; their families . . .; their attitudes . . . .' You know the litany. I don't hear anything about 'these kids' any more."

What accounts for Glendale's dramatic success? "We are data driven," explained Associate Superintendent for Curriculum and Instruction Jan

## Glendale Union District Philosophy

▼ A challenging and meaningful districtwide core curriculum should be taught to all students in the district's nine high schools.

▼ All students can learn and achieve to high standards.

▼ The development of curriculum and assessment is best accomplished by specially trained district teachers acquainted with local conditions.

▼ Locally developed assessments should be aligned with state and national standards.

Rowe. "Data is the energy that drives continuous learning." Over 20 years ago, Glendale instituted an Instructional Management System, a network of personnel and resources to promote curriculum alignment, districtwide assessments, and rigorous use of data as a catalyst for improvement. It is based on the philosophy in the box to the left.

How does Glendale put that philosophy into action? Teachers representing each of the nine high schools within a given subject area are periodically released from the classroom to participate in workshops to develop curriculum and assessments. Out of these workshops, led by curriculum coordinators, teachers produce one or more culminating, end-of-semester or end-of-year, districtwide assessments in each subject area. When it is test time in Glendale, all students across the district take the same tests in the content areas they studied. In most subjects, they take two tests, one multiple-choice and one performance-based.

## Districtwide Performance-Based Assessments

"Developing performance assessments in mathematics and science has been a new process for Glendale over the last few years," explained Science Coordinator Liz Tataseo. "We used to be more fact-oriented. Now we require students to conduct an experiment and come to conclusions. They have to understand the scientific method and demonstrate their knowledge and skills in a real context. The tasks take four to six days to complete." Mathematics performance assessments are equally challenging, requiring students to solve complex problems, show a depth of understanding, and communicate clearly about the mathematics concepts and problem-solving strategies they used.

"We are constantly trying to improve these performance assessments," Tataseo continued. Teachers and coordinators develop and fine-tune assessments together using the process illustrated in Figure 6.1. First, they establish outcomes, which are based on national and state standards. Then they design assessment models, which specify the task parameters (i.e., characteristics of the task) for the assessments. Next comes the construction of rubrics (explicit standards for student achievement). Finally, they write the assessments. Teachers often take the assessments themselves to see how they work.

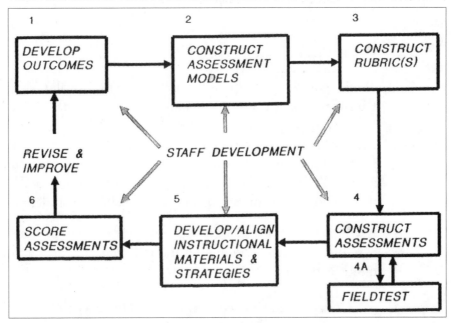

FIGURE 6.1: GLENDALE UNION'S PROCESS FOR DEVELOPING PERFORMANCE-BASED ASSESSMENTS

Typically, assessments are field-tested for the first year and then revised based on teacher feedback. Every few years, the district starts the whole cycle all over again, revising and updating curriculum and assessments to ensure accuracy, validity, and challenge to students.

## Alignment Is the Word

Developing homegrown performance assessments, as time-consuming and complex as it is, is only the beginning of a process designed to improve student learning at Glendale. What happens next has become the buzz word around Glendale: "alignment." As Mathematics Coordinator John Booth explained, "These aren't the kind of assessments that you can wait until two weeks before the test to start working on the outcomes. The entire curriculum has to be aligned if students are going to succeed. We are constantly asking ourselves, does the curriculum align with the outcomes? How can we improve instruction so students are improving?"

One place these questions get answered is during summer workshops, where teachers are paid to score performance assessments and develop instructional materials aligned to assessments. "Scoring performance assessments is one of the best professional development experiences I've ever had," claimed one Glendale High School mathematics teacher. "We learn how to grade reliably and consistently, but that's only part of it. We see how kids think. We see what they don't understand. We learn how to better teach the types of problems on the test."

## Teaching to the Test?

Teaching to the test? Is that what goes on at Glendale? Margaret Garcia-Dugan, principal at Glendale High School, loved that question. "You bet! Why wouldn't you teach to a test? What's fair about teaching one thing and testing something else? The football coach isn't going to teach the kids to play softball. The driver education teacher wouldn't have students learn the names of the parts of the car and then send them out on the road. It's just that schools don't want to be held accountable for student learning."

Accountability for student learning is what the Instructional Management System at Glendale Union is all about. Glendale defines accountability with three questions:

1. What do the district's many publics (parents, patrons, students, and educators) desire in terms of learner performance?

2. Currently, how effective are the district schools in bringing about the desired learner performance?

3. If the district schools are not as effective as desired, what should these schools be doing now to bring about the desired learner behavior? (Handout, Glendale Union High School District, n.d.)

Good data about student learning is at the core of this accountability system. Every summer, Glendale's Data Processing Department produces extensive reports that give the district a snapshot of their effectiveness. The district developed the system to meet their own reporting needs. Summaries of student performance go to the school board, principals, department heads, and individual teachers. While school results are public, individual teacher results are not. Every school learns how well students scored in each content area, how that compared to the district average, and how well they did on two important indices: the Quality Index, which measures student learning based on weighing criterion-referenced test questions by difficulty, and the Equity Index, which determines what correlation exists between mother's level of education and student achievement. Individual teachers' reports include results for each skill or concept so teachers can pinpoint strong and weak areas.

If the story stopped here, however, Glendale might not have experienced its impressive success. What matters are not the fancy printouts, but the opportunities to use them to improve. The data set in motion a process of collective reflection and goal setting focused on improving learning results. At the school level, planning teams meet periodically to analyze the data and set specific benchmarks for improving student learning, reducing dropout rates, closing the equity gap, and implementing new programs. In addition, at each school, departments meet as teams to pore over their data, set targets for improving specific student learning outcomes, and discuss what instructional strategies they will implement to reach their goal. "Data keep the conversation focused on instruction. Wilted lettuce is not what we talk about," observed Sid Bailey of Washington High School.

What do they talk about? Sheila Ringhiser, Science Department Chair at Washington High School, reflected on last year's biology team meeting: "We talked about the human systems outcome. We knew we needed to get that score up. We started talking about a particular lab that we all could incorporate. We also thought reading comprehension was a problem for some students and decided to use the reciprocal reading strategy to improve students' reading ability. To me, the best part of this process is that we can't allow even one student not to learn. We used to just accept that some students would sit back and do nothing. Now, teachers aren't going to allow that. If we have 25 students and one gets a zero, look what that does to our score. We've learned that we don't have to lose those kids. We just keep trying something different."

It didn't always work this well, leveled Principal Bailey. "When I started nine years ago, the goals teachers set for improvement were modest. They could be accomplished in a week's time. That was okay with me because we needed to build trust. Teachers didn't know if they were going to get beat up with data. I wasn't asking them to look at data and set goals so I could determine how good or bad they were and decide who I would drop the hammer on. I wanted to build ownership. I wanted them to see that when they focused on a goal, they could improve student learning. They've heard me say it a million times: all kids can learn, and teachers make the difference."

## Algebra for All

A few years ago, Mathematics Department chairs and the district Mathematics Coordinator, John Booth, started to wonder, "Why, if we really believe all kids can learn, are we teaching basic algebra, a watered-down course for kids they thought couldn't do algebra?" The district then made the decision to eliminate remedial mathematics courses in every school.

To help ensure that all students are ready for a challenging ninth-grade curriculum, the district offers a popular pre-algebra summer course. In addition, individual schools have instituted their own creative solutions to helping all students succeed in their rigorous mathematics program.

Vic Johnson, Washington High's Mathematics Department chair, explained, "We killed four sections of basic algebra, roughly 100 students spread through all the algebra courses. All the kids took the same final, and our scores went up two percentage points. The following year, we had the best scores in the district. Then we decided we were wasting our time teaching general math. We flushed that too. Our scores still went up. We used to give them bonehead math courses. Now, worst-case scenario, all of our kids end up with two years of quality mathematics. They are far better off and feel much better about themselves."

Washington High School also created special "trailer" courses for students who have not yet mastered all the objectives in Integrated Mathematics 1 (first semester) or 2 (second semester). The courses concentrate only on those objectives the students need to work on so they can catch up quickly and move on to the next semester of mathematics. Their purpose is to make students successful, not frustrated, and to move them on to the next level. In the first year of the program, all 21 students ended up with an A or B in first-year algebra. By the beginning of their sophomore year, they had caught up and were ready to start Mathematics 3 with their classmates.

Elsewhere in the district, Glendale and Apollo High Schools, "majority minority" schools serving a high percentage of low-income and ESL students, have piloted another unique approach to providing quality mathematics for all. It's called "modified continuous progress." In this program the math teachers divide the Mathematics 1-2 course into four modules, with each module designed to last one quarter (nine weeks). Students need to achieve 75 percent proficiency to be ready for the next module. If they don't master the module, they repeat it until they do. Now, after several years, the program has produced promising results. At Glendale and Apollo, data talk: both the Quality Index and the Equity Index have improved. Less than 5 percent of students do not complete the first module by their freshman year, and more students than ever are enrolling in advanced mathematics courses. Now six of the nine high schools in the district are using this approach.

# Keys to Success

Using data as effectively as they do at Glendale requires a systemic approach. You could take any piece of the Glendale program—the planning process, the trailer courses, the thorough data reports—and get nowhere without other parts of the system being in place. One of the most important of these is qualified and committed leadership. At Glendale, a district-level team, comprising the associate superintendent for curriculum and instruction, six curriculum coordinators, and the directors of vocational education, testing, and research and assessment, provide vision and direction, technical expertise, number crunching, on-site support to staff, and staff development.

Staff development is an absolute must. The district devotes 5 percent of its budget to it. Teachers spend an average of four to five days during the school year working together to develop curriculum, assessments, and new instructional strategies. Hundreds also take part in the voluntary two to three weeks of professional development offered during the summer. They learn how to score assessments, construct performance tasks, develop rubrics, write curriculum, and align curriculum, instruction, and assessment. In addition, principals receive training in how to work with data and share them in ways that promote growth and reduce fear.

That's because the principal's role is key. Data cannot be used to punish. In fact, by agreement with the teachers association, test results are not involved in teacher evaluation. Associate Superintendent Jan Rowe explained, "So much depends on how the message gets across from their administrators. The whole purpose of the assessment program is longitudinal improvement. Whatever the score, we can always do better. No one is getting fired because of one set of test scores. When this message is handled well, it takes care of the anxiety."

Teacher involvement is another key. Glendale Union's teachers are engaged in developing assessments, determining outcomes, developing curriculum, analyzing data, and setting goals. While individual teachers do not have the option of teaching whatever they like (they have to teach the district curriculum), they can teach however they like, using any instructional approach as long as it produces results.

Of course, a system like Glendale's does not sprout overnight. They've been at it for more than 20 years, starting with one area of the curriculum and slowly incorporating new subjects over time. Districts interested in moving toward a data-driven approach like Glendale's might consider starting with

## Keys to Glendale's Success

▼ Qualified and committed leadership

▼ Staff development

▼ Teacher involvement

one area of the curriculum first while investing heavily in professional and leadership development. Glendale veterans will be the first to tell you: don't up the accountability without upping the support.

*For more information about Glendale's Instructional Management System, contact Dr. Marc Becker, Director of Research, Glendale Union High School District, at (623) 435-6000.*

# EQUITY 2000: Derailing Tracking in Providence, Rhode Island

"Let's get the calculators ready to go," Carol Armour instructed as she began her 90-minute Integrated Mathematics II class at Feinstein High School in Providence, Rhode Island. Integrated Mathematics II is a challenging course that combines algebra and geometry. The students are preparing for the "Shop Till You Drop" task set, a week-long project where they will use a system of equations to discuss the best buy on combinations of jeans and sweaters. They will be charting, graphing, and writing and solving two variable equations.

"You can do this," Ms. Armour exhorts the class. "You need to reach into the brain and think. You are going to have to think about linear equations. Think if the solution is realistic. Think with common sense!"

"You can do this" was not always the prevailing attitude toward students like those who filled the tables in Carol Armour's mathematics class at Feinstein. In fact, only a few years ago many of these students would have been tracked into remedial, basic, or applied mathematics or any one of a web of courses that kept students out of the college-bound track. Now, every student in the school takes algebra and geometry. At Feinstein, they are expected to take four years of high school mathematics, culminating in the demanding Pacesetter course, a fourth-year mathematics program aimed at making the high-standards curriculum associated with the College Board's Advanced Placement program part of all high school learning. That's just the way it is!

What Ms. Armour's students don't know is that when they were entering fourth grade, the Providence Public Schools launched a systemic reform effort that could—no exaggeration—change the course of their lives. The effort is called EQUITY 2000, a program designed by the College Board. The goal of the program is to close the achievement gap between disadvantaged and advantaged students by eliminating tracking at all grade levels and in all subjects. The College Board's own research uncovered the fact that minority students who have not taken algebra or geometry are 40 to 60 percent less likely to complete college. But when they do take these gatekeeper courses, they succeed and go on to college at about the same rate as nonminority students. If EQUITY 2000 delivers on its promise, Ms. Armour's students will no longer be shut out of opportunities for higher education because they haven't taken the right mathematics courses.

After six years, there is cause for optimism in Providence. Not only is 99 percent of the student body taking algebra compared to 43 percent in 1990-91, more students are succeeding. "Our failure rate is lower than it was six years ago when we had only a select group of students taking algebra," explained Providence's former Mathematics Administrator Anthony Terceira. "What's more, enrollment in the third and fourth years of mathematics has tripled—and for only one reason: more kids think they can do it." Similar positive results have been achieved in other urban districts participating in EQUITY 2000 nationwide, including Milwaukee, Wisconsin; San Jose, California; Prince George's County, Maryland; and Nashville, Tennessee. (See Figures 5.1–5.3.)

## Components of Success

Terceira and his staff attribute their success to the systemic approach of the EQUITY 2000 program. EQUITY 2000 sites like Providence commit to implementing the following six components:

**Districtwide policy changes:** At the heart of EQUITY 2000 is a commitment to provide all students with the opportunity to achieve at high levels in all subject areas, beginning with a focus on mathematics. To put this into practice, the program requires that districts implement policies that end tracking and raise standards. As Terceira explained, "You can't ask schools to change unless there is a policy in place they can hang their hats on. The policy has to clearly articulate the absolute commitment that all kids will have access to high standards. Then you have to define who 'all kids' are."

In Providence, the district set a policy of untracked mathematics, the same algebra content for all students, and a four-year mathematics program for all students. "We started with mathematics because you have to pick your battles. You can't change a school system all at once. But we used mathematics for leverage. If that policy is in place, what else has to be in place? Pretty soon changes have to happen in other curricular areas too. Mathematics becomes the hook on which everything else has to hang," commented Terceira.

**Establishment of ongoing professional development for teachers, counselors, and principals:** A second component of EQUITY 2000 is support for school staff in changing attitudes, expectations, and methods through high-quality professional development. Former Mathematics Resource Specialist Sandra Campo explained how this happened in Providence: "Our staff development is absolutely systemic and continuous. We have two weeks

### EQUITY 2000 Components

▼ Districtwide policy changes

▼ Ongoing professional development

▼ Academic enrichment programs

▼ Increased parental involvement

▼ Formation of school-community partnerships

▼ Use of disaggregated data

of training every summer followed by nine continuous staff development activities throughout the school year. It is not another shotgun approach. Six years later, our mathematics teachers are still coming together, bringing up issues, learning new approaches. They see that this approach to professional development is different. This time there is a real commitment."

"There are three pieces to the mathematics teachers' professional development: content, pedagogy, and equity," added Claire Pollard, also a Mathematics Resource Specialist. "Equity is up front in every activity. You can't avoid the issue. You may think you don't see color, but that's not true. We worked to understand our own beliefs and multiple learning and cultural styles."

A key feature of Providence's professional development plan is to involve not only teachers, but principals and guidance counselors as well. For principals, professional development is about helping them move from being building managers to educational leaders. For guidance counselors, it involves focusing on their role as change agents and advocates for children. Head of Elementary Guidance Patricia Nailor elaborated, "Guidance counselors have been a vital part of EQUITY 2000 from the beginning, which is unusual. Counselors traditionally have been kept in the background and viewed as support. Their professional development emphasizes raising expectations of students, awareness of pedagogy and equity issues, and collaboration with mathematics teachers. Through EQUITY 2000, counselors actually took part in mathematics sessions so that we could overcome our own mathematics anxiety and increase our belief that all students could learn rigorous mathematics. Because counselors and mathematics teachers had the chance to work together, we started to break down preconceived ideas we had about each other and created teams of educators focused on teaching and learning."

**Academic enrichment programs:** A third component of EQUITY 2000 is to provide academic enrichment programs such as Saturday Academies and Summer Scholar Programs to supplement the regular course work for students who need the help. "We realize that there are children who are not going to be ready for a more rigorous mathematics program, and it's not their fault," said Terceira. "We have to provide safety nets to help those children who are underprepared, for whatever reason, so they have an equal opportunity to be successful. Anything you can do, do: before-school and after-school tutoring, community-based tutors, parents, college kids, libraries, boys and girls clubs."

The Saturday Academies are one important safety net now in place for students in Providence. Targeted to students who are having difficulty with pre-algebra, algebra, or geometry, Saturday Academies run for six weeks in the fall and spring. Students go to a college campus, where they are given computers, guidance, and rigorous mathematics. Most important, thinks Terceira, "The kids learn that we believe in them."

Another safety net is Providence's grading policy. With the recommendation of their mathematics teacher and guidance counselor, students can be given an incomplete instead of an F and the opportunity to go to summer school and work on those areas where they had difficulty. The message is "you are not done yet."

**Increased parental involvement:** Empowering parents to be effective advocates for their children is another key component of EQUITY 2000. Terceira reported on their progress toward this goal in Providence: "It's taken six years to build. But we now have a cadre of parents who are committed to the program. We used to worry, do we have enough parents? But we kept calling parents, talking about the program, offering family mathematics nights, and educating parents about the Saturday Academies. Now, if there was any danger of losing the Saturday Academies, we'd have a critical mass of parents who would fight hard for it."

**Formation of school-community partnerships:** A fifth component is enlisting the support of higher education and community organizations in working toward academic excellence for all students. In Providence, for example, the school district is collaborating with faculty at local colleges and universities to increase awareness about the needs of urban students and to better prepare teachers for work in urban schools.

**Use of disaggregated student enrollment and achievement data:** Finally, EQUITY 2000 puts the rigorous use of data to monitor progress toward reform as a top priority. Terceira explained how data have driven reform in Providence: "All of the research says that in every district, some students are underrepresented. In our case, we knew exactly who they were—children of color. First we looked at enrollment data and found that the students in high-level mathematics courses didn't represent our kids—there were very few children of color. Then we put in place a three-year plan that absolutely benchmarked 1993-94 to have every student taking algebra."

"There has to be a D-day or it never comes. You can always find a reason to do a little more of this or that. You have to set absolute times and not waiver. If you get a group of committed people, give them what they need, let them alone, and let them gather data, they will prove all kids can learn."

In Providence, D-day has come, and it looks like students, like those in Ms. Armour's mathematics class, are winning.

*For more information on EQUITY 2000, contact Dr. Patricia Nailor, Director of Elementary Guidance, Providence Public Schools, at (401) 456-1718 or visit the EQUITY 2000 Web site at www.collegeboard.org.*

# Walking the Talk in Hudson, Massachusetts

**Action steps in Hudson**

▼ Professional development

▼ Grant funding

▼ Local partnerships

▼ Collaborative decision making

▼ Community involvement

▼ Curriculum reform

Four years in "systemic reform time" is not long. But it was long enough for the Hudson (Massachusetts) Public Schools to turn their mathematics and science education programs around. Hudson doesn't have the reputation of some wealthier suburban Boston towns that surround it. In the early 1990s, it didn't have the academic results, either. When compared with 19 nearby towns, Hudson scored at the very bottom in mathematics and science performance. No more. For the last several years scores have improved until Hudson now outperforms many of its more affluent neighbors.

How did this school district do it? By walking systemic reform talk. The prime mover has been Superintendent Sheldon Berman. Under his visionary leadership, the district has taken the following actions:

▼ provided in-depth professional development in mathematics and science for virtually every teacher;

▼ leveraged thousands of dollars in grant money;

▼ forged partnerships with local research and development organizations, universities, and the Massachusetts Department of Education's State Systemic Initiative;

▼ established collaborative decision-making structures;

▼ built community support;

▼ implemented sweeping mathematics and science curriculum reform.

Guiding all these efforts is the systematic use of data to inform decision making. Here's an overview of how some reforms got under way in Hudson.

In mathematics, teachers first worked together to study state and local standards, critically examine their own curriculum, and then plan for curriculum reform, K-12. At the elementary level, Hudson schools are now several years into implementing Investigations, a problem-based mathematics curriculum, in every classroom. The middle school is now poised to implement the Connected Mathematics Project through a four-year, $60,000 grant from the Center for the Enhancement of Science and Mathematics Education (CESAME) at Northeastern University. And at the high school, teachers piloted Houghton Mifflin's Integrated Mathematics Series and are now exploring the Interactive Mathematics Program from the University of California at Berkeley.

In science, an equally ambitious process of improvement is in motion. Years of studying science standards, professional development in inquiry, and piloting of inquiry-based programs are culminating in a K–5 implementation of Full Option Science System (FOSS). "By no means are we done," said Berman. "In some ways, we are just beginning. But I feel good about what we have been able to create."

## Leaning on Data

Though Berman admitted that change is sometimes more opportunistic than planned, he and other decision makers in Hudson lean heavily on data to inform decision making and motivate change. For example, Berman used data about the district's poor performance in mathematics and science as a wake-up call to staff and the community about the need for reform. It worked.

Hudson quickly found that the old state assessment tests and standardized tests didn't provide enough of the kind of data they needed to analyze their curriculum. So they decided to administer both their own district assessments at grades 3, 5, 7, 9, and 11 and a commercially designed test that includes more open-ended questions and the use of manipulatives. "If we are going to teach that way, we are going to test that way, too," Berman explained.

Now curriculum coordination groups, comprising all teachers who teach in a content area, regularly review district test data along with state and national test results to identify strengths and weaknesses in the curriculum. From their work with these data, staff learned that they weren't teaching fractions well, from elementary on up, and took steps to better their practice. They also reanalyzed what they were doing with open-ended questions and looked at the quality of mathematics instruction for special education students. When the test came around again, they were pleased to learn that they had actually made gains in the areas targeted for improvement.

"These are not easy conversations," observed Berman. "Sometimes people don't see areas of weaknesses and prefer to stroke themselves on the back. Plus, teachers are not familiar with using data. But they are getting more practice." Now they are analyzing state test data to help them improve their programs.

Besides data about student performance, Hudson also uses teacher surveys to monitor the implementation of new programs (see **Data Tools**, DT 4.14). For example, after the first year of implementing Investigations, the district administered a survey with questions like these: "What has helped you? What do you think of the instruments? What changes are you seeing in student behavior?" Teachers, curriculum coordination groups, and the superintendent reviewed the results and used them to inform planning for the next year. Because teachers overall were enthusiastic about the units and were using even more than the district's goal, a decision was made to expand the program. The results also put to rest one major objection to the program—that it would be too difficult for "low achievers." Most teachers reported that the program was terrific for students who had not performed well with a traditional curriculum.

Using data for continuous improvement is also the driving force behind a 50-question survey the district is administering annually to teachers, high school students, and parents to assess the district's progress overall. The Hudson Leadership Team, comprising school committee members, parents, administrators, a member of the Board of Selectmen, and teachers, is using the results to help move the district forward. "These surveys give us very detailed information to track how we are doing. We added questions in mathematics and science since they are our focus areas," Berman reported.

Next steps for Hudson's data-driven improvement effort are to start analyzing student work and to nurture a culture of inquiry among teachers as well as students. Hudson has learned that once in motion the cycle of continuous improvement is hard to stop.

*For more information, contact Sheldon Berman, Superintendent, Hudson Public Schools, at (978) 567-6100.*

# Wagons Heading West in Hallowell, Maine

In the Hall-Dale School District in Hallowell, Maine, all wagons are headed west. The staff, students, and community members know who they are and what they stand for. They have five overarching goals that focus their work (see box below). They have a well-articulated and coordinated curriculum based on high academic standards—complete with benchmarks and performance indicators for each grade level. And they work hard as a community of learners to achieve all that they have set out to do to enrich students' lives. The members of this school community know what they want: they have their "eyes on the prize" and are working with determination to improve student learning.

Getting those wagons lined up wasn't easy. It was the result of a three-year process led by former Superintendent Leon Levesque and a dedicated team of administrators, teachers, and community members. "First, we had to build the foundation," Levesque explained, defining this as a set of beliefs, a vision for the future, a mission, goals, and guiding principles.

Even before Levesque arrived in the district, the Hall-Dale School-Community Coalition—a group of teachers, administrators, parents, community members, and school board members—had started to articulate a vision for the district. As the new superintendent, Levesque knew he had to understand and build on this and prior work done in the district. He interviewed past and present school board members, staff, administrators, and community members, studied documents, and held community-based focus and study groups.

While many common themes were sounded, Levesque found that Hall-Dale, like many districts, was headed east, west, north, and south all at once. "We had some 50 to 60 goals. There was a lot of energy. It

## Goals

**1. Learning**
By the year 2001, the Hall-Dale School System will have in place a well-articulated and coordinated curriculum which sets high academic standards and which provides for the assessment of learning results.

**2. Professional Development**
By the year 2001, the Hall-Dale School System will have in place a focused program for professional development to address district, school, and individual needs.

**3. Facilities**
By the year 2001, the Hall-Dale School System will be engaged in implementing a facilities plan to meet short-term and long-term district needs.

**4. Technology**
By the year 2001, the Hall-Dale School System will have in place a technology plan that supports the integration of technology with work and learning.

**5. Community**
By the year 2001, the Hall-Dale School System will be engaged in building partnerships and in making school facilities available year-round for community activities and learning.

just needed to be directed in a productive way," he observed. Over the next year, Levesque worked with the staff and community to distill a succinct set of beliefs, goals, and principles. He presented them for discussion at public meetings and staff meetings, out of which emerged a crisp document known as the "Plan for the Future."

This plan is not just words on paper. It does two things for Hall-Dale. First, it confirms and validates what they already believe and do:

▼ staff development of high quality;

▼ opportunities for parental involvement;

▼ time for staff to work and learn together;

▼ enrichment of students' lives.

Second, the plan guides decision making and action. Levesque explained, "Without this foundation, we would just move according to events. If something new, such as a reading program, came along, we might jump on it instead of asking, 'How does it fit?' "

## Articulating and Aligning the K-12 Curriculum

If this document was the foundation, Hall-Dale's curriculum work, the next phase of activity, was a major construction project. The district set out to fully articulate and align curriculum in all eight content areas within 18 months, culminating in the publication of a final product. To accomplish this and do it well, Hall-Dale had to pay attention to process as well as product. Levesque had one in mind.

The process would not be top-down. Instead, it would center on eight teacher leaders who would take charge of curriculum groups in each content area. These leaders would work directly with the superintendent, researching and drafting curriculum in their particular content areas. Every teacher and administrator would be involved in a K-12 curriculum committee. Administrators would be learners and peers, not authority figures. Parents would be involved in reviewing the works in progress. The effort would be well financed with stipends and monthly release time for teacher leaders and four release days for the whole staff. "Everyone was going to talk, smell, and breathe curriculum development," said Levesque. "That was what we were doing that year."

Over the next 18 months, the Hall-Dale community hammered out some tough issues. Since K-12 teachers had rarely worked together, it took some doing to overcome the inevitable finger pointing from school to school and forge genuine cooperation. Some teachers objected to the idea of an articulated, aligned curriculum; others saw national standards as "foreign invaders." Staff waged debates about whether curriculum should be developed by disciplines or be interdisciplinary. "People were in different places," explained Page Keeley, former Science Curriculum Coordinator. "We had a lot of discussion about instruction, about what inquiry meant, about group work, and about the support needed to implement changes."

Eventually the process paid off. What emerged was not just an elegant curriculum document, but a staff that was well educated and committed to carrying it out. "Doing the curriculum work was the best form of professional development. Instead of bringing in someone from the outside, we had to become the experts. Now the staff is equipped to carry on the work," commented Keeley.

Another big payoff was improved communication. Staff members understand what is expected of them. They can communicate better with one another because they all agree about what they are supposed to do. Blaming and finger pointing have given way to shared responsibility for student learning across the grade levels. And because of their full participation, administrators understand the standards and the implementation issues classroom teachers face.

Now that the curriculum is distributed, Hall-Dale has taken on the next set of challenges: selecting materials that align with it, providing ongoing professional development for teachers, infusing technology, and assessing how well students are learning. This is where using data will become an important part of the process. "We need to generate good data at the school level and hold ourselves accountable for our successes and failures," Levesque explained. "If a child isn't learning one way, we need to figure out what else we can do." The solid structure of beliefs and academic expectations Hall-Dale has built will make it tough for any student to fall through the cracks.

*For more information, contact Nora Murray, Superintendent, MSAD #16, at (207) 622-6351.*

# Performance-Based Learning and Assessment in Pomperaug Regional School District 15

In Mrs. Pelletier's fourth-grade classroom, students don their laboratory coats and begin their work as scientists. Today they will observe how five different mystery powders react to a series of tests. While the powders may be a mystery to the students, the expectations for the task are crystal clear. Posted on the wall is the "Classroom Assessment List: Making Observations of Mystery Powders." Six questions cue students to the specific criteria for a good observation:

▼ Did you use all of your senses?

▼ Did you use your magnifying glass correctly?

▼ Did you record only what you observed?

▼ Did you record many, detailed observations?

▼ Were your observations neat and organized?

▼ How did you do overall?

In Pomperaug Regional School District 15 in Middlebury and Southbury, Connecticut, assessment lists such as these are a hallmark of a performance-based learning and assessment system. This comprehensive reform of curriculum, instruction, and assessment has permeated virtually every classroom in the district. Assistant Superintendent Michael Hibbard described performance-based learning and assessment as "the rudder, guiding our organization in the direction of improving student learning."

At the heart of the system is the use of carefully constructed performance tasks. Performance tasks engage students in using what they know in real-life, meaningful situations. These tasks aren't add-ons, but an integral part of learning as well as a chance to assess student performance (Hibbard et al. 1996). Ranging from short activities to long-term culminating projects, performance tasks in Pomperaug are keyed to important content knowledge, process skills, and work habits in the curriculum.

Each performance task is accompanied by an assessment list, the specific criteria by which student work will be judged (see sample in Figure 6.2).

FIGURE 6.2

---

## Exhibit 2. Performance Task Assessment List for a Graph
## Elementary School

1. **Heading**
   T: I included my name and the date.
   O: I included my name and the date but they are in the wrong place.
   W: I did not include my name or the date.

2. **Title**
   T: The title tells exactly what the graph is about. The title includes a short statement of what I changed and what I measured.
   O: The title tells what the graph is about.
   W: The title is missing or it tells little.

3. **Labeling the Data**
   T: Each axis has a name that explains what that axis is and the data has units.
   O: The axes need names that are more clear and/or the data needs units.
   W: The names for the axes and/or the units for the data are missing.

4. **Selecting a Scale for Each Axis**
   T: Each axis has a scale that fits the data in the data table.
   The scales help use the whole graph well.
   O: The scales for one or both axes need to be improved.
   W: The scales are missing or they are incorrect.

5. **Drawing Lines or Bars on the Graph**
   T: The lines or bars are drawn accurately and very neatly.
   O: There are some mistakes or the work is a little messy.
   W: There are many mistakes and/or the work is very messy.

6. **Use of Space and Color**
   T: The whole graph uses the space well. Color or some other technique is used so the graph is easy to read.
   O: The space is not used too well and color or some other technique could be used better so that the graph is easier to read.
   W: The graph needs a lot of work on the use of space and color.

7. **Key or Legend**
   T: The key or legend is very clear.
   O: The key or legend is OK.
   W: The key or legend needs a lot of work.

Did I do my best work?

Terrific          OK          Needs Work

Teachers use examples of student work—both excellent and flawed—to help students clearly understand what the criteria mean.

"If performance-based learning and assessment is the rudder, assessment lists are the trim tab, creating pressure on the rudder and moving it more efficiently," Hibbard observed, extending the sailing analogy. "Lists are easy enough for teachers to create, so they feel comfortable and will use them. And they end up being a powerful tool for improving instruction."

## Bringing Everyone on Board

"Pilot projects always work. The issue is how to scale up to change the whole system," continued Hibbard, the champion of performance-based learning and assessment in Pomperaug. With Hibbard at the helm, District 15 has handled scale-up masterfully, nurturing a long-term, sustained change process. In fact, it is rare to see any change permeate as broadly and deeply as performance-based learning and assessment has in Pomperaug. Veteran teachers, new teachers, teachers at every grade level in each school in the district are articulate about the process, skillful in its use, and committed to it.

The process began in the late 1980s, when a small group of teachers attended conferences and workshops to learn about portfolios and assessment lists. By 1991, the district formed a Portfolio Leadership Team of volunteer teachers from each school and key administrators to develop the performance-based learning and assessment model further and involve more teachers in the experiment. Hibbard described these early innovators as "scouts," testing out new approaches in their classroom and encouraging a new wave of teachers, "pioneers," to come along.

By 1993-94, the district offered school-based in-service courses, had created manuals, and had a healthy pioneer group established. Gradually, over the next few years, more and more teachers grew interested in performance assessment, took courses, and participated in summer curriculum work. When enough "settlers" had joined in, they formed a critical mass, signaling a major instructional shift districtwide. Meanwhile, scouts and pioneers continued to develop by taking on leadership roles, conducting action research, and writing about and presenting their work (Hibbard et al. 1996). In addition, the district encouraged networking of teachers within a school and across schools to problem-solve, share successes, and provide leadership for the reform effort.

## Better and Better Student Work

For teachers like Kelly Pelletier, performance-based learning and assessment results in a different allocation of time. "I spend more time preparing tasks and assessment lists and less time talking and correcting students' mistakes. But the quality of student work is so much better. This is a much more efficient use of my time," Pelletier explained.

"It makes so much sense to teach kids real stuff. They get so excited," said third-grade teacher Amy Anctil. "Assessment lists take the guesswork out of the task. They are there when I'm not. They empower kids and help them become more independent."

Teachers agree that performance-assessment lists result in better student work from the outset. But that's not all. They also give students the tools they need to keep improving. Unlike a rubric, assessment lists provide students with specific feedback about each element on the list so they know exactly where they need to improve. Gone is that vague sense that "I'm not doing well but I don't have a clue how to do better." Students are also encouraged to self-assess, conference with the teacher about discrepancies between teacher and student assessment, and set goals for improvement.

"It's good to be able to self-assess," one fourth-grader explained. "Then you have your opinion, not just the teacher's. And you can check your work before you turn it in and fix it."

Consistency is another factor that contributes to improved student learning. Because tasks are keyed to dimensions that cut across grade levels and content areas (such as persuasive writing or observation), students have many opportunities to hone important skills over time, including their self-assessment skills. Students encounter assessments lists from kindergarten to twelfth grade, but the lists become less specific as students reach "performance maturity" and internalize criteria. "Our goal is to wean them from the lists," teacher Deborah McKeon Nelson explained.

Although performance tasks are challenging, they are not just for the bright students: they are used with all students, including special education students. Special education teachers applaud assessment lists for providing just the kind of structure that many special education students need. Often, special and regular education teachers design tasks together to help assure that they are appropriate for all students. When necessary, tasks and performance lists are adapted for special education students and extra coaching is provided. "We build a range into the tasks so we can challenge everyone," special education teacher Terri Thorndike noted.

## Teacher Self-Reflection

Clearly, assessment lists act as a mechanism for students' self-reflection and growth. Happily, they do the same for teachers. When teachers receive specific feedback on how well students performed a task, they are empowered to make immediate adjustments in their teaching to reach more students. High school physics teacher Jim Lehner offered this example: "I do a task with my Science-Technology-Society students where they build a reflector. The best they can do is to build a large reflector that concentrates sunlight in one spot. This year a lot of kids missed the point that you can use a large reflecting surface to collect more sunlight. The lists gave me detailed, quantified information about what the kids were getting and what they were missing. I realized that I needed to give them more examples of good reflectors, shine them on the wall, show how the pathways move, and to do more work with geometry."

### Dimensions for Science Experiments

▼ Observing and finding a question to investigate

▼ Selecting a problem/stating a hypothesis

▼ Designing an experiment to test the hypothesis

▼ Analyzing data to evaluate the hypothesis

▼ Communicating the outcome to a specific audience

▼ Troubleshooting (Hibbard et al. 1996, 91)

Assessment lists also provide teachers with data on how their classes are performing on common "dimensions" in the curriculum. District 15 uses the term "dimensions" to refer to the elements of important skills students are expected to master, such as graphing, making observations, conducting science experiments, and solving mathematics problems. Teachers derive more specific assessment lists for particular tasks from these dimensions. While teachers tailor their own tasks and assessment lists, they all teach to the same dimensions.

By collecting and analyzing assessment list data by dimension, teachers learn where their classes are strong and weak overall and how to reshape curriculum and instruction to address key weaknesses (see Figure 6.3).

"In order to teach using performance assessments, you have to be self-reflective," Anctil elaborated. "You can't just teach something and move on. If you are asking your students what they did well and what to improve on, you have to expect the same of yourself." And teachers, like students, get the advantage of feedback targeted to key pieces of content, skills, and work habits in the curriculum.

The district offers interested teachers a special opportunity to pursue their own questions about how to improve teaching and learning through their Teacher Portfolio Project. In the Portfolio Project, teachers like Linda Gedja

**FIGURE 6.3: ASSESSMENT OF NONFICTION WRITING IN SCIENCE**

Check the Dimensions of Relative Weakness for Each Student

Writing Assignment Title: _____

_____ Date: _____

Dimensions of Nonfiction Writing in Science

| Student Names | Content, Main Idea | Supporting Details | Vocabulary Used | Vocabulary Explained | Diagrams, Drawings | Extensions | Connections | Organization | English Mechanics | Neat, Presentable |
|---|---|---|---|---|---|---|---|---|---|---|
| | | | | | | | | | | |
| | | | | | | | | | | |
| | | | | | | | | | | |
| | | | | | | | | | | |
| | | | | | | | | | | |
| | | | | | | | | | | |
| | | | | | | | | | | |
| | | | | | | | | | | |
| | | | | | | | | | | |
| | | | | | | | | | | |
| | | | | | | | | | | |
| | | | | | | | | | | |
| | | | | | | | | | | |
| | | | | | | | | | | |

decide on a focus question, collect data and examples of student work over the school year, and present their conclusions. Gedja wanted to find out how to improve students' ability to design scientific experiments. She studied the curriculum, examined student performance data to see where students were having difficulty, and developed new ways to guide students in designing experiments that were both interesting to the students and of benefit to the scientific community.

## Sailing Onward

Clearly, high-quality professional development, ongoing and targeted to teachers at different levels, has been the wind in the sails, powering reform in Pomperaug. And what keeps reform on course, the compass, say Pomperaug staff, is a set of shared beliefs about learning and the characteristics of performance-based learning and assessment and a vigilant focus on the goal: improved student learning.

With Pomperaug's performance-based learning and assessment system as the rudder, District 15 is moving at a good clip toward its goal of improved student learning. Pomperaug students outperform students in socioeconomically similar school districts on both the Connecticut Academic Performance Test (CAPT), a state test for tenth-graders that combines literal understanding and performance assessment, and on the Connecticut Mastery Test (CMT), a state test administered to grades 4, 6, and 8 in reading and mathematics (Hibbard et al. 1996). (See "Determining Cause and Effect" in Chapter 4 for more on student learning results in Pomperaug.)

As for the future, most likely not all the students in Mrs. Pelletier's class will grow up to be scientists, although they are relishing their role as fourth-grade scientists. But chances are good they will graduate from Pomperaug Regional High School with the ability to use their knowledge, skills, and productive work habits to tackle problems in the real world. After all, they will have had lots of practice with that in school.

*For more information on performance-based learning and assessment, contact Pomperaug Regional School District, at (203) 758-8250 or visit the district's Web site at www.region15.org.*

# References

Adelman, Nancy, ed. 1995. *A research review: The educational uses of time.* Washington, DC: U.S. Department of Education.

Adler, Martha A. 1992. The educational status of national origin students: On an invisible track. *Equity Coalition* 3(1): 10-13.

Bernhardt, Victoria L. 1996. Data makes the difference with school reform. *Quality Digest* (September).

———. 1997. Data analysis workshop. Randolph, VT (July).

———. 1998. *Data analysis for comprehensive schoolwide improvement.* Larchmont, NY: Eye on Education.

Blanchard, Kenneth, and Spencer Johnson. 1982. *The one-minute manager.* New York: Morrow.

Campbell, Patricia B., and Jennifer N. Storo. 1996. *Whose responsibility is it? The role of administrators and counselors.* Math and Science for the Coed Classroom Series. Groton, MA: Campbell-Kibler Associates.

Castle, S. and G. D. Watts. 1992. The tyranny of time. *Doubts and Certainties: A Forum on School Transformation from the NEA National Center for Innovation* 7(2): 1–4.

Century, Jean Rose. 1994. *Making sense of the literature on equity in education.* Newton, MA: Education Development Corp. Draft.

Cleveland, Harlan. 1985. *The knowledge executive: Leadership in an information society.* New York: Dutton.

Covey, Stephen R. 1989. *The seven habits of highly effective people: Restoring the character ethic.* New York: Simon and Schuster.

Crandall, David, and Susan Loucks. 1982. *The practice profile: An all-purpose tool for program communication, staff development, evaluation, and improvement.* Andover, MA: The NETWORK, Inc.

Cushman, Kathleen. 1996. Looking collaboratively at student work: An essential toolkit. *Horace* (Coalition of Essential Schools, Brown University) 13(2): 1.

Delpit, Lisa. 1995. *Other people's children: Cultural conflict in the classroom.* New York: New Press.

Education Trust. [1996]. *Education watch: The Education Trust community data guide.* Washington, DC: Education Trust.

———. 1996. *Education watch: The 1996 Education Trust state and national data book.* Washington, DC: Education Trust.

Erickson, Lynn. 1995. *Stirring the head, heart, and soul: Redefining curriculum and instruction.* Newbury Park, CA: Corwin.

Estrin, Elise Trumball. 1993. *Alternative assessment: Issues in language, culture, and equity.* Knowledge Brief 11. San Francisco: Far West Laboratory.

Everson, Howard T., and Marlene Dunham. 1996. *Signs of success: EQUITY 2000: Preliminary evidence of effectiveness.* [New York]: College Entrance Examination Board.

Fullan, Michael. 1993. *Change forces: Probing the depths of educational reform.* Bristol, PA: Falmer.

———. 2001. *The new meaning of educational change.* 3rd ed. New York: Teachers College Press.

Gamoran, Adam. 1992. Synthesis of research: Is ability grouping equitable? *Educational Leadership* 50(2): 11-17.

Gartner, Alan, and Dorothy Kerzner Lipsky. 1987. Beyond special education: Toward a quality system for all students. *Harvard Education Review* 57(4): 367-95.

Grayson, Dolores A., and Mary D. Martin. 1997. *Generating expectations for student achievement: An equitable approach to educational excellence: Teacher handbook.* 3rd. ed. Canyon Lake, CA: GrayMill.

Greenbaum, Judith L. 1992. Special education: A changing system. *Equity Coalition* 3(1): 18-20.

Guskey, Thomas, and Dennis Sparks. 1996. Exploring the relationship between staff development and improvements. *Student Learning, the Journal of Staff Development* (Oxford, OH: National Staff Development Council) 17(4): 36.

Hall, Gene E., and Susan Loucks. 1978. Teacher concerns as a basis for facilitating and personalizing staff development. *Teachers College Record* 80(1): 36-53.

Hein, George E., and Sabra Price. 1994. *Active assessment for active science: A guide for elementary school teachers.* Portsmouth, NH: Heinemann.

Herman, Joan L., Pamela R. Aschbacher, and Lynn Winters. 1992. *A practical guide to alternative assessment.* Alexandria, VA: Association for Supervision and Curriculum Development.

Herman, Joan L., and Lynn Winters. 1992. *Tracking your school's success: A guide to sensible evaluation.* Newbury Park, CA: Corwin.

Hibbard, K. Michael, et al. 1996. *A teacher's guide to performance-based learning and assessment.* Alexandria, VA: Association for Supervision and Curriculum Development.

Hilliard, Asa III. 1991. Do we have the will to educate all children? *Educational Leadership* 49(1): 31-36.

Howard, Jeffrey. 1991. *Getting smart: The social construction of intelligence.* Lexington, MA: Efficacy Institute.

Jacobs, Heidi Hayes. 1997. *Mapping the big picture: Integrating curriculum and assessment K-12.* Alexandria, VA: Association for Supervision and Curriculum Development.

Johnson, Ruth. 1996. *Setting our sights: Measuring equity in school change.* Los Angeles: Achievement Council.

Joyce, Bruce, James Wolf, and Emily Calhoun. 1993. *The self-renewing school.* Alexandria, VA: Association for Supervision and Curriculum Development.

Kane, Michael, and Sol Pelavin. 1990. *Changing the odds: Factors increasing access to college.* New York: College Entrance Examination Board.

Lachat, Mary Ann, and Martha Williams. 1996. *Learner-based accountability: Using data to support continuous school improvement.* South Hampton, NH: Center for Resource Management. Typescript.

Lennon, Thelma, Pamela Blackwell, Cheri Bridgeforth, and Pat Cole, eds. 1996. *Pathways: School guidance and counseling in EQUITY 2000.* New York: College Entrance Examination Board.

Lezotte, Lawrence W., and Barbara C. Jacoby. 1992. *Sustainable school reform: The district context for school improvement.* Okemos, MI: Effective Schools.

Light, Richard J., Judith D. Singer, and John B. Willett. 1990. *By design: Planning research on higher education.* Cambridge, MA, and London: Harvard University Press.

Linn, Eleanor. 1992. Untracking high school mathematics. *Equity Coalition* 3(1): 26-28.

Loucks-Horsley, Susan, and Leslie F. Hergert. 1985. *An action guide for school improvement.* Alexandria, VA: Association for Supervision and Curriculum Development, and Andover, MA: The NETWORK, Inc.

Loucks-Horsley, Susan, Peter W. Hewson, Nancy Love, and Katherine E. Stiles. 1998. *Designing professional development for teachers of science and mathematics.* Thousand Oaks, CA: Corwin.

Martin, Anne. 1988. Screening, early intervention, and remediation: Obscuring children's potential. *Harvard Education Review* 58(4): 488-501.

Marzano, Robert J., and John S. Kendall. 1996. *A comprehensive guide to designing standards-based districts, schools, and classrooms.* Alexandria, VA: Association for Supervision and Curriculum Development, and Aurora, CO: Mid-continent Regional Educational Laboratory.

Meyer, Robert H. 2000. Value-added indicators: A powerful tool for evaluating science and mathematics programs and policies. *NISE Policy Brief* 3(3): 1-8.

Mid-Atlantic Eisenhower Consortium for Mathematics and Science Education. 1997. *Third International Mathematics and Science Study TIMSS: A sourcebook of 8th-grade findings*. Philadelphia: Mid-Atlantic Eisenhower Consortium for Mathematics and Science Education.

Mitchell, Ruth. 1996. *Front-end alignment: Using standards to steer educational change.* Washington, DC: Education Trust.

Mokros, Jan, Susan Jo Russell, and Karen Economopoulos. 1995. *Beyond arithmetic: Changing mathematics in the elementary classroom.* Palo Alto, CA: Dale Seymour.

National Center for Improving Science Education. 1989. *Getting started in science: A blueprint for elementary school science education.* Andover, MA: The NETWORK, Inc.

National Council of Teachers of Mathematics. 1989. *Curriculum and evaluation standards for school mathematics.* Reston, VA: National Council of Teachers of Mathematics.

———. 1995. *Assessment standards for school mathematics.* Reston, VA: National Council of Teachers of Mathematics.

———. 2000. Principles and standards for school mathematics. Reston, VA: National Council of Teachers of Mathematics.

National Research Council. 1996. *National science education standards.* Washington, DC: National Academy Press.

———. 1999. *Designing mathematics or science curriculum programs: A guide for using mathematics and science education standards.* Washington, DC: National Academy Press.

———. 2000. *Inquiry and the National Science Education Standards: A guide for teaching and learning.* Washington, DC: National Academy Press.

National Science Foundation. [1997]. *Foundations: The challenge and promise of K-8 science education reform.* Monograph series vol. 1. Arlington, VA: Division of Elementary, Secondary, and Informal Education.

National Staff Development Council. 1997. Data-driven improvement effort leads to results in Oak Park. *Results* (September): 1.

Oakes, Jeannie. 1985. *Keeping track: How schools structure inequality.* New Haven: Yale University Press.

———. 1986. Keeping track, part 1: The policy and practice of curriculum inequality. *Phi Delta Kappan* (September): 12-16.

———. 1990. *Multiplying inequalities: The effects of race, social class, and tracking on opportunities to learn mathematics and science.* Santa Monica, CA: RAND Corp.

Ogbu, J. U., and M. E. Matute-Bianchi. 1990. Understanding sociological factors: Knowledge, identity, and school adjustment. In *Beyond language: Social and cultural factors in schooling language minority students,* developed by the Bilingual Education Office, California State Department of Education, Sacramento, CA. Los Angeles: California State University, Evaluation, Dissemination, and Assessment Center.

O'Neil, John. 1992. On tracking and individual differences: A conversation with Jeannie Oakes. *Educational Leadership* 50(2): 19-21.

Patterson, Jerry L. 1993. *Leadership for tomorrow's schools.* Alexandria, VA: Association for Supervision and Curriculum Development.

Powell, Mary Jo. 1994. *Equity in the reform of mathematics and science education: A look at issues and solutions.* Executive Summary. Edited by Martha Boethel. Austin, TX: Southwest Consortium for the Improvement of Mathematics and Science Teaching.

Quaglia, Russell J. N.d. *Impacting student aspirations: Eight conditions that make a difference.* Orono, ME: National Center for Student Aspirations.

Regional Educational Laboratories. 1998. *Improving classroom assessment: A toolkit for professional developers (Toolkit98).* Portland, OR: Northwest Regional Educational Laboratory.

Rothman, Robert. 1994. Evaluation comment. *Proceedings of the 1993 CRESST Conference: Assessment questions: Equity answers.* Los Angeles: National Center for Research on Evaluation, Standards, and Student Testing.

Sacks, Peter. 2000. *Standardized minds: The high price of America's testing culture and what we can do to change it.* Cambridge, MA: Perseus Books.

Sagor, Richard. 1992. *How to conduct collaborative action research.* Alexandria, VA: Association for Supervision and Curriculum Development.

Saphier, Jon and Matthew King. 1985. Good seeds grow in strong cultures. *Educational Leadership* 42(6): 67–74.

Schmidt, William H., Curtis C. McKnight, and Senta A. Raizen. 1997. *A splintered vision: An investigation of U.S. science and mathematics education.* Dordrecht, the Netherlands: Kluwer.

Schmidt, William H., et al. 1998. *A summary of facing the consequences: Using TIMSS for a closer look at United States mathematics and science education.* Dordrecht, the Netherlands: Kluwer.

Schmoker, Michael. 1996. *Results: The key to continuous improvement.* Alexandria, VA: Association for Supervision and Curriculum Development.

Senge, Peter. 1990. *The fifth discipline: The art and practice of the learning organization.* New York: Currency/Doubleday.

Sinha, D., and R. C. Tripahti. 1994. Individualism in a collectivistic culture: A case of coexistence of opposites. In *Individualism and collectivism: Theory, method, and application*, ed. U. Kim, H. Triandis, C. Kagitcibasi, S. Choi, and G. Yoon. Thousand Oaks, CA: Sage.

Sizer, Theodore R. 1996. *Horace's hope: What works for the American high school*. New York: Houghton Mifflin.

Slavin, Robert. 1988. Synthesis of research on grouping in elementary and secondary schools. *Educational Leadership* 46(1): 67-77.

Tatum, Beverly D. 1997. *"Why are all the black kids sitting together in the cafeteria?" and other conversations about race*. New York: Basic Books.

Thompson, Charles L. and John S. Zueli. 1999. The frame and the tapestry: Standards-based reform and professional development. In *Teaching as the learning profession: Handbook of policy and practice*, ed. Linda Darling-Hammond and Gary Sykes. San Francisco: Jossey-Bass.

Tonack, De, and Ceri Dean, eds. 1997. *Change in action: Navigating and investigating the classroom using action research*. Aurora, CO: McREL.

The tracking wars: Is anyone winning? *The Harvard Education Letter* 8(3): 1-4.

U.S. Department of Education. 1994. *NAEP 1992 trends in academic progress*. Washington, DC: Government Printing Office (OERI).

———. 1996. *Pursuing excellence: A study of U.S. eighth-grade mathematics and science teaching, learning, curriculum, and achievement in international context*. NCES 97-198. Washington, DC: Government Printing Office.

———. 1998. *Pursuing excellence: A study of U.S. twelfth-grade mathematics and science achievement in international context*. NCES 98-049. Washington, DC: Government Printing Office.

———. 1999. *The TIMSS videotape classroom study: Methods and findings from an exploratory research project on eighth-grade mathematics instruction in Germany, Japan, and the United States*. NCES 1999-074. Washington, DC: Government Printing Office.

Vermont Department of Education. 1996. *Vermont's framework of standards and learning opportunities*. Montpelier, VT: Vermont Department of Education.

———. 1998. *Equity and excellence action planning guide*. Montpelier, VT: Vermont Department of Education.

Wagner, Tony. 1998. Change as collaborative inquiry: A 'constructivist' methodology for reinventing schools. *Phi Delta Kappan* (March): 512–17.

Warren, Beth, and Ann S. Rosebery. 1993. *Equity in the future tense: Redefining relationships among teachers, students, and science in linguistic minority classrooms.* Working Paper 1-93. Cambridge, MA: TERC.

Weiss, Carol H. 1998. *Evaluation.* 2nd ed. Upper Saddle River, NJ: Prentice-Hall.

Weiss, Iris R. 1997. The status of science and mathematics teaching in the United States: Comparing teacher views and classroom practice to national standards. *NISE Brief* (University of Wisconsin-Madison) 1(3): 1–7.

Weiss, Iris R. 1999. *Evaluating mathematics and science professional development programs.* Chapel Hill, NC: Horizon Research, Inc.

Weiss, Iris R., Elizabeth E. Arnold, Eric R. Banilower, and Eugene H. Soar. 2000. *Local systemic change through teacher enhancement: Year five cross-site report.* Chapel Hill, NC: Horizon Research, Inc.

Weiss, Iris R., Michael C Matti, and P. Sean Smith. 1994. *Report of the 1993 national survey of science and mathematics education.* Chapel Hill, NC: Horizon Research.

Weissglass, Julian. [1997]. *Ripples of hope: Building relationships for educational change.* Santa Barbara, CA: Center for Educational Change in Mathematics and Science, University of California.

Wellman, David. 1977. *Portraits of white racism.* Cambridge, England: Cambridge University Press.

Wheelock, Anne. 1992. The case for untracking. *Educational Leadership* 50(2): 8-18.

———. 1993. Tracking to untracking in the middle grades. *Equity and Choice* 9(2): 44-50.

Wiggins, Grant P. 1998. *Educative assessment: Designing assessments to inform and improve student performance.* San Francisco: Jossey-Bass.

Williams, Belinda, and Ellen Newcombe. 1994. Building on the strengths of urban learners. *Educational Leadership* 51(8): 75-78.

Wong-Filmore, Lily, and Lois M. Meyer. 1992. The curriculum and linguistic minorities. In *Handbook of research on curriculum,* ed. P. W. Jackson. New York: Macmillan.

# Data Tools

## Chapter 2

## Chapter 3

# Chapter 4

# Chapter 5

## A DISTRICT SELF-ASSESSMENT GUIDE FOR IMPROVING MATHEMATICS TEACHING AND LEARNING

The U.S. Department of Education offers a number of resources to support states and districts in helping students master challenging mathematics. This self-assessment guide is intended to assist stakeholders in thinking creatively about federal resources along with other state and local sources of support for improving mathematics teaching and learning.

The guide highlights key federal programs and poses questions about how their provisions can apply in the context of helping all students master challenging mathematics, with special attention to Title I, Title II, Title III, Title VI, Title VII of the Elementary and Secondary Education Act (ESEA), the Goals 2000: Educate America Act, and the recently reauthorized Individuals with Disabilities Education Act (IDEA). Addressing these questions with your colleagues, thinking through effective answers, and responding with concrete strategies are essential to achieving the goal that all students master challenging mathematics, including the foundations of algebra and geometry by the end of the 8th grade.

| Promoting Equity and Excellence: High Standards That Apply to *All* Students |
|---|

Haven't started → Fully implemented

- Does your district have a plan for ensuring that all students are given the opportunity to meet high quality state/local standards in mathematics?

- Are these standards clearly articulated both within and across the grade levels?

- Are the standards linked to professional development?

- Have you compared them against standards in other districts, states, and nations, or against the National Assessment of Educational Progress (NAEP)?

- Have you provided opportunities for parents, community members, business representatives, teachers and students to discuss your state/local standards?

- Does your district have indicators to assess how well you are providing equal access in the area of mathematics regardless of students' gender, race/ethnicity, English proficiency, or abilities?

Source: U.S. Department of Education.

Haven't started ——→ Fully implemented

- Does your district examine disaggregated student achievement data to inform your mathematics program?

- Does your district know what percent of 8th grade students take algebra or other courses including significant algebra content?

- Are materials and assessments modified to provide accommodation when necessary?

- Do schools in your district ensure that students having difficulty or those needing extra enrichment in mathematics are identified on a timely basis?

- Do schools in your district offer any before-, after-, or summer school programs in mathematics to provide students with the extra learning time they may need?

## Promoting High Quality Curricula and Instruction

Haven't started ——→ Fully implemented

- Does your district provide curriculum opportunities for 4th through 8th grade students to move beyond arithmetic to algebra, geometry, statistics, and data analysis?

- Does your district provide active and effective leadership and administrative support for mathematics education?

- Does your district have a process for evaluating the effectiveness of your mathematics program and making mid-course corrections?

- Does your mathematics curriculum develop students' understanding of concepts using multiple representations?

- Do teachers of mathematics provide frequent opportunities for students to conjecture, explain, predict, and defend their ideas in a variety of ways?

Source: U.S. Department of Education.

Haven't started ———→ Fully implemented

- Do teachers of mathematics give students opportunities to explore open-ended and non-routine problems and to experience the power and usefulness of mathematics in the world around them?

- Does your district provide appropriate textbooks, technology, and other curriculum materials that are standards-based and rigorous?

- Are your criteria for adopting curriculum materials research-based?

- Do you provide training on your adoption criteria for the individuals responsible for selecting curriculum materials?

- Have you reviewed the newest National Science Foundation (NSF) mathematics curriculum projects?

## Professional Development and Promoting High Quality Teachers

Haven't started ———→ Fully implemented

- Does your district employ teachers who are well-prepared in mathematics content and pedagogy?

- Does your district have mathematics specialists and/or master teachers who assist and mentor other faculty in mathematics instruction?

- Does your district offer administrative support and encouragement for long-term and ongoing mathematics professional development experiences for teachers?

- Does your district make available professional development institutes and networks to enable teachers to communicate with each other and become mathematical thinkers?

- Does your district provide time for teachers of mathematics at different grade levels to review, evaluate, and revise the mathematics program?

Source: U.S. Department of Education.

Haven't started → Fully implemented

- Does your district provide time for teachers to observe one another in the teaching of mathematics?

- Does your district provide regular opportunities for teachers to work together in reviewing student work?

- Does your district provide encouragement and support for teachers to participate in programs of recognition for excellence (e.g., Distinguished Educators, National Board Certification)?

- Does your district provide both general and special education staff with skills and knowledge that will help them foster the mathematics achievement of students with disabilities?

- Does your district offer professional development opportunities that promote high-quality mathematics instruction for limited English proficient students?

- Does your district use NSF programs, assistance from colleges and universities, and other forms of outside support to provide high quality professional development?

---

### Cultivating Partnerships Among Schools, Parents, and Communities

Haven't started → Fully implemented

- Does your district provide parents with clear information about students' mathematics curriculum, assessments, and proficiency levels?

- Does your district provide training to help parents assist their children in meeting higher standards in mathematics (e.g., disseminate information on the importance of mathematics for college and careers, assist parents in understanding new ways of teaching and reinforcing mathematics concepts)?

- Do schools in your district have parent-school compacts that include a discussion of mathematics education?

Source: U.S. Department of Education.

## Using Assessments for Improving Student Performance

Haven't started ———→ Fully implemented

- Does your district conduct a needs assessment specific to mathematics that is based on student achievement data relative to state/local standards?

- Are mathematics assessments aligned with goals and objectives of the curriculum and embedded in instruction?

- Does your district have improvement targets for student performance in mathematics?

- Are your students making progress toward meeting state standards in mathematics?

- Do teachers use assessment for:

  -- instructional feedback?

  -- analysis of student understanding and progress?

  -- diagnosis of student needs?

  -- assignment of grades?

  -- communication with parents?

  -- curriculum review?

## Using Available Resources Effectively

Haven't started ———→ Fully implemented

- Does your district take advantage of technical assistance from school support teams and federally funded providers such as the Comprehensive Centers, Regional Labs, the Eisenhower Consortia, and the Eisenhower National Clearinghouse to access high quality information on mathematics teaching and learning?

- Do you use college students and community members skilled in mathematics to tutor students?

Source: U.S. Department of Education.

Progress Toward Standards—A Self Assessment: Student Learning

SCHOOL/DISTRICT:_____ DATE:_____ __Math __Science __Both

Directions: Mark the box in each row that most accurately describes your school at the present time. Mark only one box in each row.

| | Maintenance | Awareness | Transition | Emergence | Predominance |
|---|---|---|---|---|---|
| 1 | ☐ Educators do not share a vision for student learning. | ☐ Educators are aware of the importance of a shared vision for student learning. | ☐ The school is developing a common vision for student learning based on a study of standards. | ☐ The school articulates a common vision for student learning based on a study of standards. | ☐ The school embraces a common vision for student learning based on careful study and extensive dialogue about standards. |
| 2 | ☐ Educators are not aware of the need to provide all students the opportunity to achieve standards through quality instruction, rigorous content, ample resources, and qualified teachers. | ☐ Educators are aware of the need to provide all students the opportunity to achieve standards through quality instruction, rigorous content, ample resources, and qualified teachers. | ☐ The school is developing a plan to provide all students the opportunity to achieve standards through quality instruction, rigorous content, ample resources, and qualified teachers. | ☐ The school has begun to implement a plan to provide all students the opportunity to achieve standards through quality instruction, rigorous content, ample resources, and qualified teachers. | ☐ The school provides all students the opportunity to achieve standards through quality instruction, rigorous content, ample resources, and qualified teachers. |
| 3 | ☐ Educators are not aware of the potential of collaborative study to improve student learning. | ☐ Educators are aware of the need to collaborate to study student learning data, reflect on practice, and improve instruction. | ☐ Groups of educators in the school occasionally collaborate to study student learning data, reflect on practice, and improve instruction. | ☐ A majority of school staff often collaborate to study student learning data, reflect on practice, and improve instruction. | ☐ School staff consistently collaborate to study student learning data, reflect on practice, and improve instruction. |
| 4 | ☐ School improvement plans are not based on student learning data. | ☐ Educators are aware of the need to base school improvement plans on student learning data. | ☐ School improvement plans are based on standardized state and national test data. | ☐ School improvement plans are based on national, state, and local sources of student learning data. | ☐ School improvement plans are based on multiple sources of disaggregated student learning data, including performance assessments. |
| 5 | ☐ School administrators do not understand or promote standards-based reform. | ☐ School administrators are aware of standards-based reform and recognize the need to promote it. | ☐ School administrators understand standards-based reform and are taking steps to implement it. | ☐ School administrators endorse standards-based reform and promote its implementation. | ☐ School administrators are committed to standards-based reform and systematically promote its full implementation. |

Evidence:

1

2

3

4

5

## Progress Toward Standards—A Self Assessment:
## Curriculum, Instruction, and Assessment

SCHOOL/DISTRICT:_____ DATE:_____ __Math __Science __Both

Directions: Mark the box in each row that most accurately describes your school at the present time. Mark only <u>one</u> box in each row.

| | Maintenance | Awareness | Transition | Emergence | Predominance |
|---|---|---|---|---|---|
| 1 | ☐ Educators are not aware of the components of a standards-based curriculum. | ☐ Educators are aware of the components of a standards-based curriculum. | ☐ The school has developed a plan for implementing standards-based curriculum and some teachers are piloting materials. | ☐ A standards-based curriculum is being implemented by a majority of educators in the school. | ☐ A standards-based curriculum and appropriate materials to support high-quality teaching and learning are being implemented throughout the school. |
| 2 | ☐ Educators are not aware of standards-based instructional practices. | ☐ Educators are aware of standards-based instructional practices. | ☐ Standards-based instructional practices are being piloted by some educators. | ☐ Standards-based instructional practices are used by a majority of educators in the school. | ☐ Standards-based instructional practices are used throughout the school. |
| 3 | ☐ Educators are not aware of standards-based assessment practices. | ☐ Educators are aware of the need to base assessments on criteria directly related to standards. | ☐ A variety of standards-based assessment practices are being piloted by some educators. | ☐ A wide variety of standards-based assessment practices are used by a majority of educators. | ☐ A wide variety of classroom assessment practices are used to gauge student achievement and shape instructional planning throughout the school. |
| 4 | ☐ Curriculum, instruction, and assessment are not aligned. | ☐ Educators are aware of the need to align curriculum, instruction, and assessment practices. | ☐ Educators begin to identify strategies for aligning curriculum, instruction, and assessment. | ☐ A majority of educators in the school are aligning curriculum, instruction, and assessment. | ☐ A coherent approach to aligning curriculum, instruction, and assessment is used throughout the school. |
| 5 | ☐ School decisions about curriculum, instruction, and assessment are not informed by data. | ☐ Educators are aware of the need to base school decisions about curriculum, instruction, and assessment on data. | ☐ The school occasionally bases decisions about curriculum, instruction, and assessment on data. | ☐ The school often bases decisions about curriculum, instruction, and assessment on data. | ☐ The school consistently bases decisions about curriculum, instruction, and assessment on data. |
| 6 | ☐ School administrators do not promote standards-based curriculum, instruction, and assessment implementation. | ☐ School administrators respond to individual educators who initiate implementation of standards-based curriculum, instruction, and assessment. | ☐ School administrators encourage individual educators to implement standards-based curriculum, instruction, and assessment. | ☐ School administrators promote schoolwide efforts to implement and align standards-based curriculum, instruction, and assessment. | ☐ School administrators systematically support schoolwide efforts to implement, align, and continuously improve standards-based curriculum, instruction, and assessment. |

Christopher-Gordon Publishers, Inc. © 2002

<u>Evidence:</u>

1

2

3

4

5

6

## Progress Toward Standards—A Self Assessment: Equity

SCHOOL/DISTRICT:_____  DATE:_____  __Math  __Science  __Both

Directions: Mark the box in each row that most accurately describes your school at the present time. Mark only one box in each row.

| | Maintenance | Awareness | Transition | Emergence | Predominance |
|---|---|---|---|---|---|
| 1 | ☐ Educators are not aware of the impact of bias and the importance of making curriculum relevant to both genders and to students' racial, class, and cultural backgrounds. | ☐ Educators are aware of the need to review the curriculum for bias and relevance. | ☐ Some educators have begun to review the curriculum for bias and relevance. | ☐ A majority of educators are revising and supplementing curriculum as needed to address bias and relevance. | ☐ The school has developed an equity plan; educators throughout the school continuously review curriculum for bias and relevance and revise and supplement the curriculum as needed to address equity issues. |
| 2 | ☐ Educators are not aware of the implications of racial, class, cultural, and gender issues in standards-based instructional practices. | ☐ Educators are aware of equity issues in standards-based instructional practices. | ☐ Equity issues are addressed in the instructional practices that are piloted by some educators. | ☐ Equity issues are addressed in the instructional practices that are used by a majority of educators in the school. | ☐ Equity issues are regularly addressed in the instructional practices used throughout the school. |
| 3 | ☐ Educators are not aware of the implications of racial, class, cultural, and gender issues in standards-based assessment practices. | ☐ Educators are aware of equity issues in standards-based assessment practices. | ☐ Equity issues are addressed in the assessment practices that are piloted by some educators. | ☐ Equity issues are addressed in the assessment practices that are used by a majority of educators in the school. | ☐ Equitable, standards-based assessment practices are used throughout the school to measure student achievement and shape instructional planning. |
| 4 | ☐ Decisions about curriculum, instruction, and assessment are not informed by data disaggregated by race, class, cultural background, and gender. | ☐ Educators are aware of the need to include equity data in school decisions about curriculum, instruction, and assessment. | ☐ The school occasionally includes equity data in decisions about curriculum, instruction, and assessment. | ☐ The school often includes equity data in decisions about curriculum, instruction, and assessment. | ☐ The school consistently includes equity data in decisions about curriculum, instruction, and assessment. |
| 5 | ☐ School administrators are not aware of equitable practices or expertise among staff. | ☐ School administrators respond to individual educators who initiate equitable practices in curriculum, instruction, and assessment. | ☐ School administrators encourage educators to address equitable practices in standards-based curriculum, instruction, and assessment. | ☐ School administrators promote equitable practices in standards-based curriculum, instruction, and assessment. | ☐ School administrators systematically support schoolwide efforts to implement, reflect, and continuously improve equitable practices. |

Evidence:

1

2

3

4

5

Progress Toward Standards—A Self Assessment: Professional Development

SCHOOL/DISTRICT:_____ DATE:_____ __Math __Science __Both

Directions: Mark the box in each row that most accurately describes your school at the present time. Mark only <u>one</u> box in each row.

| Maintenance | Awareness | Transition | Emergence | Predominance |
|---|---|---|---|---|
| 1 ☐ Professional development is self-selected and focused on educators' individual needs. | ☐ Professional development addresses the priorities of a majority of individual educators. | ☐ Professional development addresses priorities identified by the school as a whole. | ☐ Professional development is planned collaboratively by teachers and administrators to address school goals as well as individual needs. | ☐ Collegial professional development is an integral part of the school improvement planning process. |
| 2 ☐ Few professional development opportunities are provided by the school. | ☐ Professional development opportunities are a series of unfocused or disconnected events. | ☐ Formal professional development opportunities focused on standards-based teaching and learning are available to all educators. | ☐ Ongoing formal and informal professional development opportunities are focused on standards-based teaching and learning. | ☐ Professional development opportunities are focused on standards-based teaching and learning and embedded in the day-to-day work of the school. |
| 3 ☐ Minimal time or resources are available for ongoing professional development. | ☐ The school budget and schedule provide limited support for professional development. | ☐ The school budget and schedule provide some support for schoolwide professional development. | ☐ The school budget and schedule provide some support for collegial professional development through ongoing study, reflection, and dialogue. | ☐ The school budget and schedule provide resources to support the development of a professional learning community that includes all teachers and administrators. |
| 4 ☐ Data are not used to inform planning, implementation, or evaluation of professional development. | ☐ Educators are aware of the need to use data to inform planning, implementation, and evaluation of professional | ☐ The school occasionally uses data to inform planning, implementation, and evaluation of professional development. | ☐ The school often uses data to inform planning, implementation, and evaluation of professional development. | ☐ The school consistently uses data to inform planning, implementation, and evaluation of professional development. |
| 5 ☐ School administrators do not promote professional learning. | ☐ School administrators respond to individual educators who initiate professional learning opportunities. | ☐ School administrators encourage groups of educators within the school to develop a professional culture. | ☐ School administrators promote the development of some features of a schoolwide professional culture. | ☐ School administrators systematically support the development of a schoolwide professional culture where staff collaborate, reflect, experiment, and continuously learn from research and practice. |

Evidence:

1

2

3

4

5

# Consensogram

**Consensograms** *are vivid visual displays of data generated by a group. The focus can be a group's perception of commitment, belief, interest, knowledge, skill level, etc.. The questions can be generated by a facilitator, the organization, the group or several members. The consensogram offers an efficient way of gathering and displaying information from a large group that can be used immediately for processing.*

**Directions:**

1. Provide each member of the group with a post-it note for each question to be explored. (Be sure the post-its are all of the same size).

2. Display the questions for consideration on a chart or overhead.

3. Ask participants to respond to each question, based on their own perceptions, using a scaled of 0-100 (responses must be in increments of 10, with no negative numbers); and to place their response on a post-it note that will correspond to the question. **NOTE:** Numbers or colors can be useful to discriminate between questions

4. Once all participants have created their response post-its, they should place them on the prepared charts in the form of a bar graph.

5. When all responses have been posted, the group can begin processing the data.

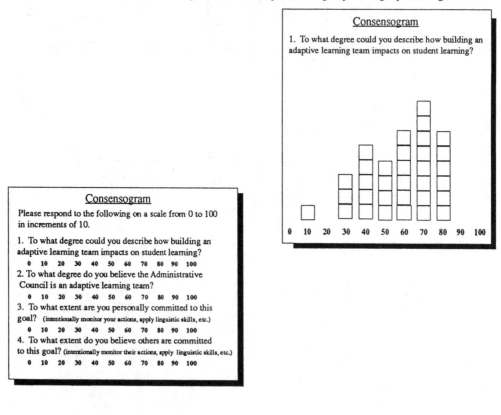

Consensogram

1. To what degree could you describe how building an adaptive learning team impacts on student learning?

0    10    20    30    40    50    60    70    80    90    100

Consensogram

Please respond to the following on a scale from 0 to 100 in increments of 10.

1. To what degree could you describe how building an adaptive learning team impacts on student learning?
0   10   20   30   40   50   60   70   80   90   100

2. To what degree do you believe the Administrative Council is an adaptive learning team?
0   10   20   30   40   50   60   70   80   90   100

3. To what extent are you personally committed to this goal? (intentionally monitor your actions, apply linguistic skills, etc.)
0   10   20   30   40   50   60   70   80   90   100

4. To what extent do you believe others are committed to this goal? (intentionally monitor their actions, apply linguistic skills, etc.)
0   10   20   30   40   50   60   70   80   90   100

Reprinted with permission of Laura Lipton and Bruce Wellman, MiraVia LCC. Based on the work of W. Edward Deming and Total Quality Management.

**Additional Sources of Data**

---
Data Source 1

**Possible Explanation**

---
Data Source 2

---
Data Source 3

## The Tuning Protocol: A Process for Reflection on Teacher and Student Work

The "tuning protocol" was developed by David Allen and Joe McDonald at the Coalition of Essential Schools primarily for use in looking closely at student exhibitions. In the outline below, unless otherwise noted, time allotments indicated are the suggested minimum for each task.

**I. Introduction** [10 minutes]. Facilitator briefly introduces protocol goals, norms and agenda. Participants briefly introduce themselves.

**II. Teacher Presentation** [20 minutes]. Presenter describes the context for student work (its vision, coaching, scoring rubric, etc.) and presents samples of student work (such as photocopied pieces of written work or video clips of an exhibition).

**III. Clarifying Questions** [5 minutes maximum]. Facilitator judges if questions more properly belong as warm or cool feedback than as clarifiers.

**IV. Pause to reflect on warm and cool feedback** [2–3 minutes maximum]. Participants make note of "warm," supportive feedback and "cool," more distanced comments (generally no more than one of each).

**V. Warm and Cool Feedback** [15 minutes]. Participants among themselves share responses to the work and its context; teacher-presenter is silent. Facilitator may lend focus by reminding participants of an area of emphasis supplied by teacher-presenter.

**VI. Reflection / Response** [15 minutes]. Teacher-presenter reflects on and responds to those comments or questions he or she chooses to. Participants are silent. Facilitator may clarify or lend focus.

**VII. Debrief** [10 minutes]. Beginning with the teacher-presenter ("How did the protocol experience compare with what you expected?"), the group discusses any frustrations, misunderstandings, or positive reactions participants have experienced. More general discussion of the tuning protocol may develop.

### Guidelines for Facilitators

1. Be assertive about keeping time. A protocol that doesn't allow for all the components will do a disservice to the presenter, the work presented, and the participants' understanding of the process. Don't let one participant monopolize.
2. Be protective of teacher-presenters. By making their work more public, teachers are exposing themselves to kinds of critiques they may not be used to. Inappropriate comments or questions should be recast or withdrawn. Try to determine just how "tough" your presenter wants the feedback to be.
3. Be provocative of substantive discourse. Many presenters may be used to blanket praise. Without thoughtful but probing "cool" questions and comments, they won't benefit from the tuning protocol experience. Presenters often say they'd have liked more cool feedback.

### Norms for Participants

1. Be respectful of teacher-presenters. By making their work more public, teachers are exposing themselves to kinds of critiques they may not be used to. Inappropriate comments or questions should be recast or withdrawn.
2. Contribute to substantive discourse. Without thoughtful but probing "cool" questions and comments, presenters won't benefit from the tuning protocol experience.
3. Be appreciative of the facilitator's role, particularly in regard to following the norms and keeping time. A tuning protocol that doesn't allow for all components (presentation, feedback, response, debrief) to be enacted properly will do a disservice both to the teacher-presenters and to the participants.

Reprinted with permission from the Coalition of Essential Schools, Inc. from *Horace*, Vol. 13, No. 2, Nov., 1996. www.worldwatch.org

## Making the Whole Student Visible: The Descriptive Review of a Child

At the Prospect Center for Education and Research in Bennington, Vermont, Patricia Carini developed one of the earliest and most influential processes for reflecting on students and their work. As the Center began to archive examples of student work from the Prospect School, an independent school founded in 1965, Carini and her staff recognized the potential for teacher learning through close collaborative looks at such work. The ensuing "Descriptive Review of a Child" comprised a series of rounds of description in which the observations of a number of participants accrue around a few focused questions.

The process aims, writes Rhoda Kanevsky in her essay condensed below, to "make the child visible" as a "unique person who is trying to make sense of the world." Guided by a facilitator, the presenting teacher describes the child; then questions and comments from other participants evoke new information and insights. The intent, she says, is not to change the child but to help the teacher see the child in a new light, and "use the child's interests and values to create harmony in the child's school life." The protocol is summarized as follows:

1. The chairperson convenes the session. The teacher-presenter gives the child's basic statistics: a pseudonym for the sake of privacy, as well as such facts as grade, age, and birth order. The chairperson describes the teacher-presenter's "focusing question" (e.g., "How can I help Jason work more productively with other children in the classroom?").

2. The presenting teacher may describe the classroom context if it would be helpful to participants: the room plan, setting, schedule, etc. Then she describes the child, including both characteristic and unusual behavior, using the prompts in the following categories:

*Physical Presence and Gesture.* Characteristic gestures and expressions: How are these visible in the child's face, hands, body attitudes? How do they vary, and in response to what circumstances (e.g., indoors and outdoors)? Characteristic level of energy: How would you describe the child's rhythm and pace? How does it vary? How would you describe the child's voice: its rhythm, expressiveness, inflection?

*Disposition.* How would you describe the child's characteristic temperament and its range (e.g., intense, even, up-and-down)? How are feelings expressed? Fully? Rarely? How do you "read" the child's feelings? Where and how are they visible? What is the child's emotional tone or "color" (e.g., vivid, bright, serene, etc.)?

*Relationships with Children and Adults.* Does the child have friends? How would you characterize those attachments? Are they consistent? Changeable? Is the child recognized within the group? How is this recognition expressed? Is the child comfortable in the group? How would you describe the child's casual, day-to-day contact with others? How does this daily contact vary? When there are tensions, how do they get resolved? How would you describe the child's relationship to you? To other adults?

*Activities and Interests.* What are the child's preferred activities? Do these reflect underlying interests that are visible to you? For example, does drawing or story writing center on recurrent and related motifs such as superhuman figures, danger and rescue, volcanoes, and other large-scale events? How would you describe the range of the child's interests? Which interests are intense, passionate? How would you characterize the child's engagement with projects (e.g., quick, methodical, slapdash, thorough)? Is the product important to the child? What is the response to mishaps, frustrations? Are there media that have a strong appeal for the child (e.g., paint, blocks, books, woodworking)?

*Formal Learning.* What is the child's characteristic approach to a new subject or process or direction? In learning, what does the child rely on (e.g., observation, memory, trial and error, steps and sequence, getting the whole picture, context)? How does that learning approach vary from subject to subject? What is the child's characteristic attitude toward learning? How would you characterize the child as a thinker? What ideas and content have appeal? Is there a speculative streak? A problem-solving one? A gift for analogy and metaphor? For image? For reason and logic? For insight? For intuition? For the imaginative leap? For fantasy? What are the child's preferred subjects? What conventions and skills come easily? Which are hard?

3. The chairperson summarizes the teacher's portrayal, calling attention to any dominant themes or patterns.

4. The chairperson asks for descriptions from others who have worked with or observed the child. The presenter may also report comments from others who are not present.

5. The chairperson briefly describes the child's previous school experience, any important medical data, and any family information directly supplied to the school by the family (not by hearsay). The teacher also reports what she knows directly from the family. Unless the family is included in the Review, the review focuses primarily on what the teacher can do to support the child.

6. After the chairperson restates the focusing question, the participants offer questions or comments. This opens out multiple perspectives and generates new information that may enhance the teacher's insights, expectations, or approach, or may even shift her focusing question itself.

7. The chairperson summarizes this new information, restates the focusing question, and asks for recommendations drawn from both the foregoing description and participants' own experiences and knowledge of other children. These recommendations focus on ways to support the child's strengths (not change the child) and create harmony in his or her school life. They may contradict or build on each other, and the teacher need not comment on them or take them. They serve as a resource for all present.

8. The chair pulls together and critiques the Review, summarizing any themes of the recommendations or follow-up plans.

*Condensed with permission from* Exploring Values and Standards: Implications for Assessment. *New York: NCREST, Teachers College, Columbia University. 1993.*

Reprinted with permission from the Coalition of Essential Schools, Inc. from *Horace,* Vol. 13, No. 2, Nov., 1996.

377

## A Yardstick for Measuring the Growth of a Team

As a group begins its life, and at several points during its growth, the leader and members might reflect on the following group characteristics and spend some time sharing the data that are collected. Through rating each characteristic, it is possible to get a general picture of the perceptions that various members have about the team and how it is developing. It is also possible to identify difficulties that may be blocking progress:

### A. Goal Clarity

| 1 | 2 | 3 | 4 | 5 |
|---|---|---|---|---|
| No apparent goals | Goal confusion | Average goal clarity | Goals mostly clear | Goals very clear |

### B. Trust and openness

| 1 | 2 | 3 | 4 | 5 |
|---|---|---|---|---|
| None | Little | Average | Considerable | Remarkable |

### C. Empathy among members

| 1 | 2 | 3 | 4 | 5 |
|---|---|---|---|---|
| None | Little | Average | Considerable | Remarkable |

### D. Balance between group task and maintenance needs

| 1 | 2 | 3 | 4 | 5 |
|---|---|---|---|---|
| None | Little | Average | Good | Excellent |

### E. Leadership needs

| 1 | 2 | 3 | 4 | 5 |
|---|---|---|---|---|
| Leadership needs not met | Some leadership needs met | Average meeting of leadership needs | Good meeting of leadership needs | Excellent meeting of leadership needs |

### F. Decision making

| 1 | 2 | 3 | 4 | 5 |
|---|---|---|---|---|
| Unable to make decisions | Inadequate decision making | Average decision making | Good decision making | Full consensus |

### G. Use of group resources (knowledges, skills, experiences)

| 1 | 2 | 3 | 4 | 5 |
|---|---|---|---|---|
| Not used | Poorly used | Average use | Well used | Fully and effectively used |

### H. Sense of belonging

| 1 | 2 | 3 | 4 | 5 |
|---|---|---|---|---|
| None | Some | Average | Good | Strong |

Reprinted by permission of Learning Innovations from *Building Systems for Professional Growth: An Action Guide* by Margaret A. Arbuckle and Lynn B. Murray and published by The Regional Laboratory for Educational Improvement of the Northeast and Islands (now Learning Innovations, a Division of WestEd, Stoneham, MA). Copyright © 1989 by Learning Innovations.

# Data Tool #DT 2-8

## Information and Analysis

| | ONE | TWO | THREE | FOUR | FIVE |
|---|---|---|---|---|---|
| **APPROACH** | Data or information about student performance and needs is not gathered in any systematic way; there is no way to figure out what needs to change at the school. | There is no systematic process, but some teacher and student information is collected and used to problem-solve and establish essential student learnings. | School collects data on student performance (e.g., attendance, achievement) and conducts surveys on student, teacher, and parent needs. The information is used to drive the strategic quality plan for school change. | There is systematic reliance on hard data (including data for subgroups) as a basis for decision making at the classroom level as well as at the school level. Changes are based on the study of data to meet the needs of students and teachers. | Information is gathered in all areas of student interaction with the school. Teachers engage students in gathering information on their own performance. Accessible to all levels, it is comprehensive in scope, and is an accurate reflection of school quality. |
| **IMPLEMENTATION** | No information is gathered with which to make changes. Student dissatisfaction with the learning process is seen as an irritation, not a need for improvement. | Some data is tracked, such as drop-out rates. Only a few individuals are asked for feedback about areas of schooling. | School collects information on students and graduates (e.g., student achievement and expectations), analyzes and uses it in conjunction with future trends for planning. Identified areas for improvement are tracked over time. | Information is used to improve the effectiveness of teaching strategies on all student learning. Students' historical performance is graphed and utilized for diagnostics. Student evaluations and performances are analyzed by teachers in all classrooms. | Innovative teaching processes that meet the needs of students are implemented to the delight of teachers, parents, and students. Information is analyzed and used to prevent student failure. Root causes are known through analyses. Problems are prevented through the use of data. |
| **OUTCOME** | Only anecdotal and hypothetical information is available about student performance, behavior and satisfaction. Problems are solved individually with short-term results. | Little data is available. Change is limited to some areas of the school and dependent upon individual teachers and their efforts. | Information collected about student and parent needs, about assessment and instructional practices is shared with the school staff, and is used to plan for change. Information helps staff understand pressing issues, how to analyze information for "root causes," and how to track for improvement. | An information system is in place. Positive trends begin to appear in many classrooms and schoolwide. There is evidence that these results are caused by understanding and effectively using data collected. | Students are delighted with the school's instructional processes and proud of their own capabilities to learn and assess their own growth. Good to excellent achievement results with all students. No student falls through the cracks. Teachers use data to predict and prevent potential problems. |

Reprinted by permission of Eye On Education (6 Depot Way, West Larchmont, NY 10538, 914-833-0551) from *The School Portfolio: A Comprehensive Framework for School Improvement.* by Victoria L. Bernhardt. Copyright © 1994 by Eye on Education, Inc.

**Figure 5.1a**
## Perceptions of Attitudes, Readiness and Commitment to Change

**Name:** _____

**School:** _____

**Date:** _____

**Role:** ___Teacher ___Administrator ___Support Staff ___Paraprofessional ___Parent ___Student

### Part I: Perceptions of Beliefs and Practices

Please take a few minutes to think about <u>your own</u> perceptions of where your school is relative to student achievement.

1. **Student Achievement**

   a) What percent of your school's staff is dissatisfied with current levels of student achievement?

   | 0% | 25% | 50% | 75% | 100% |

2. **Expectations**

   a) What percent of the students does the staff believe are capable of achieving at or above grade level in all subject areas?

   | 0% | 25% | 50% | 75% | 100% |

   b) What percent of K-12 students does the staff believe should be prepared to pursue a college or university education?

   | 0% | 25% | 50% | 75% | 100% |

   c) What percent of students does your staff believe are capable of succeeding in the college-preparatory pattern of courses required for university eligibility?

   | 0% | 25% | 50% | 75% | 100% |

3. **Aspirations For and Information About Higher Education**

   a) What percent of your student population do you believe is interested in going to a college or university after high school?

   | 0% | 25% | 50% | 75% | 100% |

   b) What percent of your student population and their parents are prepared to make well-informed decisions about college?

   | 0% | 25% | 50% | 75% | 100% |

**Figure 5.1a**
**Perceptions of Attitudes, Readiness and Commitment to Change (continued)**

4.  **Curriculum and Instruction**

    a)  What percent of your student population is learning a rigorous, challenging curriculum built around higher-order thinking skills and problem solving?

    | 0% | 25% | 50% | 75% | 100% |

    b)  What percent of the teachers in your school is investigating and trying to learn and use strategies that are proven to meet the needs of diverse student populations, e.g., cooperative learning, untracking sheltered English?

    | 0% | 25% | 50% | 75% | 100% |

5.  **School Practices**

    a)  What percent of the staff is interested in eliminating tracking and other grouping practices that can inhibit student academic achievement?

    | 0% | 25% | 50% | 75% | 100% |

    b)  What percent of the staff engages in formal discussions about current educational practices that work for *all* students?

    | 0% | 25% | 50% | 75% | 100% |

    c)  What percent of the staff shares their ideas for school improvement?

    | 0% | 25% | 50% | 75% | 100% |

## Part II: Perceptions of Support for Collegiality

Please check "Yes" or "No":

1.  Is there a climate in your school that promotes joint problem solving around the issue of raising student achievement?

    Yes _____    No _____

2.  Is time set aside on a regular basis for staff to develop and share strategies for improving student achievement?

    Yes _____    No _____

**Figure 5.1a**
**Perceptions of Attitudes, Readiness and Commitment to Change (continued)**

## Part III: Perceptions of Current School Status

On the whole, my school is: (Check the one that *most closely* describes your school.)

_____ *Not Ready*
- No consensus about the school's vision.
- No desire to change.
- Unaware of low-level curriculum and its implications for college-going.
- Satisfied with current levels of achievement.

_____ *Ready for Change*
- Building consensus about the school vision.
- Substantial desire among the staff for change.
- Efforts to create a team to lead change.
- Widespread evidence of dissatisfaction with levels of student achievement.
- Baseline data on achievement analyzed, shared and discussed.

_____ *Implementing Change*
- School vision has been developed.
- Staff development and budget reflect the vision.
- Joint problem solving on school structure, curriculum and instruction, and increasing student achievement and 4-year college-going rates.
- Changes in instructional/counseling practices beginning.
- Using data in decision making.
- Team leadership.

_____ *Beginning Evidence of Change*
- Strategies and practices are more aligned to vision.
- Higher level of staff commitment.
- Increased interest in teaching students a rigorous, balanced curriculum and courses.
- Beginning to dismantle schoolwide practices which inhibit student achievement (i.e., tracking).
- Indicators of improved student achievement exist.
- Indicators of changes in the academic culture exist.
- Monitoring plan.
- Reallocation of resources.

_____ *On the Move*
- Movement aligned with vision.
- Evidence of schoolwide belief in higher expectations for students.
- Staff initiating practices which accelerate student achievement.
- Sustained gains in student achievement.
- All students are aware of and are being prepared for 4-year college opportunities.
- Consistent and ongoing monitoring using data.
- Reallocation of resources.

## Who's in Our School/District?

School/District _____  Year _____

| | Grade | | | | Grade | | | | Grade | | | | Grade | | | | Grade | | | | Grade | | | | Total | | | |
|---|---|---|---|---|---|---|---|---|---|---|---|---|---|---|---|---|---|---|---|---|---|---|---|---|---|---|---|---|
| | Female | | Male | | Female | | Male | | Female | | Male | | Female | | Male | | Female | | Male | | Female | | Male | | Female | | Male | |
| | # | % | # | % | # | % | # | % | # | % | # | % | # | % | # | % | # | % | # | % | # | % | # | % | # | % | # | % |
| African American | | | | | | | | | | | | | | | | | | | | | | | | | | | | |
| Latino/a | | | | | | | | | | | | | | | | | | | | | | | | | | | | |
| Asian | | | | | | | | | | | | | | | | | | | | | | | | | | | | |
| Native American | | | | | | | | | | | | | | | | | | | | | | | | | | | | |
| White | | | | | | | | | | | | | | | | | | | | | | | | | | | | |
| Free/Reduced Lunch | | | | | | | | | | | | | | | | | | | | | | | | | | | | |
| At this school less than one year | | | | | | | | | | | | | | | | | | | | | | | | | | | | |
| Bilingual/ESL | | | | | | | | | | | | | | | | | | | | | | | | | | | | |
| Total | | | | | | | | | | | | | | | | | | | | | | | | | | | | |

# denotes actual number in each subgroup. % denotes percent of the total class.

## Norm-Referenced Mathematics Achievement Results
### (e.g. MAT, CTBS, etc.)

School/District _____    Year _____

| | Grade ____ Mean Score | | Grade ____ Mean Score | | Grade ____ Mean Score | | Grade ____ Mean Score | | Grade ____ Mean Score | |
|---|---|---|---|---|---|---|---|---|---|---|
| | Female Mean | Male Mean | Female Mean | Male Mean | Female Mean | Male Mean | Female Mean | Male Mean | Female Mean | Male Mean |
| Total (by gender) | | | | | | | | | | |
| African American | | | | | | | | | | |
| Latino/a | | | | | | | | | | |
| Asian | | | | | | | | | | |
| Native American | | | | | | | | | | |
| White | | | | | | | | | | |
| Free/Reduced Lunch | | | | | | | | | | |
| Bilingual/ESL | | | | | | | | | | |
| At this school less than one year | | | | | | | | | | |
| Other | | | | | | | | | | |

## Norm-Referenced Science Achievement Results

School/District _____

Year _____

| | Grade ___ Mean Score ___ | | Grade ___ Mean Score ___ | | Grade ___ Mean Score ___ | | Grade ___ Mean Score ___ | | Grade ___ Mean Score ___ | |
|---|---|---|---|---|---|---|---|---|---|---|
| | Female Mean | Male Mean | Female Mean | Male Mean | Female Mean | Male Mean | Female Mean | Male Mean | Female Mean | Male Mean |
| Total (by gender) | | | | | | | | | | |
| African American | | | | | | | | | | |
| Latino/a | | | | | | | | | | |
| Asian | | | | | | | | | | |
| Native American | | | | | | | | | | |
| White | | | | | | | | | | |
| Free/Reduced Lunch | | | | | | | | | | |
| Bilingual/ESL | | | | | | | | | | |
| At this school less than one year | | | | | | | | | | |
| Other | | | | | | | | | | |

## Standards–Based Mathematics Assessment Results ( State Tests)
### Two-Year Comparisons

Grade _____ Year _____

Mathematics _____ Topic _____ (e.g. Algebra)

| | At or above standard | | | | Slightly below standard | | | | Significantly below standard | | | |
|---|---|---|---|---|---|---|---|---|---|---|---|---|
| | Female | | Male | | Female | | Male | | Female | | Male | |
| | # | % | # | % | # | % | # | % | # | % | # | % |
| African American | | | | | | | | | | | | |
| Latino/a | | | | | | | | | | | | |
| Asian | | | | | | | | | | | | |
| Native American | | | | | | | | | | | | |
| White | | | | | | | | | | | | |
| Free/ Reduced Lunch | | | | | | | | | | | | |
| At this school less than one year | | | | | | | | | | | | |
| Other (e.g. ESL) | | | | | | | | | | | | |
| Total | | | | | | | | | | | | |

Grade _____ Year _____

Mathematics _____ Topic _____ (e.g. Algebra)

| | At or above standard | | | | Slightly below standard | | | | Significantly below standard | | | |
|---|---|---|---|---|---|---|---|---|---|---|---|---|
| | Female | | Male | | Female | | Male | | Female | | Male | |
| | # | % | # | % | # | % | # | % | # | % | # | % |
| African American | | | | | | | | | | | | |
| Latino/a | | | | | | | | | | | | |
| Asian | | | | | | | | | | | | |
| Native American | | | | | | | | | | | | |
| White | | | | | | | | | | | | |
| Free/ Reduced Lunch | | | | | | | | | | | | |
| At this school less than one year | | | | | | | | | | | | |
| Other (e.g. ESL) | | | | | | | | | | | | |
| Total | | | | | | | | | | | | |

Can be used to compare either the same students over two different years or grades (e.g. their fourth- and sixth-grade scores) or two different groups (e.g. the 1998 and 1999 students in Algebra)

## Standards-Based Science Assessment Results (State Tests)
## Two-Year Comparisons

Grade _____ Year _____

Science _____ Topic _____ (e.g. Earth Science)

Grade _____ Year _____

Science _____ Topic _____ (e.g. Earth Science)

| | At or above standard | | | | Slightly below standard | | | | Significantly below standard | | | |
|---|---|---|---|---|---|---|---|---|---|---|---|---|
| | Female | | Male | | Female | | Male | | Female | | Male | |
| | # | % | # | % | # | % | # | % | # | % | # | % |
| African American | | | | | | | | | | | | |
| Latino/a | | | | | | | | | | | | |
| Asian | | | | | | | | | | | | |
| Native American | | | | | | | | | | | | |
| White | | | | | | | | | | | | |
| Free/ Reduced Lunch | | | | | | | | | | | | |
| At this school less than one year | | | | | | | | | | | | |
| Other (e.g. ESL) | | | | | | | | | | | | |
| Total | | | | | | | | | | | | |

| | At or above standard | | | | Slightly below standard | | | | Significantly below standard | | | |
|---|---|---|---|---|---|---|---|---|---|---|---|---|
| | Female | | Male | | Female | | Male | | Female | | Male | |
| | # | % | # | % | # | % | # | % | # | % | # | % |
| African American | | | | | | | | | | | | |
| Latino/a | | | | | | | | | | | | |
| Asian | | | | | | | | | | | | |
| Native American | | | | | | | | | | | | |
| White | | | | | | | | | | | | |
| Free/ Reduced Lunch | | | | | | | | | | | | |
| At this school less than one year | | | | | | | | | | | | |
| Other (e.g. ESL) | | | | | | | | | | | | |
| Total | | | | | | | | | | | | |

Can be used to compare either the same students over two different years or grades (e.g. their fourth- and sixth-grade scores) or two different groups (e.g. the 1998 and 1999 students in Algebra)

**Analyzing Norm-Referenced Test Results by Quartile**

Name of test: _____

Date of Assessment: _____

Grade: _____

Name of school: _____

Number reported (N): _____

| Year 1 | Quartiles (% of quartile) | 1 (score of 1-25) | 2 (score of 26-50) | 3 (score of 51-75) | 4 (score of 76-99) |
|---|---|---|---|---|---|
| | Expected distribution of students | 25% | 25% | 25% | 25% |
| | Your school's distribution of scores | | | | |

| Year 2 | Quartiles (% of quartile) | 1 (score of 1-25) | 2 (score of 26-50) | 3 (score of 51-75) | 4 (score of 76-99) |
|---|---|---|---|---|---|
| | Expected distribution of students | 25% | 25% | 25% | 25% |
| | Your school's distribution of scores | | | | |

| Year 3 | Quartiles (% of quartile) | 1 (score of 1-25) | 2 (score of 26-50) | 3 (score of 51-75) | 4 (score of 76-99) |
|---|---|---|---|---|---|
| | Expected distribution of students | 25% | 25% | 25% | 25% |
| | Your school's distribution of scores | | | | |

**Questions:**

Are a disproportionate number of our lowest quartile students poor, minority, or female? _____

Are students moving out of the lowest quartile over time? _____

## Sample: Following a Cohort of Students Over Time

### Charting Standardized Achievement Scores

If the scores are matched, i.e., the students are the same from one year to the next, we can make comparisons.

A NCE score of 50 is calculated by test publishers to be the average score from one year of teaching at any grade level.

A gain of zero does not mean that nothing was learned. It means that students achieved one year's growth in one year's time (as measured by this particular test). (3rd grade to 4th grade scores)

**Matched CTBS NCE Math Scores By Class, Over Time**

**Spring 93 to Spring 96**

NCE scores can be used for comparisons because they:
- have equal intevals
- can be aggregated and averaged
- have a derived average of 50, and a standard deviation of 21.06
- can be compared from one test to another
- can be compared from one grade to another
- can be used to calculate gain scores
- match percentiles of 1 to 99
- can be converted to percentiles after analysis

Follow the same students over time, or, at minimum, the same classes.

**Typical Standardized Achievement Chart**

Most often Student Achievement scores are charted for one year, by grade level, implying that one could make meaningful comparisons from grade-to-grade, which we really cannot, because the scores do not represent the same students.

Source: Victoria Bernhardt, *Data Analysis for Comprehensive Schoolwide Improvement,* 1988.

13

## Distinctive Features:

Classroom teachers find this report useful to analyze classroom and individual strengths and needs, and to plan instruction.

A. Class or group, school building, and school system information is clearly identified, along with the norming period to which the scores are compared.

B. Students are listed in alphabetical order across the top of the report.

C. For each item, the national, system, and class percent correct, and the student response are provided to allow for easy comparisons. Correct and incorrect answers, multiple responses, and omissions are all indicated.

D. Each item on the test is grouped into skill categories. for each test and skill category, the number of test items and the percent correct for the nation, the system, and the class are reported.

E. For each item, the national, system, and class percent correct, and the student response are provided. A blank indicates that the student answered the item correctly. An Alpha character indicates the incorrect response the student selected. An asterisk indicates that multiple responses were made and an O denotes an omit.

## Iowa Tests of Basic Skills

**Service 23:**
**Class Item Response Record**

| | | | |
|---|---|---|---|
| Class/Group: | MCKENZIE | Grade: | 5 |
| Building: | WASHINGTON | Level: | 11 |
| Bldg Code: | 99C001101 | Form: | K |
| System: | PORT CHARLES | Test Date: | 4/94 |
| Norms: | SPRING | Page: | 789 |
| Order No.: | 901-A4000052-00-002 | Sheet: | 13 |

(%C = Percent Correct)

| Item No. | MATH CONCEPTS & ESTIMATION Concepts | No. Items | Avg %C Nation | Avg %C System | %C Class |
|---|---|---|---|---|---|
| | | 44 | 64 | 73 | 75 |
| | | 26 | 70 | 81 | 79 |
| | **Numeration and Operations** | 9 | 71 | 80 | 77 |
| 1 | Order Numbers | | 89 | 95 | 88 |
| 13 | Order Numbers | | 70 | 74 | 68 |
| 16 | Compare Numbers | | 79 | 79 | 84 |
| 22 | Properties of Number Systems | | 60 | 79 | 72 |
| 5 | Classify Numbers: Divisibility | | 83 | 94 | 88 |
| | Standard Form | | 82 | 91 | 96 |
| 11 | Place Value | | 65 | 79 | 76 |
| 24 | Place Value | | 46 | 67 | 72 |
| 23 | Perform Fundamental Operations | | 61 | 59 | 52 |
| | **Geometry** | 4 | 72 | 87 | 89 |
| 9 | Classify Figures | | 80 | 98 | 96 |
| 17 | Identify Figures | | 57 | 74 | 80 |
| 7 | Formulas: Perimeter | | 79 | 89 | 96 |
| | | | 70 | 87 | 84 |
| | **Measurement** | 3 | 69 | 83 | 84 |
| 15 | Estimate Measurements | | 55 | 76 | 76 |
| 18 | Identify Appropriate Units | | 74 | 85 | 84 |
| 12 | Time | | 77 | 88 | 92 |
| | **Fractions/Decimals/Percents** | 4 | 62 | 69 | 62 |
| 14 | Interpret Representations | | 68 | 65 | 60 |
| 26 | Interpret Representations | | 50 | 53 | 36 |
| 4 | Compare and Order | | 83 | 85 | 84 |
| 25 | Proportion | | 45 | 70 | 68 |

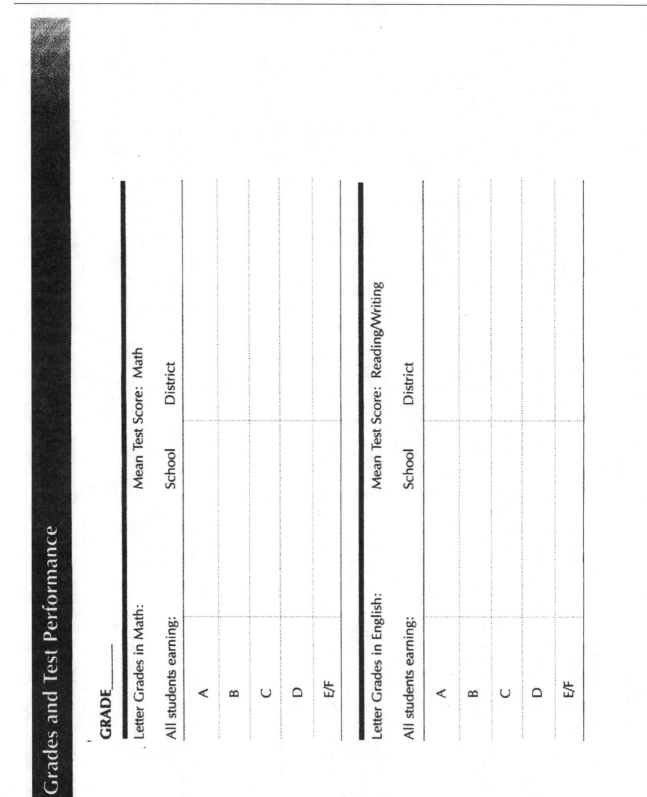

## Grades and Test Performance

**GRADE** ____

**Letter Grades in Math:** Mean Test Score: Math

| | School | District |
|---|---|---|
| All students earning: | | |
| A | | |
| B | | |
| C | | |
| D | | |
| E/F | | |

**Letter Grades in English:** Mean Test Score: Reading/Writing

| | School | District |
|---|---|---|
| All students earning: | | |
| A | | |
| B | | |
| C | | |
| D | | |
| E/F | | |

# Data Tool #DT 3-11

**Elementary/Middle School Retention Rates**

School/District _____  Year _____

| | Grade | | | | | Grade | | | | | Grade | | | | | Grade | | | | | Grade | | | | | Totals | | | |
|---|---|---|---|---|---|---|---|---|---|---|---|---|---|---|---|---|---|---|---|---|---|---|---|---|---|---|---|---|---|
| | Female | | Male | | | Female | | Male | | | Female | | Male | | | Female | | Male | | | Female | | Male | | | Female | | Male | |
| | # | % | # | % | | # | % | # | % | | # | % | # | % | | # | % | # | % | | # | % | # | % | | # | % | # | % |
| Total (by gender) | | | | | | | | | | | | | | | | | | | | | | | | | | | | | |
| African American | | | | | | | | | | | | | | | | | | | | | | | | | | | | | |
| Latino/a | | | | | | | | | | | | | | | | | | | | | | | | | | | | | |
| Asian | | | | | | | | | | | | | | | | | | | | | | | | | | | | | |
| Native American | | | | | | | | | | | | | | | | | | | | | | | | | | | | | |
| White | | | | | | | | | | | | | | | | | | | | | | | | | | | | | |
| Free/ Reduced Lunch | | | | | | | | | | | | | | | | | | | | | | | | | | | | | |
| At this school less than one year | | | | | | | | | | | | | | | | | | | | | | | | | | | | | |
| Bilingual/ESL | | | | | | | | | | | | | | | | | | | | | | | | | | | | | |
| Other | | | | | | | | | | | | | | | | | | | | | | | | | | | | | |

# denotes actual number in each subgroup. % denotes percent of the subgroup total (e.g. 10 females out of a total of 100 females equals 10%)

CHRISTOPHER-GORDON PUBLISHERS, INC. © 2002

# Data Tool #DT 3-12

## Students Overage for Grade by Two or More Years

School/District _____    Year _____

| | Grade | | | | Grade | | | | Grade | | | | Grade | | | | Grade | | | | Totals | | | |
|---|---|---|---|---|---|---|---|---|---|---|---|---|---|---|---|---|---|---|---|---|---|---|---|---|
| | Female | | Male | | Female | | Male | | Female | | Male | | Female | | Male | | Female | | Male | | Female | | Male | |
| | # | % | # | % | # | % | # | % | # | % | # | % | # | % | # | % | # | % | # | % | # | % | # | % |
| Total (by gender) | | | | | | | | | | | | | | | | | | | | | | | | |
| African American | | | | | | | | | | | | | | | | | | | | | | | | |
| Latino/a | | | | | | | | | | | | | | | | | | | | | | | | |
| Asian | | | | | | | | | | | | | | | | | | | | | | | | |
| Native American | | | | | | | | | | | | | | | | | | | | | | | | |
| White | | | | | | | | | | | | | | | | | | | | | | | | |
| Free/ Reduced Lunch | | | | | | | | | | | | | | | | | | | | | | | | |
| At this school less than one year | | | | | | | | | | | | | | | | | | | | | | | | |
| Bilingual/ESL | | | | | | | | | | | | | | | | | | | | | | | | |
| Other | | | | | | | | | | | | | | | | | | | | | | | | |

# denotes actual number in each subgroup.  % denotes percent of the subgroup total
(e.g. 10 females out of a total of 100 females equals 10%)

## Dropout Rate by Cohort

School/District _____

Year _____

| | Freshman | | | | Sophomore | | | | Junior | | | | Senior | | | | 4 Year Total | | | |
| | Female | | Male | | Female | | Male | | Female | | Male | | Female | | Male | | Female | | Male | |
| | # | % | # | % | # | % | # | % | # | % | # | % | # | % | # | % | # | % | # | % |
|---|---|---|---|---|---|---|---|---|---|---|---|---|---|---|---|---|---|---|---|---|
| Total (by gender) | | | | | | | | | | | | | | | | | | | | |
| African American | | | | | | | | | | | | | | | | | | | | |
| Latino/a | | | | | | | | | | | | | | | | | | | | |
| Asian | | | | | | | | | | | | | | | | | | | | |
| Native American | | | | | | | | | | | | | | | | | | | | |
| White | | | | | | | | | | | | | | | | | | | | |
| Free/Reduced Lunch | | | | | | | | | | | | | | | | | | | | |
| At this school less than one year | | | | | | | | | | | | | | | | | | | | |
| Bilingual/ESL | | | | | | | | | | | | | | | | | | | | |
| Other | | | | | | | | | | | | | | | | | | | | |

# denotes actual number in each subgroup. % denotes percent of the subgroup total.
(e.g. 10 females out of a total of 100 females equals 10%)

# Data Tool #DT 3-14

**Students Absent More Than 15% of the School Year**

School/District _____    Year _____

| | Grade | | | | Grade | | | | Grade | | | | Grade | | | | Grade | | | | Totals | | | |
|---|---|---|---|---|---|---|---|---|---|---|---|---|---|---|---|---|---|---|---|---|---|---|---|---|
| | Female | | Male | | Female | | Male | | Female | | Male | | Female | | Male | | Female | | Male | | Female | | Male | |
| | # | % | # | % | # | % | # | % | # | % | # | % | # | % | # | % | # | % | # | % | # | % | # | % |
| Total (by gender) | | | | | | | | | | | | | | | | | | | | | | | | |
| African American | | | | | | | | | | | | | | | | | | | | | | | | |
| Latino/a | | | | | | | | | | | | | | | | | | | | | | | | |
| Asian | | | | | | | | | | | | | | | | | | | | | | | | |
| Native American | | | | | | | | | | | | | | | | | | | | | | | | |
| White | | | | | | | | | | | | | | | | | | | | | | | | |
| Free / Reduced Lunch | | | | | | | | | | | | | | | | | | | | | | | | |
| At this school less than one year | | | | | | | | | | | | | | | | | | | | | | | | |
| Bilingual/ESL | | | | | | | | | | | | | | | | | | | | | | | | |
| Other | | | | | | | | | | | | | | | | | | | | | | | | |

# denotes actual number in each subgroup. % denotes percent of the subgroup total (e.g. 10 females out of a total of 100 females equals 10%)

# Data Tool #DT 3-15

**Discipline Referrals**

School/District _____

(More than _____ times in the _____ school year, _____ semester)
Year _____

| | Grade | | | | Grade | | | | Grade | | | | Grade | | | | Grade | | | | Totals | | | |
|---|---|---|---|---|---|---|---|---|---|---|---|---|---|---|---|---|---|---|---|---|---|---|---|---|
| | Female | | Male | | Female | | Male | | Female | | Male | | Female | | Male | | Female | | Male | | Female | | Male | |
| | # | % | # | % | # | % | # | % | # | % | # | % | # | % | # | % | # | % | # | % | # | % | # | % |
| Total (by gender) | | | | | | | | | | | | | | | | | | | | | | | | |
| African American | | | | | | | | | | | | | | | | | | | | | | | | |
| Latino/a | | | | | | | | | | | | | | | | | | | | | | | | |
| Asian | | | | | | | | | | | | | | | | | | | | | | | | |
| Native American | | | | | | | | | | | | | | | | | | | | | | | | |
| White | | | | | | | | | | | | | | | | | | | | | | | | |
| Free/ Reduced Lunch | | | | | | | | | | | | | | | | | | | | | | | | |
| At this school less than one year | | | | | | | | | | | | | | | | | | | | | | | | |
| Bilingual/ESL | | | | | | | | | | | | | | | | | | | | | | | | |
| Other | | | | | | | | | | | | | | | | | | | | | | | | |

# denotes actual number in each subgroup. % denotes percent of the subgroup total (e.g. 10 females out of a total of 100 females equals 10%)

**Putting It All Together — Student Learning Data Summary Sheet**

| Data Source | Areas of Strength | Areas for Improvement | Possible Implications for Action (CIA, Equity, Critical Supports) |
|---|---|---|---|
| | | | |
| | | | |
| | | | |
| | | | |

## Secondary Mathematics Course Taking

School/District _____     Year _____

| | General Math Female | | General Math Male | | Algebra I Female | | Algebra I Male | | Geometry Female | | Geometry Male | | Algebra II Female | | Algebra II Male | | Trigonometry Female | | Trigonometry Male | | Calculus Female | | Calculus Male | | School/Class Population Totals Female | | School/Class Population Totals Male | |
| --- | --- | --- | --- | --- | --- | --- | --- | --- | --- | --- | --- | --- | --- | --- | --- | --- | --- | --- | --- | --- | --- | --- | --- | --- | --- | --- |
| | # | % | # | % | # | % | # | % | # | % | # | % | # | % | # | % | # | % | # | % | # | % | # | % | # | % | # | % |
| Total (by gender) | | | | | | | | | | | | | | | | | | | | | | | | | | |
| African American | | | | | | | | | | | | | | | | | | | | | | | | | | |
| Latino/a | | | | | | | | | | | | | | | | | | | | | | | | | | |
| Asian | | | | | | | | | | | | | | | | | | | | | | | | | | |
| Native American | | | | | | | | | | | | | | | | | | | | | | | | | | |
| White | | | | | | | | | | | | | | | | | | | | | | | | | | |
| Free/ Reduced Lunch | | | | | | | | | | | | | | | | | | | | | | | | | | |
| At this school less than one year | | | | | | | | | | | | | | | | | | | | | | | | | | |
| Bilingual/ESL | | | | | | | | | | | | | | | | | | | | | | | | | | |
| Other | | | | | | | | | | | | | | | | | | | | | | | | | | |

# denotes actual number in each subgroup. % denotes percent of the subgroup total (e.g. 10 females out of a total of 100 females equals 10%)

## Secondary Science Course Taking

School/District _____    Year _____

| | Chemistry | | | | Computer Science | | | | Physics | | | | Advanced Science | | | | Advanced Science | | | | A. P. Science | | | | School/Class Population Totals | | | |
|---|---|---|---|---|---|---|---|---|---|---|---|---|---|---|---|---|---|---|---|---|---|---|---|---|---|---|---|---|
| | Female | | Male | | Female | | Male | | Female | | Male | | Female | | Male | | Female | | Male | | Female | | Male | | Female | | Male | |
| | # | % | # | % | # | % | # | % | # | % | # | % | # | % | # | % | # | % | # | % | # | % | # | % | # | % | # | % |
| Total (by gender) | | | | | | | | | | | | | | | | | | | | | | | | | | | | |
| African American | | | | | | | | | | | | | | | | | | | | | | | | | | | | |
| Latino/a | | | | | | | | | | | | | | | | | | | | | | | | | | | | |
| Asian | | | | | | | | | | | | | | | | | | | | | | | | | | | | |
| Native American | | | | | | | | | | | | | | | | | | | | | | | | | | | | |
| White | | | | | | | | | | | | | | | | | | | | | | | | | | | | |
| Free/ Reduced Lunch | | | | | | | | | | | | | | | | | | | | | | | | | | | | |
| At this school less than one year | | | | | | | | | | | | | | | | | | | | | | | | | | | | |
| Bilingual/ESL | | | | | | | | | | | | | | | | | | | | | | | | | | | | |
| Other | | | | | | | | | | | | | | | | | | | | | | | | | | | | |

# denotes actual number in each subgroup. % denotes percent of the subgroup total
(e.g. 10 females out of a total of 100 females equals 10%)

# Data Tool #DT 3-19

## Performance on Standardized Tests and Course Placement, by Race and Ethnicity

### Grade 8 or 9

| Top Quartile Performers | Number | Number Enrolled in Algebra I | Percentage Enrolled in Algebra I |
|---|---|---|---|
| African American | | | |
| Asian | | | |
| Latino | | | |
| Native American | | | |
| Total | | | |

| Second Quartile Performers | Number | Number Enrolled Algebra I | Percentage Enrolled in Algebra I |
|---|---|---|---|
| African American | | | |
| Asian | | | |
| Latino | | | |
| Native American | | | |
| Total | | | |

# Data Tool #DT 3-20

## Student Placement in Special Programs

School/District _____

( Special Ed. _____ Gifted and Talented _____ Advanced Placement _____ Other _____ )

Year _____

| | Grade | | | | Grade | | | | Grade | | | | Grade | | | | Grade | | | | Totals | | | |
|---|---|---|---|---|---|---|---|---|---|---|---|---|---|---|---|---|---|---|---|---|---|---|---|---|
| | Female | | Male | | Female | | Male | | Female | | Male | | Female | | Male | | Female | | Male | | Female | | Male | |
| | # | % | # | % | # | % | # | % | # | % | # | % | # | % | # | % | # | % | # | % | # | % | # | % |
| Total (by gender) | | | | | | | | | | | | | | | | | | | | | | | | |
| African American | | | | | | | | | | | | | | | | | | | | | | | | |
| Latino/a | | | | | | | | | | | | | | | | | | | | | | | | |
| Asian | | | | | | | | | | | | | | | | | | | | | | | | |
| Native American | | | | | | | | | | | | | | | | | | | | | | | | |
| White | | | | | | | | | | | | | | | | | | | | | | | | |
| Free / Reduced Lunch | | | | | | | | | | | | | | | | | | | | | | | | |
| At this school less than one year | | | | | | | | | | | | | | | | | | | | | | | | |
| Bilingual/ESL | | | | | | | | | | | | | | | | | | | | | | | | |
| Other | | | | | | | | | | | | | | | | | | | | | | | | |

# denotes actual number in each subgroup.  % denotes percent of the subgroup total (e.g. 10 females out of a total of 100 females equals 10%)

## How Well Are Teachers Prepared?

**Elementary Level** ( regular classroom _____ Special Education _____ )

| Number | Percentage of teaching staff | Number who have taken a math/science course in the last 5 years | Number who have taken a math/science workshop in the last 5 years |
|---|---|---|---|
| Not permanent (subs, temps) | | | |
| Emergency/ alternative credential | | | |
| Certified, with less than 2 years experience | | | |
| Certified, with more than 2 years experience | | | |
| All others | | | |

**Secondary Level**

| | Total course sections (Algebra I, Biology, etc.) | Number of sections taught by teachers with valid certification | Number of sections taught by teachers out of their field | Number who have taken a professional development course in the last 5 years |
|---|---|---|---|---|
| Mathematics | | | | |
| Science | | | | |
| Computers | | | | |

## Equity and Technology Checklist

| In your classroom do *all* students (male, female, different abilities).... | Yes | No | Not Sure |
|---|---|---|---|
| 1. have equal time at the computer? | ❏ | ❏ | ❏ |
| 2. take an equal number of turns at the keyboard when working in pairs or small groups? | ❏ | ❏ | ❏ |
| 3. take equal turns deciding what to enter into the computer when working in pairs or small groups? | ❏ | ❏ | ❏ |
| 4. use the computer for mathematical problem-solving (rather than only for practice with isolated skills, such as number facts)? | ❏ | ❏ | ❏ |
| 5. have opportunities to share their thinking and reasoning about the problems they solve on the computer in small groups/with the class as a whole? | ❏ | ❏ | ❏ |

| Do you.... | Yes | No | Not Sure |
|---|---|---|---|
| 1. set aside a computer (or a specific time at one computer) just for girls? | ❏ | ❏ | ❏ |
| 2. offer girls encouragement and support to try new and challenging software? | ❏ | ❏ | ❏ |
| 3. use computers for mathematical activities that draw on the interests and experience of *all* students? | ❏ | ❏ | ❏ |
| 4. let students know that computers are for everyone - no matter what gender, age, or occupation? | ❏ | ❏ | ❏ |
| 5. try to use software free of harmful gender or other stereotypes? | ❏ | ❏ | ❏ |
| 6. help parents to select software for their children that offers mathematical problem-solving experiences? | ❏ | ❏ | ❏ |
| 7. encourage parents to support their daughter's interest in and knowledge about computers? | ❏ | ❏ | ❏ |
| 8. when possible, invite women who use computers professionally to speak to your class? | ❏ | ❏ | ❏ |

By Christina Perez, from the Weaving Gender Equity into Math Reform project, TERC, 1999.

## Computer Laboratory Usage Form 1

*The purpose of this form is to give you a comprehensive picture and data about which students use the computer laboratory and how they are using it. Use the form to record observations of individual students. Provide as much information as you know about the students. You may need to check with an administrator, school secretary, counselor, or teacher to complete information for some of the categories such as income level, ability level, or language status. You can summarize these results on form 2.*

For _____ School Year    Date and Length of Observations_____

Name of School_____    School District_____

| Student (Name or an I.D.#) | Race/Ethnicity (AA, AI, API, EA, L, NI) | Sex (M, F) | Income Status (L, NL) | Ability Level (LA, HA) | Language Status (LES, NES) | Other (M, SD) | Working Status (WA, WIG) | Activity (P, PS, DnP, G, O) |
|---|---|---|---|---|---|---|---|---|
| | | | | | | | | |
| | | | | | | | | |
| | | | | | | | | |
| | | | | | | | | |
| | | | | | | | | |
| | | | | | | | | |
| | | | | | | | | |
| | | | | | | | | |
| | | | | | | | | |
| | | | | | | | | |
| TOTAL | | | | | | | | |
| Legend: | AA=African American AI=American Indian API=Asian/Pacific Islander EA=European American L=Latino NI=Not identified | M=male F=female | L=low income NL=not low income | LA=lower achieving HA=higher achieving | LES=limited Eng. speaking NES=native Eng. speaking | M=migrant SD=student w/disability | WA=working alone WIG=working in group | P=programming PS=problem solving DnP=drill and practice G=game O=other(identify) |

**Northwest Educational Technology Consortium** [http://www.netc.org/]
**Equity in Educational Technology · Last Updated : 9/18/97**

## Computer Laboratory Usage Form 2

*Use this form to summarize the results of observations recorded on form 1.*

For _____ School Year    Date and Length of Observations_____

Name of School_____    School District_____

| Student Group | Number Working Alone | Number Working with Others | Number Asking for Assistance | Number Engaged in Activity | | | | Total |
|---|---|---|---|---|---|---|---|---|
| | | | | P | PS | DP | G | |
| African American | | | | | | | | |
| American Indian | | | | | | | | |
| Asian/Pacific Islander | | | | | | | | |
| European American | | | | | | | | |
| Latino | | | | | | | | |
| Not identified | | | | | | | | |
| Female | | | | | | | | |
| Male | | | | | | | | |
| Low income | | | | | | | | |
| Not low income | | | | | | | | |
| Lower achieving | | | | | | | | |
| Higher achieving | | | | | | | | |
| Limited English speaking | | | | | | | | |
| Migrant | | | | | | | | |
| Student with disability | | | | | | | | |
| Legend: | P=programming<br>PS=problem solving, that is, the purpose is to teach or use problem-solving skills<br>DnP=drill and practice, the purpose is to practice a specific skill or set of skills over and over<br>G=game (exclusively for fun, does not have an educational purpose) | | | | | | | |

Northwest Educational Technology Consortium [http://www.netc.org/]
Equity in Educational Technology - Last Updated : 9/18/97

## Technology Course Enrollment Form

*Use this form to record the enrollment of formal courses as well as participation in other technology-related activities such as mini-courses, computer clubs, or technology fairs. Indicate the date and time of the course or activity.*

For _____ School Year     Date Completed_____

Name of School_____     School District_____

| Student Group | Number in Course 1 | Number in Course 2 | Number in Course 3 | Number in Course 4 | Number in Course 5 |
|---|---|---|---|---|---|
| African American | | | | | |
| American Indian | | | | | |
| Asian/Pacific Islander | | | | | |
| European American | | | | | |
| Latino | | | | | |
| Not identified | | | | | |
| Female | | | | | |
| Male | | | | | |
| Low income | | | | | |
| Not low income | | | | | |
| Lower achieving | | | | | |
| Higher achieving | | | | | |
| Limited English speaking | | | | | |
| Migrant | | | | | |
| Student with disability | | | | | |
| TOTAL | | | | | |

| Legend: | Course Title | Date(s) | Time(s) |
|---|---|---|---|
| | Course 1:_____ | _____ | _____ |
| | Course 2:_____ | _____ | _____ |
| | Course 3:_____ | _____ | _____ |
| | Course 4:_____ | _____ | _____ |
| | Course 5:_____ | _____ | _____ |

Northwest Educational Technology Consortium [http://www.netc.org/]
Equity in Educational Technology - Last Updated : 9/18/97

## Sample College-Going and Graduation Rate Survey

Dear _____,

We are following up on students who were juniors at (school name) _____ during the school year _____. Please check the appropriate boxes, fold over, and return to the address on the back.

_____ 1. I completed high school or a GED (Circle one).

_____ 2. I attended a two-year college.

_____ 3. I graduated from a two-year college.

_____ 4. I attended a four-year college.

_____ 5. I graduated from a four-year college.

What about your high school education prepared you well for college?

What about your high school education did not prepare you well for college?

What recommendations can you make to better prepare our students for college?

Name

(Other side of card)

Name and Address

Return to:

Your High School Address

## College–Going and Graduation Rates

School/District _____     Year _____

| | Received h. s. diploma or GED | | | | Attended a 2-year college | | | | Graduated from a 2-year college | | | | Attended a 4-year college | | | | Graduated from a 4-year college | | | |
|---|---|---|---|---|---|---|---|---|---|---|---|---|---|---|---|---|---|---|---|---|
| | Female | | Male | | Female | | Male | | Female | | Male | | Female | | Male | | Female | | Male | |
| | # | % | # | % | # | % | # | % | # | % | # | % | # | % | # | % | # | % | # | % |
| Total (by gender) | | | | | | | | | | | | | | | | | | | | |
| African American | | | | | | | | | | | | | | | | | | | | |
| Latino/a | | | | | | | | | | | | | | | | | | | | |
| Asian | | | | | | | | | | | | | | | | | | | | |
| Native American | | | | | | | | | | | | | | | | | | | | |
| White | | | | | | | | | | | | | | | | | | | | |
| Free/ Reduced Lunch | | | | | | | | | | | | | | | | | | | | |
| At this school less than one year | | | | | | | | | | | | | | | | | | | | |
| Bilingual/ESL | | | | | | | | | | | | | | | | | | | | |
| Other | | | | | | | | | | | | | | | | | | | | |

.# denotes actual number in each subgroup. % denotes percent of the subgroup total (e.g. 10 females out of a total of 100 females equals 10%)

# STUDENTS SPEAK
## My Education and My Future
## Grades 3-5

**Please mark your answers like this** ∎
**DO NOT cross** X
**or check** √

USE NO. 2 PENCIL ONLY

**Dear Student:** *We made this survey to find out how you feel about your school, your classmates, and yourself. Your answers will help us make school a better place for you to learn. There are no right or wrong answers. Please be honest, no one will know your answers. If you do not want to do this, please return the survey to the teacher.*

**Please be sure to fill in the answer neatly!**

## I. Background Information

**1. How old are you?**

- □ 7 □ 10
- □ 8 □ 11
- □ 9 □ 12
- □ 13

**2. Are you a girl or a boy ?**

- □ Girl
- □ Boy

**3. What grade are you in?**

- □ 3rd
- □ 4th
- □ 5th

## II. How often each week do you spend time doing the things listed below?

| | | Often | Sometimes | Never |
|---|---|---|---|---|
| 4. | Homework | □ | □ | □ |
| 5. | Playing with friends after school | □ | □ | □ |
| 6. | Playing sports or doing hobbies | □ | □ | □ |
| 7. | Reading for fun (books, magazines) | □ | □ | □ |
| 8. | Watching TV or playing video games | □ | □ | □ |
| 9. | Doing things you enjoy with your family | □ | □ | □ |
| 10. | Doing chores or helping around the house | □ | □ | □ |

## III. Please fill in your answers for each question.

| | | Always | Often | Sometimes | Never |
|---|---|---|---|---|---|
| 11. | Students say things that hurt or insult me. | □ | □ | □ | □ |
| 12. | I like my teachers. | □ | □ | □ | □ |
| 13. | I believe I can always improve. | □ | □ | □ | □ |
| 14. | My teachers allow me to explore topics I find interesting. | □ | □ | □ | □ |
| 15. | I like to learn new things. | □ | □ | □ | □ |
| 16. | Teachers make learning fun. | □ | □ | □ | □ |
| 17. | I am a leader. | □ | □ | □ | □ |
| 18. | I set goals for myself. | □ | □ | □ | □ |
| 19. | Teachers listen to what I say. | □ | □ | □ | □ |

| | | Always | Often | Sometimes | Never |
|---|---|---|---|---|---|
| 20. | My teachers want me to do well. | A ☐ | O ☐ | S ☐ | N ☐ |
| 21. | My teachers tell me when I do a good job when I try my best | A ☐ | O ☐ | S ☐ | N ☐ |
| 22. | We work on many projects in class. | A ☐ | O ☐ | S ☐ | N ☐ |
| 23. | I like it when we do different types of activities in class. | A ☐ | O ☐ | S ☐ | N ☐ |
| 24. | I have fun at school. | A ☐ | O ☐ | S ☐ | N ☐ |
| 25. | Teachers expect me to make good decisions. | A ☐ | O ☐ | S ☐ | N ☐ |

## III.   Please fill in your answers for each question.

| | | Always | Often | Sometimes | Never |
|---|---|---|---|---|---|
| 26. | I think doing homework is important. | A ☐ | O ☐ | S ☐ | N ☐ |
| 27. | I like helping others. | A ☐ | O ☐ | S ☐ | N ☐ |
| 28. | I think of my teachers as friends. | A ☐ | O ☐ | S ☐ | N ☐ |
| 29. | Doing well in school is important to me. | A ☐ | O ☐ | S ☐ | N ☐ |
| 30. | My teachers ask lots of questions during class. | A ☐ | O ☐ | S ☐ | N ☐ |
| 31. | It's okay to be different. | A ☐ | O ☐ | S ☐ | N ☐ |
| 32. | I set a good example for others to follow. | A ☐ | O ☐ | S ☐ | N ☐ |
| 33. | I am responsible for my actions. | A ☐ | O ☐ | S ☐ | N ☐ |
| 34. | I know I can be anything I want to be. | A ☐ | O ☐ | S ☐ | N ☐ |
| 35. | In class we work together in groups. | A ☐ | O ☐ | S ☐ | N ☐ |
| 36. | My teachers care about me. | A ☐ | O ☐ | S ☐ | N ☐ |
| 37. | I am good at many things. | A ☐ | O ☐ | S ☐ | N ☐ |
| 38. | I ask lots of questions. | A ☐ | O ☐ | S ☐ | N ☐ |
| 39. | Teachers like it when I try something new. | A ☐ | O ☐ | S ☐ | N ☐ |
| 40. | I get excited about going to school. | A ☐ | O ☐ | S ☐ | N ☐ |
| 41. | I am a good decision maker. | A ☐ | O ☐ | S ☐ | N ☐ |
| 42. | I see myself being successful in the future. | A ☐ | O ☐ | S ☐ | N ☐ |
| 43. | I am proud of my school. | A ☐ | O ☐ | S ☐ | N ☐ |
| 44. | I try my best in school. | A ☐ | O ☐ | S ☐ | N ☐ |
| 45. | I think about going to college. | A ☐ | O ☐ | S ☐ | N ☐ |
| 46. | I have friends to talk to at school. | A ☐ | O ☐ | S ☐ | N ☐ |
| 47. | I think about what I want to be when I get older. | A ☐ | O ☐ | S ☐ | N ☐ |

## IV.   When I need help or advice I go to…

| | | Always | Often | Sometimes | Never |
|---|---|---|---|---|---|
| 48. | My parents | A ☐ | O ☐ | S ☐ | N ☐ |
| 49. | My techers | A ☐ | O ☐ | S ☐ | N ☐ |
| 50. | My school counselor | A ☐ | O ☐ | S ☐ | N ☐ |
| 51. | My friends | A ☐ | O ☐ | S ☐ | N ☐ |
| 52. | My brothers and sisters | A ☐ | O ☐ | S ☐ | N ☐ |
| 53. | My grandparents | A ☐ | O ☐ | S ☐ | N ☐ |

## V.   When you think about your future, how important are the following things?

| | | Very Important | Important | Not Important |
|---|---|---|---|---|
| 54. | Making lots of money | VI ☐ | I ☐ | NI ☐ |
| 55. | Being happy | VI ☐ | I ☐ | NI ☐ |
| 56. | Going to college | VI ☐ | I ☐ | NI ☐ |
| 57. | Having a good job | VI ☐ | I ☐ | NI ☐ |
| 58. | Having fun | VI ☐ | I ☐ | NI ☐ |
| 59. | Having a family | VI ☐ | I ☐ | NI ☐ |

## MAP Q

### HIGH SCHOOL PHYSICS CURRICULUM MAP

| | CONTENT | SKILLS | ASSESSMENT |
|---|---|---|---|
| **SEPTEMBER** | Measuring systems<br>Uncertainties in measurement<br><br>Vector addition | Make measurements in SI units<br>Present the results of an experiment as a lab report<br><br>Use a computer graphing program<br><br>Add vectors using trigonometry<br><br>Use significant figures in collecting and manipulating data<br><br>Analyze graphs of data for slope and the equation of the line | Written lab reports<br>Tests: problems, multiple choice, essay<br>Lab performance |
| **OCTOBER** | Linear motion<br><br>Vector addition<br><br>Acceleration of gravity | Vector addition continued<br><br>Analyze the effect of forces on motion<br><br>Use algebra to solve equations for motion<br><br>Represent the motion of a body as position vs. Time and velocity vs. Time graphs from lab data<br><br>Determine the acceleration of gravity in the lab | Written lab reports<br>Tests: problems, multiple choice, essay<br>Lab performance<br><br>Scientist report (library research)<br><br>Oral presentation of group problem-solving activity |
| **NOVEMBER** | Newton's Laws of Motion<br><br>Forces<br><br>Torque | Add force vectors using trigonometry as well as in the lab<br><br>Draw free body diagrams to isolate the forces acting on a body<br><br>For a body in equilibrium, show that EA. = 0 and write equations to represent this<br><br>Analyze force problems involving friction, inclines, and torques. | Written lab reports<br>Tests: problems, multiple choice, essay<br>Lab performance<br><br>Lab report written in the IMRAD form |
| **DECEMBER** | Motion in two dimensions<br><br>Centripetal forces<br><br>Gravitation | ID Real and fictitious forces<br><br>Use algebra to solve sets of equations relating the vertical and horizontal components of 2D motion<br><br>Describe gravitation as one of the forces of nature | Written lab reports<br>Tests: problems, multiple choice, essay<br>Lab performance<br><br>Design problem "10m vehicle" |

## MAP Q, continued

## HIGH SCHOOL PHYSICS CURRICULUM MAP

| | CONTENT | SKILLS | ASSESSMENT |
|---|---|---|---|
| JANUARY | Work | To relate work, energy, and power | Written lab reports |
| | Energy, potential & kinetic | | Tests: problems, multiple choice, essay |
| | Momentum | Write equations representing the law of conservation on momentum for systems | Lab performance |
| | | | Midterm Exam |
| FEBRUARY | Kinetic Theory | Write equations to describe the exchange of heat in a system including any phase changes which may occur. | Written lab reports |
| | Heat | | Tests: problems, multiple choice, essay |
| | | Relate the structure of matter to the properties of the different phases of matter | Lab performance |
| MARCH | Waves | Predict the results of wave interactions | Written lab reports |
| | Sound | | Tests: problems, multiple choice, essay |
| | Light | Analyze a system with moving source or observer to predict the change in frequency of an emitted sound using Doppler effect concepts | Lab performance |
| | | | Design project |
| | | Relate the properties of light to its dual nature | |
| APRIL | Electrostatics | Use the laws of electrostatics to predict the results of induction and conduction effects on charged bodies | Written lab reports |
| | Current Electricity | | Tests: problems, multiple choice, essay |
| | | | Lab performance |
| | | Interpret and analyze field diagrams | IMRAD lab report |
| | | | Field diagram analysis |
| MAY | DC circuits | Use Ohm's and Kirchoff's laws to analyze solve circuit diagrams | Written lab reports |
| | Magnetism | | Tests: problems, multiple choice, essay |
| | Nuclear Physics | Set up circuits in the laboratory | Lab performance |
| | | Evaluate the benefits vs. the risks of nuclear energy and radioisotope use in terms of the properties of radiation | Position paper RE nuclear energy |
| | | | Circuit diagram analysis |
| JUNE | Astronomy | Complete the assignments and projects in the Astronomy packet and prepare a portfolio of these activities | Compile portfolio of astronomy assignments |
| | | | FINAL EXAM |

## CURRICULUM

The curriculum is the district's plan for instruction. In detail, the curriculum specifies what mathematics students need to know and be able to do, and it includes examples of activities and resources designed to lead students to the achievement of school and district goals.

Does the K-12 mathematics curriculum:

1. Follow developmentally appropriate goals and objectives?
☐ Yes ☐ No
Ⓐ Ⓕ Ⓢ Ⓝ

2. Reflect state and national standards and objectives?
☐ Yes ☐ No
    a) the CMT?
☐ Yes ☐ No
    b) the CAPT?
☐ Yes ☐ No
    c) the "Curriculum and Evaluation Standards" of the NCTM?
☐ Yes ☐ No
    d) the forthcoming Connecticut Mathematics Curriculum Framework and the forthcoming Connecticut State Department of Education Guide to K-12 Program Development in Mathematics?
☐ Yes ☐ No

3. Reflect the collective thinking of teachers, administrators, mathematicians and other users of mathematics, and parents?
☐ Yes ☐ No
Ⓐ Ⓕ Ⓢ Ⓝ

4. Include a process for ongoing development and evaluation?
☐ Yes ☐ No
Ⓐ Ⓕ Ⓢ Ⓝ

5. Include instructional guides for teachers?
☐ Yes ☐ No
Ⓐ Ⓕ Ⓢ Ⓝ

6. Exist in sufficient quantity that copies are available in every classroom?
☐ Yes ☐ No
Ⓐ Ⓕ Ⓢ Ⓝ

7. Require that all students have equal opportunities to engage in worthwhile mathematical tasks?
☐ Yes ☐ No
Ⓐ Ⓕ Ⓢ Ⓝ

8. Connect instruction to real life experience?
☐ Yes ☐ No
Ⓐ Ⓕ Ⓢ Ⓝ

9. Articulate content logically, both at grade level and across grade levels?
☐ Yes ☐ No
Ⓐ Ⓕ Ⓢ Ⓝ

10. Arrange instructional content sequentially, moving from concrete, to pictorial, to symbolic?
☐ Yes ☐ No
Ⓐ Ⓕ Ⓢ Ⓝ

A = Always   F = Frequently   S = Sometimes   N = Never

11. Relate mathematics content to previous learning?  ☐ Yes ☐ No  Ⓐ Ⓕ Ⓢ Ⓝ

12. Relate mathematics to other curriculum content areas?  ☐ Yes ☐ No  Ⓐ Ⓕ Ⓢ Ⓝ

13. Specify that instruction be activity based?  ☐ Yes ☐ No  Ⓐ Ⓕ Ⓢ Ⓝ

14. Specify routine use of manipulatives in all grades?  ☐ Yes ☐ No  Ⓐ Ⓕ Ⓢ Ⓝ

15. Include activities that accommodate various student learning styles?  ☐ Yes ☐ No  Ⓐ Ⓕ Ⓢ Ⓝ

16. Include activities that develop critical and creative thinking skills?  ☐ Yes ☐ No  Ⓐ Ⓕ Ⓢ Ⓝ

17. Include non-routine problem-solving activities?  ☐ Yes ☐ No  Ⓐ Ⓕ Ⓢ Ⓝ

18. Include activities that engage student interest and help students develop appreciation for the power and beauty of mathematics?  ☐ Yes ☐ No  Ⓐ Ⓕ Ⓢ Ⓝ

19. Include activities that provide students with opportunities to conjecture, explain, predict, and defend their ideas in a variety of ways?  ☐ Yes ☐ No  Ⓐ Ⓕ Ⓢ Ⓝ

20. Include activities that require students to use mathematical language, vocabulary, and notation to represent ideas, describe relationships, and model situations?  ☐ Yes ☐ No  Ⓐ Ⓕ Ⓢ Ⓝ

21. Include activities that incorporate the use of calculators and computers into instruction in order to assist students in discovering and investigating mathematical concepts and to solve problems?  ☐ Yes ☐ No  Ⓐ Ⓕ Ⓢ Ⓝ

A = Always   F = Frequently   S = Sometimes   N = Never

# Data Tool #DT 4-3

## Things I Expect to See the Students Doing in Mathematics Classroom

Student-to-student communication

Active participation

Problem solving rather than rote activity

Students using manipulatives and constructions

Applications

Use of a variety of strategies

Students posing nontrivial questions

Making connections to the real world

Having fun

Keeping journals; doing reflective thinking

Explaining

Engaged in learning new things

Showing satisfaction through involvement

Exhibiting a sense of accomplishment

Being confident in giving/defending answers

Some disequilibrium

Student-teacher interaction (extended discourse)

Student risk-taking in class (to revise, defend, etc.)

Non-threatening learning environment

Reprinted by permission of Mathematics Renaissance from *Investigating Mathematics Reform: Data Gathering Toolkit* prepared by the staff of the Mathematics Renaissance. Copyright © 1996 by Mathematics Renaissance.

# Data Tool #DT 4-4

## What Are Students Doing [in Math Class]?

Some things one might observe in an inquiry-based classroom:

1. Interacting with each other, as well as working independently, just as adults do.

2. Working in teams to challenge and defend possible solutions. Students help each other to learn.

3. Working in groups to test solutions to problems, with each group member highly involved.

4. Communicating mathematical ideas to one another through examples, demonstrations, models, drawings, and logical arguments.

5. Using textbooks as one of many resources. Students also should know how and when to use manipulatives (such as blocks and balances) and technology (such as calculators and computers) as problem-solving tools.

6. Applying math to real-life problems and not just practicing a collection of isolated skills. Students spend lots of time solving complex problems.

7. Seeking a best solution among several solutions to a problem. Students can explain the different ways they reach these solutions and can defend the choice of one over another.

Reprinted by permission of Mathematics Renaissance from *Investigating Mathematics Reform: Data Gathering Toolkit* prepared by the staff of the Mathematics Renaissance. Copyright © 1996 by Mathematics Renaissance.

CHAPTER 10   Identifying Inquiry in the Classroom

## INQUIRY INDICATORS
## WHAT ARE THE STUDENTS DOING?

**On-the-Run Reference Guide to the Nature of Elementary Science**

Imagine yourself in an inquiry classroom. What would you expect to see? These guidelines from the Vermont Elementary School/Continuous Assessment Project were created by observing students as they did "hands-on, minds-on" exploration in the classroom. "The intent is not to use the guide as a checklist," they said, "but to use it as a statement of what we value in the areas of science process, science dispositions, and science content development."

When students are doing inquiry-based science, an observer will see that:

Students View Themselves as Active
Participants in the Process of Learning

1. They look forward to doing science.
2. They demonstrate a desire to learn more.
3. They seek to collaborate and work cooperatively with their peers.
4. They are confident in doing science; they demonstrate a willingness to modify ideas, take risks, and display healthy skepticism.
5. They respect individuals and differing points of view.

Students Accept an "Invitation to Learn"
and Readily Engage in the Exploration Process

1. They exhibit curiosity and ponder observations.
2. They take the opportunity and time to try out and persevere with their own ideas.

Students Plan and Carry Out Investigations

1. They design a fair test as a way to try out their ideas, not expecting to be told what to do.
2. They plan ways to verify, extend, or discard ideas.
3. They carry out investigations by handling materials with care, observing, measuring, and recording data.

Students Communicate Using a Variety of Methods

1. They express ideas in a variety of ways: journals, reporting out, drawing, graphing, charting, etc.

419

2. They listen, speak, and write about science with parents, teachers, and peers.
3. They use the language of the processes of science.
4. They communicate their level of understanding of concepts that they have developed to date.

## Students Propose Explanations and Solutions and Build a Store of Concepts

1. They offer explanations both from a "store" of previous experience and from knowledge gained as a result of ongoing investigation.
2. They use investigations to satisfy their own questions.
3. They sort out information and decide what is important (what does and doesn't work).
4. They are willing to revise explanations and consider new ideas as they gain knowledge (build understanding).

## Students Raise Questions

1. They ask questions—verbally or through actions.
2. They use questions that lead them to investigations that generate or redefine further questions and ideas.
3. They value and enjoy asking questions as an important part of science.

## Students Use Observations

1. They observe carefully, as opposed to just looking.
2. They see details, seek patterns, detect sequences and events; they notice changes, similarities, and differences.
3. They make connections to previously held ideas.

## Students Critique Their Science Practices

1. They create and use quality indicators to assess their own work.
2. They report and celebrate their strengths and identify what they'd like to improve upon.
3. They reflect with adults and their peers.

Adapted from materials created by the Vermont Elementary Science Project and the Continuous Assessment in Science Project, ©1995.  Courtesy of Gregg Humphrey.

# INQUIRY INDICATORS
# WHAT ARE THE TEACHERS DOING?

**The Role of the Teacher in the Inquiry Classroom**

In the inquiry classroom, the teacher's role becomes less involved with direct teaching and more involved with modeling, guiding, facilitating, and continually assessing student work. Teachers in inquiry classrooms must constantly adjust levels of instruction to the information gathered by that assessment.

The teacher's role is more complex, including greater responsibility for creating and maintaining conditions in which children can build understanding. In this capacity, the teacher is responsible for developing student ideas and maintaining the learning environment.

Besides the process skills that the student must hone in the inquiry classroom, there are also skills a teacher must develop in order to support student learning of scientific ideas. When you enter an inquiry classroom, you may see that the:

Teachers Model Behaviors and Skills

1. They show children how to use new tools or materials.
2. They guide students in taking more and more responsibility in investigations.
3. They help students design and carry out skills of recording, documenting, and drawing conclusions.

Teachers Support Content Learning

1. They help students form tentative explanations while moving toward content understanding.
2. They introduce tools and materials and scientific ideas appropriate to content learning.
3. They use appropriate content terminology, as well as scientific and mathematical language.

Teachers Use Multiple Means of Assessment

1. They are sensitive to what children are thinking and learning, and identify areas in which children are struggling.
2. They talk to children, ask questions, make suggestions, share, and interact.

## Innovation Configuration Continuum: NCTM Evaluation Standard - Instruction

### Component 1: Displaying Content Accuracy and Developmental Appropriateness

| (4) | (3) | (2) | (1) |
|---|---|---|---|
| Teacher typically uses completely accurate content, and with sensitivity to students' developmental levels and mathematical maturity. | Teacher typically uses accurate content, sometimes with sensitivity to students' developmental levels and mathematical maturity. | Teacher uses inaccurate content, and typically in a manner not developmentally appropriate. | Teacher seldom uses accurate content or developmentally appropriate methods of delivery. |

### Component 2: Employing Realistic Contexts and Constructivist Approaches

| (4) | (3) | (2) | (1) |
|---|---|---|---|
| Teacher typically employs realistic contexts that incorporate student experiences, and encourages students to explore, investigate, and discuss ideas. | Teacher typically sets instruction in a realistic context, but provides little time for students to explore and discuss their own ideas. | Teacher sometimes uses realistic context for instruction, but typically allows no time for student-directed exploration or discussion. | Teacher seldom employs realistic contexts or allows any time for student exploration or discussion. |

### Component 3: Maintaining Facilitative Environment

| (4) | (3) | (2) | (1) |
|---|---|---|---|
| Teacher typically assumes several instructional roles - explaining, modeling so students see and understand, and encouraging students reflection. | Teacher typically assumes more than one instructional role and explains so that students understand, but usually does not model or encourage student reflection. | Teacher typically lectures and/or provides notes to students, encouraging little interaction or student reflection. | Teacher typically lectures and provides no opportunities for student interaction. |

### Component 4: Emphasizing Concepts, Logical Connections, and Relationships

| (4) | (3) | (2) | (1) |
|---|---|---|---|
| Teacher typically emphasizes strong conceptual frameworks and multiple representations and translations of ideas, and presents mathematics as an integrated body of logically related topics. | Teacher typically emphasizes concepts rather than arbitrary rules, occasionally uses multiple representations of ideas, and sometimes presents mathematics as an integrated body of study. | Teacher equally emphasizes concepts and arbitrary rules, seldom uses more than one way to represent an idea, and presents few connections or relationships between mathematical concepts. | Teacher typically emphasizes collections of arbitrary rules to be memorized, uses one or no representation for ideas, and presents no logical connections between mathematical topics. |

### Component 5: Encouraging Problem Solving, Reasoning, and Communication

| (4) | (3) | (2) | (1) |
|---|---|---|---|
| Teacher typically provides high-quality opportunities for students to engage in problem solving, reasoning, and communicating mathematically.. | Teacher occasionally provides high-quality opportunities for students to engage in problem solving, reasoning, and communicating mathematically.. | Teacher seldom provides high-quality opportunities for students to engage in problem solving, reasoning, and communicating mathematically.. | Teacher does not provide opportunities for students to engage in problem solving, reasoning, and communicating mathematically.. |

McREL Eisenhower High Plains Consortium for Mathematics and Science

# SURVEY OF CLASSROOM PI

IN

## ELEMENTARY SCHOOL
# MATHEMATICS

Thank you for your time and patience in completing this survey. The survey was designed with mathematics educators representing a number of states, including your own. We hope the results will help teachers and schools in improving curriculum and support for mathematics education. Each school will receive a report on the results of this survey. Please read each question and the possible responses carefully, and then mark your response by filling in the appropriate circle in the response section.

Please use #2 pencil in responding to this survey.

A joint project of the Council of Chief State School Officers and the National Institute for Science Education funded by the National Science Foundation

## INSTRUCTIONAL ACTIVITIES IN MATHEMATICS

*Listed below are some questions about what students in the target class do in mathematics. For each activity, pick one of the choices (0, 1, 2, 3) to indicate the percentage of instructional time that students are doing each activity. In responding, please think of an average student in this class.*

**What percentage of mathematics instructional time in the target class do students:**

> **NOTE: No more than two '3's , or four '2's should be reported for this set of items.**

| | None | Less than 25% | 25% to 33% | More than 33% |
|---|---|---|---|---|
| 34 Collect or analyze data. | ⓪ | ① | ② | ③ |
| 35 Maintain and reflect on a mathematics portfolio of their own work. | ⓪ | ① | ② | ③ |
| 36 Use hands-on materials or manipulatives (e.g., counting blocks, geometric shapes, algebraic tiles). | ⓪ | ① | ② | ③ |
| 37 Engage in mathematical problem solving (e.g., computation, story-problems, mathematical investigations). | ⓪ | ① | ② | ③ |
| 38 Work in pairs or small groups. | ⓪ | ① | ② | ③ |
| 39 Do a mathematics activity with the class **outside** the classroom. | ⓪ | ① | ② | ③ |
| 40 Use computers, calculators, or other educational technology to learn mathematics. | ⓪ | ① | ② | ③ |

**When students in the target class are engaged in *problem-solving activities* as part of mathematics instruction, what percentage of that time do students:**

> **NOTE: No more than two '3's , or four '2's should be reported for this set of items.**

| | None | Less than 25% | 25% to 33% | More than 33% |
|---|---|---|---|---|
| 41 Complete computational exercises or procedures from a text or a worksheet. | ⓪ | ① | ② | ③ |
| 42 Solve word problems from a textbook or worksheet. | ⓪ | ① | ② | ③ |
| 43 Solve novel mathematical problems. | ⓪ | ① | ② | ③ |
| 44 Write an explanation to a problem using several sentences. | ⓪ | ① | ② | ③ |
| 45 Apply mathematical concepts to real or simulated "real-world" problems. | ⓪ | ① | ② | ③ |
| 46 Make estimates, predictions, guesses, or hypotheses. | ⓪ | ① | ② | ③ |
| 47 Analyze data to make inferences or draw conclusions. | ⓪ | ① | ② | ③ |
| 48 Other: _____ | ⓪ | ① | ② | ③ |

Reprinted by permission of Council of Chief State School Officers. Material was supported by a grant from the National Science Foundation, Division of Research, Evaluation and Communication.

**When students in the target class work in** *pairs or small groups* **as part of mathematics instruction, what percentage of that time do students:**

> **NOTE: No more than two '3's , or four '2's should be reported for this set of items.**

| | None | Less than 25% | 25% to 33% | More than 33% |
|---|---|---|---|---|
| 49 Talk about ways to solve mathematics problems. | ⓪ | ① | ② | ③ |
| 50 Complete written assignments from the textbook or worksheets. | ⓪ | ① | ② | ③ |
| 51 Work on an assignment, report, or project that takes longer than one week to complete. | ⓪ | ① | ② | ③ |
| 52 Work on a writing project where group members help to improve each others' (or the group's) work. | ⓪ | ① | ② | ③ |
| 53 Review assignments, problems, or prepare for a test or quiz. | ⓪ | ① | ② | ③ |
| 54 Other: _____ | ⓪ | ① | ② | ③ |

**When students in the target class are engaged in activities that involve the** *use of hands-on materials* **, what percentage of that time do students:**

> **NOTE: No more than two '3's , or four '2's should be reported for this set of items.**

| | None | Less than 25% | 25% to 33% | More than 33% |
|---|---|---|---|---|
| 55 Work with hands-on materials such as counting blocks, geometric shapes, or algebraic tiles to understand concepts. | ⓪ | ① | ② | ③ |
| 56 Measure objects using tools such as rulers, scales, or protractors. | ⓪ | ① | ② | ③ |
| 57 Build models or charts. | ⓪ | ① | ② | ③ |
| 58 Collect data by counting, observing, or conducting surveys. | ⓪ | ① | ② | ③ |
| 59 Present information to students concerning a mathematical idea or project. | ⓪ | ① | ② | ③ |
| 60 Other: _____ | ⓪ | ① | ② | ③ |

Reprinted by permission of Council of Chief State School Officers. Material was supported by a grant from the National Science Foundation, Division of Research, Evaluation and Communication.

## USE OF CALCULATORS, COMPUTERS AND OTHER EQUIPMENT

**When students in the target class are engaged in activities that involve the** *use of calculators, computers, or other educational technology* **as part of mathematics instruction, what percentage of that time do students:**

> **NOTE: No more than two '3's , or four '2's should be reported for this set of items.**

| | None | Less than 25% | 25% to 33% | More than 33% |
|---|---|---|---|---|
| 61  Learn facts or practice procedures. | ⓪ | ① | ② | ③ |
| 62  Use sensors and probes. | ⓪ | ① | ② | ③ |
| 63  Retrieve or exchange data or information (e.g., using the Internet). | ⓪ | ① | ② | ③ |
| 64  Display and analyze data. | ⓪ | ① | ② | ③ |
| 65  Develop geometric concepts. | ⓪ | ① | ② | ③ |
| 66  Take a test or quiz. | ⓪ | ① | ② | ③ |
| 67  Use individualized instruction or tutorial software. | ⓪ | ① | ② | ③ |

**For Items 68-71, indicate how often the average student uses each of the following types of equipment in this mathematics class:**

| | Not Available | Available, but rarely used | Used less than 7 times per year | Used 7 to 36 times per year | Used Weekly |
|---|---|---|---|---|---|
| 68  Math manipulatives (e.g., pattern blocks, algebraic tiles) | ⓪ | ① | ② | ③ | ④ |
| 69  Measuring tools (e.g., rulers, protractors, scales) | ⓪ | ① | ② | ③ | ④ |
| 70  Calculators | ⓪ | ① | ② | ③ | ④ |
| 71  Graphing calculators | ⓪ | ① | ② | ③ | ④ |

Reprinted by permission of Council of Chief State School Officers. Material was supported by a grant from the National Science Foundation, Division of Research, Evaluation and Communication.

## ASSESSMENTS

**For items 72-79, indicate how often you use each of the following strategies when assessing students in the target mathematics class.**

| | None | 1 - 4 times per year | 1 - 3 times per month | 1 - 3 times per week | 4 - 5 times per week |
|---|---|---|---|---|---|
| 72 Objective items (e.g., multiple choice, true/false) | ⓪ | ① | ② | ③ | ④ |
| 73 Short answer questions such as performing a mathematical procedure | ⓪ | ① | ② | ③ | ④ |
| 74 Extended response item for which student must explain or justify solution | ⓪ | ① | ② | ③ | ④ |
| 75 Performance tasks or events (e.g., hands-on activities) | ⓪ | ① | ② | ③ | ④ |
| 76 Individual or group demonstration, presentation | ⓪ | ① | ② | ③ | ④ |
| 77 Mathematics projects | ⓪ | ① | ② | ③ | ④ |
| 78 Portfolios | ⓪ | ① | ② | ③ | ④ |
| 79 Systematic observation of students | ⓪ | ① | ② | ③ | ④ |

## INSTRUCTIONAL INFLUENCES

**For items 80-89, indicate the degree to which each of the following influences what you teach in the target mathematics class.**

| | N/A | Strong Negative Influence | Somewhat Negative Influence | Little or No Influence | Somewhat Positive Influence | Strong Positive Influence |
|---|---|---|---|---|---|---|
| 80 Your state's curriculum framework or content standards | ⓪ | ① | ② | ③ | ④ | ⑤ |
| 81 Your district's curriculum framework or guidelines | ⓪ | ① | ② | ③ | ④ | ⑤ |
| 82 Textbook / instructional materials | ⓪ | ① | ② | ③ | ④ | ⑤ |
| 83 State test | ⓪ | ① | ② | ③ | ④ | ⑤ |
| 84 District test | ⓪ | ① | ② | ③ | ④ | ⑤ |
| 85 National mathematics education standards | ⓪ | ① | ② | ③ | ④ | ⑤ |
| 86 Your experience in pre-service preparation | ⓪ | ① | ② | ③ | ④ | ⑤ |
| 87 Students' special needs | ⓪ | ① | ② | ③ | ④ | ⑤ |
| 88 Parents/community | ⓪ | ① | ② | ③ | ④ | ⑤ |
| 89 Preparation of students for next grade or level | ⓪ | ① | ② | ③ | ④ | ⑤ |

Reprinted by permission of Council of Chief State School Officers. Material was supported by a grant from the National Science Foundation, Division of Research, Evaluation and Communication.

## CLASSROOM INSTRUCTIONAL PREPARATION

**For items 90-107 , please indicate how well prepared you are now to:**

| | | Not well prepared | Somewhat prepared | Well prepared | Very well prepared |
|---|---|---|---|---|---|
| 90 | Teach mathematics at your assigned level. | ⓪ | ① | ② | ③ |
| 91 | Use/manage cooperative learning groups in mathematics. | ⓪ | ① | ② | ③ |
| 92 | Integrate mathematics with other subjects. | ⓪ | ① | ② | ③ |
| 93 | Provide mathematics instruction that meets mathematics standards (district, state, or national). | ⓪ | ① | ② | ③ |
| 94 | Use a variety of assessment strategies (including objective and open-ended formats). | ⓪ | ① | ② | ③ |
| 95 | Teach estimation strategies. | ⓪ | ① | ② | ③ |
| 96 | Teach problem solving strategies. | ⓪ | ① | ② | ③ |
| 97 | Select and/or adapt instructional materials to implement your written curriculum. | ⓪ | ① | ② | ③ |
| 98 | Teach mathematics with the use of manipulative materials, such as counting blocks, geometric shapes, and so on. | ⓪ | ① | ② | ③ |
| 99 | Teach students with physical disabilities. | ⓪ | ① | ② | ③ |
| 100 | Help students document and evaluate their own mathematics work. | ⓪ | ① | ② | ③ |
| 101 | Teach classes for students with diverse abilities. | ⓪ | ① | ② | ③ |
| 102 | Teach mathematics to students from a variety of cultural backgrounds. | ⓪ | ① . | ② | ③ |
| 103 | Teach mathematics to students who have limited English proficiency. | ⓪ | ① | ② | ③ |
| 104 | Teach students who have a learning disability which impacts mathematics learning. | ⓪ | ① | ② | ③ |
| 105 | Encourage participation of females in mathematics. | ⓪ | ① | ② | ③ |
| 106 | Encourage participation of minorities in mathematics. | ⓪ | ① | ② | ③ |
| 107 | Involve parents in the mathematics education of their children. | ⓪ | ① | ② | ③ |

Reprinted by permission of Council of Chief State School Officers. Material was supported by a grant from the National Science Foundation, Division of Research, Evaluation and Communication.

**TEACHER OPINIONS**

**Please indicate your opinion about each of the statements below:**

| | Strongly disagree | Disagree | Neutral / undecided | Agree | Strongly agree |
|---|---|---|---|---|---|
| 108 Students learn mathematics best when they ask a lot of questions. | ⓪ | ① | ② | ③ | ④ |
| 109 Students master and retain mathematical algorithms more efficiently through repeated practice than through the use of applications and simulations. | ⓪ | ① | ② | ③ | ④ |
| 110 Calculators use should be incorporated only after the mastery of basic arithmetic facts. | ⓪ | ① | ② | ③ | ④ |
| 111 All students can learn challenging content in mathematics. | ⓪ | ① | ② | ③ | ④ |
| 112 Students learn mathematics best in classes with students of similar abilities. | ⓪ | ① | ② | ③ | ④ |
| 113 It is important for students to learn basic mathematics skills before solving problems. | ⓪ | ① | ② | ③ | ④ |
| 114 I really enjoy teaching mathematics. | ⓪ | ① | ② | ③ | ④ |
| 115 I am supported by colleagues to try out new ideas in teaching mathematics. | ⓪ | ① | ② | ③ | ④ |
| 116 I receive little support from the school administration for teaching mathematics. | ⓪ | ① | ② | ③ | ④ |
| 117 Mathematics teachers in this school regularly share ideas and materials. | ⓪ | ① | ② | ③ | ④ |
| 118 Mathematics teachers in this school regularly observe each other teaching classes. | ⓪ | ① | ② | ③ | ④ |
| 119 I have many opportunities to learn new things about mathematics or mathematics teaching in my present job. | ⓪ | ① | ② | ③ | ④ |
| 120 I am required to follow rules at this school that conflict with my best professional judgment about teaching and learning mathematics. | ⓪ | ① | ② | ③ | ④ |
| 121 Most mathematics teachers in this school contribute actively to making decisions about the mathematics curriculum. | ⓪ | ① | ② | ③ | ④ |
| 122 I have adequate time during the regular school week to work with my peers on mathematics curriculum or instruction. | ⓪ | ① | ② | ③ | ④ |
| 123 I have adequate curriculum materials available for mathematics instruction. | ⓪ | ① | ② | ③ | ④ |
| 124 Absenteeism is a problem in my class. | ⓪ | ① | ② | ③ | ④ |
| 125 Mobility of students in and out of our school is a problem. | ⓪ | ① | ② | ③ | ④ |

Reprinted by permission of Council of Chief State School Officers. Material was supported by a grant from the National Science Foundation, Division of Research, Evaluation and Communication.

## Expectations for Students in Mathematics

**Memorize Facts, Definitions, Formulas**

Recite basic mathematics facts

Recall mathematics terms & definitions

Recall formulas and computational procedures

**Communicate Understanding of Mathematical Concepts**

Communicated mathematical ideas

Use representations to model mathematical ideas

Explain findings and results from data analysis strategies

Develop/explain relationships between concepts

Show or explain relationships between models, diagrams, and/or other representations

**Perform Procedures**

Use numbers to count, order, denote

Do computational procedures or algorithms

Follow procedures/instructions

Solve equations/formulas/routine word problems

Organize or display data

Read or produce graphs and tables

Execute geometric constructions

**Conjecture, Generalize, Prove**

Determine the truth of a mathematical pattern or proposition

Write formal or informal proofs

Recognize, generate or create patterns

Find a mathematical rule to generate a pattern or number sequence

Make and investigate mathematical conjectures

Identify faulty arguments or misrepresentations

Identify faulty arguments or misrepresentations of data

Reason inductively or deductively

**Solve Non-routine Problems/Make Connections**

Apply and adapt a variety of appropriate strategies to solve non-routine problems

Apply mathematics in contexts outside of mathematics

Analyze data, recognize patterns

Synthesize content and ideas from several sources

**Response Codes for Time on Topic**

**0=None, not covered**

**1=Slight coverage** (less than one class/lesson)

**2=Moderate coverage** (one to five classes/lessons)

**3=Sustained coverage** (more than five classes/lessons)

**Response Codes for Expectations for Students**

**0=No emphasis** (Not a performance goal for this topic)

**1=Slight emphasis** (Less than 25% of time on this topic)

**2=Moderate emphasis** (25% to 33% of time on this topic)

**3=Sustained emphasis** (more than 33% of time on this topic)

Reprinted by permission of Council of Chief State School Officers. Material was supported by a grant from the National Science Foundation, Division of Research, Evaluation and Communication.

**Time on Topic** — **Middle School Mathematics Topics** — **Expectations for Students in Mathematics**

| \<none\> | ¹ Number sense / Properties / Relationships | Memorize Facts, Definitions, Formulas | Communicate Understanding of Mathematical Concepts | Perform Procedures | Conjecture, Generalize, Prove | Solve Non-Routine Problems/Make Connections |
|---|---|---|---|---|---|---|
| ⓪ ① ② ③ | 101 Place value | ⓪ ① ② ③ | ⓪ ① ② ③ | ⓪ ① ② ③ | ⓪ ① ② ③ | ⓪ ① ② ③ |
| ⓪ ① ② ③ | 102 Whole numbers | ⓪ ① ② ③ | ⓪ ① ② ③ | ⓪ ① ② ③ | ⓪ ① ② ③ | ⓪ ① ② ③ |
| ⓪ ① ② ③ | 103 Operations | ⓪ ① ② ③ | ⓪ ① ② ③ | ⓪ ① ② ③ | ⓪ ① ② ③ | ⓪ ① ② ③ |
| ⓪ ① ② ③ | 104 Fractions | ⓪ ① ② ③ | ⓪ ① ② ③ | ⓪ ① ② ③ | ⓪ ① ② ③ | ⓪ ① ② ③ |
| ⓪ ① ② ③ | 105 Decimals | ⓪ ① ② ③ | ⓪ ① ② ③ | ⓪ ① ② ③ | ⓪ ① ② ③ | ⓪ ① ② ③ |
| ⓪ ① ② ③ | 106 Percents | ⓪ ① ② ③ | ⓪ ① ② ③ | ⓪ ① ② ③ | ⓪ ① ② ③ | ⓪ ① ② ③ |
| ⓪ ① ② ③ | 107 Ratio, proportion | ⓪ ① ② ③ | ⓪ ① ② ③ | ⓪ ① ② ③ | ⓪ ① ② ③ | ⓪ ① ② ③ |
| ⓪ ① ② ③ | 108 Patterns | ⓪ ① ② ③ | ⓪ ① ② ③ | ⓪ ① ② ③ | ⓪ ① ② ③ | ⓪ ① ② ③ |
| ⓪ ① ② ③ | 109 Real numbers | ⓪ ① ② ③ | ⓪ ① ② ③ | ⓪ ① ② ③ | ⓪ ① ② ③ | ⓪ ① ② ③ |
| ⓪ ① ② ③ | 110 Exponents, scientific notation | ⓪ ① ② ③ | ⓪ ① ② ③ | ⓪ ① ② ③ | ⓪ ① ② ③ | ⓪ ① ② ③ |
| ⓪ ① ② ③ | 111 Factors, multiples, divisibility | ⓪ ① ② ③ | ⓪ ① ② ③ | ⓪ ① ② ③ | ⓪ ① ② ③ | ⓪ ① ② ③ |
| ⓪ ① ② ③ | 112 Odds, evens, primes, composites | ⓪ ① ② ③ | ⓪ ① ② ③ | ⓪ ① ② ③ | ⓪ ① ② ③ | ⓪ ① ② ③ |
| ⓪ ① ② ③ | 113 Estimation | ⓪ ① ② ③ | ⓪ ① ② ③ | ⓪ ① ② ③ | ⓪ ① ② ③ | ⓪ ① ② ③ |
| ⓪ ① ② ③ | 114 Order of operations | ⓪ ① ② ③ | ⓪ ① ② ③ | ⓪ ① ② ③ | ⓪ ① ② ③ | ⓪ ① ② ③ |
| ⓪ ① ② ③ | 115 Relationships between operations | ⓪ ① ② ③ | ⓪ ① ② ③ | ⓪ ① ② ③ | ⓪ ① ② ③ | ⓪ ① ② ③ |
| ⓪ ① ② ③ | 116 Mathematical properties (e.g., distributive property) | ⓪ ① ② ③ | ⓪ ① ② ③ | ⓪ ① ② ③ | ⓪ ① ② ③ | ⓪ ① ② ③ |

**Time on Topic** — **Middle School Mathematics Topics** — **Expectations for Students in Mathematics**

| \<none\> | ² Measurement | Memorize Facts, Definitions, Formulas | Communicate Understanding of Mathematical Concepts | Perform Procedures | Conjecture, Generalize, Prove | Solve Non-Routine Problems/Make Connections |
|---|---|---|---|---|---|---|
| ⓪ ① ② ③ | 201 Use of measuring instruments | ⓪ ① ② ③ | ⓪ ① ② ③ | ⓪ ① ② ③ | ⓪ ① ② ③ | ⓪ ① ② ③ |
| ⓪ ① ② ③ | 202 Theory (arbitrary, standard units, unit size) | ⓪ ① ② ③ | ⓪ ① ② ③ | ⓪ ① ② ③ | ⓪ ① ② ③ | ⓪ ① ② ③ |
| ⓪ ① ② ③ | 203 Conversions | ⓪ ① ② ③ | ⓪ ① ② ③ | ⓪ ① ② ③ | ⓪ ① ② ③ | ⓪ ① ② ③ |
| ⓪ ① ② ③ | 204 Metric (SI) system | ⓪ ① ② ③ | ⓪ ① ② ③ | ⓪ ① ② ③ | ⓪ ① ② ③ | ⓪ ① ② ③ |
| ⓪ ① ② ③ | 205 Length, perimeter | ⓪ ① ② ③ | ⓪ ① ② ③ | ⓪ ① ② ③ | ⓪ ① ② ③ | ⓪ ① ② ③ |
| ⓪ ① ② ③ | 206 Area, volume | ⓪ ① ② ③ | ⓪ ① ② ③ | ⓪ ① ② ③ | ⓪ ① ② ③ | ⓪ ① ② ③ |
| ⓪ ① ② ③ | 207 Surface Area | ⓪ ① ② ③ | ⓪ ① ② ③ | ⓪ ① ② ③ | ⓪ ① ② ③ | ⓪ ① ② ③ |
| ⓪ ① ② ③ | 208 Direction, Location, Navigation | ⓪ ① ② ③ | ⓪ ① ② ③ | ⓪ ① ② ③ | ⓪ ① ② ③ | ⓪ ① ② ③ |
| ⓪ ① ② ③ | 209 Angles | ⓪ ① ② ③ | ⓪ ① ② ③ | ⓪ ① ② ③ | ⓪ ① ② ③ | ⓪ ① ② ③ |
| ⓪ ① ② ③ | 210 Circles (e.g,. pi, radius, area) | ⓪ ① ② ③ | ⓪ ① ② ③ | ⓪ ① ② ③ | ⓪ ① ② ③ | ⓪ ① ② ③ |
| ⓪ ① ② ③ | 211 Mass (weight) | ⓪ ① ② ③ | ⓪ ① ② ③ | ⓪ ① ② ③ | ⓪ ① ② ③ | ⓪ ① ② ③ |
| ⓪ ① ② ③ | 212 Time, temperature | ⓪ ① ② ③ | ⓪ ① ② ③ | ⓪ ① ② ③ | ⓪ ① ② ③ | ⓪ ① ② ③ |

Reprinted by permission of Council of Chief State School Officers. Material was supported by a grant from the National Science Foundation, Division of Research, Evaluation and Communication.

431

**Time on Topic**   **Middle School Mathematics Topics**   **Expectations for Students in Mathematics**

| \<none\> | | ³ Data Analysis / Probability / Statistics | Memorize Facts, Definitions, Formulas | Communicate Understanding of Mathematical Concepts | Perform Procedures | Conjecture, Generalize, Prove | Solve Non-Routine Problems/Make Connections |
|---|---|---|---|---|---|---|---|
| ⓪ ① ② ③ | 301 | Bar graph, histogram | ⓪ ① ② ③ | ⓪ ① ② ③ | ⓪ ① ② ③ | ⓪ ① ② ③ | ⓪ ① ② ③ |
| ⓪ ① ② ③ | 302 | Pie charts, circle graphs | ⓪ ① ② ③ | ⓪ ① ② ③ | ⓪ ① ② ③ | ⓪ ① ② ③ | ⓪ ① ② ③ |
| ⓪ ① ② ③ | 303 | Pictographs | ⓪ ① ② ③ | ⓪ ① ② ③ | ⓪ ① ② ③ | ⓪ ① ② ③ | ⓪ ① ② ③ |
| ⓪ ① ② ③ | 304 | Line graphs | ⓪ ① ② ③ | ⓪ ① ② ③ | ⓪ ① ② ③ | ⓪ ① ② ③ | ⓪ ① ② ③ |
| ⓪ ① ② ③ | 305 | Stem and Leaf plots | ⓪ ① ② ③ | ⓪ ① ② ③ | ⓪ ① ② ③ | ⓪ ① ② ③ | ⓪ ① ② ③ |
| ⓪ ① ② ③ | 306 | Scatter plots | ⓪ ① ② ③ | ⓪ ① ② ③ | ⓪ ① ② ③ | ⓪ ① ② ③ | ⓪ ① ② ③ |
| ⓪ ① ② ③ | 307 | Box plots | ⓪ ① ② ③ | ⓪ ① ② ③ | ⓪ ① ② ③ | ⓪ ① ② ③ | ⓪ ① ② ③ |
| ⓪ ① ② ③ | 308 | Mean, median, mode | ⓪ ① ② ③ | ⓪ ① ② ③ | ⓪ ① ② ③ | ⓪ ① ② ③ | ⓪ ① ② ③ |
| ⓪ ① ② ③ | 309 | Line of best fit | ⓪ ① ② ③ | ⓪ ① ② ③ | ⓪ ① ② ③ | ⓪ ① ② ③ | ⓪ ① ② ③ |
| ⓪ ① ② ③ | 310 | Quartiles, percentiles | ⓪ ① ② ③ | ⓪ ① ② ③ | ⓪ ① ② ③ | ⓪ ① ② ③ | ⓪ ① ② ③ |
| ⓪ ① ② ③ | 311 | Sampling, Sample spaces | ⓪ ① ② ③ | ⓪ ① ② ③ | ⓪ ① ② ③ | ⓪ ① ② ③ | ⓪ ① ② ③ |
| ⓪ ① ② ③ | 312 | Simple probability | ⓪ ① ② ③ | ⓪ ① ② ③ | ⓪ ① ② ③ | ⓪ ① ② ③ | ⓪ ① ② ③ |
| ⓪ ① ② ③ | 313 | Compound probability | ⓪ ① ② ③ | ⓪ ① ② ③ | ⓪ ① ② ③ | ⓪ ① ② ③ | ⓪ ① ② ③ |
| ⓪ ① ② ③ | 314 | Combinations and permutations | ⓪ ① ② ③ | ⓪ ① ② ③ | ⓪ ① ② ③ | ⓪ ① ② ③ | ⓪ ① ② ③ |
| ⓪ ① ② ③ | 315 | Summarize data in a table or graph | ⓪ ① ② ③ | ⓪ ① ② ③ | ⓪ ① ② ③ | ⓪ ① ② ③ | ⓪ ① ② ③ |

**Time on Topic**   **Middle School Mathematics Topics**   **Expectations for Students in Mathematics**

| \<none\> | | ⁴ Algebraic Concepts | Memorize Facts, Definitions, Formulas | Communicate Understanding of Mathematical Concepts | Perform Procedures | Conjecture, Generalize, Prove | Solve Non-Routine Problems/Make Connections |
|---|---|---|---|---|---|---|---|
| ⓪ ① ② ③ | 401 | Absolute value | ⓪ ① ② ③ | ⓪ ① ② ③ | ⓪ ① ② ③ | ⓪ ① ② ③ | ⓪ ① ② ③ |
| ⓪ ① ② ③ | 402 | Use of variables | ⓪ ① ② ③ | ⓪ ① ② ③ | ⓪ ① ② ③ | ⓪ ① ② ③ | ⓪ ① ② ③ |
| ⓪ ① ② ③ | 403 | Evaluation of formulas | ⓪ ① ② ③ | ⓪ ① ② ③ | ⓪ ① ② ③ | ⓪ ① ② ③ | ⓪ ① ② ③ |
| ⓪ ① ② ③ | 404 | One-step equations | ⓪ ① ② ③ | ⓪ ① ② ③ | ⓪ ① ② ③ | ⓪ ① ② ③ | ⓪ ① ② ③ |
| ⓪ ① ② ③ | 405 | Coordinate Plane | ⓪ ① ② ③ | ⓪ ① ② ③ | ⓪ ① ② ③ | ⓪ ① ② ③ | ⓪ ① ② ③ |
| ⓪ ① ② ③ | 406 | Patterns | ⓪ ① ② ③ | ⓪ ① ② ③ | ⓪ ① ② ③ | ⓪ ① ② ③ | ⓪ ① ② ③ |
| ⓪ ① ② ③ | 407 | Multi-step equations | ⓪ ① ② ③ | ⓪ ① ② ③ | ⓪ ① ② ③ | ⓪ ① ② ③ | ⓪ ① ② ③ |
| ⓪ ① ② ③ | 408 | Inequalities | ⓪ ① ② ③ | ⓪ ① ② ③ | ⓪ ① ② ③ | ⓪ ① ② ③ | ⓪ ① ② ③ |
| ⓪ ① ② ③ | 409 | Linear, non-linear relations | ⓪ ① ② ③ | ⓪ ① ② ③ | ⓪ ① ② ③ | ⓪ ① ② ③ | ⓪ ① ② ③ |
| ⓪ ① ② ③ | 410 | Rate of change/slope/line | ⓪ ① ② ③ | ⓪ ① ② ③ | ⓪ ① ② ③ | ⓪ ① ② ③ | ⓪ ① ② ③ |
| ⓪ ① ② ③ | 411 | Operations on polynomials | ⓪ ① ② ③ | ⓪ ① ② ③ | ⓪ ① ② ③ | ⓪ ① ② ③ | ⓪ ① ② ③ |
| ⓪ ① ② ③ | 412 | Factoring | ⓪ ① ② ③ | ⓪ ① ② ③ | ⓪ ① ② ③ | ⓪ ① ② ③ | ⓪ ① ② ③ |
| ⓪ ① ② ③ | 413 | Square roots & radicals | ⓪ ① ② ③ | ⓪ ① ② ③ | ⓪ ① ② ③ | ⓪ ① ② ③ | ⓪ ① ② ③ |
| ⓪ ① ② ③ | 414 | Operations on radicals | ⓪ ① ② ③ | ⓪ ① ② ③ | ⓪ ① ② ③ | ⓪ ① ② ③ | ⓪ ① ② ③ |
| ⓪ ① ② ③ | 415 | Rational expressions | ⓪ ① ② ③ | ⓪ ① ② ③ | ⓪ ① ② ③ | ⓪ ① ② ③ | ⓪ ① ② ③ |
| ⓪ ① ② ③ | 416 | Functions and relations | ⓪ ① ② ③ | ⓪ ① ② ③ | ⓪ ① ② ③ | ⓪ ① ② ③ | ⓪ ① ② ③ |
| ⓪ ① ② ③ | 417 | Quadratic equations | ⓪ ① ② ③ | ⓪ ① ② ③ | ⓪ ① ② ③ | ⓪ ① ② ③ | ⓪ ① ② ③ |
| ⓪ ① ② ③ | 418 | Systems of equations | ⓪ ① ② ③ | ⓪ ① ② ③ | ⓪ ① ② ③ | ⓪ ① ② ③ | ⓪ ① ② ③ |
| ⓪ ① ② ③ | 419 | Systems of inequalities | ⓪ ① ② ③ | ⓪ ① ② ③ | ⓪ ① ② ③ | ⓪ ① ② ③ | ⓪ ① ② ③ |
| ⓪ ① ② ③ | 420 | Matrices, determinants | ⓪ ① ② ③ | ⓪ ① ② ③ | ⓪ ① ② ③ | ⓪ ① ② ③ | ⓪ ① ② ③ |
| ⓪ ① ② ③ | 421 | Complex numbers | ⓪ ① ② ③ | ⓪ ① ② ③ | ⓪ ① ② ③ | ⓪ ① ② ③ | ⓪ ① ② ③ |

Reprinted by permission of Council of Chief State School Officers. Material was supported by a grant from the National Science Foundation, Division of Research, Evaluation and Communication.

**Time on Topic**    *Middle School Mathematics Topics*        ***Expectations for Students in Mathematics***

| Time on Topic <none> | # | Geometric Concepts | Memorize Facts, Definitions, Formulas | Communicate Understanding of Mathematical Concepts | Perform Procedures | Conjecture, Generalize, Prove | Solve Non-Routine Problems/Make Connections |
|---|---|---|---|---|---|---|---|
| ⓪ ① ② ③ | 501 | Basic terminology | ⓪ ① ② ③ | ⓪ ① ② ③ | ⓪ ① ② ③ | ⓪ ① ② ③ | ⓪ ① ② ③ |
| ⓪ ① ② ③ | 502 | Points, lines, rays, and vectors | ⓪ ① ② ③ | ⓪ ① ② ③ | ⓪ ① ② ③ | ⓪ ① ② ③ | ⓪ ① ② ③ |
| ⓪ ① ② ③ | 503 | Patterns | ⓪ ① ② ③ | ⓪ ① ② ③ | ⓪ ① ② ③ | ⓪ ① ② ③ | ⓪ ① ② ③ |
| ⓪ ① ② ③ | 504 | Congruence | ⓪ ① ② ③ | ⓪ ① ② ③ | ⓪ ① ② ③ | ⓪ ① ② ③ | ⓪ ① ② ③ |
| ⓪ ① ② ③ | 505 | Similarity | ⓪ ① ② ③ | ⓪ ① ② ③ | ⓪ ① ② ③ | ⓪ ① ② ③ | ⓪ ① ② ③ |
| ⓪ ① ② ③ | 506 | Triangles | ⓪ ① ② ③ | ⓪ ① ② ③ | ⓪ ① ② ③ | ⓪ ① ② ③ | ⓪ ① ② ③ |
| ⓪ ① ② ③ | 507 | Quadrilaterals | ⓪ ① ② ③ | ⓪ ① ② ③ | ⓪ ① ② ③ | ⓪ ① ② ③ | ⓪ ① ② ③ |
| ⓪ ① ② ③ | 508 | Circles | ⓪ ① ② ③ | ⓪ ① ② ③ | ⓪ ① ② ③ | ⓪ ① ② ③ | ⓪ ① ② ③ |
| ⓪ ① ② ③ | 509 | Angles | ⓪ ① ② ③ | ⓪ ① ② ③ | ⓪ ① ② ③ | ⓪ ① ② ③ | ⓪ ① ② ③ |
| ⓪ ① ② ③ | 510 | Polygons | ⓪ ① ② ③ | ⓪ ① ② ③ | ⓪ ① ② ③ | ⓪ ① ② ③ | ⓪ ① ② ③ |
| ⓪ ① ② ③ | 511 | Polyhedra | ⓪ ① ② ③ | ⓪ ① ② ③ | ⓪ ① ② ③ | ⓪ ① ② ③ | ⓪ ① ② ③ |
| ⓪ ① ② ③ | 512 | Models | ⓪ ① ② ③ | ⓪ ① ② ③ | ⓪ ① ② ③ | ⓪ ① ② ③ | ⓪ ① ② ③ |
| ⓪ ① ② ③ | 513 | Spatial reasoning, 3-D relationships | ⓪ ① ② ③ | ⓪ ① ② ③ | ⓪ ① ② ③ | ⓪ ① ② ③ | ⓪ ① ② ③ |
| ⓪ ① ② ③ | 514 | Symmetry | ⓪ ① ② ③ | ⓪ ① ② ③ | ⓪ ① ② ③ | ⓪ ① ② ③ | ⓪ ① ② ③ |
| ⓪ ① ② ③ | 515 | Transformations (e.g., flips, turns) | ⓪ ① ② ③ | ⓪ ① ② ③ | ⓪ ① ② ③ | ⓪ ① ② ③ | ⓪ ① ② ③ |
| ⓪ ① ② ③ | 516 | Pythagorean Theorem | ⓪ ① ② ③ | ⓪ ① ② ③ | ⓪ ① ② ③ | ⓪ ① ② ③ | ⓪ ① ② ③ |
| ⓪ ① ② ③ | 517 | Simple trigonometric ratios | ⓪ ① ② ③ | ⓪ ① ② ③ | ⓪ ① ② ③ | ⓪ ① ② ③ | ⓪ ① ② ③ |

| Time on Topic <none> | # | Instructional Technology | Memorize Facts, Definitions, Formulas | Communicate Understanding of Mathematical Concepts | Perform Procedures | Conjecture, Generalize, Prove | Solve Non-Routine Problems/Make Connections |
|---|---|---|---|---|---|---|---|
| ⓪ ① ② ③ | 601 | Use of calculators | ⓪ ① ② ③ | ⓪ ① ② ③ | ⓪ ① ② ③ | ⓪ ① ② ③ | ⓪ ① ② ③ |
| ⓪ ① ② ③ | 602 | Graphing calculators | ⓪ ① ② ③ | ⓪ ① ② ③ | ⓪ ① ② ③ | ⓪ ① ② ③ | ⓪ ① ② ③ |
| ⓪ ① ② ③ | 603 | Computers and internet | ⓪ ① ② ③ | ⓪ ① ② ③ | ⓪ ① ② ③ | ⓪ ① ② ③ | ⓪ ① ② ③ |

## END OF SURVEY
## Thank you for your participation!

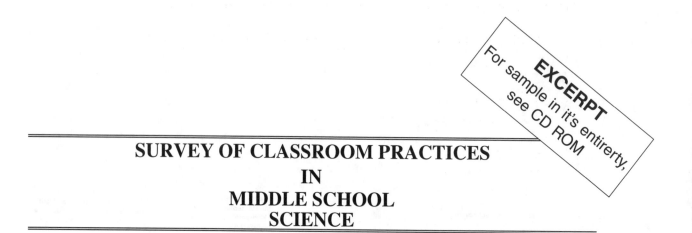

**EXCERPT**
For sample in it's entirerty, see CD ROM

# SURVEY OF CLASSROOM PRACTICES
# IN
# MIDDLE SCHOOL
# SCIENCE

Thank you for your time and patience in completing this survey. The survey was designed with science educators from around the country. We hope the results will help teachers and schools in improving curriculum and support for science education. Each school will receive a report on the results of this survey. Please read each question and the possible responses carefully, and then mark your response by filling in the appropriate circle in the response section.

A joint project of the Council of Chief State School Officers, the Regional Alliance for Mathematics and Science Education, and the Wisconsin Center for Education Research funded by the National Science Foundation

## INSTRUCTIONAL ACTIVITIES IN SCIENCE

*Listed below are some questions about what students in the target class do in science. For each activity, pick one of the choices (0,1,2,3) to indicate the percentage of instructional time that students are engaged in the activity identified. In responding, please think of an average student in the target class.*

**What percentage of science instructional time in the target class do students:**

NOTE: No more than two '3's , or four '2's should be recorded for this set of items.

|  | None | Less than 25% | 25% to 33% | More than 33% |
|---|---|---|---|---|
| 34 Collect information about science. | ⓪ | ① | ② | ③ |
| 35 Maintain and reflect on a science portfolio of their own work. | ⓪ | ① | ② | ③ |
| 36 Write about science. | ⓪ | ① | ② | ③ |
| 37 Do a laboratory activity, investigation, or experiment in class. | ⓪ | ① | ② | ③ |
| 38 Work in pairs or small groups (non-laboratory). | ⓪ | ① | ② | ③ |
| 39 Do a science activity with the class **outside** the classroom or science laboratory. | ⓪ | ① | ② | ③ |
| 40 Use computers, calculators or other educational technology to learn science. | ⓪ | ① | ② | ③ |

**When students in the target class are engaged in** *laboratory activities, investigations, or experiments* **as part of science instruction, what percentage of that lab time do students:**

NOTE: No more than two '3's , or four '2's should be recorded for this set of items.

|  | None | Less than 25% | 25% to 33% | More than 33% |
|---|---|---|---|---|
| 41 Follow step-by-step directions. | ⓪ | ① | ② | ③ |
| 42 Use science equipment or measuring tools to collect data. | ⓪ | ① | ② | ③ |
| 43 Change something in a experiment to see what will happen. | ⓪ | ① | ② | ③ |
| 44 Design ways to solve a problem. | ⓪ | ① | ② | ③ |
| 45 Make guesses, predictions, or hypotheses. | ⓪ | ① | ② | ③ |
| 46 Draw conclusions from science data. | ⓪ | ① | ② | ③ |
| 47 Formulate questions to be tested. | ⓪ | ① | ② | ③ |
| 48 Review the work of others. | ⓪ | ① | ② | ③ |

Reprinted by permission of Council of Chief State School Officers. Material was supported by a grant from the National Science Foundation, Division of Research, Evaluation and Communication.

**When students in the target class work in** *pairs or small groups* **as part of science instruction, what percentage of that time do students:**

> **NOTE: No more than two '3's , or four '2's should be recorded for this set of items.**

| | None | Less than 25% | 25% to 33% | More than 33% |
|---|---|---|---|---|
| 49 Talk about ways to solve science problems. | ⓪ | ① | ② | ③ |
| 50 Complete written assignments from the textbook or workbook. | ⓪ | ① | ② | ③ |
| 51 Write results or conclusions of a laboratory activity. | ⓪ | ① | ② | ③ |
| 52 Work on an assignment, report or project that takes longer than one week to complete. | ⓪ | ① | ② | ③ |
| 53 Work on a writing project or portfolio where group members help to improve each others' (or the group's) work. | ⓪ | ① | ② | ③ |
| 54 Review assignments or prepare for a quiz or test. | ⓪ | ① | ② | ③ |

**When students in the target class** *collect information* **about science from books, magazines, computers, or other sources, what percentage of that time do students:**

> **NOTE: No more than two '3's , or four '2's should be recorded for this set of items.**

| | None | Less than 25% | 25% to 33% | More than 33% |
|---|---|---|---|---|
| 55 Ask questions to improve understanding. | ⓪ | ① | ② | ③ |
| 56 Organize and display the information in tables or graphs. | ⓪ | ① | ② | ③ |
| 57 Make a prediction based on the information or data. | ⓪ | ① | ② | ③ |
| 58 Discuss different conclusions from the information or data. | ⓪ | ① | ② | ③ |
| 59 List positive (pro) and negative (con) reactions to the information. | ⓪ | ① | ② | ③ |
| 60 Reach conclusions or decisions based upon the information or data. | ⓪ | ① | ② | ③ |

Reprinted by permission of Council of Chief State School Officers. Material was supported by a grant from the National Science Foundation, Division of Research, Evaluation and Communication.

## USE OF CALCULATORS, COMPUTERS AND OTHER EQUIPMENT

**When students in the target class are engaged in activities that involve the** *use of calculators, computers, or other educational technology* **as part of science instruction, what percentage of that time do students:**

> NOTE: No more than two '3's , or four '2's should be recorded for this set of items.

| | None | Less than 25% | 25% to 33% | More than 33% |
|---|---|---|---|---|
| 61 Learn facts or practice procedures | ⓪ | ① | ② | ③ |
| 62 Use sensors and probes (e.g., CBL's) | ⓪ | ① | ② | ③ |
| 63 Retrieve or exchange data or information (e.g. using the Internet) | ⓪ | ① | ② | ③ |
| 64 Display and analyze data | ⓪ | ① | ② | ③ |
| 65 Solve problems using simulations | ⓪ | ① | ② | ③ |
| 66 Take a test or quiz | ⓪ | ① | ② | ③ |
| 67 Use individualized instruction or tutorial software | ⓪ | ① | ② | ③ |

**For Items 68-71, indicate how often the average student uses each of the following types of equipment in this science class:**

| | Not Available | Available, but rarely used | Used less than 7 times per year | Used 7 to 36 times per year | Used Weekly |
|---|---|---|---|---|---|
| 68 Computer/lab interfacing devices | ⓪ | ① | ② | ③ | ④ |
| 69 Running water in laboratories | ⓪ | ① | ② | ③ | ④ |
| 70 Electrical outlets in laboratories | ⓪ | ① | ② | ③ | ④ |
| 71 Other lab equipment (e.g., scales, balances) | ⓪ | ① | ② | ③ | ④ |

Reprinted by permission of Council of Chief State School Officers. Material was supported by a grant from the National Science Foundation, Division of Research, Evaluation and Communication.

## ASSESSMENTS

**For items 72-79, indicate how often you use each of the following strategies when assessing students in the target science class.**

| | | None | 1 - 4 times per year | 1 - 3 times per month | 1 - 3 times per week | 4 - 5 times per week |
|---|---|---|---|---|---|---|
| 72 | Objective items (e.g., multiple choice, true/false) | ⓪ | ① | ② | ③ | ④ |
| 73 | Short answer (e.g. fill-in-the-blank) | ⓪ | ① | ② | ③ | ④ |
| 74 | Extended response item for which student must explain or justify answer | ⓪ | ① | ② | ③ | ④ |
| 75 | Performance tasks or events (e.g. hands-on activities) | ⓪ | ① | ② | ③ | ④ |
| 76 | Individual or group demonstration, presentation | ⓪ | ① | ② | ③ | ④ |
| 77 | Science projects | ⓪ | ① | ② | ③ | ④ |
| 78 | Portfolios | ⓪ | ① | ② | ③ | ④ |
| 79 | Systematic observation of students | ⓪ | ① | ② | ③ | ④ |

## INSTRUCTIONAL INFLUENCES

**For Items 80-89, indicate the degree to which each of the following influences what you teach in the target science class.**

| | | N/A | Strong Negative Influence | Somewhat Negative Influence | Little or no Influence | Somewhat Positive Influence | Strong Positive Influence |
|---|---|---|---|---|---|---|---|
| 80 | Your state's curriculum framework or content standards | ⓪ | ① | ② | ③ | ④ | ⑤ |
| 81 | Your district's curriculum framework or guidelines | ⓪ | ① | ② | ③ | ④ | ⑤ |
| 82 | Textbook/instructional materials | ⓪ | ① | ② | ③ | ④ | ⑤ |
| 83 | State test | ⓪ | ① | ② | ③ | ④ | ⑤ |
| 84 | District test | ⓪ | ① | ② | ③ | ④ | ⑤ |
| 85 | National science education standards | ⓪ | ① | ② | ③ | ④ | ⑤ |
| 86 | Your experience in pre-service preparation | ⓪ | ① | ② | ③ | ④ | ⑤ |
| 87 | Students' special needs | ⓪ | ① | ② | ③ | ④ | ⑤ |
| 88 | Parents/community | ⓪ | ① | ② | ③ | ④ | ⑤ |
| 89 | Prepare students for next grade or level | ⓪ | ① | ② | ③ | ④ | ⑤ |

Reprinted by permission of Council of Chief State School Officers. Material was supported by a grant from the National Science Foundation, Division of Research, Evaluation and Communication.

## CLASSROOM INSTRUCTIONAL PREPARATION

**For items 90-106, please indicate how well prepared you are now to:**

| | | Not well prepared | Somewhat prepared | Well prepared | Very well prepared |
|---|---|---|---|---|---|
| 90 | Teach science at your assigned level. | ⓪ | ① | ② | ③ |
| 91 | Use/manage cooperative learning groups in science. | ⓪ | ① | ② | ③ |
| 92 | Integrate science with other subjects. | ⓪ | ① | ② | ③ |
| 93 | Provide science instruction that meets science standards (district, state, or national). | ⓪ | ① | ② | ③ |
| 94 | Use a variety of assessment strategies (including objective and open-ended formats). | ⓪ | ① | ② | ③ |
| 95 | Use mathematics in science. | ⓪ | ① | ② | ③ |
| 96 | Manage a class of students who are using hands-on or laboratory activities. | ⓪ | ① | ② | ③ |
| 97 | Take into account students' prior conceptions about natural phenomena when planning curriculum and instruction. | ⓪ | ① | ② | ③ |
| 98 | Teach students with physical disabilities. | ⓪ | ① | ② | ③ |
| 99 | Help students document and evaluate their own science work. | ⓪ | ① | ② | ③ |
| 100 | Teach classes with students with diverse abilities. | ⓪ | ① | ② | ③ |
| 101 | Teach science to students from a variety of cultural backgrounds. | ⓪ | ① | ② | ③ |
| 102 | Teach science to students who have limited English proficiency. | ⓪ | ① | ② | ③ |
| 103 | Teach students who have a learning disability which impacts science learning. | ⓪ | ① | ② | ③ |
| 104 | Encourage participation of females in science. | ⓪ | ① | ② | ③ |
| 105 | Encourage participation of minorities in science. | ⓪ | ① | ② | ③ |
| 106 | Involve parents in the science education of their children. | ⓪ | ① | ② | ③ |

Reprinted by permission of Council of Chief State School Officers. Material was supported by a grant from the National Science Foundation, Division of Research, Evaluation and Communication.

## TEACHER OPINIONS

Please indicate your opinion about each of the statements below:

| | | Strongly disagree | Disagree | Neutral / undecided | Agree | Strongly agree |
|---|---|---|---|---|---|---|
| 107 | Activity-based science experiences are not worth the time and expense for what students learn. | ⓪ | ① | ② | ③ | ④ |
| 108 | The testing program in my state/district dictates what science I teach. | ⓪ | ① | ② | ③ | ④ |
| 109 | Laboratory-based science classes are more effective than non-laboratory classes. | ⓪ | ① | ② | ③ | ④ |
| 110 | All students can learn challenging content in science. | ⓪ | ① | ② | ③ | ④ |
| 111 | Students learn science better in classes with students of similar abilities. | ⓪ | ① | ② | ③ | ④ |
| 112 | It is important for students to learn basic scientific terms and formulas before learning underlying concepts and principles. | ⓪ | ① | ② | ③ | ④ |
| 113 | I really enjoy teaching science. | ⓪ | ① | ② | ③ | ④ |
| 114 | I am supported by colleagues to try out new ideas in teaching science. | ⓪ | ① | ② | ③ | ④ |
| 115 | I receive little support from the school administration for teaching science. | ⓪ | ① | ② | ③ | ④ |
| 116 | Science teachers in this school regularly share ideas and materials. | ⓪ | ① | ② | ③ | ④ |
| 117 | Science teachers in this school regularly observe each other teaching classes. | ⓪ | ① | ② | ③ | ④ |
| 118 | I have many opportunities to learn new things about science or science teaching in my present job. | ⓪ | ① | ② | ③ | ④ |
| 119 | I am required to follow rules at this school that conflict with my best professional judgment about teaching and learning science. | ⓪ | ① | ② | ③ | ④ |
| 120 | Most science teachers in this school contribute actively to make decisions about the science curriculum. | ⓪ | ① | ② | ③ | ④ |
| 121 | I have adequate time during the regular school week to work with my peers on science curriculum instruction. | ⓪ | ① | ② | ③ | ④ |
| 122 | I have adequate curriculum materials available for science instruction. | ⓪ | ① | ② | ③ | ④ |
| 123 | Absenteeism is a problem in my class. | ⓪ | ① | ② | ③ | ④ |
| 124 | Mobility of students in and out of our school is a problem. | ⓪ | ① | ② | ③ | ④ |

Reprinted by permission of Council of Chief State School Officers. Material was supported by a grant from the National Science Foundation, Division of Research, Evaluation and Communication.

## Expectations for Students in Science

**Memorize**
- Facts
- Definitions, Terms
- Formulas

**Understand Concepts**
- Explain concepts
- Observe and explain teacher demonstrations
- Explain procedures and methods of science and inquiry
- Organize and display data in tables or charts

**Perform Procedures**
- Make observations
- Collect and record data
- Use appropriate tools
- Make measurements, do computations
- Execute procedures

**Conduct Experiments**
- Generate questions, make predictions
- Plan and design experiments
- Test effects of different variables
- Draw conclusions
- Communicate investigations & explanations

**Analyze Information**
- Classify and compare data
- Analyze data, recognize patterns
- Infer from data, draw conclusions

**Apply Concepts & Make Connections**
- Use and integrate concepts
- Apply to real-world situations
- Build or revise theory
- Make generalizations

### Response Codes for Time on Topic

**0=None, not covered**
**1=Slight coverag** (less than one class/lesson)
**2=Moderate coverag** (one to five classes/lessons)
**3=Sustained coverag** (more than five classes/lessons)

### Response Codes for Expectations of Students

**0=No emphasi** (Not a performance goal for this topic)
**1=Slight emphasi** (Less than 25% of time on this topic)
**2=Moderate emphasi** (25% to 33% of time on this topic)
**3=Sustained emphasi** (more than 33% of time on this topic)

| Time on Topic | | Middle School Science | Memorize | Understand Concepts | Perform Procedures | Conduct Experiments | Analyze Information | Apply Concepts |
|---|---|---|---|---|---|---|---|---|
| \<none\> | 1 | Nature of Science | Memorize | Understand Concepts | Perform Procedures | Conduct Experiments | Analyze Information | Apply Concepts |
| 0 1 2 3 | 101 | Scientific habits of mind (e.g. reasoning, evidence-based conclusions, skepticism) | 0 1 2 3 | 0 1 2 3 | 0 1 2 3 | 0 1 2 3 | 0 1 2 3 | 0 1 2 3 |
| 0 1 2 3 | 102 | Scientific method (e.g., observation, experimentation, analysis, theory development and reporting) | 0 1 2 3 | 0 1 2 3 | 0 1 2 3 | 0 1 2 3 | 0 1 2 3 | 0 1 2 3 |
| 0 1 2 3 | 103 | Issues of diversity, culture, ethnicity, race, gender in science | 0 1 2 3 | 0 1 2 3 | 0 1 2 3 | 0 1 2 3 | 0 1 2 3 | 0 1 2 3 |
| 0 1 2 3 | 104 | History of scientific innovations | 0 1 2 3 | 0 1 2 3 | 0 1 2 3 | 0 1 2 3 | 0 1 2 3 | 0 1 2 3 |
| 0 1 2 3 | 105 | Ethical issues in science | 0 1 2 3 | 0 1 2 3 | 0 1 2 3 | 0 1 2 3 | 0 1 2 3 | 0 1 2 3 |
| \<none\> | 2 | Science and Technology | Memorize | Understand Concepts | Perform Procedures | Conduct Experiments | Analyze Information | Apply Concepts |
| 0 1 2 3 | 201 | Design a solution or product, implement a design | 0 1 2 3 | 0 1 2 3 | 0 1 2 3 | 0 1 2 3 | 0 1 2 3 | 0 1 2 3 |
| 0 1 2 3 | 202 | Relationship between scientific inquiry and technological design | 0 1 2 3 | 0 1 2 3 | 0 1 2 3 | 0 1 2 3 | 0 1 2 3 | 0 1 2 3 |
| 0 1 2 3 | 203 | Technological benefits, trade-offs and consequences | 0 1 2 3 | 0 1 2 3 | 0 1 2 3 | 0 1 2 3 | 0 1 2 3 | 0 1 2 3 |
| \<none\> | 3 | Science, Health and Environment | Memorize | Understand Concepts | Perform Procedures | Conduct Experiments | Analyze Information | Apply Concepts |
| 0 1 2 3 | 301 | Personal health, behavior, disease, nutrition | 0 1 2 3 | 0 1 2 3 | 0 1 2 3 | 0 1 2 3 | 0 1 2 3 | 0 1 2 3 |
| 0 1 2 3 | 302 | Environmental health, pollution, waste disposal, resources, conservation | 0 1 2 3 | 0 1 2 3 | 0 1 2 3 | 0 1 2 3 | 0 1 2 3 | 0 1 2 3 |
| 0 1 2 3 | 303 | Resources, conservation | 0 1 2 3 | 0 1 2 3 | 0 1 2 3 | 0 1 2 3 | 0 1 2 3 | 0 1 2 3 |
| 0 1 2 3 | 303 | Natural and Human-caused hazards | 0 1 2 3 | 0 1 2 3 | 0 1 2 3 | 0 1 2 3 | 0 1 2 3 | 0 1 2 3 |

Reprinted by permission of Council of Chief State School Officers. Material was supported by a grant from the National Science Foundation, Division of Research, Evaluation and Communication.

## Expectations for Students in Science

**Memorize**
- Facts
- Definitions, Terms
- Formulas

**Understand Concepts**
- Explain concepts
- Observe and explain teacher demonstrations
- Explain procedures and methods of science and inquiry
- Organize and display data in tables or charts

**Perform Procedures**
- Make observations
- Collect and record data
- Use appropriate tools
- Make measurements, do computations
- Execute procedures

**Conduct Experiments**
- Generate questions, make predictions
- Plan and design experiments
- Test effects of different variables
- Draw conclusions
- Communicate investigations & explanations

**Analyze Information**
- Classify and compare data
- Analyze data, recognize patterns
- Infer from data, draw conclusions

**Apply Concepts & Make Connections**
- Use and integrate concepts
- Apply to real-world situations
- Build or revise theory
- Make generalizations

---

*Response Codes for Time on Topic*

**0=None, not covered**
**1=Slight coverag** (less than one class/lesson)
**2=Moderate coverag** (one to five classes/lessons)
**3=Sustained coverag** (more than five classes/lessons)

*Response Codes for Expectations of Students*

**0=No emphasi** (Not a performance goal for this topic)
**1=Slight emphasi** (Less than 25% of time on this topic)
**2=Moderate emphasi** (25% to 33% of time on this topic)
**3=Sustained emphasi** (more than 33% of time on this topic)

---

| Time on Topic | | Middle School Science | Memorize | Understand Concepts | Perform Procedures | Conduct Experiments | Analyze Information | Apply Concepts |
|---|---|---|---|---|---|---|---|---|
| <none> | 4 | Measurement & Calculation in Science | | | | | | |
| ⓪ ① ② ③ | 401 | The International System | ⓪ ① ② ③ | ⓪ ① ② ③ | ⓪ ① ② ③ | ⓪ ① ② ③ | ⓪ ① ② ③ | ⓪ ① ② ③ |
| ⓪ ① ② ③ | 402 | Mass & Weight | ⓪ ① ② ③ | ⓪ ① ② ③ | ⓪ ① ② ③ | ⓪ ① ② ③ | ⓪ ① ② ③ | ⓪ ① ② ③ |
| ⓪ ① ② ③ | 403 | Length | ⓪ ① ② ③ | ⓪ ① ② ③ | ⓪ ① ② ③ | ⓪ ① ② ③ | ⓪ ① ② ③ | ⓪ ① ② ③ |
| ⓪ ① ② ③ | 404 | Volume | ⓪ ① ② ③ | ⓪ ① ② ③ | ⓪ ① ② ③ | ⓪ ① ② ③ | ⓪ ① ② ③ | ⓪ ① ② ③ |
| ⓪ ① ② ③ | 405 | Time | ⓪ ① ② ③ | ⓪ ① ② ③ | ⓪ ① ② ③ | ⓪ ① ② ③ | ⓪ ① ② ③ | ⓪ ① ② ③ |
| ⓪ ① ② ③ | 406 | Temperature | ⓪ ① ② ③ | ⓪ ① ② ③ | ⓪ ① ② ③ | ⓪ ① ② ③ | ⓪ ① ② ③ | ⓪ ① ② ③ |
| ⓪ ① ② ③ | 407 | Accuracy & Precision | ⓪ ① ② ③ | ⓪ ① ② ③ | ⓪ ① ② ③ | ⓪ ① ② ③ | ⓪ ① ② ③ | ⓪ ① ② ③ |
| ⓪ ① ② ③ | 408 | Significant Digits | ⓪ ① ② ③ | ⓪ ① ② ③ | ⓪ ① ② ③ | ⓪ ① ② ③ | ⓪ ① ② ③ | ⓪ ① ② ③ |
| ⓪ ① ② ③ | 409 | Derived Units | ⓪ ① ② ③ | ⓪ ① ② ③ | ⓪ ① ② ③ | ⓪ ① ② ③ | ⓪ ① ② ③ | ⓪ ① ② ③ |
| ⓪ ① ② ③ | 410 | Conversion Factors | ⓪ ① ② ③ | ⓪ ① ② ③ | ⓪ ① ② ③ | ⓪ ① ② ③ | ⓪ ① ② ③ | ⓪ ① ② ③ |
| ⓪ ① ② ③ | 411 | Density | ⓪ ① ② ③ | ⓪ ① ② ③ | ⓪ ① ② ③ | ⓪ ① ② ③ | ⓪ ① ② ③ | ⓪ ① ② ③ |
| <none> | 5 | Components of Living Systems | Memorize | Understand Concepts | Perform Procedures | Conduct Experiments | Analyze Information | Apply Concepts |
| ⓪ ① ② ③ | 501 | Cell structure / function | ⓪ ① ② ③ | ⓪ ① ② ③ | ⓪ ① ② ③ | ⓪ ① ② ③ | ⓪ ① ② ③ | ⓪ ① ② ③ |
| ⓪ ① ② ③ | 502 | Cell Theory | ⓪ ① ② ③ | ⓪ ① ② ③ | ⓪ ① ② ③ | ⓪ ① ② ③ | ⓪ ① ② ③ | ⓪ ① ② ③ |
| ⓪ ① ② ③ | 503 | Cell Response | ⓪ ① ② ③ | ⓪ ① ② ③ | ⓪ ① ② ③ | ⓪ ① ② ③ | ⓪ ① ② ③ | ⓪ ① ② ③ |
| ⓪ ① ② ③ | 504 | Genes | ⓪ ① ② ③ | ⓪ ① ② ③ | ⓪ ① ② ③ | ⓪ ① ② ③ | ⓪ ① ② ③ | ⓪ ① ② ③ |
| ⓪ ① ② ③ | 505 | Organs | ⓪ ① ② ③ | ⓪ ① ② ③ | ⓪ ① ② ③ | ⓪ ① ② ③ | ⓪ ① ② ③ | ⓪ ① ② ③ |
| ⓪ ① ② ③ | 506 | Organ Systems | ⓪ ① ② ③ | ⓪ ① ② ③ | ⓪ ① ② ③ | ⓪ ① ② ③ | ⓪ ① ② ③ | ⓪ ① ② ③ |

Reprinted by permission of Council of Chief State School Officers. Material was supported by a grant from the National Science Foundation, Division of Research, Evaluation and Communication.

## Expectations for Students in Science

### Memorize
Facts
Definitions, Terms
Formulas

### Understand Concepts
Explain concepts
Observe and explain teacher demonstrations
Explain procedures and methods of science
  and inquiry
Organize and display data in tables or charts

### Perform Procedures
Make observations
Collect and record data
Use appropriate tools
Make measurements, do computations
Execute procedures

### Conduct Experiments
Generate questions, make predictions
Plan and design experiments
Test effects of different variables
Draw conclusions
Communicate investigations & explanations

### Analyze Information
Classify and compare data
Analyze data, recognize patterns
Infer from data, draw conclusions

### Apply Concepts & Make Connections
Use and integrate concepts
Apply to real-world situations
Build or revise theory
Make generalizations

---

#### Response Codes for Time on Topic

**0=None, not covered**
**1=Slight coverag** (less than one class/lesson)
**2=Moderate coverag** (one to five classes/lessons)
**3=Sustained coverag** (more than five classes/lessons)

#### Response Codes for Expectations of Students

**0=No emphasi** (Not a performance goal for this topic)
**1=Slight emphasi** (Less than 25% of time on this topic)
**2=Moderate emphasi** (25% to 33% of time on this topic)
**3=Sustained emphasi** (more than 33% of time on this topic)

---

| Time on Topic | Middle School Science | Memorize | Understand Concepts | Perform Procedures | Conduct Experiments | Analyze Information | Apply Concepts |
|---|---|---|---|---|---|---|---|
| <none> | 6 Botany | Memorize | Understand Concepts | Perform Procedures | Conduct Experiments | Analyze Information | Apply Concepts |
| 0 1 2 3 | 601 Nutrition/Photosynthesis | 0 1 2 3 | 0 1 2 3 | 0 1 2 3 | 0 1 2 3 | 0 1 2 3 | 0 1 2 3 |
| 0 1 2 3 | 602 Vascular System | 0 1 2 3 | 0 1 2 3 | 0 1 2 3 | 0 1 2 3 | 0 1 2 3 | 0 1 2 3 |
| 0 1 2 3 | 603 Reproduction | 0 1 2 3 | 0 1 2 3 | 0 1 2 3 | 0 1 2 3 | 0 1 2 3 | 0 1 2 3 |
| 0 1 2 3 | 604 Growth/development/behavior | 0 1 2 3 | 0 1 2 3 | 0 1 2 3 | 0 1 2 3 | 0 1 2 3 | 0 1 2 3 |
| 0 1 2 3 | 605 Health & disease | 0 1 2 3 | 0 1 2 3 | 0 1 2 3 | 0 1 2 3 | 0 1 2 3 | 0 1 2 3 |
| <none> | 7 Animal Biology | Memorize | Understand Concepts | Perform Procedures | Conduct Experiments | Analyze Information | Apply Concepts |
| 0 1 2 3 | 701 Nutrition | 0 1 2 3 | 0 1 2 3 | 0 1 2 3 | 0 1 2 3 | 0 1 2 3 | 0 1 2 3 |
| 0 1 2 3 | 702 Circulation | 0 1 2 3 | 0 1 2 3 | 0 1 2 3 | 0 1 2 3 | 0 1 2 3 | 0 1 2 3 |
| 0 1 2 3 | 703 Excretion | 0 1 2 3 | 0 1 2 3 | 0 1 2 3 | 0 1 2 3 | 0 1 2 3 | 0 1 2 3 |
| 0 1 2 3 | 704 Respiration | 0 1 2 3 | 0 1 2 3 | 0 1 2 3 | 0 1 2 3 | 0 1 2 3 | 0 1 2 3 |
| 0 1 2 3 | 705 Growth/development/behavior | 0 1 2 3 | 0 1 2 3 | 0 1 2 3 | 0 1 2 3 | 0 1 2 3 | 0 1 2 3 |
| 0 1 2 3 | 706 Health & disease | 0 1 2 3 | 0 1 2 3 | 0 1 2 3 | 0 1 2 3 | 0 1 2 3 | 0 1 2 3 |
| 0 1 2 3 | 707 Skeletal & muscular system | 0 1 2 3 | 0 1 2 3 | 0 1 2 3 | 0 1 2 3 | 0 1 2 3 | 0 1 2 3 |
| 0 1 2 3 | 708 Nervous & endocrine system | 0 1 2 3 | 0 1 2 3 | 0 1 2 3 | 0 1 2 3 | 0 1 2 3 | 0 1 2 3 |
| <none> | 8 Human Biology | Memorize | Understand Concepts | Perform Procedures | Conduct Experiments | Analyze Information | Apply Concepts |
| 0 1 2 3 | 801 Nutrition/Digestive System | 0 1 2 3 | 0 1 2 3 | 0 1 2 3 | 0 1 2 3 | 0 1 2 3 | 0 1 2 3 |
| 0 1 2 3 | 802 Circulatory System (Blood) | 0 1 2 3 | 0 1 2 3 | 0 1 2 3 | 0 1 2 3 | 0 1 2 3 | 0 1 2 3 |
| 0 1 2 3 | 803 Excretory System | 0 1 2 3 | 0 1 2 3 | 0 1 2 3 | 0 1 2 3 | 0 1 2 3 | 0 1 2 3 |
| 0 1 2 3 | 804 Respiration & Respiratory System | 0 1 2 3 | 0 1 2 3 | 0 1 2 3 | 0 1 2 3 | 0 1 2 3 | 0 1 2 3 |
| 0 1 2 3 | 805 Growth/development/behavior | 0 1 2 3 | 0 1 2 3 | 0 1 2 3 | 0 1 2 3 | 0 1 2 3 | 0 1 2 3 |
| 0 1 2 3 | 806 Health & disease | 0 1 2 3 | 0 1 2 3 | 0 1 2 3 | 0 1 2 3 | 0 1 2 3 | 0 1 2 3 |
| 0 1 2 3 | 807 Skeletal & muscular system | 0 1 2 3 | 0 1 2 3 | 0 1 2 3 | 0 1 2 3 | 0 1 2 3 | 0 1 2 3 |
| 0 1 2 3 | 808 Nervous & endocrine system | 0 1 2 3 | 0 1 2 3 | 0 1 2 3 | 0 1 2 3 | 0 1 2 3 | 0 1 2 3 |

## Expectations for Students in Science

**Memorize**
- Facts
- Definitions, Terms
- Formulas

**Understand Concepts**
- Explain concepts
- Observe and explain teacher demonstrations
- Explain procedures and methods of science and inquiry
- Organize and display data in tables or charts

**Perform Procedures**
- Make observations
- Collect and record data
- Use appropriate tools
- Make measurements, do computations
- Execute procedures

**Conduct Experiments**
- Generate questions, make predictions
- Plan and design experiments
- Test effects of different variables
- Draw conclusions
- Communicate investigations & explanations

**Analyze Information**
- Classify and compare data
- Analyze data, recognize patterns
- Infer from data, draw conclusions

**Apply Concepts & Make Connections**
- Use and integrate concepts
- Apply to real-world situations
- Build or revise theory
- Make generalizations

---

### Response Codes for Time on Topic

**0=None, not covered**
**1=Slight coverag** (less than one class/lesson)
**2=Moderate coverag** (one to five classes/lessons)
**3=Sustained coverag** (more than five classes/lessons)

### Response Codes for Expectations of Students

**0=No emphasi** (Not a performance goal for this topic)
**1=Slight emphasi** (Less than 25% of time on this topic)
**2=Moderate emphasi** (25% to 33% of time on this topic)
**3=Sustained emphasi** (more than 33% of time on this topic)

---

**Time on Topic** — Middle School Science — **Expectations for Students in Science**

| Time on Topic | | Topic | Memorize | Understand Concepts | Perform Procedures | Conduct Experiments | Analyze Information | Apply Concepts |
|---|---|---|---|---|---|---|---|---|
| ⓪①②③ | 9 | Evolution | | | | | | |
| ⓪①②③ | 901 | Evidence for Evolution | ⓪①②③ | ⓪①②③ | ⓪①②③ | ⓪①②③ | ⓪①②③ | ⓪①②③ |
| ⓪①②③ | 902 | Modern Evolutionary Theory | ⓪①②③ | ⓪①②③ | ⓪①②③ | ⓪①②③ | ⓪①②③ | ⓪①②③ |
| ⓪①②③ | 903 | Human Evolution | ⓪①②③ | ⓪①②③ | ⓪①②③ | ⓪①②③ | ⓪①②③ | ⓪①②③ |
| ⓪①②③ | 904 | Classification | ⓪①②③ | ⓪①②③ | ⓪①②③ | ⓪①②③ | ⓪①②③ | ⓪①②③ |
| ⓪①②③ | 905 | Natural Selection | ⓪①②③ | ⓪①②③ | ⓪①②③ | ⓪①②③ | ⓪①②③ | ⓪①②③ |
| ⓪①②③ | 906 | Adaptation & Variation | ⓪①②③ | ⓪①②③ | ⓪①②③ | ⓪①②③ | ⓪①②③ | ⓪①②③ |
| ⓪①②③ | 10 | Reproduction & Development | | | | | | |
| ⓪①②③ | 1001 | Mitotic/Meiotic Cell Division | ⓪①②③ | ⓪①②③ | ⓪①②③ | ⓪①②③ | ⓪①②③ | ⓪①②③ |
| ⓪①②③ | 1002 | Asexual Reproduction | ⓪①②③ | ⓪①②③ | ⓪①②③ | ⓪①②③ | ⓪①②③ | ⓪①②③ |
| ⓪①②③ | 1003 | Inherited Traits | ⓪①②③ | ⓪①②③ | ⓪①②③ | ⓪①②③ | ⓪①②③ | ⓪①②③ |
| ⓪①②③ | 1004 | Sexual Reproduction & Development in Plants | ⓪①②③ | ⓪①②③ | ⓪①②③ | ⓪①②③ | ⓪①②③ | ⓪①②③ |
| ⓪①②③ | 1005 | Sexual Reproduction & Development in Animals | ⓪①②③ | ⓪①②③ | ⓪①②③ | ⓪①②③ | ⓪①②③ | ⓪①②③ |
| ⓪①②③ | 1006 | Sexual Reproduction & Development in Humans | ⓪①②③ | ⓪①②③ | ⓪①②③ | ⓪①②③ | ⓪①②③ | ⓪①②③ |
| ⓪①②③ | 11 | Ecology | | | | | | |
| ⓪①②③ | 1101 | Food Chains/Webs | ⓪①②③ | ⓪①②③ | ⓪①②③ | ⓪①②③ | ⓪①②③ | ⓪①②③ |
| ⓪①②③ | 1102 | Competition & Cooperation | ⓪①②③ | ⓪①②③ | ⓪①②③ | ⓪①②③ | ⓪①②③ | ⓪①②③ |
| ⓪①②③ | 1103 | Energy Flow Relationships | ⓪①②③ | ⓪①②③ | ⓪①②③ | ⓪①②③ | ⓪①②③ | ⓪①②③ |
| ⓪①②③ | 1104 | Ecological Succession | ⓪①②③ | ⓪①②③ | ⓪①②③ | ⓪①②③ | ⓪①②③ | ⓪①②③ |
| ⓪①②③ | 1105 | Ecosystems | ⓪①②③ | ⓪①②③ | ⓪①②③ | ⓪①②③ | ⓪①②③ | ⓪①②③ |
| ⓪①②③ | 1106 | Populations | ⓪①②③ | ⓪①②③ | ⓪①②③ | ⓪①②③ | ⓪①②③ | ⓪①②③ |

Reprinted by permission of Council of Chief State School Officers. Material was supported by a grant from the National Science Foundation, Division of Research, Evaluation and Communication.

# Data Tool #DT 4-9

## Science and Social Sciences
# P R O G R A M   A S S E S S M E N T

> ### THIS FORM IS REQUIRED FOR ALL TEACHERS
> **Failure to accurately fill out this form may postpone the arrival of future orders.**

Please carefully answer each of the following **required** questions. This information is regularly reported to principals and district administration.

**What were the estimated student contact hours accrued during this unit?** (These hours may include direct science lessons and/or presented in an integrated context.) _____

**How successful were you in implementing this instructional unit?** (Use rubric below to answer this question.)

| Circle One | DESCRIPTORS |
|:---:|---|
| 1 | I did not use this unit. |
| 2 | I taught a few of the lessons/activities in this unit. |
| 3 | I taught this entire unit. |
| 4 | I used this unit as a central focus of instruction in my classroom. I taught the entire unit and I included several additional learning opportunities for my students. My students effectively showed mastery of the objectives of this unit. |
| 5 | I used this unit and the content/concepts contained in it as the central focus of instruction. I integrated the objectives of this unit with other instructional outcomes taught to my students. |

# Data Tool #DT 4-10

Math Committee

Dear Teachers,

We are taking a survey regarding the use of math manipulatives. We need your input concerning the following manipulatives.

|  | Use | Never Use | Would Use If Properly Trained |
|---|---|---|---|
| 1. Pattern Blocks |  |  |  |
| 2. Pentominoes |  |  |  |
| 3. Fraction Circles |  |  |  |
| 4. Geoboards |  |  |  |
| 5. Unifix Cubes |  |  |  |
| 6. Tiles (Squares) |  |  |  |
| 7. Tangrams |  |  |  |
| 8. Geometry templates |  |  |  |

# EVALUATION OF STAFF DEVELOPMENT: HOW DO YOU KNOW IT TOOK?[1]

## Susan F. Loucks, Marge Melle

In the past several years, staff development has begun to emerge as a valuable means for improving schools, upgrading the skills of educational personnel, and providing opportunities for their personal growth. As staff development gains value, however, the evaluation of staff development programs is all but stagnated. Those in charge still rely primarily on reports of participant satisfaction to determine the success of their programs, be they awareness sessions, workshops, institutes, or individual consultations. While the perceptions of participants yield valuable information, they are not valid indicators of whether staff development has made a difference.

In this article we present several alternatives to satisfaction questionnaires. We describe how we and our colleagues have been able to determine whether anything has changed as a result of staff development programs – how we can tell whether they "took" with the participants who were involved.

Since 1973, work at the Texas Research and Development Center for Teacher Education has focused on what happens to individuals (teachers, administrators, college faculty) as they try out new practices, as they implement innovations.[2] In 1976 a collaborative effort was begun with the Jefferson County, Colorado, Public Schools, to design and test an approach

[1] The research reported in this article was conducted by the Research and Development Center for Teacher Evaluation at the University of Texas under a contract with the National Institute of Education. The opinions expressed here, however, are those of the authors and do not represent those of the funding agency.

[2] In this article, we see staff development as a vehicle for helping people improve what they are doing. These improvements take the form of a new practice, program, process – an "innovation" in its broadest sense. Thus we use the words practice, program and innovation interchangeably. We know from experience that the techniques we describe can be used with a wide range of practices: from a simple strategy for asking different kinds of questions, to a large, complex alternative school. Thus the techniques are useful for staff developers whose job it is to help teachers "improve" their practice in the broadest sense of the term.

to implementing new curricula that relied on staff development with the support of school and district resources. The approach, aimed at meeting the developmental needs of teachers and administrators, was used in a three-year effort to implement a revision of the upper-elementary science curriculum in approximately eighty elementary schools. The effort was monitored continuously through the use of several techniques developed by both collaborating partners. We were able to keep track of three things:

- how teachers' *concerns* about the program changed as it was implemented,

- how teachers' familiarity with and sophistication in *use* of the program changed, and

- to what extent teachers were using each of the program's *components*.

In other articles we and our colleagues have described in detail the staff development design used and the specific findings resulting from its use (Hall *et al.*, 1980; Loucks and Pratt, 1979). In this article we concentrate on the concepts and the tools we used for evaluating the effort, with just enough about the design and some examples of the findings to make the evaluation come alive. *Here we concentrate on how we determined the actual effects of staff development on teachers in classrooms.*

## The Design for Implementing the Revised Curriculum

Briefly, the revised curriculum combined a "hands-on," inquiry approach to science instruction with behavioral objectives and assessment techniques. The new teacher's guide included all necessary procedures, references to materials and equipment, and accompanying worksheets.

The eighty elementary schools in the district were divided into three groups, each beginning implementation at roughly six-month intervals, so that training and resources could be concentrated on a manageable number of teachers and schools at a time. The staff development plan called for activities spread out over a year and designed so they answered the kinds of questions teachers were asking *when* they were asking them. First, the science department was to create awareness of the new curriculum and provide information about inservice activities at a short faculty meeting two to three months before inservice. Subsequently, three full-day released-time inservice sessions were planned for teachers in each phase over a nine-month period. These inservices provided "hands-on" experiences with each unit in the curriculum, plus sessions on such topics as classroom management and discussion techniques.

The framework for the implementation design was the Concerns-Based Adoption Model (CBAM) (Hall, Wallace and Dossett, 1973), a model which views the change process from the perspective of the individual teacher.

The CBAM is based on the assumption that change is a lengthy, complex and highly personal experience, and that implementation can only be accomplished when the different needs of teachers are met as they emerge.

Two dimensions of the CBAM were utilized in the evaluation of the science implementation. Stages of Concern (see Figure 1) formed the basis for staff development and support activities. Early stages of Awareness, Informational, and Personal concerns (SoC 0, 1, 2), known to be dominant in the beginning of any change effort, were attended to in small, close-knit faculty meetings prior to implementation. Management (Stage 3) concerns, known to emerge as teachers first begin to use a new curriculum, were addressed in the inservice sessions. Because higher Stages of Concern (Stages 4, 5, 6) are known to emerge only with experience and time, few activities in the implementation were targeted at these concerns. However, several self-paced modules aimed at student-oriented needs (such as the implications of Piaget's work for science instruction) were made available during inservice sessions. In general, however, the implementation effort was targeted at lowering Informational, Personal, and Management concerns (SoC 1, 2, 3).

### Figure 1
### Stages of Concern: Typical Expressions of Concern About the Innovation
(Hall and Loucks, 1978)

| Stages of Concern | Expressions of Concern |
|---|---|
| 6　Refocusing | I have some ideas about something that would work even better. |
| 5　Collaboration | I am concerned about relating what I am doing with what other instructors are doing. |
| 4　Consequence | How is my use affecting kids? |
| 3　Management | I seem to be spending all my time in getting material ready. |
| 2　Personal | How will using it affect me? |
| 1　Informational | I would like to know more about it. |
| 0　Awareness | I am not concerned about it (the innovation). |

Levels of Use (see Figure 2), describing the behaviors of teachers as they become increasingly more familiar with and skilled in using a program, provided district staff with a tool for goal-setting and informed implementation planning. It was decided early in the effort that the district goal was to have teachers at least at a Routine Level of Use (LoU IVA) at the completion of the implementation.

### Figure 2
### Levels of Use of the Innovation: Typical Behaviors
(Hall, Loucks, Rutherford and Newlove, 1975)

| Level of Use | Behavioral Indices of Level |
|---|---|
| IV　Renewal | The user is seeking more effective alternatives to the established use of the innovation. |
| V　Integration | The user is making deliberate efforts to coordinate with others in using the innovation. |
| IVB　Refinement | The user is making changes to increase outcomes. |
| IVA　Routine | The user is making few or no changes and has an established pattern of use. |
| III　Mechanical | The user is making changes to better organize use of the innovation. |
| II　Preparation | The user is preparing to use the innovation. |
| I　Orientation | The user is seeking out information about the innovation. |
| O　Nonuse | No action is being taken with respect to the innovation. |

### Monitoring Implementation

During the course of the implementation effort, three methodologies were used to assess its effects. Stages of Concern and Levels of Use data were collected five times during the three-year implementation. A third methodology, developed by the science department and district evaluators, identified program components and used these as the basis for measuring the extent of implementation in another set of schools. We describe each concept below, the measurement procedures we used, and some sample findings.

Susan F. Loucks, Marge Melle 107

**Figure 3**
**Sample Concerns Profiles for Two Teachers**

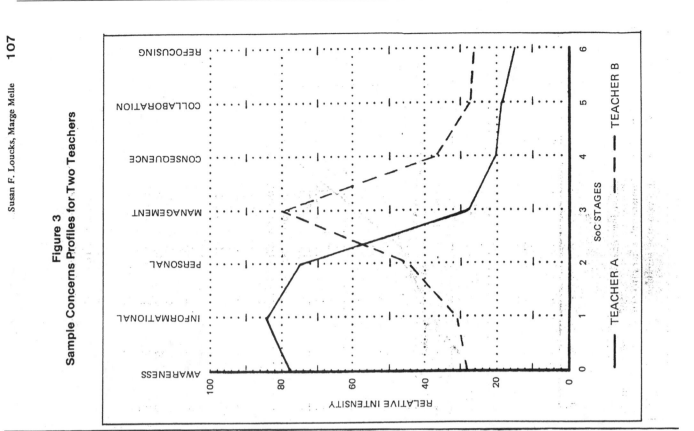

## Stages of Concern

We collected Stages of Concern data using the 35-item Stage of Concern (SoC) Questionnaire (Hall, George and Rutherford, 1977). This 15-minute instrument allows teachers to describe how much concern they feel about different aspects of a new program. It results in a profile of the intensity of concern they feel on each of the seven stages.

Stages of Concern data gave us a clear sense of teachers' needs related to the revised curriculum at any one point in time, and so they were a valuable formative evaluation tool. We could retarget resources, reformulate training designs, and deliver individualized assistance based on individual teacher profiles. Figure 3 provides examples of two teacher profiles. Teacher A (typical of profiles we found *before* inservice had taken place) wanted more information (what is it?) and had questions about personal impact (how will it affect me?); while Teacher B (representative of some of the profiles we found in Jefferson County Schools after inservice) was having problems managing the new program (will I ever get this organized? where do I find the time to set up?). Both sets of concerns suggested specific kinds of information and/or assistance that would have been most relevant to each teacher.

Stages of Concern data aggregated for each school also gave us clues to the influences at the school-level. For example, we found several school profiles that looked like Teacher B's profile. This we found was most often due to a lack of principal commitment to the new program, which resulted in consumable supplies not being reordered, facilities and classes scheduled in such a way that science instruction was difficult, and supply closets that were always in disarray. School profiles allowed us to quickly recognize which schools needed special assistance.

Similarly, district-wide concerns profiles assisted the planning of staff development activities and the overall assessment of whether the plan was having the desired effect. Figure 4 shows a representative sample of teachers from several schools. The solid line indicates concerns well before inservice took place. This first measurement suggested the need for an orientation session, describing the new curriculum and providing basic information. The dashed line represents concerns after inservice had occurred. Information and Personal concerns had decreased without an increase in Management concerns (indicating a successful round of inservices which helped teachers use the curriculum without these typical kinds of problems). The dotted line, one year after implementation, shows a gradual increase in concern about the program's effects on students, another positive sign that the staff development effort had helped focus teachers in productive ways.

This article originally appeared in *The Journal of Staff Development*, April 1982. Reprinted by permission of the National Staff Development Council, 1998.

## Levels of Use

We used a second monitoring tool, Levels of Use (LoU), to determine how teachers were using the new program, how comfortable, skilled and sensitive to students they were in its use. A focused interview procedure, taking approximately 20 minutes, allowed assignment of a single LoU to a teacher (Loucks, Newlove and Hall, 1976).

Levels of Use data also provided formative evaluation information: how were teachers behaving with the new curriculum? An individual teacher's score suggested information or assistance needed, giving guidance to staff development efforts. A look at how the Levels of Use of a sample of teachers changed over time (see Figure 5) illustrates a progression from nonuse to use, and from disorganized first use to the establishment of a routine.

### Figure 5
### Levels of Use Distribution for a Sample of Jefferson County Teachers

|  | O | I | II | III | IVA | IVB | V | VI |  |
|---|---|---|---|---|---|---|---|---|---|
| One year before inservice | 80 | 14 | 1 | 3 | 0 | 0 | 0 | 1 | N = 69 |
| One month before inservice | 12 | 16 | 63 | 4 | 6 | 0 | 0 | 0 | N = 51 |
| Three months after inservice | 8 | 14 | 6 | 42 | 22 | 4 | 2 | 2 | N = 50 |
| Fifteen months after inservice | 16 | 2 | 0 | 25 | 41 | 12 | 2 | 2 | N = 51 |

As with Stages of Concern, Levels of Use proved a valuable tool for monitoring change due to the staff development effort, and for determining finally whether the effort had been successful.

## Assessing Components of the Program

A final way we used to determine the effect of the staff development program on teachers was to look at how their behaviors changed with respect to the revised curriculum. To do so, it was necessary to define the program carefully, describing each component as to how it might look in the classroom.

This evaluation technique differed from Stages of Concern and Levels of Use in that an instrument had to be developed especially for the science curriculum.[3] In the paragraphs that follow we describe the development of a procedure for describing and assessing the Jefferson County science curriculum, and the several ways the procedure was used.

[3]With concerns and use, the instruments are generic and can be used for any new practice, simply by focusing the teacher when expressing concerns and describing use.

### Figure 4
### Changes in Concern Over Time for a Group of Jefferson County Teachers

Before inservice

Immediately after inservice

One year after inservice

This article originally appeared in *The Journal of Staff Development*, April 1982. Reprinted by permission of the National Staff Development Council, 1998.

450

Susan F. Loucks, Marge Melle    **111**

## Figure 6 (Continued)

reflects attention to seasonal demands, sharing of materials, and maximum utilization of space and personnel. Before each unit is taught, overall planning for that unit takes place.

III. Program components over which the teacher has the major influence for implementation in the classroom:

9. *Class time in science is used effectively* (time on task). At least 75% of the class time is devoted to exploration, pupil interaction, recording data, discussions and listening to each other. An efficient management system for distribution and clean-up of materials is evident.

10. *Teacher-student interaction facilitates the program.* Using the students' language, the teacher shares with students the objectives of the units. Discussion techniques include: neutral rewarding, wait time, questions above recall level, maximized use of student-student discussion; and data sharing.

11. *The classroom environment and arrangement facilitates student-student interaction in small groups.* Furniture and materials are arranged in order to facilitate small group interaction. Student behaviors include sharing of materials, listening to each other, working together towards a group goal, and interacting with each other (cooperative learning). Students are task-oriented most of the time.

12. *The instruction in one classroom follows the stages of the learning cycle in science: exploration, concept formation, concept application.*

Implementation of the components of the curriculum was assessed during the second year of use. Interviews and classroom observations were conducted by specially trained certified teachers and by staff members from the evaluation and science departments. In eleven schools, each grade three through six teacher who taught science was interviewed extensively and observed for a total science class on three separate occasions. In addition, the principal and library media specialist for each school were interviewed. A complete description of the study and detailed findings are found in the evaluation report (Darnell, 1979).

The data gathered helped answer several questions about the effect of the staff development program in helping teachers use the curriculum. As shown in Figure 8, it was possible to see clearly how teachers were using each component. Teacher and school profiles enabled staff developers to "troubleshoot" components that were giving teachers problems, either for lack of information, skill, equipment, time or support. For example, in Winter Elementary (Figure 8), most teachers were not assessing science instruction to the extent suggested in the Guide (Component 3). In this particular case, teachers were not clear about how to do the actual

---

**110**    The Journal of Staff Development

Twelve components of the elementary science program were identified and described in their ideal form. We clustered these twelve components into three categories. These components and categories are described in Figure 6. Once the program components were defined, detailed descriptions of each were written in order to ultimately measure as objectively as possible the extent to which each component was in place in any one classroom. The behaviors were placed on a 5-point Likert scale: 1 – outside the intended program; 2-3 – getting a good start; 4 – well on the way; 5 – best practices in operation. An illustration appears in Figure 7. Instruments and data recording sheets for use in monitoring the extent of implementation of the program as defined by the twelve components were developed by the district's Department of Evaluation (Darnell, 1979). These included a classroom observation checklist and focused interviews for teachers, the principal, and media specialist.

## Figure 6
## Components of the Science Program

I. Program components over which district policy or procedure appear to have the major influence for implementation in the classroom:

1. *The recommended percentage of teaching time during the day is devoted to science.* An average of 15% of the student's day (10% for third grade) should be devoted to science.

2. *Science is taught according to the district guide.* During the school year the teacher teaches all units, all objectives of each unit, and 90% of the activities.

3. *Students' learning is assessed according to the district science guide.* According to a review of each unit, the teacher uses the guide assessments with students 85% of the time.

4. *Basic skills, as differentiated by the continuum in each curriculum area, are being integrated into the science program.* The basic skills keyed in the guide are being *introduced* or stressed in their *subject area* time allotment while they are being *reinforced* during science instruction.

5. *The outdoors is used as a classroom when recommended.* Whenever outdoor activities are recommended as part of a unit, they are always included.

II. Program components over which the building principal and the teacher building and classroom:

6. *All materials, equipment, and media are available.* Appropriate commercial guides and the district guide are available for use. Enough materials are available for individual or small group usage. A storage system of logical sequence is established.

7. *Principals have arranged for release of teachers for the total inservice training package and have allocated financial support to the program.*

8. *Long and short-range planning is evident.* The year's schedule is written out and being implemented by the teacher or the team. This schedule

**Figure 8**
**Sample Building Summary Sheet**

| | 1 Outside Intended Program | 2 Getting a Good Start | 3 | 4 Well on the Way | 5 Best Practices Working |
|---|---|---|---|---|---|
| 1. Time is devoted to science | ** | ** | ** | * | ** |
| 2. Science is taught according to R-1 Guide | *** | ** | | * | |
| 3. Assessment of pupil learning | *** | ** | * | | |
| 4. Integration of basic skills | * | ***** | | | |
| 5. The outdoor classroom is used as recommended | | ** | * | ** | ** |
| 6. Recommended materials, equipment and media are available | | | *** | *** | * |
| 7. Inservicing and financial arrangements have been made | ** | | *** | *** | |
| 8. Long and short range planning | *** | *** | *** | ** | |
| 9. Use of class time | | *** | **** | ** | |
| 10. Teacher-Pupil interaction facilitates program | ** | **** | **** | ** | |
| 11. Classroom environment facilitates program | | *** | *** | *** | ** |
| 12. Instruction is sequenced to facilitate the guided inquiry learning approach | ** | *** | **** | *** | |

\* = one teacher    All grade 3, 4, 5, 6 teachers

School ____ Winter Elementary

Teacher ____

assessments, and so were rarely doing any evaluation of student effort. Staff developers were able to present a short workshop to teachers, clarifying what the assessments required and giving concrete examples of how to observe and record student progress.

---

**Figure 7**
**Example of a Component Described**

Is Science Taught According to R-1 Guide?

| Outside Intended Program — 1 | Getting a Good Start — 2 ——— 3 | Well on Way — 4 | Best Practices Working — 5 |
|---|---|---|---|

**1 — Outside Intended Program**

**A** During the school year the teacher covers less than 85% of the objectives and activities.
The teacher may or may not cover units in the guide. If units are taught, more activities are omitted than included.

**B** Objectives or activities are not sequenced.
Objectives may be used but teacher-made activities are used mainly to accomplish the objectives.

**C** Supplementary media is frequently used in addition to or to the exclusion of hands-on activities.

**2 — Getting a Good Start**

**A** During the school year 85% of the objectives and 85% of the activities are taught. The teacher covers the units as written and spends the allotted time (see #1). Some units may be abbreviated because an extra amount of time was spent on another unit.

**B** The teacher can:
• Point in the guide to the objective that is currently being taught.
• Describe what objectives and activities went before and what objectives will come after current activities.

**C** Teacher uses supplementary media sparingly.

**4 — Well on Way / 5 — Best Practices Working**

**A** During the school year the teacher teaches all units, all objectives of each unit and 90% of the activities. At the end of some objectives teacher uses Optional Activities to extend the unit with small groups of students.

**B** The teacher can relate what objective is being studied and how the activity pertains to accomplishing the objective. He/she can relate what objectives preceded and will succeed the objective being taught.

**C** Teacher uses supplementary media sparingly and can demonstrate how supplements which are used support the objectives being taught.

**Figure 9**
**Percent of Implementation of the Revised Elementary Science Program for Component # 10**

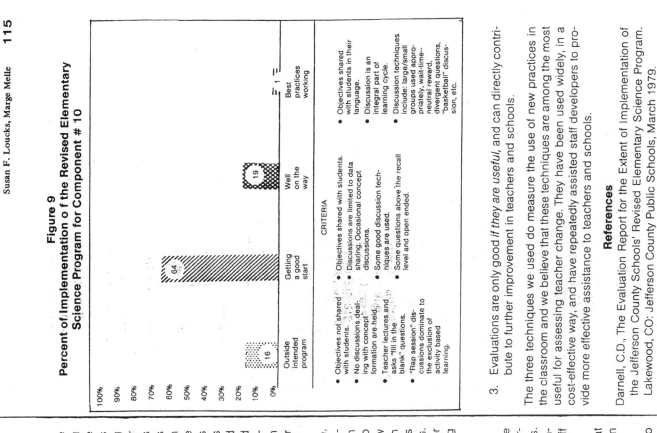

**114**

Every school had a profile summarizing teachers' use of the science curriculum. This enabled staff developers to work closely with building principals and teachers to diagnose needs and help meet them. In some cases it was as straightforward as presenting a special workshop (as in Winter Elementary), delivering additional equipment, or helping reschedule classes so that teachers had access to a special room for science or a planning period before science to prepare. In other cases the data provoked some healthy dialogues about why things were done as they were, and who had ultimate responsibility for student learning. In one case, for example, a low score for teachers on time allotted for science (Component 1) resulted in an affirmation that the staff had made a conscious decision to cut back on science in order to devote more time to basic skills instruction. In another case, however, the same data (little time allotted for science) described teachers who simply did not like "the mess and bother" and so were ignoring the district direction. Some principal pressure combined with tips on how to avoid "the mess and bother" resulted in teachers not only teaching the units, but being excited because their students seemed to be benefiting.

Finally, component profiles were made up for the district-wide sample. These enabled staff developers to see the success of their efforts. Histograms such as Figure 9 described what percent of teachers fell in each category of use. Component 10, considered by district staff to be critical to the success of the curriculum for students, showed minimal use. Few teachers (1%) were facilitating student experimentation and discussion in an exemplary way. From these data district staff learned that the inservices they were offering were not helping teachers acquire these particular skills. One result of this finding was a series of workshop opportunities for teachers which helped them maximize student inquiry and interaction using special grouping strategies.

In the Jefferson County staff development effort, we found the three evaluation techniques described in this article very useful in both understanding and monitoring the effect of the effort on teachers and schools. The techniques themselves, Stages of Concern, Levels of Use, and Component Assessment, underscore the strong beliefs we share about staff development evaluation:

1. The "proof of the pudding" for staff development efforts aimed at helping teachers develop new skills and/or use new practices lies in *whether those practices are then used in the classroom.*

2. The only way to find out about change in classroom practice is to *interact individually with each teacher to find out, and*

3. Evaluations are only good *if they are useful,* and can directly contribute to further improvement in teachers and schools.

The three techniques we used do measure the use of new practices in the classroom and we believe that these techniques are among the most useful for assessing teacher change. They have been used widely, in a cost-effective way, and have repeatedly assisted staff developers to provide more effective assistance to teachers and schools.

### References

Darnell, C.D., The Evaluation Report for the Extent of Implementation of the Jefferson County Schools' Revised Elementary Science Program. Lakewood, CO: Jefferson County Public Schools, March 1979.

## Summary

Hall, G.E., George A.A., & Rutherford, W.L., Measuring Stages of Concern About the Innovation: A Manual for Use of the SoC Questionnaire. Austin: Research and Development Center for Teacher Education, The University of Texas, 1977.

Hall, G.E. & Loucks, S.F., Teacher Concerns as a Basis for Facilitating and Personalizing Staff Development. *Teachers College Record*, September 1978, Vol. 80, No. 1, pp. 36-53.

Hall, G.E., Loucks, S.F., Rutherford, W.L., & Newlove, B.N., Levels of Use of the Innovation: A Framework for Analyzing Innovation Adoption. *The Journal of Teacher Education*, 1975, Vol. 26, No. 1, pp. 52-56.

Hall, G.E., Wallace, R.C., & Dossett, W.A., A Developmental Conceptualization of the Adoption Process Within Educational Institutions. Austin: Research and Development Center for Teacher Education, The University of Texas, 1973.

Hall, G.E., et. al., Making Change Happen: A Case Study of School District Implementation. Austin: Research and Development Center for Teacher Education, The University, 1980.

Jefferson County Schools, *A Principal's Handbook for Elementary Science*. Lakewood, CO: Jefferson County Public Schools, 1979.

Loucks, S.F., & Pratt, M. Effective Curriculum Change Through a Concerns-based Approach to Planning and Staff Development. *Educational Leadership*, December 1979, Vol. 37, No. 3, pp. 212-215.

Loucks, S.F., Newlove, B.W., & Hall, G.E. Measuring Levels of Use of the Innovation: A Manual for Trainers, Interviewers, and Raters. Austin: Research and Development Center for Teacher Education, The University of Texas, 1975.

**117** Susan F. Loucks, Marge Melle

*Susan Loucks – Susan is currently on the staff of THE NETWORK, Inc. in Andover, Massachusetts where she directs projects in the areas of evaluation, training, program validation, research and technical assistance. She recently moved from Austin, Texas where she spent nine years at the Research and Development Center for Teacher Education conducting research on the change process and training in applications of the research to schools. Her academic background includes a B.A. in geology from the State University of New York at Binghamton, and an M.A. and Ph.D. in curriculum and instruction from the University of Texas at Austin. She has written extensively in the areas of program implementation and evaluation, staff development and school improvement.*

*Marge Melle – Marge did her undergraduate work at the University of Colorado where she majored in psychology. She received her M.A. in Science Education from the University of Northern Colorado, and has earned graduate credit since then in organizational development work. She worked as an elementary school teacher and library media specialist before becoming the specialist in charge of elementary science in Jefferson County Public Schools. Her current emphasis is on developing a program for primary students which integrates science, social studies, career education, health education, environmental education, and some language arts.*

This article originally appeared in *The Journal of Staff Development*, April 1982. Reprinted by permission of the National Staff Development Council, 1998.

Form Approval  OMB No: 3145-0136  Expires:  August 2001

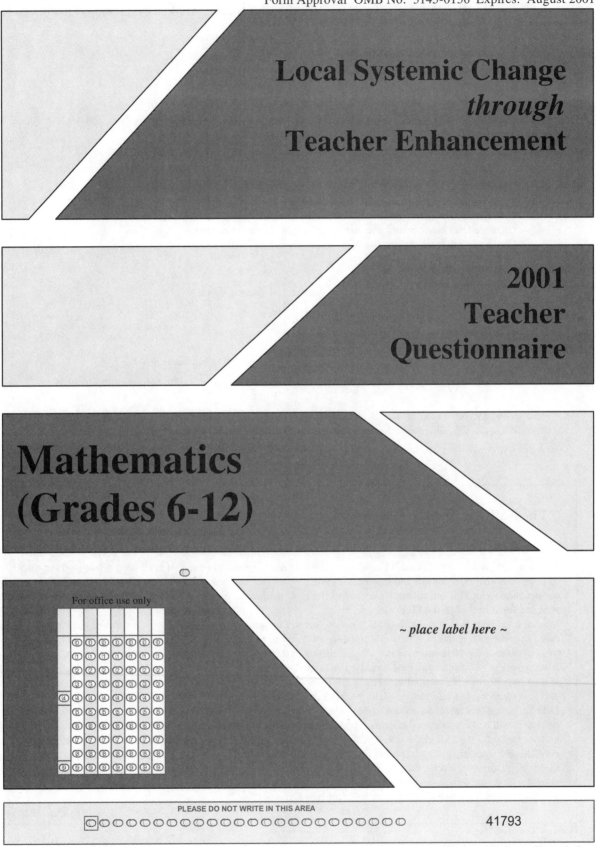

# Local Systemic Change *through* Teacher Enhancement

## 2001 Teacher Questionnaire

# Mathematics (Grades 6-12)

For office use only

~ *place label here* ~

PLEASE DO NOT WRITE IN THIS AREA

41793

Horizon Research, Inc.

National Science Foundation

**Instructions:** Please use a #2 pencil to complete this questionnaire. Darken ovals completely, but do not stray into adjacent ovals. Be sure to erase completely any stray marks.

## A. Teacher Demographic Information

1. Are you:

   ○ Male
   ○ Female

2. Race - Are you: (Darken one or more.)

   ○ American Indian or Alaskan Native    ○ Hispanic or Latino
   ○ Asian                                ○ Native Hawaiian or Other Pacific Islander
   ○ Black or African-American            ○ White

3. Describe your educational background: (Darken all ovals that apply.)

   ○ Undergraduate major in mathematics or mathematics education
   ○ Undergraduate minor in mathematics or mathematics education
   ○ Graduate-level major or minor in mathematics or mathematics education
   ○ Certification to teach mathematics
   ○ None of the above

4. How many years have you taught prior to this school year? (Darken one oval.)

   | 0-2 | 3-5 | 6-10 | 11-15 | 16-20 | 21-25 | 26 or more |
   |-----|-----|------|-------|-------|-------|------------|
   | ○   | ○   | ○    | ○     | ○     | ○     | ○          |

5. When did you last complete a mathematics course for college credit? (Darken one oval.)

   ○ In the last 5 years    ○ 6-10 years ago    ○ 11-20 years ago    ○ More than 20 years ago

6. Have you taught one or more classes of advanced mathematics in the last three years, e.g., algebra II / trigonometry, pre-calculus, calculus, discrete mathematics, abstract or linear algebra? (Darken one oval.)

   ○ Yes    ○ No

---

### The National Science Foundation's Local Systemic Change (LSC) through Teacher Enhancement Program's Core Evaluation

You have been selected to participate in the nationwide evaluation of the federally-funded Local systemic Change (LSC) program. LSC is a National Science Foundation Teacher Enhancement program that is currently funding more than 50 local projects that offer science and mathematics professional development to teachers around the country. **The cover letter accompanying this questionnaire identifies the LSC project in your area, as well as the instructional materials that are the forces of that LSC project.**

Several times over the course of the LSC, each project will administer questionnaires to a sample of teachers who are targeted to participate in the local project's professional development activities. Note that you may be asked to complete this questionnaire even if you have not yet participated in the project's professional development; your response is important, regardless of whether you have already participated. A small number of randomly-selected teachers in each project is asked to provide additional information in interviews, sometimes in conjunction with a classroom visit. In order to continue receiving federal funding, each LSC project must participate in this national evaluation.

Data collection procedures have been developed to ensure high-quality data and protect teacher confidentiality. Your responses will be kept strictly confidential; they will be combined with the responses of the other teachers in your project and used only for the LSC evaluation. The name label and numbering on this questionnaire are used to help local projects deliver questionnaires to the proper teachers and follow up with teachers who have not responded; no information identifying individual teachers will be reported under any circumstances. After you complete the questionnaire, you should remove the name label and return the questionnaire as specified by your local LSC project. Additional information about privacy, as well as public burden, is provided on page 7 of this questionnaire.

## B. Teacher Opinions and Preparedness

7. Please provide your opinion about each of the following statements.
   (Darken one oval on each line.)

| | Strongly Disagree | Disagree | No Opinion | Agree | Strongly Agree |
|---|---|---|---|---|---|
| a. Students generally learn mathematics best in classes with students of similar abilities. | ① | ② | ③ | ④ | ⑤ |
| b. I feel supported by colleagues to try out new ideas in teaching mathematics. | ① | ② | ③ | ④ | ⑤ |
| c. Mathematics teachers in this school have a shared vision of effective mathematics instruction. | ① | ② | ③ | ④ | ⑤ |
| d. Mathematics teachers in this school regularly share ideas and materials related to mathematics. | ① | ② | ③ | ④ | ⑤ |
| e. Mathematics teachers in this school are well-supplied with materials for investigative mathematics instruction. | ① | ② | ③ | ④ | ⑤ |
| f. I have time during the regular school week to work with my peers on mathematics curriculum and instruction. | ① | ② | ③ | ④ | ⑤ |
| g. I have adequate access to calculators for teaching mathematics. | ① | ② | ③ | ④ | ⑤ |
| h. I have adequate access to computers for teaching mathematics. | ① | ② | ③ | ④ | ⑤ |
| i. I enjoy teaching mathematics. | ① | ② | ③ | ④ | ⑤ |
| j. I am well-informed about the NCTM *Standards* for the grades I teach. | ① | ② | ③ | ④ | ⑤ |
| k. The mathematics program in this school is strongly supported by local organizations, institutions, and/or businesses. | ① | ② | ③ | ④ | ⑤ |

8. In the left section, please rate each of the following in terms of its **importance** for effective mathematics instruction in the grades you teach. In the right section, please indicate how **prepared** you feel to do each one.
   (Darken one oval in each section on each line.)

| | Importance | | | | Preparation | | | |
|---|---|---|---|---|---|---|---|---|
| | Not Important | Some-what Important | Fairly Important | Very Important | Not Adequately Prepared | Some-what Prepared | Fairly Well Prepared | Very Well Prepared |
| a. Provide concrete experience before abstract concepts. | ① | ② | ③ | ④ | ① | ② | ③ | ④ |
| b. Develop students' conceptual understanding of mathematics. | ① | ② | ③ | ④ | ① | ② | ③ | ④ |
| c. Take students' prior understanding into account when planning curriculum and instruction. | ① | ② | ③ | ④ | ① | ② | ③ | ④ |
| d. Practice computational skills and algorithms. | ① | ② | ③ | ④ | ① | ② | ③ | ④ |
| e. Make connections between mathematics and other disciplines. | ① | ② | ③ | ④ | ① | ② | ③ | ④ |
| f. Have students work in cooperative learning groups. | ① | ② | ③ | ④ | ① | ② | ③ | ④ |
| g. Have students participate in appropriate hands-on activities. | ① | ② | ③ | ④ | ① | ② | ③ | ④ |
| h. Engage students in inquiry-oriented activities. | ① | ② | ③ | ④ | ① | ② | ③ | ④ |
| i. Have students prepare project/laboratory/research reports. | ① | ② | ③ | ④ | ① | ② | ③ | ④ |
| j. Use calculators. | ① | ② | ③ | ④ | ① | ② | ③ | ④ |
| k. Use computers. | ① | ② | ③ | ④ | ① | ② | ③ | ④ |
| l. Engage students in applications of mathematics in a variety of contexts. | ① | ② | ③ | ④ | ① | ② | ③ | ④ |
| m. Use performance-based assessment. | ① | ② | ③ | ④ | ① | ② | ③ | ④ |
| n. Use portfolios. | ① | ② | ③ | ④ | ① | ② | ③ | ④ |
| o. Use informal questioning to assess student understanding. | ① | ② | ③ | ④ | ① | ② | ③ | ④ |

PLEASE DO NOT WRITE IN THIS AREA

41793

9. My principal: (Darken one oval on each line.)

| | Strongly Disagree | Disagree | No Opinion | Agree | Strongly Agree |
|---|---|---|---|---|---|
| a. Encourages me to select mathematics content and instructional strategies that address individual students' learning. | ① | ② | ③ | ④ | ⑤ |
| b. Accepts the noise that comes with an active classroom. | ① | ② | ③ | ④ | ⑤ |
| c. Encourages the implementation of current national standards in mathematics education. | ① | ② | ③ | ④ | ⑤ |
| d. Encourages innovative instructional practices. | ① | ② | ③ | ④ | ⑤ |
| e. Enhances the mathematics program by providing me with needed materials and equipment. | ① | ② | ③ | ④ | ⑤ |
| f. Provides time for teachers to meet and share ideas with one another. | ① | ② | ③ | ④ | ⑤ |
| g. Encourages me to observe exemplary mathematics teachers. | ① | ② | ③ | ④ | ⑤ |
| h. Encourages teachers to make connections across disciplines. | ① | ② | ③ | ④ | ⑤ |
| i. Acts as a buffer between teachers and external pressures (e.g., parents). | ① | ② | ③ | ④ | ⑤ |

10. Are you the mathematics department chair for your school? (Darken one oval.)

   ○ No (continue with Question 11)
   ○ Yes (skip to Question 12)
   ○ Our school does not have a mathematics department chair (skip to Question 12)

11. My department chair: (Darken one oval on each line.)

| | Strongly Disagree | Disagree | No Opinion | Agree | Strongly Agree |
|---|---|---|---|---|---|
| a. Encourages me to select mathematics content and instructional strategies that address individual students' learning. | ① | ② | ③ | ④ | ⑤ |
| b. Accepts the noise that comes with an active classroom. | ① | ② | ③ | ④ | ⑤ |
| c. Encourages the implementation of current national standards in mathematics education. | ① | ② | ③ | ④ | ⑤ |
| d. Encourages innovative instructional practices. | ① | ② | ③ | ④ | ⑤ |
| e. Enhances the mathematics program by providing me with needed materials and equipment. | ① | ② | ③ | ④ | ⑤ |
| f. Provides time for teachers to meet and share ideas with one another. | ① | ② | ③ | ④ | ⑤ |
| g. Encourages me to observe exemplary mathematics teachers. | ① | ② | ③ | ④ | ⑤ |
| h. Encourages teachers to make connections across disciplines. | ① | ② | ③ | ④ | ⑤ |

12. Many teachers feel better prepared to teach some mathematics topics than others. How well prepared do you feel to teach each of the following topics at the grade levels you teach, whether or not they are currently included in your curriculum? (Darken one oval on each line.)

| | Not Adequately Prepared | Somewhat Prepared | Fairly Well Prepared | Very Well Prepared |
|---|---|---|---|---|
| a. Estimation | ① | ② | ③ | ④ |
| b. Measurement | ① | ② | ③ | ④ |
| c. Pre-algebra | ① | ② | ③ | ④ |
| d. Algebra | ① | ② | ③ | ④ |
| e. Patterns and relationships | ① | ② | ③ | ④ |
| f. Geometry and spatial sense | ① | ② | ③ | ④ |
| g. Functions (including trigonometric functions) and pre-calculus concepts | ① | ② | ③ | ④ |
| h. Data collection and analysis | ① | ② | ③ | ④ |
| i. Probability | ① | ② | ③ | ④ |
| j. Statistics (e.g., hypothesis tests, curve fitting and regression) | ① | ② | ③ | ④ |
| k. Topics from discrete mathematics (e.g., combinatorics, graph theory, recursion) | ① | ② | ③ | ④ |
| l. Mathematical structures (e.g., vector spaces; groups, rings, fields) | ① | ② | ③ | ④ |
| m. Calculus | ① | ② | ③ | ④ |
| n. Technology (calculators, computers) in support of mathematics | ① | ② | ③ | ④ |

Horizon Research, Inc.

3

13. Within the arena of mathematical processes, many teachers feel better prepared to guide and help develop student learning in some domains than others. How well prepared do you feel to provide guidance in the following, at the grade levels you teach? (Darken one oval on each line.)

| | Not Adequately Prepared | Somewhat Prepared | Fairly Well Prepared | Very Well Prepared |
|---|---|---|---|---|
| a. Problem solving | ① | ② | ③ | ④ |
| b. Reasoning and proof | ① | ② | ③ | ④ |
| c. Communication (written and oral) | ① | ② | ③ | ④ |
| d. Connections within mathematics and from mathematics to other disciplines | ① | ② | ③ | ④ |
| e. Multiple representations (e.g., concrete models, and numeric, graphical, symbolic, and geometric representations) | ① | ② | ③ | ④ |

14. Please indicate how well prepared you feel to do each of the following. (Darken one oval on each line.)

| | Not Adequately Prepared | Somewhat Prepared | Fairly Well Prepared | Very Well Prepared |
|---|---|---|---|---|
| a. Lead a class of students using investigative strategies. | ① | ② | ③ | ④ |
| b. Manage a class of students engaged in hands-on/project-based work. | ① | ② | ③ | ④ |
| c. Help students take responsibility for their own learning. | ① | ② | ③ | ④ |
| d. Recognize and respond to student diversity. | ① | ② | ③ | ④ |
| e. Encourage students' interest in mathematics. | ① | ② | ③ | ④ |
| f. Use strategies that specifically encourage participation of females and minorities in mathematics. | ① | ② | ③ | ④ |
| g. Involve parents in the mathematics education of their students. | ① | ② | ③ | ④ |

15. Please rate the effect of each of the following on your mathematics instruction. (Darken one oval on each line.)

| | Inhibits Effective Instruction | | Neutral or Mixed | | Encourages Effective Instruction | N/A Don't Know |
|---|---|---|---|---|---|---|
| a. State and/or district curriculum frameworks. | ① | ② | ③ | ④ | ⑤ | Ⓝ |
| b. State and/or district testing policies and practices. | ① | ② | ③ | ④ | ⑤ | Ⓝ |
| c. Counseling department policies and practices. | ① | ② | ③ | ④ | ⑤ | Ⓝ |
| d. College placement tests. | ① | ② | ③ | ④ | ⑤ | Ⓝ |
| e. Quality of available instructional materials. | ① | ② | ③ | ④ | ⑤ | Ⓝ |
| f. Access to calculators for mathematics instruction. | ① | ② | ③ | ④ | ⑤ | Ⓝ |
| g. Access to computers for mathematics instruction. | ① | ② | ③ | ④ | ⑤ | Ⓝ |
| h. Funds for purchasing equipment and supplies for mathematics. | ① | ② | ③ | ④ | ⑤ | Ⓝ |
| i. System of managing instructional resources at the district or school level. | ① | ② | ③ | ④ | ⑤ | Ⓝ |
| j. Time available for teachers to plan and prepare lessons. | ① | ② | ③ | ④ | ⑤ | Ⓝ |
| k. Time available for teachers to work with other teachers. | ① | ② | ③ | ④ | ⑤ | Ⓝ |
| l. Time available for teacher professional development. | ① | ② | ③ | ④ | ⑤ | Ⓝ |
| m. Importance that the school places on mathematics. | ① | ② | ③ | ④ | ⑤ | Ⓝ |
| n. Consistency of mathematics reform efforts with other school/district reforms. | ① | ② | ③ | ④ | ⑤ | Ⓝ |
| o. Public attitudes toward reform. | ① | ② | ③ | ④ | ⑤ | Ⓝ |

16. How many of your students' parents do each of the following? (Darken one oval on each line.)

| | None | A Few | | About 1/2 | | Almost All |
|---|---|---|---|---|---|---|
| a. Volunteer to assist with class activities. | ⓪ | ① | ② | ③ | ④ | ⑤ |
| b. Donate money or materials for classroom instruction. | ⓪ | ① | ② | ③ | ④ | ⑤ |
| c. Attend parent-teacher conferences. | ⓪ | ① | ② | ③ | ④ | ⑤ |
| d. Attend school activities such as PTA meetings and Family Mathematics nights. | ⓪ | ① | ② | ③ | ④ | ⑤ |
| e. Voice support for the use of an investigative approach to mathematics instruction. | ⓪ | ① | ② | ③ | ④ | ⑤ |
| f. Voice support for traditional approaches to mathematics instruction. | ⓪ | ① | ② | ③ | ④ | ⑤ |

Horizon Research, Inc.                    4

## C.  Your Mathematics Teaching

17. Which of the following are you currently teaching?
(Darken each oval that applies.)
   ○ Middle school mathematics
   ○ High school mathematics

**Questions 18-20 ask about your mathematics teaching.  Please answer for your first middle/high school mathematics class of the day.**

18. What grade level is this class? (Darken one oval.)   ○ Middle school mathematics      ○ High school mathematics

19. About how often do **you** do each of the following in your mathematics instruction in this class?  (Darken one oval on each line.)

| | Never | Rarely (e.g., a few times a year) | Sometimes (e.g., once or twice a month) | Often (e.g., once or twice a week) | All or almost all mathematics lessons |
|---|---|---|---|---|---|
| a. Use the LSC-designated instructional materials (see cover letter) as the basis of mathematics lessons. | ① | ② | ③ | ④ | ⑤ |
| b. Introduce content through formal presentations. | ① | ② | ③ | ④ | ⑤ |
| c. Arrange seating to facilitate student discussion. | ① | ② | ③ | ④ | ⑤ |
| d. Use open-ended questions. | ① | ② | ③ | ④ | ⑤ |
| e. Require students to explain their reasoning when giving an answer. | ① | ② | ③ | ④ | ⑤ |
| f. Encourage students to communicate mathematically. | ① | ② | ③ | ④ | ⑤ |
| g. Encourage students to explore alternative methods for solutions. | ① | ② | ③ | ④ | ⑤ |
| h. Encourage students to use multiple representations (e.g., numeric, graphic, geometric, etc.). | ① | ② | ③ | ④ | ⑤ |
| i. Allow students to work at their own pace. | ① | ② | ③ | ④ | ⑤ |
| j. Help students see connections between mathematics and other disciplines. | ① | ② | ③ | ④ | ⑤ |
| k. Use assessment to find out what students know before or during a unit. | ① | ② | ③ | ④ | ⑤ |
| l. Embed assessment in regular class activities. | ① | ② | ③ | ④ | ⑤ |
| m. Assign mathematics homework. | ① | ② | ③ | ④ | ⑤ |
| n. Read and comment on the reflections students have written in their notebooks or journals. | ① | ② | ③ | ④ | ⑤ |

20. About how often do **students** in this class take part in each of the following types of activities as part of their mathematics instruction?  (Darken one oval on each line.)

| | Never | Rarely (e.g., a few times a year) | Sometimes (e.g., once or twice a month) | Often (e.g., once or twice a week) | All or almost all mathematics lessons |
|---|---|---|---|---|---|
| a. Participate in student-led discussions. | ① | ② | ③ | ④ | ⑤ |
| b. Participate in discussions with the teacher to further mathematical understanding. | ① | ② | ③ | ④ | ⑤ |
| c. Work in cooperative learning groups. | ① | ② | ③ | ④ | ⑤ |
| d. Make formal presentations to the class. | ① | ② | ③ | ④ | ⑤ |
| e. Read from a mathematics textbook in class. | ① | ② | ③ | ④ | ⑤ |
| f. Read other (non-textbook) mathematics-related materials in class. | ① | ② | ③ | ④ | ⑤ |
| g. Practice routine computations/algorithms. | ① | ② | ③ | ④ | ⑤ |
| h. Review homework/worksheet assignments. | ① | ② | ③ | ④ | ⑤ |
| i. Use mathematical concepts to interpret and solve word problems. | ① | ② | ③ | ④ | ⑤ |
| j. Work on solving a real-world problem. | ① | ② | ③ | ④ | ⑤ |
| k. Share ideas or solve problems with each other in small groups. | ① | ② | ③ | ④ | ⑤ |
| l. Engage in hands-on mathematical activities. | ① | ② | ③ | ④ | ⑤ |
| m. Play mathematics games. | ① | ② | ③ | ④ | ⑤ |
| n. Follow specific instructions in an activity or investigation. | ① | ② | ③ | ④ | ⑤ |
| o. Design or implement their own investigation. | ① | ② | ③ | ④ | ⑤ |
| p. Work on models or simulations. | ① | ② | ③ | ④ | ⑤ |
| q. Work on extended mathematics investigations or projects (a week or more in duration). | ① | ② | ③ | ④ | ⑤ |
| r. Participate in field work. | ① | ② | ③ | ④ | ⑤ |

PLEASE DO NOT WRITE IN THIS AREA

◉○○○○○○○○○○○○○○○○○○○○○○○○○○○○    41793

Horizon Research, Inc.                                  5

20. (continued)

| | Never | Rarely (e.g., a few times a year) | Sometimes (e.g., once or twice a month) | Often (e.g., once or twice a week) | All or almost all mathematics lessons |
|---|---|---|---|---|---|
| s. Record, represent and/or analyze data. | ① | ② | ③ | ④ | ⑤ |
| t. Write a description of a plan, procedure or problem-solving process. | ① | ② | ③ | ④ | ⑤ |
| u. Write reflections in a notebook or journal. | ① | ② | ③ | ④ | ⑤ |
| v. Use calculators or computers for learning or practicing skills. | ① | ② | ③ | ④ | ⑤ |
| w. Use calculators or computers to develop conceptual understanding. | ① | ② | ③ | ④ | ⑤ |
| x. Use calculators or computers as a tool (e.g., spreadsheets, data analysis). | ① | ② | ③ | ④ | ⑤ |
| y. Work on portfolios. | ① | ② | ③ | ④ | ⑤ |
| z. Take short-answer tests (e.g., multiple choice, true/false, fill-in-the-blank). | ① | ② | ③ | ④ | ⑤ |
| aa. Take tests requiring open-ended responses (e.g., descriptions, justifications of solutions). | ① | ② | ③ | ④ | ⑤ |
| bb. Engage in performance tasks for assessment purposes. | ① | ② | ③ | ④ | ⑤ |

## D. LSC Professional Development

**Questions 21-27 refer to the NSF-supported Local Systemic Change (LSC) program. Please refer to the cover letter accompanying this questionnaire for information about the LSC project activities and designated materials in your district. If you have not yet participated in LSC professional development, darken this oval ○ and skip to Question 26.**

21. To what extent is each of the following true of LSC mathematics-related professional development in your district? (Darken one oval on each line.)

| | Not at all | | | | To a great extent |
|---|---|---|---|---|---|
| a. I am involved in planning my mathematics-related professional development. | ① | ② | ③ | ④ | ⑤ |
| b. I am encouraged to develop an individual professional development plan to address my needs and interests related to mathematics education. | ① | ② | ③ | ④ | ⑤ |
| c. I am given time to work with other teachers as part of my professional development. | ① | ② | ③ | ④ | ⑤ |
| d. I am given time to reflect on what I've learned and how to apply it to the classroom. | ① | ② | ③ | ④ | ⑤ |
| e. I receive support as I try to implement what I've learned. | ① | ② | ③ | ④ | ⑤ |

22. Approximately how many **total hours** have you spent on formal, LSC-provided professional development in mathematics/mathematics education **since the LSC project began**? (Darken one oval.)

○ 0      ○ 10-19      ○ 40-59      ○ 80-99      ○ 130-159      ○ 200 or greater
○ 1-9    ○ 20-39      ○ 60-79      ○ 100-129    ○ 160-199

23. Please indicate the number of times you have participated in each of the following activities **during this school year**. (Darken one oval on each line.)

| | 0 | 1-2 | 3-4 | 5-6 | 7 or more |
|---|---|---|---|---|---|
| a. Participated in an LSC academic year study group/discussion group. | ① | ② | ③ | ④ | ⑤ |
| b. Was "coached" on my teaching by an LSC teacher leader/staff person based on a classroom observation. | ① | ② | ③ | ④ | ⑤ |
| c. Received assistance from an LSC "teacher leader" in my school. | ① | ② | ③ | ④ | ⑤ |
| d. Received assistance from an LSC staff person in my district. | ① | ② | ③ | ④ | ⑤ |
| e. Received assistance from an LSC-designated mathematician/mathematics educator from a college/university/museum/industry. | ① | ② | ③ | ④ | ⑤ |
| f. Read messages in a Listserv discussion sponsored by the LSC. | ① | ② | ③ | ④ | ⑤ |
| g. Posted messages to a Listserv discussion sponsored by the LSC. | ① | ② | ③ | ④ | ⑤ |

Horizon Research, Inc.                    6

24. How would you rate the overall quality of the LSC professional development? (Darken one oval.)

| Very Poor | Poor | Fair | Good | Very Good | Excellent |
|:---:|:---:|:---:|:---:|:---:|:---:|
| ○ | ○ | ○ | ○ | ○ | ○ |

25. To what extent has participation in LSC mathematics-related professional development increased your: (Darken one oval on each line.)

|  | Not at all | | | | To a great extent |
|---|:---:|:---:|:---:|:---:|:---:|
| a. Mathematics content knowledge. | ① | ② | ③ | ④ | ⑤ |
| b. Understanding of how children think about/learn mathematics. | ① | ② | ③ | ④ | ⑤ |
| c. Ability to implement high-quality mathematics instructional materials. | ① | ② | ③ | ④ | ⑤ |

26. How many mathematics classes are you currently teaching that use the materials designated by your LSC (see cover letter) as the primary instructional materials? (Darken one oval.)

- ○ None
- ○ One
- ○ Two
- ○ Three
- ○ Four
- ○ Five
- ○ Six or more

27. Have you been identified as a teacher leader for your district's NSF-supported LSC project?

- ○ Yes
- ○ No

**Thank you very much for participating in this survey!**

*Privacy Act and Public Burden Statements*  The information requested on this survey is solicited under the authority of the National Science Foundation Act of 1950, as amended. The information from this data collection will be retained as part of the Privacy Act System of Records in accordance with the Privacy Act of 1974. Data submitted will be used in accordance with the criteria established by NSF for monitoring research and education grants, and in response to Public Law 99-383 and 24 USC 1885c. The information requested may be disclosed to qualified researchers and contractors in order to coordinate programs and to a Federal agency, court or party in a court or Federal administrative proceeding if the government is a party. Information may be added to and maintained by the Education and Training System of Records 63 Federal Register 264, 272 (January 5, 1998).

Public reporting burden for this collection of information is estimated to average 20 minutes per response, including the time for reviewing instructions. Send comments regarding this burden estimate, or any other aspect of this collection of information, including suggestions for reducing this burden, to Suzanne Plimpton, Reports Clearance Officer, Systems and Services Branch, Division of Administrative Services, National Science Foundation, 4201 Wilson Blvd., Arlington, VA 22230. An agency may not conduct or sponsor, and a person is not required to respond to, a collection of information unless it displays a currently valid OMB control number. The OMB number for this survey is 3145-0136.

DesignExpert™ by NCS    Printed in U.S.A.    Mark Reflex® EW-210957-1:654321    HR06
PLEASE DO NOT WRITE IN THIS AREA

41793

462

Doc.Ref.:ICC881/NRC418

## Section C

## OPPORTUNITY TO LEARN
### (Science) EXCERPT

For a full set of these surveys, see Boston College TIMSS web site at www.steep.bc.edu/timss.

In this section, a set of exercises on various science topics are presented, and you are asked to indicate whether you have taught or will teach the topic to your science class this year.

Please remember, "your science class" refers to the class which is identified on the cover of this questionnaire, and which will be tested as part of TIMSS in your school.

Available Topics

I.      Earth Features: Composition
II.     Earth Features: Landforms
III.    Earth Features: Bodies of Water
IV.     Earth Features: Bodies of Water
V.      Earth Features: Atmosphere
VI.     Earth Features: Rocks and Soils
VII.    Human Biology
VIII.   Human Biology
IX.     Energy Types, Sources, and Conversions
X.      Energy Types, Sources, and Conversions
XI.     Energy Types, Sources, and Conversions
XII.    Data Analysis

Source: IEA Third International Mathematics and Science Study, Teacher Questionnaire (Science).

Doc.Ref.:ICC881/NRC418

# VI. EARTH FEATURES: ROCKS AND SOILS

*The following exercises illustrate the above topic. These exercises, or ones like them, might be used to assess students' learning of this topic.*

A.  Which layer in the diagram contains the most organic material?

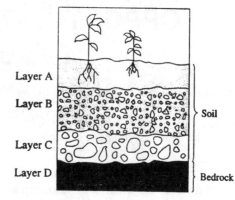

B.  The presence of igneous rock in an area would indicate that the area once had...?

C.  Rock that is made of material that has settled to the bottom of lakes and oceans and been compressed and hardened is...?

**1.  Is anything done in your science class that would enable your students to complete similar exercises that address this topic?**

*Check one:* ☐ Yes ☐ No

**If YES...**  *Check as many as apply.*

a)  Something was done EARLIER this year. ................................................. ☐
b)  Something is CURRENTLY in progress. ................................................. ☐
c)  Something will be done LATER this year. ................................................. ☐

**If NO...**  *Check as many as apply.*

d)  The topic was covered in the curriculum for an EARLIER grade. ............ ☐
e)  Although the topic is in the curriculum for THIS grade, I will not cover it. ☐
f)  The topic is covered in the curriculum for a LATER grade. ...................... ☐
g)  To my knowledge, this topic is NOT INCLUDED in the curriculum. ...... ☐
h)  I DO NOT KNOW whether this topic is covered in any other grade. ........ ☐

**2.  If you were to develop a test for your science class that assesses this particular science topic, which of the above items would you consider appropriate for the test?**

*Check all that apply.*

A ☐      B ☐      C ☐      none ☐

**3.  Are students likely to encounter this topic <u>outside</u> of school this year?**

*Check one:* ☐ Yes ☐ No

Source: IEA Third International Mathematics and Science Study, Teacher Questionnaire (Science).

Doc.Ref.:ICC881/NRC418

# Section D

# Pedagogical Approach

To better understand what teachers <u>believe</u> about how science is best taught, we are asking you to respond to two out of the three following hypothetical teaching situations. Several possible approaches are presented for each situation. Some of the situations may involve topics that are tangential to your current teaching field, and therefore, may or may not be likely to occur in your classes. Nevertheless, we are interested in what you <u>believe</u> would be the best approach or sequence of approaches to help students learn in these situations regardless of whether they may occur in your classes.

- Respond to the two situations with the science content most similar to your background and experience

- Imagine yourself in each situation.

- Assume that there are no time or equipment constraints.

*For item 1:*

- Indicate how strongly you agree or disagree with each of the four statements made about the teaching approach presented.

*For items 2 and 3:*

- Choose what you believe, based on your own principles and beliefs, to be the best approach or sequence of approaches to help students learn.

- Number the boxes next to each approach in the order in which you would consider using them. If you would use only one approach, place a '1' in that box only. Write zero in blank the box for any approach you would not consider using.

*Remember, respond to only two of the next three items: 1, 2, and 3.*

*Source:* IEA Third International Mathematics and Science Study, Teacher Questionnaire (Science).

Doc.Ref.:ICC881/NRC418

1.  **A teacher began instruction on a new topic in energy (e.g., chemical energy, mechanical energy, energy in life or earth processes). The first thing the teacher did was ask the students "What do you think energy is?" Student responses ranged from very accurate to quite incorrect. What is your opinion about this approach?**

*Check one box only in each line.*

| | strongly disagree | disagree | agree | strongly agree |
|---|---|---|---|---|
| a) This approach should be avoided because some students might get confused by other students' inaccurate ideas about energy. ............... | ☐ | ☐ | ☐ | ☐ |
| b) The teacher should have begun instruction by first explaining what energy is......................... | ☐ | ☐ | ☐ | ☐ |
| c) This approach was useful because the teacher became aware of the students' ideas about energy ................................................. . | ☐ | ☐ | ☐ | ☐ |
| d) The teacher should have begun instruction with a demonstration of the effects of energy followed by a discussion of the concept of energy. ................................................ | ☐ | ☐ | ☐ | ☐ |

*Source:* IEA Third International Mathematics and Science Study, Teacher Questionnaire (Science).

Doc.Ref.:ICC881/NRC418

2.  A student puts his hand in the water in the class aquarium and says, "Look! My hand swells up in the water. See how much bigger than normal it is?" Although the student's hand does appear to be larger than normal when in the water, the student's reasoning is not an accurate explanation of this phenomenon.

**If you were working with a class in which you suspected many students shared the belief stated by the student above and if there were no time constraints on what you might do in responding to this, what approach or sequence of approaches do you believe would best help students learn?**

*Place a '1' in the box next to the approach you believe to be the best. If you believe other approaches would also be acceptable, place a number in the box next to each one indicating the order in which you would consider using it. You need not choose more than one approach. Write a zero in the box for any approach you do not consider acceptable.*

a)  I would explain to the students how water affects the angles of reflection making an object appear larger than it really is. ................................. ☐

b)  I would ask the class questions about how the different objects in the aquarium appear in and out of the water to lead them to understand that the above explanation is inaccurate. ............................................. ☐

c)  I would give the students an experiment to do measuring the size of different objects both outside and in several different places inside the aquarium to generate data contrary to the above statement ...................... ☐

d)  I would ask the students to design and conduct an experiment on the size of objects outside and inside an aquarium that would help them decide whether the explanation above is correct. ............................. ☐

e)  I would have the students read relevant information from their textbooks. ................................................................................ ☐

f)  I would demonstrate an experiment or show a filmstrip on how water affects the appearance of objects which would provide a basis for arriving at a more accurate explanation. ....................................... ☐

g)  I would have the students compare their ideas about why objects would appear to be different sizes inside and outside of the aquarium in a discussion. ............................................................................. ☐

**h)  Which of the approaches listed above do you believe to be the least acceptable approach?**
*Place the letter (a - g) of that approach in the box.* ........................... ☐

*Source:* IEA Third International Mathematics and Science Study, Teacher Questionnaire (Science).

Doc.Ref.:ICC881/NRC418

3. A boy in class says, "I already have two brothers, so my mother's next baby probably will be a girl." This idea is quite different from how human inheritance works.

**If you were working with a class in which you suspected many students shared the belief stated by the student above and if there were no time constraints on what you might do in responding to this, what approach or sequence of approaches do you believe would best help students learn?**

*Place a '1' in the box next to the approach you believe to be the best. If you believe other approaches would also be acceptable, place a number in the box next to each one indicating the order in which you would consider using it. You need not choose more than one approach. Write a zero in the box for any approach you do not consider acceptable.*

a) I would give the students a more accurate explanation of how human inheritance works. .........................................................................

b) I would ask the class questions that lead students to understand that the above idea is inaccurate. ...........................................................

c) I would have students collect data about inheritance from their class-mates .................................................................................................

d) I would ask the students to design and conduct an investigation on human inheritance that would help them decide whether the idea above is correct. ......................................................................................

e) I would have the students read relevant information from their text-books. .................................................................................................

f) I would use some data to demonstrate how inheritance works which would provide a basis for arriving at a more accurate explanation. .........

g) I would have the students compare their ideas about how human inherit-ance works by discussing this topic. ..........................................................

**h) Which of the approaches listed above do you believe to be the least acceptable approach?**
*Place the letter (a - g) of that approach in the box. ...........................*

**THANK YOU for the thought, time and effort you have put into completing this questionnaire.**

*Source:* IEA Third International Mathematics and Science Study, Teacher Questionnaire (Science).

**1998** *Investigations* **Survey**                                     **Page 1**

Name _____

Grade _____  School _____

1.    Please indicate below the *Investigations* units you have used or plan to use this
       school year, your years of teaching experience with each unit, including this
       school year, and your overall evaluation of the effectiveness of each unit.

| Name of Unit | Years of Experience | Evaluation of Effectiveness |
|---|---|---|
| | | Low                                    High |
| _____ | _____ | 1  2  3  4  5 |
| _____ | _____ | 1  2  3  4  5 |
| _____ | _____ | 1  2  3  4  5 |
| _____ | _____ | 1  2  3  4  5 |
| _____ | _____ | 1  2  3  4  5 |
| _____ | _____ | 1  2  3  4  5 |
| _____ | _____ | 1  2  3  4  5 |
| _____ | _____ | 1  2  3  4  5 |

2.    What percent of your math instruction relies on *Investigations*, from 0 to 100%?

1998 Investigations Survey

Name _____

4.  What has been most helpful to you in implementing Investigations?

5.  What additional professional development or support would be of assistance to you as you move toward full implementation of Investigations?

6.  How has the program made a difference in your own understanding of mathematics?

7.  In what ways has your teaching of mathematics changed as a result of the program?

8.  Has your comfort with or confidence in the program evolved since your initial engagement? What accounts for either your increased self-confidence or continued discomfort?

9.  What are the challenges that the program poses from the points of view of pedagogy, management, or understanding?

10. How have your students' understanding of mathematics concepts and their ability to articulate their ideas changed as a result of Investigations?

11. What impact, if any, has the program had on children who we might perceive as either gifted or challenged in mathematics?

12. What feedback have you received from parents regarding Investigations?

# CLASSROOM OBERVATION PROTOCOL

Following is a set of practices we would expect to see in a classroom where Framework-Aligned mathematics is being taught. Note that not all practices are appropriate in every lesson. Rate each of these practices on a scale from 1 to 5 and indicate the rating in the space to the left of each practice.

School: _____

Teacher: _____

Class/Grade: _____

| 1 | 2 | 3 | 4 | 5 | NA |
|---|---|---|---|---|---|
| not observed | | some | | observed a great deal | |

_____Curricular materials are selected that are challenging as well as accessible to all students.

_____There is a balance of higher order thinking and mathematical reasoning, development of conceptual understanding, and skill building in small group discussion and work.

_____There is a balance of higher order thinking and mathematical reasoning, development of conceptual understanding, and skill building in whole class discussion and work.

_____Students are expected to explain their thinking and share their ideas.

_____Students work in small, heterogeneous groups to maximize opportunities for meaningful learning.

Reprinted by permission of Judy Mumme, CAMS, from *CAMS Evaluation MR Classroom Observation Protocol* by Steven Cohen.

_____Teachers give instruction in and reinforce cooperative learning strategies.

_____Groups are diverse in terms of gender, language, ethnicity, and 'ability'.

_____*Groups give presentations to the class on their findings during group investigations, often using posters or models.

_____Calculators, manipulatives, and other materials are available at all times.

_____*Students are asked to communicate their understandings both orally and in writing.

_____There are concluding discussions in which students take the lead or play a highly significant role.

_____*Individually, students are given opportunities to demonstrate mathematical growth by doing quality large-scale work that is complete in that it demonstrates mathematical power through: higher-order mathematical thinking, clear communication using multiple ways of representing ideas, mathematics content, and appropriate mathematical tools and techniques.

_____*Assessment is used to evaluate student work, and not students.

_____*There is a tradition of draft, feedback, and revision for submitted written work.

_____*Portfolios of student work are periodically reviewed and refined.

_____Students develop their own algorithms.

*These items may be difficult to assess during a single observation. If possible, double check these items with teacher and student responses during interviews.

## 2000–2001 Local Systemic Change
## Pre-Classroom Observation Interview

After you have expressed appreciation to the teacher for allowing you to observe the class, and answered any questions s/he might have about confidentiality, the incentive system, etc.; ask the following questions:

1.   What has this class been doing in mathematics/science recently?

     PROBES:    What unit are you working on?
                 What instructional materials are you using[*]?

2.   What do you anticipate doing in your mathematics/science class on the day I will be observing?

     PROBE:     What do you hope students will learn as a result of the work you have planned?

3.   What is the next step for this class?

4.   Is there anything in particular that I should know about the group of students that I will be observing?

---

[*] Note that the evaluator will need to be thoroughly conversant with the instructional materials designated for use by the LSC in order to complete the observation ratings.

> **NOTE:** This form is included for information purposes only. Evaluators will need to complete the form on the Web.

## 2000–2001 Local Systemic Change Classroom Observation Protocol[1]

### BACKGROUND INFORMATION

Project _____     Date of Observation _____

LSC ID[2] _____     Time of Observation:

Start _____     End _____

Subject Observed[3] _____     Observer _____

Grade Level _____     Observer's Role in Project:

___ Lead Evaluator

___ Other Certified Observer

### SECTION ONE: CONTEXTUAL BACKGROUND AND ACTIVITIES

In this section, please fill in the circles that best describe the class. *For each item, be sure to fill in all responses that apply.*

#### I. Classroom Demographics and Context

**A. What is the total number of students in the class at the time of the observation?**
- ○ 15 or fewer
- ○ 16–20
- ○ 21–25
- ○ 26–30
- ○ 31 or more

**B. What is the approximate percentage of white (not Hispanic origin) students in this class?**
- ○ 0–10 percent
- ○ 11–25 percent
- ○ 26–50 percent
- ○ 51–75 percent
- ○ 76–100 percent

**C. Indicate the *teacher's*:**
1. Gender
   - ○ Male     ○ Female
2. Race/Ethnicity
   - ○ African-American (not Hispanic origin)
   - ○ American Indian or Alaskan Native
   - ○ Asian or Pacific Islander
   - ○ Hispanic
   - ○ White (not Hispanic origin)
   - ○ Other

**D. If applicable, indicate the *teacher aide's*:**
1. Gender
   - ○ Male     ○ Female
2. Race/Ethnicity
   - ○ African-American (not Hispanic origin)
   - ○ American Indian or Alaskan Native
   - ○ Asian or Pacific Islander
   - ○ Hispanic
   - ○ White (not Hispanic origin)
   - ○ Other

---

[1] Be sure you have read the "2000–2001 Local Systemic Change Classroom Observations: Guidelines for Evaluators" and have completed the "Pre-Classroom Observation Interview" before observing the class.

[2] Use the LSC ID number as indicated in the Classroom Observation Sample provided by HRI.

[3] In mathematics/science projects observe the subject for which the teacher was sampled.

**E.   Rate the adequacy of the physical environment.**

1.   Classroom resources:

| ○ | ○ | ○ | ○ | ○ |
|---|---|---|---|---|
| 1 | 2 | 3 | 4 | 5 |

Sparsely equipped                                    Rich in resources

2.   Classroom Space:

| ○ | ○ | ○ | ○ | ○ |
|---|---|---|---|---|
| 1 | 2 | 3 | 4 | 5 |

Crowded                                              Adequate space

3.   Room arrangement:

| ○ | ○ | ○ | ○ | ○ |
|---|---|---|---|---|
| 1 | 2 | 3 | 4 | 5 |

Inhibited interactions                               Facilitated interactions
among students                                       among students

## II.   Lesson Description

**In a paragraph or two, describe the lesson you observed.**  Include where this lesson fits in the overall unit of study.  Be sure to include enough detail to provide a context for your ratings of this lesson and also to allow you to recall the details of this lesson when needed in future years for longitudinal analysis.

## III.   Purposes of Lesson

**A.   Indicate the *major[4] content area(s)* of this lesson or activity.**

○   1.   Numeration and number theory
○   2.   Computation
○   3.   Estimation
○   4.   Measurement
○   5.   Patterns and relationships
○   6.   Pre-algebra
○   7.   Algebra
○   8.   Geometry and spatial sense
○   9.   Functions (including trigonometric functions) and pre-calculus concept
○   10.   Data collection and analysis
○   11.   Probability
○   12.   Statistics (e.g., hypothesis tests, curve-fitting, and regression)
○   13.   Topics from discrete mathematics (e.g., combinatorics, graph theory, recursion)
○   14.   Mathematical structures (e.g., vector spaces, groups, rings, fields)

○   16.   Life Science
          (please specify: _____)
○   17.   Physical science
          (please specify: _____)
○   18.   Earth/space sciences
          ○   a.   Astronomy
          ○   b.   Oceanography
          ○   c.   Geology
          ○   d.   Meteorology
          ○   e.   Environmental sciences
○   19.   Engineering and design principles
○   20.   History of mathematics/science

○   21.   None of the above (please explain)

---

[4]   "Major" means was used or addressed for a substantial portion of the lesson; if you were describing the lesson to someone, this feature would help characterize it.

**B.** Indicate the *primary intended purpose(s)* of this lesson or activity based on the pre- and/or post-observation interviews with the teacher.

- ○ 1. Identifying prior student knowledge
- ○ 2. Introducing new concepts
- ○ 3. Developing conceptual understanding
- ○ 4. Reviewing mathematics/science concepts
- ○ 5. Developing problem-solving skills
- ○ 6. Learning mathematics/science processes, algorithms, or procedures
- ○ 7. Learning vocabulary/specific facts
- ○ 8. Practicing computation for mastery
- ○ 9. Developing appreciation for core ideas in mathematics/science
- ○ 10. Developing students' awareness of contributions of scientists/mathematicians of diverse backgrounds
- ○ 11. Assessing student understanding

## IV. Instructional Materials

**A. Is this lesson based on instructional materials designated for use by this LSC?**

○ Yes    ○ No, SKIP to Part V below

**B. Indicate the *single* set of LSC-designated instructional materials intended to form the basis of this lesson (e.g., FOSS; Insights; STC; Investigations in Number, Data, and Space; Connected Math; IMP; SEPUP), based on the information provided in the pre-observation interview.**

Please specify.
_____

**C. How closely did the lesson adhere to the instructions provided in the teacher's manual?**

○ Exactly, SKIP to Part V below
○ Almost totally    ○ Mostly    ○ Somewhat    ○ A little    ○ Hardly at all

**D. How did the modifications affect the quality of the lesson design?**

○ Helped a lot    ○ Helped a little    ○ Neutral    ○ Hurt a little    ○ Hurt a lot

## V. Classroom Instruction

**A. Indicate the *major[5] way(s)* in which student activities were structured.**

○ As a whole group    ○                    As small groups    ○ As pairs    ○ As individuals

**B. Indicate the *major[5] way(s)* in which students engaged in class activities.**

○ Entire class was engaged in the same activities at the same time.
○ Groups of students were engaged in different activities at the same time (e.g., centers).

---

[5] "Major" means was used or addressed for a substantial portion of the lesson; if you were describing the lesson to someone, this feature would help characterize it.

**C. Indicate the *major*[6] *activities* of students in this lesson.** When choosing an "umbrella" category, be sure to indicate subcategories that apply as well. (For example, if you mark "listened to a presentation," indicate by whom.)

- O 1. Listened to a presentation:
  - O a. By teacher (would include: demonstrations, lectures, media presentations, extensive procedural instructions)
  - O b. By student (would include informal, as well as formal, presentations of their work)
  - O c. By guest speaker/"expert" serving as a resource

- O 2. Engaged in discussion/seminar:
  - O a. Whole group
  - O b. Small groups/pairs

- O 3. Engaged in problem solving/investigation:
  - O a. Worked with manipulatives
  - O b. Played a game to build or review knowledge/skills
  - O c. Followed specific instructions in an investigation
  - O d. Had some latitude in designing an investigation

  - O e. Recorded, represented and/or analyzed data
  - O f. Recognized patterns, cycles or trends
  - O g. Evaluated the validity of arguments or claims
  - O h. Provided an informal justification or formal proof

- O 4. Engaged in reading/reflection/written communication about mathematics or science:
  - O a. Read about mathematics/science
  - O b. Answered textbook/worksheet questions
  - O c. Reflected on readings, activities, or problems individually or in groups
  - O d. Prepared a written report
  - O e. Wrote a description of a plan, procedure, or problem-solving process
  - O f. Wrote reflections in a notebook or journal

- O 5. Used technology/audio-visual resource:
  - O a. To develop conceptual understanding
  - O b. To learn or practice a skill
  - O c. To collect data (e.g., probeware)
  - O d. As an analytic tool (e.g., spreadsheets or data analysis)
  - O e. As a presentation tool
  - O f. For word processing or as a communications tool (e.g., e-mail, Internet, Web)

- O 6. Other activities
  - O a. Arts and crafts activity
  - O b. Listened to a story
  - O c. Wrote a poem or story
  - O d. Other (Please specify.) _____

---

[6] "Major" means was used or addressed for a substantial portion of the lesson; if you were describing the lesson to someone, this feature would help characterize it.

**D. Comments**

Please provide any additional information you consider necessary to capture the activities or context of this lesson. Include comments on any feature of the class that is so salient that you need to get it "on the table" right away to help explain your ratings; for example, the class was interrupted by a fire drill, the kids were excited about an upcoming school event, or the teacher's tone was so warm (or so hostile) that it was an overwhelmingly important feature of the lesson.

## SECTION TWO: RATINGS

In Section One of this form, you documented what occurred in the lesson. In this section, you are asked to rate each of a number of key indicators in four different categories, from 1 (not at all) to 5 (to a great extent). You may list any additional indicators you consider important in capturing the essence of this lesson and rate these as well. Use your "Ratings of Key Indicators" (Part A) to inform your "Synthesis Ratings" (Part B). It is important to indicate in "Supporting Evidence for Synthesis Ratings" (Part C) what factors were most influential in determining your synthesis ratings and to give specific examples or quotes to illustrate those factors.

Note that any one lesson is not likely to provide evidence for every single indicator; use 6, "Don't know" when there is not enough evidence for you to make a judgment. Use 7, "N/A" (Not Applicable) when you consider the indicator inappropriate given the purpose and context of the lesson. Section Two concludes with ratings of the likely impact of instruction, and a capsule description of the lesson.

## I. Design

|  | Not at all | | | | To a great extent | Don't know | N/A |
|---|---|---|---|---|---|---|---|

### A. Ratings of Key Indicators

1. The design of the lesson incorporated tasks, roles, and interactions consistent with investigative mathematics/science.  1 2 3 4 5 | 6 | 7

2. The design of the lesson reflected careful planning and organization.  1 2 3 4 5 | 6 | 7

3. The instructional strategies and activities used in this lesson reflected attention to students' experience, preparedness, and/or learning styles.  1 2 3 4 5 | 6 | 7

4. The resources available in this lesson contributed to accomplishing the purposes of the instruction.  1 2 3 4 5 | 6 | 7

5. The instructional strategies and activities reflected attention to issues of access, equity, and diversity for students (e.g., cooperative learning, language-appropriate strategies/materials).  1 2 3 4 5 | 6 | 7

6. The design of the lesson encouraged a collaborative approach to learning.  1 2 3 4 5 | 6 | 7

7. Adequate time and structure were provided for "sense-making."  1 2 3 4 5 | 6 | 7

8. Adequate time and structure were provided for wrap-up.  1 2 3 4 5 | 6 | 7

9. Formal assessments of students were consistent with investigative mathematics/science.  1 2 3 4 5 | 6 | 7

10. Design for future instruction takes into account what transpired in the lesson.  1 2 3 4 5 | 6 | 7

11. _____  1 2 3 4 5

### B. Synthesis Rating

| 1 | 2 | 3 | 4 | 5 |
|---|---|---|---|---|
| Design of the lesson not at all reflective of best practice in mathematics/science education | | | | Design of the lesson extremely reflective of best practice in mathematics/science education |

### C. Supporting Evidence for Synthesis Rating

## II. Implementation

| | | Not at all | | | | To a great extent | Don't know | N/A |
|---|---|---|---|---|---|---|---|---|

### A. Ratings of Key Indicators

1. The instruction was consistent with the underlying approach of the instructional materials designated for use by the LSC.

    1  2  3  4  5    6    7

2. The instructional strategies were consistent with investigative mathematics/science.

    1  2  3  4  5    6    7

3. The teacher appeared confident in his/her ability to teach mathematics/science.

    1  2  3  4  5    6    7

4. The teacher's classroom management style/strategies enhanced the quality of the lesson.

    1  2  3  4  5    6    7

5. The pace of the lesson was appropriate for the developmental levels/needs of the students and the purposes of the lesson.

    1  2  3  4  5    6    7

6. The teacher took into account prior knowledge of students.

    1  2  3  4  5    6    7

7. The teacher's questioning strategies were likely to enhance the development of student conceptual understanding/problem solving (e.g., emphasized higher order questions, appropriately used "wait time," identified prior conceptions and misconceptions).

    1  2  3  4  5    6    7

8. The lesson was modified as needed based on teacher questioning or other student assessments.

    1  2  3  4  5    6    7

9. _____

    1  2  3  4  5

### B. Synthesis Rating

| 1 | 2 | 3 | 4 | 5 |
|---|---|---|---|---|
| Implementation of the lesson not at all reflective of best practice in mathematics/science education | | | | Implementation of the lesson extremely reflective of best practice in mathematics/science education |

### C. Supporting Evidence for Synthesis Rating

## III. Mathematics/Science Content

### A. Ratings of Key Indicators

| | | Not at all | | | | To a great extent | Don't know | N/A |
|---|---|---|---|---|---|---|---|---|
| 1. | The mathematics/science content was significant and worthwhile. | 1 | 2 | 3 | 4 | 5 | 6 | 7 |
| 2. | The mathematics/science content was appropriate for the developmental levels of the students in this class. | 1 | 2 | 3 | 4 | 5 | 6 | 7 |
| 3. | Students were intellectually engaged with important ideas relevant to the focus of the lesson. | 1 | 2 | 3 | 4 | 5 | 6 | 7 |
| 4. | Teacher-provided content information was accurate. | 1 | 2 | 3 | 4 | 5 | 6 | 7 |
| 5. | The teacher displayed an understanding of mathematics/science concepts (e.g., in his/her dialogue with students). | 1 | 2 | 3 | 4 | 5 | 6 | 7 |
| 6. | Mathematics/science was portrayed as a dynamic body of knowledge continually enriched by conjecture, investigation analysis, and/or proof/justification. | 1 | 2 | 3 | 4 | 5 | 6 | 7 |
| 7. | Elements of mathematical/science abstraction (e.g., symbolic representations, theory building) were included when it was important to do so. | 1 | 2 | 3 | 4 | 5 | 6 | 7 |
| 8. | Appropriate connections were made to other areas of mathematics/science, to other disciplines, and/or to real-world contexts. | 1 | 2 | 3 | 4 | 5 | 6 | 7 |
| 9. | The degree of "sense-making" of mathematics/science content within this lesson was appropriate for the developmental levels/needs of the students and the purposes of the lesson. | 1 | 2 | 3 | 4 | 5 | 6 | 7 |
| 10. | _____ | 1 | 2 | 3 | 4 | 5 | | |

### B. Synthesis Rating

| 1 | 2 | 3 | 4 | 5 |
|---|---|---|---|---|
| Mathematics/science content of lesson not at all reflective of current standards for mathematics/science education | | | | Mathematics/science content of lesson extremely reflective of current standards for mathematics/science education |

### C. Supporting Evidence for Synthesis Rating

481

## IV. Classroom Culture

### A1. Ratings of Key Indicators

| | Not at all | | | | To a great extent | Don't know | N/A |
|---|---|---|---|---|---|---|---|
| 1. Active participation of all was encouraged and valued. | 1 | 2 | 3 | 4 | 5 | 6 | 7 |
| 2. There was a climate of respect for students' ideas, questions, and contributions. | 1 | 2 | 3 | 4 | 5 | 6 | 7 |
| 3. Interactions reflected collegial working relationships among students (e.g., students worked together, talked with each other about the lesson). | 1 | 2 | 3 | 4 | 5 | 6 | 7 |
| 4. Interactions reflected collaborative working relationships between teacher and students. | 1 | 2 | 3 | 4 | 5 | 6 | 7 |
| 5. The climate of the lesson encouraged students to generate ideas, questions, conjectures, and/or propositions. | 1 | 2 | 3 | 4 | 5 | 6 | 7 |
| 6. Intellectual rigor, constructive criticism, and the challenging of ideas were evident. | 1 | 2 | 3 | 4 | 5 | 6 | 7 |
| 7. _____ | 1 | 2 | 3 | 4 | 5 | | |

### A2. Respect for Diversity

Based on the culture of a classroom, observers are generally able to make inferences about the extent to which there is an appreciation of diversity among students (e.g., their gender, race/ethnicity, and/or cultural background). While direct evidence that reflects particular sensitivity or insensitivity toward diversity is not often observed, we would like you to document any examples you do see. If any examples were observed, please check here ☐ and describe below:

### B. Synthesis Rating

| 1 | 2 | 3 | 4 | 5 |
|---|---|---|---|---|
| Classroom culture interfered with student learning | | | | Classroom culture facilitated the learning of all students |

### C. Supporting Evidence for Synthesis Rating

## V. Overall Ratings of the Lesson

### A. Likely Impact of Instruction on Students' Understanding of Mathematics/Science

While the impact of a single lesson may well be limited in scope, it is important to judge whether the lesson is likely to help move students in the desired direction. For this series of ratings, consider all available information (i.e., your previous ratings of design, implementation, content, and classroom culture, and the pre- and post-observation interviews with the teacher) as you assess the likely impact of this lesson. Feel free to elaborate on ratings with comments in the space provided.

Select the response that best describes your overall assessment of the *likely effect* of this lesson in each of the following areas.

| | Negative effect | | Mixed or neutral effect | | Positive effect | Don't know | N/A |
|---|---|---|---|---|---|---|---|
| 1. Students' understanding of mathematics/science as a dynamic body of knowledge generated and enriched by investigation. | O | O | O | O | O | O | O |
| 2. Students' understanding of important mathematics/science concepts. | O | O | O | O | O | O | O |
| 3. Students' capacity to carry out their own inquiries. | O | O | O | O | O | O | O |
| 4. Students' ability to apply or generalize skills and concepts to other areas of mathematics/science, other disciplines, and/or real-life situations. | O | O | O | O | O | O | O |
| 5. Students' self-confidence in doing mathematics/science. | O | O | O | O | O | O | O |
| 6. Students' interest in and/or appreciation for the discipline. | O | O | O | O | O | O | O |

**Comments (optional):**

## B. Capsule Description of the Quality of the Lesson

In this final rating of the lesson, consider all available information about the lesson, its context and purpose, and your own judgment of the relative importance of the ratings you have made. Select the capsule description that best characterizes the lesson you observed. Keep in mind that this rating is *not* intended to be an average of all the previous ratings, but should encapsulate your overall assessment of the quality and likely impact of the lesson. Please provide a brief rationale for your final capsule description of the lesson in the space provided.

○ **Level 1: Ineffective Instruction**

There is little or no evidence of student thinking or engagement with important ideas of mathematics/science. Instruction is *highly unlikely* to enhance students' understanding of the discipline or to develop their capacity to successfully "do" mathematics/science. Lesson was characterized by either (select one below):

○ **Passive "Learning"**

Instruction is pedantic and uninspiring. Students are passive recipients of information from the teacher or textbook; material is presented in a way that is inaccessible to many of the students.

○ **Activity for Activity's Sake**

Students are involved in hands-on activities or other individual or group work, but it appears to be activity for activity's sake. Lesson lacks a clear sense of purpose and/or a clear link to conceptual development.

○ **Level 2: Elements of Effective Instruction**

Instruction contains some elements of effective practice, but there are *serious problems* in the design, implementation, content, and/or appropriateness for many students in the class. For example, the content may lack importance and/or appropriateness; instruction may not successfully address the difficulties that many students are experiencing, etc. Overall, the lesson is *very limited* in its likelihood to enhance students' understanding of the discipline or to develop their capacity to successfully "do" mathematics/science.

○ **Level 3: Beginning Stages of Effective Instruction** (Select one below.)
○ Low 3      ○ Solid 3      ○ High 3

Instruction is purposeful and characterized by quite a few elements of effective practice. Students are, at times, engaged in meaningful work, but there are *weaknesses*, ranging from substantial to fairly minor, in the design, implementation, or content of instruction. For example, the teacher may short-circuit a planned exploration by telling students what they "should have found"; instruction may not adequately address the needs of a number of students; or the classroom culture may limit the accessibility or effectiveness of the lesson. Overall, the lesson is *somewhat limited* in its likelihood to enhance students' understanding of the discipline or to develop their capacity to successfully "do" mathematics/science.

○ **Level 4: Accomplished, Effective Instruction**

Instruction is purposeful and engaging for most students. Students actively participate in meaningful work (e.g., investigations, teacher presentations, discussions with each other or the teacher, reading). The lesson is well-designed and the teacher implements it well, but adaptation of content or pedagogy in response to student needs and interests is limited. Instruction is *quite likely* to enhance most students' understanding of the discipline and to develop their capacity to successfully "do" mathematics/science.

○ **Level 5: Exemplary Instruction**

Instruction is purposeful and all students are highly engaged most or all of the time in meaningful work (e.g., investigation, teacher presentations, discussions with each other or the teacher, reading). The lesson is well-designed and artfully implemented, with flexibility and responsiveness to students' needs and interests. Instruction is *highly likely* to enhance most students' understanding of the discipline and to develop their capacity to successfully "do" mathematics/science.

**Please provide your rationale for the capsule rating:**

## 2000–2001 Local Systemic Change
## Post-Classroom Observation Interview

After you have expressed appreciation to the teacher for allowing you to observe the class, ask the following questions:

1.  Were there any ways in which the lesson was different from what you had planned?

2.  What did this lesson tell you about what your students are learning and still need to learn in mathematics/science?

    PROBE:      How do you plan to further assess the students' learning?

3.  What challenges have you faced in encouraging your students to be actively engaged in this mathematics/science class?

    PROBE:      How have you approached these challenges?

4.  What is the next step for this class?

Taking Charge of Change

## Concerns Questionnaire

Name _____

In order to identify these data, please give us the last four digits of your Social Security number:

_____

The purpose of this questionnaire is to determine what people who are using or thinking about using various programs are concerned about at various times during the innovation adoption process. The items were developed from typical responses of school and college teachers who ranged from no knowledge at all about various programs to many years experience in using them. Therefore, *a good part of the items on this questionnaire may appear to be of little relevance or irrelevant to you at this time*. For the completely irrelevant items, please circle "0" on the scale. Other items will represent those concerns you do have, in varying degrees of intensity, and should be marked higher on the scale. For example:

| | 0 | 1 | 2 | 3 | 4 | 5 | 6 | 7 |
|---|---|---|---|---|---|---|---|---|
| This statement is very true of me at this time. | 0 | 1 | 2 | 3 | 4 | 5 | 6 | 7 |
| This statement is somewhat true of me now. | 0 | 1 | 2 | 3 | 4 | 5 | 6 | 7 |
| This statement is not at all true of of me at this time. | 0 | 1 | 2 | 3 | 4 | 5 | 6 | 7 |
| This statement seems irrelevant to me. | 0 | 1 | 2 | 3 | 4 | 5 | 6 | 7 |

Please respond to the items in terms of *your present concerns*, or how you feel about your involvement or potential involvement with _____ (please specify the innovation. We do not hold to any one definition of this program, so please think of it in terms of *your own perceptions* of what it involves. Remember to respond to each item in terms of *your present concerns* about your involvement or potential involvement with the above named innovation.

Thank you for taking time to complete this task.

\* \* \*

| 0 | | 1 | 2 | 3 | 4 | | 5 | | 6 | | 7 |
|---|---|---|---|---|---|---|---|---|---|---|---|
| irrelevant | | Not true of me now | | | Somewhat true of me now | | | | | | Very true |

| | 0 | 1 | 2 | 3 | 4 | 5 | 6 | 7 |
|---|---|---|---|---|---|---|---|---|
| 1. I am concerned about students/attitudes toward this innovation. | 0 | 1 | 2 | 3 | 4 | 5 | 6 | 7 |
| 2. I now know of some other approaches that might work better. | 0 | 1 | 2 | 3 | 4 | 5 | 6 | 7 |
| 3. I don't even know what the innovation is. | 0 | 1 | 2 | 3 | 4 | 5 | 6 | 7 |
| 4. I am concerned about not having enough time to organize myself each day. | 0 | 1 | 2 | 3 | 4 | 5 | 6 | 7 |
| 5. I would like to help other faculty in their use of the innovation. | 0 | 1 | 2 | 3 | 4 | 5 | 6 | 7 |
| 6. I have a very limited knowledge about the innovation. | 0 | 1 | 2 | 3 | 4 | 5 | 6 | 7 |
| 7. I would like to know the effect of reorganization on my professional status. | 0 | 1 | 2 | 3 | 4 | 5 | 6 | 7 |
| 8. I am concerned about conflict between my interests and my responsibilities. | 0 | 1 | 2 | 3 | 4 | 5 | 6 | 7 |
| 9. I am concerned about revising my use of the innovation. | 0 | 1 | 2 | 3 | 4 | 5 | 6 | 7 |
| 10. I would like to develop working relationships with both our faculty and outside faculty using this innovation. | 0 | 1 | 2 | 3 | 4 | 5 | 6 | 7 |
| 11. I am concerned about how the innovation affects students. | 0 | 1 | 2 | 3 | 4 | 5 | 6 | 7 |
| 12. I am not concerned about this innovation. | 0 | 1 | 2 | 3 | 4 | 5 | 6 | 7 |

| | 0 | 1 | 2 | 3 | 4 | 5 | 6 | 7 |
|---|---|---|---|---|---|---|---|---|
| 13. I would like to know who will make the decisions in the new system. | 0 | 1 | 2 | 3 | 4 | 5 | 6 | 7 |
| 14. I would like to discuss the possibility of using the innovation. | 0 | 1 | 2 | 3 | 4 | 5 | 6 | 7 |
| 15. I would like to know what resources are available if we decide to adopt this innovation. | 0 | 1 | 2 | 3 | 4 | 5 | 6 | 7 |
| 16. I am concerned about my inability to manage all the innovation requires. | 0 | 1 | 2 | 3 | 4 | 5 | 6 | 7 |
| 17. I would like to know how my teaching or administration is supposed to change. | 0 | 1 | 2 | 3 | 4 | 5 | 6 | 7 |
| 18. I would like to familiarize other departments or persons with the progress of this new approach. | 0 | 1 | 2 | 3 | 4 | 5 | 6 | 7 |
| 19. I am concerned about evaluating my impact on students. | 0 | 1 | 2 | 3 | 4 | 5 | 6 | 7 |
| 20. I would like to revise the innovation's instructional approach. | 0 | 1 | 2 | 3 | 4 | 5 | 6 | 7 |
| 21. I am completely occupied with other things. | 0 | 1 | 2 | 3 | 4 | 5 | 6 | 7 |
| 22. I would like to modify our use of the innovation based on the experiences of our students. | 0 | 1 | 2 | 3 | 4 | 5 | 6 | 7 |
| 23. Although I don't know about this innovation, I am concerned about things in the area. | 0 | 1 | 2 | 3 | 4 | 5 | 6 | 7 |
| 24. I would like to excite my students about their part in this approach. | 0 | 1 | 2 | 3 | 4 | 5 | 6 | 7 |
| 25. I am concerned about time spent working with nonacademic problems related to this innovation. | 0 | 1 | 2 | 3 | 4 | 5 | 6 | 7 |
| 26. I would like to know what the use of the innovation will require in the immediate future. | 0 | 1 | 2 | 3 | 4 | 5 | 6 | 7 |
| 27. I would like to coordinate my effort with others to maximize the innovation's effects. | 0 | 1 | 2 | 3 | 4 | 5 | 6 | 7 |
| 28. I would like to have more information on time and energy commitments required by this innovation. | 0 | 1 | 2 | 3 | 4 | 5 | 6 | 7 |
| 29. I would like to know what other faculty are doing in this area. | 0 | 1 | 2 | 3 | 4 | 5 | 6 | 7 |
| 30. At this time, I am not interested in learning about this innovation. | 0 | 1 | 2 | 3 | 4 | 5 | 6 | 7 |
| 31. I would like to determine how to supplement, enhance, or replace the innovation. | 0 | 1 | 2 | 3 | 4 | 5 | 6 | 7 |
| 32. I would like to use feedback from students to change the program. | 0 | 1 | 2 | 3 | 4 | 5 | 6 | 7 |
| 33. I would like to know how my role will change when I am using the innovation. | 0 | 1 | 2 | 3 | 4 | 5 | 6 | 7 |
| 34. Coordination of tasks and people is taking too much of my time. | 0 | 1 | 2 | 3 | 4 | 5 | 6 | 7 |
| 35. I would like to know how this innovation is better than what we have now. | 0 | 1 | 2 | 3 | 4 | 5 | 6 | 7 |

## 2000–2001 Local Systemic Change
## Teacher Interview[1]

1. What grade(s) do you teach?

2. This district is involved in an NSE supported local systemic change initiative.[2]

   To what extent have you participated in those activities (i.e., number of hours/days since becoming involved in the project)?[3]

   PROBE for both summer and academic year activities.

3. How do you feel about the professional development provided by the LSC?

4. How has the LSC affected you and your teaching?

   Probe for examples of changes.

5. What specific characteristics of the LSC have been most helpful to you?

6. What aspects have been least helpful? Why?

7. What else do you need in order to continue improving your mathematics (science) instruction?

8. Sometimes school and district policies and practices facilitate reform. At other times they get in the way. Are there any policies or practices in your school or district that you believe will help you in making the changes suggested by the LSC?

9. Are there any policies or practices that you believe will limit your ability to make the changes suggested by the LSC?

---

[1] This protocol should be used for teacher interviews in all projects, except those in the Final Year. Baseline Year projects *do not* conduct teacher interviews as part of the core evaluation.

[2] You may want to use the local name for the LSC instead of, or in addition to, mentioning NSF, perhaps even giving examples of specific activities.

[3] Only treated teachers who have participated in 20 or more hours of professional development have been included in the random sample for teacher interviews.

For teachers who have been identified as teacher leaders for the LSC:
(If teacher is not a designated teacher leader, SKIP to Question 11.)

10. How well prepared do you feel to carry out your role as a teacher leader in the LSC?

    PROBE for specific examples of preparedness and how that came to be.

11. Do you have any other comments you would like to share?

# Data Tool #DT 4-19

## Student Interview Protocol

This interview may be used with individuals or groups of students. Please note any other demographic information about the student(s) that you feel is relevant {e.g., gender, ethnicity, socio-economic status, home language(s), etc.}.

Discuss confidentiality with the student(s). Let them know that nothing they say will be repeated in a way that is attributable to them, and if this is a group interview, that they should not repeat anything said by other students during the interview.

1. What is the grade level and math class of the student(s)?
2. Give an example of an instance where you felt you were really challenged, and learned from that experience.
   - What would make math/science more challenging for you?
   - How often do you feel that you are unable to do the mathematics because it is too hard or confusing? Give any examples.
3. Give an example of where in real life you will use the math you are learning in class. Do you think your math work has anything to do with "real life"?
   - Do you use math outside the classroom? Can you give examples?
4. Do you work with other students in groups? What kind of groups (e.g., small group, large group, pairs, etc.)?
   - Do you feel that group work helps you learn better or not? Give examples.
5. Has your teacher taught you about how to work cooperatively in groups?
   - What has s/he said to you about how to work in groups?
6. How much does your teacher usually lead the class?

Reprinted by permission of Judy Mumme, CAMS, from *CAMS Evaluation Interview Protocol* by Steven Cohen.

Sample Student Interview Questions

What projects have you done?

How often do you work on a project alone? in a group?

What kinds of problems have you solved?

How often do you solve difficult but interesting problems for which there are often many possible answers?

How often do you do research outside the classroom with fellow students?

Are there resources, such as books, computers and other materials at your school to help you with your projects?

How often do you talk about mathematics with a group of students in your class?

What oral reports or presentations have you given in your class? How often?

What kind of work do you put in your portfolio? Why?

What type of homework do you usually do?

Can you suggest ways to better show how and what you know?

Other comments or suggestions?

## 1996 Local Systemic Change
## Classroom Artifact Collection: Full Set
## Instructions for Teachers

## Overview

Your school district is involved in a science/mathematics professional development project funded through the National Science Foundation's Local Systemic Change through Teacher Enhancement (LSC) Program. The national evaluation of LSC projects includes a number of standardized data collection activities that will enable NSF to see the impact and progress of projects in districts across the country. Contributions from individual teachers are a valuable and essential part of this national evaluation.

We would like you to contribute to the LSC evaluation by providing a sample of "artifacts" from your classroom. Everything you submit will be kept confidential. These materials will not be used to evaluate you or your teaching. We hope that these items are readily accessible and will not take long for you to gather, organize, and briefly explain. We welcome any suggestions for simplifying or improving this process.

## Classroom Artifact Instructions

The first step is selecting an instructional unit that you have taught during the current academic year. (Your LSC project's evaluator will tell you whether a science or a mathematics unit should be used.) Select a unit that you feel exemplifies your most successful teaching and is indicative of the direction in which you are moving as a professional. From this unit, provide the items described below. Use the enclosed colored summary sheets as dividers to organize the items in your packet.

**I. Cover Sheet**

Complete the general information at the top of this sheet. The checklist at the bottom will help you organize your materials. Before submitting your packet to the project evaluator, please use the checklist to make certain all the requested materials are included.

**II. Contextual Information**

Briefly answer the six questions to provide the context of your selected unit. The questions will guide your description of your instructional goals and the student assessments you have used. If you prefer, you may word-process your answers and include them on a separate sheet. Your answers should be brief; if more contextual information is needed, the project evaluator will contact you.

**III. Sample Lesson**

From the selected unit, choose the lesson that best exemplifies the content and strategies used in the unit. The lesson may have been taught in a single class session or over the course of several class sessions. Submit the lesson in whatever form you choose, e.g., a written lesson plan, a detailed summary of the lesson, or a videotape of the class session(s). Include student worksheets or handouts, and if available, examples of student work, if these will help to clarify the lesson's focus or activities.

**IV. Sample Assessment**

Provide an example of an assessment "instrument," such as instructions for a student project/portfolio, a performance task, a test given during or at the end of the unit, or any other assessment tool you have used.

**V. Student Work Samples on Selected Assessment**

If at all possible, please include examples of several students' work on the assessment submitted for Item IV. Include any comments, ratings or grades that were assigned.

## Classroom Artifact Collection: Full Set
## I.  Cover Sheet

**Directions to Teachers:**
Please include this cover sheet with the classroom artifacts you provide for the LSC Project core evaluation.

State: _____     Teacher: _____

District: _____     Class/Grade Level: _____

School: _____     Date: _____

Instructional Unit     Class Time Spent On

Title: _____     Instructional Unit: _____

**Checklist:**

Please check off each item you have enclosed in this classroom artifact packet:

☐     I. This cover sheet

☐     II. Contextual information

☐     III. Sample lesson

☐     IV. Sample assessment

☐     V. Student work samples on selected assessment

## Classroom Artifact Collection: Full Set
## II.  Contextual Information

1.  Please give a brief description of this instructional unit.  What were your goals and expectations for students in this unit?

2.  Briefly describe what the students had experienced prior to the selected lesson and what the class did next.

3.  What are the qualities of the lesson you have provided that made it successful for you and your students?

4.  Where does the assessment you have provided fit in the sequence of unit activities?

5.  In what other ways have you assessed your students in this unit, either formally or informally?

6.  How are the lesson and assessment you have provided similar to other lessons and assessments you generally use with your students?  How are they different from others you use?

## Classroom Artifact Collection: Full Set
## III.  Sample Lesson

Teacher:  _____

Instructional unit:  _____

Number of class sessions for lesson:  _____

Time period covered by lesson:  _____

Format of artifact:  _____
    (lesson plan, lesson summary, video, other)

Additional artifacts included:  _____
    (worksheets, handouts, etc.)


Use this space to add any additional information you feel would help
to communicate the essence of the lesson you have selected.

# Classroom Artifact Collection: Full Set
## IV.  Sample Assessment

Teacher: _____

Instructional unit: _____

Topic of assessment: _____

Type of assessment: _____
   (quiz, unit test, project, performance task, etc.)

Time allowed for students to complete: _____

Use this space to add any additional information you feel would help to communicate the essence of the assessment you have selected.

## Classroom Artifact Collection: Full Set

## V. Student Work Samples
## on Selected Assessment

Teacher: _____

Instructional unit: _____

Number of student samples: _____

Teacher feedback included?    Yes    No

If so, what kind? _____
    (grade, comments, rubric score, etc.)

Use this space to add any additional information you feel would help to communicate the essence of the student work samples you have selected.

## Figure 9.4 Peer Review and Self-Assessment Checklist

| | | Wow! | Good | Refine | Redo |
|---|---|---|---|---|---|
| Authentic: | A contextually faithful encounter with the "doing" of a subject. | ☐ | ☐ | ☐ | ☐ |
| | • The work engages students in experiences and challenges that replicate or simulate the tasks, demands, and situations encountered "in the field." | ☐ | ☐ | ☐ | ☐ |
| | • The performance and production challenges are genuine. They assess whether students can fashion a quality product or performance in ways that adults are "tested" (e.g., oral reports, conducting an experiment, juried exhibits of artwork, judging the adequacy of a design, developing policy, etc.). | ☐ | ☐ | ☐ | ☐ |
| | • The tasks involve real problems, not (merely) drills or exercises. (If a novice-level course, some of the work is authentic in that it is scaffolded performance or apprenticeship.) | ☐ | ☐ | ☐ | ☐ |
| | • Primary sources and/or first-hand research are expected. | ☐ | ☐ | ☐ | ☐ |
| Meaningful: | The work will be appropriate to the intellectual interests, prior experience, and levels of (diverse) students. | ☐ | ☐ | ☐ | ☐ |
| | • The design results in genuine intellectual challenges that are nonetheless accessible to students. | ☐ | ☐ | ☐ | ☐ |
| | • The work is aptly scaffolded, simplified, or adjusted for the developmental needs of students. | ☐ | ☐ | ☐ | ☐ |
| Rigorous: Likely to Yield Understanding | Content, competency, work design, and performance standards are high. | ☐ | ☐ | ☐ | ☐ |
| | • The materials used and ideas focused on are challenging; and the lessons, assignments, and assessments demand quality work from students. | ☐ | ☐ | ☐ | ☐ |
| | • The work of the unit/course focuses on worthy topics, issues, texts, problems—big ideas, essential questions. | ☐ | ☐ | ☐ | ☐ |
| Responsive: | The design allows room for diverse abilities, interests, and unanticipatable reactions, and for emerging student interests. | ☐ | ☐ | ☐ | ☐ |
| | • The design of the work leaves room for adjustment, by both teacher and students, based on emerging performance difficulties. | ☐ | ☐ | ☐ | ☐ |
| | • The work can be done by students with diverse learning styles and talents without compromising rigor. | ☐ | ☐ | ☐ | ☐ |
| | • The calendar leaves ample room for students to follow up on questions, interests, problems, etc. that emerge from the work requirements and performance. | ☐ | ☐ | ☐ | ☐ |

## Figure 9.4 Continued

| | | Wow! | Good | Refine | Redo |
|---|---|---|---|---|---|
| **Coherent:** | The unit or course has a clear and obvious logic to the *student*. | ☐ | ☐ | ☐ | ☐ |
| | • Assignments and assessment tasks lead "naturally" to others. The work of the unit(s) builds, from the simple to the complex—not just as activities, texts, or lessons strung together. | ☐ | ☐ | ☐ | ☐ — |
| | • Despite surprises, twists, and turns about how the work will ultimately play out, the student is never confused about where the work is headed in terms of overarching focus on final work requirements. (In narrative terms, students sense the movement toward a resolution of *known* purposes, issues, and tensions at work in the syllabus "story-line"). | ☐ | ☐ | ☐ | ☐ |
| **Engaging:** | The work requirements, experiences, and lessons are thought provoking and generative of deepening interest and quality work. | ☐ | ☐ | ☐ | ☐ |
| | • The activities pique student curiosity; they take the student beyond merely enjoyable actions and opinion-offering to inquiries and performance demands that cause depth of thought and the desire to do tasks well. | ☐ | ☐ | ☐ | ☐ |
| | • The work is rich enough and accommodating of levels enough that it will likely engage all students, not just the most able, the most dutiful, or only those able to delay gratification. | ☐ | ☐ | ☐ | ☐ |
| **Effective:** | The work requirements and incentives are such that we should expect atypically good performance results based on this design. | ☐ | ☐ | ☐ | ☐ |
| | • The assessment tasks and standards are so clearly spelled out (while challenging), and the design so effectively builds toward them that we can expect across-the-board fine performance, if students attend to the requirements. | ☐ | ☐ | ☐ | ☐ |
| | • Modeling and feedback opportunities are part of the design. | ☐ | ☐ | ☐ | ☐ |
| **Feasible:** | The work requirements are such that the unit will *work* in the time/syllabus/grade level proposed and is not dependent upon an unrealistically ideal school context. | ☐ | ☐ | ☐ | ☐ |
| | • The unit will work in the time/syllabus/grade level allotted. | ☐ | ☐ | ☐ | ☐ |
| | • The unit can be successful without impossibly unrealistic school conditions (though some structural changes may be required in scheduling, interdisciplinary courses, etc.). | ☐ | ☐ | ☐ | ☐ |
| **Efficient:** | The work requirements are such that the unit takes up the right amount of time and energy, given the overall course and program priorities and objectives. | ☐ | ☐ | ☐ | ☐ |

## Alternative Assessment Evaluation Form

| | Yes | Somewhat | No |
|---|---|---|---|
| **1. Content/Skill Coverage and Correct Method** | 3 | 2 | 1 |

**The assessment:**
- Clearly states skills and content to be covered
- Correctly uses alternative assessment to measure these skills and content
- Avoids irrelevant and/or unimportant content
- Deals with enduring themes or significant knowledge
- Matches statements of coverage to task content and performance criteria

| | | | |
|---|---|---|---|
| **2. Performance Criteria:** | 3 | 2 | 1 |

- Include everything of importance and omit irrelevant features of performance
- State criteria clearly and provide samples of student work to illustrate them
- Are stated generally, especially if the intent is use as an instructional tool
- Are analytical trait, especially if the intent is use as an instructional tool

| | | | |
|---|---|---|---|
| **3. Performance Tasks:** | 3 | 2 | 1 |

**General:**
- Elicit the desired performances or work;
- Recreate an "authentic" context for performance
- Exemplify good instruction
- Are reviewed by others (students, peers, experts)

**Sampling/Representativeness/Generalizability:**
- Cover the content or skill area well; results can be generalized
- Sample performance in a way that is representative of what a student can do

**Bias and Distortion:**
- Avoid factors that might get in the way of student ability to demonstrate what they know and can do

|  | Yes | Somewhat | No |
|---|---|---|---|
| **4. Fairness and Rater Bias** | 3 | 2 | 1 |

**Performance Tasks:**
- Have content and context that are equally familiar, acceptable, and appropriate for students in all group
- Tap knowledge and skills all students have had adequate time to acquire in class
- Are as free as possible of cultural, ethnic, or gender stereotypes
- Are as free as possible of language barriers

**Performance Criteria and Rater Training:**
- Ensure that irrelevant features of performance do not influence how other, supposedly independent, features are judged
- Ensure that knowledge of the type of student does not influence judgments about performance quality
- Ensure that knowledge of individual students does not affect judgments about performance quality

|  | Yes | Somewhat | No |
|---|---|---|---|
| **5. Consequences** | 3 | 2 | 1 |

**The assessment:**
- Communicates appropriate messages
- Results in acceptable effects on students, teachers, and others
- Is worth the instructional time devoted to it; students learn something from doing the assessment and/or using the performance criteria
- Provides information relevant to the decisions being made
- Is perceived by students and teachers as valid

|  | Yes | Somewhat | No |
|---|---|---|---|
| **6. Cost and Efficiency** | 3 | 2 | 1 |

**The assessment:**
- Is cost efficient—the results are worth the investment
- Is practical/"do-able"

FIGURE 3.2
## Stimulus Questions Derived from the Reasoning Processes of Dimensions 3 and 4

| Stimulus Question | Reasoning Process | Dimension |
|---|---|---|
| Do you want to determine how certain things are similar and different? | Comparing | 3 |
| Do you want to organize things into groups? Do you want to identify the rules or characteristics that have been used to form groups? | Classifying | 3 |
| Are there specific pieces of information that you want to draw conclusions about? | Induction | 3 |
| Are there specific rules you see operating here? Are there things that you know must happen? | Deduction | 3 |
| Are there errors in reasoning you want to describe? Are there errors being performed in a process? | Error Analysis | 3 |
| Is there a position you want to defend on a particular issue? | Constructing Support | 3 |
| Do you see a relationship that no one else has seen? What is the abstract pattern or theme that is at the heart of the relationship? | Abstracting | 3 |
| Are there differing perspectives on an issue you want to explore? | Analyzing Perspectives | 3 |
| Is there an important decision that should be studied or made? | Decision Making | 4 |
| Is there some new idea or new theory that should be described in detail? | Definitional Investigation | 4 |
| Is there something that happened in the past that should be studied? | Historical Investigation | 4 |
| Is there a possible or hypothetical event that should be studied? | Projective Investigation | 4 |
| Do you want to describe how some obstacle can be overcome? | Problem Solving | 4 |
| Is there a prediction you want to make and then test? | Experimental Inquiry | 4 |
| Is there something you want to improve upon? Is there something new you want to create? | Invention | 4 |

Reprinted by permission of McREL (Mid-continent Research for Education and Learning), from *Assessing Student Outcomes: Performance Assessment Using the Dimensions of Learning Model* by Robert J. Marzano, Debra Pickering, and Jay McTighe. Copyright © 1993 by McREL.

REPORT CARDS WITH NO GRADES: MOVING TOWARD THE FUTURE

---

## FIGURE 7.1
## A Report Card with No Overall Grades

**Name:** Al Einstein
**Address:** 1111 E. McSquare Dr.
**City:** Relativity, CO 80000
**Grade Level:** 11

**Course Titles:**
Algebra II and Trigonometry    Physical Education
Advanced Placement Physics    Chorus
U.S. History    Geography
American Literature

### Standards Rating

| Algebra II and Trigonometry | | (1) | (2) | (3) | (4) |
|---|---|---|---|---|---|
| Mathematics Standard 1: | Numeric Problem Solving | 1.75 | | | |
| Mathematics Standard 2: | Computation | | | | |
| Mathematics Standard 3: | Measurement | | 2.5 | | |
| Mathematics Standard 4: | Geometry | | 2.75 | | |
| Mathematics Standard 5: | Probability | | 2.5 | | |
| Mathematics Standard 6: | Functions | 1.0 | | | |
| Mathematics Standard 7: | Data Analysis | | 2.25 | | |
| Reasoning Standard: | Decision Making | | 2.5 | | |
| Communication Standard: | Written | 1.25 | | | |
| Communication Standard: | Oral | 1.5 | | | |
| Nonachievement Factor: | Effort | 1.5 | | | |

**Mathematics Achievement: 2.13**    Overall: 1.95

| Advanced Placement Physics | | (1) | (2) | (3) | (4) |
|---|---|---|---|---|---|
| Science Standard 1: | Structure/Properties of Matter | | | | 4.0 |
| Science Standard 2: | Energy Types | | | | 3.75 |
| Science Standard 3: | Motion | | | | 4.0 |
| Science Standard 4: | Forces | | | | 4.0 |
| Reasoning Standard: | Experimental Inquiry | | | | 4.0 |
| Reasoning Standard: | Problem Solving | | | | 4.0 |
| Communication Standard: | Audience | 1.0 | | | |
| Nonachievement Factor: | Behavior | | | 3.25 | |

**Science Achievement: 3.94**    Overall: 3.73

| U.S. History | | (1) | (2) | (3) | (4) |
|---|---|---|---|---|---|
| History Standard 1: | Civilization and Society | | 2.0 | | |
| History Standard 2: | Exploration & Colonization | | | 3.25 | |
| History Standard 3: | Revolution and Conflict | | | | 4.0 |
| History Standard 4: | Industry and Commerce | | 2.75 | | |
| History Standard 5: | Forms of Government | | 2.5 | | |
| Reasoning Standard: | Comparing and Contrasting | | | 3.5 | |
| Reasoning Standard: | Making Deductions | | | | 4.0 |
| Communication Standard: | Written | 1.5 | | | |
| Nonachievement Factor: | Behavior | | | 3.25 | |

**History Achievement: 2.9**    Overall: 3.0

TRANSFORMING CLASSROOM GRADING

## FIGURE 7.1 *(continued)*

**Standards Rating**

### American Literature

| Standard | Description | Rating (1)–(4) |
|---|---|---|
| Language Arts Standard 1: | The Writing Process | 2.5 |
| Language Arts Standard 2: | Usage, Style, and Rhetoric | 3.25 |
| Language Arts Standard 3: | Research: Process & Product | 3.75 |
| Language Arts Standard 4: | The Reading Process | |
| Language Arts Standard 5: | Reading Comprehension | |
| Language Arts Standard 6: | Literary/Text Analysis | 2.5 |
| Language Arts Standard 7: | Listening and Speaking | 2.25 |
| Language Arts Standard 8: | The Nature of Language | |
| Language Arts Standard 9: | Literature | 1.25 |
| Reasoning Standard: | Analyzing Relationships | 3.75 |
| Nonachievement Factor: | Attendance | 2.5 |
| Nonachievement Factor: | Behavior | 2.5 |

**Lang. Arts Achievement: 2.58**     Overall: 2.65

### Physical Education

| Standard | Description | Rating (1)–(4) |
|---|---|---|
| Physical Education Standard 1: | Move't Forms: Theory & Pract. | 2.25 |
| Physical Education Standard 2: | Motor Skill Development | 3.75 |
| Physical Education Standard 3: | Physical Fitness: Appreciation | 3.0 |
| Physical Education Standard 4: | Physical Fitness: Application | 2.5 |
| Reasoning Standard: | Problem Solving | 3.25 |
| Nonachievement Factor: | Attendance | 2.75 |
| Nonachievement Factor: | Behavior | 2.5 |
| Nonachievement Factor: | Effort | 1.5 |

**Phys. Ed. Achievement: 2.88**     Overall: 2.75

### Chorus

| Standard | Description | Rating (1)–(4) |
|---|---|---|
| Music Standard 1: | Vocal Music | 3.75 |
| Music Standard 2: | Instrumental Music | 3.75 |
| Music Standard 3: | Music Composition | 3.25 |
| Music Standard 4: | Music Theory | 2.25 |
| Music Standard 5: | Music Appreciation | 4.0 |
| Reasoning Standard: | Classifying | 2.75 |
| Communication Factor: | Written | 3.25 |

**Music Achievement: 3.40**     Overall: 3.33

### Geography

| Standard | Description | Rating (1)–(4) |
|---|---|---|
| Geography Standard 1: | Places and Regions | 2.25 |
| Geography Standard 2: | Human Systems | 3.5 |
| Geography Standard 3: | Physical Systems | 3.75 |
| Geography Standard 4: | Uses of Geography | 2.75 |
| Geography Standard 5: | Environment and Society | 3.75 |
| Geography Standard 6: | The World in Spatial Terms | 2.25 |
| Reasoning Standard: | Making Deductions | 3.5 |
| Nonachievement Factor: | Effort | 2.75 |

**Geography Achievement: 3.04**     Overall: 3.06

*The Checklist:*
# Assessing the Tracking Practices in your School

*by Eleanor Linn and Norma Barquet*

THIS informal survey is intended for a multicultural, gender-representative cross-section of your school community including teachers, students, administrators, parents and support staff. They should be involved in the survey planning process. Some questions will require gathering additional information. The results of this assessment should stimulate discussion on the status of tracking in your school.

**Directions:** Answer each question with: Y for Yes, S for Somewhat, N for No, and D for Don't Know or Doesn't Apply. Try to answer every question.

## District Policy and School Culture

____ 1. Does your school district's policy establish a democratic view of education where all students regardless of socio-economic status, gender, race or ethnicity are expected to achieve high standards of social and academic performance?

____ 2. Has a survey of school culture or climate been undertaken to ensure that every student has the necessary personal and academic support to achieve the district's expectations?

## School/Program/Classroom Organization

____ 3. Are all classes free of tracking and ability grouping?

____ 4. Are the needs of high- and low-achieving students (i.e., gifted and talented and special education) met within the regular class setting?

____ 5. Are all students required to take more than two years of math and science at the high school level?

## Evaluation Procedures

____ 6. Are students assessed in a language in which they can best demonstrate their cognitive abilities and subject area knowledge?

____ 7. Have assessment instruments been analyzed for cultural, gender, or linguistic bias?

____ 8. Are Individualized Educational Programs (IEP) and other special education plans thoroughly reviewed at least once a year?

____ 9. Are open-ended questions, essay-writing, portfolios, and performance-based tests used in the evaluation process?

____ 10. Is the criteria for evaluating and grading students consistent throughout the school program?

____ 11. Do school staff members use special consultants to aid in assessing students with special needs (i.e., bilingual psychologists for bilingual students, etc.)?

## Student Placement

____ 12. Are parents regularly informed and actively involved in the placement decisions that affect their children?

____ 13. Is the grouping of students for instructional purposes flexible, temporary, and intended to accelerate learning?

____ 14. Do parents and students have the option to accept, reject, or request a specific placement in a class or program?

____ 15. Do special education students exit special education programs on a regular basis to be mainstreamed?

____ 16. Are within-class groups heterogeneous in nature and reconstituted several times a year?

____ 17. Are students who have academic difficulties given the necessary support to avoid grade retention?

## Curriculum and Instruction

____ 18. Are critical thinking, expository writing, and oral presentations an integral part of all student programs?

____ 19. Do all students have a chance to read and critique challenging and highly interesting material?

____ 20. Are cooperative learning techniques used with groups of students of all ages and supported in all classrooms?

____ 21. Is language instruction infused in all programs so that students for whom English is not their first language can thrive?

____ 22. Are various learning styles, such as verbal, musical, logical-mathematical, spatial, kinesthetic, and inter-personal included and valued in most classroom activities?

____ 23. Is persistence taught, valued, and rewarded in all classes?

____ 24. Is small class size a goal at all levels of the school program?

## Student Participation

____ 25. Are girls, students with low socio-economic status, minorities, physically disabled, and limited-English speaking students represented in leadership roles such as student council and student government?

____ 26. Are minority students and girls actively recruited to participate in extracurricular activities, including enrichment programs such as math club and science olympiad?

____ 27. Are curricular, co-curricular, and extra-curricular activities and programs monitored for proportionate involvement of girls and students of color?

____ 28. Is there an active recruitment and support program to get all students involved in intellectually challenging academic courses and programs?

## Staff Expectations

____ 29. Do teachers really believe that all students can achieve social and academic excellence?

____ 30. Are there support groups to help students who lack the confidence to take certain courses?

____ 31. Do staff avoid using terms such as "bright students," "able learners," "college bound," "remedial," "lower track," and "L.D." to refer to specific groups of students?

____ 32. Have all staff received inservice training to facilitate working with diverse groups, using cooperative learning techniques, and matching teaching/learning styles?

## Distribution of Resources

____ 33. Do all students regardless of gender, race, national origin, and disability have equal access to computers, graphing calculators and other forms of sophisticated equipment and technology?

____ 34. Are special programs and classes such as bilingual education and special education centrally located in the school building?

____ 35. Do girls' sports, bilingual and special education classes, and other programs targeted to girls and minorities have equal access to the most desirable facilities, schedule time, and other resources in the school?

____ 36. Are the most experienced and motivated teachers assigned to programs throughout the school regardless of the level of classes they teach or the sports they coach?

____ 37. Are African Americans, national-origin language minorities, and women fairly represented in all job classifications?

____ 38. Are adequate numbers of up-to-date, interesting textbooks and curricular materials purchased on an equitable basis for all students in all programs?

## Final Results of School Experiences

____ 39. Are drop out rate data collected and analyzed annually by race/gender/ethnicity?

____ 40. Have students been followed after graduation to see what kinds of jobs and education they have pursued to determine the school's success in preparing students?

### Scoring the Checklist:

1. Count the number of Y, S, N, and D answers separately.

2. Give the following value to the corresponding letter answers: Y=2; S=1; N=0.

3. Add the total number of points for Y, S and N answers. This is your score.

4. You should not have more than 8 D answers.

**60-80 points**    *Fantastico!* Your school is a place where students feel they have equal status, equal access, and an equal chance to succeed. Recognize your successes, share them with others, and celebrate them. Continue to monitor, adjust and evaluate your practices to improve and maintain excellence and equity in your school. Keep up the good work!

**30-59 points**    You are on the right track. Your school is either currently involved in de-tracking or the tracking practices are not as pervasive as in many other schools. Analyze the areas where you wrote "No" and begin to discuss ways to increase flexibility and access to your programs and practices. Encourage your staff to read and discuss the articles in this issue. Continuously assess your status and keep focused!

**0-31 points**    You have much work to do. The practices in your school are probably sifting and sorting students based on a number of inequitable criteria. This can result in a lack of access and educational benefits for whole groups of students. Begin by encouraging your school staff to read and discuss the articles in this issue. Select one area which needs immediate attention and engage those who would be most affected in the change process. Once change is under way you can select another area to work on. Make sure that changes become institutionalized. Continue to monitor, adjust and evaluate your programs and practices. *Bonne chance et bon courage!*

<u>Get Ready, Get Set: A Readiness Assessment for Untracking</u>

As your school moves to reduce tracking, provide greater access to valued knowledge for all students, and close learning gaps, you will need to think about your school's preparation for change and assess your strengths and needs for resources. This assessment can help you identify the next steps your school can take to challenge all students in multiple-ability classes.

Based on your best knowledge, rate your school in relation to the following conditions for untracking as:

* (<u>Stage 1</u>) Strongly disagree: ("We've hardly begun to think about it.")

* (<u>Stage 2</u>) Somewhat disagree: ("We have some awareness and a few individual teachers have tried this.")

* (<u>Stage 3</u>) Somewhat agree: ("We've outlined the next steps to take and identified the resources we all need to make this happen.")

* (<u>Stage 4</u>) Strongly agree: ("We are confident that this condition is in place and will support teachers ready for change. We're still learning how, but we're ready!")

---

1. We have had in-depth conversations about our core beliefs, our goals for student learning, and our responsibilities for student achievement.

    1     2     3     4

2. Our school vision communicates our belief that all students will learn at high levels, and we have defined this vision in terms of what all students will know and be able to do when they leave our school.

    1     2     3     4

3. We have a leadership team in place that is prepared to explain and promote this vision among all parents and concerned citizens.

    1     2     3     4

4. Our school is organized into teams of teachers who have regular time to talk to one another.

    1     2     3     4

5. Even if not everyone agrees, a significant number of staff—in one grade, team, or department— are willing to pilot the heterogeneous sections of the curriculum so that all students are at least in grade-level courses with equal access to high-content curriculum.

1    2    3    4

6. Staff have opportunities for ongoing professional development to help them communicate high expectations to all students and build a variety of learning experiences into their classes to help all students meet "high content" goals.

1    2    3    4

7. Staff development opportunities are intensive, sustained, and focused on content that enriches learning for all students.

1    2    3    4

8. Our faculty feels confident that we can offer the interesting content, pace, and challenge of the "top" to heterogeneous classes in a way that addresses the individual needs of all students.

1    2    3    4

9. We have redesigned teaching and learning to build in different means for students to learn and demonstrate complex knowledge and higher order skills through, for example, thematic interdisciplinary units, integrated language arts and discussion -based learning, math in context, and active, hands-on projects.

1    2    3    4

10. Teachers of heterogeneous classes have access to a rich variety of materials for student learning including a standards-based curriculum specifically designed for diverse learners.

1    2    3    4

11. We have put supports such as teacher coaching, cross-age tutoring, double classes, extra help programs, or pre-teaching in place so that weaker students can succeed in heterogeneous classes.

1    2    3    4

12. We have considered how to redesign curriculum-based assessments at the classroom level so that we assess what students know and are able to do based on real performance.

1    2    3    4

13. Our guidance counselors are prepared to assume the role of "opportunity-expanders" rather than "gatekeepers."

1    2    3    4

14. Our school has reassessed our school communications, document, and routines to expand learning opportunities for all and foster a democratic school culture.

1    2    3    4

15. Our school has maximized opportunities for positive contact among various groups of students in all aspects of school life, both academic and extracurricular.

1    2    3    4

16. Our school has facilitated risk-taking of teachers by waiving or modifying teacher evaluations or through other incentives during the early stages of change.

1    2    3    4

17. Can you think of other considerations that bear on your school's readiness for untracking?

Anne Wheelock: 3/94

## Action Steps for Untracking

After discussing the results of the "readiness assessment" in small groups and as a whole faculty, schools can work to identify three areas that require attention. List in order of importance to develop proposals for strengthening schools' capacity to change.

1. Area for attention:

   Proposed action and expected outcome:

   Resources needed:

2. Area for attention:

   Proposed action and expected outcome:

   Resources needed:

3. Area for attention:

   Proposed action and expected outcome:

   Resources needed:

```
Observation Sheet for
Verbal Interaction Assessment
```

Directions
    For each category indicated, tally the teacher comments directed at boys and girls. Refer to the definition of each category if necessary

|  | Teachers Comments Directed at: | | | |
|---|---|---|---|---|
|  | Boys | Total | Girls | Total |
| **I. Praise** | | | | |
| A. Academic | ___ | ___ | ___ | ___ |
| B. Nonacademic | ___ | ___ | ___ | ___ |
| **II. Academic Criticism** | | | | |
| A. Intellectual quality | ___ | ___ | ___ | ___ |
| B. Effort | ___ | ___ | ___ | ___ |
| **III. Nonacademic Criticism** | | | | |
| A. Mild | ___ | ___ | ___ | ___ |
| B. Harsh | ___ | ___ | ___ | ___ |
| **IV. Questions** | | | | |
| A. Low level | ___ | ___ | ___ | ___ |
| B. High level | ___ | ___ | ___ | ___ |
| **V. Academic Intervention** | | | | |
| A. Facilitative | ___ | ___ | ___ | ___ |
| B. Disruptive | ___ | ___ | ___ | ___ |

From *Building Gender Fairness in Schools* by Beverly Stitt. Copyright © 1988 by the Board of Trustees, Southern Illinois University. Reprinted by permission of the publisher, Southern Illinois University Press.

Observation Categories

I. **Praise**
   A. **Academic.** Rewards and reinforcement given for the intellectual quality of work: Good answer. You've written a very interesting report. Your evaluation of the problem is excellent.
   B. **Nonacademic.** All rewards and reinforcements not directed to the intellectual quality of academic work: You're being nice and quiet today. That's an attractive dress. That's a very neatly written paper.

II. **Academic Criticism**
   A. **Intellectual quality.** Critical remarks directed at the lack of intellectual quality of work: Perhaps math isn't a good field for you. Is this experiment too difficult for you? You don't seem able to grasp this material.
   B. **Effort.** Comments attributing academic failure to lack of effort: You're not trying hard enough. I know you can do the work if you put your mind to it and study harder.

III. **Nonacademic Criticism**
   A. **Mild.** Negative comments that reprimand violations of conduct, rules, forms, behavior, and other nonacademic areas: Tom, stay in line. Sally, quiet down. Jim, your paper is too messy.
   B. **Harsh.** These negative comments make scenes and attract attention. They are louder, often longer, and always stronger than mild criticism: Tom, get back in line; I've had more than enough from you today; stay in line or suffer the consequences; move. Harriet, the rules are quite straightforward, and you are talking again and disturbing others, for violating the rules, you are to stay after class today for one hour in the detention hall.

IV. **Questions**
   A. **Low-level.** Questions that require memory on the part of the student: When did Columbus arrive in the Americas? Who was the fifth president? What is the name of this color?
   B. **High-level.** Questions that require higher intellectual processes and ask the student to use information, not just memorize it: In your opinion, why did Columbus come to America? Analyze the causes of the Vietnam War. Determine the range of possible answers in this quadratic equation. How would you evaluate this painting? Can you apply the rules of supply and demand to the following example? How would you write your own personal statement on human rights?

V. **Academic Intervention**
   A. **Facilitative.** Behaviors that facilitate learning by providing students with suggestions, hints, and cues to encourage and enable them to complete the task for themselves. The teacher helps, but the student does the work: Think of yesterday's formula, and try to do that problem again. Double check your facts. Your explanation isn't complete; review the purpose of the law, and then try it again. Watch me do this experiment, then you try it again by yourself.
   B. **Disruptive.** Comments that prevent or short-circuit success because the teacher intrudes and takes over the process. The teacher does the task for the student. When the teacher provides the answer instead of the direction, this category is tallied: Let me do that for you. That's wrong—the answer is 14. You're way off base; watch me do it.

## SURVEY OF MATHEMATICS TEACHERS

1. What summer institutes have you attended?

   | | | |
   |---|---|---|
   | ____ | Summer | 1997 |
   | ____ | Summer | 1998 |
   | ____ | Summer | 1999 |

2. What courses do you usually teach? (Place an X in the space next to the course name. Circle the grade level of the students to whom you teach that course; indicate the number of class periods taught per course.)

   | Course Name | Grade Level | # of Class Periods Taught |
   |---|---|---|
   | ____ General Math | 6  7  8  9  10  11  12 | _____ |
   | ____ Pre-Algebra | 6  7  8  9  10  11  12 | _____ |
   | ____ Algebra | 6  7  8  9  10  11  12 | _____ |
   | ____ Geometry | 6  7  8  9  10  11  12 | _____ |
   | ____ Trigonometry | 6  7  8  9  10  11  12 | _____ |
   | ____ Pre-Calculus | 6  7  8  9  10  11  12 | _____ |
   | ____ Calculus | 6  7  8  9  10  11  12 | _____ |
   | ____ Special Populations | 6  7  8  9  10  11  12 | _____ |
   | ____ Other | 6  7  8  9  10  11  12 | _____ |

3. In your classes, do you teach students how to use a calculator? (Circle one.)

   1 — Yes, in all classes
   2 — Yes, in some classes
   3 — No (Skip to Question 4)

4. How do you allow students in your classes to use calculators? (Circle one.)

   1 — Classwork only
   2 — Classwork and homework
   3 — Classwork, homework. and tests
   4 — Classwork and tests
   5 — Homework and tests
   6 — Homework only
   7 — Tests only

Reprinted by permission of the Pelavin Research Center of the American Institutes for Research. Summer 1993.

SURVEY OF MATHEMATICS TEACHERS
Page 2

5.     If you don't allow students to take a calculator home for use in their homework assignments, why? (Circle one.)

       1 — Inappropriate for students to do homework with a calculator
       2 — Not enough calculators for all my students
       3 — Some students wouldn't return them
       4 — Both 2 and 3
       5 — Other (Please explain: _____)
       6 — Already allow students to take calculators home

6.     In your classes, do your students work in groups to solve problems? (Circle one.)

       1 — Yes, in all classes
       2 — Yes, in some classes
       3 — No (Skip to Question 9)

7.     How frequently do you have students work in groups to solve problems? (Circle one.)

       1 — Less frequently than once a week
       2 — Once a week
       3 — Two or three times a week
       4 — Four or five times a week
       5 — More frequently than once a day

8.     What is the average size of a problem-solving group? (Circle one.)

       1 — 2 -3  students
       2 — 3 -4  students
       3 — 4 -5  students
       4 — 5+ students

9.     How successful are your students at group problem-solving? (Circle one.)

       1 — Very successful
       2 — Fairly successful
       3 — Somewhat successful
       4 — Not successful

Reprinted by permission of the Pelavin Research Center of the American Institutes for Research.  Summer 1993.

SURVEY OF MATHEMATICS TEACHERS
Page 3

10.     During the past academic year, did you:

(a)     Discuss postsecondary opportunities with poor or
        minority students?                                      yes ___      no ___
(b)     Discuss postsecondary opportunities with
        parents/family of poor or minority students?           yes ___      no ___
(c)     Use manipulatives to teach mathematics?                 yes ___      no ___

11.     Please estimate the percent of students in your school who take pre-algebra
        before entering high school.

                _____ %

12.     Please estimate the percent of students in your school who are capable of taking
        and passing a course in pre-algebra before entering high school.

                _____ %

13.     Please estimate the percent of students in your school who take algebra before
        entering high school.

                _____ %

14.     Please estimate the percent of students in your school who are capable of taking
        and passing a course in algebra.

                _____ %

15.     Please estimate the percent of students in your school who are capable of taking
        and passing geometry.

                _____ %

Reprinted by permission of the Pelavin Research Center of the American Institutes for Research. Summer 1993.

SURVEY OF MATHEMATICS TEACHERS
Page 4

16. Please estimate the percent of students in your school who are capable of taking and passing mathematics courses beyond geometry (such as algebra II, trigonometry, or calculus).

_____ %

17. Please estimate the percent of students in your school who, if finances were not an issue, are capable of going on to college upon graduation from high school. (Include two- and four- year schools; exclude proprietary schools.)

_____ %

18. Please estimate the percent of students in your school who are capable of graduating from college.

_____ %

19. For each activity listed below, specify the frequency with which you worked with other <u>teachers</u> during the past year:

|  |  | Never | Rarely | Sometimes | Frequently |
|---|---|---|---|---|---|
| (1) | Developing and implementing activities designed to motivate students to achieve in mathematics | 1 | 2 | 3 | 4 |
| (2) | Developing and implementing activities designed to increase students' awareness of college requirements, knowledge of the college admissions process, or knowledge of sources of financial aid | 1 | 2 | 3 | 4 |
| (3) | Helping individual students with school work | 1 | 2 | 3 | 4 |
| (4) | Helping individual students resolve discipline problems | 1 | 2 | 3 | 4 |

Reprinted by permission of the Pelavin Research Center of the American Institutes for Research. Summer 1993.

SURVEY OF MATHEMATICS TEACHERS
Page 5

20.  For each activity listed below, specify the frequency with which you worked with <u>counselors</u> during the past year:

|  |  | Never | Rarely | Sometimes | Frequently |
|---|---|---|---|---|---|
| (1) | Developing and implementing activities designed to motivate students to achieve in mathematics | 1 | 2 | 3 | 4 |
| (2) | Developing and implementing activities designed to increase students' awareness of college requirements, knowledge of the college admissions process, or knowledge of sources of financial aid | 1 | 2 | 3 | 4 |
| (3) | Helping individual students with school work | 1 | 2 | 3 | 4 |
| (4) | Helping individual students resolve discipline problems | 1 | 2 | 3 | 4 |

21.  Do you have any additional comments you would like to add?

Reprinted by permission of the Pelavin Research Center of the American Institutes for Research. Summer 1993.

SURVEY OF MATHEMATICS TEACHERS
Page 6

*The following questions are optional. Your responses may be useful in a subsequent analysis. If you do provide this information, know that it is much appreciated and that your personal identification will be protected.*

22.   What is your gender? (Circle one.)

1 — Male
2 — Female

23.   What is your age?

_____ years

24.   What is your racial/ethnic group? (Circle one.)

1 — Native American
2 — Asian
3 — Black (not Hispanic)
4 — Hispanic
5 — White (not Hispanic)
6 — Other (please specify) _____

25.   Do you speak a language other than English? (Circle one.)

1— Yes
2— No

26.   a. What is the highest academic degree you have received? (Circle one.)

1 — B.A./B.S.
2 — M.A./M.S.
3 — Ph.D.
4 — Other (please specify) _____

Reprinted by permission of the Pelavin Research Center of the American Institutes for Research. Summer 1993.

SURVEY OF MATHEMATICS TEACHERS
Page 7

b. In what field is your bachelor's degree?  (If your degree is in a multiple fields, indicate your primary field)

1 — Mathematics
2 — General education
3 — Social sciences (e.g., psychology, sociology, economics, political science)
4 — Other sciences (e.g., biology, chemistry, geology, physics, engineering)
5 — Humanities (e.g., English, philosophy, fine arts, foreign languages)
6 — Other (please specify) _____

c. If you have an advanced degree, In what field ~ this degree? (If your degree is in multiple fields. indicate your primary field)

1 — Mathematics
2 — General education
3 — Social sciences (e.g., psychology, sociology, economics, political science)
4 — Other sciences (e.g., biology, chemistry, geology, physics, engineering)
5 — Humanities (e.g., English, philosophy, fine arts, foreign languages)
6 — Other (please specify) _____
7 — I do not have an advanced degree

27.  Are you credentialed to teach mathematics in your state? (Circle one.)

1 - Yes
2 - No

28.  How many years of teaching experience do you have?

_____ years

29.  How long have you taught in your current school district?

_____ years

30.  How long have you taught mathematics?

_____ years

Reprinted by permission of the Pelavin Research Center of the American Institutes for Research.  Summer 1993.

SURVEY OF MATHEMATICS TEACHERS
Page 8

31.     a. Have you ever taught pre-algebra?  (Circle one.)

        1 — Yes
        2 — No (Skip to Question 32)

        b. If yes, for how long?

        _____ years

32.     a. Have you ever taught algebra?  (Circle one.)
        1 — Yes
        2 — No (Skip to Question 33)


        b. If yes, for how long?

        _____ years


33.     a. Have you ever taught geometry?  (Circle one.)
        1 — Yes
        2 — No (Skip to Question 34)

        b. If yes, for how long?

        _____ years

34.     a. Have you ever taught mathematics courses beyond geometry (such as
        algebra II, trigonometry, or calculus)?

    .   b. If yes, for how long?

        _____ years


*Thank you for taking the time to complete this survey.*

## SURVEY OF MILWAUKEE GUIDANCE COUNSELORS

(address correction requested.)

Date: _____

1.  What grade students do you counsel? (Circle all that apply.)

    5   6   7   8   9   10   11   12

2.  Please estimate the percent of students in your school who take pre-algebra before entering high school.

    _____%

3.  Please estimate the percent of students in your school who are capable of taking and passing a course in pre-algebra before entering high school.

    _____%

Reprinted by permission of the Pelavin Research Center of the American Institutes for Research. Summer 1992.

Survey of Milwaukee Guidance Counselors
Page 2

4.    (If the answer to Question 3 is less than 100%.) What are the major reasons that more students are not able to take and pass pre-algebra? (Select the top three answers and rank them in order of importance (1-3) in the blank spaces provided: "1" being the most important)

\_\_\_\_\_    Student skills and preparation (e.g., weak mathematic skills, weak problem solving skills, weak conceptual/abstract reasoning skills, poor language skills, etc.)

\_\_\_\_\_    Student abilities (e.g., not smart enough, lack ability, etc.)

\_\_\_\_\_    Student study habits (e.g., poor study skills, poor study habits, lack of motivation, etc.)

\_\_\_\_\_    Social supports (e.g., no role models, lack of parental support or discipline, family problems, negative peer pressure, etc.)

\_\_\_\_\_    School structures (e.g., inconsistent curriculum, tracking, availability of courses, etc.)

\_\_\_\_\_    Teachers' abilities (e.g., inappropriate teaching methods, etc.)

\_\_\_\_\_    Teachers' attitudes (e.g., bias, discrimination, etc.)

\_\_\_\_\_    Other (Please specify: _____
_____)

5.    Do you think it is possible to take a student who is unprepared for pre-algebra successfully through a pre-algebra course in one year? In other words, can teachers make up for deficiencies in a student's preparation and teach the pre-algebra material in one year? (Circle one.)

1- Yes

2- No

Survey of Milwaukee Guidance Counselors
Page 3

6.  Please estimate the percent of students in your school who are capable of taking and passing a course in algebra.

    _____%

7.  (If the answer to Question 6 is less than 100%.) What are the major reasons that more students are not able to take and pass algebra? (Select the top three answers and rank them in order of importance (1-3) in the blank spaces provided: "1" being the most important.)

    _____  Student skills and preparation (e.g., weak mathematic skills, weak problem solving skills, weak conceptual/abstract reasoning skills, poor language skills, etc.)

    _____  Student abilities (e.g., not smart enough, lack ability, etc.)

    _____  Student study habits (e.g., poor study skills, poor study habits, lack of motivation, etc.)

    _____  Social supports (e.g., no role models, lack of parental support or discipline, family problems, negative peer pressure, etc.)

    _____  School structures (e.g., inconsistent curriculum, tracking, availability of courses, etc.)

    _____  Teachers' abilities (e.g., inappropriate teaching methods, etc.)

    _____  Teachers' attitudes (e.g., bias, discrimination, etc.)

    _____  Other (Please specify: _____)
    _____

Reprinted by permission of the Pelavin Research Center of the American Institutes for Research. Summer 1992.

Survey of Milwaukee Guidance Counselors
Page 4

8.  Please estimate the percent of student in your school who are capable of taking and passing a course in geometry.

    _____%

9.  (If the answer to Question 8 is less than 100%.) What are the major reasons that more students are not able to take and pass geometry? (Select the top three answers and rank them in order of importance (1-3) in the blank spaces provided: "1" being the most important.)

    _____ Student skills and preparation (e.g., weak mathematic skills, weak problem solving skills, weak conceptual/abstract reasoning skills, poor language skills, etc.)

    _____ Student abilities (e.g., not smart enough, lack ability, etc.)

    _____ Student study habits (e.g., poor study skills, poor study habits, lack of motivation, etc.)

    _____ Social supports (e.g., no role models, lack of parental support or discipline, family problems, negative peer pressure, etc.)

    _____ School structures (e.g., inconsistent curriculum, tracking, availability of courses, etc.)

    _____ Teachers' abilities (e.g., inappropriate teaching methods, etc.)

    _____ Teachers' attitudes (e.g., bias, discrimination, etc.)

    _____ Other (Please specify: _____

    _____)

Reprinted by permission of the Pelavin Research Center of the American Institutes for Research. Summer 1992.

Survey of Milwaukee Guidance Counselors
Page 5

10. Please estimate the percent of students in your school who are capable of going on to college. (include two- and four-year schools; exclude proprietary schools.)

11. (If the answer to Question 10 is less than 100%.) What is the major reason that more students are not capable of going on to college? (Select the top three answers and rank them in order of importance (1-3) in the blank spaces provided: "1" being the most important.)

_____ Student skills and preparation (e.g., weak mathematic skills, weak problem solving skills, weak conceptual/abstract reasoning skills, poor language skills, etc.)

_____ Student abilities (e.g., not smart enough, lack ability, etc.)

_____ Student study habits (e.g., poor study skills, poor study habits, lack of motivation, etc.)

_____ Social supports (e.g., no role models, lack of parental support or discipline, family problems, negative peer pressure, etc.)

_____ School structures (e.g., inconsistent curriculum, tracking, availability of courses, etc.)

_____ Counselors' abilities (e.g., do not inform students about college requirements, admission process, or financial aid, etc.)

_____ Counselors' attitudes (e.g., bias, discrimination, etc.)

_____ Other (Please specify: _____)

12. Please estimate the percent of students in your school who are capable of graduating from college.

_____%

Reprinted by permission of the Pelavin Research Center of the American Institutes for Research. Summer 1992.

Survey of Milwaukee Guidance Counselors
Page 6

13. Please estimate the percent of students in your school who are aware of the entrance requirements for four-year public colleges and universities in your state.

_____%

14. a. Do students at your school have access to information or activities concerning college entrance requirements? (Circle one.)

1- Yes
2- No      (Skip to Question 15)

b. If yes, indicate which information or activities your school offers to inform students about college entrance requirements. (Check all that apply.)

_____ Individual counseling

_____ Group counseling

_____ College resource center

_____ College readiness programs (e.g., TIP, Pave the Way, Project Able, etc.)

_____ College visits or college fairs

_____ Financial aid workshops

_____ Information for parents (e.g., Parents' Night, or other activity or method for providing information to parents)

_____ Career Day/career testing/career counseling

_____ Other (Please specify: _____
_____)

15. Please estimate the percent of students in your school who, with financial aid, could afford to attend a four-year public college or university in your state.

_____%

Reprinted by permission of the Pelavin Research Center of the American Institutes for Research. Summer 1992.

Survey of Milwaukee Guidance Counselors
Page 7

16.     Please estimate the percent of students in your school who are aware of the various college financial aid sources available to them.

_____%

17.     a.      Do students at your school have access to information or activities concerning college financial aid? (Circle one.)

1- Yes

2- No

        b.      If yes, please indicate which activities or information your school offers to inform students about financial aid. (Check all that apply.)

_____ Individual counseling

_____ Group counseling

_____ College resource center

_____ College readiness programs (e.g., TIP, Pave the Way, Project Able, etc.)

_____ College visits or college fairs

_____ Financial aid workshops

_____ Information for parents (e.g., Parents Night, or other activity or method for providing information to parents)

_____ Career Day/career testing/career counseling

_____ Other (Please specify: _____

_____ )

Survey of Milwaukee Guidance Counselors
Page 8

. Please estimate the percent of students in your school who are aware of the various steps in the college admissions process.

_____%

19. a. Do students in your school have access to information concerning the college admissions process? (Circle one.)

1- Yes

2- No   (Skip to Question 20)

b. If yes, please indicate how information concerning the college admissions process is made available to students. (Check all that apply.)

_____ Individual counseling

_____ Group counseling

_____ College resource center

_____College readiness programs (e.g., TIP, Pave the Way, Project Able, etc.)

_____ College visits or college fairs

_____ Financial aid workshops

_____ Information for parents (e.g., Parents Night, or other activity or method for providing information to parents)

_____ Career Day/career testing/career counseling

_____ Other (Please specify: _____

_____)

Survey of Milwaukee Guidance Counselors
Page 9

20    a.    Does your school offer any college awareness activities specifically for economically disadvantaged or minority students? (Circle one.)

1- Yes

2- No

b.    If yes, please indicate which activities your school offers to economically disadvantaged or minority students? (Check all that apply.)

_____ Individual counseling

_____ Group counseling

_____ College resource center

_____ College readiness programs (e.g., TIP, Pave the Way, Project Able, etc.)

_____ College visits or college fairs

_____ Financial aid workshops or assistance with completing forms

_____ Information about minority fellowships

_____ Minority speakers in classrooms/assemblies

_____ Information for parents (e.g., Parents Night, or other activity or method for providing information to parents)

_____ Career Day/career testing/career counseling

_____ Other (Please specify: _____)

Reprinted by permission of the Pelavin Research Center of the American Institutes for Research. Summer 1992.

Survey of Milwaukee Guidance Counselors
Page 10

21     a.     Does your school offer college awareness activities specifically for the parents/ family of economically disadvantaged or minority students? (Circle one.)

          1- Yes

          2- No        (Skip to Question 22)

      b.     If yes, please indicate which activities your school offers to parents/family of economically disadvantaged or minority students? (Check all that apply.)

      _____ Individual counseling

      _____ Group counseling

      _____ College resource center

      _____College readiness programs (e.g., TIP, Pave the Way, Project Able, etc.)

      _____ College visits or college fairs

      _____ Financial aid workshops or assistance with completing forms

      _____ Information about minority fellowships

      _____ Minority speakers in classrooms/ assemblies

      _____ Information for parents (e.g., Parents Night, or other activity or method for providing information to parents)

      _____ Career Day/career testing/career counseling

      _____ Other (Please specify: _____
                           _____)

22.     Do you have any additional comments you would like to make?

Reprinted by permission of the Pelavin Research Center of the American Institutes for Research. Summer 1992.

## Figure 5.7
## Characteristics of High-Performing and Low-Performing Counseling Programs

Directions: Circle the number that you think best reflects the performance of your school's/district's counseling programs and explain why.

| Low-Performing Programs | How is My School Doing? (1 = low, 5= high) | High-Performing Programs | Why? |
|---|---|---|---|
| A set of loosely related services performed almost exclusively by counselors. | 1 2 3 4 5 | A well-defined planning process that leads to well-coordinated services for all students. | |
| Students "fall through the cracks." | 1 2 3 4 5 | An ongoing monitoring system is set up to constantly assess student performance and provide services where needed. | |
| Counselor operates in isolation from the school, community, and district. | 1 2 3 4 5 | Counselor serves constructively on teams in planning for improvement of student achievement. | |
| No coordinated planning process to provide for the needs of students; plans are viewed as a bureaucratic requirement. | 1 2 3 4 5 | Planning process involves everyone in the school community: students, parents, teachers, administrators, and counselors. | |
| Little district support | 1 2 3 4 5 | District provides services and support to schools by:<br>• providing technical assistance in their assessment of needs and evaluation.<br>• providing special allocations of resources to schools serving large numbers of low-income and underrepresented students.<br>• periodically reviewing school plans.<br>• identifying elements that should be coordinated across and among schools. | |
| Make no use of data to analyze and improve the learning of students on a regular basis. | 1 2 3 4 5 | Use data on a regular basis to analyze and improve the learning of students. | |
| Individual progress of underrepresented students is not monitored and /or data is not available or easily accessible. | 1 2 3 4 5 | Counselors actively monitor the progress of underrepresented students in college-preparatory classes by analyzing access and success data and provide assistance and intervention when needed. | |
| No attention is paid to research. | 1 2 3 4 5 | Counselors analyze and share research information on tracking, retention, and heterogeneous grouping. | |
| Counselors are not viewed as "change agents" in schools. | 1 2 3 4 5 | Counselors demonstrate leadership skills as "change agents" in schools. | |

Form designed by Phyllis J. Hart.

# Data Tool #DT 5-7

## Student Gender Equity Survey

1. If I told my friends that I wanted to have a career that uses science, they would say...

2. If someone told me that girls can not have careers that use science, I would tell them...

3. When I get to high school and have a choice about whether or not to learn more science, I will probably decide...

4. If I were a science teacher and I could teach sceince any way I wanted to, I would probably teach science by...

5. What I want the most from this science class this year is...

6. I wish my science teacher...

7. I would like to learn more about science, because in the future...

8. When I am asked to be the leader in my lab group, I...

9. In some science classes, the teacher makes most of the decisions about what to study and how to learn; in other science classes the students make most of the decisions about what to study and how to learn. In my science class...

10. In my science class, the girls...

11. In my science class, the boys...

12. What I like the most about my science class is...

13. My parents think my science class...

14. My science teacher thinks I...

Mid-continent Regional Educational Laboratory (1997, May). *Change in Action: Navigating and Investigating the Classroom Using Action Research. Reports of Twenty-Two Teacher Research Projects.* Aurora, CO: Aurora. Reprinted With Permission of McREL.

## GUIDELINES FOR EVALUATING MATHEMATICS BOOKS FOR BIAS

Compiled by Marylin A. Hulme

### A: Check the Text

1. Are there examples of word problems using both girls and boys? If so, what topics are they dealing with? Separately or together?

2. Compare the number of females and males depicted in word problems dealing with recipes, cooking, sewing and other home-based skills, including mowing lawns and gardening. Is there a balance? Are their roles stereotyped?

3. Compare the number of females and males presented in word problems as active in the world of work outside the home. Are they working in a wide variety of careers? Are their roles stereotyped? What about their salaries?

4. Are girls generally depicted in math problems as consumers, and boys as producers? ·

5. What language is used to address women and men? To refer to them? When names are used, so they represent diverse cultural groups?

6. Is the text free of sexist/racist language?

### B: Check the Illustrations

7. Compare the number of boys and girls pictured *doing* as opposed to *watching* activities.

8. Are there members of diverse cultural groups depicted as active in the illustrations? Are there women and men from such groups?

9. What type of activities are girls and women involved in?

10. What type of activities are boys and men involved in?

### C: And, in Conclusion

11. Do the texts include the contributions to the field of mathematics made by women and by members of culturally diverse groups?

12. Do the total references to boys and men in illustrations and texts greatly outnumber the total references to girls and women.

13. Is mathematics clearly shown to be fundamentally important to many different careers, even if at first it appears that mathematics is not involved?

14. Are there inferences, however unintentional, that boys are generally more competent in mathematics than girls, and that mathematics is more important to their futures than to girls' futures?

Reprinted by permission of Marylin A. Hulme and the Feminist Press. From *Guidelines for Evaluating Mathematics Books for Bias*, compiled by Marilyn A. Hulme, published by the Equity Assistance Center, New York University, 1996. Based on *Checklists for Counteracting Race and Sex Bias in Eductional Materials*, compiled by Martha P. Cotera, published by WEEA Publishing Center, Educational Development Center, Newton, MA, 1982; and Non-Sexist Curricular Materials for Elementary Schools, by Laurie Olsen Johnson, published by the Feminist Press at the City University of New York (Copyright © 1974 by Larie Olsen Johnson).

# GUIDELINES FOR EVALUATING SCIENCE BOOKS FOR STEREOTYPING

Compiled by Marylin A. Hulme

## A: Check the Illustrations

1. Compare the number of girls and boys pictured *doing* experiments.

2. Compare the number of girls and boys pictured *watching* experiments.

3. Compare the number of women and men pictured in the role of researcher (e.g. conducting experiments).

4. Are members of diverse cultural groups depicted as active in the illustrations? Are there women and men from such groups?

5. a) What are the types of experiments shown with girls? What type of activities?
   b) What are the types of experiments shown with boys? What type of activities?

## B: Check the Text

6. Are there examples of experiments or written problems using girls and boys? As investigators? If so, how many are girls and how many are boys? Together?

7. What language is used to address women and men? To refer to them?

8. Are girls generally depicted as consumers, and boys as producers?

9. Is the text free of sexist/racist language?

10. Are there inferences, however unintentional, that boys are more competent in science than girls?

## C: And, in Conclusion

11. How is the "doing of science" depicted - involving teamwork, or a solitary occupation?

12. Do texts include the contributions to the field of science made by women and by members of culturally diverse groups?

13. Do total references to boys and men in illustrations and text greatly outnumber total references to girls and women?

Reprinted by permission of Marylin A. Hulme and the Feminist Press. From *Guidelines for Evaluating Mathematics Books for Bias*, compiled by Marilyn A. Hulme, published by the Equity Assistance Center, New York University, 1996. Based on *Checklists for Counteracting Race and Sex Bias in Educational Materials*, compiled by Martha P. Cotera, published by WEEA Publishing Center, Educational Development Center, Newton, MA, 1982; and Non-Sexist Curricular Materials for Elementary Schools, by Laurie Olsen Johnson, published by the Feminist Press at the City University of New York (Copyright © 1974 by Larie Olsen Johnson

## Diversity in the Classroom: A Checklist

This checklist is designed to help teachers and other educators effectively identify and respond to diversity in the classroom. It focuses on various aspects of the classroom environment, including curriculum materials, teaching strategies and teacher/student behaviors.

### Teaching Materials

_____ Are contributions and perspectives of women and cultures other than EuroAmericans integrated into textbooks and other curriculum materials?

_____ Are women, ethnic minorities and people of diverse socioeconomic classes and religions portrayed in a nonstereotypical manner?

_____ Do the resource materials include appropriate information about religion when religion is integral to the context of the subject?

_____ Do textbooks or curriculum materials focus on "famous people," usually those of privileged class status; or are the accomplishments and hard work of poor and working-class people given equal focus and respect?

_____ Do the resource materials include cultures represented by families in your school and community?

_____ Do English-language learners have access to resources in their native languages?

_____ Are teaching materials selected that allow all students to participate and feel challenged and successful?

### Teacher As Role Model: Questions To Ask Yourself

_____ Am I knowledgeable about the religious, cultural, linguistic and socioeconomic backgrounds of my students and people in my community?

_____ In my own life, do I model respect for, and inclusion of, people who are different (religion, race, language, abilities, socioeconomic class)?

_____ Do students perceive me as sincerely interested in, and respectful of, contributions made by women and the many ethnic, religious, racial and socioeconomic groups that make up the country?

_____ Do I know where to find resources on diversity issues regarding race, ethnicity, religion, class, language, disability, gender and sexual orientation?

_____ Do I respectfully accommodate students with disabilities in my classroom?

_____ Do I recognize and acknowledge the value of languages other than standard English?

_____ Can I recognize and constructively address value conflicts based on race, religion or socioeconomic class?

### Teacher/Student Interactions

_____ Am I careful not to prejudge a student's performance based on cultural differences, socioeconomic status or gender?

_____ Do I promote high self-esteem for all children in my classroom? Do I help each child to feel good about who he or she is?

_____ Do I encourage students to understand and respect the feelings of others who are different from them?

_____ Do my students see me as actively confronting instances of stereotyping, bias and discrimination when they occur?

_____ Given what I ask students to talk or write about, do I avoid placing value on spending money, or having money or major consumer products?

_____ Do I put myself in the place of the language minority student and ask, "How would I feel in this classroom?"

_____ Do I make an effort to learn some words in the home languages of my English-language learners?

_____ Am I conscious of the degree and type of attention I am giving to members of each gender in classroom interactions? Do I have an equitable system for calling on students?

_____ Do I use gender-neutral language?

_____ Do I teach about religion, rather than teaching religion or ignoring religion altogether? When teaching about religion, do I:

- place religion within an historical and cultural context?

- use opportunities to include religion in history, literature and music?

- avoid making qualitative comparisons among religions?

- avoid soliciting information about the religious affiliations or beliefs of my students?

## Teaching Children To Be Proactive

_____ Do I teach children to identify instances of prejudice and discrimination?

_____ Do I help my students to develop proper responses to instances of prejudice and discrimination?

## General Strategies

_____ Do I involve parents and other community members in helping children develop greater understanding of the benefits and challenges of living in a culturally diverse society?

_____ Do I inform parents of my multicultural, anti-bias curriculum?

_____ Do I support and encourage the hiring of minority teachers and staff?

_____ Do I build a secure and supportive atmosphere by creating a noncompetitive classroom environment?

_____ Do I use opportunities such as current events to discuss different cultures and religions?

_____ Do I provide students with opportunities to problem-solve issues of inclusiveness?

_____ Do I use activities that demonstrate how the privilege of groups of higher economic status is directly connected to the lack of privilege of lower socioeconomic status people?

_____ Do I have students examine and analyze the representation of class, race, gender, ability and language differences in media and their community?

_____ Do I recognize that tracking reinforces classism and is counterproductive to student learning at all ability levels?

_____ Do I utilize children's literature to help students understand and empathize with individuals who have experienced prejudice and discrimination and to discuss important social issues?

---

| Northwest Consortium for Mathematics and Science Teaching |
| --- |

## Science and Mathematics for All:
### Developing and Implementing a Shared Vision

*Equity in Mathematics and Science Checklist*

Consider each question and check the box that corresponds to the **best** answer you can provide at this time. Answer all questions.

| A. Does your school/district... | Yes | No | Not Sure |
| --- | :---: | :---: | :---: |
| 1. compare science and mathematics achievement test data by gender ethnicity? | ☐ | ☐ | ☐ |
| 2. monitor science and mathematics course enrollments by gender and ethnicity? | ☐ | ☐ | ☐ |
| 3. monitor participation in mathematics and science extracurricular activities by gender and ethnicity? | ☐ | ☐ | ☐ |
| 4. have stated goals which target equitable gender and ethnic participation and performance? | ☐ | ☐ | ☐ |
| 5. have an intervention plan for achieving and maintaining the stated equity goals? | ☐ | ☐ | ☐ |
| 6. involve teachers in the development and implementation of the goals and intervention plan? | ☐ | ☐ | ☐ |
| 7. involve parents in the development and implementation of the goals and intervention plan? | ☐ | ☐ | ☐ |
| 8. have an effective peer support and/or tutoring program? | ☐ | ☐ | ☐ |
| 9. provide career education programs that emphasize the importance of mathematics and science? | ☐ | ☐ | ☐ |
| 10. provide programs and materials to help elementary parents and teachers capitalize on young students' natural interest and positive attitudes for mathematics and science? | ☐ | ☐ | ☐ |
| 11. hire and support female and minority mathematics and science teachers? | ☐ | ☐ | ☐ |
| 12. provide assistance for those who are "science or math anxious"? | ☐ | ☐ | ☐ |

| B. In the Classroom do you... | Yes | No | Not Sure |
| --- | :---: | :---: | :---: |
| 1. include in the mathematics program, the use of manipulatives that facilitate the understanding of concepts? | ☐ | ☐ | ☐ |
| 2. use an activity-based, student centered science program? | ☐ | ☐ | ☐ |

3. provide regular opportunities for girls and minorities to master computer concepts and skills? ☐ ☐ ☐

4. monitor mathematics and science instructional materials for sexism and racism? ☐ ☐ ☐

5. incorporate into the curriculum the historical and contemporary contributions of women and minorities to mathematics and science? ☐ ☐ ☐

6. monitor your questioning patterns and techniques by gender and ethnicity? ☐ ☐ ☐

7. use classroom displays that reflect the involvement of women and minorities in science and mathematics? ☐ ☐ ☐

8. provide frequent opportunities for students to interact with women and minority role models who are involved in science and mathematics in school and/or careers? ☐ ☐ ☐

9. use diagnostic instruments that provide information about students' learning styles? ☐ ☐ ☐

| **C. Does your professional development include...** | Yes | No | Not Sure |
|---|---|---|---|
| 1. ongoing staff development programs that promote activity based science? | ☐ | ☐ | ☐ |
| 2. ongoing staff development programs that promote the mathematics instruction exemplified in the NCTM standards? | ☐ | ☐ | ☐ |
| 3. inservice programs on cognition and learning styles? | ☐ | ☐ | ☐ |
| 4. opportunities to network with other educators in your school, district or region who share your equity goals? | ☐ | ☐ | ☐ |
| 5. staff development programs on teacher expectations and their role in promoting equity? | ☐ | ☐ | ☐ |
| 6. instructional experiences on how to recognize and handle bias in materials? | ☐ | ☐ | ☐ |

**Analyzing Your Responses.**

Take a good look at your responses. Those questions you answered with "yes" probably indicate areas where equitable practices are in place. The "not sure" answers are areas that deserve more attention and require further investigation so that you can respond in a more definite manner. The questions that prompted a "no" answer likely indicate areas that must be targeted in any attempt to improve the participation and achievement of girls and minorities in science and mathematics.

Reprinted by permission of Learning Innovations from *Facilitating Systemic Change in Science and Mathematics Education: A Professional Developer's Tool-Kit*, Field Test Version, by the Regional Laboratory Network Program (now Learning Innovations, a Division of WestEd, Stoneham, MA) and adapted by the Northwest Consortium for Mathematics and Science Teaching in

Profile of an Equitable Math and Science Classroom and Teacher

## Profile of an Equitable Math and Science Classroom and Teacher

**Components:**

Introduction
Physical Environment
Curriculum
Language
Teaching Methodology
Behavior Management
Academic Evaluation
Classroom Integration

Joy Wallace
Vermont Institute for Science, Mathematics and Technology
November 10, 1993 Version.
Based on "Profile of an Equitable Classroom," 1991, The NETWORK, Inc.

*P.O.Box 310, Randolph Center, Vermont 05061 Phone:802-728-4108/4635 Fax: 728-3026*

## Profile of an Equitable Math and Science Classroom and Teacher

### Introduction

The following are Standards and guidelines for an equitable mathematics and science teacher and classroom. Each section defines the category and describes factors for promoting maximum student learning in mathematics and science. Classroom characteristics and teacher behaviors included in "Profile of an Equitable Math and Science Classroom and Teacher" reflect current research of effective teaching and learning, as well as a focus on promoting equity.

It is important to remember that the teacher and a classroom do not exist in isolation, but are part of a larger context that includes school and district policies and practices, administrative support of equity, other teachers, peer influences on students and parental involvement. Therefore, this deals with only part of the total picture.

From Columbia Education Center by Joy Wallace, August 1997 version. Based on "Profile of an Equitable Classroom," 1991, The NETWORK, Inc. Used by permission of Joy Wallace, Columbia Educ. Center, Portland, Oregon, 503-760-2346.

## Profile of an Equitable Math and Science Classroom and Teacher

### Physical Environment

**Definition:** The physical environment of the classroom includes:

- displays on bulletin boards,
- posters and presentations used to decorate the room,
- greetings and messages posted on walls, and
- configuration of desks and arrangement of room.

### Ideal:

A. Wall displays show both male and female representatives of various races, cultures and physical disabilities actively engaged in science and mathematics activities -- from historical to present.

B. Wall displays invite and support interest in science and mathematics of all students.

C. Seating arrangements and placement of furniture are flexible and facilitate the integration of all members of the class into learning activities.

D. Classroom environment encourages movement of the teacher to be close to all students.

E. Classroom environment is barrier free.

F. The teacher extends student learning beyond the walls of the classroom into the community through partnerships with businesses, parents and community groups.

From Columbia Education Center by Joy Wallace, August 1997 version. Based on "Profile of an Equitable Classroom," 1991, The NETWORK, Inc. Used by permission of Joy Wallace, Columbia Educ. Center, Portland, Oregon, 503-760-2346.

## Profile of an Equitable Math and Science Classroom and Teacher

### Curriculum

**Definition:** The curriculum of a classroom includes:

- formal and informal content taught through lessons,
- all activities related to lessons, and
- all aspects of the teacher's program.

**Ideal:**

A. Math and science activities and lessons are multicultural. They identify contributions of various cultures to math and science, and present various cultural perspectives about math and science topics.

B. Information is presented by the teacher using a variety of methods that appeal to all students and invite the participation of under-represented students.

C. The teacher organizes math and science instruction to insure that students learn to cooperate with students who are different.

D. The teacher encourages and enables students to examine science and mathematics from a variety of cultural perspectives.

E. The teacher carefully selects textbooks and resource materials from an equity perspective. If biases exist, the teacher discusses them with students, including how biased materials can effect learning.

F. The teacher has an extensive background in mathematics and/or science content.

G. The teacher is very secure with teaching mathematics and science content and can creatively utilize various methods of content presentation.

H. The teacher designs rigorous mathematics and/or science lessons that challenge all students.

I. The teacher involves parents in the mathematics and/or science learning of students.

J. The teacher includes learning activities that will develop skills, such as spatial skills, that have disparate development in students.

From Columbia Education Center by Joy Wallace, August 1997 version. Based on "Profile of an Equitable Classroom," 1991, The NETWORK, Inc. Used by permission of Joy Wallace, Columbia Educ. Center, Portland, Oregon, 503-760-2346.

## Profile of an Equitable Math and Science Classroom and Teacher

### Language

**Definition**: The language of the classroom includes:

- the language and style of language used by the teacher, and
- the language and style of language the teacher allows students to use.

**Ideal**:

A. The teacher uses inclusionary terms for people in all written and oral communication. Inclusionary terms DO NOT assign positions to a specific gender, race or ethnicity (i.e. fireman vs. firefighter or "the student, he" vs. "the students, they" or "the student, he or she").

B. The teacher consciously uses oral or written examples of women involved in science and mathematics activities.

C. The teacher works with students to develop inclusionary language and encourages its use.

D. The teacher does not allow any verbal harassment of one student by another.

E. The teacher discusses the negative impact of derogatory terms in reference to race, gender, ethnicity, physical disability and sexual preference, and how this effects the learning environment.

F. The teacher integrates current linguistic use into his/her language patterns, such as changing "handicapped" to "disabled" and changing "Black Heritage" to "African American Heritage".

From Columbia Education Center by Joy Wallace, August 1997 version. Based on "Profile of an Equitable Classroom," 1991, The NETWORK, Inc. Used by permission of Joy Wallace, Columbia Educ. Center, Portland, Oregon, 503-760-2346.

## Profile of an Equitable Math and Science Classroom and Teacher

### Teaching Methodology

**Definition**: The teaching methodology in the classroom includes:

- style of presentation,
- time devoted to presentation, and
- method of attention directed at students.

**Ideal**:

A. The teacher provides the same amount of teaching attention to all students.

B. The teacher varies the type of teaching attention to meet students' needs and learning styles.

C. The teacher ensures the equal participation of all students in classroom discussions through various methods.

D. The teacher uses a variety of presentation styles during mathematics and science lessons to keep all students engaged and involved in learning.

E. The teacher analyzes interactions with students for differential patterns and takes action to counteract and balance differences.

F. The teacher is knowledgeable of various methods for presenting content.

G. The teacher keeps updated on new teaching methods through staff development and reading.

H. The teacher collaborates and discusses teaching methods with colleagues.

I. The teacher utilizes inquiry as a mode for student learning.

J. The teacher uses math manipulatives and/or science experiments to promote learning by all students.

K. The teacher actively engages all students in discussion in science and math lessons, paying careful attention to the involvement of less verbal, aggressive students.

L. The teacher uses small groups to promote the verbal participation of all in discussions of math and science.

M. The teacher encourages students to take more math and science courses, and to get involved in informal math and science learning activities, such as events at science museums, etc.

N. The teacher prevents passive non-participation of students by engaging all students in discussions.

O. The teacher makes sure that all students set up and use science and math equipment.

## Profile of an Equitable Math and Science Classroom and Teacher

### Behavior Management

**Definition:** The behavior management of the classroom includes:

- style the teacher uses to control student behavior,
- time the teacher takes to control student behavior, and
- methods used by the teacher to control student behavior.

### Ideal:

A. The teacher explicitly informs students in advance of acceptable and unacceptable behavior in the science and mathematics classroom.

B. The teacher explicitly informs students in advance of the consequences of behavior.

C. The teacher regularly praises students equally for good behavior.

D. The teacher is consistent when applying behavior management techniques.

E. The teacher DOES NOT allow any student to harass another student in any way.

From Columbia Education Center by Joy Wallace, August 1997 version. Based on "Profile of an Equitable Classroom," 1991, The NETWORK, Inc. Used by permission of Joy Wallace, Columbia Educ. Center, Portland, Oregon, 503-760-2346.

## Profile of an Equitable Math and Science Classroom and Teacher

### Academic Evaluation

**Definition:** The academic evaluation of the classroom includes:

- style and systems used by the teacher to assess student performance,
- style and systems used by the teacher to evaluate student performance, and
- style and systems used by the teacher to report student academic performance.

**Ideal:**

A. The teacher has high academic expectations for all students and expectations for students are not influenced by students' race, gender, ethnicity or physical disability.

B. The teacher has analyzed personal biases that may influence expectations for students.

C. The teacher communicates high academic expectations to all students.

D. The teacher praises students for the intellectual quality of their math and science work, irrespective of the student's race, gender, national origin or physical disability from a set of criteria which has been announced to the students.

E. The teacher uses a variety of methods of authentic assessment to evaluate student performance.

F. The teacher experiments with different methods of authentic assessment, keeps track of the effective methods and continuously tries to improve classroom assessment.

From Columbia Education Center by Joy Wallace, August 1997 version. Based on "Profile of an Equitable Classroom," 1991, The NETWORK, Inc. Used by permission of Joy Wallace, Columbia Educ. Center, Portland, Oregon, 503-760-2346.

## Profile of an Equitable Math and Science Classroom and Teacher

### Classroom Integration

**Definition:** Classroom integration includes:

- structure used to facilitate student social and academic cooperation, and
- activities used to facilitate student social and academic cooperation.

**Ideal:**

A. The teacher utilizes a variety of reaming activities in math and science that will help students to learn from one another and work together effectively.

B. The teacher integrates students of all learning styles and abilities into heterogeneous groups.

C. The teacher structures math and science activities to promote the development among all students of leadership skills

D. The teacher encourages students to identify and analyze their participation and involvement in groups, and to develop strategies for increasing effectiveness.

# Index

# About the Author

Nancy Love is a Senior Associate at TERC, in Cambridge, MA, where she works with Regional Alliance for Mathematics and Science Education. A seasoned professional developer and author, Love consults with schools and educators nationally in designing effective professional development, understanding change, and using data effectively. In 1999, she co-authored the book *Global Perspectives for Local Action: Using TIMSS to Improve U.S. Mathematics and Science Education: A Professional Development Guide*, published by the National Research Council (NRC), and with co-author Susan Mundry, trained a cadre of national facilitators to disseminate the findings of the NRC.

Before coming to TERC, Love worked with a team from the National Institute for Science Education (NISE) to co-author the highly acclaimed book *Designing Professional Development for Teachers of Science and Mathematics* with Susan Loucks-Horsley, Peter Hewson, and Kathy Stiles. As the former Director of the Massachusetts Facilitator Project and Cooperative Learning Services at The NETWORK, Inc, she has twelve years of experience disseminating nationally validated programs and supporting school improvement. She has also served as adjunct faculty at Salem and Worcester State Colleges and taught in inner-city and alternative high schools.